GRID COMPUTING – TECHNOLOGY AND APPLICATIONS, WIDESPREAD COVERAGE AND NEW HORIZONS

Edited by **Soha Maad**

Grid Computing – Technology and Applications, Widespread Coverage and New Horizons
Edited by Soha Maad

Published by InTech

Janeza Trdine 9, 51000 Rijeka, Croatia

Publishing Process Manager Dejan Grgur

Technical Editor Teodora Smiljanic

Cover Designer InTech Design Team

Additional hard copies can be obtained from orders@intechopen.com

Grid Computing – Technology and Applications, Widespread Coverage and New Horizons
Edited by Soha Maad
p. cm.
ISBN 978-953-51-0604-3

For EU product safety concerns:
IN TECH d.o.o., Prolaz Marije Krucifikse Kozulić 3, 51000 Rijeka, Croatia,
info@intechopen.com or visit our website at intechopen.com.

Meet the editor

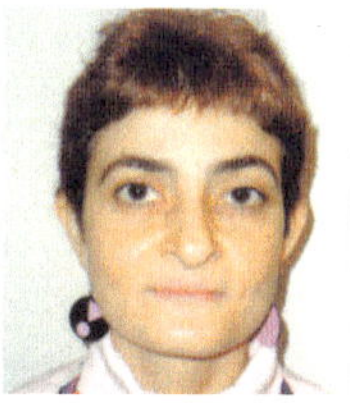

Dr Soha Maad is the founder and manager of IGROW EEIG (Integrated Technologies and Services for Sustainable Growth European Economic Interest Grouping) at INVENT Dublin City University, Ireland. Dr Maad obtained her PhD from the University of Warwick, UK. She has 12 years of research experience in the application of Information and Communication Technologies, including Grid and High Performance Computing to various domains. Dr Maad is an Associate Honorary Member of HRB Centre for Primary Care Research, Royal College of Surgeons, Ireland. She worked as a research fellow at Trinity College Dublin and University College Cork, Ireland; INRIA, France, and was an ERCIM fellow at Fraunhofer Institute of Media Communication, Germany.

Contents

Preface XI

Section 1 Advances in Grid Computing - Workflow 1

Chapter 1 **w-TG: A Combined Algorithm to Optimize the Runtime of the Grid-Based Workflow Within an SLA Context 3**
Dang Minh Quan, Joern Altmann and Laurence T. Yang

Chapter 2 **On the Effect of Applying the Task Clustering for Identical Processor Utilization to Heterogeneous Systems 29**
Hidehiro Kanemitsu, Gilhyon Lee, Hidenori Nakazato, Takashige Hoshiai and Yoshiyori Urano

Section 2 Advances in Grid Computing - Resources Management 47

Chapter 3 **Resource Management for Data Intensive Tasks on Grids 49**
Imran Ahmad and Shikharesh Majumdar

Chapter 4 **A New Approach to Resource Discovery in Grid Computing 71**
Leyli Mohammad Khanli, Saeed Kargar and Ali Kazemi Niari

Chapter 5 **Task Scheduling in Grid Environment Using Simulated Annealing and Genetic Algorithm 89**
Wael Abdulal, Ahmad Jabas, S. Ramachandram and Omar Al Jadaan

Section 3 Advances in Grid Computing - Parallel Execution 111

Chapter 6 **Efficient Parallel Application Execution on Opportunistic Desktop Grids 113**
Francisco Silva, Fabio Kon, Daniel Batista, Alfredo Goldman, Fabio Costa and Raphael Camargo

Chapter 7 **Research and Implementation of Parallel Cache Model Through Grid Memory 135**
Qingkui Chen, Lichun Na, He Jia, Song Lin Zhuang and Xiaodong Ding

Chapter 8 **Hierarchy-Aware Message-Passing in the Upcoming Many-Core Era 151**
Carsten Clauss, Simon Pickartz, Stefan Lankes and Thomas Bemmerl

Section 4 Grid Applications 179

Chapter 9 **Grid Computing in High Energy Physics Experiments 181**
Dagmar Adamová and Pablo Saiz

Chapter 10 **Using Grid Computing for Constructing Ternary Covering Arrays 221**
Himer Avila-George, Jose Torres-Jimenez, Abel Carrión and Vicente Hernández

Chapter 11 **Grid Infrastructure for Domain Decomposition Methods in Computational ElectroMagnetics 241**
Olivier Terzo, Pietro Ruiu, Lorenzo Mossucca, Matteo Alessandro Francavilla and Francesca Vipiana

Chapter 12 **Characterization of Hepatic Lesions Using Grid Computing (Globus) and Neural Networks 267**
Sheng Hung Chung and Ean Teng Khor

Section 5 International Widespread of Grid Technology 281

Chapter 13 **Applications Exploiting e-Infrastructures Across Europe and India Within the EU-IndiaGrid Project 283**
Alberto Masoni and Stefano Cozzini

Section 6 New Horizons for Grid Technology 309

Chapter 14 **Open Development Platform for Embedded Systems 311**
E. Ostúa, A. Muñoz, P. Ruiz-de-Clavijo, M.J. Bellido, D. Guerrero and A. Millán

Chapter 15 **Potential of Grid Technology for Embedded Systems and Applications 325**
Mona Abo El-Dahb and Yoichi Shiraishi

Preface

Grid research, rooted in distributed and high performance computing, started in mid-to-late 1990s when scientists around the world acknowledged the need to establish an infrastructure to support their collaborative research on compute and data intensive experiments. Soon afterwards, national and international research and development authorities realized the importance of the Grid and gave it a primary position on their research and development agenda. The importance of the Grid was translated into large funding from various national and international sources, channeled to various Grid projects around the world aiming at building the so-called global infrastructure for e-Science. Selected key projects, such as EGEE (Enabling Grids For E-sciencE) in Europe and Globus in the United States, played a key role in developing this infrastructure.

The first generation Grid, referred to as Grid 1.0, was intended to coordinate resource sharing and problem solving in dynamic, multi-institutional virtual organizations. The sharing is not primarily file exchange but rather direct access to computers, software, data, and other resources, as is required by a range of collaborative problem-solving and resource-brokering strategies emerging in industry, science, and engineering. Following Grid 1.0, Web 2.0 emerged as a more user-friendly successor of Grid1.0. Grid 3.0 attempts to establish a merge between the web and Grid technologies to leverage the potential of the web in addressing the challenges faced by Grid 1.0 to deliver a user friendly infrastructure for high performance computing and collaboration. The EU vision of the next generation Grid is a service oriented knowledge utility infrastructure serving the needs of various application domains.

Grid research supported by national, regional, European, and international funding within the framework of various projects explored various themes including: Grid interoperability, Grid workflows, Grid security management, Grid universal accessibility, high end visualization using the Grid and for the Grid, social and economic modelling for Grid interoperability and Grid universal accessibility, the virtualisation of Grid resources, data management solutions for the Grid, Grid portability, Grid interactivity, and Grid usability in various application domains.

The Grid evolved from tackling data and compute-intensive problems, to addressing global-scale scientific projects, connecting businesses across the supply chain, and is aiming towards becoming a World Wide Grid that is integrated in our daily routine activities. The future vision of the next generation Grid is a Service Oriented Knowledge Utility capable of delivering knowledge to users and enabling resource sharing, collaboration and business transactions across individuals and organizations.

This book tells a story of a great potential, a continued strength, and widespread international penetration of Grid computing. It overviews the latest advances in the field and traces the evolution of selected Grid applications. The book highlights the international widespread coverage and unveils the future potential of the Grid.

This book is divided into six sections:

The first three sections overview latest advances in Grid computing including: Grid workflow (chapters 1 and 2), resources management (chapters 3, 4, and 5), and parallel execution (chapters 6, 7 and 8).

Section four considers selected key Grid applications including high-energy physics, constructing ternary covering arrays, computational electromagnetic, and medical applications including Hepatic Lesions.

Section five highlights the international widespread penetration and coverage of the Grid and presents success Grid stories from Europe and India.

Section six unveils the potential and horizon of the Grid in future applications including embedded systems and the design of inverter power supply.

The book is targeted at researchers and practitioners in the field of Grid computing and its application in various domains. Researchers will find some of the latest thinking in the Grid field and many examples of the state-of-the-art technologies and use across domain verticals. Both researchers who are just beginning in the field and researchers with experience in the domain should find topics of interest. Furthermore, practitioners will find the theory, new techniques, and standards that can increase the uptake of Grid technologies and boost related industry supply and demand. Many chapters consider applications and case studies that provide useful information about challenges, pitfalls, and successful approaches in the practical use of Grid technology. The chapters were written in such a way that they are interesting and understandable for both groups. They assume some background knowledge of the domain, but no specialist knowledge is required. It is possible to read each chapter on its own.

The book can be also used as a reference to understand the various related technology challenges, identified by regional research and development authorities, within the various research framework programs. The latter are intended to create lead markets in Information and Communication Technologies and to enact regional development plans.

Many people contributed to the realization of this book in different ways. First of all, we would like to thank the authors. They have put in considerable effort in writing their chapters. We are very grateful to the technical editors who contributed valuable efforts and dedicated time to improving the quality of the book. Furthermore, we would like to thank Dejan Grgur, Mia Macek, Natalia Reinic, and all members of the Editorial Collegiums at InTech for giving us the opportunity to start this book in the first place and their support in bringing the book to publication.

Dr. Soha Maad
Manager, IGROW Integrated Technologies and Services for Sustainable Growth
European Economic Interest, Grouping (EEIG) Invent DCU, Dublin City University,
Glasnevin, Dublin,
Ireland

Section 1

Advances in Grid Computing - Workflow

1

w-TG: A Combined Algorithm to Optimize the Runtime of the Grid-Based Workflow Within an SLA Context

Dang Minh Quan[1], Joern Altmann[2] and Laurence T. Yang[3]
[1]*Center for REsearch And Telecommunication Experimentation for NETworked Communities*
[2]*Technology Management, Economics, and Policy Program, Department of Industrial Engineering, College of Engineering, Seoul National University*
[3]*Department of Computer Science, St. Francis Xavier University*
[1]*Italy*
[2]*South Korea*
[3]*Canada*

1. Introduction

In the Grid Computing environment, many users need the results of their calculations within a specific period of time. Examples of those users are weather forecasters running weather forecasting workflows, and automobile producers running dynamic fluid simulation workflow Lovas et al. (2004). Those users are willing to pay for getting their work completed on time. However, this requirement must be agreed on by both, the users and the Grid provider, before the application is executed. This agreement is contained in the Service Level Agreement (SLA) Sahai et al. (2003). In general, SLAs are defined as an explicit statement of expectations and obligations in a business relationship between service providers and customers. SLAs specify the a-priori negotiated resource requirements, the quality of service (QoS), and costs. The application of such an SLA represents a legally binding contract. This is a mandatory prerequisite for the Next Generation Grids.

However, letting Grid-based workflows' owners work directly with resource providers has two main disadvantages:

- The user has to have a sophisticated resource discovery and mapping tools in order to find the appropriate resource providers.
- The user has to manage the workflow, ranging from monitoring the running process to handling error events.

To free users from this kind of work, it is necessary to introduce a broker to handle the workflow execution for the user. We proposed a business model Quan & J. Altmann (2007) for the system as depicted in Figure 1, in which, the SLA workflow broker represents the user as specified in the SLA with the user. This controls the workflow execution. This includes mapping of sub-jobs to resources, signing SLAs with the services providers, monitoring, and error recovery. When the workflow execution has finished, it settles the accounts, pays the service providers and charges the end-user. The profit of the broker is the difference. The value-added that the broker provides is the handling of all the tasks for the end-user.

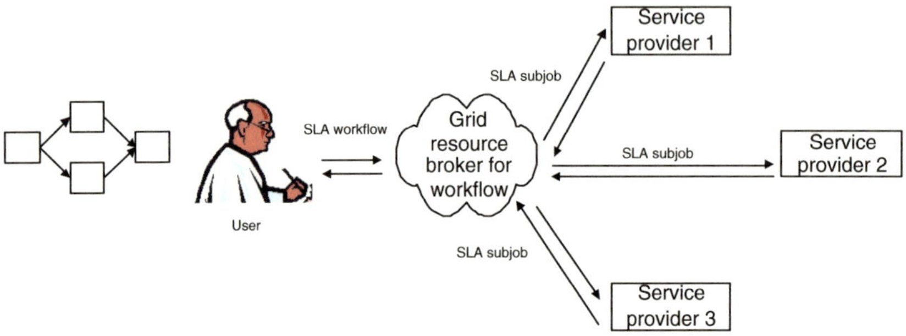

Fig. 1. Stakeholders and their business relationship

We presented a prototype system supporting SLAs for the Grid-based workflow in Quan et al. (2005; 2006); Quan (2007); Quan & Altmann (2007). Figure 2 depicts a sample scenario of running a workflow in the Grid environment.

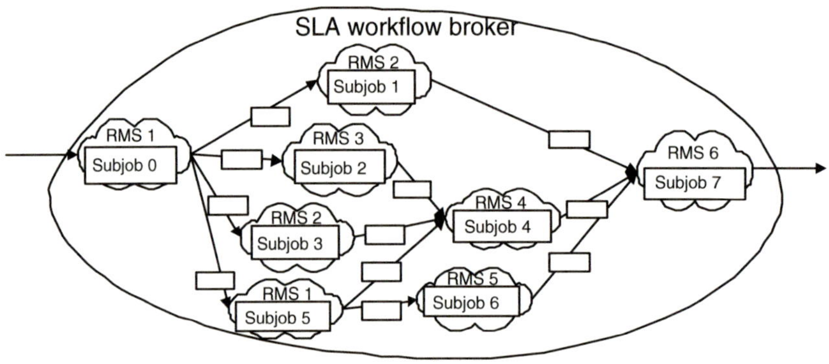

Fig. 2. A sample running Grid-based workflow scenario

In the system handling the SLA-based workflow, the mapping module receives an important position. Our ideas about Grid-based workflow mapping within the SLA context have 3 main scenarios.

- Mapping heavy communication Grid-based workflow within the SLA context, satisfying the deadline and optimizing the cost Quan et al. (2006).
- Mapping light communication Grid-based workflow within the SLA context, satisfying the deadline and optimizing the cost Quan & Altmann (2007).
- Mapping Grid-based workflow within the SLA context with execution time optimization.

The requirement of optimizing the execution time emerges in several situations.

- In the case of catastrophic failure, when one or several resource providers are detached from the grid system at a time, the ability to finish the workflow execution on time as stated in the original SLA is very low and the ability to be fined because of not fulfilling SLA is nearly 100%. Within the SLA context, which relates to business, the fine is usually very high and increases with the lateness of the workflow's finished time. Thus, those sub-jobs, which form an workflow, must be mapped to the healthy RMSs in a way, which minimizes the workflow finishing time Quan (2007).

- When the Grid is busy, there are few free resources. In this circumstance, finding a feasible solution meeting the user's deadline is a difficult task. This constraint equals to find an optimizing workflow execution time mapping solution. Even when the mapping result does not meet the preferred deadline, the broker can still use it for further negotiation with the user.

The previous work proposed an algorithm, namely the w-Tabu Quan (2007), to handle this problem. In the w-Tabu algorithm, a set of referent solutions, which distribute widely over the search space, is created. From each solution in the set, we use the Tabu search to find the local minimal solution. The Tabu search extends the local search method by using memory structures. When a potential solution has been determined, it is marked as "taboo" so that the algorithm does not visit that solution frequently. However, this mechanism only searches the area around the referent solution. Thus, many areas containing good solutions may not be examined by the w-Tabu algorithm and thus, the quality of the solution is still not as high as it should be.

In this book chapter, we propose a new algorithm to further improve the quality of the mapping solution. The main contribution of the book chapter includes:

- An algorithm based Genetic algorithm called the w-GA algorithm. According to the character of the workflow, we change the working mechanism of the crossover and mutation operations. Thus, the algorithm could find a better solution than the standard GA algorithm with the same runtime.
- An analysis the strong and weak points of w-GA algorithm compared to the w-Tabu algorithm. We do an extensive experiment in order to see the quality of w-GA algorithm in performance and runtime.
- An combined algorithm, namely w-TG. We propose a new algorithm by combining the w-GA algorithm and the w-Tabu algorithm. The experiment shows that the new algorithm finds out solutions about 9% greater than the w-Tabu algorithm.

In the early state of the business Grid like now, there are not so many users or providers and the probability of numerous requests coming at a time is very low. Moreover, even when the business Grid becomes crowd, there are many periods that only one SLA workflow request coming at a time. Thus, in this book chapter, we assume the broker handles one workflow running request at a time. The extension of mapping many workflows at a time will be the future work.

The chapter is organized as follows. Sections 2 and 3 describe the problem and the related works respectively. Section 4 presents the w-GA algorithm. Section 5 describes the performance experiment, while section 6 introduces the combined algorithm w-TG and its performance. Section 7 concludes the book chapter with a short summary.

Sjs	cpu	speed (Mhz)	stor (GB)	exp	rt (slot)	S-sj	D-sj	data (GB)
0	128	1000	30	2	16	0	1	1
1	64	1000	20	1	13	0	2	4
2	128	1000	30	2	14	0	3	6
3	128	1000	30	2	5	0	5	10
4	128	1000	30	2	8	1	7	3
5	32	1000	10	0	13	2	4	2
6	64	1000	20	1	16	3	4	8
7	128	1000	30	2	7	4	7	4
						5	4	3
						5	6	6
Workflow starting slot: 10						6	7	6

Table 1. Sample workflow specification

2. Problem statement

2.1 Grid-based workflow model

Like many popular systems handling Grid-based workflows Deelman et al. (2004); Lovas et al. (2004); Spooner et al. (2003), our system is of the Directed Acyclic Graph (DAG) form. The user specifies the required resources needed to run each sub-job, the data transfer between sub-jobs, the estimated runtime of each sub-job, and the expected runtime of the whole workflow. In this book chapter, we assume that time is split into slots. Each slot equals a specific period of real time, from 3 to 5 minutes. We use the time slot concept in order to limit the number of possible start-times and end-times of sub-jobs. Moreover, a delay of 3 minutes is insignificant for the customer. Table 1 presents the main parameters including sub-job specifications and data transfer specifications of the sample workflow in Figure 2. The sub-job specification includes the number of CPU (cpu), the CPU speed (speed), the amount of storage (stor), the number of experts (exp), the required runtime (rt). The data transfer specification includes the source sub-job (S-sj), the destination sub-job (D-sj), and the number of data (data). It is noted that the CPU speed of each sub-job can be different. However, we set it to the same value for the presentation purposes only.

2.2 Grid service model

The computational Grid includes many High Performance Computing Centers (HPCCs). The resources of each HPCC are managed by a software called local Resource Management System (RMS)[1]. Each RMS has its own unique resource configuration, the number of CPUs, the amount of memory, the storage capacity, the software, the number of experts, and the service price. To ensure that the sub-job can be executed within a dedicated time period, the RMS must support an advance resource reservation such as CCS Hovestadt (2003). Figure 3 depicts an example of an CPU reservation profile of such an RMS. In our model, we reserve three main types of resources: CPU, storage, and expert. The addition of further resources is straightforward.

[1] In this book chapter, RMS is used to represent the cluster/super computer as well as the Grid service provided by the HPCC.

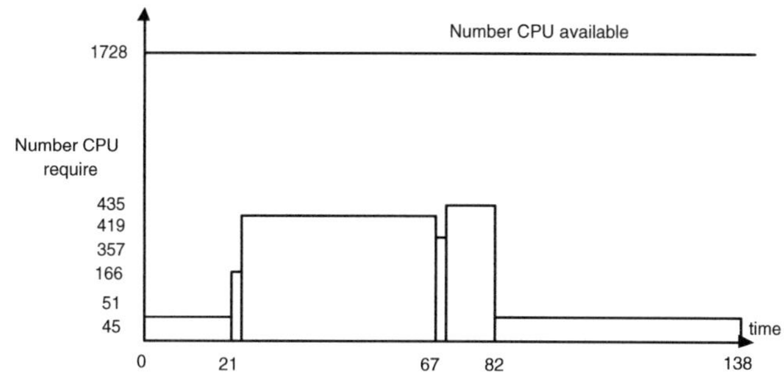

Fig. 3. A sample CPU reservation profile of a local RMS

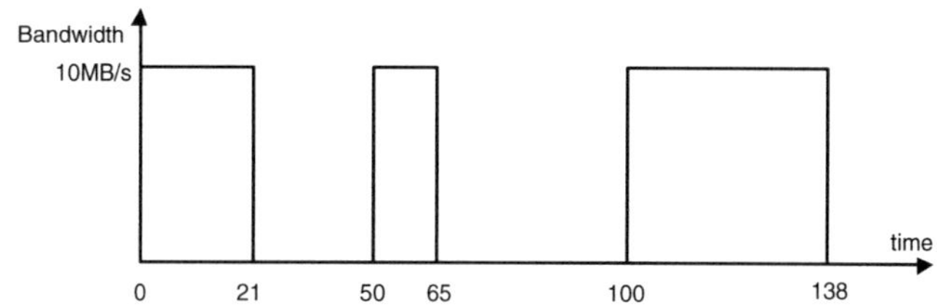

Fig. 4. A sample bandwidth reservation profile of a link between two local RMSs

If two output-input-dependent sub-jobs are executed on the same RMS, it is assumed that the time required for the data transfer equals zero. This can be assumed since all compute nodes in a cluster usually use a shared storage system such as NFS or DFS. In all other cases, it is assumed that a specific amount of data will be transferred within a specific period of time, requiring the reservation of bandwidth.

The link capacity between two local RMSs is determined as the average available capacity between those two sites in the network. The available capacity is assumed to be different for each different RMS couple. Whenever a data transfer task is required on a link, the possible time period on the link is determined. During that specific time period, the task can use the entire capacity, and all other tasks have to wait. Using this principle, the bandwidth reservation profile of a link will look similar to the one depicted in Figure 4. A more realistic model for bandwidth estimation (than the average capacity) can be found in Wolski (2003). Note, the kind of bandwidth estimation model does not have any impact on the working of the overall mechanism.

Table 2 presents the main resource configuration including the RMS specification and the bandwidth specification of the 6 RMSs in Figure 2. The RMS specification includes the number of CPU (cpu), the CPU speed in Mhz (speed), the amount of storage in GB (stor), the number of expert (exp). The bandwidth specification includes the source RMS (s), the destination RMS (d), and the bandwidth in GB/slot (bw). For presentation purpose, we assume that all reservation profiles are empty. It is noted that the CPU speed of each RMS can be different. We set it to the same value for the presentation purposes only.

2.3 Problem specification

The formal specification of the described problem includes following elements:

ID	cpu	speed	stor	exp	s	d	bw	s	d	bw
1	256	1000	3000	4	1	2	1	2	1	1
2	128	1000	2000	3	1	3	3	3	1	3
3	256	1000	3000	4	1	4	2	4	1	2
4	256	1000	3000	4	1	5	3	5	1	3
5	256	1000	3000	4	1	6	2	6	1	2
6	64	1000	1000	2	2	3	1	3	2	1
					2	4	1	4	2	1
					2	5	3	5	2	3
					2	6	2	6	2	2
					3	4	1	4	3	1
					3	5	3	5	3	3
					3	6	1	6	3	1
					4	5	2	5	4	2
					4	6	3	6	4	3
					5	6	1	6	5	1

Table 2. Sample RMS configurations

- Let R be the set of Grid RMSs. This set includes a finite number of RMSs, which provide static information about controlled resources and the current reservations/assignments.
- Let S be the set of sub-jobs in a given workflow including all sub-jobs with the resource and runtime requirements.
- Let E be the set of edges in the workflow, which express the dependency between the sub-jobs and the necessity for data transfers between the sub-jobs.
- Let K_i be the set of resource candidates of sub-job s_i. This set includes all RMSs, which can run sub-job s_i, $K_i \subset R$.

Based on the given input, the required solution includes two sets defined in Formula 1 and 2.

$$M = \{(s_i, r_j, start, stop) | s_i \in S, r_j \in K_i\} \tag{1}$$

$$N = \{(e_{ik}, start, stop) | e_{ik} \in E\} \tag{2}$$

If the solution does not have a start, stop slot for each s_i, it becomes a configuration as defined in Formula 3.

$$a = \{(s_i, r_j) | s_i \in S, r_j \in K_i\} \tag{3}$$

A feasible solution must satisfy following conditions:

- **Criterion 1:** All $K_i \neq \emptyset$. There is at least one RMS in the candidate set of each sub-job.
- **Criterion 2:** The dependencies of the sub-jobs are resolved and the execution order remains unchanged.
- **Criterion 3:** The capacity of an RMS must equal or greater than the requirement at any time slot. Each RMS provides a profile of currently available resources and can run many sub-jobs of a single flow both sequentially and in parallel. Those sub-jobs, which run on the same RMS, form a profile of resource requirement. With each RMS r_j running sub-jobs of the Grid workflow, with each time slot in the profile of available resources and profile of

resource requirements, the number of available resources must be larger than the resource requirement.

- **Criterion 4:** The data transmission task e_{ki} from sub-job s_k to sub-job s_i must take place in dedicated time slots on the link between the RMS running sub-job s_k to the RMS running sub-job s_i. $e_{ki} \in E$.

The goal is to minimize the makespan of the workflow. The makespan is defined as the period from the desired starting time until the finished time of the last sub-job in the workflow. In addition to the aspect that the workflow in our model includes both parallel and sequential sub-jobs, the SLA context imposes the following distinguishing characteristics.

- An RMS can run several parallel or sequential sub-jobs at a time.
- The resources in each RMS are reserved.
- The bandwidth of the links connecting RMSs is reserved.

To check for the feasibility of a configuration, the mapping algorithm must go through the resource reservation profiles and bandwidth reservation profile. This step needs a significant amount of time. Suppose, for example, that the Grid system has m RMS, which can satisfy the requirement of n sub-jobs in a workflow. As an RMS can run several sub-jobs at a time, finding out the optimal solution needs (m^n) loops for checking the feasibility. It can be easily shown that the optimizing of the execution time of the workflow on the Grid as described above is an NP hard problem Black et al. (1999). Previous experiment results have shown that with the number of sub-jobs equaling 6 and number of RMSs equaling 20, the runtime to find out the optimal solution is exponential Quan et al. (2007).

3. Related works

The mapping algorithm for Grid workflow has received a lot of attentions from the scientific community. In the literature, there are many methods to mapping a Grid workflow to Grid resource within different contexts. Among those, the old but well-known algorithm Condor-DAGMan from the work of Condor (2004) is still used in some present Grid systems. This algorithm makes local decisions about which job to send to which resource and considers only jobs, which are ready to run at any given instance. Also, using a dynamic scheduling approach, Duan et al. (2006) and Ayyub et al. (2007) apply many techniques to frequently rearrange the workflow and reschedule it in order to reduce the runtime of the workflow. Those methods are not suitable for the context of resource reservation because whenever a reservation is canceled, a fee is charged. Thus, frequent rescheduling may lead to a higher running workflow cost.

Deelman et al. (2004) presented an algorithm which maps Grid workflows onto Grid resources based on existing planning technology. This work focuses on coding the problem to be compatible with the input format of specific planning systems and thus transferring the mapping problem to a planning problem. Although this is a flexible way of gaining different destinations, which includes some SLA criteria, significant disadvantages regarding the time-intensive computation, long response times and the missing consideration of Grid-specific constraints appeared.

In Mello et al. (2007), Mello et. al. describe a load balancing algorithm addressed to Grid computing environment called RouteGA. The algorithm uses GA techniques to provide an equal load distribution based on the computing resources capacity. Our work is different from the work of Mello et. al. in two main aspects.

- While we deal with workflow, the work in Mello et al. (2007) considers a group of single jobs but with no dependency among them.
- In our work, The resources are reserved, whereas Mello et al. (2007) does not consider the resource reservation context.

Related to the mapping task graph to resources, there is also the multiprocessor scheduling precedence-constrained task graph problem Gary et al. (1979); Kohler et al. (1974). As this is a well-known problem, the literature has recorded a lot of methods for this issue, which can be classified into several groups Kwok et al. (1999). The classic approach is based on the so-called list scheduling technique Adam et al. (1974); Coffman et al. (1976). More recent approaches are the UNC (Unbounded Number of Clusters) Scheduling Gerasoulis et al. (1992); Sarkar (1989), the BNP (Bound Number of Processors) Scheduling Adam et al. (1974); Kruatrachue et al. (1987); Sih et al. (1993), the TDB (Task Duplication Based) Scheduling Colin et al. (1991); Kruatrachue et al. (1988), the APN (Arbitrary Processor Network) Scheduling Rewini et al. (1990), and the genetic Hou et al. (1994); Shahid et al. (1994). Our problem differs from the multiprocessor scheduling precedence-constrained task graph problem in many factors. In the multiprocessor scheduling problem, all processors are similar, but in our problem, RMSs are heterogeneous. Each task in our problem can be a parallel program, while each task in the other problem is a strictly sequential program. Each node in the other problem can process one task at a time while each RMS in our problem can process several sub-jobs at a time. For these reasons, we cannot apply the proposed techniques to our problem because of the characteristic differences.

In recent works Berman et al. (2005); Blythe et al. (2005); Casanova et al. (2000); Ma et al. (2005), authors have described algorithms which concentrate on scheduling the workflow with parameter sweep tasks on Grid resources. The common destination of those algorithms is optimizing the makespan, defined as the time from when execution starts until the last job in the workflow is completed. Subtasks in this kind of workflow can be group in layers and there is no dependency among subtasks in the same layer. All proposed algorithms assume each task as a sequential program and each resource as a compute node. By using several heuristics, all those algorithms perform the mapping very quickly. Our workflow with the DAG form can also be transformed to the workflow with parameter sweep tasks type, and thus we have applied all those algorithms to our problem.

Min-min algorithm

Min-min uses the Minimum MCT (Minimum Completion Time) as a measurement, meaning that the task that can be completed the earliest is given priority. The motivation behind Min-min is that assigning tasks to hosts that will execute them the fastest will lead to an overall reduced finished time Berman et al. (2005); Casanova et al. (2000). To adapt the min-min algorithm to our problem, we analyze the workflow into a set of sub-jobs in sequential layers. Sub-jobs in the same layer do not depend on each other. With each sub-job in the sequential layer, we find the RMS which can finish sub-job the earliest. The sub-job in the layer which has the earliest finish time, then, will be assigned to the determined RMS. A more detailed description about the algorithm can be seen in Quan (2007).

Max-min algorithm

Max-min's metric is the Maximum MCT. The expectation is to overlap long-running tasks with short-running ones Berman et al. (2005); Casanova et al. (2000). To adapt the max-min algorithm to our problem, we analyze the workflow into a set of sub-jobs in sequential layers. Sub-jobs in the same layer do not depend on each other. With each sub-job in the sequential layer, we find the RMS which can finish sub-job the earliest. The sub-job in the layer which has the latest finish time, will be assigned to the determined RMS. A more detailed description about the algorithm can be seen in Quan (2007).

Suffer algorithm

The rationale behind sufferage is that a host should be assigned to the task that would "suffer" the most if not assigned to that host. For each task, its sufferage value is defined as the difference between its best MCT and its second-best MCT. Tasks with a higher sufferage value take precedence Berman et al. (2005); Casanova et al. (2000). To adapt a suffer algorithm to our problem, we analyze the workflow into a set of sub-jobs in sequential layers. Sub-jobs in the same layer do not depend on each other. With each sub-job in the sequential layer, we find the earliest and the second-earliest finish time of the sub-job. The sub-job in the layer which has the highest difference between the earliest and the second-earliest finish time will be assigned to the determined RMS. A more detailed description about the algorithm can be seen in Quan (2007).

GRASP algorithm

In this approach a number of iterations are made to find the best possible mapping of jobs to resources for a given workflow Blythe et al. (2005). In each iteration, an initial allocation is constructed in a greedy phase. The initial allocation algorithm computes the tasks whose parents have already been scheduled on each pass, and consider every possible resource for each such task. A more detailed description about the algorithm can be seen in Quan (2007).

w-DCP algorithm

The DCP algorithm is based on the principle of continuously shortening the longest path (also called critical path (CP)) in the task graph by scheduling tasks in the current CP to an earlier start time. This principal was applied for scheduling workflows with parameter sweep tasks on global Grids by Tianchi Ma et al in Ma et al. (2005). We proposed a version of DCP algorithm to our problem in Quan (2007).

The experiment results show that the quality of solutions found by those algorithm is not sufficient Quan (2007). To overcome the poor performance of methods in the literature, in the previous work Quan (2007), we proposed the w-Tabu algorithm. An overview of w-Tabu algorithm is presented in Algorithm 1.

The assigning sequence is based on the latest start_time of the sub-job. Sub-jobs having smaller latest start time will be assigned earlier. Each solution in the reference solutions set can be thought of as the starting point for the local search so it should be spread as widely as possible in the searching space. To satisfy the space spread requirement, the number of similar map $sub - job : RMS$ between two solutions, must be as small as possible. The improvement procedure based on the Tabu search has some specific techniques to reduce the computation time. More information about w-Tabu algorithm can be seen in Quan (2007).

Algorithm 1 w-Tabu algorithm

```
Determine assignning sequence for all sub-jobs of the workflow
Generate reference solution set
for all solution in reference set do
    Improve the solution as far as possible with the modified Tabu search
end for
Pick the solution with best result
```

4. w-GA algorithm

4.1 Standard GA

The standard application of GA algorithm to find the minimal makespan of a workflow within an SLA context is presented in Algorithm 2. We call it the n-GA algorithm.

Algorithm 2 n-GA algorithm

```
Determine assigning sequence for all sub-jobs of the workflow
Generate reference configuration set
while num_mv < max do
    Evaluate the makespan of each configuration
    a"= best configuration
    Add a" to the new population
    while the new population is not enough do
        Select parent couple configurations according to their makespan
        Crossover the parent with a probability to form new configurations
        Mutate the new configuration with a probability
        Put the new configuration to the new population
    end while
    num_mv ← num_mv + 1
end while
return a"
```

Determining the assigning sequence

The sequence of determining runtime for sub-jobs of the workflow in an RMS can also affect the final makespan, especially in the case of many sub-jobs in the same RMS. Similar to w-Tabu algorithm, the assigning sequence is based on the latest *start_time* of the sub-job. Sub-jobs having the smaller latest start time will be assigned earlier. The complete procedure can be seen in Quan (2007). Here we outline some main steps. We determine the earliest and the latest start time for each of the sub-jobs of the workflow under ideal conditions. The time period to do data transferring among sub-jobs is computed by dividing the amount of data over a fixed bandwidth. The latest start/stop time for each sub-job and each data transfer depends only on the workflow topology and the runtime and not on the resources context. Those parameters can be determined by using conventional graph algorithms.

Generating the initial population

In the n-GA algorithm, the citizen is encoded as described in Figure 5. We use this convention encoding as it naturally presents a configuration and thus, it is very convenient to evaluate the timetable of the solution.

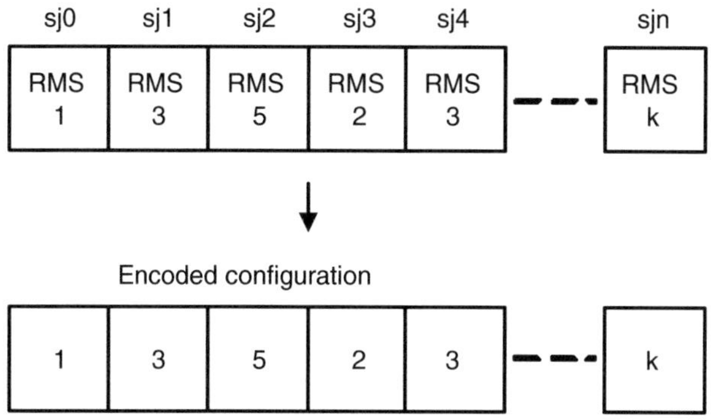

Fig. 5. The encoded configuration

Each sub-job has different resource requirements and there are a lot of RMSs with different resource configurations. The initial action is finding among those heterogeneous RMSs the suitable RMSs, which can meet the requirement of the sub-job. The matching between the sub-job's resource requirement and the RMS's resource configuration is done by several logic checking conditions in the WHERE clause of the SQL SELECT command. This work will satisfy Criterion 1. The set of candidate lists is the configuration space of the mapping problem.

The crossover operation of the GA will reduce the distance between two configurations. Thus, to be able to search over a wide search area, the initial population should be distributed widely. To satisfy the space spreading requirement, the number of the same map sub-job:RMS between two configurations must be as small as possible. We apply the same algorithm for creating the initial set of the configuration in Quan (2007). The number of the member in the initial population set depends on the number of available RMSs and the number of sub-jobs.

For example, from Table 1 and 2, the configuration space of the sample problem is presented in Figure 6a. The initial population will be presented in Figure 6b.

Determining the makespan

The fitness value is based on the makespan of the workflow. In order to determine the makespan of a citizen, we have to calculate the timetable of the whole workflow. The algorithm for computing the timetable is presented in Algorithm 3. The start and stop time of the sub-job is determined by searching the resource reservation profile. The start and stop time of data transfer is determined by searching the bandwidth reservation profile. This procedure will satisfy Criteria 2 and 3 and 4.

After determining the timetable, we have a solution. With our sample workflow, the solution of the configuration 1 in Figure 6b including the timetable for sub-jobs and the time table for data transfer is presented in Table 3. The timetable for sub-jobs includes the RMS and the start, stop time of executing the sub-job. The timetable for data transfer includes the source and destination sub-jobs (S-D sj), source and destination RMS (S-D rms), and the start and stop time of performing the data transfer. The makespan of this sample solution is 64.

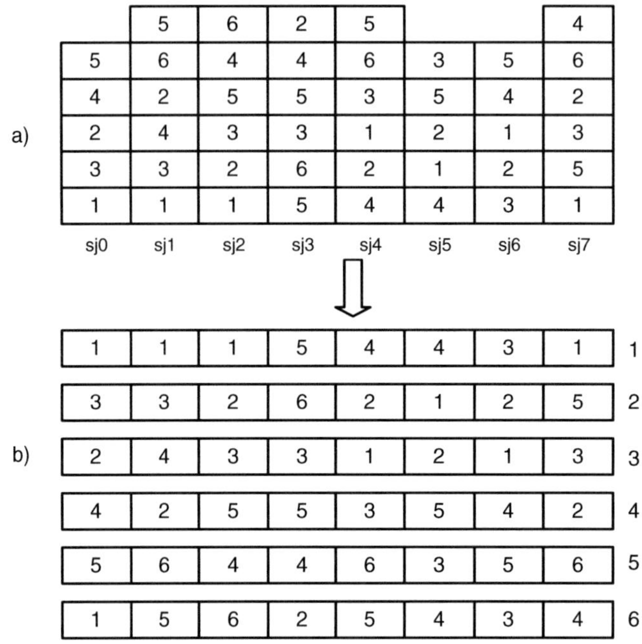

Fig. 6. Sample of forming the initial population

Algorithm 3 Determining timetable algorithm

for Each sub-job k following the assign sequence **do**
    Determine set of assigned sub-jobs Q, which having output data transfer to the sub-job k
    for Each sub-job i in Q **do**
        min_st_tran=end_time of sub-job i +1
        Search in reservation profile of link between RMS running sub-job k and RMS running sub-job i to determine start and end time of data transfer task with the start time > min_st_tran
    end for
    min_st_sj=max end time of all above data transfer +1
    Search in reservation profile of RMS running sub-job k to determine its start and end time with the start time > min_st_sj
end for

Crossover and mutation

Parents are selected according to the roulette wheel method. The fitness of each configuration = $1/makespan$. Firstly, the sum L of all configuration fitness is calculated. Then, a random number l from the interval $(0, L)$ is generated. Finally, we go through the population to sum the fitness p. When p is greater than l, we stop and return to the configuration where we were.

The crossover point is chosen randomly. For the purpose of demonstration, we use the sample workflow in Figure 2. Assume that we have a parents and a crossover point as presented in Figure 7a. The child is formed by copying from two parts of the parents. The result is presented in Figure 7b. The mutation point is chosen randomly. At the mutation point, r_j of s_i

Sjs	RMS	start-stop	S-D sj	S-D rms	start-stop
0	1	10-25	0-1	1-1	0-0
1	1	26-29	0-2	1-1	0-0
2	1	30-42	0-3	1-5	26-27
3	5	28-32	0-5	1-4	26-30
4	4	44-51	1-7	1-1	0-0
5	4	31-43	2-4	1-4	43-43
6	3	50-65	3-4	5-4	33-36
7	1	68-74	4-7	4-1	52-53
			5-4	4-4	0-0
			5-6	4-3	44-49
			6-7	3-1	66-67

Table 3. Sample solution timetable

is replaced by another RMS in the candidate RMS set. It is noted that the probability of having a mutation with a child is low, ranging approximately from 0.5% to 1%. The final result is presented in Figure 7c.

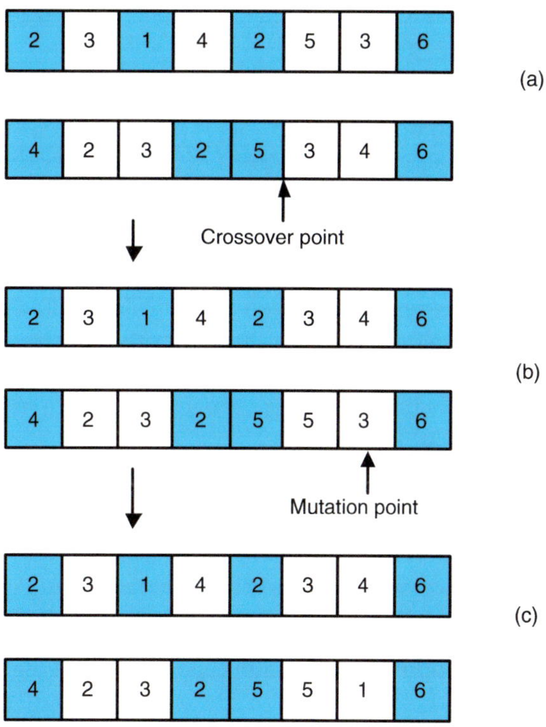

Fig. 7. Standard GA operations

4.2 Elimination of the standard GA

We did several experiments with n-GA and the initial result was not satisfactory. The algorithm has long runtime and presents low quality solutions. We believe that the reason for this is located in we do the crossover and mutation operations. In particular, we do not carefully consider the critical path of the workflow. The runtime of the workflow depends mainly on the execution time of the critical path. With a defined solution and timetable, the critical path of a workflow is defined with the algorithm as described in Algorithm 4.

Algorithm 4 Determining critical path algorithm

1: Let C is the set of sub-jobs in the critical path
2: Put last sub-job into C
3: *next_subjob*=last sub-job
4: **repeat**
5:     *prev_subjob* is determined as the sub-job having latest finished data output transfer to *next_subjob*
6:     Put *prev_subjob* into C
7:     *next_sj* = *prev_subjob*
8: **until** *prev_sj*= first sub-job

We start with the last sub-job determined. The next sub-job of the critical path will have the latest finish data transfer to the previously determined sub-job. The process continues until the next sub-job becomes the first sub-job.

The purpose of the crossover operation in the n-GA algorithm is creating new solutions in the hope that they are superior to the old one. In the crossover phase of the GA algorithm, when the sub-jobs of the critical path are not moved to other RMSs, the old critical path will have very low probability of being shortened. Thus, the overall makespan of the workflow has a low probability of improvement.

The primary purpose of the mutation operation is to maintain genetic diversity from one generation of a population of chromosomes to the next. In particular, it allows the algorithm to avoid local minima by preventing the population of chromosomes from becoming too similar to each other. When the sub-jobs of the critical path are not moved to other RMSs, the old critical path will have very low probability of being changed. Thus, the mutation operation does not have as good effect as it should have.

With the standard GA algorithm, it is always possible that the above situation happens and thus creates a long convergent process. We can see an example scenario in Figure 7. Assume that we select a parent as presented in Figure 7a. Using the procedure in Algorithm 4, we know the critical path of each solution which is marked by colour boxes. After the crossover and mutation operation as described in Figure 7b, 7c, the old critical path remains the same.

To overcome this elimination, we propose an algorithm called the w-GA algorithm.

4.3 w-GA algorithm

The framework of the w-GA algorithm is similar to the n-GA algorithm. We focus on the crossover and mutation operations. Assume that we selected a parent such as in Figure 7(a), the following steps will be taken.

Step 1: Determine the critical path of each solution. The procedure to determine this is described in Algorithm 4. In each solution of our example, the sub-jobs joined with the critical path are marked with color. The sub-jobs joined with the critical path in solution 1 include 0, 2, 4, 7. The sub-jobs joined the critical path in solution 2 include 0, 3, 4, 7.

Step 2: Form the critical set. The critical set includes sub-jobs have appeared in both critical paths. With our example, the critical set includes sub-jobs 0, 2, 3, 4, 7.

Step 3: Create derived configurations. The derived configuration is extracted from the old one by getting only sub-jobs which have appeared in the critical set. After this step, the two new configurations of the example are presented in Figure 8.

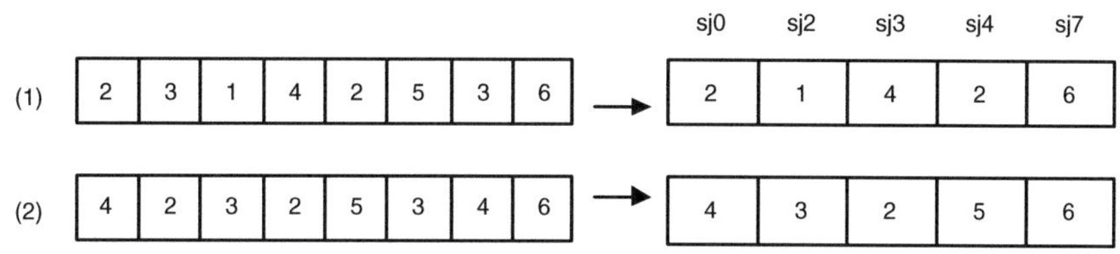

Fig. 8. The new derived configurations

Step 4: Exchange assignment if there is improvement signal. A couple $(s_i : r_j | s_i \in S, r_j \in K_i)$ is called an assignment. Assume that $(s1_i : r_j)$ is an assignment of the derived configuration 1, and $(s2_i : r_k)$ is an assignment of the derived configuration 2. If we change $(s1_i : r_j)$ to $(s1_i : r_k)$ and the finished time of the data transfer from the sub-job $s1_i$ to the next sub-job in the critical path is decreased, we say that the improvement signal appears. Without the improvement signal, the critical path cannot be shortened and the *makespan* cannot be improved. The algorithm for doing the exchange assignment is presented in Algorithm 5.

Algorithm 5 Exchange assignment algorithm

$imp\_signal \leftarrow 0$
for each sub-job s_i in the critical set **do**
  $(s1_i : r_j)$ change to $(s1_i : r_k)$
  if has improving signal **then**
    $imp\_signal \leftarrow 1$
  else
    $(s1_i : r_k)$ change to $(s1_i : r_j)$
  end if
  $(s2_i : r_k)$ change to $(s2_i : r_j)$
  if has improving signal **then**
    $imp\_signal \leftarrow 1$
  else
    $(s1_i : r_j)$ change to $(s1_i : r_k)$
  end if
end for

With each sub-job, we exchange the RMS between two configurations. If the exchange indicates an improvement signal, we keep the change. Otherwise, we return to the old assignment.

If there are some changes in either of the two configurations, we move to step 5. If there is no change, we move to step 4. In our example, the possible changes could be presented in Figure 9.

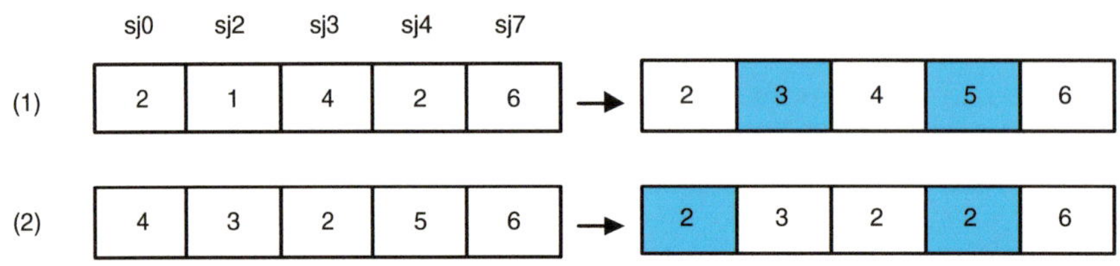

Fig. 9. Derived configurations after exchanging

Step 5: Do crossover. When there is no change with step 4 we do a normal crossover with the two derived configurations. This procedure is presented in Figure 10.

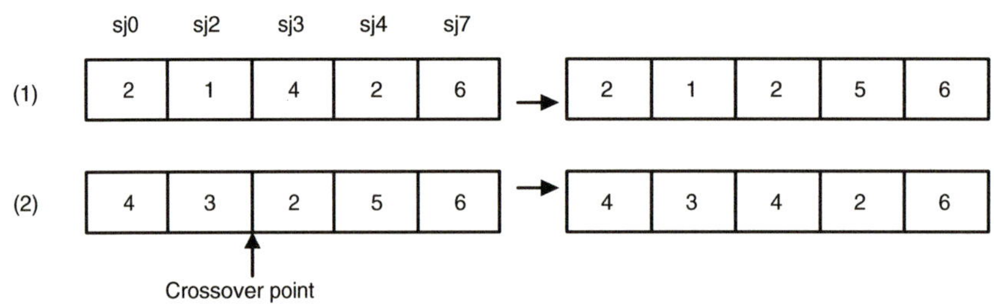

Fig. 10. Normal crossover operations

Step 6: Do mutation. The mutation is done on the derived configuration with no successful change. With each selected configuration, the mutation point is chosen randomly. At the mutation point, r_j of s_i is replaced by another RMS in the candidate RMS set. Like the normal GA algorithm, the probability to do mutation with a configuration is small. We choose a random selection because the main purpose of mutation is to maintain genetic diversity from one generation of a population of chromosomes to the next. If we also use mutation to improve the quality of the configuration, the operation mutation needs a lot of time. Our initial experiment shows that the algorithm cannot find a good solution within the allowable period.

Step 7: Reform the configuration. We return the derived configurations to the original configurations to have the new configurations. With our example, assume that step 4 is successful so we have two new derived configurations as in Figure 9. The new configurations are presented in Figure 11.

5. w-GA performance and discussion

The goal of the experiment is to measure the feasibility of the solution, its *makespan* and the time needed for the computation. The environment used for the experiments is rather standard and simple (Intel Duo 2,8Ghz, 1GB RAM, Linux FC5).

To do the experiment, we generated 18 different workflows which:

- Have different topologies.

(1)	2	3	3	4	5	5	3	6
(2)	2	2	3	2	2	3	4	6

Fig. 11. Newly created configurations

- Have a different number of sub-jobs with the number of sub-jobs being in the range from 7 to 32.
- Have different sub-job specifications. Without loss of generality, we assume that each sub-job has the same CPU performance requirement.
- Have different amounts of data transfer.

The runtime of each sub-job in each type of RMS is assigned by using Formula 4.

$$rt_j = \frac{rt_i}{\frac{pk_i+(pk_j-pk_i)*k}{pk_i}} \tag{4}$$

With pk_i, pk_j is the performance of a CPU in RMS r_i, r_j respectively and rt_i is the estimated runtime of the sub-job with the resource configuration of RMS r_i. k is the speed up control factor. Within the performance experiment, in each workflow, 60% of the number of sub-jobs have $k = 0.5$, 30% of the number of sub-jobs have $k = 0.25$, and 10% of the number of sub-jobs have $k = 0$.

The complexity of the workflow depends on the number of sub-job in the workflow. In the experiment, we stop at 32 sub-jobs for a workflow because it is much greater than the size of the recognized workflows. As far as we know, with our model of parallel task sub-job, most existing scientific workflows as described by Ludtke et al. Ludtke et al. (1999), Berriman et al. Berriman et al. (2003) and Lovas et al. Lovas et al. (2004) include just 10 to 20 sub-jobs.

As the difference in the static factors of an RMS such as OS, CPU speed and so on can be easily filtered by SQL query, we use 20 RMSs with the resource configuration equal to or even better than the requirement of sub-jobs. Those RMSs have already had some initial workload in their resource reservation and bandwidth reservation profiles. In the experiment, 30% of the number of RMS have CPU performance equals to the requirement, 60% of the number of RMS have CPU performance which is 100% more powerful than requirement, 10% of the number of RMS have CPU performance which is 200% more powerful than requirement.

We created 20 RMSs in the experiment because it closely parallels the real situation in Grid Computing. In theory, the number of sites joining a Grid can be very large. However, in reality, this number is not so great. The number of sites providing commercial service is even smaller. For example, the Distributed European Infrastructure for Supercomputing Applications (DEISA) has only 11 sites. More details about the description of resource configurations and workload configurations can be seen at the address: http://it.i-u.de/schools/altmann/DangMinh/desc_expe2.txt.

Sjs	0	100	200	400	600	800	1000
Simple level experiment							
7	56	52	52	52	52	52	52
8	187	55	55	55	55	55	55
9	93	71	64	64	64	64	64
10	81	56	56	56	56	56	56
11	229	65	65	65	65	65	65
12	88	88	88	88	88	88	88
13	149	52	52	52	52	52	52
Intermediate level experiment							
14	218	149	149	149	149	115	115
15	243	185	185	185	185	185	185
16	196	180	180	180	180	180	170
17	73	49	49	49	49	49	49
18	269	207	144	144	144	144	144
19	216	87	87	86	86	86	86
20	248	151	151	151	151	151	151
Advance level experiment							
21	76	37	37	37	37	37	37
25	289	262	217	217	214	205	204
28	276	229	201	76	76	76	76
32	250	250	250	250	250	205	205

Table 4. w-GA convergent experiment results

5.1 Time to convergence

To study the convergence of the w-GA algorithm, we do three levels of experiments according to the size of the workflow. At each level, we use the w-GA to map workflows to the RMSs. The maximum number of generations is 1000. The best found *makespan* is recorded at 0, 100, 200, 400, 600, 800 and 1000 generations. The result is presented in Table 4.

From the data in the Table 4, we see a trend that the w-GA algorithm needs more generations to convergence when the size of the workflow increases.

At the simple level experiment, we map workflow having from 7 to 13 sub-jobs to the RMSs. From this data, we can see that the w-GA converges to the same value after fewer than 200 generations in most case.

At the intermediate level of the experiment where we map a workflow having from 14 to 20 sub-jobs to the RMSs, the situation is slightly different than the simple level. In addition to many cases showing that the w-GA converges to the same value after fewer than 200 generations, there are some cases where the algorithm found a better solution after 600 or 800 generations.

When the size of the workflow increases from 21 to 32 sub-jobs as in the advanced level experiment, converging after fewer than 200 generations happens in only one case. In other cases, the w-GA needs from 400 to more than 800 generations.

5.2 Performance comparison

We have not noticed a similar resource model or workflow model as stated in Section 2. To do the performance evaluation, in the previous work we implemented the w-DCP, Grasp, minmin, maxmin, and suffer algorithms to our problem Quan (2007). The extensive experiment result is shown in Figure 12.

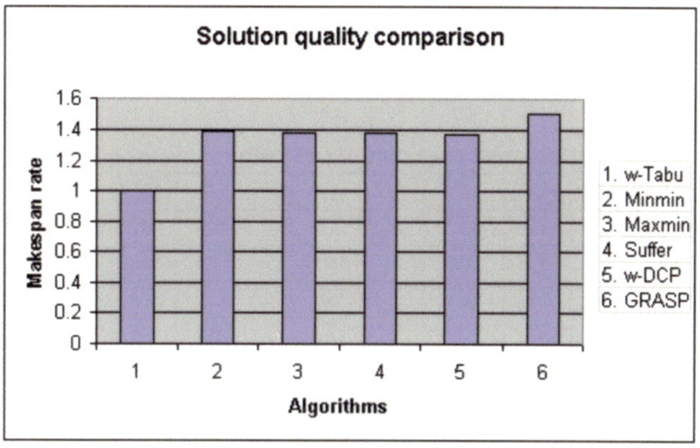

Fig. 12. Overall performance comparison among w-Tabu and other algorithms
Quan (2007)

The experiment result in Figure 12 shows that the w-Tabu algorithm has the highest performance. For that reason, we only need to consider the w-Tabu algorithm in this work. To compare the performance of the w-GA algorithm with other algorithms, we map 18 workflows to RMSs using the w-GA, the w-Tabu, and the n-GA algorithms. Similar to the experiment studying the convergence of the w-GA algorithm, this experiment is also divided into three levels according to the size of the workflow. With the n-GA algorithm, we run it with 1000 generations. With w-GA algorithm, we run it with 120 generations and 1000 generations and thus we have the w-GA1000 algorithm and the w-GA120 algorithm respectively. The purpose of running the w-GA at 1000 generations is for theoretical purpose. We want to see the limit performance of w-GA and n-GA within a long enough period. Thus, with the theoretical aspect, we compare the performance of the w-GA1000, the w-Tabu and the n-GA1000 algorithms. The purpose of running w-GA at 120 generations is for practical purposes. We want to compare the performance of the w-Tabu algorithm and the w-GA algorithm in the same runtime. With each mapping instance, the *makespan* of the solution and the runtime of the algorithm are recorded. The experiment results are presented in Table 5.

In three levels of the experiments, we can see the domination of the w-GA1000 algorithm. In the whole experiment, w-GA1000 found 14 better and 3 worse solutions than did the n-GA1000 algorithm and the w-Tabu algorithm. The overall performance comparison in average relative value is presented in Figure 13. From this Figure, we can see that the w-GA1000 is about 21% better than the w-Tabu and the n-GA1000 algorithms. The data in the Table 5 and Figure 13 also show an equal performance between the w-Tabu and the n-GA1000 algorithms.

	w-GA 1000		w-GA 120		w-Tabu		n.GA 1000	
Sjs	Mksp	Rt	Mksp	Rt	Mksp	Rt	Mksp	Rt
Simple level experiment								
7	52	20	52	2	56	2	67	19
8	55	25	55	3	144	2	67	23
9	64	29	71	3	79	1	79	24
10	56	31	56	4	81	3	94	27
11	65	39	65	4	102	4	160	37
12	88	45	88	5	58	2	62	39
13	52	48	52	5	54	3	65	44
Intermediate level experiment								
14	115	40	149	4	154	3	128	37
15	185	43	185	5	81	4	85	40
16	170	47	180	5	195	3	195	44
17	49	54	49	6	54	4	63	49
18	144	52	207	5	171	5	144	48
19	86	51	87	5	201	5	150	47
20	151	60	151	6	193	4	205	57
Advance level experiment								
21	37	74	37	8	37	7	47	70
25	204	59	262	6	195	8	195	55
28	76	108	229	11	86	7	105	105
32	205	111	250	12	250	10	239	106

Table 5. Performance comparison among w-GA and other algorithms

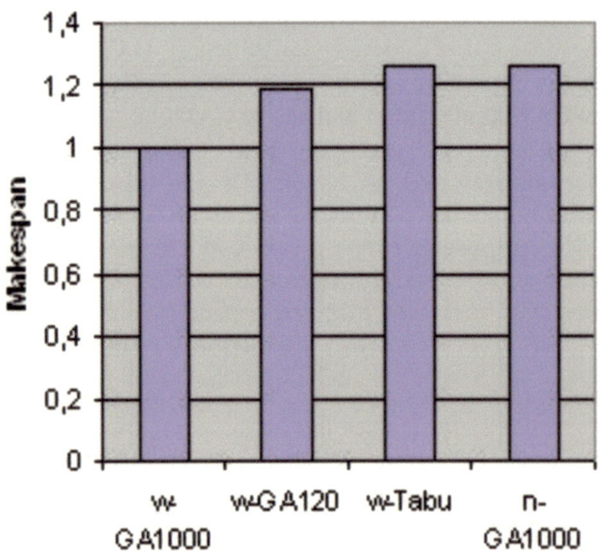

Fig. 13. Overall performance comparison among w-GA and other algorithms

With the runtime aspect, the runtime of the w-GA1000 algorithm is slightly greater than the n-GA1000 algorithm because the w-GA is more complicated than the n-GA. However, the runtime of both the w-GA1000 and the n-GA1000 are much, much longer when compare to the runtime of w-Tabu algorithm. On average, the runtime of the w-GA1000 and the n-GA1000 are 10 times longer than the runtime of the w-Tabu algorithm.

The long runtime of the w-GA1000 and the n-GA1000 is the great disadvantage for them to be employed in the real environment. In practice, thought, the broker scheduling a workflow for 1 or 2 minutes is not acceptable. As the w-Tabu algorithm needs only from 1 to 10 seconds, we run the w-GA algorithm at 120 generations so it has relatively the same runtime as w-Tabu algorithm. As the n-GA algorithm does not have a good performance even at 1000 generations, we will not consider it within the practical framework. In particular, we focus on comparing the performance of the w-GA120 and the w-Tabu algorithm.

From the data in Table 5, we see a trend that the w-GA120 decreases its performance compared to the w-Tabu when the size of the workflow increases.

At the simple level and intermediate level of the experiment, the quality of the w-GA120 is better than the quality of the w-Tabu algorithm. The w-GA algorithm found 3 worse solutions and 11 better solutions than the w-Tabu algorithm.

However, at the advance level experiment, the quality of the w-GA120 is not acceptable. Apart from one equal solution, the w-GA120 found more worse solutions than the w-Tabu algorithm. This is because of the large search space. With a small number of generations, the w-GA cannot find high quality solutions.

6. The combined algorithm

From the experiment results of the w-GA120 and w-Tabu algorithms, we have noted the following observations.

- The w-Tabu algorithm has runtime from 1 to 10 seconds and this range is generally acceptable. Thus, the mapping algorithm could make use of the maximum value of allowed time period, i.e 10 seconds in this case, to find the highest possible quality solution.
- Both the w-GA and the w-Tabu found solutions with great differing quality in some cases. This means in some case the w-GA found a very high quality solution but the w-Tabu found very low quality solutions and vice versa.
- When the size of the workflow is very big and the runtime of the w-GA and the w-Tabu to find out solution also reaches the limit, the quality of the w-GA120 is not as good as the w-Tabu algorithm.

From these observations, we propose an other algorithm combining the w-GA120 and the w-Tabu algorithm. The new algorithm called w-TG is presented in Algorithm 6.

From the experiment data in Table 5, the runtime of the w-TG algorithm is from 4 to 10 seconds. We run the w-GA with 120 generations in all cases for two reasons.

- If the size of the workflow is large, increasing the number of generations will significantly increase the runtime of the algorithm. Thus, this runtime may exceed the acceptable range.

Algorithm 6 w-TG algorithm

if the size of the workflow <= 20 **then**
    Call w-GA120 to find solution a1
    Call w-Tabu to find solution a2
    $a'' \leftarrow better(a1, a2)$
else
    Call w-Tabu to find solution a''
end if
return a''

- If the size of the workflow is small, the algorithm has high probability of convergence within a small number of generations. The data in Table 4 also supports this idea.

To examine the performance of the w-TG algorithm, we do an extensive experiment in order to make a comparison with the w-GA and the w-Tabu algorithm. For this experiment, we keep the topology of 18 workflows as in the experiment in Section 4 but change the configuration of sub-jobs in each workflow. With each topology we created 5 different workflows. Thus, we have a total 90 different workflows.

Those workflows are mapped to the RMSs using the w-GA, the w-Tabu and the w-TG algorithms. The *makespan* of the solution and the runtime of the algorithm are then recorded. From the experiment data, the runtime of all algorithms is from 1 to 12 seconds. The average performance of each algorithm is presented in Figure 14 and Figure 15.

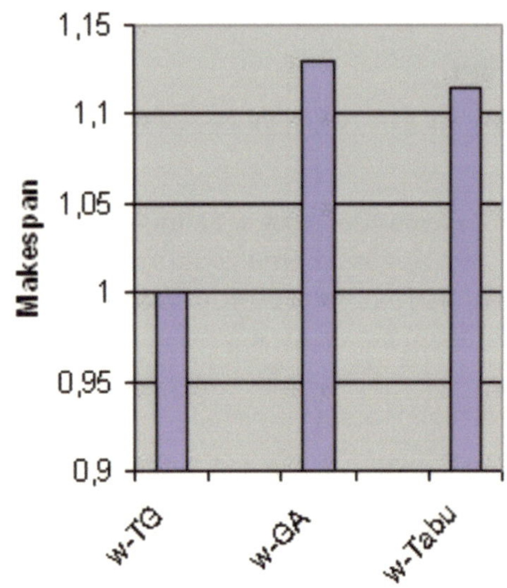

Fig. 14. Performance comparison when the size of each workflow less than or equal to 20

Figure 14 presents the comparison of the average *makespan* in relative value when all the workflows in the experiment have the number of sub-job less than or equal to 20. We want to see the performance of the equal combination part of the w-TG algorithm. As can be seen from Figure 14, the w-TG algorithm has the highest performance. The w-TG algorithm found solutions 11% better than the w-Tabu algorithm and 12% better than the w-GA120 algorithm.

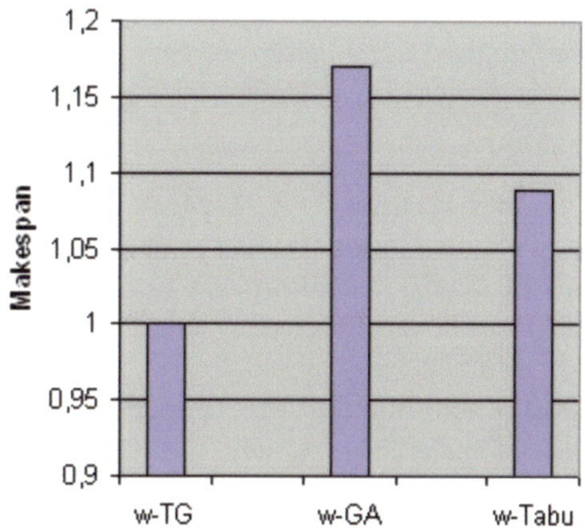

Fig. 15. Performance comparison when the size of each workflow less than or equal to 32

We make the average comparison with all 90 workflows, and the overall result of this is presented in Figure 15. As with the workflow having the number of sub-jobs more than 20, the quality of the w-TG algorithm is equal to the quality of the w-Tabu algorithm. Thus the better rate of the w-TG compared to the w-Tabu is reduced by about 9%. In contrast, as the quality of the w-GA algorithm is not as good with a workflow having the number of sub-jobs more than 20. Thus the worse rate of the w-GA algorithm compared to the w-TG algorithm is an increase to 17%.

We can also see that the performance of the w-GA120 compared to the w-Tabu in this experiment is not as high as in the experiment of Section 5.2. This means that the performance of the w-GA120 fluctuates with different scenarios. However, in any case, the combined algorithm still has good performance.

7. Conclusion

In this book chapter we presented the modified Genetic Algorithm and its combination with the w-Tabu algorithm to form a new algorithm called w-TG to solve the problem of optimizing runtime of the Grid-based workflows within the SLA context. In our work, the distinguishing characteristic is that each sub-job of a workflow can be either a sequential or parallel program. In addition, each grid service can handle many sub-jobs at a time and its resources are reserved. The w-Tabu algorithm creates a set of referent solutions, which distribute widely over the search space, and then searches around those points to find the local minimal solution. We proposed a special genetic algorithm to map workflow to the Grid resources called w-GA. In the w-GA algorithm, we applied many dedicated techniques for workflow within the crossover and mutation operations in order to improve the searching quality. The experiment showed that both the w-GA and the w-Tabu found solutions with great differing quality in some cases. When the size of the workflow is very big and the runtime of the w-GA and the w-Tabu to find out solution also reaches the limit, the quality of the w-GA is not as good as the w-Tabu algorithm. The combined algorithm can fix the disadvantage of the individual algorithms. Our performance evaluation showed that the combined algorithm created solution of equal or better quality than the previous algorithm and requires the same range of computation time period. The latter is a decisive factor for the applicability of the proposed method in real environments.

8. References

Adam, T. L., Chandy, K. M. and Dickson, J. R., 1974, A comparison of list scheduling for parallel processing systems. *Communication of the ACM*, 17, 685-690.

Ayyub, S. and Abramson, D. (2007) 'GridRod - A Service Oriented Dynamic Runtime Scheduler for Grid Workflows'. *Proceedings of the 21st ACM International Conference on Supercomputing*, pp. 43-52.

Berman *et al.* 2005 'New Grid Scheduling and Rescheduling Methods in the GrADS Project', *International Journal of Parallel Programming*, Vol. 33, pp.209-229.

Berriman, G. B., Good, J. C., Laity, A. C. (2003) 'Montage: a Grid Enabled Image Mosaic Service for the National Virtual Observatory', *ADASS*, Vol. 13, pp.145-167.

P. E. Black, "Algorithms and Theory of Computation Handbook", CRC Press LLC, 1999.

Blythe *et al.* 2005 'Task Scheduling Strategies for Workflow-based Applications in Grids', *Proceeding of the IEEE International Symposium on Cluster Computing and the Grid (CCGrid 2005)*, pp.759-767.

Casanova, H., Legrand, A., Zagorodnov, D. and Berman, F. 2000 'Heuristics for Scheduling Parameter Sweep applications in Grid environments', *Proceeding of the 9th HeterogeneousComputing workshop (HCW'2000)*, pp.292–300.

Coffman, E. G., 1976, Computer and Job-Shop Scheduling Theory. John Wiley and Sons, Inc., New York, NY.

Colin, J. Y. and Chretienne, P., 1991, Scheduling with small computation delays and task duplication. *Operation Research*, 39, 680-684.

CondorVersion 6.4.7 Manual. www.cs.wisc.edu/condor/manual/v6.4 [10 December 2004].

Deelman, E., Blythe, J., Gil, Y., Kesselman, C., Mehta, G., Patil, S., Su, M., Vahi, K. and Livny, M. (2004) 'Pegasus : Mapping Scientific Workflows onto the Grid', *Proceedings of the 2nd European Across Grids Conference*, pp.11-20.

Duan, R., Prodan, R., Fahringer, T. (2006) 'Run-time Optimization for Grid Workflow Applications', *Proceedings of the 7th IEEE/ACM International Conference on Grid Computing (Grid'06)*, pp. 33-40.

Elmagarmid, A.K. (1992) *Database Transaction Models for Advanced Applications*, Morgan Kaufmann.

Gary, M. R. and Johnson, D. S., 1979, Computers and Intractability: A Guide to the theory of NP-Completeness. W. H. Freeman and Co.

Georgakopoulos, D., Hornick, M., and Sheth, A. (1995) 'An Overview of Workflow Management: From Process Modeling to Workflow Automation Infrastructure', *Distributed and Parallel Databases*, Vol. 3, No. 2, pp.119-153.

Gerasoulis, A. and Yang, T., 1992, A comparison of clustering heuristics for scheduling DAG's on multiprocessors. *J. Parallel and Distributed Computing*, 16, 276-291.

Hou, E. S. H., Ansari, N., and Ren, H., 1994, A genetic algorithm for multiprocessor scheduling. *IEEE Transactions on Parallel and Distributed Systems*, 5, 113-120.

Hovestadt, M. (2003) 'Scheduling in HPC Resource Management Systems:Queuing vs. Planning', *Proceedings of the 9th Workshop on JSSPP at GGF8*, LNCS, pp.1-20.

Hsu, M. (ed.) (1993) *Special Issue on Workflow and Extended Transaction Systems,* IEEE Data Engineering, Vol. 16, No. 2.

Kohler, W. H. and Steiglitz, K., 1974, Characterization and theoretical comparison of branch-and-bound algorithms for permutation problems. *Journal of ACM,* 21, 140-156.

Kruatrachue, B. and Lewis, T. G., 1987, Duplication Scheduling Heuristics (DSH): A New Precedence Task Scheduler for Parallel Processor Systems. Oregon State University, Corvallis, OR.

Kruatrachue , B., and Lewis, T., 1988, Grain size determination for parallel processing. *IEEE Software,* 5, 23-32.

Kwok Y. K. and Ahmad, I., 1999, Static scheduling algorithms for allocating directed task graphs to multiprocessors. *ACM Computing Surveys (CSUR),* 31, 406-471.

Lovas, R., Dózsa, G., Kacsuk, P., Podhorszki, N., Drótos, D. (2004) 'Workflow Support for Complex Grid Applications: Integrated and Portal Solutions', *Proceedings of 2nd European Across Grids Conference,* pp.129-138.

Ludtke, S., Baldwin, P. and Chiu, W. (1999) 'EMAN: Semiautomated Software for High-Resolution Single-Particle Reconstructio' , *Journal of Structure Biology,* Vol. 128, pp. 146–157.

Ma, T. and Buyya, R. 2005 'Critical-Path and Priority based Algorithms for Scheduling Workflows with Parameter Sweep Tasks on Global Grids', *Proceeding of the 17th International Symposium on Computer Architecture and High Performance Computing (SBAC-PAD 2005), IEEE CS Press,* pp.251-258.

Mello, R. F., Filho J. A. A., Senger, L. J., Yang, L. T. (2007) 'RouteGA: A Grid Load Balancing Algorithm with Genetic Support', *Proceedings of the 21st International Conference on Advanced Networking and Applications, (AINA 2007), IEEE CS Press,* pp.885-892.

Quan, D.M., Kao, O. (2005) 'On Architecture for an SLA-aware Job Flows in Grid Environments', *Journal of Interconnection Networks,* Vol. 6, No. 3, pp.245-264.

Quan, D.M., Hsu, D. F. (2006) 'Network based resource allocation within SLA context', *Proceedings of the GCC2006,* pp. 274-280.

Quan, D.M., Altmann, J. (2007) 'Business Model and the Policy of Mapping Light Communication Grid-Based Workflow Within the SLA Context', *Proceedings of the International Conference of High Performance Computing and Communication (HPCC07),* pp.285-295.

Quan, D.M. (2007) 'Error recovery mechanism for grid-based workflow within SLA context', *Int. J. High Performance Computing and Networking,* Vol. 5, No. 1/2, pp.110-121.

Quan, D.M., Altmann, J. (2007) 'Mapping of SLA-based Workflows with light Communication onto Grid Resources', *Proceedings of the 4th International Conference on Grid Service Engineering and Management (GSEM 2007),* pp.135-145

Quan, D.M., Altmann, J. (2007) 'Mapping a group of jobs in the error recovery of the Grid-based workflow within SLA context', *Proceedings of the 21st International Conference on Advanced Networking and Applications, (AINA 2007), IEEE CS Press,* pp.986-993.

Rewini , H. E. and Lewis, T. G., 1990, Scheduling parallel program tasks onto arbitrary target machines. *Journal of Parallel and Distributed Computing,* 9, 138-153.

Shahid, A., Muhammed, S. T. and Sadiq, M., 1994, GSA: scheduling and allocation using genetic algorithm. Paper presented at the Conference on European Design Automation, Paris, France, 19-23 September.

Sahai, A., Graupner, S., Machiraju, V. and Moorsel, A. 2003 'Specifying and Monitoring Guarantees in Commercial Grids through SLA', *Proceeding of the 3rd IEEE/ACM CCGrid2003*, pp.292–300.

Sarkar, V., 1989, Partitioning and Scheduling Parallel Programs for Multiprocessors. MIT Press, Cambridge, MA.

Sih, G. C., and Lee, E. A., 1993, Declustering: a new multiprocessor scheduling technique. *IEEE Transactions on Parallel and Distributed Systems*, 4, 625-637.

Singh, M. P. and Vouk, M. A. (1997) *Scientific Workflows: Scientific Computing Meets Transactional Workflows*, http://www.csc.ncsu.edu/faculty/mpsingh/papers/databases/workflows/sciworkflows.html

Spooner, D. P., Jarvis, S. A., Cao, J., Saini, S. and Nudd, G. R. (2003) 'Local Grid Scheduling Techniques Using Performance Prediction', IEEE Proceedings - Computers and Digital Techniques, pp.87–96.

Yu, J., Buyya R. (2005) 'A taxonomy of scientific workflow systems for grid computing', *SIGMOD Record*, Vol. 34, No. 3, pp.44-49.

Fischer, L. *Workflow Handbook 2004*, Future Strategies Inc., Lighthouse Point, FL, USA.

Wolski, R. (2003) 'Experiences with Predicting Resource Performance On-line in Computational Grid Settings', *ACM SIGMETRICS Performance Evaluation Review*, Vol. 30, No. 4, pp.41-49.

2

On the Effect of Applying the Task Clustering for Identical Processor Utilization to Heterogeneous Systems

Hidehiro Kanemitsu[1], Gilhyon Lee[1], Hidenori Nakazato[2], Takashige Hoshiai[2] and Yoshiyori Urano[2]
[1]*Graduate School of Global Information and Telecommunication Studies, Waseda University*
[2]*Global Information and Telecommunication Institute, Waseda University*
Japan

1. Introduction

Actual task execution models over the networked processors, e.g., cluster, grid and utility computing have been studied and developed for maximizing the system throughput by utilizing computational resources. One of major trends in task execution types is to divide the required data into several pieces and then distribute them to workers like "master-worker model". In contrast to such a data intensive job, how to divide a computational intensive job into several execution units for parallel execution is under discussion from theoretical points of view. If we take task parallelization into account in a grid environment such as a computational grid environment, an effective task scheduling strategy should be established. In the light of combining task scheduling concepts and grid computing methodologies, heterogeneity with respect to processing power, communication bandwidth and so on should be incorporated into a task scheduling strategy. If we assume the situation where multiple jobs are being submitted in the unknown number of computational resources over the Internet, objective functions can be considered as follows: (i) Minimization of the schedule length (the time duration from per each job, (ii) Minimization of the completion time of the last job, (iii) Maxmization of the degree of contribution to the total speed up ratio for each computational resources. As one solution for those three objective functions, in the literature(Kanemitsu, 2010) we proposed a method for minimizing the schedule length per one job with a small number of computational resources (processors) for a set of identical processors. The objective of the method is "utilization of computational resources". The method is based on "task clustering" (A. Gerasoulis, 1992), in which tasks are merged into one "cluster" as an execution unit for one processor. As a result, several clusters are generated and then each of which becomes one assignment unit. The method proposes to impose the lower bound for every cluster size to limit the number of processors. Then the literature theoretically showed the near-optimal lower bound to minimize the schedule length.

However, which processor should be assigned to a cluster is not discussed because the proposal assumes identical processors. If we use one of conventional cluster assignment methods such as CHP(C. Boeres, 2004), triplet(B. Cirou, 2001), and FCS(S. Chingchit, 1999), almost all processors may be assigned to clusters because they try to achieve the maximum task parallelism to obtain the minimized schedule length. Thus, the third objective function may not be achieved by those cluster assignment strategies.

In this chapter, we propose a method for deriving the lower bound of the cluster size in heterogeneous distributed systems and a task clustering algorithm. From results of experimental simulations, we discuss the applicability of the proposal to obtain better processor utilization.

The remainder of this chapter is organized as follows. Sec. 2 presents other conventional approaches related to task clustering for heterogeneous distributed systems, and sec. 3 presents our assumed model, then the lower bound of the cluster size is derived in sec. 4. Sec. 5 presents a task clustering algorithm which adopts the lower bound shown in sec. 4. Experimental results are shown in sec. 6, and finally we present conclusion and future works in sec. 7.

2. Related works

In a distributed environment, where each processor is completely connected, task clustering(A. Gerasoulis, 1992; T. Yang, 1994; J. C. Liou, 1996) has been known as one of task scheduling methods. In a task clustering, two or more tasks are merged into one cluster by which communication among them is localized, so that each cluster becomes one assignment unit to a processor. As a result, the number of clusters becomes that of required processors. On the other hand, if we try to perform a task clustering in a heterogeneous distributed system, the objective is to find an optimal processor assignment, i.e., which processor should be assigned to the cluster generated by a task clustering. Furthermore, since the processing time and the data communication time depend on each assigned processor's performance, each cluster should be generated with taking that issue into account. As related works for task clustering in heterogeneous distributed systems, CHP(C. Boeres, 2004), Triplet(B. Cirou, 2001), and FCS(S. Chingchit, 1999) have been known.

CHP(C. Boeres, 2004) firstly assumes that "virtual identical processors", whose processing speed is the minimum among the given set of processors. Then CHP performs task clustering to generate a set of clusters. In the processor assignment phase, the cluster which can be scheduled in earliest time is selected, while the processor which has possibility to make the cluster's completion time earliest among other processors is selected. Then the cluster is assigned to the selected processor. Such a procedure is iterated until every cluster is assigned to a processor. In CHP algorithm, an unassigned processor can be selected as a next assignment target because it has no waiting time. Thus, each cluster is assigned to different processor, so that many processors are required for execution and therefore CHP can not lead to the processor utilization.

In Triplet algorithm(B. Cirou, 2001), task groups, each of which consists of three tasks, named as "triplet" according to data size to be transferred among tasks and out degree of each task. Then a cluster is generated by merging two triplets according to its execution time and data transfer time on the fastest processor and the slowest processor. On the other hand, each processor is grouped as a function of its processing speed and communication bandwidth, so that several processor groups are generated. As a final stage, each cluster is assigned to a processor groups according to the processor group's load. The processor assignment policy in

Triplet is that one cluster is assigned a processor groups composed of two or more processors. Thus, such a policy does not match with the concept of processor utilization.

In FCS algorithm(S. Chingchit, 1999), it defines two parameters, i.e., β: total task size to total data size ratio (where task size means that the time unit required to execute one instruction) for each cluster and τ: processing speed to communication bandwidth ratio for each processor. During task merging steps are performed, if β of a cluster exceeds τ of a processor, the cluster is assigned to the processor. As a result, the number of clusters depends on each processor's speed and communication bandwidth. Thus, there is one possibility that "very small cluster" is generated and then FCS can not match with the concept of processor utilization.

3. Assumed model

3.1 Job model

We assume a job to be executed among distributed processor elements (PEs) is a Directed Acyclic Graph (DAG), which is one of task graphs. Let $G^s_{cls} = (V_s, E_s, V^s_{cls})$ be the DAG, where s is the number of task merging steps(described in sec. 3.2), V_s is the set of tasks after s task merging steps, E_s is the set of edges (data communications among tasks) after s task merging steps, and V^s_{cls} is the set of clusters which consists of one or more tasks after s task merging steps. An i-th task is denoted as n^s_i. Let $w(n^s_i)$ be a size of n^s_i, i.e., $w(n^s_i)$ is the sum of unit times taken for being processed by the reference processor element. We define data dependency and direction of data transfer from n^s_i to n^s_j as $e^s_{i,j}$. And $c(e^s_{i,j})$ is the sum of unit times taken for transferring data from n^s_i to n^s_j over the reference communication link.

One constraint imposed by a DAG is that a task can not be started execution until all data from its predecessor tasks arrive. For instance, $e^s_{i,j}$ means that n^s_j can not be started until data from n^s_i arrives at the processor which will execute n^s_j. And let $pred(n^s_i)$ be the set of immediate predecessors of n^s_i, and $suc(n^s_i)$ be the set of immediate successors of n^s_i. If $pred(n^s_i) = \emptyset$, n^s_i is called START task, and if $suc(n^s_i) = \emptyset$, n^s_i is called END task. If there are one or more paths from n^s_i to n^s_j, we denote such a relation as $n^s_i \prec n^s_j$.

3.2 Task clustering

We denote the i-th cluster in V^s_{cls} as $cls_s(i)$. If n^s_k is included in $cls_s(i)$ by "the $s+1$ th task merging", we formulate one task merging as $cls_{s+1}(i) \leftarrow cls_s(i) \cup \{n^s_k\}$. If any two tasks, i.e., n^s_i and n^s_j, are included in the same cluster, they are assigned to the same processor. Then the communication between n^s_i and n^s_j is localized, so that we define $c(e^s_{i,j})$ becomes zero. Task clustering is a set of task merging steps, that is finished when certain criteria have been satisfied.

Throughout this chapter, we denote that $cls_s(i)$ is "linear" if and only if $cls_s(i)$ contains no independent task(A. Gerasoulis, 1993). Note that if one cluster is linear, at least one path among any two tasks in the cluster exists and task execution order is unique.

3.3 System model

We assume that each PE is completly connected to other PEs, with non-identical processing speeds and communication bandwidths The set of PEs is expressed as $P = \{P_1, P_2, \ldots, P_m\}$,

Parameter	Definition
$top_s(i)$	$\{n_k^s \mid \forall n_l^s \in pred(n_k^s) s.t., n_l^s \notin cls_s(i)\} \cup \{START\ Tasks \in cls_s(i)\}.$
$in_s(i)$	$\{n_k^s \mid \exists n_l^s \in pred(n_k^s) s.t., n_l^s \notin cls_s(i)\} \cup \{START\ Tasks \in cls_s(i)\}.$
$out_s(i)$	$\{n_k^s \mid \exists n_l^s \in suc(n_k^s) s.t., n_l^s \notin cls_s(i)\} \cup \{END\ Tasks \in cls_s(i)\}.$
$btm_s(i)$	$\{n_k^s \mid \forall n_l^s \in suc(n_k^s), s.t., n_l^s \notin cls_s(i)\} \cup \{END\ Tasks \in cls_s(i)\}.$
$desc(n_k^s, i)$	$\{n_l^s \mid n_k^s \prec n_l^s, n_l^s \in cls_s(i)\} \cup \{n_k^s\}$
$S(n_k^s, i)$	$\sum_{n_l^s \in cls_s(i)} t_p(n_l^s, \alpha_p) - \sum_{n_l^s \in desc(n_k^s, i)} t_p(n_l^s, \alpha_p)$
$tlevel(n_k^s)$	$\begin{cases} \max\limits_{n_l^s \in pred(n_k^s)} \{tlevel(n_l^s) + t_p(n_l^s, \alpha_p) + t_c(e_{l,k}, \beta_{q,p})\}, \ if\ n_k^s \in top_s(i). \\ TL_s(i) + S(n_k^s, i),\ otherwise. \end{cases}$
$TL_s(i)$	$\max\limits_{n_k^s \in top_s(i)} \{tlevel(n_k^s)\}$
$blevel(n_k^s)$	$\max\limits_{n_l^s \in suc(n_k^s)} \{t_p(n_k^s, \alpha_p) + t_c(e_{k,l}^s, \beta_{p,q}) + blevel(n_l^s)\}$
$level(n_k^s)$	$tlevel(n_k^s) + blevel(n_k^s)$
$BL_s(i)$	$\max\limits_{n_k^s \in out_s(i)} \{S(n_k^s, i) + blevel(n_k^s)\}$
$LV_s(i)$	$TL_s(i) + BL_s(i) = \max\limits_{n_k^s \in cls_s(i)} \{level(n_k^s)\}$
ϕ_s	$\{\ldots, < cls_s(i), P_p >, \ldots\}$
$sl_w(G_{cls}^s, \phi_s)$	$\max\limits_{cls_s(i) \in V_{cls}^s} \{LV_s(i)\}$

Table 1. Parameter Definition Related to $sl_w(G_{cls}^s)$ (Here $n_k^s \in cls_s(i)$).

and let the set of processing speeds as $alpha$, i.e., $\alpha = \{\alpha_1, \alpha_2, \ldots, \alpha_m\}$. Let the set of communication bandwidths as β, i.e.,

$$\beta = \begin{pmatrix} \infty & \beta_{1,2} & \beta_{1,3} & \cdots & \beta_{1,m} \\ \beta_{2,1} & \infty & \beta_{2,3} & \cdots & \beta_{2,m} \\ \beta_{3,1} & \beta_{3,2} & \infty & \cdots & \beta_{3,m} \\ \vdots & \vdots & \vdots & \vdots & \vdots \\ \beta_{m,1} & \beta_{m,2} & \beta_{m,3} & \cdots & \infty \end{pmatrix}. \quad (1)$$

$\beta_{i,j}$ means the communication bandwidth from P_i to P_j. The processing time in the case that n_k^s is processed on P_i is expressed as $t_p(n_k^s, \alpha_i) = w(n_k^s)/\alpha_i$. The data transfer time of $e_{k,l}^s$ over $\beta_{i,j}$ is $t_c(e_{i,j}^s, \beta_{k,l}) = c(e_{i,j}^s)/\beta_{k,l}$. This means that both processing time and data transfer time are not changed with time, and suppose that data transfer time within one PE is negligible.

4. Processor utilization

4.1 The indicative value for the schedule length

The schedule length depends on many factors, i.e., execution time for each task, communication time for each data exchanged among tasks, execution order after the task scheduling, processing speed, and communication bandwidth. Furthermore, whether a data transfer time can be localized or not depends on the cluster structure. The proposed method is that a cluster is generated after the lower bound of the cluster size (the total execution time of every task included in the cluster) has been derived. The lower bound is decided when the indicative value for the schedule length is minimized. In this chapter, the indicative value is defined as $sl_w(G^s_{cls}, \phi_s)$, that means the indicative value for the schedule length after s task merging steps and ϕ_s is the set of mapping between PEs and clusters after s task merging steps. $sl_w(G^s_{cls}, \phi_s)$ is the maximum value of the execution path length which includes both task execution time and data transfer time, provided that each task is scheduled as late as possible and every data from its immediate predecessors has been arrived before the scheduled time (its start time). Table 1 shows notations and definitions for deriving $sl_w(G^s_{cls}, \phi_s)$. In the table, assigned PEs for $cls_s(i)$ and $cls_s(j)$ are P_p and P_q, respectively. And suppose $n^s_k \in cls_s(i), n^s_l \in cls_s(j)$. In table 1, especially $S(n^s_k, i)$ means the degree of increase of execution time by independent tasks for n^s_k. Threrfore, the smaller $S(n^s_k, i)$, the earlier n^s_k can be scheduled. The task n^s_k which dominates $sl_w(G^s_{cls}, \phi_s)$ (In the case of $sl_w(G^s_{cls}, \phi_s) = level(n^s_k)$) means that the schedule length may be maximized if n^s_k is scheduled as late as possible.

Example 1. *Fig. 1 shows one example for deriving $sl_w(G^s_{cls}, \phi_s)(s = 5)$. In the figure, there are two PEs, i.e., P_1 and P_2. The DAG has two clusters, i.e., $cls_5(1)$ and $cls_5(4)$ after 5 task merging steps. In (a), numerical values on tasks and edges mean the time unit to be processed on the reference PE and the time unit to be transferred among reference PEs on the reference communication bandwidth. On the other hand, (b) corresponds to the state that $cls_5(1)$ and $cls_5(4)$ have been assigned to P_1 and P_2, respectively. The bottom are shows the derivation process for $sl_w(G^5_{cls}, \phi_5)$. From the derivation process, it is shown that the schedule length may be maximized if n^5_2 is scheduled as late as possible.*

4.2 Relationship between $sl_w(G^s_{cls}, \phi_s)$ and the schedule length

Our objective is to minimize $sl_w(G^s_{cls}, \phi_s)$ with maintaining the certain size of each cluster for processor utilization. The schedule length can not be known before scheduling every task, we must estimate it by using $sl_w(G^s_{cls}, \phi_s)$. Thus, it must be proved that $sl_w(G^s_{cls}, \phi_s)$ can effect on the schedule length. In this section, we show that minimizing $sl_w(G^s_{cls}, \phi_s)$ leads to minimizing the schedule length to some extent. In this section we present that relationship between Table 2 shows notations for showing characteristics of $sl_w(G^s_{cls}, \phi_s)$. In an identical processor system, provided that every processor speed and communication bandwidth are 1, no processor assignment policy is needed. Thus, let $sl_w(G^s_{cls}, \phi_s)$ in an identical processor system as $sl_w(G^s_{cls})$. In the literature (Kanemitsu, 2010), it is proved that minimizing $sl_w(G^s_{cls})$ leads to minimizing the lower bound of the schedule length as follows.

Lemma 1. *In an identical processor system, let $\Delta sl^{s-1}_{w,up}$ which satisfies $sl_w(G^s_{cls}) - cp \leq \Delta sl^{s-1}_{w,up}$ and be derived before s task merging steps. Then we obtain*

$$sl(G^s_{cls}) \geq \frac{sl_w(G^s_{cls}) - \Delta sl^{s-1}_{w,up}}{1 + \frac{1}{g_{min}}}, \tag{2}$$

where cp and g_{min} are defined in table 2, and $sl(G^s_{cls})$ is the schedule length after s task merging steps. ■

As for $\Delta sl^{s-1}_{w,up}$, it is defined in the literature (Kanemitsu, 2010). Furthermore, it can be proved that the upper bound of the schedule length can be reduced by reducing $sl_w(G^s_{cls})$ by the following lemma.

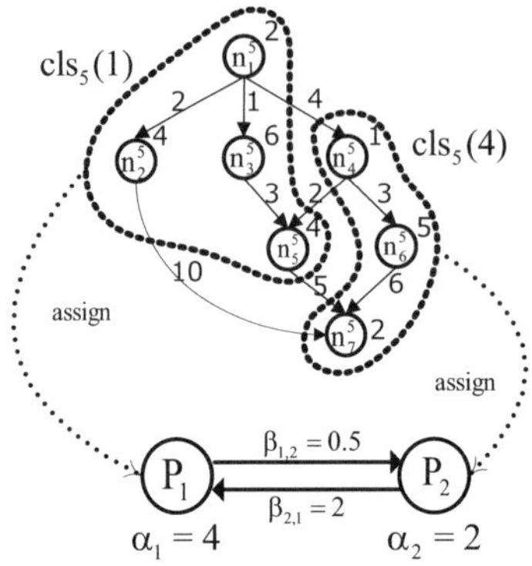

(a) After 5 tesk merging steps have been done.

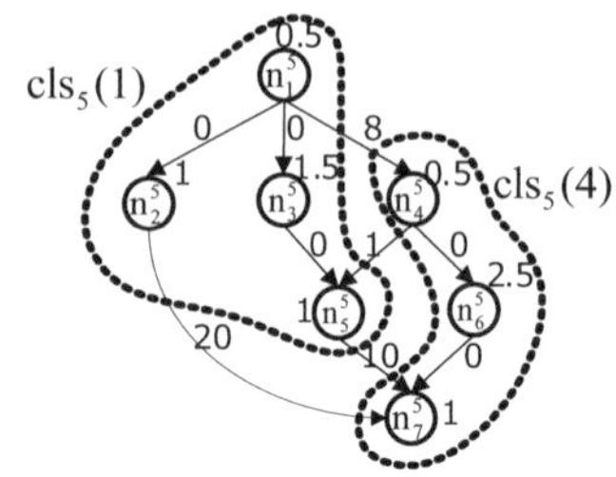

(b) After processor assignments have been done.

$top_5(1)=\{n_1^5\}, top_5(4)=\{n_4^5\},$

$in_5(1)=\{n_1^5,n_5^5\}, in_5(4)=\{n_4^5,n_7^5\}$

$out_5(1)=\{n_1^5,n_2^5,n_5^5\}, out_5(4)=\{n_4^5,n_7^5\}$

$btm_5(1)=\{n_2^5,n_5^5\}, btm_5(4)=\{n_7^5\}$

------ $cls_5(1)$ section------

$TL_5(1)=tlevel(n_1^5)=0,$

$tlevel(n_2^5)=TL_5(1)+S(n_2^5,1)=0+t_p(n_1^5,\alpha_1)+t_p(n_3^5,\alpha_1)+t_p(n_5^5,\alpha_1)=3,$

$blevel(n_2^5)=t_p(n_2^5)+t_c(e_{2,7}^5,\beta_{1,2})+blevel(n_7^5)=1+20+1=22,$

$level(n_2^5)=25,$

$tlevel(n_3^5)=TL_5(1)+S(n_3^5,1)=0+t_p(n_1^5)+t_p(n_2^5)=0.5+1=1.5,$

$blevel(n_3^5)=t_p(n_3^5)+t_c(e_{3,5}^5,\beta_{1,2})+blevel(n_5^5)=1.5+0+1+10+1=13.5,$

$level(n_3^5)=15,$

$S(n_1^5,1)=0,$

$$blevel(n_1^5)=t_p(n_1^5)+\max\{blevel(n_2^5),blevel(n_3^5),t_c(e_{1,4}^5,\beta_{1,2})+blevel(n_4^5)\}$$
$$=0.5+\max\{22,13.5,8+13.5\}=22.5=level(n_1^5),$$

$tlevel(n_5^5)=TL_5(1)+S(n_5^5,1)=0+t_p(n_1^5)+t_p(n_2^5)+t_p(n_3^5)=3,$

$blevel(n_5^5)=4+5+2=12,$

$level(n_5^5)=15,$

$$BL_5(1)=\max_{n_k^5\in out_5(1)}\{S(n_k^5,1)+blevel(n_k^5)\}$$
$$=S(n_2^5,1)+blevel(n_2^5)=25,$$

$LV_5(1)=TL_5(1)+BL_5(1)=level(n_2^5)=25.$

------ $cls_5(1)$ section END------

------ $cls_5(4)$ section------

$TL_5(4)=tlevel(n_4)=0.5+8=8.5,$

$tlevel(n_6)=TL_5(4)+t_p(n_4^5)=8.5+0.5=9,$

$$blevel(n_4^5)=t_p(n_4^5)+\max\{1+blevel(n_5^5),blevel(n_6^5)\}$$
$$=0.5+\max\{1+12,3.5\}=13.5$$

$level(n_4^5)=22,$

$tlevel(n_7^5)=TL_5(4)+t_p(n_4^5)+t_p(n_6^5)=8.5+0.5+2.5=11.5,$

$blevel(n_7^5)=1,$

$level(n_7^5)=12.5,$

$$BL_5(4)=\max_{n_k^5\in out_5(4)}\{S(n_k^5,4)+blevel(n_k^5)\}$$
$$=S(n_4^5,4)+blevel(n_4^5)=0+13.5=13.5,$$

$LV_5(4)=TL_5(4)+BL_5(4)=level(n_4^5)=8.5+13.5=22.$

------ $cls_5(4)$ section END------

$sl_w(G_{cls}^5,\phi)=\max\{LV_5(1),LV_5(4)\}=LV_5(1)=level(n_2^5)=25.$

Fig. 1. Example of $sl_w(G_{cls}^5, \phi_5)$ derivation.

Lemma 2. *In an identical processor system, if* $sl(G_{cls}^S) \leq cp$, *then we obtain*

$$sl(G_{cls}^S) \leq sl_w(G_{cls}^S) + \max_{p \in G_{cls}^0} \left\{ \sum_{\substack{n_k^0, n_l^0 \in p, \\ n_k^0 \in pred(n_l^0)}} c(e_{k,l}^0) \right\}. \blacksquare \tag{3}$$

Proof. In $seq_s^{\prec}$, some edges are localized and others may be not localized. Furthermore, edges in $seq_s^{\prec}$ do not always belong to the critical path. Then we have the following relationship.

$$-\max_{p\in G_{cls}^{0}}\left\{\sum_{\substack{n_k^0,n_l^0\in p,\\ n_k^0\in pred(n_l^0)}} c(e_{k,l}^0)\right\} \leq sl_w(G_{cls}^S) - cp. \tag{4}$$

Also, only in the case of $sl(G_{cls}^S) \leq cp$, we have the following rlationship.

$$\begin{aligned}
& sl_w(G_{cls}^S) - cp \leq sl_w(G_{cls}^S) - sl(G_{cls}^S) \\
\Leftrightarrow & -\max_{p\in G_{cls}^{0}}\left\{\sum_{\substack{n_k^0,n_l^0\in p,\\ n_k^0\in pred(n_l^0)}} c(e_{k,l}^0)\right\} \leq sl_w(G_{cls}^S) - sl(G_{cls}^S) \\
\Leftrightarrow & \; sl(G_{cls}^S) \leq sl_w(G_{cls}^S) + \max_{p\in G_{cls}^{0}}\left\{\sum_{\substack{n_k^0,n_l^0\in p,\\ n_k^0\in pred(n_l^0)}} c(e_{k,l}^0)\right\}.
\end{aligned} \tag{5}$$

□

From lemma 1 and 2, it is concluded that in an identical processor system the schedule length can be minimized if $sl_w(G_{cls})$ is minimized.

As a next step, we show the relationship between $sl_w(G_{cls}^s, \phi_s)$ and the schedule length in a heterogeneous distributed system. The following lemma is proved in the literature (Sinnen, 2007).

Lemma 3. In an identical processor system, we have

$$cp_w \leq sl(G_{cls}^s).\blacksquare \tag{6}$$

In a heterogeneous distributed system, we assume the state like fig. 2, i.e., at the initial state every task is assigned a processor with the fastest and the widest communication bandwidth (let the processor as P_{max}). In fig. 2 (a), each task belongs to respective processor. Furthermore, we virtually assign P_{max} to each task to decide the processing time for each task and the data transfer time among any two tasks. Let the mapping as ϕ_0. Under the situation, we have the following corollary.

Corollary 1. *In a heterogeneous distributed system, let $cp_w(\phi_0)$ as the one with the mapping ϕ_0 in the table 2. Then we have*

$$cp_w(\phi_0) \leq sl(G_{cls}^s, \phi_s).\blacksquare \tag{7}$$

As for the relationship between cp and cp_w, in the literature (Sinnen, 2007), the following is proved.

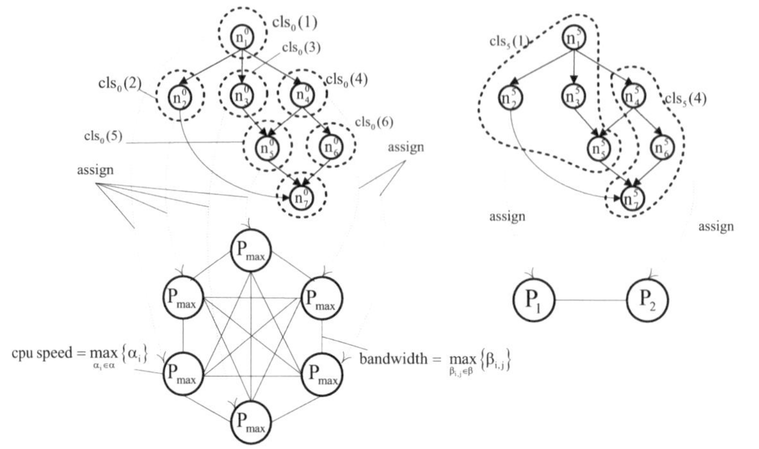

(a) Initial state (DAG : G^0_{cls}, Assignment : ϕ_0). (b) The state after task clustering (DAG : G^s_{cls}, Assignment : ϕ_s).

Fig. 2. Assumed condition during cluster generation procedures.

Parameter	Definition
p	One path of G^0_{cls}, i.e., $\{n^0_0, n^0_1, n^0_2, \ldots, n^0_k\} \cup \{e^0_{0,1}, e^0_{1,2}, \ldots e^0_{k-1,k}\}$, by which a sequence $< n^0_0, n^0_1, n^0_2, \ldots, n^0_k >$ is constructed, where $e^0_{l-1,l} \in E_0$, n^0_0 is a START task and n^0_k is an END task.
$seq^{\prec}_s$	One path in which every task belongs to seq_s.
$seq^{\prec}_s(i)$	Set of subpaths in each of which every task in $cls_s(i)$ belongs to $seq^{\prec}_s$.
$proc(n^s_k)$	The processor to which n^s_k has been assigned.
cp	$\max\limits_{p}\left\{\sum\limits_{n^0_k \in p} w(n^s_k) + \sum\limits_{e^0_{k,l} \in p} c(e^s_{k,l})\right\}.$
$cp(\phi_s)$	$\max\limits_{p}\left\{\sum\limits_{n^s_k \in p} t_p(n^s_k, \alpha_p) + \sum\limits_{e^s_{k,l} \in p} t_c(c(e^s_{k,l}), \beta_{p,q})\right\}$, where n^s_k, n^s_l are assigned to P_p, P_q.
cp_w	$\max\limits_{p \in G^0_{cls}}\left\{\sum\limits_{n^0_k \in p} w(n^0_k)\right\}.$
$cp_w(\phi_s)$	$\max\limits_{p \in G^s_{cls}}\left\{\sum\limits_{n^s_k \in p} t_p(n^s_k, \alpha_p)\right\}$
$g_{\min}$	$\min\limits_{n^0_k \in V^0_{cls}}\left\{\dfrac{\min\limits_{n^0_j \in pred(n^0_k)}\{w(n^0_j)\}}{\max\limits_{n^0_j \in pred(n^0_k)}\{c(e^0_{j,k})\}}, \dfrac{\min\limits_{n^0_l \in suc(n^0_k)}\{w(n^0_l)\}}{\max\limits_{n^0_l \in suc(n^0_k)}\{c(e^0_{k,l})\}}\right\}.$
$g_{\max}$	$\max\limits_{n^0_k \in V^0_{cls}}\left\{\dfrac{\max\limits_{n^0_j \in pred(n^0_k)}\{w(n^0_j)\}}{\min\limits_{n^0_j \in pred(n^0_k)}\{c(e^0_{j,k})\}}, \dfrac{\max\limits_{n^0_l \in suc(n^0_k)}\{w(n^0_l)\}}{\min\limits_{n^0_l \in suc(n^0_k)}\{c(e^0_{k,l})\}}\right\}.$

Table 2. Parameter Definitions which are used in analysis on $sl_w(G^s_{cls}, \phi_s)$.

Lemma 4. *In an identical processor system, by using g_{min} defined in table 2, we have*

$$cp \leq \left(1 + \frac{1}{g_{min}}\right) cp_w. \blacksquare \tag{8}$$

By using lemma 4, in a heterogeneous distributed system, the following is derived.

Corollary 2. *In a heterogeneous distributed system, we have*

$$cp(\phi_s) \leq \left(1 + \frac{1}{g_{min}(\phi_s)}\right) cp_w(\phi_s). \blacksquare \tag{9}$$

From corollary 1, the following is derived.

Corollary 3. *In a heterogeneous distributed system, we have*

$$cp_w(\phi_0) \leq cp_w(\phi_s) \leq sl(G^s_{cls}, \phi_s). \blacksquare \tag{10}$$

From corollary 2 and 3, the following theorem is derived.

Thorem 4.1. *In a heterogeneous distributed system, let the DAG after s task merging steps as G^s_{cls}. And assume every cluster in V^s_{cls} is assigned to a processor in P. Let the schedule length as $sl(G^s_{cls}, \phi_s)$. If we define $\Delta sl^{s-1}_{w,up}$ that satisfies $sl_w(G^s_{cls}, \phi_s) - cp(\phi_0) \leq \Delta sl^{s-1}_{w,up}$, the following relationship is derived.*

$$sl(G^s_{cls}, \phi_s) \geq \frac{sl_w(G^s_{cls}, \phi_s) - \Delta sl^{s-1}_{w,up}}{1 + \frac{1}{g_{min}(\phi_0)}}. \tag{11}$$

Proof. From the assumption and corollary 2, we have

$$sl_w(G^s_{cls}, \phi_s) - \left(1 + \frac{1}{g_{min}(\phi_0)}\right) cp_w(\phi_0) \leq \Delta sl^{s-1}_{w,up}. \tag{12}$$

Also, from corollary 3, we obtain $cp_w(\phi_0) \leq sl(G^s_{cls}, \phi_s)$. Thus if this is applied to (12), we have

$$sl_w(G^s_{cls}, \phi_s) - \left(1 + \frac{1}{g_{min}(\phi_0)}\right) sl(G^s_{cls}, \phi_s) \leq \Delta sl^{s-1}_{w,up} \tag{13}$$

$$\Leftrightarrow \tag{14}$$

$$sl(G^s_{cls}, \phi_s) \geq \frac{sl_w(G^s_{cls}, \phi_s) - \Delta sl^{s-1}_{w,up}}{1 + \frac{1}{g_{min}(\phi_0)}}. \tag{15}$$

□

Assume that $\Delta sl^{s-1}_{w,up}$ is the value which is decided after $s - 1$ task merging steps. Since

$$cp(\phi_0) = sl_w(G^0_{cls}, \phi_0), \tag{16}$$

this value is an upper bound of increase in terms of $sl_w(G^s_{cls}, \phi_s)$ and can be defined in any policy, e.g., the slowest processor is assigned to each cluster and so on. However, at least $\Delta sl^{s-1}_{w,up}$ must be decided before s task merging steps. From the theorem, it can be said that reducing $sl_w(G^s_{cls}, \phi_s)$ leads to reduction of the lower bound of the schedule length in a heterogeneous distributed system.

As for the upper bound of the schedule length, the following theorem is derived.

Thorem 4.2. *In a heterogeneous distributed sytem, if and only if* $sl(G^s_{cls}, \phi_s) \le cp(\phi_0) = sl(G^0_{cls}, \phi_0)$*, we have*

$$sl(G^s_{cls}, \phi_s) \le sl_w(G^s_{cls}, \phi_s) + \zeta - \lambda - \mu, \tag{17}$$

where

$$\zeta = \max_p \left\{ \sum_{\substack{n^0_k, n^0_l \in p, \\ n^0_k \in pred(n^0_l), \\ t_c(e^s_{k,l}, \max_{\beta_{i,j}\in\beta}\{\beta_{i,j}\})=0}} t_c(e^0_{k,l}, \max_{\beta_{i,j}\in\beta}\left\{\beta_{i,j}\right\}) \right\}, \tag{18}$$

$$\lambda = \min_p \left\{ \sum_{\substack{n^0_k \in p, \\ proc(n^s_k)=p_m}} \left(t_p(n^s_k, \alpha_m) - t_p(n^0_k, \max_{\alpha_i \in \alpha}\{\alpha_i\}) \right) \right\}, \tag{19}$$

$$\mu = \min_p \left\{ \sum_{\substack{n^0_k, n^0_l \in p, proc(n^s_k)=P_i, \\ proc(n^s_l)=P_j, \\ n^0_k \in pred(n^0_l)}} \left(t_c(e^s_{k,l}, \beta_{i,j}) - t_c(e^0_{k,l}, \max_{\beta_{i,j}\in\beta}\left\{\beta_{i,j}\right\}) \right) \right\}. \tag{20}$$

p and $proc(n^0_k)$ are defined in table 2. That is, ζ, λ, μ is derived by scanning every path in the DAG.

Proof. After s task merging steps, there may be both localized edges and not localized edges which compose $sl_w(G^s_{cls}, \phi_s)$. Obviously, we have $sl_w(G^0_{cls}, \phi_0) = cp(\phi_0)$, such edges are not always ones which belongs to $cp(\phi_0)$. Therefore the lower bound of $sl_w(G^s_{cls}, \phi_s) - cp(\phi_0)$ can be derived by three factors, i.e., decrease of the data transfer time by localization in one path, increase of the processing time by task merging steps (from ϕ_0 to ϕ_s), and increase of data transfer time for each unlocalized edges (from ϕ_0 to ϕ_s). The localized data transfer time is derived by taking the sum of localized data transfer time for one path. On the other hand, if increase of the processing time is derived by taking the minimum of the sum of increase of task processing time from ϕ_0 to ϕ_s for each path, this value is λ or more. The unlocalized data transfer time is expressed as μ. Then we have

$$-\zeta + \lambda + \mu \le sl_w(G^s_{cls}, \phi_s) - cp(\phi_0). \tag{21}$$

If $sl(G^s_{cls}, \phi_s) \leq cp(\phi_0) = sl(G^0_{cls}, \phi_0)$, we obtain

$$-\zeta + \lambda + \mu \leq sl_w(G^R_{cls}, \phi_R) - sl(G^R_{cls}, \phi_R) \tag{22}$$

$$\Leftrightarrow sl(G^R_{cls}, \phi_R) \leq sl_w(G^R_{cls}, \phi_R) + \zeta - \lambda - \mu. \tag{23}$$

□

Theorem 4.2 is true if we adopt a clustering policy such that $sl(G^s_{cls}, \phi_s) \leq sl(G^{s-1}_{cls}, \phi_{s-1})$. From theorem 4.1 and 4.2, it can be concluded that reducing the $sl_w(G^s_{cls}, \phi_s)$ leads to the reduction of the schedule length in a heterogeneous distributed system. Thus, the first objective of our proposal is to minimize $sl_w(G^s_{cls}, \phi_s)$.

4.3 The lower bound of each cluster size

To achieve processor utilization, satisfying only "$sl_w(G^s_{cls}, \phi_s)$ minimization" not enough, because this value does not guarantee each cluster size. Thus, in this section we present how large each cluster size should be. In the literature (Kanemitsu, 2010), the lower bound of each cluster size in an identical processor system is derived as follows.

$$\delta_{opt} = \sqrt{cp_w \max_{n^0_k \in V_0} \left\{ \frac{\max_{n^0_l \in V^0_{cls}} \{w(n^0_l)\}}{g_{\max}} \right\}}. \tag{24}$$

(24) is the lower bound of each cluster size when $sl_w(G^R_{cls})$ can be minimized, provided that every cluster size is above a certain threshold, δ. And R corresponds to the number of merging steps when every cluster size is δ_{opt} or more. If taking the initial state of the DAG in a heterogeneous system into account, δ_{opt} is expressed by $\delta_{opt}(\phi_0)$ as follows.

$$\delta_{opt}(\phi_0) = \sqrt{cp_w(\phi_0) \max_{n^0_l \in V_0} \left\{ \frac{\max_{n^0_l \in V_0} \left\{ t_p(n^0_l, \max_{\alpha_i \in \alpha} \{\alpha_i\}) \right\}}{g_{\max}(\phi_0)} \right\}}. \tag{25}$$

By imposing $\delta_{opt}(\phi_0)$, it can be said that at least $sl_w(G^0_{cls}, \phi_0)$ can be minimized. However, for $s \geq 1$ $sl_w(G^s_{cls}, \phi_s)$ can not always be minimized by $\delta_{opt}(\phi_0)$, because the mapping of each cluster and each processor is changed and then $sl_w(G^s_{cls}, \phi_s)$ is not equal to $sl_w(G^0_{cls}, \phi_0)$. In this chapter, one heuristic of our method is to impose the same lower bound ($\delta_{opt}(\phi_0)$) for every cluster which will be generated by the task clustering.

5. Task clustering algorithm

5.1 Overview of the algorithm

In the previous section, we presented how large each cluster size should be set for processor utilization. In this section, we present the task clustering algorithm with incorporating the following two requirements.

1. Every cluster size is $\delta_{opt}(\phi_0)$ or more.

2. Minimize $sl_w(G^R_{cls}, \phi_R)$, where R is the total number of merging steps until the first requirement is satisfied.

Fig. 3 shows the task clustering algorithm. At first, the mapping ϕ_0 is applied to every task. Then $\delta_{opt}(\phi_0)$ is derived. Before the main procedures, two sets are defined, i.e., UEX_s and RDY_s. UEX_s is the set of clusters whose size is smaller than $\delta_{opt}(\phi_0)$, and RDY_s is defined as follow.

$$RDY_s = \{cls_s(r) | cls_s(r) \in UEX_s, pred(n^s_{r'}) = \emptyset, cls_s(r) = \{n^s_{r'}\}\} \cup \left\{ \begin{array}{l} cls_s(r) | cls_s(r) \in UEX_s, cls_s(q) \notin UEX_s, \\ n^s_{q'} \in cls_s(q), n^s_{q'} \in pred(n^s_{r'}) \; for \; \forall n^s_{r'} \in top_s(r) \end{array} \right\}. \quad (26)$$

RDY_s is the set of clusters whose preceding cluster sizes are $\delta_{opt}(\phi_0)$ or more. That is, the algorithm tries to merge each cluster in top-to-bottom manner.

The algorithm is proceeded during $UEX_s \neq \emptyset$, which implies that at least one cluster in UEX_s exists. At line 3, one processor is selected by a processor selection method, e.g., by CHP(C. Boeres, 2004) (In this chapter, we do not present processor selection methods). At line 4, one cluster is selected as $pivot_s$, which corresponds to "the first cluster for merging". Once the $pivot_s$ is selected, "the second cluster for merging", i.e., $target_s$ is needed. Thus, during line 5 to 7, procedures for selecting $target_s$ and merging $pivot_s$ and $target_s$ are performed. After those procedures, at line 7 RDY_s is updated to become RDY_{s+1}, and $pivot_s$ is also updated to become $pivot_{s+1}$. Procedures at line 6 and 7 are repeated until the size of $pivot_s$ is $\delta_{opt}(\phi_0)$ or more. The algorithm in fig. 3 has common parts with that of the literature (Kanemitsu, 2010), i.e., both algorithms use $pivot_s$ and $target_s$ for merging two clusters until the size of $pivot_s$ exceeds a lower bound of the cluster size. However, one difference among them is that the algorithm in fig. 3 keeps the same $pivot_s$ during merging steps until its size exceeds $\delta_{opt}(\phi_0)$, while the algorithm in (Kanemitsu, 2010) selects the new $pivot_s$ in every merging step. The reason of keeping the same $pivot_s$ is to reduce the time complexity in selection for $pivot_s$, which requires scanning every cluster in RDY_s. As a result, the number of scanning RDY_s can be reduced with compared to that of (Kanemitsu, 2010).

5.2 Processor assignment

In the algorithm presented in fig. 3, the processor assignment is performed before selecting $pivot_s$. Suppose that a processor P_p is selected before the $s+1$th merging step. Then we assume that P_p is assigned to every cluster to which P_{max} is assigned, i.e., no actual processor has been assigned. By doing that, we assume that such unassigned clusters are assigned to "an identical processor system by P_p" in order to select $pivot_s$. Fig. 4 shows an example of the algorithm. In the figure, (a) is the state of ϕ_2, in which the size of $cls_2(1)$ is $\delta_{opt}(\phi_0)$ or more. Thus, $RDY_2 = \{cls_2(3) = \{n^2_3\}, cls_2(4) = \{n^2_4\}, cls_2(7) = \{n^2_7\}\}$. The communication bandwidth from P_1 to P_{max} is set as $\min_{1 \leq q \leq m, 1 \neq q} \{\beta_{1,q}\}$ in order to regard communication bandwidth between an actual processor and P_{max} bottleneck in the schedule length. In (b), it is assumed that every cluster in UEX_2 is assigned to P_p after P_p is selected. Bandwidths among P_p are set as $\min_{1 \leq q \leq m, p \neq q} \{\beta_{p,q}\}$ to estimate the $sl_w(G^2_{cls}, \phi_2)$ of the worst case. Therefore, $pivot_2$(in this case, $cls_2(3)$) is selected by deriving LV value for each cluster in RDY_2, provided that such a mapping state. After (b), if the size of $cls_3(3)$ is smaller than $\delta_{opt}(\phi_0)$, every cluster in UEX_3 is still assigned to P_p to maintain the mapping state. In (d) if the size of $cls_4(3)$

INPUT: G^0_{cls}
OUTPUT: G^R_{cls}
Set the mapping ϕ_0 to the input DAG.
Define UEX_s as a set of clusters whose size is under $\delta_{opt}(\phi_0)$;
Define RDY_s as a set of clusters which statisies eq. (26).;
For each $n_k \in V$, let $n^0_k \leftarrow n_k, cls_0(k) = \{n^0_k\}$ and put $cls_0(k)$ into V^0_{cls}.
Derive $\delta_{opt}(\phi_0)$ by eq. (25).
$E_0 \leftarrow E, UEX_0 \leftarrow V^0_{cls}, RDY_0 \leftarrow \{cls_0(k) | cls_0(k) = \{n^0_k\}, pred(n^0_k) = \emptyset\}$;
WHILE $UEX_s \neq \emptyset$ **DO**
  select a processor P_p from P;
  $pivot_s \leftarrow getPivot(RDY_s)$;
  WHILE size of $pivot_s < \delta_{opt}(\phi_0)$ **DO**
    $target_s \leftarrow getTarget(pivot_s)$;
    $RDY_{s+1} \leftarrow merging(pivot_s, target_s)$ and update $pivot_s$;
  ENDWHILE
ENDWHILE
RETURN G^R_{cls};

Fig. 3. Procedures for the Task Clustering.

exceeds $\delta_{opt}(\phi_0)$, the mapping is changed i.e., clusters in UEX_4 are assigned to P_{max} to select the new $pivot_4$ for generating the new cluster.

5.3 Selection for $pivot_s$ and $target_s$

As mentioned in 5.1, one objective of the algorithm is to minimize $sl_w(G^R_{cls}, \phi_R)$. Therefore, in RDY_s, $pivot_s$ should have maximum LV value (defined in table 1), because such a cluster may dominate $sl_w(G^s_{cls}, \phi_s)$ and then $sl_w(G^{s+1}_{cls}, \phi_{s+1})$ after $s+1$ th merging may became lower than $sl_w(G^s_{cls}, \phi_s)$. Our heuristic behined the algorithm is that this policy for selecting $pivot_s$ can contribute to minimize $sl_w(G^R_{cls}, \phi_R)$. The same requirement holds to the selection of $target_s$, i.e., $target_s$ should be the cluster which dominates LV value of $pivot_s$. In fig. 4 (b), $cls_2(3)$ having the maximum LV value in RDY_2 is selected. Then n^2_6, i.e., $cls_2(6)$ dominating $LV_2(3)$ is selected as $target_2$. similarly in (c) n^3_5, i.e., $cls_3(5)$ dominating $LV_3(3)$ is selected as $target_3$.

5.4 Merging $pivot_s$ and $target_s$

After $pivot_s$ and $target_s$ have been selected, the merging procedure, i.e.,

$$pivot_{s+1} \leftarrow pivot_s \cup target_s \tag{27}$$

is performed. This procedure means that every cluster in $target_s$ is included in $pivot_{s+1}$. Then $pivot_s$ and $target_s$ are removed from UEX_s and RDY_s. After this merging step has been performed, clusters satisfying requirements for RDY_{s+1}(in eq. (26)) are included in RDY_{s+1}. Furthermore, every cluster's LV value is updated for selecting $pivot_{s+1}$ and $target_{s+1}$ before the next merging step.

6. Experiments

We conducted the experimental simulation to confirm advantages of our proposal. Thus, we compared with other conventional methods in terms of the following points of view.

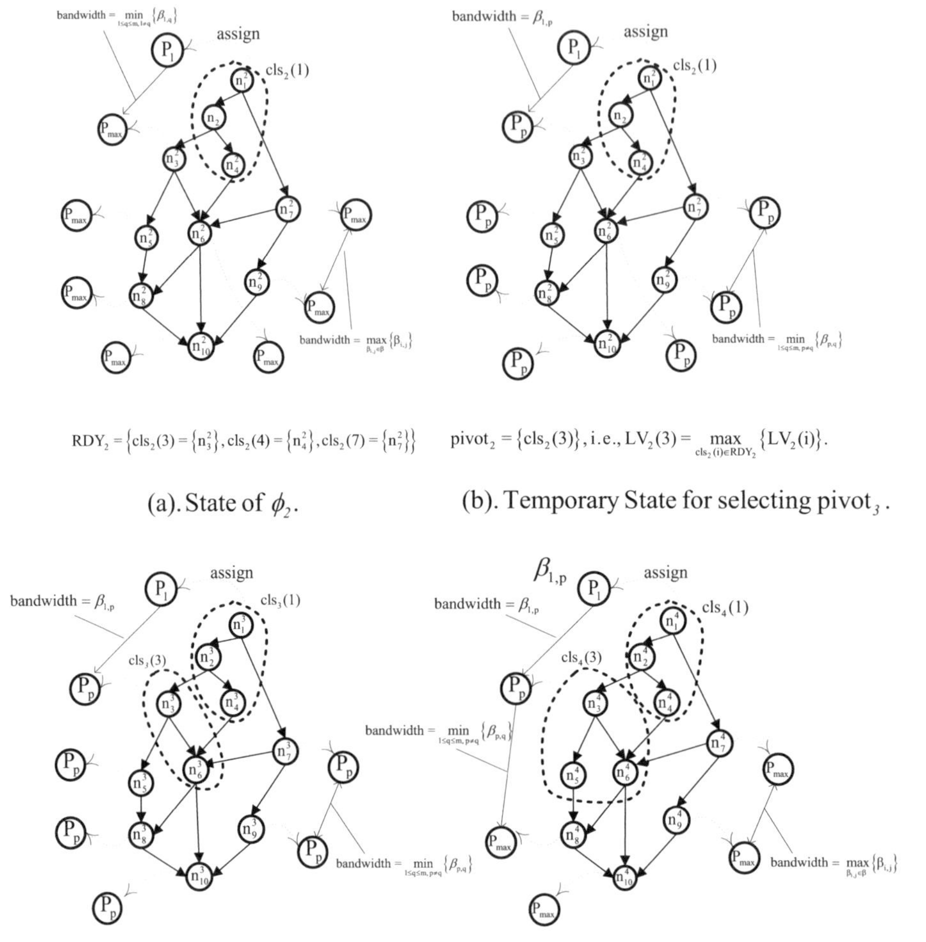

(a). State of ϕ_2. (b). Temporary State for selecting $pivot_3$.

(c). The size of $cls_3(3) < \delta_{opt}(\phi_0)$. (d). State of ϕ_4, and the size of $cls_4(3) \geq \delta_{opt}(\phi_0)$.

Fig. 4. Example of the Task Clustering Algorithm.

1. Whether minimizing $sl_w(G^R_{cls}, \phi_R)$ leads to minimzing the schedule length or not.

2. The range of applicability by imposing $\delta_{opt}(\phi_0)$ as the lower bound of every cluster size.

We showed by theorem 4.1 and 4.2 that both the lower bound and the upper bound of the schedule length can be expressed by $sl_w(G^s_{cls}, \phi_s)$. Thus, in this experiment we confirm that the actual relationship between the schedule length and $sl_w(G^s_{cls}, \phi_s)$.

6.1 Experimental environment

In the simulation, a random DAG is generated. In the DAG, each task size and each data size are decided randomly. Also CCR (Communication to Computation Ratio)(Sinnen, 2005; 2007) is changed from 0.1 to 10. The max to min ratio in terms of data size and task size is set to 100.

Also we decided the Parallelism Factor (PF) is defined as ρ, taking values of 0.5, 1.0, and 2.0 (H. Topcuoglu, 2002). By using PF, the depth of the DAG is defined as $\frac{\sqrt{|V_0|}}{\rho}$.

The simulation environment was developed by JRE1.6.0_0, the operating system is Windows XP SP3, the CPU architecture is Intel Core 2 Duo 2.66GHz, and the memory size is 2.0GB.

6.2 Comparison about $sl_w(G^R_{cls}, \phi_R)$ and the schedule length

In this experiment, we compared $sl_w(G^R_{cls}, \phi_R)$ and the schedule length to confirm the validity of theorem 4.1 and 4.2. Comparison targets are as follows.

No.	α	β	CCR	$\lvert V^R_{cls}\rvert$	$sl_w(G^R_{cls}, \phi_R)$ Ratio			$sl(G^R_{cls}, \phi_R)$ Ratio		
					A	B	C	A	B	C
1	5	5	0.1	168	1.000	1.054	1.097	1.000	1.018	1.123
2			1.0	56	1.000	1.241	1.391	1.000	1.131	1.209
3			5.0	34	1.000	1.320	1.514	1.000	1.140	1.288
4			10.0	19	1.000	1.378	1.611	1.000	1.219	1.341
5	5	10	0.1	160	1.000	1.072	1.105	1.000	1.012	1.073
6			1.0	49	1.000	1.203	1.419	1.000	1.144	1.248
7			5.0	30	1.000	1.355	1.428	1.000	1.172	1.301
8			10.0	16	1.000	1.329	1.503	1.000	1.237	1.344
9	10	5	0.1	150	1.000	1.032	1.066	1.000	1.016	1.071
10			1.0	47	1.000	1.177	1.284	1.000	1.097	1.198
11			5.0	41	1.000	1.209	1.615	1.000	1.173	1.291
12			10.0	26	1.000	1.482	1.598	1.000	1.227	1.302
13	10	10	0.1	187	1.000	1.069	1.044	1.000	1.044	1.050
14			1.0	67	1.000	1.292	1.157	1.000	1.179	1.132
15			5.0	44	1.000	1.344	1.419	1.000	1.203	1.297
16			10.0	28	1.000	1.461	1.433	1.000	1.272	1.301

Table 3. Comparison of $sl_w(G^R_{cls}, \phi_R)$ and the Schedule Length in Random DAGs($|V_0| = 1000$).

No.	α	β	CCR	$\lvert V^R_{cls}\rvert$	$sl_w(G^R_{cls}, \phi_R)$ Ratio			$sl(G^R_{cls}, \phi_R)$ Ratio		
					A	B	C	A	B	C
1	5	5	0.1	351	1.000	1.032	1.041	1.000	1.021	1.049
2			1.0	144	1.000	1.193	1.241	1.000	1.098	1.142
3			5.0	78	1.000	1.216	1.266	1.000	1.126	1.172
4			10.0	44	1.000	1.272	1.371	1.000	1.190	1.193
5	5	10	0.1	346	1.000	1.048	1.044	1.000	1.013	1.013
6			1.0	136	1.000	1.177	1.233	1.000	1.133	1.152
7			5.0	75	1.000	1.242	1.385	1.000	1.152	1.189
8			10.0	41	1.000	1.238	1.411	1.000	1.273	1.206
9	10	5	0.1	344	1.000	1.022	1.037	1.000	1.044	1.031
10			1.0	135	1.000	1.093	1.133	1.000	1.086	1.099
11			5.0	72	1.000	1.203	1.192	1.000	1.173	1.162
12			10.0	39	1.000	1.288	1.370	1.000	1.234	1.221
13	10	10	0.1	367	1.000	1.017	1.041	1.000	1.013	1.011
14			1.0	149	1.000	1.188	1.241	1.000	1.076	1.081
15			5.0	80	1.000	1.279	1.339	1.000	1.147	1.175
16			10.0	46	1.000	1.341	1.367	1.000	1.198	1.201

Table 4. Comparison of $sl_w(G^R_{cls}, \phi_R)$ and the Schedule Length in FFT DAGs($|V_0| = 2048$).

A. At first, the lower bound of the cluster size is derived as $\delta_{opt}(\phi_0)$. Then the task clustering algorithm in fig. 4 is performed, while processor assignment policy is based on CHP(C. Boeres, 2004).

B. The lower bound of the cluster size is derived as $\delta_{opt}(\phi_0)$. Then the task clustering policy is based on "load balancing" (J. C. Liou, 1997), while processor assignment policy is based on CHP(C. Boeres, 2004), in which merging step for generating one cluster is proceeded until the cluster size exceeds $\delta_{opt}(\phi_0)$.

C. The lower bound of the cluster size is derived as $\delta_{opt}(\phi_0)$. Then the task clustering policy is random-basis, i.e., two clusters smaller than $\delta_{opt}(\phi_0)$ are selected randomly to merge into one larger cluster, while processor assignment policy is based on CHP(C. Boeres, 2004), in which merging step for generating one cluster is proceeded until the cluster size exceeds $\delta_{opt}(\phi_0)$.

The difference between A, B and C is how to merge clusters, while they have the common lower bound for the cluster size and the common processor assignment policy. We compared $sl_w(G^R_{cls}, \phi_R)$ and the schedule length by averaging them in 100 random DAGs.

Table 3 and 4 show comparison results in terms of $sl_w(G^R_{cls}, \phi_R)$ and the schedule length. The former is the result in the case of random DAGs. On the other hand, the latter is the result in the case of FFT DAGs. In both tables, α corresponds to max-min ratio for processing speed in P, and β corresponds to max-min ratio for communication bandwidth in P. "$sl_w(G^R_{cls}, \phi_R)$ Ratio" and "$sl(G^R_{cls}, \phi_R)$ Ratio" correspond to ratios to "A", i.e., a value larger than 1 means that $sl_w(G^R_{cls}, \phi_R)$ or $sl(G^R_{cls}, \phi_R)$ is larger than that of "A". In table 3, it can be seen that both $sl_w(G^R_{cls}, \phi_R)$ and $sl(G^R_{cls}, \phi_R)$ in "A" are better than "B" and "C" as a whole. Especially, the larger CCR becomes, the better both $sl_w(G^R_{cls}, \phi_R)$ and $sl(G^R_{cls}, \phi_R)$ in "A" become. It can not be seen that noteworthy characteristics related to $sl_w(G^R_{cls}, \phi_R)$ and $sl(G^R_{cls}, \phi_R)$ with varying the degree of heterogeneity (i.e., α and β). The same results hold to table 4. From those results, it can be concluded that minimizing $sl_w(G^R_{cls}, \phi_R)$ leads to minimizing the schedule length as theoretically proved by theorem 4.1 and 4.2.

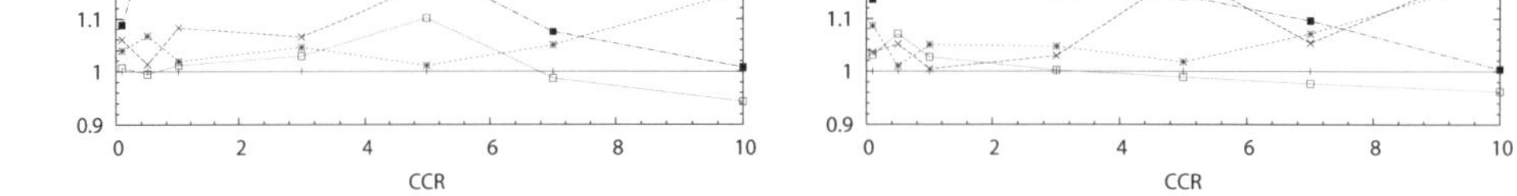

(a) $(\alpha, \beta) = (5, 5)$

(b) $(\alpha, \beta) = (10, 10)$

Fig. 5. Optimality for the Lower Bound of the Cluster Size.

6.3 Applicabiligy of $\delta_{opt}(\phi_0)$

In this experiment, we confirmed that how optimal the lower bound of the cluster size, $\delta_{opt}(\phi_0)$ derived by eq. (25). Comparison targets in this experiment are based on "A" at sec. 6.2, but only the lower bound of the cluster size is changed, i.e., $\delta_{opt}(\phi_0)$, $0.2\delta_{opt}(\phi_0)$, $0.5\delta_{opt}(\phi_0)$, $1.5\delta_{opt}(\phi_0)$, and $2.0\delta_{opt}(\phi_0)$. The objective of this experiment is to confirm the range of applicability of $\delta_{opt}(\phi_0)$, due to the fact that $\delta_{opt}(\phi_0)$ is not a value when $sl_w(G^s_{cls}, \phi_s)$ can be minimized for $1 \leq s$. Fig. 5 shows comparison results in terms of the optimality of $\delta_{opt}(\phi_0)$. (a) corresponds to the case of the degree of heterogeneity $(\alpha, \beta) = (5, 5)$, and (b) corresponds to $(10, 10)$. From (a), it can be seen that $\delta_{opt}(\phi_0)$ takes the best schedule length than other cases during CCR takea from 0.1 to 5.0. However, when CCR is 7 or more, $1.5\delta_{opt}(\phi_0)$ takes the best schedule length. This is because $\delta_{opt}(\phi_0)$ may be too small for a data intensive DAG. Thus, it can be said that $1.5\delta_{opt}(\phi_0)$ is more appropriate size than $\delta_{opt}(\phi_0)$ when CCR exceeds a certain value. On the other hand, in (b), the larger CCR becomes, the better the schedule length by case of $1.5\delta_{opt}(\phi_0)$ becomes. However, during CCR is less than 3.0, $\delta_{opt}(\phi_0)$ can be the best lower bound of the cluster size. As for other lower bounds, 2.0 $\delta_{opt}(\phi_0)$ has the local maximum value of the schedule length ratio when CCR takes from 0.1 to 2.0 in both figures. Then in larger CCR, the schedule length ratio decreases because such size becomes more appropriate for a data intensive DAG. On the other hand, in the case of $0.25\delta_{opt}(\phi_0)$, the schedule length ratio increases with CCR. This means that $0.25\delta_{opt}(\phi_0)$ becomes smaller for a data intensive DAG with CCR increases.

From those results, it can be said that the lower bound for the cluster size should be derived according to the mapping state. For example, if the lower bound can be adjusted as a function of each assigned processor's ability (e.g., the processing speed and the communication bandwidth), the better schedule length may be obtained. For example in this chapter the lower bound is derived by using the mapping state of ϕ_0. Thowever, by using the other mapping state, we may be obtain the better schedule length. To do this, it must be considered that which mapping state has good effect on the schedule length. This point of view is an issue in the future works.

7. Conclusion and future works

In this chapter, we presented a policy for deciding the assignment unit size to a processor and a task clustering for processor utilization in heterogeneous distributed systems. We defined the indicative value for the schedule length for heterogeneous distributed systems. Then we theoretically proved that minimizing the indicative value leads to minimization of the schedule length. Furthermore, we defined the lower bound of the cluster size by assuming the initial mapping state. From the experimental results, it is concluded that minimizing the indicative value has good effect on the schedule length. However, we found that the lower bound of the cluster size should be adjusted with taking an assigned processor's ability into account.

As a future work, we will study on how to adjust the lower bound of the cluster size for obtaining the better schedule length and more effective processor utilization.

8. References

A. Gerasoulis and T. Yang., A Comparison of Clustering Heuristics for Scheduling Directed Acyclic Graphs on Multiprocessors, *Journal of Parallel and Distributed Computing*, Vol. 16, pp. 276-291, 1992.

T. Yang and A. Gerasoulis., DSC: Scheduling Parallel Tasks on an Unbounded Number of Processors, *IEEE Trans. on Parallel and Distributed Systems*, Vol. 5, No. 9 pp. 951-967, 1994.

J. C. Liou, M. A. Palis., An Efficient Task Clustering Heuristic for Scheduling DAGs on Multiprocessors, *Procs. of the 8th Symposium on Parallel and Distributed Processing*,October, 1996.

Hidehiro Kanemitsu, Gilhyon Lee, Hidenori Nakazato, Takashige Hoshiai, and Yoshiyori Urano, Static Task Cluster Size Determination in Homogeneous Distributed Systems, *Software Automatic Tuning: from concepts to state-of-the-art results*, Springer-Verlag (ISBN: 1441969349), pp. 229 – 252, 2010.

C. Boeres, J. V. Filho and V. E. F. Rebello, A Cluster-based Strategy for Scheduling Task on Heterogeneous Processors, *Procs. of the 16th Symposium on Computer Architecture and High Performance Computing (SBAC-PAD'04)*, pp.214 – 221, 2004.

B. Cirou, E. Jeannot, Triplet : a Clustering Scheduling Algorithm for Heterogeneous Systems, *Procs. of 2001 International Conference on Parallel Processing Workshops (ICPPW'01)*, pp. 231 – 236, 2001.

S. Chingchit, M. Kumar and L.N. Bhuyan, A Flexible Clustering and Scheduling Scheme for Efficient Parallel Computation, *Procs. of the 13th International and 10th Symposium on Parallel and Distributed Processing*, pp. 500 – 505, 1999.

O. Sinnen and L. A. Sousa., Communication Contention in Task Scheduling, *IEEE Trans. on Parallel and Distributed Systems*, Vol. 16, No. 6., pp. 503-515, 2005.

O. Sinnen., Task Scheduling for Parallel Systems, *Wiley*, 2007.

A. Gerasoulis and T. Yang., On the Granularity and Clustering of Directed Acyclic Task Graphs, *IEEE Trans. on Parallel And Distributed Systems*, Vol. 4, No. 6, June, 1993.

H. Topcuoglu, S. Hariri, M. Y. Wu. : Performance-Effective and Low-Complexity Task Scheduling for Heterogeneous Computing, , *IEEE Trans. on Parallel and Distributed Systems*, Vol. 13, No. 3 pp. 260-274, 2002.

J. C. Liou and M. A. Palis., A Comparison of General Approaches to Multiprocessor Scheduling, *Procs. of the 11th International Symposium on Parallel Processing*, pp. 152 – 156, 1997.

Section 2

Advances in Grid Computing - Resources Management

3

Resource Management for Data Intensive Tasks on Grids

Imran Ahmad and Shikharesh Majumdar
Carleton University, Ottawa, Canada

1. Introduction

The ubiquitous Internet as well as the availability of powerful computers and high-speed network technologies as low-cost commodity components are changing the way computing is carried out. It becomes more feasible to use widely distributed computers for solving large-scale problems, which cannot often be effectively dealt without using a single existing powerful supercomputer. In terms of computations and data requirements, these problems are often resource intensive due to their size and complexity. They may also involve the use of a variety of heterogeneous resources that are not usually available in a single location. This led to the emergence of what is known as Grid computing. Grid computing enables sharing of heterogeneous distributed resources across different administrative and geographical boundaries [3]. By sharing these distributed resources, many complex distributed tasks can be performed in a cost effective way. The way the resources are allocated to tasks holds a pivotal importance for achieving satisfactory system performance [4]. To perform efficiently, the resource allocation algorithm has to take into account many factors, such as, the system and workload conditions, type of the task to be performed and the requirements of the end user.

To devise more efficient allocation algorithms, it may be useful to classify the given tasks into predefined types based on similarities in their predicted resource needs or workflows. This classification of tasks into various types provides the possibility to customize the allocation algorithm according to a particular group of similar tasks. This chapter presents an effective resource management middleware developed for a type of resource-intensive tasks classified as Processable Bulk Data Transfer (PBDT) tasks. The common trait among PBDT tasks is the transfer of a very large amount of data which has to be processed in some way before it can be delivered from a source node to a set of designated sink nodes (Ahmad, I & Majumdar, S. , 2008). Typically, these tasks can be broken down into parallel sub-tasks, called jobs. Various multimedia and High Energy Physics (HEP) applications can be classified as PBDT tasks. The processing operation involved in these tasks may be as simple as applying a compression algorithm to a raw video file in a multimedia application; or, as complex as isolating information about particles pertaining to certain wavelengths in High Energy Physics (HEP) experimentations [22][25]. Performing PBDT tasks requires both computing power and large bandwidths for data transmission. To perform such resource-intensive tasks, in recent years, research has been conducted in devising effective resource management middleware which has led to the creation of various efficient technologies. In order to provide a satisfactory performance, these systems must optimize the overall execution time (or makespan) of the resource-intensive tasks. This requires efficient allocation of the resources for the sub-tasks (called jobs in this paper) of the PBDT tasks at the individual machines of the network of nodes.

The problem of optimally scheduling these sub-tasks is a well-known NP complete problem [12]. To tackle it, various heuristics-based algorithms that can generate near-optimal solutions to optimization problems in polynomial times are devised. In this chapter a Bi-level Grid Resource Management System abbreviated as BiLeG is presented, in which the decision-making module is divided into two separate sub-modules. The upper level decision-making module is called the Task & Resource Pool Selector (TRPS). It selects a task from the given bag-of-tasks for which resources are to be assigned and chooses a partition of resources available for this chosen task (called the resource-pool of this task) which is typically a subset of all the resources available. The lower level decision-making module is called the Resource Allocator (RA), which uses an assignment algorithm to decide how the resources(from the chosen resource-pool) are allocated to the jobs, in a given task. Various algorithms can be used at RA whereas various policies can be deployed at TRPS. A particular combination of a TRPS policy and a RA scheduling algorithm deployed at a time is called an allocation-plan which determines the resource allocation for each task in the given bag-of-tasks. The following notation is used in this paper to write an allocation-plan: TRPS Policy, RA-Algorithm>. Investigating the choice of the most appropriate allocation-plan under a specific set of workload and system conditions is the focus of this chapter.

The main contributions of this paper are summarized.

1. It proposes the ATSRA algorithm and two extensions based on constraints relaxation technique.
   Based on simulation, it analyses the performance of the proposed algorithms for different number of available Grid nodes.
2. The experimental results capture the trade-off between accuracy in resource allocation and scheduling overhead both of which affect the overall system performance. The chapter discusses under which circumstances the proposed original algorithm or its extensions should be used.

The rest of the paper is organized as follows. In Section 2, different approaches to resource allocation of tasks on Grids are presented. In Section 3, PBDT tasks are described. In Section 4, the problem being solved is defined and an overview of the proposed system is presented. In Section 5 policies are described. In Section 6, the concept of Architectural Templates is described. In Section 7, a Linear Programming (LP) based algorithm and its extensions are described that can be used to perform PBDT tasks. In Section 8, experimental results are presented. Finally, in Section 9, the chapter is concluded.

2. Approaches to resource allocation of tasks on grids

Different researchers have taken various approaches to resource allocation of Tasks on Grids. The approaches to allocate resources in Grids can be divided into three broad categories.

1. Traditional Schedulers and Resource Brokers
2. Policy based Resource Allocation
3. Workflow based Resource Allocation

Each of these approaches is discussed in a following subsection.

2.1 Traditional schedulers and resource brokers

One of the traditional approaches is to use a Grid resource broker which selects suitable resources by interacting with various middleware services. Venugopal describes such a Grid resource broker that discovers computational and data resources running diverse middleware through distributed discovery services [12]. However, any mechanism for breaking a given task into parallel jobs for processing, is not present.

YarKhan and Dongarra [22] have also performed scheduling experiments in a Grid environment using simulated annealing. To evaluate the schedules generated by the simulated annealing algorithm they use a Performance Model, a function specifically created to predict the execution time of the program. Generating such a Performance Model requires detailed analysis of the program to be scheduled.

Another effort worth mentioning is Grid Application Development Software (GrADS) Project [2]. At the heart of the GrADS architecture is an enhanced execution environment which continually adapts the application to changes in the Grid resources, with the goal of maintaining overall performance at the highest possible level. A number of resource allocation algorithms can be used at GrADS to schedule a given bag-of-tasks in Grid environments. Due to the NP-complete nature of the resource allocation problem the majority of proposed solutions are heuristic algorithms [14] [18] [20].

2.2 Policy based resource allocation

For resource allocation in Grids, some researchers have also proposed policy based resource allocation techniques. Sander et al. [12] propose a policy based architecture for QoS configuration for systems that comprise different administrative domains in a Grid. They focus on making decisions when users attempt to make reservations for network bandwidth across several administrative network domains that are controlled by a bandwidth broker. The bandwidth broker acts as an allocator and establishes an end-to-end signalling process that chooses the most efficient path based on the available bandwidth. The work presented in [13] is concerned with data transmission costs only; whereas the research presented in this research needs to consider both computation and communication costs associated with the PBDT tasks. Verma. et al. [19] has also proposed a technique in which resource allocation is performed based on a predefined policy. But in this research, the resource allocation is not based on any performance measure.

2.3 Workflow based resource allocation

Many recent efforts have focused on scheduling of workflows in Grids. [16] presents a QoS-based workflow management system and a scheduling algorithm that match workflow applications with resources using event condition action rules. Pandey and Buyya have worked on scheduling scientific workflows using various approaches in the context of their

GridBus workflow management effort [11] [23]. [23] has developed an architecture to specify and to schedule workflows under resource allocation constraints. Also, many of the data Grid projects that support distributed processing of remote data have proposed workflow scheduling [11] [21].

3. Processable Bulk Data Transfer (PBDT) tasks

PBDT tasks require bulk transfer of processed data. Such data transfers are typical in multimedia systems and HEP experiments. For example in [1], 650MB of data was transferred on an average from a source to a set of sink nodes. High communication and computing times in PBDT tasks effectively amortizes the overhead of the LP-based algorithm used for optimization of the system performance. A PBDT task is characterized by the following three characteristics.

1. The task involves large data transfer that has to be processed in some way before it can be used at the sink nodes. The large amount of data involved in the PBDT differentiates it from the compute intensive tasks where data usually consists of is only the parameters of the remote functions invoked. This implies that the data communication costs cannot be ignored while scheduling a PBDT task.
2. Cost of data processing is proportional to the length of the raw data file.
3. The unprocessed raw file is such that it can be either processed as a whole or be divided into multiple partitions. If divided into partitions, each partition can be processed independently. The resultant processed partitions can later be combined to generate the required processed file. Consider a source file F, of size L. F can be partitioned into k disjoint partitions, with data sizes of $\{L_1, L_2 \ldots L_k\}$, such that

$$L = \sum_{i=1}^{k} L_i \tag{1}$$

Then for a PBDT task, the length of the required processed file is given by

$$L^{\sim} = \sum_{i=1}^{k} \varepsilon L_i \tag{2}$$

where ε_i is a processing factor which is the ratio of the size of the processed partition and that of the original partition.

PBDT tasks are increasingly becoming important. They are used in various multimedia, high-energy physics and medical applications. The following section explains two of the practical examples of PBDT tasks.

3.1 Particle physics data grids

Particle Physics Data Grids (PPDG) is a colloboratory project concerned with providing next-generation infrastructure for high-energy and nuclear physics experiments. One of the important requirements of PPDG is to deal with the enormous amount of data that is created during high-energy physics experiments that must be analyzed by large groups of specialists. Data storage, replication, job scheduling, resource management and security components of the Grid must be integrated for use by the physics collaborators. Processing these tasks require huge computing capabilities and fast communication capabilities. Grid computing is used for processing PPDG tasks that can be classified as a PBDT task.

3.2 Multimedia encoding

Multimedia encoding is required for applying a specific codec to a video [27]. Conventional methods use a single system for the conversion. The compression of the raw captured video data into an MPEG-1 or MPEG-2 data stream can take an enormous amount of time, which increases with higher quality conversions. Depending on the quality level of the video capture, the data required for a typical one hour tape can create over 10 GB of video data, which needs to be compressed to approximately 650 MB to fit on a VideoCD. The compression stage is CPU intensive, since it matches all parts of adjacent video frames looking for similar sub-pictures, and then creates an MPEG data stream encoding the frames. At higher quality levels, more data is initially captured and enhanced algorithms, which consume more time, are used. The compression process can take a day or more, depending on the quality level and the speed of the system being used. For commercial DVD quality, conversions are typically done by a service company that has developed higher quality conversion algorithms which may take considerable amount of time to execute. Grid technology is ideal for improving the process of video conversion.

4. Overall system architecture

In this research we have focused on the problem of allocating resources for a given bag of PBDT tasks. The bag-of-tasks consists of a set of independent PBDT tasks all of which must be executed successfully. The Grid system consists of n nodes. Collectively, these n nodes are represented by a set Δ. Each individual PBDT task in the given bag-of-tasks may be divided into a number of sub-tasks called *jobs* which can be executed in parallel, independent of each other. As discussed, PBDT tasks are resource-intensive tasks that use a large amount of computing resources and communication bandwidth. Usually, if a node starts processing a PBDT task, pre-emption of this task is counter-productive as it wastes the effort of transferring the raw-data file to the concerned node. Also, due to excessive demand of computing power, a node is assumed to handle the processing of only one PBDT task at a time. In this research we have made the following two assumptions regarding the running of constituent jobs of a task on Grid nodes.

1. Once a job starts executing on a Grid node, it cannot be pre-empted.
2. Only one job can be executed on a Grid node at a time.

For the cost analysis of the purposed architecture, we have measured *cost* by the time (in seconds) spent in performing a particular communication or computation job. We have chosen one megabyte as a unit of data. When a particular node i accesses data in node j, the communication cost of transporting a data unit from node i to node j is designated by d(i,j). It is assumed that the communication costs are metrics, meaning that they are non-negative, represented by Cp_m which is the cost of processing a unit of data. Set of all the nodes in the system is represented by Δ. To represent the computing costs, a vector of $|\Delta|$ dimensions denoted by $[C_p]$ is used which holds the values of the computing costs of all the nodes in the system. A matrix $[C_c]$ of dimensions $|\Delta|$ x $|\Delta|$ denotes the values of the communication costs between all the nodes in the system. The objective of this research is to assign resources to tasks in such a manner that the total cost in executing the given bag-of-tasks is minimized; where the total cost is defined as the total time spent by a task at all the resources it has used during its execution. Total cost indicates the total resource usage for executing a task and hence the minimization of the total cost is a system objective.

The BiLeG resource management system consists of two decision-making modules; a lower level decision-making module called Resource Allocator (RA) and a higher level decision-making module called Task Resource Pool Selector (TRPS). TRPS selects a task T_i from the given bag of PBDT tasks and allocates it a resource-pool which is a subset of all resources available. A resource-pool of a particular task T_i is represented by Γ_i, where $\Gamma_i \subseteq \Delta$. RA allocates resources for a particular task T_i chosen from its associated resource-pool Γ_i.

Each PBDT task consists of an unprocessed raw-data file, information about the processing operation that is required to be performed on the raw-data file and a set of sink nodes where the processed file is to be delivered. The source node groups the submitted tasks into a bag-of-tsks (Fig. 1, Step-1) and initiates the processing by sending "initiate" signal to the TRPS Fig. 1 , Step-2). TRPS determines how many Grid resources are reserved (Fig. 1 , Step-3) by interacting with the Grid Computing Environment. This set of reserved nodes is represented by Δ. TRPS determines a resource-pool Γ_i for each of the tasks T_i. Not all the Grid nodes reserved are available or visible to an individual task T_i in the bag-of-tasks, T. Typically, each task has a different resource-pool selected by TRPS according to the TRPS policy used. For an individual task, using all the resources of the resource-pool may not be the best option for its most efficient execution. A TRPS resource selection policy is deployed at TRPS and determines the way in which TRPS chooses a resource-pool for each individual task. The policy uses the existing system state and resource availability in making its decision.

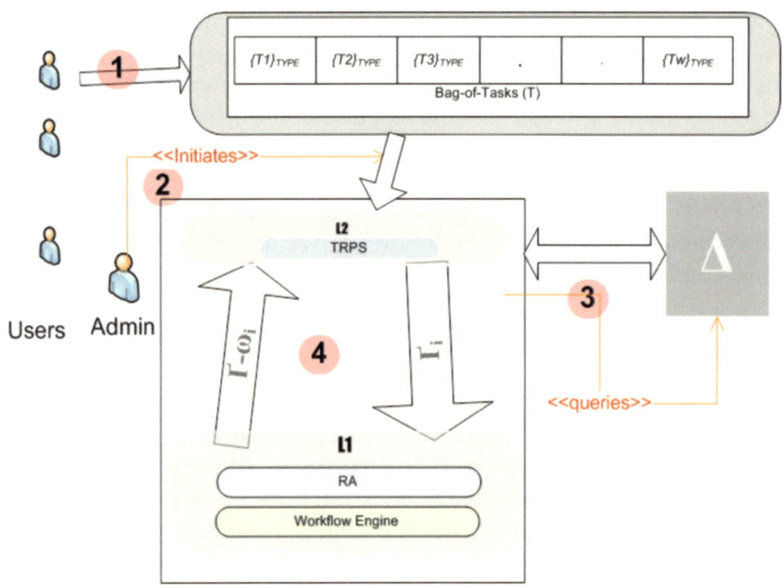

Fig. 1. BiLeG Architecture

From the resource-pool Γ_i allocated by TRPS to T_i, the lower level decision-making module (RA) chooses a set of resources that are used to perform T_i. This set of resources is denoted by ω_i. For different systems, different resource allocation algorithm may be best suited at RA. The remaining set of resources (Γ_i - ω_i) are returned to TRPS. Based on the resources chosen by the algorithm, RA divides a particular task into various jobs. RA specifies the details of the jobs in a file which is called the *workflow* of a Task, T_i. BiLeG architecture includes a software component called *workflow engine* which is designed to execute all the constituent jobs of a Task. The workflow engine is implemented as service and is responsible for running all the constituent jobs associated with a particular Task.

A combination of a TRPS policy and an RA algorithm is called an *Allocation Plan(AP)* and is represented by AP{<Policy>,<Algorithm>}. This paper explores the factors that determine the choice of the most efficient allocation plan for a given bag-of-tasks.

Note that the visibility of RA for a particular task is limited to its resource-pool. RA is myopic in nature and is not concerned with the overall system performance optimization. The objective of RA is to optimize the performance for a particular task only. TRPS is concerned with global system performance and has the responsibility to choose an appropriate resource-pool for each of the tasks and pass it on to RA. RA assigns a set of resources from the resource-pool passed to it by TRPS.

It can be observed that In the BiLeG architecture, by dividing the overall system into two independent decision-making modules and by assigning both decision-making modules separate responsibilities; we divide the problem of scheduling the tasks in the given bag-of-tasks into three different sub-problems:

1. Determination of the task execution order at TRPS
2. Selection of resource-pool
3. Resource allocation for each constituent job in the given bag-of-tasks at RA.

These three sub-problems may be solved by three independent algorithms. The division into three independent sub-problems makes the architecture customizable. It also provides finer-grade control over the resource allocation for the given bag-of-tasks and helps improving the stated optimization objective.

5. TRPS resoruce selection policy

A TRPS resource selection policy is used at the upper decision making module to select the resource-pool for each task. It can be either *static* or *dynamic* in nature. A TRPS policy is said to be static if mapping between tasks and their corresponding resource-pools is established before the system starts executing tasks and it is dynamic if these mappings are established during runtime according to the current availability of the resources. Two static TRPS policies considered in this paper are presented in this section. Dynamic TRPS polices are discussed available in [6].

5.1 Static Resource-Pool--Single Partition (SRP_{SP}) policy

In SRP_{SP}, the TRPS algorithm has two phases, a *mapping phase* and *an execution phase.*

The mapping phase (Fig. 2) is performed before the execution of the first task. Each task in T has a given resource-pool Δ. Thus, for each task $T_i \epsilon T$ and $\Gamma_i = \Delta$. In *Mapping* phase, a mapping between each task and the most appropriate set of resources it needs, is determined. To create this mapping, TRPS iteratively calls the algorithm at RA for each task in T.

In the *Execution Phase,* the first task in set T is executed first. TRPS iterates through all the tasks in T and chooses the next task for which the complete set of resources needed is available. All the tasks, for which each resource allocated by RA is available start executing. All the tasks, for which all the resources allocated by Resource Allocator are not yet available, wait in a queue. Once a task is complete, it is removed from T. The resources released by task are now added to the free resource set and the queue of waiting tasks is checked again to see whether the resource demand of any of these tasks can be satisfied. If all the resources of a particular are now available it starts execution and the next task in the waiting queues is checked and so on. The resources released by the task are now added to the resource set. The queue of waiting tasked is checked again in a First-In-First-Out (FIFO) order to see whether the resource demand of any of the tasks can be satisfied. When T={}, it means that all tasks have been assigned resources.

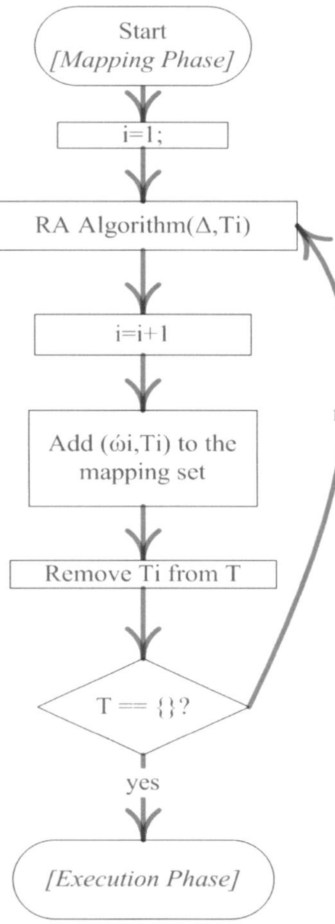

Fig. 2. Mapping Phase of Static Resource Pool Policies

5.2 Static Resource-Pool-Single Partition with Backfilling (SRP_{SP}+BF) policy

SRP_{SP}+BF is an improvement of SRP_{SP}. A drawback of SRP_{SP} is that the performance of the system may deteriorate due to two factors. First, there is the contention for resources, as each task has to wait until the complete set of resources it has been assigned to during the mapping phase becomes available. Second, there is the presence of unused resources that are not utilized at all; as it is possible that some resources may not become a part of mapping of any task. Thus, at a particular instance there may be resources that are available but are not being utilized while tasks are waiting in a queue (as the complete resource-pools associated with the tasks waiting in the queue are not available.)

The *mapping phase* of SRP_{SP}+BF is similar to SRP_{SP}. In the *execution phase*, SRP_{SP}+BF starts just like SRP_{SP}. Once all the tasks for which the resources are available have started to execute, the SRP_{SP}+BF tries to take advantage of the unused resource set by combining them into a single resource-pool. This resource-pool is given to the first task that is waiting in the queue and is it is passed to the Resource Allocator for the resource assignment. This process is called called *backfilling*. Backfilling is repeated till there is no unused resource in the system.

6. Architectural templates for RA

This section presents the concept of Architectural Templates that are used by the resource allocation algorithm deployed at the RA. In addition to deciding on how to decompose a task into its constituent jobs, an Architectural Template divides the available resources into different entities and assigns each of them a specialized role. We have identified the following five roles that can be assigned to the entities:

1. **Source:** A single Grid node where the raw data file of T_i is located.
2. **Sink:** A set of Grid nodes where the processed file is to be delivered.
3. **Compute-Farm:** A set of Grid nodes dedicated to process the raw data file in parallel.
4. **Data-Farm:** A set of Grid nodes used for replicating the data.
5. **Egress Node:** A node where files are combined after being processed at the compute-farm.

Note that a particular node may be part of a different entity at different times. For example a resource may be best utilized in a compute-farm for processing a particular job at one time, thus being a part of the compute-farm entity. But the same node may be used more effectively in a data-farm for processing a job in another task at another time; thus being a part of a data-farm entity. For each type of a task a set of appropriate templates is given as an input to the Resource Allocator. In this paper we have assumed the same set of templates described later can be used for every task in the bag-of-tasks. Thus, an Architectural Template specifies the structure of the suggested functional domains in which available resources are to be divided. This section briefly discusses a set of templates suitable for PBDT tasks.

6.1 2-Tier Architectural Templates

In 2-Tier Templates only the source and the sink nodes are used for both processing and data transfer. There are two different types of 2 tier Templates: 2-Tier-a and 2-Tier-b. In a 2-Tier-a Template, the source node is used for data processing. Fig. 3 (a) shows the process, if 2-Tier-a architecture is used in a system. TRPS co-ordinates with the Task RA (1) and gives it a PBDT task and a resource pool (which is the set of all available nodes for this task). Task RA sends an acknowledgment signal back to TRPS (2). The Task Workflow Engine, deployed at Lower Level, L1, signals the source node to start the processing of data at the source node (3_1). The raw data file is processed at source node (3_2), and is delivered to each of the sink nodes (3_{31} to 3_{3k}). After the transfer of processed data is completed, each of the k sink nodes sends an acknowledgment to the Task Workflow Engine to indicate that the processed file have reached the sink nodes(shown by (4_1) to (4_k)). Once all the k sink nodes have sent completion signals to RA, RA sends the signal to TRPS to indicate that the task has been completed (5).

2-Tier-b Architectural Template is similar to 2-Tier-a (shown in Fig. 3 (b)). The important difference is that instead of using the source node, the data processing job is done at each of the sink nodes (3_{31} to 3_{3k} in Fig. 3 (b)).

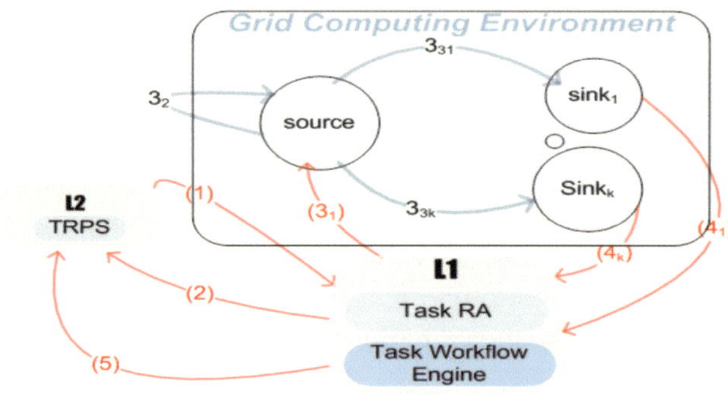

(a)

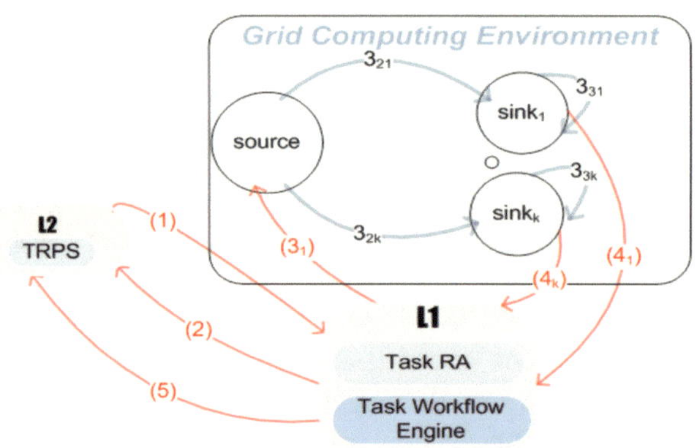

(b)

Fig. 3. (a) 2-Tier-a Architecture (b) 2-Tier-b Architecture

6.2 4-tier Architectural templates

In a 4-tier Architectural Template, the resource pool of the given task (representing the set of available resources for the given task selected by TRPS) is grouped in two domains a compute-farm and a data-farm. Both a compute-farm and a data-farm have a specific role (see Fig. 4). The role the compute-farm is to process the data. Once all the data is processed, it is combined at the Egress node. The role of the data-farm is to replicate this processed data at chosen nodes to optimize its transfer to the sink nodes. Initially, TRPS co-ordinates with the RA and gives it a PBDT task and a corresponding resource pool (1). After running the resource allocation algorithm, RA generates the workflow of the given task T_i which indicates that which of the nodes from the provided resource pool will be used. RA returns $\acute{\omega}_i$ back to TRPS indicating which of the resources are planned to be used for the execution of task T_i (2). The Task Workflow Engine initiates the process (3). Once processing of the data is completed at the compute-farm nodes, these partitions are transferred to a special node called Egress Node where they are combined to produce the required processed file. The Egress Node sends a signal to the Task Workflow Engine (4) to indicate the completion of this stage.

The responsibility of the Egress node is to make sure that all the partitions of the raw data file associated with T_i have been successfully processed. Even if a small portion of data gets missing or corrupted due to any unforeseen error, the resultant processed file formed by the combination of the constituent processed files may be become invalid. In practical environments catching such error at earlier stage is often desirable as the Task Workflow Engine can re-initiate the processing of faulty data partition only. If Egress node is not present, the system is not able to catch such errors at early stages and in case of an error in the processing of one of the partitions, the resultant processed file becomes invalid. In this case the only way to recover is to restart the whole process again from the scratch which would be considerable wastage of both time and resources.

From Egress, this processed data is transferred to the data nodes chosen by the algorithm in the workflow. From there it is delivered to each of the k sink nodes. Once the processed data is delivered to all sink nodes, Task Workflow Engine is notified (5_1 to 5_k) which, in turn, notifies the TRPS (6) to indicate the completion of the task. Note that in compute-farm partitions of raw data files are transferred. But in data-farm complete processed files (not partitions) are transferred and replicated. 3-tier Architectural Template (having a compute-farm, but no data-farm or Egress node) is not discussed in this paper. If data-farm is not required, 3-tier Architectural Template can be used instead of a 4-tier Template.

7. RA Algorithms

In this section ATSRA algorithms are described which enable RA to assign resources to T_i within the resource pool, $\acute{\Gamma}_i$, allocated to it by TRPS. ATSRA algorithms are based on Linear Programming which is a popular technique for solving optimization problems [12][13]. It models an optimization problem as a set of linear expressions composed of input parameters and output parameters. The LP solver starts by creating a problem instance of the model by assigning values to the input parameters[16][17]. The problem instance is then subjected to an objective function, which is also required to be a linear expression. The values of the output variables, which collectively represent the optimal solution, are determined for the best value of the objective function. Based on this approach three algorithms are presented in this section which can be deployed at RA. Each of the ATSRA algorithms has the following two stages.

Stage-1: Selection of the most appropriate Architectural Template, AT_i for T_i.

Stage-2: Allocation of the resources for AT_i (if not done in stage 1.)

7.1 $ATSRA_{org}$ algorithm

A summary of the $ATSRA_{org}$ algorithm is presented. The algorithm is explained in more detail in the following section.

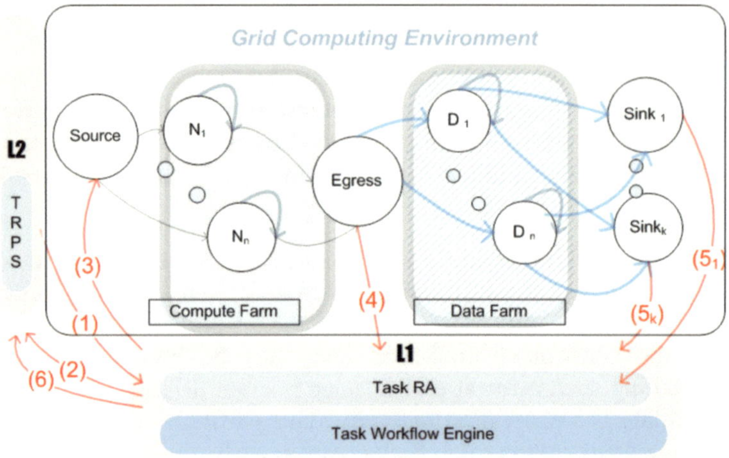

Fig. 4. 4-Tier Architecture

Summary of $ATSRA_{org}$ algorithm
1 *initialize*
2 *calculate* $cost_{2\text{-Tier-a}}$ *and* $cost_{2\text{-Tier-b}}$
3 $cost_{min} = min(cost_{2\text{-Tier-a}}, cost_{2\text{-Tier-b}})$
4 *calcuate* $cost_{4\text{-Tier}}$
5 *If* $cost_{4\text{-Tier}} < cost_{min}$
6 $cost_{min}=cost_{4\text{-tier}}$
7 *choose Architectural Template associated with* $cost_{min}$
8 *Allocate resources for Architectural Template associated with* $cost_{min}$

First, cost associated with each of the Architectural Templates is calculated and the template having the minimum amount of total cost is chosen. The Architectural Template Selection phase starts with calculating the costs associated with the simplest of the templates. For PBDT tasks described in this paper, it starts with the 2-tier architectures.

If L is the size of the raw data file in MB, n_{src} is the source node, n_{sink_i} is the ith sink node, ξ is the processing factor associated with the given task T_i, Cp_{src} is the CPU processing cost per data unit at the source node, then total cost of performing the given PBDT task using 2-Tier-a architecture is

$$cost_{2\text{-Tier-a}} = L\left\{ \sum_{i=1}^{k} \xi d(n_{src}, n_{sink_i}) + Cp_{src} \right\} \quad (3)$$

If Cp_{Sink_k} is the cost of processing per data unit at the kth sink node then the total cost of performing a PBDT task using a 2-Tier-b architecture is given by

$$cost_{2\text{-Tier-b}}=L[\textstyle\sum_{i=1}^{k}\{d(n_{src}, sink_k) + \xi Cp_{Sink_k}\}] \quad (4)$$

For 4-tier cost calculations, the cost function is formulated as a mixed integer/linear programming (MILP) problem which is an LP problem with the additional restriction that certain variables must take integer values. MILP problems are generally h0arder to solve than LP problems [11]. If n_{src} is the source node, n_{sink_j} is the jth sink node, n_{egress} is the egress node and p is the number of partitions of the raw data file (as mentioned in its metadata); then for 4-tier Architectural Templates, the cost can be formulated as:

$$cost_{4\text{-}tier} = \min L \begin{bmatrix} \sum_{j=1}^{n} \frac{1}{p}\{Cp_j + d(n_{src}, n_j) + \varepsilon d(n_j, n_{egress})\}x_i \\ + \varepsilon \sum_{i=1}^{n} d(n_{egress}, n_i)y_i + \varepsilon \sum_{i=1}^{n} \sum_{j=1}^{k} d\left(n_i, n_{sink_j}\right) w_{ij} \end{bmatrix} \tag{5}$$

where x_i is a binary variable which is 1 if a particular node n_i is assigned to compute-farm and is 0 otherwise. Similarly y_i is a node assignment binary variable for the data-farm. It is 1, if a node is used for replication in the data-farm and is 0 otherwise. Variable w_{ij} is the *fraction* of the processed file that a sink gets from a particular node in data-farm. Note that we are considering $PBDT_{fixed\text{-}par}$ task with equal partitions, and each of these partitions at compute-farm has a length of L/p.

The feasibility of a particular assignment is determined by the following constraints.

1. $\sum_{i=1}^{n} w_{ij} = 1 \qquad \forall j = 1\ to\ k$
2. $\sum_{i=1}^{n} x_i = p$
3. $x_i \in \{0,1\}$
4. $y_i \in \{0,1\}$
5. $w_{ij} \leq y_i \qquad i \in \Gamma, j \in S$
6. $w_{ij} \geq 0 \qquad i \in \Gamma, j \in S$

The first constraint specifies that the sum of all parts of the files being transferred from the data-farm to a particular sink node should add up to form the full length of the file. The second constraint specifies that the number of nodes used in the compute-farm should be equal to the number of partitions of the raw data file of the given task. The third and the fourth constraints ensure that both x_i and y_i are binary variables. The fifth constraint makes sure that the solution proposed by the algorithm has a non-zero value of w_{ij}, if and only if $y_i>0$. For example, consider a certain node n_3 and for a particular sink node s_7. w_{37} (that represents the portion of the total processed file that s_7 gets from n_3) should only have a non-zero value if $y_3=1$ (that is y_3 is being used as a node in data-farm). The last constraint prevents negative values for w_{ij}.

$$\text{Let} \quad \tilde{Cp_j} = Cp_j + d(n_{src}, n_j) + \varepsilon d(n_j, n_{egress}) \tag{6}$$

Then $\tilde{Cp_j}$ represents the total cost of sending a unit data to a node in compute-farm, processing it and sending it to the egress node. From Equation (5) and Equation (6)

$$cost_{4\text{-}tier} = \min L \left[\frac{1}{p} \sum_{j=1}^{n} \tilde{Cp_j} x_i + \varepsilon \sum_{i=1}^{n} d(n_{egress}, n_i) y_i + \varepsilon \sum_{i=1}^{n} \sum_{j=1}^{k} d(n_i, Sink_j) w_{ij}\right] \tag{7}$$

The input of the ATSRA algorithms are the computing cost vector [C_p] and the communication cost matrix [C_c. The output is the *solution matrix* which represents the values of solution variables, i.e.

x_i, y_i $\forall i = 1$ to n
w_{ij} $\forall i = 1$ to n, j=1 to k

It is important to note that there is nothing that prevents a node to be part of both compute-farm and data-farm. For example if the solution matrix has x_3=1 and y_3=1 and then n_3 is used both in data-farms and compute-farms. Once the costs calculated with all the Architectural Templates are calculated, the minimum of them is chosen. If $cost_{min} = cost_{4\text{-tier}}$, then resources are allocated according the values of the variables in solution matrix.

7.2 ATSRA$_{SSR}$ algorithm

For small number of nodes, ATSRA$_{org}$ algorithm performs well. But as the number of nodes increases the time taken by the algorithm to run becomes considerable. ATSRA$_{SSR}$ is proposed to improve performance for large number of nodes. It is based on finding a lower bound for the cost minimization problem formulated in Equation (7). The basic idea is to replace a "difficult" minimization problem by a simpler minimization problem whose optimal value is at least as small as $cost_{4\text{-tier}}$.

For the "relaxed" problem to have this property, there are two possibilities.

1. Enlarge the set of feasible solutions so that one optimizes. If the set of feasible solutions is represented by P, then it means to find P' such that $P \subseteq P'$.

OR

2. Replace the minimum objective function of Equation (7) by a function that has the same or a smaller value everywhere.

For the ATSRA$_{SSR}$, we have chosen the first approach. We formulate a new optimization problem called the relaxation of the original problem, using the same objective function but a larger feasible region P' that includes P as a subset. Because P' contains P, any solution which belongs to P, also belongs to P' as well. This relaxed cost is denoted by $cost_{4\text{-tier-relaxed}}$.. Tenlarge the set of feasible solutions, constraint relaxation technique is used. In ATSRA$_{SSR}$, the constraint relaxation technique is used at the Architectural Template selection stage only. Once an Architectural Template has been chosen, exact LP formulation is used for resource allocation. It is thus named as ATSRA Single Stage Relaxation (SSR) or ATSRA$_{SSR}$, as the constraint relaxation is applied only to first stage of the algorithm.

Summary of ATSRA $_{SSR}$ algorithm
1 *initialize*
2 *calculate* $cost_{2\text{-Tier-a}}$ *and* $cost_{2\text{-Tier-b}}$
3 $cost_{min} = min(cost_{2\text{-Tier-a}}, cost_{2\text{-Tier-b}})$
4 *calcuate* $cost_{4\text{-Tier-relaxed}}$
5 *If* $cost_{4\text{-Tier-relaxed}} < cost_{min} <$
6 *goto step 9*
7 *else*
calculate $cost_{4\text{-Tier}}$
8 $cost_{min} = min(cost_{4\text{-Tier}}, cost_{min})$
9 *choose Architectural Template associated with* $cost_{min}$
10 *Allocate resources for Architectural Template associated with* $cost_{min}$

The $ATSRA_{SSR}$ starts by calculating the costs associated with 2- tier Architectural Templates 2a and 2b, using Equations (3) and (4). The minimum of these two is called as $cost_{min}$. For 4-tier Architectural Templates, instead of calculating exact $cost_{4\text{-tier}}$, $cost_{4\text{-tier-relaxed}}$ is calculated. For constraint relaxation, the fifth constraint (i.e. $w_{ij} \leq y_i$) is dropped.

7.3 $ATSRA_{BSR}$ algorithm

In $ATSRA_{BSR}$ algorithm we apply relaxation of the constraints at both Architectural Template Selection and resource allocation stages.

A summary of $ATSRA_{BSR}$ is as follows:

Summary of $ATSRA_{BSR}$ algorithm
1 initialize
2 calculate $cost_{2\text{-Tier-a}}$ *and* $cost_{2\text{-Tier-b}}$
3 $cost_{min} = min(cost_{2\text{-Tier-a}}, cost_{2\text{-Tier-b}})$
4 calcuate $cost_{4\text{-Tier-relaxed}}$
5 If $cost_{4\text{-Tier-relaxed}} < cost_{min}$
6 $cost_{min} = cost_{4\text{-tier-relaxed}}$
7 choose Architectural Template associated with $cost_{min}$
8 Allocate resources for Architectural Template associated with $cost_{min}$

The important thing to note is that in $ATSRA_{BSR}$, the constraint relaxation technique is used at both the Architectural Template selection stage and the relaxed solution matrix is used for actual resource allocation. For relaxation, constraints 3 and 4 are replaced by

$$3' \quad 0 \leq x_i \leq 1$$
$$4' \quad 0 \leq y_i \leq 1$$

Note that the constraint relaxed in $ATSRA_{SSR}$ produces an invalid solution matrix. By dropping fifth constraint (i.e. $w_{ij} \leq y_i$), the variable w_{ij} can be assigned a non-zero value even if the corresponding data-farm node y_i is not assigned. Thus the resultant solution matrix cannot be used in resource allocation. But in $ATSRA_{SSR}$, we are using this relaxation only for the selection of Architectural Template and if 4-tier is chosen then the exact LP formulation is used for actual resource allocation. For $ATSRA_{BSR}$, we have chosen such constraints for relaxation that do not produce an invalid solution matrix. Thus the same resultant solution matrix is used for resources allocation as well.

Note that as we move from $ATSRA_{org}$ to $ATSRA_{SSR}$ and then to $ATSRA_{BSR}$, following are some of the considerations.

1. Time complexity of algorithm is reduced.
2. Imprecision in Resource Allocation increases.

The decrease in algorithm running time is the benefit of using this relaxation

8. Results experimental

This paper uses the following performance metrics.

Makespan total ($t_{ms\text{-}total}$): The time in seconds required for completing all the tasks in the given bag-of-tasks, T.

Makespan non-scheduling ($t_{ms\text{-}nonSch}$): The time in seconds required for completing all the tasks in T, *excluding* the time taken by scheduling algorithm.

Scheduling algorithm running time (t_{sch}): Total time in seconds taken by the scheduling algorithm to schedule all the given resources.

Total cost (t_{cost}). Sum of the time in seconds for which all the resources are utilized in performing the bag-of-tasks T.

To analyze the performance of the proposed RA algorithms, a simulation based investigation is performed. Various performance metrics described earlier were captured at the end of each simulation. Each experiment was repeated enough number of times to produce a confidence interval of ±5% for each performance metric at a confidence level of 95%. The workload chosen for these experiments is a bag-of-tasks consisting of 32 $PBDT_{fixed\text{-}par}$ tasks. Each of these tasks models the encoding of a raw multimedia file which is to be processed and delivered to a set of sink nodes. The choice of the raw data file is based on a typical animation movie described in [2]. The size of the raw data files of each of the tasks in the given bag-of-tasks is an important workload parameter. A detailed study of the characteristics of similar real-world tasks was carried out. The true representative probability distribution of the sizes of the raw or unprocessed data files used in similar tasks has been a subject of discussion over the years in the research community. Researchers seem to be split over characterizing it either with a Pareto or with Log-normal distribution. After careful analysis the Pareto distribution seems to be a better representative of PBDT multimedia workloads and is thus used. Another important parameter for the workload is the value of p, which is the number of partitions in which raw data files can be divided. This value is included in the metadata of each of the raw data file of the given tasks. The value of p depends on the structure of the raw data file and the type of processing required for it. For example, if a raw data file of multimedia animation contains 20 sub-sequences, each of which has to be processed as a single partition, then this task has a p of 20. The number of partitions (referred to as sub-sequences in the description of the movie rendering project presented in [1]) for each raw file varies from 1 to 30. We have used a uniform distribution [1-30] for modeling the number of partitions in each raw multimedia file. The mean of the raw data files is fixed at 650MB.

For performance analysis of the proposed algorithms total number of nodes of the Grid system is increased. Number of Grid nodes is directly related to the time-complexity of the deployed algorithm. All other parameters related to workload and system conditions are kept constant.

Fig. 5 shows the performance of three RA algorithms ($ATSRA_{org}$, $ATSRA_{SSR}$ and $ATSRA_{BSR}$) with SRP_{sp} deployed at the TRSP. Fig. 5(a) shows the time taken by each of the algorithm to run. It can be that for small number of nodes, there is not much difference in the scheduling time taken be these three algorithms. The time taken by the $ATSRA_{org}$ algorithm rises sharply as number of nodes is increased more than 32. It can be observed that for $ATSRA_{BSR}$, t_{sch} does not rise sharply. Fig. 6(b) shows the value of Makespan non-scheduling ($t_{ms\text{-}nonSch}$) for each of the proposed algorithms as the number of nodes is increased. It is clear that $ATSRA_{org}$ has the lowest value of $t_{ms\text{-}nonSch}$ for all values of n. This is expected as by using all

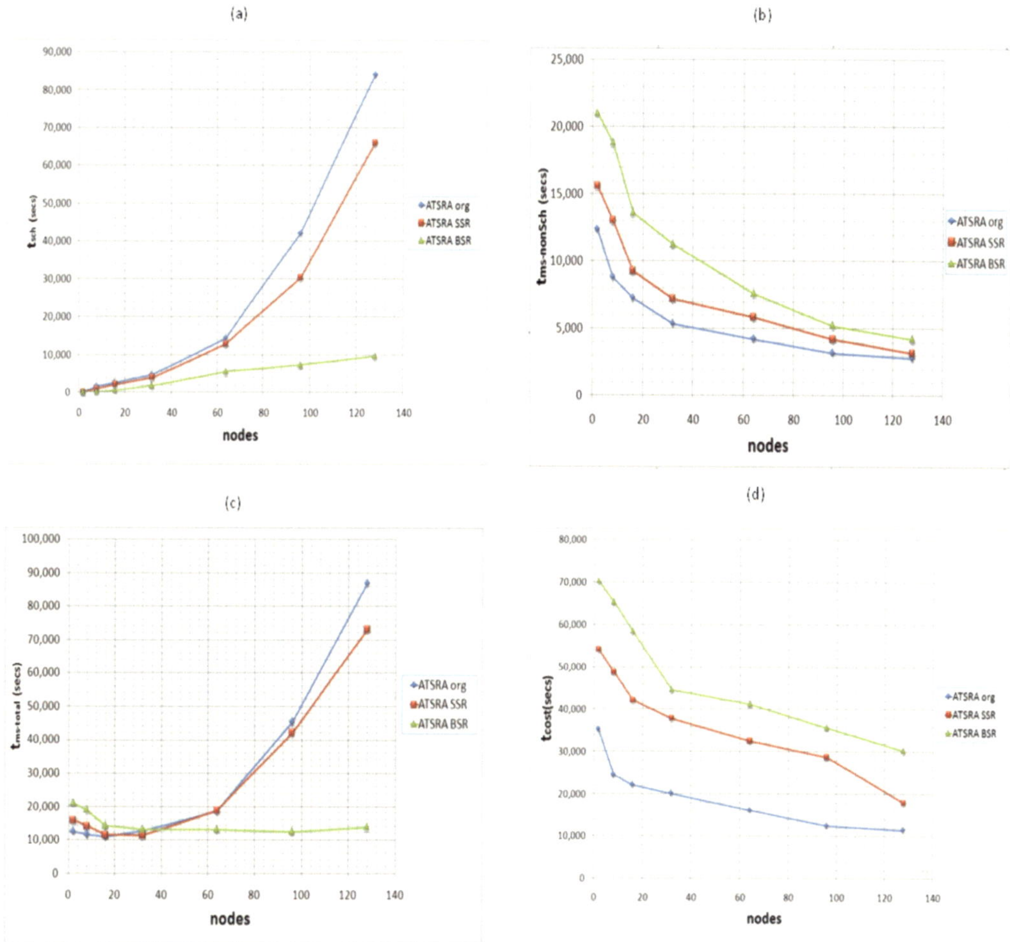

Fig. 5. Performance with SRP_{sp} chosen at TRPS (a) Scheduling Algorithm Running time (b) Makespan non-Scheduling time (c) Makespan Total (d) Total Cost

constraints associated with the LP formulation, we are allocating the resource with the highest precision and it this allocation is expected to be efficient. As constraint relaxation is applied at stage one of the algorithms in $ATSRA_{SSR}$, $t_{ms\text{-}nonSch}$ increases. It further increases for $ATSRA_{BSR}$ in which constraint relaxation is applied at both stage of the algorithm. Fig. 6(d) shows the total cost (t_{cost}) for each of the three algorithms. $ATSRA_{org}$ has the lowest t_{cost} as we are allocating the resources with highest precision. This is followed by $ATSRA_{SSR}$ and $ATSRA_{BSR}$. The overall makespan time, $t_{ms\text{-}total}$ shown in Fig. 5(c) includes both the scheduling time and the execution time for the bag-of-tasks. It captures the tradeoff between $t_{ms\text{-}noSch}$ and t_{sch} presented in Fig. 5(b) and 5(a) respectively. For a very small number of nodes the scheduling overhead for the $ATSRA_{org}$ is small and $t_{ms\text{-}nonsch}$ is the lowest and as a result the best $t_{ms\text{-}total}$ is achieved. For a large number of nodes, the scheduling overhead for $ATSRA_{org}$ is very high and the benefit of using a better resource allocation is offset by the overhead and its performance deteriorates. $ATSRA_{BSR}$ that exhibits the smallest scheduling overhead for a large number of nodes (see Fig. 5(a)) demonstrates the best $t_{ms\text{-}total}$ (see Fig.

5(c)). It is interesting to see that $ATSRA_{SSR}$ produces the best $t_{ms\text{-}total}$ for a range of intermediate values of the number of Grid nodes. The accuracy of resource allocation for $ATSRA_{SSR}$ lies between that achieved with $ATSRA_{org}$ and $ATSRA_{BSR}$. For a small number of nodes, t_{sch} of $ATSRA_{SSR}$ is comparable to that of $ATSRA_{org}$; whereas the $t_{ms\text{-}nonSch}$ achieved by $ATSRA_{SSR}$ is inferior to that achieved by $ATSRA_{org}$. Thus if the number of nodes is small, $ATSRA_{SSR}$ is inferior to that of $ATSRA_{org}$.

For a large number of nodes, although $ATSRA_{SSR}$ gives rise to a lower scheduling overhead than $ATSRA_{BSR}$, the advantage is offset by the much lower execution time produced by $ATSRA_{BSR}$. The net effect is that $t_{ms\text{-}total}$ achieved by $ATSRA_{SSR}$ is inferior to that of $ATSRA_{BSR}$ for a large number of nodes.

Fig. 6 shows the performance of ATSRA algorithms when SRP_{sp} +BF is deployed at TRPS. As in the case of Fig. 5(c) the best $t_{ms\text{-}total}$ is achieved by $ATSRA_{BSR}$ for larger numbers of nodes; whereas $ATSRA_{org}$ demonstrates the best performance for a lower number of nodes. $ATSRA_{SSR}$ demsonstrates a slightly higher $t_{ms\text{-}total}$ than $ATSRA_{org}$ when the number of Grid nodes is small. Although the total makespan achieved by it is better than $ATSRA_{org}$ at higher number of nodes, it is higher than that achieved by $ATSRA_{BSR}$. The relative performances of the three algorithms captured in Fig. 6(a) , Fig. 6(b) and Fig. 6(d) are the same as those displayed in Fig. 5(a), Fig. 5(b) and Fig. 5(d) respectively. $ATSRA_{org}$ demonstrates the best in $t_{ms\text{-}nonSch}$ and t_{cost} followed by $ATSRA_{SSR}$ and $ATSRA_{BSR}$; whereas the smallest scheduling overhead is achieved with $ATSRA_{BSR}$ and $ATSRA_{org}$ demonstrates the highest scheduling overhead. The rationale for such a behavior has been provided in the discussion presented earlier for Fig. 5(a) Fig. 5(b) and Fig. 5(d). Note that although the shapes of the graphs in Fig. 5(a) and Fig. 6(a) are similar, the value of t_{sh} for a given number of nodes in Fig 6(a) is higher than the value of t_{sh} for the same number of nodes in Fig. 5(a). This is because in SRP_{sp} +BF backfilling is used which increases scheduling overheads. While the relative performance of $ATSRA_{org}$, $ATSRA_{SSR}$ and $ATSRA_{BSR}$ remains almost the same, this additional scheduling overhead has shifted the graphs upwards in Fig. 6(a) as compared to Fig. 5(a).

For $ATSRA_{org}$ and $ATSRA_{SSR}$ algorithms and any given number of nodes, the $t_{ms\text{-}nonSch}$ achieved with SRPsp +BF is observed to be smaller than that achieved SRP_{sp} (see Fig. 5 (b) and Fig. 6(b). This demonstrates the effectiveness of using backfilling that can increase the concurrency of task execution. Except for the case in which the number of Grid nodes is 128, a similar behavior is observed with $ATSRA_{BSR}$.

Comparing $t_{ms\text{-}total}$ achieved with SRP_{sp} (Fig. 5(c)) and SRP_{sp} +BF (Fig. 6(c)), we observe that for any given ATSRA algorithm, the total makespan achieved by SRPsp +BF is superior to that achieved by SRPsp when the number of nodes is small. For higher number of nodes, SRP_{sp} +BF demonstrates an inferior performance. This becauseat smaller number of nodes concurrent execution of tasks may be severely limited with SRP_{sp} because many tasks may not be able to get all their resources at the same time. With the use of backfilling this problem is alleviated as RA is run for each waiting task with the set of unused resources as the resource pool. However, this problem with task concurrency is not that severe at higher number of nodes. Thus, SRP_{sp} +BF that re-runs RA multiple times and incurs a higher scheduling overhead demonstrates an inferior performance as the potential performance benefit due to backfilling is offset by the overhead.

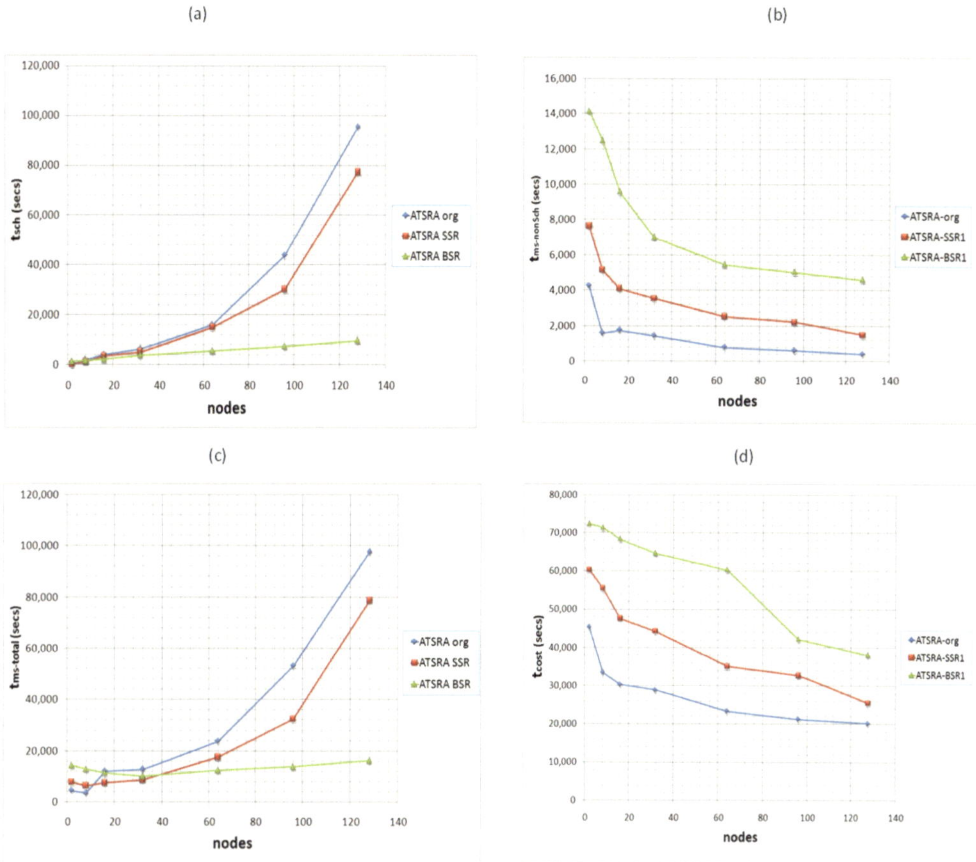

Fig. 6. Performance with SRP_{sp}+BF chosen at TRPS (a) Scheduling Algorithm Running time (b) Makespan non-Scheduling time (c) Makespan Total (d) Total Cost

9. Summary and conclusion

In this chapter, by using BiLeG an allocation-plan is devised which reflects the overall resource allocation strategy comprising two parts; a policy used at the higher decision making module, TRPS, which has the responsibility to select a resource-pool for each of the tasks; and a resource allocation algorithm used at the lower decision making module, RA, which actually assigns resources from the resource-pool selected by TRPS for a particular PBDT task. Three RA algorithms and six TRPS policies have been proposed in this chapter forming different allocation-plans. The suitability of various allocation-plans under different sets of system and workload parameters has been explored.

Detailed study of the various trade-offs, implicit in the use of different allocation-plans, is the focal points of this chapter. The most suitable allocation-plan not only depends on various workload and system parameters, it also depends on the user requirements and the hardware available. It can be seen that from the performance perspective various trade-offs exist among different allocation-plans and understanding these trade-offs in depth is the focus of the experiments conducted in this chapter.

For the choice of an appropriate allocation-plan, two of the important considerations that came out of these experimental results are the size of the Grid and the performance metric chosen for optimization. Generally, from the results obtained from the experiments conducted in chapter, it can be concluded that if an allocation-plan tries to minimize one of the performance metrics, it tends to yield higher values of the other performance metrics. For example, <SRP_{sp},$ATSRA_{org}$> always gives the lowest value of t_{cost} but it also yields one of the highest values for $t_{ms\text{-}WOH}$, especially for a large number of nodes. At RA, the trade-offs associated with reducing the accuracy of the ATSRA algorithm by relaxing some of the constraints in the LP formulation have been studied. The combination of the proposed RA algorithms and TRPS policies gives rise to various allocation-plans. These allocation-plans can be used under a wide variety of system and workload parameters to maximize the use of available resources according to a pre-determined optimization objective.

Although the research summarized in this chapter has focused primarily on the Grid systems, the proposed BiLeG architecture can also be used in a Cloud Computing environment. Cloud Computing environments are often classified as public and private Cloud environments [3]. The private Cloud environment is better suited for the BiLeG architecture; as a private Cloud environment uses a dedicated computing infrastructure that provides hosted services to a limited number of users behind a firewall and can, thus, more easily incorporate mechanisms to accurately predict the computing and communication costs.

The algorithms presented in this chapter are based on a dedicated resource environment. To adapt the BiLeG architecture to shared environments, more research is required. For example, in order to use it in a shared resource environment, mechanisms to accurately predict the unit communication and processing times are needed to be incorporated in the BiLeG architecture. Also, in a shared environment, investigating the impact of various types of communication models, such as many-to-one and one-to-many forms, an important direction for the future research.

10. References

[1] http://enterprise.amd.com/Downloads/Industry/Multimedia

[2] http://www.gridtoday.com/grid/638845.html.

[3] Abbas A. Grid Computing: A Practical Guide to Technology and Applications, Charles River Media , 2004.

[4] Ahmad I. and Majumdar S. Policies for Efficient Allocation of Grid Resources using a Bi-level Decision-making Architecture of "Processable" Bulk Data. Department of Systems and Computer Engineering, Carleton University, 2007.

[5] Ahmad I. and Majumdar S. An adaptive high performance architecture for "processable" bulk data transfers on a Grid. In 2nd International Conference on Broadband Networks (Broadnets). (3-7 Oct. 2005). IEEE, Boston, MA, USA, 2005, 1482-91.

[6] Ahmad I. and Majumdar S. Efficient Allocation of Grid Resources Using a Bi-level Decision-Making Architecture for "Processable" Bulk Data. On the Move to Meaningful Internet Systems 2007: CoopIS, DOA, ODBASE, GADA, and IS, (2007), 1313-1321.

[7] Allcock B., Chervenak A., Foster I., Kesselman C. and Livny M. Data Grid tools: enabling science on big distributed data. Journal of Physics: Conference Series, 16, 1 (2005), 571-5.

[8] Bunn J. and Newman H. Data-intensive Grids for high energy physics. In Berman G. and Hey E. eds.Grid Computing: Making the Global Infrastructure a Reality. John Wiley & Sons, Inc., New York, 2003.

[9] Berman F., Casanova H., Chien A., Cooper K., Dail H., Dasgupta A., Deng W., Dongarra J., Johnsson L., Kennedy K., Koelbel C., Liu B., Liu X., Mandal A., Marin G., Mazina M., Mellor-Crummey J., Mendes C., Olugbile A., Patel M., Reed D., Shi Z., Sievert O., Xia H. and YarKhan A. New Grid scheduling and rescheduling methods in the GrADS project. International Journal of Parallel Programming, 33, 2-3 (06 2005), 209-29.

[10] Candler W. and Townsley R. A linear two-level programming problem, Computers & Operations Research, 9, 1 (1982), 59-76.

[11] Chvatal V. Linear Programming. W.H. Freeman and Company Press, 1980.

[12] Devpura A. Scheduling Parallel and Single Batch Machines to Minimize Total Weighted Tardiness. Ph.D. Dissertation, Computer Science Department, Arizona State University, 2003.

[13] Dimitris Bertsimas, John N. Tsitsiklis. Introduction to Linear Programming. Athena Scientific, Belmont, Massachusetts, 1998.

[14] Downey A. B. Lognormal and Pareto distributions in the Internet. Comput. Commun., 28, 7 (05/02 2005), 790-801.

[15] Foster I. and Kesselman C. The Grid: Blueprint for a Future Computing Infrastructure. Morgan Kaufmann Publishers, USA, 1999.

[16] Gzara F. Large scale integer programming: A novel solution method and application. McGill University, 2004.

[17] Jeong S., Chan-Hyun Youn and Hyoug-Jun Kim. Optimal file replication scheme (CO-RLS) for data Grids. In Anonymous 6th International Conference on Advanced Communication Technology. (9-11 Feb. 2004). IEEE, Phoenix Park, South Korea, 2004, 1055-9.

[18] Foster I., Kesselman C., Lee C., Lindell B., Nahrstedt K. and Roy A. A distributed resource management architecture that supports advance reservations and co-allocation. In Anonymous Proceedings of IWQoS'99 - Seventh International Workshop on Quality of Service. (31 May-4 June 1999). IEEE, London, UK, 1999, 27-36.

[19] M. Elayeb. Efficient Data Scheduling For Real-Time Large Scale Data Intensive Distributed Applications. (Masters Dissertation, The Ohio State University).

[20] Mathur K. and Puri M. C. A bilevel bottleneck programming problem. European Journal of Operational Research, 86, 2 (10/19 1995), 337-344.

[21] Sander V., Adamson W. A., Foster I. and Roy A. End-to-end provision of policy information for network QoS. In 10th IEEE International Symposium on High Performance Distributed Computing. (7-9 Aug. 2001). IEEE Comput. Soc, San Francisco, CA, USA, 2001, 115-26.

[22] Sundaram B. and Chapman B. M. XML-based policy engine framework for usage policy Allocation in Grids. In Proceedings. (18 Nov. 2002). Springer-Verlag, Baltimore, MD, USA, 2002, 194-8.

[23] Vazhkudai S. Enabling the co-allocation of Grid data transfers. In Fourth International Workshop on Grid Computing. (17 Nov. 2003). IEEE Comput. Soc, Phoenix, AZ, USA, 2003, 44-51.

[24] Venugopal S. Scheduling Distributed Data-Intensive Applications on Global Grids. Ph.D. Dissertation, Department of Computer Science and Software Engineering, The University of Melbourne, 2006.
[25] Verma D., Sahu S., Calo S., Beigi M. and Chang I. A policy service for Grid computing. In Proceedings (18 Nov. 2002). Springer-Verlag, Baltimore, MD, USA, 2002, 243-55.
[26] Wu J., Savoie M., Campbell S., Zhang H., Bachmann G. V. and St Arnaud B. Customer-managed end-to-end lightpath provisioning. International Journal of Network Allocation, 15, 5 (2005), 349-62.
[27] Yang K., Galis A. and Todd C. Policy-based active Grid Allocation architecture. In Towards Network Superiority. (27-30 Aug. 2002). IEEE, Singapore, 2002, 243-8.

4

A New Approach to Resource Discovery in Grid Computing

Leyli Mohammad Khanli[1],
Saeed Kargar[2] and Ali Kazemi Niari[2]
[1]*C.S. Dept., University of Tabriz*
[2]*Islamic Azad University, Tabriz Branch*
Iran

1. Introduction

The grid computing systems are one of great developments in the field of engineering and computer science and provide a clear future in the global use of various optimal distributed resources (hardware and software). Therefore with expanding grid systems and the importance of finding suitable resources for users (Foster & Kesselman, 2003), while saving time and space, resource discovery algorithms are very important. If one algorithm with less traffic and without reference to unnecessary nodes in a shorter time, can find the appropriate resource for users, it will significantly increase the efficiency of the system.

There are many approaches to resource discovery, such as flooding-based and random-based. These approaches decrease the system efficiency, because the users' requests pass through many unnecessary paths and create additional traffic. Therefore it is not suitable for a grid environment with numerous nodes.

Another approach is resource discovery tree using bitmap (Chang & Hu, 2010). This method decreases some disadvantages of previous methods such as unnecessary traffic and heavy load, and furthermore the cost of update is low. But in this method, users' requests are also sent to unnecessary nodes, so in a grid environment with numerous nodes and requests, the reference to unnecessary nodes will create additional and heavy traffic and decrease the efficiency of the system.

In this work, we use a weighted tree for resource discovery (Khanli & Kargar, 2011). We only use one bitmap for the identification of available resources in nodes and also resources of children and their descendant nodes. The users' request must be transformed into this bitmap. We record a footprint of resources in nodes. When a user's query reaches every node, we can use this footprint to access the directly appropriate resource without visiting additional and unnecessary nodes and no time is consumed. We compare our algorithm with other algorithms and show that our algorithm is very efficient.

We discuss the previous works about the resource discovery in Section 2. In Section 3, we explain our proposed mechanism. Section 4 details the diagrams for comparing our method with previous methods, and finally, Section 5 contains conclusions.

2. A brief history of the resource discovery in grid

There are different methods for resource discovery in grid environment. Centralized resource discovery approaches (Berman et al., 2003; Chien et al., 2003; Foster & Kesselman, 1997; Germain et al., 2000; Mutka & Livny, 1987; Neary et al., 1999) are one of the mechanisms which suffer from single point of failure and bottlenecks.

Most of the methods in resource discovery tend to peer to peer (Al-Dmour & Teahan, 2005; Ali et al., 2005; Basu et al., 2005; Bharambe et al., 2004; Cai & Hwang, 2007; Iamnitchi et al., 2002; Koo et al., 2006; Nejdl et al., 2002; Oppenheimer et al., 2004; Shen, 2009; Talia et al., 2006; Zerfiridis & Karatza, 2003) which for example use super-peer (Mastroianni et al., 2005) or hierarchical (Liu et al., 2006) models. Apart from similarities between grid and peer to peer systems (Iamnitchi & Talia, 2005), they have critical differences in the field of security, users, applications, scale and etc. (Trunfio et al., 2007).

In the grid some methods use resource brokers to match the user's request with available resources (Bradley et al., 2006). They can consider some factors including software /hardware capabilities, network bandwidth, resource cost and so forth.

Yuhui Deng et al. (2009) suggested a peer to peer model for resource discovery which uses ant colony optimization (ACO). The main idea of this method was inspired from ants, which search their environment for food.

Xue-Sheng Qi et al. (2006) suggested a mechanism which can find multi-accessible resources and choose one of them, which uses a table. When a user wants to use the resource, reservation table will be checked. If the desired resource does not exist, it will be added to the table and the resource will be reserved.

Another method for resource discovery problems would be semantic communities (Li & Vuong, 2005; Li, 2010; Nazir et al., 2005; Zhu et al., 2005; Zhuge, 2004) which allows the grid nodes to communicate with no requirement to a central visiting point.

In (Li, 2010), Li proposes a semantics-aware topology construction method where queries propagate between semantically related nodes. To route the query, it constructs and uses the Resource Distance Vector (RDV) routing table (RDVT).

Gregor Pipan (2010), used TRIPOD overlay network for resource discovery which is based on a hybrid overlay network. He also used a K-Tree. The recommended TRIPOD overlay in this method is especially designed for resource discovery, which is combined two structures in an overlay and also used synthetic coordinate system.

Tangpongprasit et al. (2005) proposed an algorithm which uses the reservation algorithm for finding suitable resources in a grid environment. In the forward path, if there are any resources, they will be saved and reserved, in the backward path, one of them will be selected (if more than one resource has been reserved) and added to the request.

In (2006), Ramos and de Melo propose a structure of master and slave. A master does the updating and the slave restores the information from the machine.

In (2010), Chang and Hu proposed a resource discovery tree using bitmap for grids. It uses two bitmaps called the "index bitmap" and "local resource bitmap", and the other bitmap would be the "attribute counter". The local resource bitmap registers information about the local resources of nodes and the index bitmap registers the information about its children nodes which exist in the nodes that have child (non-leaf nodes). In this method, the users' query at first becomes AND with the local resource bitmap and if there is no local resource in the node, it becomes AND with the index bitmap. If the result is a nonzero number, the query will be forwarded to all children until reaching the target node. If the result of the AND operation is zero, it means that there are no resource in children and the query will be sent to the father node.

There are some differences between our algorithm and the other ones:

Our algorithm uses a tree structure in which the edges have weight. The advantage of our method is that any node in our weighted tree has a unique path, so the user's query against all of previous methods is not sent to the extra and unnecessary paths. We can directly reach the target node using a resource footprint which is stored in nodes. Furthermore, for resource discovery we only use one bitmap in every node which is for the storing of information about its local resources and the resources of its children and descendant. Also it preserves a footprint of resources and if we need a resource which is available in its children or descendant, we can directly and without any referring to unnecessary and extra nodes, reach the target node. This method significantly reduces the system traffic and increases the performance of system.

3. Our proposed method

Here, we introduce a weighted tree structure for resource discovery. In this method, like (Chang & Hu, 2010) (explain in previous section) we use one bitmap except several bitmaps will replace one bitmap with different contents. In the current method, we will allocate to any kind of resource two positions of bitmap, where one of them is the "counter" and another is the "path". A user's request should be changed into this form. There will be one bitmap in every node in which the user's query will be multiplied by this bitmap position to a position in order that the availability of matched resources would be investigated. If the current node contains the requested resource, so the requested resource is found, otherwise if it does not contain the requested resource or have the requested resource in its children and descendant, the query will be sent to the father node. However, if the node does not contain the requested resource but it is available in one of its children or descendant, the target node can be found directly and without any referring to extra nodes using the information stored in this node and weighted edges. Therefore, our offered method decreases unnecessary referrals to other nodes and reduces the additional traffic, so the time is saved and the ability of resource discovery is improved.

Due to the existence of different resources in the grid environment and also the various types of resources (attributes), the resources and their attributes should be identified in our bitmap. This bitmap has positions that numbers will be stored in. The length of the bitmap depends on the attributes of each resource. For example, if our expected resource is an operating system (OS), the different types of operating systems that are used in our grid environment determine the length of our bitmap. If the types of operating systems are XP, Linux, Unix and MacOS, our bitmap will have six positions. Actually, we allocate two positions for each type in the bitmap: the counter and path. All of the users' queries should be transformed into this form. Fig. 1, shows a sample of this bitmap that contains the XP operating system in the related node.

Fig. 1. A sample of OS type bitmap.

A node having a special resource locates the numbers 01 in two related positions. Number 0 is for counter and because this resource exists in the node itself, so the number would be 0 and the next one (Number 1) indicates the availability of resources in this node (path). Another position would be 0 indicating that no resources would be available in the node or its children. Each node in our tree contains such a bitmap at the first step and in the next steps the contents of these positions will be changed.

Our algorithm would be on a tree in which a weight will be allocated to any edge by the father nodes, i.e. each node allocates a special binary number to each child depending on the number of children. This node can determine the number of weight bits using following simple formula:

$$y = \left\lceil \log_2^n \right\rceil$$

where n is the number of children of this node, and y is at least the number of bits that should be allocated to edges as weight.

In Fig. 2, we show a weighted tree with its nodes and local resources which is regarded as the first step in constructing a weighted tree with local resources of nodes without considering the resources of children. In Fig. 3, we show same tree after gathering the children information by the father nodes which is the final form of the resource discovery tree. Now we describe the construction of the final form of a tree with an example.

Suppose that our expected resource is an operating system (OS) as Fig. 1, depicts. Each pair position is representative of one type of resource (which here is one type of OS). In Fig. 2, node K has operating system XP (01 in the last two positions), node J has operating system Linux, node F has operating system MacOS etc. The weight of edges is also written on the edges. As said before, these weights, for example 0 between node A and node B is a number in which node A is considered for node B in its memory. Now these nodes should form the final form of the tree in order that the users' requested resources can be found.

For example, we explain the method of gathering information of children and construct the final form of the bitmap in node E. First consider nodes J, K and L. Node E as the father node, takes bitmaps of these three nodes, and analysis them, storing the final information on its bitmap. Suppose that node E takes the information of nodes J, K and L. First we begin from lower positions (from right to left). The first pair position of nodes J, K and L are removed. Two of them contain 00 and the other one contains 01, node E itself has 00, so there is only one resource that is located in node K, which should be registered in the first pair position of node E. Because this resource information is received through a path with weight 01, so we write in the first position the path that the resource information comes from, i.e. 01. We transform this binary number to a decimal number and then record. If the second position which is the counter, increased by two units, namely it would be 2 (increased two units because the weights of node E are two bits). Finally, two numbers, 2 and 1 are registered in the first two positions of node E.

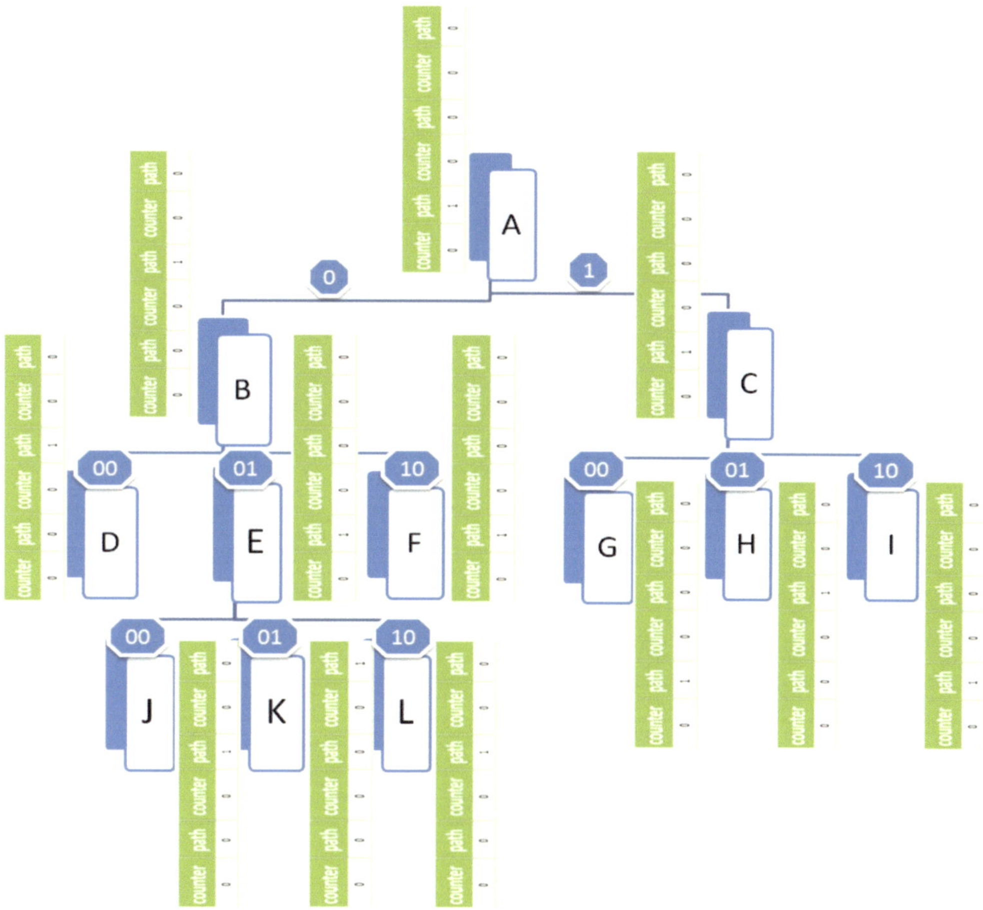

Fig. 2. Our proposed tree before gathering the children information.

Now the next two positions of nodes J, K and L are surveyed (related to the Linux operating system). Two positions related to node K, are 0 0, and nodes J and L are 0 1, meaning that nodes J and L own this resource and the information of one of these resources should be registered in the bitmap of the father node (E). In our method, any one whose counter shows a small number indicates an association with higher levels of the tree. In this case both of them are equal, so we choose one of them randomly (node J). Finally, two numbers, 2 and 0 are registered in the second two positions of node E.

In the next two positions, because node E owns this resource, there is no need for the resource information of children to be replaced by its own resource information. So, these two positions remain as 0 and 1.

The remaining nodes are made in this way using the suggested method. We show in Fig. 3, all related information and our resource discovery tree is formed as mentioned.

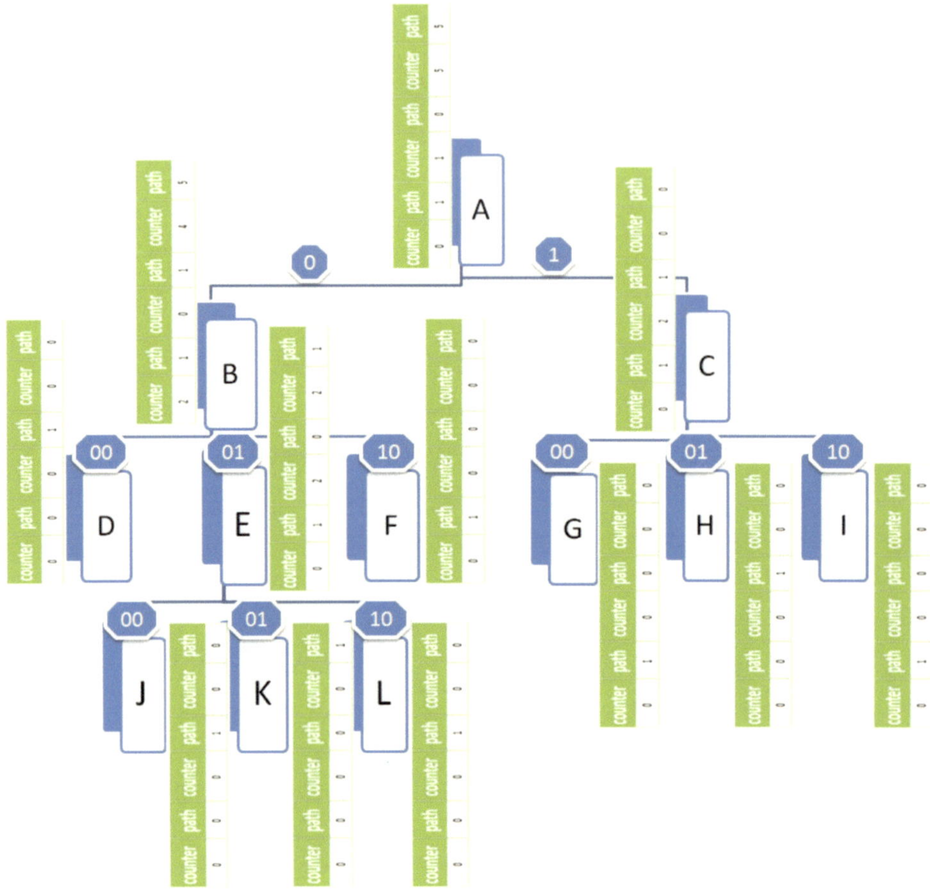

Fig. 3. Our proposed tree after gathering the children information.

3.1 Resource discovery

When any user sends his request to one of the nodes of our resource discovery tree which should be in the form of bitmaps stored in nodes, i.e. in the previous tree structure, the user's query should be in the form of a bitmap with the length of six positions (Fig. 4). The user should allocate number 1 in the pair position (1 1) related to the resource he requires. In Fig. 5, we show the method of resource discovery.

counter	path	counter	path	counter	path
0	0	0	0	1	1

Fig. 4. A sample of query bitmap.

Suppose that a user needs the operating system XP. The user should create a query in the form of a bitmap that has been shown in Fig. 4. All positions of the query bitmap are multiplied with the stored bitmap in the nodes. If the result is 0, the query will be sent to the father node. Otherwise the resulted numbers will be used for resource discovery.

Suppose in this example, the query is first sent to node H. All positions are multiplied with each other and the result would be 0. So, the request will be sent to its father node i.e. C (as Fig. 5). In node C, all positions of request are multiplied with the stored bitmap in this node and the result again would be 0. So the request will be sent to its father node i.e. A. It is observed that the result of multiplication in the node would be the numbers except 0 (5 5). So, number 5 should be changed into a binary number with length 5 so the result is 00101. Using this binary number, we can directly obtain the node which contains the requested resource; the binary number is taken through left to right and goes forward in the edges of the path. The result node would be the target node. Fig. 5 shows this search which resulted in the resource discovery in node K. As soon as a number except zero is achieved, we can directly refer to the destination node without any referring to an extra and unnecessary node.

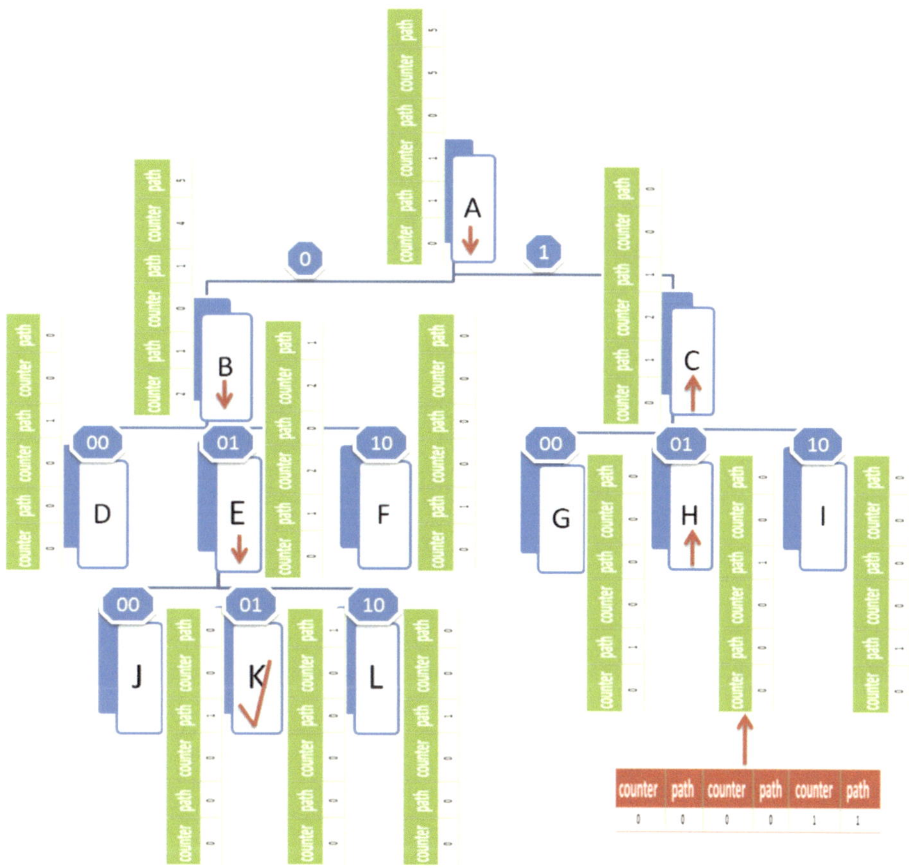

Fig. 5. An example of resource discovery in our weighted tree.

3.2 Improvement the method in a real grid environment

In the current method, the weight of edges in each node is identified and after changing into a decimal number, they are stored in their related places.

The method can be corrected in a real grid environment, because if we suppose a real grid environment with many nodes and edges, the number of 0 and 1s which are to be attached to each other will be large and in storing or converting them into their equivalent decimal, a very large number will result (maybe incomputable).

The solution would be that for storing 0 and 1s, we suppose a threshold number. When a node takes information from its children nodes, including the bitmap, the node first takes the contents of this bitmap then converts the contents of the path position to its equivalent binary number (in the length of counter) and attaches the weight of edge. If the resulted binary number is larger than threshold, this node instead of storing this large number, supposes that the node which this a large number comes from there, is a target node, namely this resource exists in this node, and so stores just the related weight of the edge in the counter, and in fact, the counter in the bitmap starts again. Then this information is sent to the father node and the above operation again will be performed.

Now, when the request reaches one of the nodes and is directed to the target node, a comparison should be made in the target node to identify if the stored number in the target node is 0 and 1, which means the resource is available in this node, otherwise the existing number moves forward of the target node and the above operation again will be performed. Fig. 6, shows this method with threshold = 2 bit, that when the length of bits becomes large in node B from 2 bits, so node B supposes that node C is a target node and stores the address of node C in its bitmap, and in fact from node B the counter will start again.

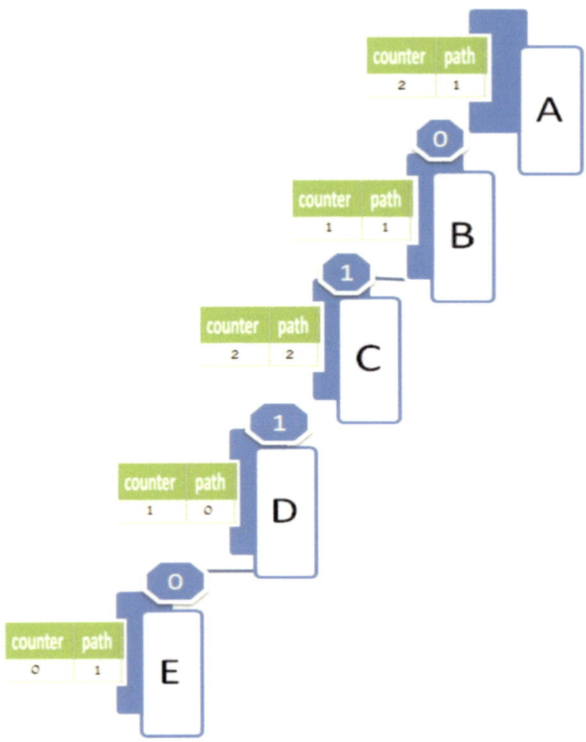

Fig. 6. An example of resource discovery tree with threshold = 2.

Another problem is the large number of the participating nodes and heterogeneity of their available resources. A user may need several resources which may send them in the form of several query bitmaps. It means that a lot of information will not be sent in the form of a unique query. But, we should identify the queries in nodes, i.e. if the query reached, relates to resource 1 or resource 2 etc. (for example OS, CPU, . . .).

We can add some bits to any query bitmap to identify the resource. For example, if there are 16 types of resources in our grid environment, we can add 4 bits to any query bitmap, in order that the receiver can identify with which resource the bitmap should be compared to. This enables us to manage several resources in the grid environment.

3.3 Complexity analysis

Here, the time and space complexities for our method will be investigated. We suppose that there are n nodes and r resources in the grid environment. Every resource has a attributes and the length of the bitmap would be b bits (Chang & Hu, 2010). Also assume the maximum number of children for a node would be m.

3.3.1 Time complexity

Our method applies to a tree structure. Users send their requests to one of the nodes and the request moves in the tree paths for the proper resource to be found. The consumed time includes the required time for computations and communications.

The computation time would be the time consumed in every node to compare the query bitmap with local bitmaps. So, we can calculate the number of nodes visited in resource discovery in our tree for computation time.

The latter would be the time lost between nodes to send a query. Here we can also calculate the number of links. The number of links and visited nodes in resource discovery would be in the same order in tree paths, so both times are supposed the same. One of these times would be larger depending on the network conditions and type of nodes. Because most nodes in the grid environment are of good computation power, but are located in distant intervals in various networks, in the following we assume the communication time through a link is larger than the computation time in a node.

In Our method like (Chang & Hu, 2010), the worst case in the resource discovery is the number of visited links from a leaf node upward to the root then downward to another leaf node. Therefore, the time complexity for our method will be $O(\log^{n}{}_{m})$ in the worst case.

3.3.2 Space complexity

To calculate the space complexity, every node in our tree requires $2 \times r \times a \times b$ places for the path bitmap (any attribute needs two places in the path bitmap) and $r \times a \times b$ places for the counter bitmap and (m + 1) links. Like (Chang & Hu, 2010), if supposing that every place and each link needs 32 bits, the total number of bits required is $n \times (32 \times (2 \times r \times a \times b + r \times a \times b + (m + 1))) = O(nrab + nm)$.

3.4 Update method

For updating, an extra bitmap called a "counter bitmap" will be used. The number of positions in this bitmap depends on the number of types of resources in the grid environment. For example, if there are 5 kinds of operating systems, this counter bitmap will also have 5 positions. The current bitmap represents the number of resources existing in children or descendant of that node.

The method is that the user places two 1s in pair positions which are requested for that resource, and if the request reaches a node, multiplies with the bitmap present in that node until it reaches a node in which its multiplication result would be a number except zero. Using these two numbers and the weight of edges, the target will be found. In the update method, when a request reaches a node with information opposite zero, numbers are removed from the pair positions of that node and two number 0s are placed in two positions which the numbers are removed from and this process will be continued in the path nodes until reaching the target node. When reaching the target node, the numbers 0 and 1 available in two related positions would be 0 and 0.

If the expected resource is to be delivered to the user, no node must have access to the resource address, in other words another user cannot use it. In the current method, the path nodes wait some time after the user's query makes some changes in their path and counter bitmaps, until a message is received from the same path to which the user's query had been sent, to update the changed positions (0 0). If the period of time (time out) ends, this node restores its previous information to the related places.

Otherwise it receives a bitmap. First, this node investigates the pair positions which have been changed in its bitmap. If it contains the information of a resource, puts the contents of the mentioned pair positions in a related place in its bitmap and sends this to its father node and the father node again iterates the process, and because it observes that the contents of these two positions are opposite zero, it tries to reach the root which then the tree is updated.

In the next state, the pair positions that have arrived from the child contain the address of no resource (to be 0 0), so the node checks the contents of the related position in its counter bitmap. If this position is zero, it means that there is no resource in the children and descendant of this node and the bitmap will be sent to its father node, otherwise if this position is any number except zero, there will at least be information related to the expected resource in one of its children. So, this node takes from its children, the path bitmaps, and finds the address of considered resource from one of children, and replaces it with the removed pair positions and then delivers the path bitmap to its father node and the father node, there will be no need to collect the information of children and only the path bitmap which when the contents of its two positions is changed moves to the root node until it stops. In Fig. 7, we show an example of update. Suppose that there are two types of resources in this grid environment, so our path bitmap will have 4 positions and the counter bitmap 2 positions. If a request sent to node B, as (Fig. 7), the result of multiplication of this request with the path bitmap of node B would be zero and the request will be sent to the father node i.e. node A, there is a resource in address 3 6 (110).

The request removes 3 6 from path bitmap of node A, and also decreases by one unit the contents of the related position in the counter bitmap. Then the request goes to node C and the process continues. Finally, it reaches node F, the target node, so its contents which have been 0 1 will be 0 0 and it reserves this resource.

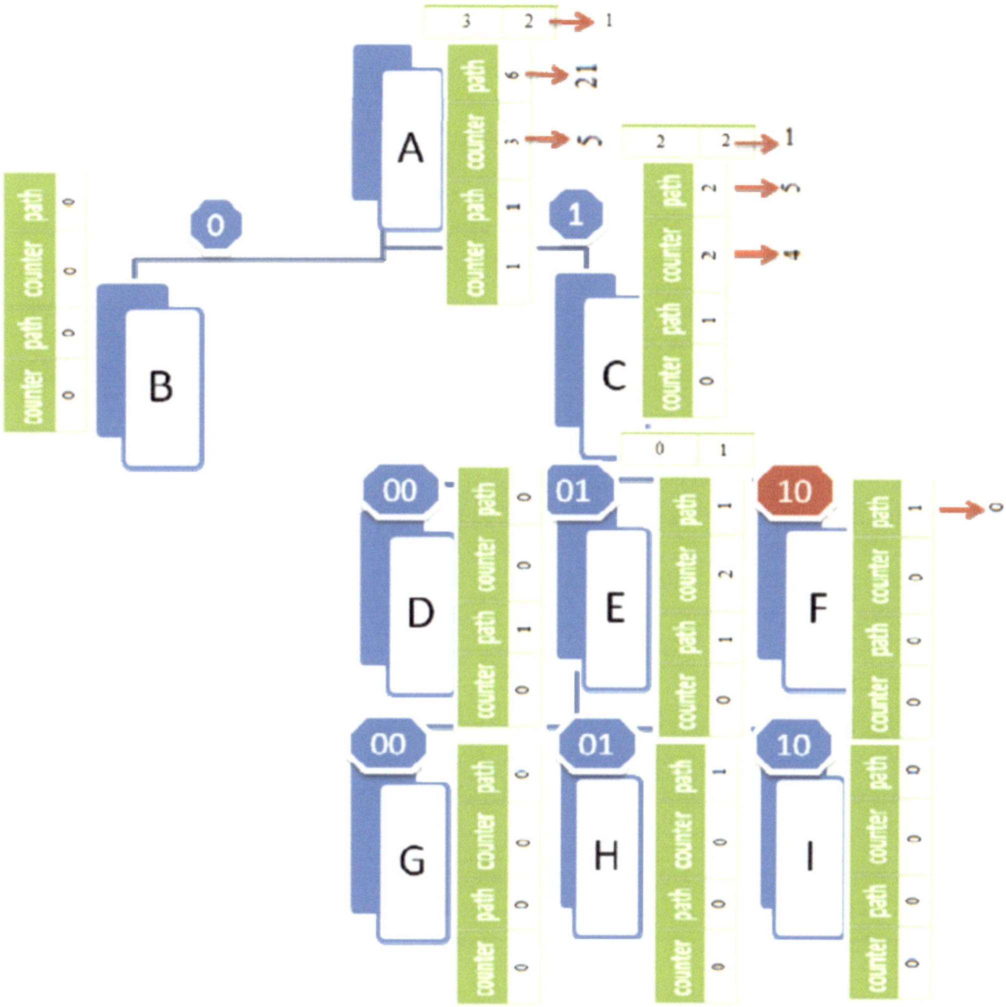

Fig. 7. An example of tree update.

In the update path, node F sends its changed bitmap to node C. If this information does not reach before the time that node C has been considered, node C restores its bitmap to the previous state, otherwise node C, after receiving the bitmap of node F, investigates the condition of removed pair positions and checks the related position of these pair positions in the counter bitmap which is 1 in node C (a nonzero number), so for the information of a resource available in one of the children of node C (nodes D or E), node C takes the information of the children nodes (except a child which has taken that changed bitmap (here node F)). Finally, node C, places numbers 4 and 5 in the condition of removed positions after investigating the information of nodes D and E. So, the bitmap will be sent to node A. Node A after observing that the contents of related pair positions are nonzero, sees there is no need to collect the information of the children, and with this information, updates its previous information. In our update method, information of children is gathered only in one of levels, and all through the path, just visited by one node in any level of tree.

4. Simulation results

In this section, we compare our simulation results with the recommended algorithm in (Chang & Hu, 2010), flooding-based approach and the algorithm proposed in (Marzolla et al., 2005; Marzolla et al., 2007) (MMO). In the first simulation tests, the total number of nodes which are visited during in the resource discovery and in updating are compared with algorithm (Chang & Hu, 2010) for 400 queries. In the second experiment, the nodes which queries send during resource discovery for the flooding-based approach, MMO algorithm and resource discovery tree algorithm, are shown and compared with our method.

As we know, for calculating the traffic which a method causes, we can calculate the number of links which are occupied for resource discovery or updating in the method. If the number of links visited for resource discovery or updating in a method is lower, the method has lower traffic and would be more efficient.

In the next simulation tests, the traffic in our method which is caused by the increased number of tree nodes in resource discovery and updating is indicated and the results are obtained for different nodes with 300 and 1000 queries. In the last simulation, we observe that the traffic caused in our method would be lower than other methods. This test is performed supposing there are 300 queries for different nodes, and the flooding-based, MMO, resource discovery tree and our methods are compared.

4.1 Simulation settings

We performed the simulation in the MATLAB environment. Our resource discovery tree is a full n-ary tree. It means that any non leaf node should have exactly n children. According to Mastroianni et al. (2007), and Chang & Hu (2010), we also assume that the resource discovery tree for simulation has height 4.

In the first experiment tests, we compare our algorithm with a resource discovery tree with a different number of index servers. Like (Chang & Hu, 2010), in this experiment there are 200 nodes in resource discovery tree and we perform this experiment with 180 queries.

We place the resources randomly in each node and then queries are sent through tree paths and compare the number of nodes that visited in each method. In Fig. 8, the difference between the number of visited nodes with two methods are observed. In this experiment, the number of visited nodes is investigated with changing the number of index servers. For example, when the number of index servers in tree is 10, so there are 10 nodes in level 1 and 190 nodes in level 2 (19 children for each node in level 1) for a tree with height 3. Because our method in the forward path just visits one node in every level so in Figs. 8, the simulations related to our method almost show the fix values.

In the second simulation tests, we assume there are 300 queries and a tree with height 4. In Fig. 9, we compare the number of nodes that queries send in our algorithm with the resource discovery tree and show that the number of nodes visited in our proposed method is lower than the previous method.

In the third simulation tests, we show the total number of nodes that were visited in the resource discovery path and for tree updating with assume 400 queries and different number of nodes for our method and compare with the other one. In Fig. 10, it is indicated that in our algorithm, fewer nodes are visited compared with the previous one.

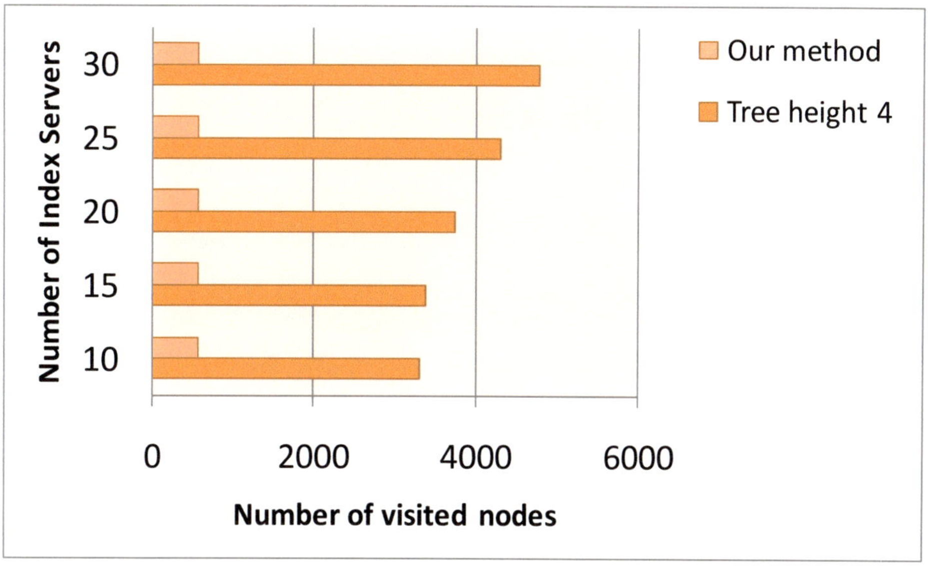

Fig. 8. The number of nodes that queries are forwarded to for 180 queries.

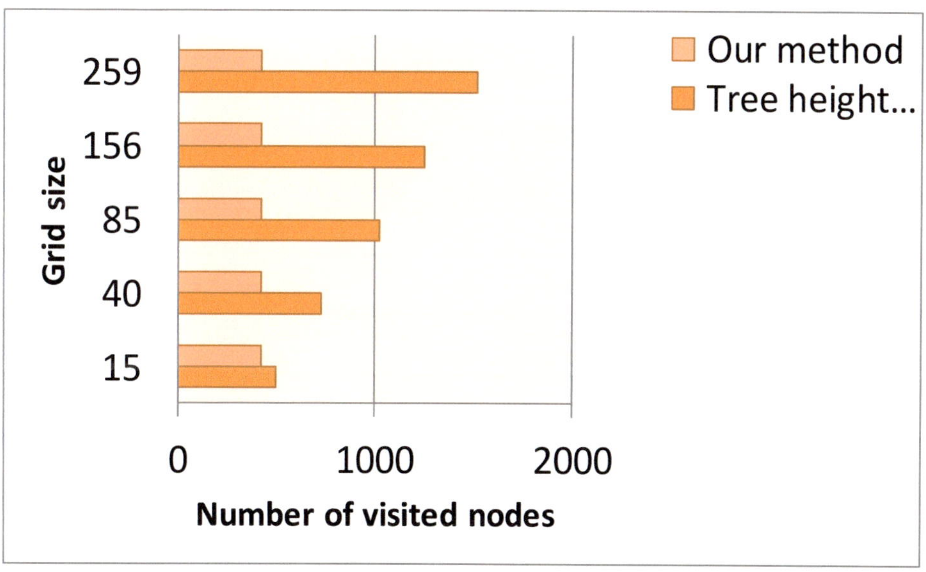

Fig. 9. The number of nodes that queries are forwarded to.

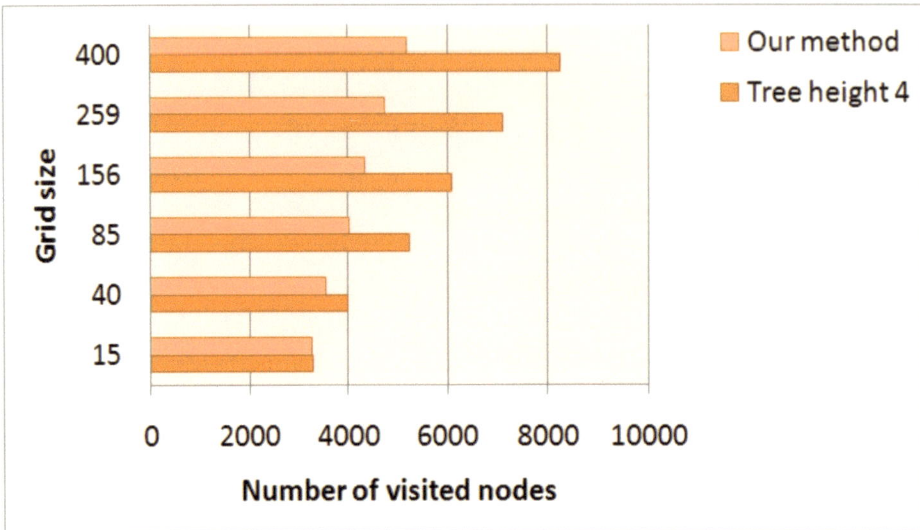

Fig. 10. Total number of nodes that are visited in resource discovery and updates.

In the next simulation tests, our method is compared with flooding-based method, MMO and resource discovery tree algorithm. In the current experiment supposing that there are 300 queries, in Fig. 11, it is indicated that the average number of nodes that queries are sent to is lower than other methods in our proposed method. The test is performed in a tree with height 4.

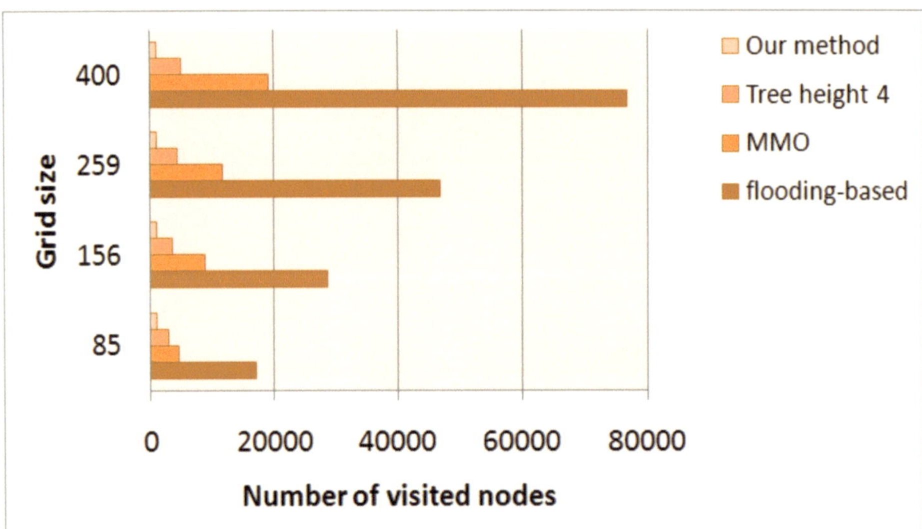

Fig. 11. Average number of nodes that queries are forwarded to using different methods.

In the next simulation tests, the number of occupied links in our method during the resource discovery phase and update phase is observed for different nodes with 300 and 1000 queries. In Fig. 12, we show the occupied links (traffic) for resource discovery and updating for 300 (Fig. 12) and 1000 queries (Fig. 13).

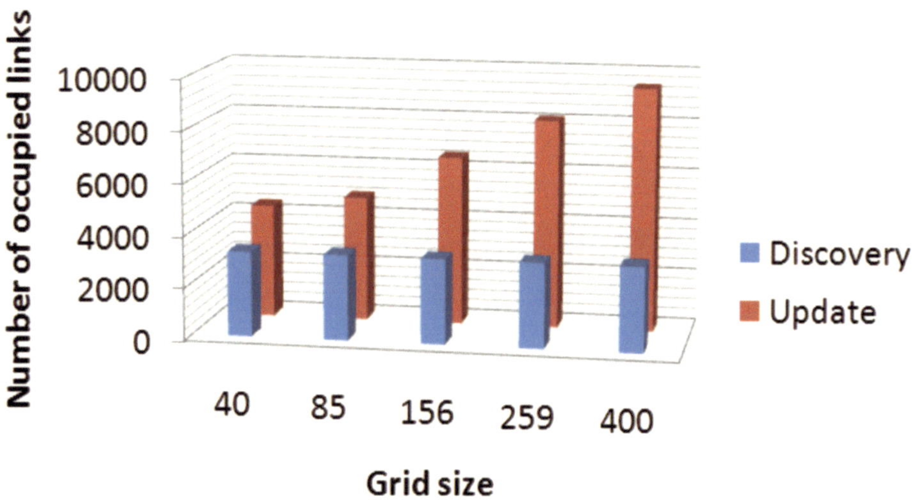

Fig. 12. Number of links that resource discovery queries and updates are forwarded to for 300 queries.

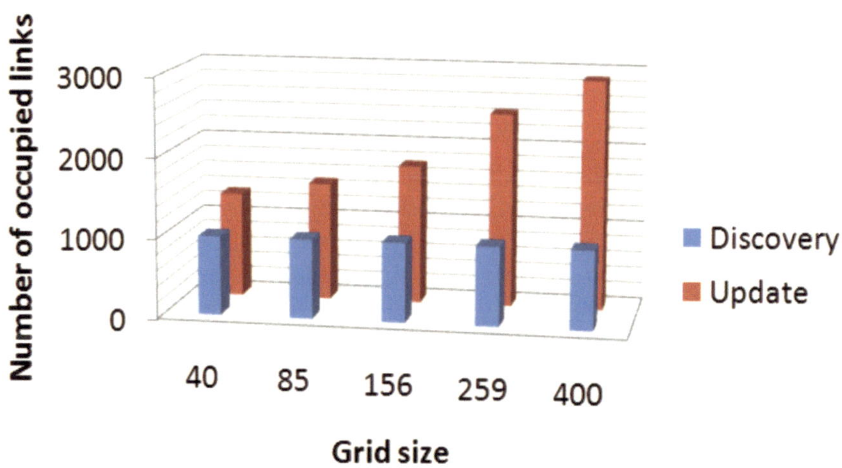

Fig. 13. Number of links that resource discovery queries and updates are forwarded to for 1000 queries.

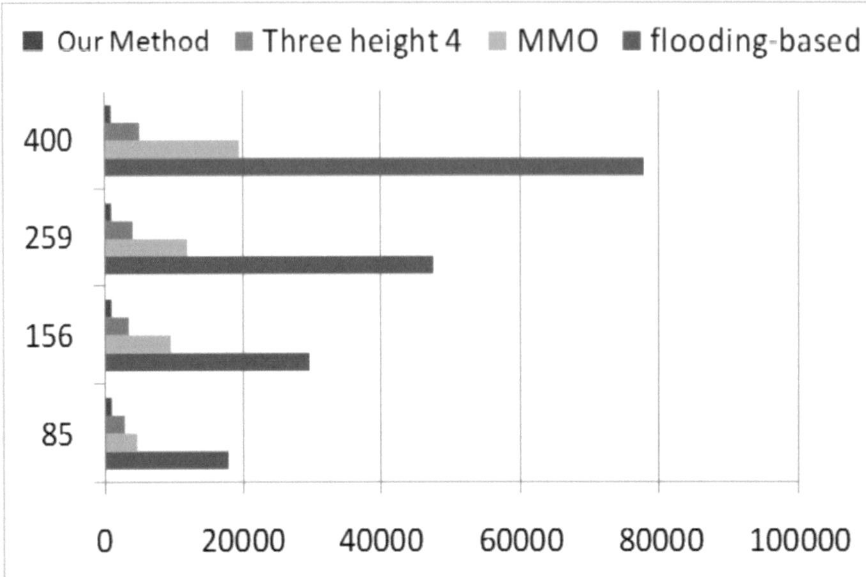

Fig. 14. Number of links that are visited by resource discovery queries for 300 queries.

In the last experiment, we supposed that there are 300 queries, and we show the visited links (traffic) which are caused during resource discovery in our method and compared with flooding-based, MMO and the resource discovery tree and for different numbers of nodes. In Fig. 14, we can see the traffic caused in our method is lower than other methods

5. Conclusions and future work

In this work, we use a tree structure in which the edges have weight. The advantage of our method is that any node in our weighted tree has a unique path, so the user's query against all of previous methods is not sent to the extra and unnecessary paths. We can directly reach the target node using a resource footprint which is stored in nodes.

Furthermore, for resource discovery we only use one bitmap in every node which is for the storing of information about its local resources and the resources of its children and descendant. Also it preserves a footprint of resources and if we need a resource which is available in its children or descendant, we can directly and without any referring to unnecessary and extra nodes, reach the target node. This method significantly reduces the system traffic and increases the performance of system.

We compare our algorithm with previous algorithms using simulations and results and show that the number of nodes visited in our resource discovery algorithm is less than that for other algorithms, and the difference would be significant with an increase in the number of nodes. Also the cost of update in our proposed algorithm is low.

In future, if we could a present a technique that could locate several heterogeneous resources (with different attributes) of a grid environment in smaller forms with a lower volume, or placed in one bitmap involving some factors, for example allocated costs for resources etc., we could improve the algorithm.

6. References

Al-Dmour, N.A. & Teahan, W.J. (2005). Peer-to-Peer protocols for resource discovery in the grid, in: *Parallel and Distributed Computing and Networks*, Innsbruck, Austria.

Ali, K.; Datta, S.; Aboelaze, M. (2005). Grid resource discovery using small world overlay graphs, in: Proceedings of the 18th IEEE Canadian Conference on Electrical and Computer Engineering.

Basu, S.; Banerjee, S.; Sharma, P.; Lee, S. (2005). NodeWiz: peer-topeer resource discovery for grids, in: 5th International Workshop on Global and Peer-to-Peer Computing (GP2PC) in Conjunction with CCGrid.

Berman, F. & et al. (2003). Adaptive computing on the grid using AppLeS, TPDS 14 (4).

Bharambe, A.R.; Agrawal, M. & Seshan, S. (2004). Mercury: Supporting scalable multiattribute range queries, in: *Proc. of ACM SIGCOMM*, pp. 353–366.

Bradley, A.; Curran, K.; Parr, G., (2006). Discovering resource in computational GRID environments. Journal of Supercomputing 35, 27–49.

Cai, M. & Hwang, K. (2007). Distributed aggregation algorithms with load- balancing for scalable grid resource monitoring, in: *Proc. of IPDPS.*

Chang, R.-S. & Hu, M.-S. (2010). A resource discovery tree using bitmap for grids, *Future Gener. Comput. Syst.* 26 29–37.

Chien, A.; Calder, B.; Elbert, S. & Bhatia, K. (2003). Entropia: Architecture and performance of an enterprise desktop grid system, J. Parallel Distrib. Comput. 63 (5).

Deng, Y.; Wang, F.; Ciura, A. (2009). Ant colony optimization inspired resource discovery in P2P Grid systems, J Supercomput 49: 4–21.

Foster, I. & Kesselman, C. (1997). Globus: A metacomputing infrastructure toolkit, *Int. J. High Perform. Comput. Appl.* 2 115–128.

Foster, I. & Kesselman, C. (2003). The Grid 2: Blueprint for a New Computing Infrastructure, Morgan Kaufmann Publishers Inc., San Francisco, CA.

Germain, C.; Neri, V.; Fedak, G.; Cappello, F. (2000). XtremWeb: Building an experimental platform for global computing, in: Proc. of IEEE/ACM Grid, December.

Iamnitchi, A.; Foster, I.; Nurmi, D. C. (2002). A peer-to-peer approach to resource location in grid environments, in: Proceedings of the 11th Symposium on High Performance Distributed Computing, Edinburgh, UK, August.

Iamnitchi, A. & Talia, D. (2005). P2P computing and interaction with Grids, *Future Gener. Comput. Syst.* 21 (3) 331–332.

Khanli, L.M. & Kargar, S. (2011). FRDT: Footprint Resource Discovery Tree for grids, Future Gener. Comput. Syst. 27 148–156.

Koo, S.G.M.; Kannan, K. & Lee, C.S.G. (2006). On neighbor selection strategy in hybrid Peer-to-Peer networks, *Future Gener. Comput. Syst.* 22, 732–741.

Li, J. (2010). Grid resource discovery based on semantically linked virtual organizations, *Future Gener. Comput. Syst.* 26, 361–373.

Li, J. & Vuong, S. (2005). Grid resource discovery using semantic communities, in: *Proceedings of the 4th International Conference on Grid and Cooperative Computing*, Beijing, China

Liu, H.; Luo, P. & Zeng, Z. (2006). A structured hierarchical P2P model based on a rigorous binary tree code algorithm, *Future Gener. Comput. Syst.*

Marzolla, M.; Mordacchini, M. & Orlando, S. (2005). Resource discovery in a dynamic environment, in: *Proceedings of the 16th International Workshop on Database and Expert Systems Applications*, DEXA'05, pp. 356–360.

Marzolla, M.; Mordacchini, M. & Orlando, S. (2007). Peer-to-peer systems for discovering resources in a dynamic grid, *Parallel Comput.* 33 (4–5) 339–358.

Mastroianni, C.; Talia, D. & Verta, O. (2005). A super-peer model for resource discovery services in large-scale grids, *Future Gener. Comput. Syst.* 21 (8) 1235–1248.

Mastroianni, C.; Talia, D. & Versta, O. (2007). Evaluating resource discovery protocols for hierarchical and super-peer grid information systems, in: *Proceedings of the 15th EUROMICRO International Conference on Parallel, Distributed and Network-Based Processing*, PDP'07, pp. 147–154.

Mutka, M.; Livny, M. (1987). Scheduling remote processing capacity in a workstation processing bank computing system, in: Proc. of ICDCS, September.

Nazir, F.; Ahmad, H.F.; Burki, H.A.; Tarar, T.H.; Ali, A. & Suguri, H. (2005). A Resource Monitoring and Management Middleware Infrastructure for Semantic Resource Grid, SAG 2004, in: LNCS, vol. 3458, pp. 188–196.

Neary, M.O.; Brydon, S.P.; Kmiec, P.; Rollins, S. & Capello, P. (1999). JavelinCC: Scalability issues in global computing, *Future Gener. Comput. Syst.* J. 15 (5–6), 659–674.

Nejdl, W.; Wolf, B.; Qu, C.; Decker, S.; SIntek, M.; Naeve, A.; Nilsson, M.; Palmer, M.; Risch, T.; Edutella. (2002). A P2P networking infrastructure based on RDF, in: Proceedings of the WWW2002, May 7–11, Honolulu, Hawaii, USA, pp. 604–615.

Oppenheimer, O.; Albrecht, J.; Patterson, D.; Vahdat, A. (2004). Scalable wide-area resource discovery, Technical Report TR CSD04-1334, Univ. of California.

Pipan, G. (2010). Use of the TRIPOD overlay network for resource discovery, Future Generation Computer Systems 26, 1257_1270.

Qi, X.S.; Li, K.L. & Yao, F.J. (2006). A time-to-live based multi-resource reservation algorithm on resource discovery in Grid environment, in: *Proceedings of the 2006 1st International Symposium on Pervasive Computing and Applications*, pp. 189–193.

Ramos, T.G. & de Melo, A.C.M.A. (2006). An extensible resource discovery mechanism for grid computing environments, in: *Proceedings of the Sixth IEEE International Symposium on Cluster Computing and the Grid*, CCGRID'06, pp. 115–122.

Shen, H. (2009). A P2P-based intelligent resource discovery mechanism in Internetbased distributed systems, *J. Parallel Distrib. Comput.* 69, 197–209.

Talia, D.; Trunfio, P.; Zeng, J. & Högqvist, M. (2006). A DHT-based Peer-to-Peer framework for resource discovery in grids. Technical Report TR-0048, Univ. of California.

Tangpongprasit, S.; Katagiri, T.; Honda, H. & Yuba, T. (2005). A time-to-live based reservation algorithm on fully decentralized resource discovery in grid computing, *Parallel Comput.* 31 (6) 529–543.

Trunfio, P.; Talia, D.; Papadakis, H.; Fragopoulou, P.; Mordacchini, M.; Pennanen, M.; Popov, K.; Vlassov, V. & Haridi, S. (2007). Peer-to-Peer resource discovery in Grids: Models and systems, *Future Gener. Comput. Syst.* 23, 864–878.

Zerfiridis, K.G.; Karatza, H.D. (2003). Centralized and decentralized service Discovery on a peer-to-peer Network - a simulation study, in: Proceedings of the Sixth United Kingdom Simulation Society Conference, UKSim 2003, Cambridge, England, 9th–11th April, pp. 171–177.

Zhu, C.; Liu, Z.; Zhang, W.; Xiao, W.; Xu, Z. & Yang, D. (2005). Decentralized grid resource discovery based on resource information community, *J. Grid Comput.*

Zhuge, H. (2004). Semantics, resource and grid, Future Gener. Comput. Syst. 20 (1) 1–5.

5

Task Scheduling in Grid Environment Using Simulated Annealing and Genetic Algorithm

Wael Abdulal[1], Ahmad Jabas[1], S. Ramachandram[1] and Omar Al Jadaan[2]
[1]*Department of Computer Science and Engineering, Osmania University*
[2]*Medical and Health Sciences University*
[1]*India*
[2]*United Arab Emirates*

1. Introduction

Grid computing enables access to geographically and administratively dispersed networked resources and delivers functionality of those resources to individual users. Grid computing systems are about sharing computational resources, software and data at a large scale. The main issue in grid system is to achieve high performance of grid resources. It requires techniques to efficiently and adaptively allocate tasks and applications to available resources in a large scale, highly heterogeneous and dynamic environment.

In order to understand grid systems, three terms are reviewed as shown below:

1. **Virtualization**: The Virtualization term in grids refers to seamless integration of geographically distributed and heterogeneous systems, which enables users to use the grid services transparently. Therefore, they should not be aware of the location of

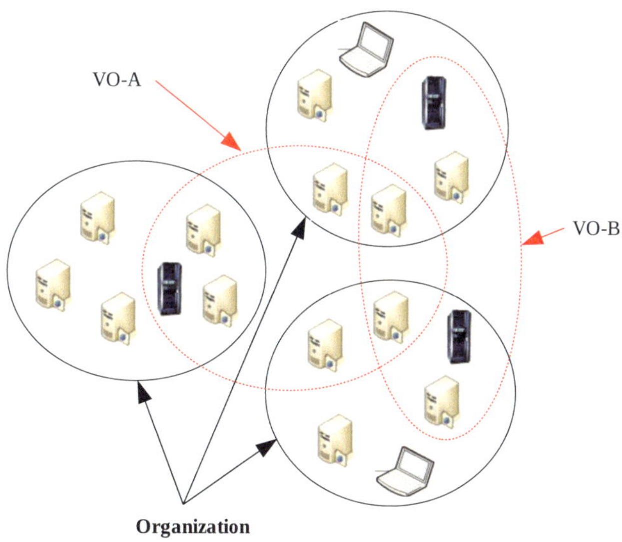

Fig. 1. Two virtual organizations are formed by combining a three real organizations

computing resources and have to submit their service request at just one point of entry to the grid system. Foster introduced the concept of Virtual Organization (VO) (Foster et al., 2001). He defines VO as a *"dynamic collection of multiple organizations providing flexible, secure, coordinated resource sharing"*. Figure 1 shows three actual organizations with both computational and data resources to share across organizational boundaries. Moreover, the same figure forms two VOs, A and B, each of them can have access to a subset of resources in each of the organizations (Moallem, 2009). Virtualization is a mechanism that improves the usability of grid computing systems by providing environment customization to users.

2. **Heterogeneity**: The organizations that form part of VO may have different resources such as hardware, operating system and network bandwidth. Accordingly, VO is considered as a collection of heterogeneous resources of organizations.
3. **Dynamism**: In the grid system, organizations or their resources can join or leave VO depending on their requirements or functional status.

Grid systems provide the ability to perform higher throughput computing by usage of many networked computers to distribute process execution across a parallel infrastructure. Nowadays, organizations around the world are utilizing grid computing in such diverse areas as collaborative scientific research, drug discovery, financial risk analysis, product design and 3−D seismic imaging in the oil and gas industry (Dimitri et al., 2005).

Interestingly, task scheduling in grid has been paid a lot of attention over the past few years. The important goal of task scheduling is to efficiently allocate tasks as fast as possible to avialable resources in a global, heterogeneous and dynamic environment. Kousalya pointed out that the grid scheduling consists of three stages: First, resource discovery and filtering. Second, resource selection and scheduling according to certain objective. Third, task submission. The third stage includes the file staging and cleanup (Kousalya & Balasubramanie, 2009; 2008). High performance computing and high throughput computing are the two different goals of grid scheduling algorithm. The main aim of the high performance computing is to minimize the execution time of the application. Allocation of resources to a large number of tasks in grid computing environment presents more difficulty than in conventional computational environments.

The scheduling problem is well known NP-complete (Garey & Johnson, 1979). It is a combinatorial optimization problem by nature. Many algorithms are proposed for task scheduling in grid environments. In general, the existing heuristic mapping can be divided into two categories (Jinquan et al., 2005):

First, online mode, where the scheduler is always in ready mode. Whenever a new task arrives to the scheduler, it is immediately allocated to one of the existing resources required by that task. Each task is considered only once for matching and scheduling.

Second, batch mode, the tasks and resources are collected and mapped at prescheduled time. This mode takes better decision because the scheduler knows the full details of the available tasks and resources. This chapter proposes a heuristic algorithm that falls in batch mode Jinquan et al. (2005).

However, this chapter studies the problem of minimizing makespan, i.e., the total execution time of the schedule in grid environment. The proposed Mutation-based Simulated Annealing (MSA) algorithm is proved to have high performance computing scheduling algorithm. MSA algorithm will be studied for random and Expected Time to Compute (ETC) Models.

2. Related works

One salient issue in grid is to design efficient schedulers, which will be used as a part of middleware services to provide efficient planning of users' tasks to grid resources. Various scheduling approaches that were suggested in classical parallel systems literature are adopted for the grid systems with appropriate modifications. Although these modifications made them suitable for execution in grid environment, these approaches failed to deliver on the performance factor. For this reason, Genetic Algorithm (GA) and Simulated Annealing (SA) algorithm, among others, used to solve difficulties of task scheduling in grid environment. They gave reasonable solutions comparing with classical scheduling algorithms. GA solutions for grid scheduling are addressed in several works (Abraham et al., 2000; Carretero & Xhafa, 2006; Abraham et al., 2008; Martino & Mililotti, 2002; Martino, 2003; Y. Gao et al., 2005). These studies ignored how to speed up convergence and shorten the search time of GA.

Furthermore, SA algorithm was studied in previous works Fidanova (2006); Manal et al. (2011). These works show important results and high quality solutions indicating that SA is a powerful technique and can be used to solve grid scheduling problem. Moreover, Jadaan, in Jadaan et al. (2009; 2010; 2011), exposed the importance of rank in GA.

The authors Wook& Park (2005) proved that both GA and SA algorithms have complementary strengths and weaknesses, accordingly, they proposed a new SA-selection to enhance GA performance to solve combinatorial optimization problem. The population size which they use is big that makes time consumed by algorithm large, specially when problem size increases. While Kazem tried to solve a static task scheduling problem in grid computing using a modified SA (Kazem et al., 2008). Prado propose a fuzzy scheduler obtained by means of evolving a fuzzy scheduler to improve the overall response time for the entire workflow (Prado et al., 2009). Rules of this evolutionary fuzzy system is obtained using genetic learning process based on Pittsburgh approach.

Wael proposed an algorithm that minimizes makespan, flowtime and time to release as well as it maximizes reliability of grid resources (Wael & Ramachandram, 2011). It takes transmission time and waiting time in resource queue into account. It uses stochastic universal sampling selection and single exchange mutation to outperform other GAs.

Lee et al. (2011) provided Hierarchical Load Balanced Algorithm (HLBA) for Grid environment. He used the system load as a parameter in determining a balance threshold. the scheduler adapts the balance threshold dynamically when the system load changes. The loads of resource are CPU utilization, network utilization and memory utilization.

P.K. Suri & Singh Manpreet (2010) proposed a Dynamic Load Balancing Algorithm (DLBA) which performs an intra-cluster and inter cluster load balancing. Intra-cluster load balancing is performed depending on the Cluster Manager (CM). CM decides whether to start the local balancing based on the current workload of the cluster which is estimated from the resources below it. Inter-cluster load balancing is done when some CMs fail to balance their workload. In this case, the tasks of the overloaded cluster will be transferred to another cluster which is underloaded. In order to check the cluster overloading, they introduced a balanced threshold. If the load of cluster is larger than balanced threshold, load balancing will be executed. The value of balanced threshold is fixed. Therefore, the balanced threshold is not appropriate for the dynamic characteristics in the grid system.

Chang et al. (2009) introduced Balanced Ant Colony Optimization algorithm (BACO) to choose suitable resources to execute tasks according to resources status. The pheromone update functions perform balancing to the system load. While local pheromone update function updates the status of the selected resource after tasks assignment. Global pheromone update the status of each resource for all tasks after completion of all tasks.

In this chapter MSA maintains two solutions at a time, and it uses single exchange mutation operator as well as random-MCT heuristic (demonstrated in subsection 5.2).

Previous works, namely, Wael et al. (2009c;b;a) considered the minimization of the makespan using GA based on Rank Roullete Wheel Selection (RRWSGA). They use standard deviation of fitness function as a termination condition of the algorithm. The aim of using standard deviation is to shorten the the time consumed by the algorithm with taking into account reasonable performance of Computing resources (97%).

Yin introduced GA which used standard deviation less than (0.1) as stopping criterion to limit the number of iterations of GA (Yin et al., 2007). This algorithm has drawbacks such as low quality solutions (almost same as low quality solutions of standard GA), generating initialization population randomly (even though the time consumed by algorithm is small comparing with standard GA), and mutation depends on exchange of every gene in the chromosome. This mutation will destroy the good information in subsequent chromosomes in next generations. In order to illustrate the usefulness of this work, next section explains the motivation behind it.

3. Motivation

The motivation of this chapter is to develop a grid scheduling algorithm that can introduce a high utilization of grid resources, speed up convergence to the optimal or sub-optimal solution, shorten time consumed by algorithm as much as possible, improve load balancing of grid resources to the best optimization level, and minimize the schedule length, i.e., makespan.

The quality of solution produced by Yin's algorithm for grid scheduling is low. In other words, Yin proposed GA where mutation with all genes of chromosome are changed (Yin et al., 2007). This type of mutation is not always suitable to solve complex optimization problem such as grid task scheduling. It destroys the information in the chromosomes and does not help to find the optimal or near-optimal solution for the problem at hand. Moreover, the population's initialization of Yin's algorithm is generated randomly without using any heuristic in initialization phase of GA. The heuristics allow GA to search closer to the optimal solution area reducing the time consumed by an algorithm to reach the reasonable level of solution.
The four subfigures 2(a), 2(b), 2(c) and 2(d) show that the single exchange mutation (two genes exchanges), represented by dashed curves, approaches the optimal solution faster than the all genes changed mutation, represented by straight curves, in terms of the number of generations. Furthermore, subfigures 2(c) and 2(d) highlight the importance of using heuristic algorithm random-MCT (demonstrated in subsection 5.2) at the initialization stage of GA.

In this chapter, two models are introduced in term of random initialization of tasks and resources. First, Random Model (RM), which follows the uniform distribution in generating the matrix EET_{ij} with low-value ranges for computing capacities of resources and the workload of tasks. Second model, Expected Time to Compute (ETC) 11, in which the workload of tasks and computing resource capacity are generated randomly, in different ranges, low and

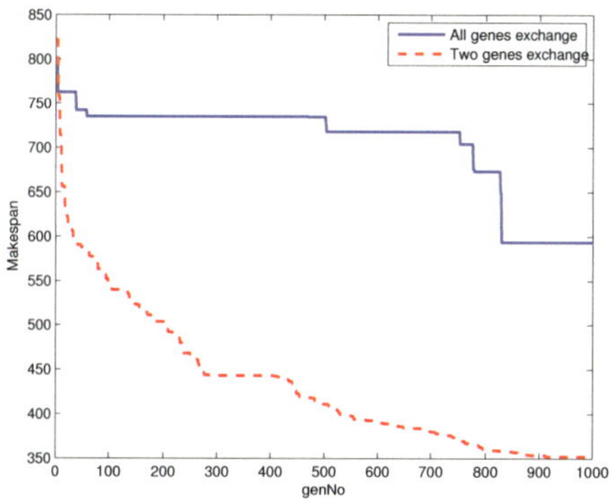

(a) Makespan results with one point crossover and random initialization of GA

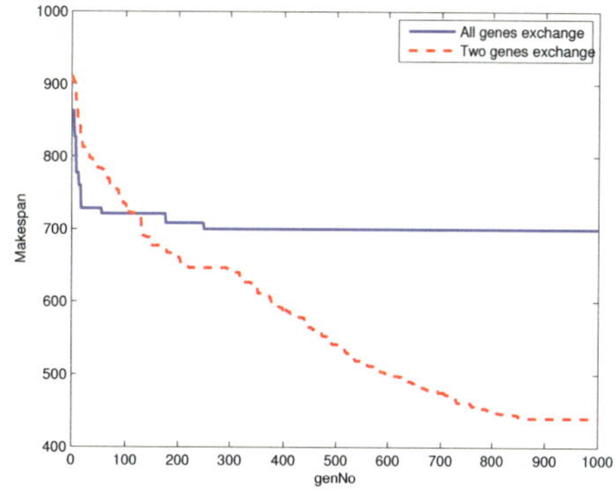

(b) Makespan results with two points crossover and random initialization of GA

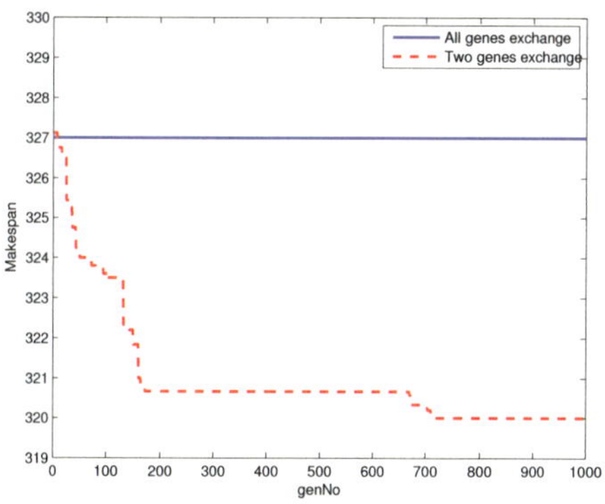

(c) Makespan results with Random-MCT and one point crossover

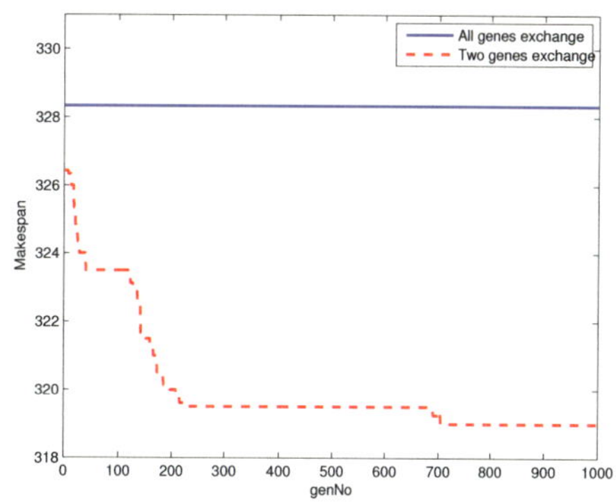

(d) Makespan results with Random-MCT and two points crossover

Fig. 2. Makespan results of experiment 8 (mentioned in table 3) which consists of 1000 tasks and 50 resources with one/two point(s) crossover, with/without Random-MCT, and two/all genes exchanged.

high. Figure 3 shows the relationships among RM and ETC models, on one hand, and both algorithms RGSGCS and MSA, on the another hand.

Fig. 3. The relationship among RM/ETC model and the RGSGCS/MSA

4. Problem formulation

For any problem formulation is fundamental issue which help to understand the problem at hand. This chapter considers a grid with sufficient arriving tasks to GA for scheduling. Let N be the total number of tasks to be scheduled and W_i, where $i = 1, 2, \cdots, N$, be the workload of each task in number of cycles. The workload of tasks can be obtained by analyzing historical data, such as determining the data size of a waiting task. Let M be the total number of computing resources and CP_j, where $j = 1, 2, \cdots, M$, be the computing capacity of each resource expressed in number of cycles per unit time. The Expected Execution Time EET_{ij} of task T_i on resource R_j is defined in the following formula:

$$EET_{ij} = \frac{W_i}{CP_j} \tag{1}$$

5. Rank Genetic Scheduler for Grid Computing Systems (RGSGCS) algorithm

GA is a robust search technique that allows a high-quality solution to be derived from a large search space in polynomial time, by applying the principle of evolution. In other words, GA is used to solve optimization problems by imitating the genetic process of biological organisms (Goldberg, 1989). In GA, a potential solution to a specific problem is represented as a chromosome containing a series of genes. A set of chromosomes make up population. GA evolves the population, that generates an optimal solution, using selection, crossover and mutation operators.

Therefore, GA combines the exploitation of best solutions from past searches with the exploration of new regions of the solution space. Any solution in the search space of the problem is represented by a chromosome.

RGSGCS is GA for solving task scheduling in grid environment. It is presented in the algorithm 2 and the flowchart 5, ((Wael et al., 2010) and (Wael et al., 2011)).

In order to successfully apply RGSGCS to solve the problem at hand, one needs to determine the following :

1. The representation of possible solutions, or the chromosomal encoding.
2. The fitness function which accurately represents the value of the solution.
3. Genetic operators (i.e., selection, crossover, Mutation and Elitism) which have to be used and the parameter values (population size, probability of applying operators, maximum number of generatons, etc.), which are suitable.

The main steps in RGSGCS are as follows:

5.1 Chromosome representation of RGSGCS algorithm

In GA, a chromosome is represented by a series of genes. Each gene, in turn, represents an index of computing resource R_j as shown below:

$$Chromosome = gene_i(R_j) \tag{2}$$

Where $i = 1, 2, \cdots, N$, and $j = 1, 2, \cdots, M$. Figure 4 shows an example of the chromosome's representation consists of three resources and thirteen tasks.

Task No.	1	2	3	4	5	6	7	8	9	10	11	12	13
Resource No.	1	3	1	3	2	2	3	1	2	1	3	2	2

Fig. 4. Task-Resource Representation for the Grid Task Scheduling Problem

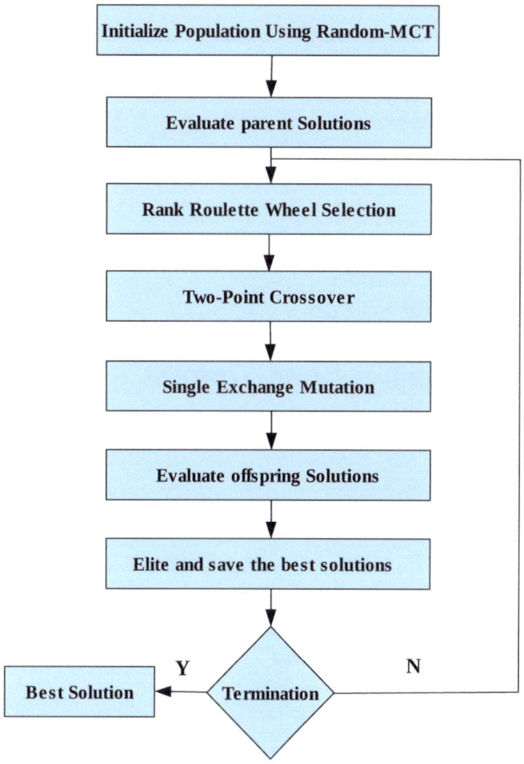

Fig. 5. Flow Chart of RGSGCS Algorithm

5.2 Population initialization of RGSGCS algorithm

One of the important steps in GA is initialization of population. This initialization supports GA to find best solutions within the available search space. In this step, in GA, if bad solutions are generated randomly, the algorithm provides bad solutions or local optimal solutions. To overcome the posed problem, generating individuals using well-known heuristics in the initial step of the algorithm is required. These heuristics generate near-optimal solutions and the meta-heuristic algorithm combines these solutions in order to obtain better final solutions.

Scheduling heuristics such as Min-Min, Minimum Completion Time (MCT), Minimum Execution Time (MET) (Braun et al., 2001), are proposed for independent tasks. Most of these heuristics are based on the following two assumptions.

First, the expected execution time EET_{ij} is deterministic and does not vary with time.

Second, each task has exclusive use of the resource. Traditional MCT heuristic assigns each task to the resource that completes it earliest. The new algorithm, Random-MCT, is described below: For the first tasks in the grid, which their number equals to total resources number in the grid, the resources are assigned randomly. The remaining tasks in the grid are assigned according to earliest finishing time. Where RT_j is the Ready Time of resource j. The time complexity of Random-MCT heuristic is O($M.N$). After completion of RGSGCS's initialization, the evaluation phase is introduced.

Algorithm 1 Random-MCT

for $Ti = 1$ *to* M tasks in the grid **do**
    for all resources R_j in the grid **do**
        $C_{ij} = EET_{ij} + RT_j$
        find resource R_p randomly for T_i
        attach T_i to R_p
    end for
end for
for remaining tasks T_i in the grid **do**
    for all resources R_j in the grid **do**
        $C_{ij} = EET_{ij} + RT_j$
        find resource R_p which will finish T_i earliest
        attach T_i to R_p
    end for
end for

Algorithm 2 RGSGCS

Generate Initial Population P of size $N1$ using Random-MCT (algorithm 1).
for $g = 1$ to $MaximumGenerations$ **do**
      Calculate the fitness of each chromosome using equations (3, 4 and 5)
    Generate offspring Population from P
     {Rank based Roulette Wheel Selection
      Recombination and Mutation
      Calculate the fitness of each chromosome using equations (3, 4 and 5) }
    (elitism) Select the members of the combined population based on minimum fitness, to make the population P of the next generation.
end for

5.3 The evaluation phase of RGSGCS algorithm

The evaluation phase evaluates the quality of resulted schedule depending on a fitness equation. The fitness equation must be devised to determine the quality of a given chromosome instance and always returns a single numerical value. In this chapter, the fitness function is the makespan, i.e., the minimum completion time of the last finishing task. In other words, makspan is the schedule length. The main goal is to maximize the throughput of the grid by minimizing makespan through an intelligent load balancing. The makespan is calculated using the equations 3 and 4.While the fitness function is expressed as in equation 5.

$$C_m = \sum_n EET_{n,m} \tag{3}$$

$$makespan = Max\{C_m\} \tag{4}$$

$$fitness = makespan \tag{5}$$

Where $m = 1, 2, \cdots, M$; $n = 1, 2, \cdots, N$; M is the total number of resources; and N is the total number of tasks. C_m is the sum of EET of each task T_n assigned to resource R_m, which denotes the completion time of the last task on resource. After the completion of the evaluation Phase, selection phase is used.

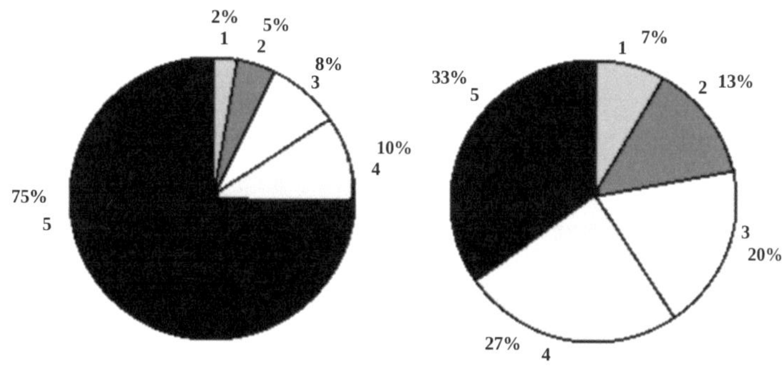

(a) Roulette Wheel Selection (b) Rank Selection

Fig. 6. Example of Roulette Wheel Selection and Rank Selection

5.4 Rank Roulette Wheel Selection (RRWS) of RGSGCS algorithm

This phase chooses chromosomes from a population for later breeding (crossover). RRWS combines the advantages of two types of selections, namely, Rank Selection (RS) and Roulette Wheel Selection (RWS).

5.4.1 Roulette Wheel Selection (RWS) of GA

GA uses proportional selection. The population of the next generation is determined by n independent random experiments; the probability that chromosome xi is selected from the pool $(x1, x2, \cdots, xm)$ to be a member of the next generation at each experiment is given by the following equation:

$$RP(c) = \frac{Fitness(c)}{\sum_{n}^{N} Fitness}; \qquad (6)$$

This process is also called roulette wheel selection. Where each chromosome of the population is represented by a slice that is directly proportional to the chromosome's fitness. A selection step is a spin of the wheel, which in the long run tends to eliminate the least fit population chromosomes. Figure 6 (a) explains the selection method of (RWS) (Obitko, 1998). A roulette wheel where are placed all chromosomes in the population, every chromosome has its place big accordingly to its fitness function. The procedure now is to assign to each chromosome a part of roulette wheel then spin the wheel n time to select n individuals.

5.4.2 Rank Selection (RS) of GA

RWS has problem when the fitness value differs very much. In RS (as shown in figure 6 (b)) the worst value has fitness value equals to 1, the second worst value equals to 2, $\cdots$, etc, and the best will have fitness value equals to N (Obitko, 1998).

Therefore, the RGSGCS's selection process is accomplished by applying RRWS (Wael et al., 2009c; Jadaan et al., 2009), RRWS orders the chromosome's fitness values of population in ascending order, and save this order in array, say *Rank*. After that, it associates the probability shown in equation(7) with each individual chromosome, calculates cumulative proportion of each chromosome, and selects solutions from the population by repeated random sampling based on cumulative proportion.

$$RP(c) = \frac{Rank(c)}{\sum_{n}^{N} Rank}; \tag{7}$$

RRWS determines how many and which individuals will be kept in the next generation. Next, crossover operator and mutation operator are explained.

5.5 Two-point crossover operator of RGSGCS algorithm

Two-point crossover operator (figure 7) controls how to exchange genes between individuals. Two chromosomes are selected randomly from mating pool. Where the middle part in each chromosome is reversed between two parent chromosomes. It is applied to the chromosomes from selection phase. After that, the mutation operator allows for random gene alteration of

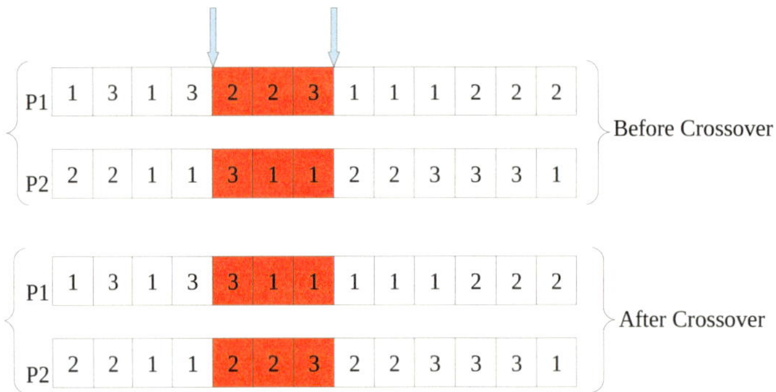

Fig. 7. Two-Point Crossover Operator

an individual.

5.6 Single exchange mutation operator of RGSGCS algorithm

In this phase, single exchange mutation operator (figure 8) is applied to the output of crossover phase. Mutation operator exchanges only two genes according to a mutation rate P_m. It is useful to avoid premature convergence of GA.

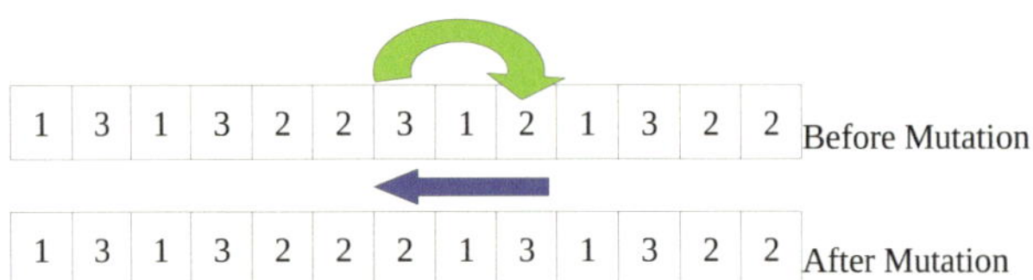

Fig. 8. One Exchange Mutation Operator

5.7 Elitism of RGSGCS algorithm

Besides the standard genetic operators (i.e., crossover and mutation operators). The elitism Phase is used finally to preserve the best candidates for the next generation, so that the algorithm always converges to the global optimum. It combines the parent population with the modified population (the candidates generated by crossover and Mutation operators), and takes the best chromosomes. After this phase, the algorithm continues to the next iteration. The algorithm terminates after it reaches the maximum generations number.

6. Time complexity analysis of RGSGCS algorithm

Time complexity analysis of RGSGCS algorithm can be analyzed step by step as shown in table 1. From table 1 time complexity of RGSGCS algorithm is expressed as: $O(Q.PS.N.M)$. Where PS is population size, and Q is Maximum number of iterations of RGSGCS algorithm.

Phase	Complexity
Initialization	$O(PS.M.N)$
Selection	$O(PS^2 + PS.log(PS) + 2PS)$
Crossover	$O(PS.N)$
Mutation	$O(PS)$
Evaluation	$O(2.PS.N.M)$
Elitisim	$O(PS + PS.log(PS))$
RGSGCS algorithm	$O(Q.PS.N.M)$

Table 1. Time complexity analysis of RGSGCS algorithm

7. Mutation based simulated annealing algorithm for minimizing makespan in grid computing systems (MSA)

SA is a global optimization technique. It derived from the concept of metallurgy which crystallizes the liquid to the required temperature. Traditional SA, as shown in figure 9 (Akella, 2009), explores globally, spending more time in regions which on average have fitter solutions. In the later stages, the search is confined to a small area, and SA optimizes within that area. In these final stages, it is similar to local search.

Instead of population which is used in GA, two solutions are maintained in MSA algorithm at a time.

Interestingly, MSA works iteratively keeping two tentative chromosomes at every iteration. For the first iteration, single exchange mutation operator is applied to initial chromosome, with different genes to produce two new solutions. For the remaining iterations, First chromosome is generated from the previous one by applying single exchange mutation operator to it, while the second chromosome is generated by applying single exchange mutation operator to initial chromosome (generated by Random-MCT algorithm 1), and each one either replaces it or not depending on acceptance criterion. The acceptance criterion works as follows: the old and the new solutions have an associated makespan *Makespan*, determined by a fitness function. If the new solution is better than the old one, then it will replace it, if it is worse, it replaces it with probability P. This probability depends on the difference between their *Makespan* values and control parameter T named temperature. This acceptance criterion provides a way of escaping from local minimum. Therefore, the probability of moving to the new solution decreases exponentially as its fitness gets worse, and also temperature gets lower. Usually temperature is gradually decreased so that uphill movements (for minimization problem) become less and less as the run progresses.

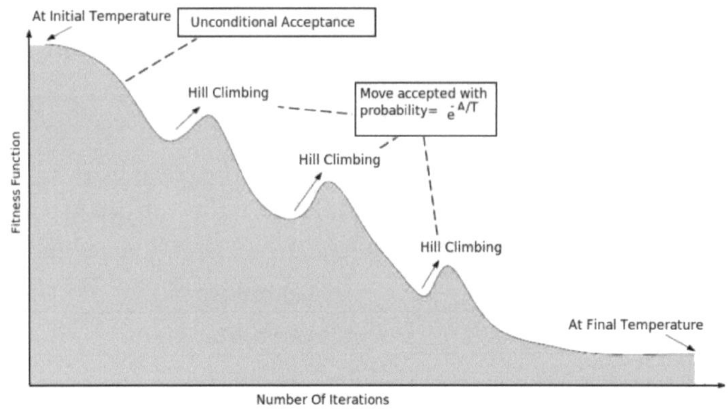

Fig. 9. Convergence of Simulated Annealing.

In single exchange mutation operator, it picks up two genes of a chromosome selected randomly, then exchanges resource indices between them if these indices are not the same vaue (Wael et al., 2011). The MSA algorithm is described by algorithm 3. In the traditional SA,

Algorithm 3 MSA

Choose an initial chromosome $s \in S$ using Random-MCT
$i = 0, s^* = s, T_{initial} = 1000, best = Makespan(s)$
$t_i = T_{initial}$
repeat
    Generate chromosome $s1 \in Neighbor(s)$ by using Single Exchange mutation.
    Apply using Single Exchange mutation on initial chromosome s to generate chromosome $s2$.
    Calculate $Makespan(s1)$ and $Makespan(s2)$.
    for $l = 1$ to 2 **do**
        Δ=exp$(\frac{Makespan(s_l)-Makespan(s)}{t_i})$
        if random[0,1] $< \Delta$ **then**
            $s = s_l$
        else
            if Makespan(s_l) $>$ best **then**
                $s^*=s_l$
                $s = s^*$
                $best = Makespan(s^*)$
            end if
        end if
    end for
    t_{i+1}=$t_i \times 0.99$;
until *Neighbours* is reached
return s^*, and best $Makespan(s^*)$ // Where *Makespan* is makespan value of candidate chromosome.

only one neighborhood solution is created in each temperature. The main difference between MSA and traditional SA is that MSA creates two neighborhood solutions in each temperature using single exchange mutation, and selects one of them according to the probability and the fitness function. Applying this modification to the traditional SA causing MSA algorithm to find better solutions in less average time. Note that in table 2 stopping criterion is refered as the total number of *Neighbours*. As *Neighbours* increases, more solutions will be evaluated and larger areas of the search space may be searched. This enhances MSA chances to find the global optimum.

In order to make additional comparison with other algorithms, Min-Min algorithm is chosen as a benchmark because most related works evaluated this algorithm (Wael et al., 2011). The idea of algorithm Min-Min is as follows: calculate the shortest execution time of every task, select the shortest task to match a resource, then delete the task. Repeat the steps until all tasks finished. This algorithm takes $O(N^2.M)$ time. While computational time complexity of MSA algorithm is expressed as O($M.N$+$Q.M.N$) or O($Q.M.N$), where Q is total number of MSA iterations.

8. Performance analysis of RGSGCS and MSA

In order to measure the final schedule of both algorithms MSA, and RGSGCS, the following parameters are used:

First, Load Balancing Factor LBF, which is in the following equation:

$$LBF = \frac{Makespan}{mean(C_m)} - 1 \tag{8}$$

Note that LBF measures load balancing of an algorithm's solution, when LBF minimizes, algorithm's quality is better. Finally, when LBF equals to zero the load balancing of algorithm's solution is optimal. MSA algorithm needs to spend very less time to come up with an optimal solution. Second, average resource utilization is given by the following equation:

$$U = \frac{mean(C_m)}{Makespan} \tag{9}$$

Where $m = 1, 2, \cdots, M$. However, according to the simulation results, it is proved that MSA is effective in speeding up convergence while providing an optimal result.

9. Simulation results Of RGSGCS and MSA

The simulation results of algorithms RGSGCS, MSA and Min-Min of RM are shown in table 3 for eight different experiments. The reason of testing experimenting is to explore the dynamic behavior of grid environment. For the experiment 1, workloads of tasks are $(6, 12, 16, 20, 24, 28, 30, 36, 40, 42, 48, 52, 60)$ cycles, and the computing capacities of resources are $(4, 3, 2)$ Cycle Per Unit Time(CPUT). The computing capacities of resources, experiments 2 to 8 in the table 3, diverse randomly from 2 to 8 CPUT for each resource. Furthrmore, the workload of tasks ranges randomly from 10 to 150 cycles. The parameters of MSA and RGSGCS are listed in table 2. MSA, Min-Min and RGSGCS are simulated using MATLAB. In table 3, the values of makespan, average time and LBF for both algorithms RGSGCS and MSA are compiled together for purpose of comparison. Table 3 and figures(10 (a), (b) and (c)) lay out that:

The average gains in time of MSA expressed as percentages are 97.66%, 91.03%, 96.83%, 89.6%, 93.35%, 90.95%, 92% and 92.29% for experiments 1 upto 8 respectively. Hence the total average gain in time for all the experiments is 92.964%.

RGSGCS algorithm	Parameters
Crossover Rate	0.8
Mutation Rate	0.1
Population Size for experiment 1	20
Population Size for experiment 2	80
Population Size for experiment 3	150
Population Size for experiment 4	250
Maximum Generations for experiments from 1 up to 3	1000
Population Size for experiments from 5 up to 8	TasksNo.
Maximum Generations for experiments from 4 up to 8	1500
MSA algorithm	
Stopping Criterion for experiments 1 and 2	$M * N$*100
Stopping Criterion for experiment 3	$M * N$*20
Stopping Criterion for experiment 4	$M * N$*10
Stopping Criterion for experiments 5 up to 8	$M * N$*5
Initial Temperature	1000
Cooling rate	0.99

Table 2. Parameters used in RGSGCS/MSA

MSA algorithm has reduction in makespan value equals to eighteen (18) when it is compared with algorithm Min-Min and equals to three (3) when it is compared with algorithm RGSGCS. Moreover, *LBF* values of algorithms MSA, Min-Min and RGSGCS are in ranges [0–1.53], [6.4–29.56] and [0–8.12] respectively.

From results discussed above, it can be concluded that MSA algorithm dynamically optimizes output schedule closer to global optimal solution.

Note that the MSA algorithm outperforms RGSGCS algorithm within very less time to run the algorithm. Depending on SA algorithm and random-MCT heuristic, MSA algorithm is powerful when it is compared with RGSGCS algorithm, while RGSGCS algorithm has less convergence to the optimal solution.

The results of the comparison among algorithms RGSGCS , Min-Min and MSA in each experiment in the table 3, prove that MSA algorithm provides an effective way to enhance the search performance, because it obtains an optimal schedule within a short time along with high resource utilization.

Notably, the solutions of MSA algorithm are high quality and can be used for realistic scheduling in grid environment. The simulation results are consistent with the performance analysis in section 8, which clarifies that the improvement to the evolutionary process is reasonable and effective.

10. Improvment in time consumed by algorithm of RGSGCS and MSA

According to the table 3, two genes exchanged in single exchange mutation has shown good performance in both algorithms RGSGCS and MSA. Moreover, the times taken by both algorithms RGSGCS and MSA are still big, and it is useful to get reasonable results along with less time consumed by algorithms RGSGCS and MSA. One way to do this is to assign

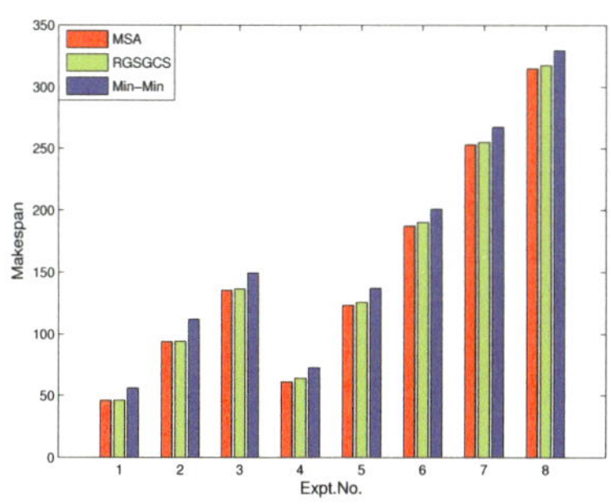

(a) Makespan values of MSA, Min-Min and RGSGCS

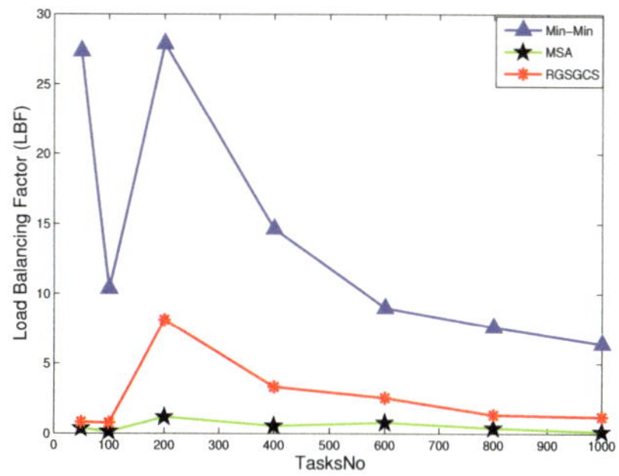

(b) *LBF* values of MSA, Min-Min and RGSGCS

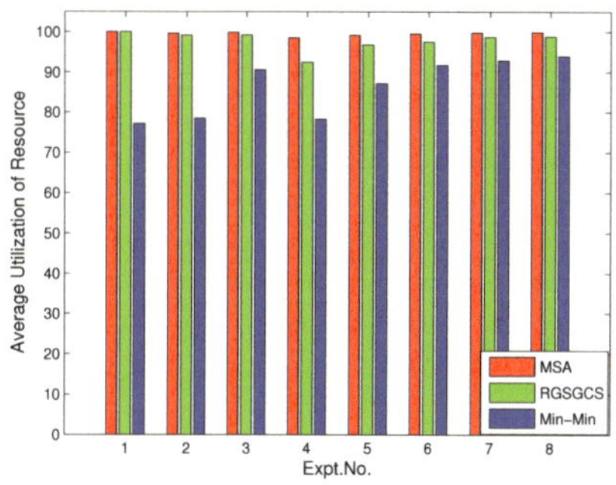

(c) Utilization of Resource of MSA, Min-Min and RGSGCS

Fig. 10. Simulation Results of Random model

probability of crossover, probability of mutation, ppopulation size and maximum generations number to the values 1 , 1, 50 and 1000, respectively in the experiments in table 3. Table 4 dispays new values of solution for both algorithms MSA and RGSGCS. This table provides the results of MSA algorithm for two different termination criterions, namely $T < e^{-300}$ for MSA(1) and $T < e^{-50}$ for MSA(2). Note that, in tables 3, 4, MR denotes reduction in makespan, which is difference between makespan values for both algorithms RGSGCS and MSA. Two experiments 9 and 10 are added to ensure scalability of both algorithms MSA and RGSGCS.

11. ETC model

The Expected Time to Compute (ETC) model is another model can also test performance of MSA algorithm. Interestingly, ETC matrix model allows to capture important characteristics of task scheduling. For example, ETC model introduces possible inconsistencies among tasks and resources in grid system by assigning a large value to $ETC(t, m)$ to indicate that task t is incompatible with resource m.

Moreover, ETC matrix considers three factors: task heterogeneity, resource heterogeneity and consistency. The task heterogeneity depends upon the various execution times of the

Algo.	*Makespan*	Time	*LBF*	*MR*	*Utilization*
	experiment 1 (13 tasks,3 resources)				
MSA	46	0.43	0		100
Min-Min	56	0.012	29.56	10	77.18
RGSGCS	46	18.38	0	0	100
	experiment 2 (50 tasks,10 resources)				
MSA	94	5.78	0.317		99.68
Min-Min	112	0.072	27.35	18	78.5
RGSGCS	94.33	64.44	0.81	0.33	99.196
	experiment 3 (100 tasks, 10 resources)				
MSA	135.5	4.5	0.063		99.94
Min-Min	149.5	0.077	10.35	14	90.62
RGSGCS	136.5	142.1	0.75	1	99.25
	experiment 4 (200 tasks, 50 resources)				
MSA	61.14	41.12	1.53		98.49
Min-Min	72.5	0.36	27.87	11.36	78.2
RGSGCS	64	395	8.12	2.86	92.49
	experiment 5 (400 tasks, 50 resources)				
MSA	123.33	67.86	0.823		99.18
Min-Min	137.2	2.92	14.62	13.87	87.24
RGSGCS	125.75	1021	3.32	2.42	96.78
	experiment 6 (600 tasks, 50 resources)				
MSA	187.5	142.58	0.452		99.55
Min-Min	201	8.92	8.98	13.5	91.76
RGSGCS	190.5	1575	2.54	3	97.52
	experiment 7 (800 tasks, 50 resources)				
MSA	253.167	248.7	0.235		99.76
Min-Min	267.37	21.66	7.6	14.203	92.94
RGSGCS	255	2826	1.33	1.833	98.69
	experiment 8 (1000 tasks, 50 resources)				
MSA	315	380.14	0.108		99.89
Min-Min	329.5	41.46	6.4	14.5	93.98
RGSGCS	317.6	4928	1.19	2.6	98.82

Table 3. Simulation Results of MSA, Min-Min and RGSGCS with probability of crossover, probability of mutation, population size and maximum generations number values taken from table 2.

tasks. The two possible values are defined high and low. Similarly the resource heterogeneity depends on the running time of a particular task across all the resources and again has two values: high and low.

In the real scheduling, three different ETC consistencies are possible. They are consistent, inconsistent and semi-consistent. The instances of benchmark problems are classified into twelve (12) different types of ETC matrices, they are generated from model of Braun (Braun et al., 2001). Each type is obtained by calculating the average value of makespan of ten runs of each algorithm except Min-Min algorithm which it runs just once by default. The

Algo.	*Makespan*	Time	*LBF*	*MR*	*Utilization*
	experiment 1 (13 tasks,3 resources)				
MSA(1)/MSA(2)	46/46.5	5.49/0.964	0/1.45		100/98.57
RGSGCS	46	5.84	0	0/0.5	100
	experiment 2 (50 tasks,10 resources)				
MSA(1)/MSA(2)	94/94	7.277/1.31	0.34/0.32		99.63/99.68
RGSGCS	94	10.28	0.33	0/0	99.67
	experiment 3 (100 tasks, 10 resources)				
MSA(1)/MSA(2)	135.5/135.5	9.33/1.64	0.05/04		99.95/99.96
RGSGCS	136	16.39	0.38	0.5/0.5	99.63
	experiment 4 (200 tasks, 50 resources)				
MSA(1)/MSA(2)	61.5/64	31.66/5.587	2.66/6.37		97.79/94.01
RGSGCS	65	42.46	7.7	3.5/1	92.285
	experiment 5 (400 tasks, 50 resources)				
MSA(1)/MSA(2)	123.33/126	57.92/10.167	0.97/2.76		99.04/97.31
RGSGCS	127.75	76.01	2.42	4.42/1.75	95.46
	experiment 6 (600 tasks, 50 resources)				
MSA(1)/MSA(2)	188/192.5	84.02/14.78	0.66/2.86		99.34/97.22
RGSGCS	190.62	107.44	3.12	2.62/-1.88	97.89
	experiment 7 (800 tasks, 50 resources)				
MSA(1)/MSA(2)	255/261	109.9/19.23	0.69/2.86		99.32/97.22
RGSGCS	259	139.41	5.83	4/-2	97.52
	experiment 8 (1000 tasks, 50 resources)				
MSA(1)/MSA(2)	316/319	136.23/23.876	0.4/1.3		99.6/98.69
RGSGCS	318	170.81	1.13	2/-1	98.88
	experiment 9 (2000 tasks, 50 resources)				
MSA(1)/MSA(2)	629/635	268.23/46.94	0.37/1.1		99.63/98.9
RGSGCS	630	329.36	0.63	1/-5	99.38
	experiment 10 (3000 tasks, 50 resources)				
MSA(1)/MSA(2)	948/953	402.8/70.62	0.47/0.84		99.53/99.17
RGSGCS	947.33	488.68	0.48	-0.67/-5.67	99.52

Table 4. Simulation Results of MSA and RGSGCS with probability of crossover, probability of mutation, population size and maximum generations number equal to 1 , 1, 50 and 1000, respectively.

instances depend upon the above three factors as task heterogeneity, resource heterogeneity and consistency. Instances are labeled as u-x-yyzz where:

1. u - is a uniform distribution, used to generate the matrix.
2. x - is a type of consistency.
   (a) c - consistent. An ETC matrix is said to be consistent if a resource *Ri* execute a task Ti faster than the resource *Rk* and *Ri* executes all other tasks faster than *Rk*.
   (b) s - semi consistent. A semiconsistent ETC matrix is an inconsistent matrix which has a sub matrix of a predefined size.
   (c) i - inconsistent. An ETC matrix is said to be inconsistent if a resource Ri executes some tasks faster than Rj and some slower.

3. yy - is used to indicate the heterogeneity of the tasks(hi-high, lo-low).
4. zz - is used to indicate the heterogeneity of the resources (hi-high, lo-low).

All the instances consist of 512 tasks and 16 resources. This Model is studied for the following algorithms:

1. GANoX algorithm is the same algorithm 2, but without using crossover operator. Single exchange mutation is used at probability of mutation equals to one.
2. PRRWSGA algorithm is the same algorithm 2, probability of crossover equals to 0.8, probability of Mutation equals to 0.01, and full chromosome will be altered.
3. MSA-ETC is the same algorithm 3. Initial chromosome can be taken as the best run of 1000 runs of the algorithm 1. Moreover, stopping criterion which is used equals to $(M \times N \times 20)$;
4. Min-Min algorithm is pointed out in section 7.

Maximum Generation is 1000 and Population Size is 50 for both algorithms GANoX and PRRWSGA. It can be seen from figures 11 (a), (b) and (c), and table 5, that MSA-ETC has superior performance on all remaining algorithms, namely, Min-Min, GANoX, and PRRWSGA, in terms of *LBF*, *Makespan*, *ResourceUtilization*, and time taken by the algorithm. Saving in average time is about 90%, except when it is compared with Min-Min.

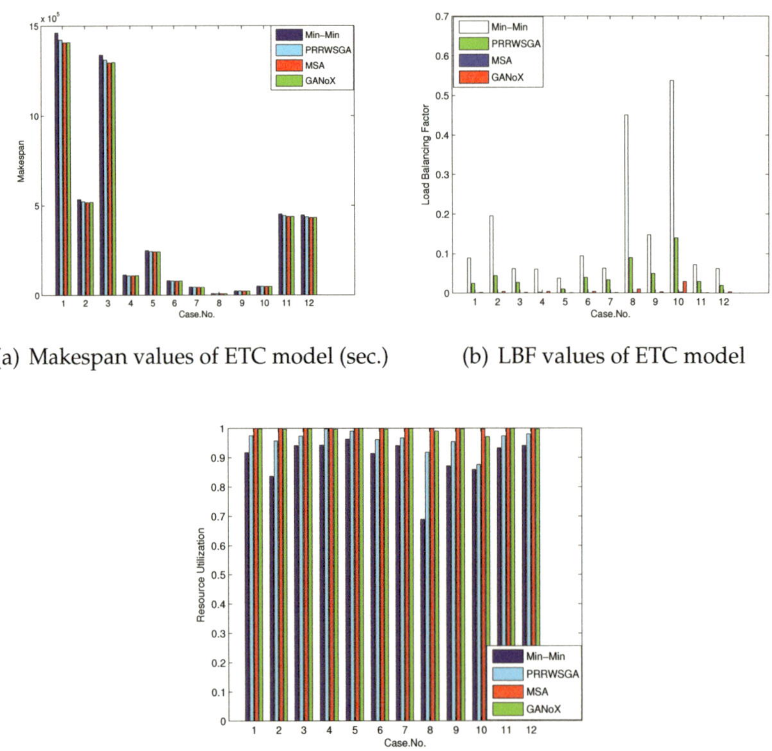

(a) Makespan values of ETC model (sec.)

(b) LBF values of ETC model

(c) Resource Utilization values of ETC model

Fig. 11. Simulation Results of ETC model

Furthermore, the resource utilization value in range [0.9975-0.9999], and LBF value in range [0.0025-0.000085]. From the analysis of time complexity of RGSGCS algorithm in the table 1,

ETC matrix / Algo.	Min-Min	MSA-ETC	GANoX	PRRWSGA
$u-c-hihi$	1462108.59	1407383.05	1408816.72	1423161.96
$u-i-hihi$	534521.65	517909.73	518207.61	522950.76
$u-s-hihi$	1337720.25	1295674.81	1297192.19	1311406.26
$u-c-hilo$	114600.52	110549.32	110774.58	110661.56
$u-i-hilo$	250758.61	243168.05	243295.24	244844.35
$u-s-hilo$	83094.47	80568.32	80680.07	81423.61
$u-c-lolo$	47104.35	45800.13	45822.55	46398.43
$u-i-lolo$	8659.29	8422.85	8430.91	8483.34
$u-s-lolo$	23337.57	22546.96	22561.49	22841.92
$u-c-lohi$	51556.38	49786.42	49907.59	50254.31
$u-i-lohi$	452016.81	438583.36	438728.74	443424.34
$u-s-lohi$	445906.75	431898.36	432666.09	437031.44
LBF	0.5379-0.0385	0.0025-0.000085	0.03-0.0008	0.14-0.002
$ResourceUtilization$	0.8365-0.963	0.9975-0.9999	0.971-0.999	0.876-0.99

Table 5. Simulation Results of ETC Model of Min-Min, MSA-ETC, GANoX, and PRRWSGA

the time complexity of GANoX algorithm and PRRWSGA algorithm is O($Q.PS.M.N$), and for MSA-ETC algorithm is O($Q.M.N$).

As a result, MSA-ETC has less time complexity when it is compared with both algorithms GANoX and PRRWSGA. In the study, the algorithm is designed and compared to different grid environments. Using MSA-ETC it can get good workload balancing results.

The proposed MSA-ETC algorithm can consistently find better schedules for several benchmark problems as compared to other techniques in the literature.

12. Conclusion

This chapter studies problem of minimizing makespan in grid environment. The MSA algorithm introduces a high throughput computing scheduling algorithm. Moreover, it provides solutions for allocation of independent tasks to grid computing resources, and speeds up convergence. As a result load balancing for MSA algorithm is higher than RGSGCS algorithm, and the gain of MSA algorithm in average time consumed by an algorithm is higher than RGSGCS algorithm for both RM and ETC models, which makes MSA algorithm very high QoS and more preferable for realistic scheduling in grid environment.

The initialization of MSA algorithm plays important role to find a good solution and to reduce the time consumed by algorithm.

Furthermore, the improvments on the performance of MSA algorithm, and RGSGCS, give another salient feature, which reduces the time consumed by algorithm to the low reasonable level.

Regarding MSA algorithm for ETC Model, MSA algorithm has superior performance among other algorithms along with resource utilization and load balancing factor values.

Other benefits of MSA algorithm include robustness and scalability features. the disadvantage of MSA algorithm is that flowtime is higher more than Min-Min, RGSGCS, and GANoX.

It can be concluded that MSA algorithm is a powerful technique to solve problem of minimizing makespan in grid environment with less time to be consumed by the intended algorithm.

13. References

A. A. P. Kazem, A. M. Rahmani, & H. H. Aghdam. A modified simulated annealing algorithm for static task scheduling in grid computing. In: *The International Conference on Computer Science and Information Technology*, September 2008, pp. (623-627), IEEE, ISBN 978-0-7695-3308-7, Singapore.

Abdulal, W., Jadaan, O. A, Ahmad Jabas, A. & S. Ramachandram. Genetic algorithm for grid scheduling using best rank power. In: *IEEE Nature & Biologically Inspired Computing (NaBIC 2009)*, December 2009, pp. (181-186), IEEE, ISBN 978-1-4244-5053-4, Coimbatore, India.

Abdulal, W., Jabas, A., Jadaan, O. A. & S. Ramachandram. An improved rank-based genetic algorithm with limited iterations for grid scheduling. In: *IEEE Symposium on Industrial Electronics and Applications (ISIEA2009)*, October 2009, pp. (215-220), IEEE, ISBN 978-1-4244-4681-0. Kuala Lumpur, Malaysia.

Abdulal, W., Jadaan, A. O., Jabas, A., Ramachandram, S., Kaiiali M. & C.R. Rao. Rank-based genetic algorithm with limited iterations for grid scheduling. In: *The First IEEE International Conference on Computational Intelligence, Communication Systems, and Networks (CICSyN2009)*, July 2009. pp. (29-34), ISBN 978-0-7695-3743-6, Indore, India.

Abdulal, W. & S. Ramachandram. Reliability-Aware Genetic Scheduling Algorithm in Grid Environment. In: *IEEE International Conference on Communication Systems and Network Technologies*, June 2011, pp. (673-677), IEEE, ISBN 978-0-7695-4437-3/11, Katra, Jammu, India.

Abdulal, W., Jadaan, O. A., Jabas, A.& S. Ramachandram. Mutation Based Simulated Annealing Algorithm for Minimizing Makespan in Grid Computing Systems. In: *IEEE International Conference on Network and Computer Science (ICNCS 2011)*. April 2011, Vol. 6. pp. (90-94), IEEE, ISBN 978-1-4244-8679-3, Kanyakumari, India.

Abdulal, W., Jadaan, o. A., Jabas, A. & S. Ramachandram. Rank based genetic scheduler for grid computing systems. In: *IEEE International Conference on Computational Intelligence and Communication Networks (CICN2010)*, Nov. 2010, pp. (644-649), IEEE, ISBN 978-1-4244-8653-3, Bhopal, India.

Abraham, A., Rajkumar Buyya & Baikunth Nath. Nature's heuristics for scheduling jobs on computational grids. In: *8th IEEE International Conference on Advanced Computing and Communications (ADCOM2000)*. `www.buyya.com/papers/nhsjcg.pdf`, pp. (45-52).

Akella, P. `http://www.ecs.umass.edu/ece/labs/vlsicad/ece665/slides/SimulatedAnnealing.ppt`.

Braun, Tracy D. and Siegel, Howard Jay and Beck, Noah and Bölöni, Lasislau L. and Maheswaran, Muthucumara and Reuther, Albert I. and Robertson, James P. and Theys, Mitchell D. and Yao, Bin and Hensgen, Debra and Freund, Richard F. A comparison of eleven static heuristics for mapping a class of independent tasks onto heterogeneous distributed computing systems, In: *Journal of Parallel Distributing Computing*. June 2001, pp. (810-837), ISSN 0743-7315.

C. Wook Han & J. Il Park. SA-selection-based genetic algorithm for the design of fuzzy controller. In: *International Journal of Control, Automation, and Systems*, 2005, Vol. 3, pp. (236-243).

Carretero, J. & Xhafa, F. Using Genetic Algorithms for Scheduling Jobs in Large Scale Grid Applications. In: *Journal of Technological and Economic Development*. `http://citeseer.ist.psu.edu/`, 2006, Vol. 12, pp. (11-17). ISSN 1392-8619 print/ISSN 1822-3613 Online.

Dimitri Bevc, Sergio, E. Zarantonello, Neena Kaushik, & Iulian Musat. (2005). Grid computing for energy exploration. `http://www.ogf.org`.

Fatos Xhafa, Enrique Alba, Bernabé Dorronsoro, Bernat Duran, & Abraham, A. Efficient batch job scheduling in grids using cellular memetic algorithms. In: *Studies in Computational Intelligence*. Springer-Verlag, 2008, pp. (273-299), Berlin, Heidelberg

Fidanova, S. Simulated annealing for grid scheduling problem. In: *International Symposium on Modern Computing*, 2006, Vol. 0, pp. (41-45).

Foster, I., Kesselman, C. & Steven Tuecke. The Anatomy of the Grid. (2001). In: *International Journal of Supercomputer Applications*.

Garey, Michael R. and Johnson, David S. Computers and Intractability: A Guide to the Theory of NP-Completeness. In: *W. H. Freeman & Co.*, ISSN 0716710455, New York, NY, USA

Goldberg, D. E. In: *Genetic Algorithms in Search, Optimization, and Machine Learning*, Addison-Wesley, ISBN 0-201-15767-5, New York.

Jinquan, Z., Lina, Ni. & Changjun, J. A Heuristic Scheduling Strategy for Independent Tasks on Grid. In: *Eighth International Conference on High-Performance Computing in Asia-Pacific Region*, IEEE Computer Society, 2005, pp. (588-593). ISBN 0-7695-2486-9, Washington, DC, USA.

Kesselman, C., & Foster, I. In: *The Grid: Blueprint for a Future Computing Infrastructure*, Morgan Kaufmann Publishers.

K. Kousalya and P. Balasubramanie. To Improve Ant Algorithm's Grid Scheduling Using Local Search. In: *International Journal Of Computational Cognition* `http://www.yangsky.com/ijcc/pdf/ijcc747.pdf`. Vol. 7, No. 4, Dec. 2009. pp. (47–57).

K. Kousalya and P. Balasubramanie. Ant Algorithm for Grid Scheduling Powered by Local Search. In: *International Journal Of Open Problems Compt. Math.*. `www.ijopcm.org/files/IJOPCM(vol.1.3.5.D.8).pdf`. Vol. 1, No. 3, Dec. 2008, pp. (222-240).

Moallem, A. Using Swarm Intelligence for Distributed Job Scheduling on the Grid. `http://library.usask.ca/theses/available/etd-04132009-123250/unrestricted/thesis.pdf`. In: *University of Saskatchewan*, March 2009.

Omar Al Jadaan, L. Rajamani, & C. Rao. Parameterless penalty function for solving constrained evolutionary optimization. In: *Hybrid Intelligent Models and Applications*, IEEE, pp. (56-63).

Omar Al Jadaan, Jabas, A., Abdulal, W., Rajamani, L., Zaiton, E., Rao, C.R. & C.R. Rao. Engineering Case Studies Using Parameterless Penalty Non-dominated Ranked Genetic Algorithm. In: *The First IEEE International Conference on Computational Intelligence, Communication Systems, and Networks (CICSyN2009)*, July 2009. pp. (51-56), ISBN 978-0-7695-3743-6, Indore, India.

Omar Al Jadaan, Wael Abdulal, Hameed, M.A, & Ahmad Jabas. & C.R. Rao. Enhancing Data Selection Using Genetic Algorithm. In: *2010 International Conference on Computational Intelligence and Communication Networks (CICN)*, Nov. 2010. pp. (434 - 439), ISBN 978-1-4244-8653-3 , Bhopal, India.

Omar Al Jadaan, Alla Alhaffa, Wael Abdulal & Ahmad Jabas. Rank Based Genetic Algorithm for solving the Banking ATMś Location Problem using convolution. In: *2011 IEEE Symposium on Computers & Informatics (ISCI)*, March 2011. pp. (6–11), ISBN 978-1-61284-689-7, Kuala Lumpur, Malaysia.

Obitko, M. (1998). http://www.obitko.com/tutorials/genetic-algorithms/selection.php.

P.K. Suri & Singh Manpreet. An efficient decentralized load balancing algorithm for grid. In: *IEEE 2nd International Advance Computing Conference*. IEEE, pp. (10-13), ISBN 978-1-4244-4790-9 , Patiala, India.

Prado, R. P. and Galán, S. García and Yuste, A. J. and Expósito, J. E. and Santiago, A. J. and Bruque, S .Evolutionary Fuzzy Scheduler for Grid Computing. In: *Proceedings of the 10th International Work-Conference on Artificial Neural Networks: Part I: Bio-Inspired Systems: Computational and Ambient Intelligence IWANN '09*, Springer-Verlag, pp. (286–293). ISBN 978-3-642-02477-1, Berlin, Heidelberg.

Ruay-Shiung Chang, Jih-Sheng Chang, & Po-Sheng Lin. An ant algorithm for balanced job scheduling in grids. In: *Future Generation Computer Systems*. Vol. 25, pp. (20-27), ISSN 0167-739X.

Suliman, M. O., Vellanki S.S. Kumar, & Abdulal, W. Optimization of Uncertain Construction Time-Cost Trade off Problem Using Simulated Annealing Algorithm. In: *World Congress on information and Communication Technologies*, Dec. 2011.

V. D. Martino & M. Mililotti. Scheduling in a grid computing environment using genetic algorithm. In: *The 16th IEEE International Parallel and Distributed Processing Symposium*, April 2002. pp. (235-239). ISBN 0-7695-1573-8.

V. D. Martino. Sub Optimal Scheduling in a Grid Using Genetic Algorithms. In: *Seventeenth International Symposium on Parallel and Distributed Processing*. ftp://ftp.cs.umanitoba.ca/pub/IPDPS03, 2003, IEEE Computer Society, ISBN 0-7695-1926-1, Washington, DC, USA.

Y. Gao, H. Rong, & J. Z. Huang. Adaptive grid job scheduling with genetic algorithms. In: *Future Generation Computer Systems*, January 2005, Vol. 21, No. 1, Elsevier Science Publishers, pp. (151-161).

Yin, Hao and Wu, Huilin and Zhou, Jiliu. An Improved Genetic Algorithm with Limited Iteration for Grid Scheduling. In: *Sixth International Conference on Grid and Cooperative Computing*. IEEE Computer Society, pp. (221-227), ISBN 0-7695-2871-6, Washington, DC, USA.

Yun-Han Lee, Seiven Leu, &Ruay-Shiung Chang. Improving job scheduling algorithms in a grid environment. In: *Future Generation Computer Systems*. Vol. 27, pp. (991-998), ISSN 0167-739X.

Section 3

Advances in Grid Computing - Parallel Execution

6

Efficient Parallel Application Execution on Opportunistic Desktop Grids

Francisco Silva[1], Fabio Kon[2], Daniel Batista[2], Alfredo Goldman[2], Fabio Costa[3] and Raphael Camargo[4]
[1]*Universidade Federal do Maranhão*
[2]*Universidade de São Paulo*
[3]*Universidade Federal de Goiás*
[4]*Universidade Federal do ABC*
Brazil

1. Introduction

The success of grid systems can be verified by the increasing number of middleware systems, actual production grids, and dedicated forums that appeared in recent years. The use of grid computing technology is increasing rapidly, reaching more scientific fields and encompassing a growing body of applications (Grandinetti, 2005; Wilkinson, 2009).

A grid might be seen as a way to interconnect clusters that is much more convenient than the construction of huge clusters. Another possible approach for conceiving a grid is the opportunistic use of workstations of regular users. The focus of an opportunistic grid middleware is not on the integration of dedicated computer clusters (e.g., Beowulf) or supercomputing resources, but on taking advantage of idle computing cycles of regular computers and workstations that can be spread across several administrative domains.

In a desktop grid, a large number of regular personal computers are integrated for executing large-scale distributed applications. The computing resources are heterogeneous in respect to their hardware and software configuration. Several network technologies can be used on the interconnection network, resulting in links with different capacities in respect to properties such as bandwidth, error rate, and communication latency. The computing resources can also be spread across several administrative domains. Nevertheless, from the user viewpoint, the computing system should be seen as a single integrated resource and be easy to use.

If the grid middleware follows an opportunistic approach, resources do not need to be dedicated for executing grid applications. The grid workload will coexist with local applications executions, submitted by the nodes regular users. The grid middleware must take advantage of idle computing cycles that arise from unused time frames of the workstations that comprise the grid. By leveraging the idle computing power of existing commodity workstations and connecting them to a grid infrastructure, the grid middleware allows a better utilization of existing computing resources and enables the execution of computationally-intensive parallel applications that would otherwise require expensive cluster or parallel machines.

Over the last decade, opportunistic desktop grid middleware developers have been constructing several approaches for allowing the execution of different application classes, such as: (a) sequential applications, where the task to be run is assigned to a single grid node; (b) parametric or bag-of-tasks applications, where several copies of a task are assigned to different grid nodes, each of them processing a subset of the input data independently and without exchanging data; (c) tightly coupled parallel applications, whose processes exchange data among themselves using message passing or shared memory abstractions.

Due to the heterogeneity, high scalability and dynamism of the execution environment, providing efficient support for application execution on opportunist grids comprises a major challenge for middleware developers, that must provide innovative solutions for addressing problems found in areas, such as:

Support for a variety of programming models, which enables the extension of the benefits of desktop grids to a larger array of application domains and communities, such as in scientific and enterprise computing, and including the ability to run legacy applications in an efficient and reliable way. Important programming models to consider include message-passing standards, such as MPI (MPI, 2009), BSP (Bisseling, 2004; Valiant, 1990), distributed objects, publish-subscribe, and mobile agents. In this chapter we will concentrate on the support for parallel application models, in particular MPI and BSP, but also pointing to the extensions of grid management middleware to support other programming models.

Resource management, which encompasses challenges such as how to efficiently monitor a large number of highly distributed computing resources belonging to multiple administrative domains. On opportunistic grids, this issue is even harder due to the dynamic nature of the execution environment, where nodes can join and leave the grid at any time due to the use of the non-dedicated machines by their regular (non-grid) users.

Application scheduling and execution management, which also includes monitoring, that must provide user-friendly mechanisms to execute applications in the grid environment, to control the execution of jobs, and to provide tools to collect application results and to generate reports about current and past situations. Application execution management should encompass all execution models supported by the middleware.

Fault tolerance, that comprises a major requirement for grid middleware as grid environments are highly prone to failures, a characteristic amplified on opportunistic grids due their dynamism and the use of non-dedicated machines, leading to a non-controlled computing environment. An efficient and scalable failure detection mechanism must be provided by the grid middleware, along with a means for automatic application execution recovery, without requiring human intervention.

In this chapter, we will provide a comprehensive description of reputable solutions found in the literature to circumvent the above described problems, emphasizing the approaches adopted in the InteGrade[1] (da Silva e Silva et al., 2010) middleware development, a multi-university effort to build a robust and flexible middleware for opportunistic grid computing. InteGrade's main goal is to be an opportunistic grid environment with support for tightly-coupled parallel applications. The next section gives an overview of grid application programming models and provides an introduction to the InteGrade grid middleware, discussing its support for executing parallel applications over a desktop grid platform.

[1] Homepage: `http://www.integrade.org.br`

Next, we will concentrate in two central issues in the development of an opportunistic grid infrastructure: application scheduling and execution management and fault tolerance.

2. Application programming models

A programming model is a necessary underlying feature of any computing system. Programming models provide well-defined constructs to build applications and are a key element to enable interoperation of application components developed by third parties. A programming model can be tied to a given programming language or it can be a higher-level abstraction layered on top of the language. In the latter case, different application components can be built using different programming languages, and the programming model, as long as properly implemented by a platform, serves as the logical bridge between them. In the heterogeneous environment of computing grids, the need for such high-level programming models is even more evident as there can be many different types of machine architecture and programming languages, all needing to be integrated as part of a seamless environment for distributed applications.

While it is largely acknowledged that no one-size-fits-all solution exists when it comes to programming models, one can argue that some programming models are best suited for particular kinds of problems than others (Lee & Talia, 2003). Considering that grid computing environments can be used to run different kinds of applications in different domains, such as e-science, finance, numeric simulation and, more generally, virtual organizations, it follows that having a variety of programming model to choose from may be an important factor. A number of well-known programming models have been investigated for grid computing, including, but not limited to, remote procedure calls (as in RPC and RMI), tuple spaces, publish-subscribe, message passing, and Web services, as well as enhancements of such models with non-functional properties such as fault tolerance, dependability and security (Lee & Talia, 2003). Note that a main emphasis of programming models for grid computing is on communication abstractions, which is due to the fact that interaction among distributed application components is a key issue for grid applications.

The InteGrade middleware offers a choice of programming models for computationally intensive distributed parallel applications, MPI (Message Passing Interface), and BSP (Bulk Synchronous Parallel) applications. It also offers support for sequential and bag-of-tasks applications. The remainder of this section presents the basic concepts of the InteGrade middleware and its support for parallel programming models.

2.1 Introduction to the InteGrade grid middleware

The basic architectural unit of an InteGrade grid is a cluster, a collection of machines usually connected by a local network. Clusters can be organized in a hierarchy, enabling the construction of grids with a large number of machines. Each cluster contains a *cluster manager* node that hosts InteGrade components responsible for managing cluster resources and for inter-cluster communication. Other cluster nodes are called *resource providers* and export part of their resources to the grid. They can be either shared with local users (e.g., secretaries using a word processor) or dedicated machines. The cluster manager node, containing InteGrade management components, must be a stable machine, usually a server, but not necessarily dedicated to InteGrade execution only. In case of a cluster manager failure, only its managed cluster machines will become unavailable. Figure 1 shows the basic components that enable application execution.

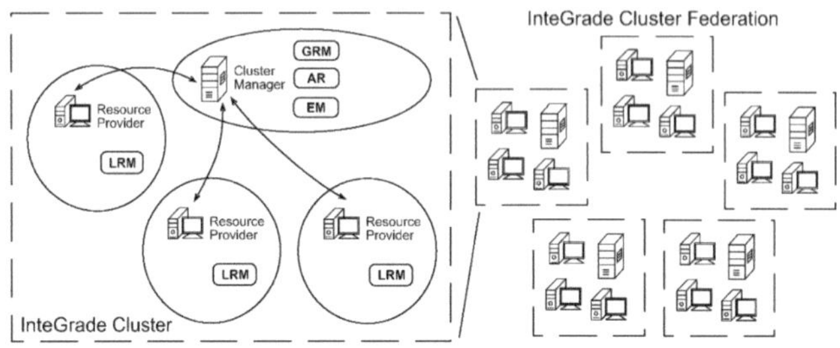

Fig. 1. InteGrade architecture.

Application Repository (AR): before being executed, an application must be previously registered with the Application Repository. This component stores the application description (metadata) and binary code.

Application Submission and Control Tool (ASCT): a graphical user interface that allows users to browse the content of the Application Repository, submit applications, and control their execution. Alternatively, applications can be submitted via the **InteGrade Grid Portal**, a Web interface similar to ASCT.

Local Resource Manager (LRM): a component that runs on each cluster node, collecting information about the state of resources such as memory, CPU, disk, and network. It is also responsible for instantiating and executing applications scheduled to the node.

Global Resource Manager (GRM): manages cluster resources by receiving notifications of resource usage from the LRMs in the cluster (through an information update protocol) and runs the scheduler that allocates tasks to nodes based on resource availability; it is also responsible for communication with GRMs in other clusters, allowing applications to be scheduled for execution in different clusters. Each cluster has a GRM and, collectively, the GRMs form the Global Resource Management service. We assume that the cluster manager node where the GRM is instantiated has a valid IP address and firewalls are configured to allow TCP traffic on the port used by the GRM. Network administrators establishing a Virtual Organization can, optionally, make use of ssh tunnels in order to circumvent firewalls and NAT boxes.

Execution Manager (EM): maintains information about each application submission, such as its state, executing node(s), input and output parameters, submission and termination timestamps. It also coordinates the recovery process in case of application failures.

Since grids are inherently more vulnerable to security threats than traditional systems, as they potentially encompass a large number of users, resources, and applications managed by different administrative domains, InteGrade encompass an opinion-based grid security model called Xenia. Xenia provides an authorization and authentication system and a security API that allows developers to access a security infrastructure that provides facilities such as digital signatures, cryptography, resource access control and access rights delegation. Using Xenia, we developed a secure Application Repository infrastructure, which provides authentication, secure communication, authorization, and application validation. A more detailed description of InteGrade security infrastructure can be found on de Ribamar Braga Pinheiro Júnior (2008); de Ribamar Braga Pinheiro Júnior et al. (2006).

2.2 InteGrade support for parallel applications

Executing computationally intensive parallel applications on dynamic heterogeneous environments, such as computational grids, is a daunting task. This is particularly true when using non-dedicated resources, as in the case of opportunistic computing, where one uses only the idle periods of the shared machines. In this scenario, the execution environment is typically highly dynamic, with resources periodically leaving and joining the grid. When a resource becomes unavailable, due to a failure or simply because the machine owner requests its use, the system needs to perform the necessary steps to restart the tasks on different machines. In the case of BSP or MPI parallel applications, the problem is even worse, since all processes that comprise the application may need to be restarted from a consistent distributed checkpoint.

2.2.1 InteGrade BSP applications

InteGrade's support for executing BSP applications adheres to the Oxford BSP API [2], targeted for the C language. Thus, an application based on the Oxford BSPlib can be executed over InteGrade with little or even no modification of its source code, requiring only its recompilation and linkage with the appropriate InteGrade libraries.

A BSP computation proceeds in a series of global supersteps. Each superstep comprises three ordered stages: (1) *concurrent computation*: computations take place on every participating process. Each process only uses values stored on its local memory. Computations are independent in the sense that they occur asynchronously of all others; (2) *communication*: at this stage, the processes exchange data between themselves; (3) *barrier synchronization*: when a process reaches this point (the barrier), it waits until all other processes have finished their communication actions. The synchronization barrier is the end of a superstep and the beginning of another one.

InteGrade's implementation of the BSP model uses CORBA (OMG, 2011) for inter-process communication. CORBA has the advantage of being an easier and cleaner communication environment, shortening development and maintenance time and facilitating system evolution. Also, since it is based on a binary protocol, the performance of CORBA-based communication is an order of magnitude faster than the performance of technologies based on XML, requiring less network bandwidth and processing power. On the shared grid machines, InteGrade uses OiL ((Maia et al., 2006)), a very light-weight version of a CORBA ORB that imposes a small memory footprint. Nevertheless, CORBA usage is completely transparent to the InteGrade application developer, who only uses the BSP interface (Goldchleger et al., 2005).

InteGrade's BSPLib associates to each process of a parallel application a *BspProxy*. The *BspProxy* is a CORBA servant responsible for receiving related communications from other processes, such as a virtual shared address read or write, or the receipt of messages signaling the end of the synchronization barrier. The creation of *BspProxies* is entirely handled by the library and is totally transparent to users.

The first created process of a parallel application is called *Process Zero*. Process Zero is responsible for assigning an unique identifier to each application process, broadcasting the

[2] The Oxford BSP Toolset `http://www.bsp-worldwide.org/implmnts/oxtool`

CORBA IORs of each process to allow them to communicate directly, and coordinating synchronization barriers. Moreover, *Process Zero* executes its normal computation on behalf of the parallel application.

On InteGrade, the synchronization barriers of the BSP model are used to store checkpoints during execution, since they provide global, consistent points for application recovery. In this way, in the case of failures, it is possible to recover application execution from a previous checkpoint, which can be stored in a distributed way as described in Section 4.3.1. Application recovery is also available for sequential, bag-of-tasks, and MPI applications.

2.2.2 Integrade MPI applications

Support for parallel applications based on MPI is achieved in InteGrade through MPICH-IG (Cardozo & Costa, 2008), which in turn is based on MPICH2[3], an open source implementation of the second version of the MPI standard, MPI2 (MPI, 1997). MPICH-IG adapts MPICH2 to use InteGrade's LRM and EM instead of the MPI daemon (MPD) to launch and manage MPI applications. It also uses the application repository to retrieve the binaries of MPI applications, which are dynamically deployed just prior to launch, instead of requiring them to be deployed in advance, as with MPICH2. MPI applications can thus be dispatched and managed in the same way as BSP or sequential applications.

In order to adapt MPICH2 to run on InteGrade, two of its interfaces were re-implemented: the *Channel Interface* (CI) and the *Process Management Interface* (PMI). The former is required to monitor a sockets channel to detect and treat failures. The latter is necessary to couple the management of MPI applications with InteGrade's Execution Manager (EM), adding functions for process location and synchronization.

Regarding communication among an application's tasks, MPICH-IG uses the MPICH2 Abstract Device Interface (ADI) to abstract away the details of the actual communications mechanisms, enabling higher layers of the communications infrastructure to be independent from them. In this way, we implemented two underlying communications channels: a CORBA-based one, for tasks running on different, possibly heterogeneous, networks, and a more efficient one, based on sockets, for tasks that reside in a single cluster.

Another feature of MPICH-IG, in contrast with conventional MPI platforms, refers to the recovery of individual application tasks after failures. This prevents the whole application from being restarted from scratch, thus contributing to reduce the makespan of application execution. Application recovery is supported by monitoring the execution state of tasks. Faulty tasks are then resumed on different grid nodes, selected by the GRM. Task recovery is implemented using system-level checkpoints. While other MPI platforms focus specifically on fault-tolerance and recovery, notably MPICH-V (Bosilca et al., 2002), they usually rely on homogeneous, dedicated, clusters. MPICH-IG removes this limitation to enable the dynamic scheduling of non-dedicated machines.

These features also favor MPICH-IG when compared to other approaches to integrate MPI into grid computing environments, such as MPICH-G2 (Karonis et al., 2003). In common to MPICH-G2 is the ability to run MPI applications on large scale heterogeneous environments, as well as the ability to switch from one communications protocol to another, depending on the relative location of the application tasks. However, MPICH-IG's ability to use

[3] http://www.mcs.anl.gov/research/projects/mpich2/

non-dedicated resources in an opportunistic way further contributes to scale up the amount of available resources. In addition, MPICH-IG enables legacy MPI applications to be transparently deployed on an InteGrade grid, without the need to modify their source code.

3. Application scheduling and execution management

Grid scheduling is a decision making process involving resources belonging to multiple administrative domains. As usual, this process includes a resource search for running applications. However, unlike traditional schedulers for distributed and parallel systems, grid schedulers have no control over the resources and applications in the system. Thus, it is necessary to have components that allow, among other features, resource discovery, monitoring and storage of information regarding resources and applications, mechanisms to allow access to different administrative domains and, depending on the adopted scheduling strategy, an approach for estimating the resources performance and the prediction of the applications execution times.

According to Schopf et al. (Schopf, 2004), a grid scheduling process can be broadly divided into three stages: filtering and resource discovery, resource selection, and preparing the environment for application execution. In the first stage, the grid scheduler creates a filter to select resources based on the restrictions and preferences provided by users during the application submission process. An information system usually provides a set of static and dynamic data about the available resources in the grid, such as their CPU capacity, the amount of available memory, and the network delay for delivering packets. Depending on the adopted scheduling heuristic, a cost estimator can sort the resources according to their efficiency to perform a certain type of code by using an analytic benchmark. In the second stage of the scheduling process, the scheduler will generate the applications mapping to resources in accordance with the system objectives, such as to minimize the response time of applications or to maximize the number of applications completed per time unit (throughput) (Dong & Akl, 2006; Zhu, 2003). In the third stage, a component running on the selected grid resource receives the application sent by the grid scheduler and prepares the environment for its execution by, for example, transferring the files containing the application input data.

A grid scheduling system can be organized in different schemes, according to different interests regarding performance and scalability (Subramani et al., 2002):

- Centralized: in this model, the scheduler maintains information about all administrative domains. All applications are submitted to the scheduler. Based on the queue of submitted applications and the information of all administrative domains, it makes the scheduling decisions.
- Hierarchical: in this scheme, each domain has its own local scheduler that are interconnected in a hierarchical structure. A request for an application execution that can not be handled with the locally available resources is sent up in the hierarchy, reaching an scheduler that has a broader view of the grid resources.
- Distributed: in this model, each domain has its own scheduler and the schedulers regularly consult each other to collect updated information about local loads. An application submitted for a given domain can then be transferred for execution in another domain that is less burdened.

3.1 Grid scheduling algorithms

A scheduling algorithm determines how the applications should be distributed for execution and how resources should be used, according to the system performance goals and the provided information. However, task mapping to a set of heterogeneous resources is a well known NP-complete problem (El-Rewini et al., 1994; Ibarra & Kim, 1977).

Scheduling algorithms can be grouped into two modes: batch and on-line (Maheswaran et al., 1999). In the on-line scheduling mode, a task is mapped to a machine as soon as it arrives to the scheduler. In the batch mode, tasks are not mapped as they arrive. Instead, they are placed inside a data structure called a meta-task and are mapped only in predefined interval times, called mapping events. In this way, batch algorithms can compare the task's resource requirements for performing better mappings.

Dong and Akl (Dong & Akl, 2006) describe scheduling algorithms commonly used in grid computing environments, among which we highlight the following:

Work Queue (WQ) is an on-line algorithm that assigns each task to the next machine that becomes available. If multiple machines become available simultaneously, one is randomly chosen. This algorithm maps only one task to a single resource. WQ does not use any specific information regarding the application or the grid resources and is particularly useful for systems where the main objective is to maximize the resources usage, instead of minimizing the execution time of individual tasks. Depending on the implementation, this algorithm may need to check the status of all m grid resources to find out which machines are available. Thus, the scheduling complexity of this algorithm is $O(m)$. An extension of this algorithm, called WQR, uses a replication mechanism. This variant is used by the OurGrid middleware [4].

Minimum Conclusion Time (MCT) is an on-line heuristic that assigns each task to the machine with the shorter expected completion time to accomplish it. The completion time corresponds to the sum of the time necessary for the machine to become available (in case it is already running another tasks) plus the time that it will take in order to execute the task. This algorithm can map more than one task per resource. The mapping complexity is $O(m)$, since as a task arrives, all grid machines are examined for determining the one having the shortest expected conclusion time for its execution.

Min-min is a batch heuristic based on MCT. This algorithm takes as input parameters a set of unmapped tasks M (meta-task) and a set of grid machines R. At its first step, the algorithm computes the completion time of each task in M for every machine in R. Next, the algorithm searches for the lowest completion time for each task. Min-min then selects the task with the minimum completion time among all tasks in M and assigns it to the machine in which this performance is expected to be obtained. The mapped task is removed from the meta-task M, and the algorithm increments the expected available time of the chosen grid resource considering the time to run the newly mapped task. This process is repeated until there are no more tasks left to be scheduled. As MCT, min-min also maps more than one task per node. Being m the number of tasks in M and r the amount of resources contained in R, computing the completion time of each task in all machines will take $O(mr)$. The loop is repeated m times, leading to a total cost of $O(m^2r)$.

[4] `http://www.ourgrid.org`

Task Grouping is an algorithm for scheduling applications comprising a large amount of short-duration tasks. In this case, scheduling and distributing each individual task would overload the system during the tasks transfer to grid resources. The algorithm groups the application's tasks according to their computation sizes and the processing power of the grid resources. Each group is sent to a single resource, reducing the required transmission overhead for task transferring.

Algorithms such as min-min and MCT need to compute how long it would take for running applications on grid resources. This information can be estimated by prediction algorithms (Liu, 2004), which usually follow two basic approaches. The first approach calculates an application estimated execution time based on stored records of previous runs of the same or similar applications. The second approach is based on knowledge regarding the application execution model, which are usually parallel applications with divisible workloads (MPI or PVM). The application code is analyzed, estimating the execution time of each task according to the capacity of the grid resources. An example of this latter approach is the PACE (Performance Analysis and Characterization Environment).

3.2 InteGrade application scheduling

The InteGrade scheduling algorithm (Goldchleger et al., 2004) follows an on-line approach. It uses a filter to select resources based on constraints and preferences provided by users during the process of submitting applications. Constraints define minimum requirements for the selection of machines, such as hardware and software platforms, resource requirements such as minimum memory requirements. Preferences define the order used for choosing the resources, like rather executing on a faster CPU than on a slower one. The tasks that make up an application are then mapped to the nodes according to the ordered list of resources. If requirements and preferences are not specified, the algorithm maps the tasks to random chosen grid resources. The algorithm can map more than one task per node.

3.2.1 InteGrade resource availability prediction

The success of an opportunistic grid depends on a good scheduler. An idle machine is available for grid processing, but whenever its local users need their resources back, grid applications executing at that machine must either migrate to another grid machine or abort and possibly restart at another node. In both cases, there is considerable loss of efficiency for grid applications. A solution is to avoid such interruptions by scheduling grid tasks on machines that are expected to remain idle for the duration of the task.

InteGrade predicts each machine's idle periods by locally performing Use Pattern Analysis of machine resources at each machine on the grid, as described in Finger et al. (2008; 2010). Currently, four different types resource are monitored: CPU use, RAM availability, disk space, and swap space.

Use pattern analysis deals with *machine resource use objects*. Each object is a vector of values representing the time series of a machine's resource use. The sampling of a machine's resource use is performed at a fixed rate (once every 5 minutes) and grouped into objects covering 48 hours with a 24-hour overlap between consecutive objects. InteGrade employ 48-hour long objects so as to have enough past information to be used in the runtime prediction phase.

The Use Pattern Analysis performs unsupervised machine learning (Barlow, 1999; Theodoridis & Koutroumba, 2003) to obtain a fixed number of *use classes*, where each class is represented by its *prototypical* object. The idea is that each class represents a frequent use pattern, such as a busy work day, a light work day or a holiday. As in most machine learning processes, there are two phases involved in the process, which in the InteGrade architecture are implemented by a module called Local Use Pattern Analyzer (LUPA), as follows.

The Learning Phase. Learning is performed off-line, using 60 objects collected by LUPA during the machine regular use. A clustering algorithm (Everitt et al., 2001) is applied to the training data, such that each cluster corresponds to a use class, represented by a prototypical object, which is obtained by averaging over the elements of the class. Learning can occur only when there is a considerable mass of data. InteGrade approach requires at least two months of data. As data collection proceeds, more data and more representative classes are obtained.

The Decision Phase. There is one LUPA module per machine on the grid. Requests are sent by the scheduler specifying the amount of resources (CPU, disk space, RAM, etc.) and the expected duration needed by an application to be executed at that machine. The LUPA module decides whether this machine will be available for the expected duration, as explained below. LUPA is constantly keeping track of the current use of resources. For each resource, it focuses on the recent history, usually the last 24 hours, and computes a distance between the recent history and each of the use classes learned during the training phase. This distance takes into account the time of the day in which the request was made, so that the recent history is compared to the corresponding times in the use classes. The class with the smallest distance is the *current use class*, which is used to predict the availability in the near future. If all resources are predicted to be available, then the application is scheduled to be executed; otherwise, it is rejected.

3.3 Application management: a mobile agents approach

In distributed systems such as opportunistic grids, failures can occur due to several factors, most of them related to resource heterogeneity and distribution. These failures together with the use of the resources by its owners modify grid resource availability (i.e. resources can be active, busy, off-line, crashed, etc.). An opportunistic grid middleware should be able to monitor and detect such changes, rescheduling applications across the available resources, and dynamically tuning the fault tolerance mechanisms to better adapt to the execution environment.

When dealing with bag-of-tasks like applications, one interesting approach may be the use of mobile agents (Pham & Karmouch, 1998), which allows the implementation of dynamic fault tolerance mechanisms based on task replication and checkpointing. A task replica is a copy of the application binary that runs independently of the other copies. Through these mechanisms a middleware may be capable of migrating tasks when nodes fail and coordinate task replicas and its checkpoints in a rational manner, keeping only the most advanced checkpoint and by migrating slow replicas. This dynamically improves application execution, compensates the misspent of resources introduced by the task replication and solves scalability issues.

These mechanisms compose a feedback control system (Goel et al., 1999; Steere et al., 1999), gathering and analyzing information about the execution progress and adjusting its behavior accordingly. Agents are suitable for opportunistic environments due to intrinsic characteristics such as:

1. *Cooperation*: agents have the ability to interact and cooperate with other agents; this can be explored for the development of complex communication mechanisms among grid nodes;
2. *Autonomy*: agents are autonomous entities, meaning that their execution goes on without any or with little intervention by the clients that started them. This is an adequate model for submission and execution of grid applications;
3. *Heterogeneity*: several mobile agent platforms can be executed in heterogeneous environments, an important characteristic for better use of computational resources among multi-organization environments;
4. *Reactivity*: agents can react to external events, such as variations on resources availability;
5. *Mobility*: mobile agents can migrate from one node to another, moving part of the computation being executed, helping to balance the load on grid nodes;

The InteGrade research group has been investigating the use of the agent paradigm for developing a grid software infrastructure since 2004, leading to the MobiGrid (Barbosa & Goldman, 2004; Pinheiro et al., 2011) and MAG (Mobile Agents for Grids) (Lopes et al., 2005) projects that are based on the InteGrade middleware.

4. Application execution fault-tolerance

On opportunistic grids, application execution can fail due to several reasons. System failures can result not only from an error on a single component but also from the usually complex interactions between the several grid components that comprise a range of different services. In addition to that, grid environments are extremely dynamic, with components joining and leaving the system at all times. Also, the likelihood of errors occurring during the execution of an application is exacerbated by the fact that many grid applications will perform long tasks that may require several days of computation.

To provide the necessary fault tolerance functionality for grid environments, several services must be available, such as: (a) **failure detection:** grid nodes and applications must be constantly monitored by a failure detection service; (b) **application failure handling:** various failure handling strategies can be employed in grid environments to ensure the continuity of application execution; and (c) **stable storage:** execution states that allow recovering the pre-failure state of applications must be saved in a data repository that can survive grid node failures. Those basic services will be discussed on the following sections.

4.1 Failure detection

Failure detection is a very important service for large-scale opportunistic grids. The high rate of churn makes failures a frequent event and the capability of the grid infrastructure to efficiently deal with them has a direct impact on its ability to make progress. Hence, failed nodes should be detected quickly and the monitoring network should itself be reliable, so as to ensure that a node failure does not go undetected. At the same time, due to the scale and geographic dispersion of grid nodes, failure detectors should be capable of disseminating information about failed nodes as fast and reliably as possible and work correctly even when no process has a globally consistent view of the system. Moreover, the non-dedicated nature of opportunistic grids requires that solutions for failure detection be very lightweight in terms of network bandwidth consumption and usage of memory and CPU cycles of resource provider machines. Besides all of these requirements pertaining to the functioning of failure detectors, they must also be easy to set-up and use; otherwise they might be a source of design and configuration errors. It is well-known that configuration errors are a common cause of grid failures (Medeiros et al., 2003). The aforementioned requirements are hard to meet as a whole and, to the best of our knowledge, no existing work in the literature addresses all of them. This is not surprising, as some goals, e.g., a reliable monitoring network and low network bandwidth consumption, are inherently conflicting. Nevertheless, they are all real issues that appear in large-scale opportunistic grids, and reliable grid applications are expected to deal with them in a realistic setting.

4.1.1 InteGrade failure detection

The InteGrade failure detection service (Filho et al., 2008) includes a number of features that, when combined and appropriately tuned, address all the above challenges while adopting reasonable compromises for the ones that conflict. The most noteworthy features of the proposed failure detector are the following: (i) a gossip- or infection-style approach (van Renesse et al., 1998), meaning that the network load imposed by the failure detector scales well with the number of processes in the network and that the monitoring network is highly reliable and descentralized; (ii) self-adaptation and self-organization in the face of changing network conditions; (iii) a crash-recover failure model, instead of simple crash; (iv) ease of use and configuration; (v) low resource consumption (memory, CPU cycles, and network bandwidth).

InteGrade's failure detection service is completely decentralized and runs on every grid node. Each process in the monitoring network established by the failure detection service is monitored by K other processes, where K is an administrator-defined parameter. This means that for a process failure to go undetected, all the K processes monitoring it would need to fail at the same time. A process r which is monitored by a process s has an open TCP connection with it through which it sends heartbeat messages and other kinds of information. If r perceives that it is being monitored by more than K processes, it can cancel the monitoring relationship with one or more randomly chosen processes. If it is monitored by more than K processes, it can select one or more random processes to start monitoring it. This approach yields considerable gains in reliability (Filho et al., 2009) at a very low cost in terms of extra control messages.

InteGrade's failure detector automatically adapts to changing network conditions. Instead of using a fixed timeout to determine the failure of a process, it continuously outputs the probability that a process has failed based on the inter-arrival times of the last W heartbeats and the time elapsed since the last heartbeat was received, where W is an administrator-defined parameter. The failure detector can then be configured to take recovery actions whenever the failure probability reaches a certain threshold. Multiple thresholds can be set, each one triggering a different recovery action, depending on the application requirements.

InteGrade employs a reactive and explicit approach to disseminate information about failed processes. This means that once a process learns about a new failure it automatically sends this information to J randomly-chosen processes that it monitors or that monitor it. The administrator-defined parameter J dictates the speed of dissemination. According to Ganesh et al. (2003), for a system with N processes, if each process disseminates a piece of information to $(\log n) + c$ randomly chosen processes, the probability that the information does not reach every process in the system is $e^{(-e^{(-c)})}$, with $n \rightarrow \infty$. For $J = 7$, this probability is less than 0.001. On the other hand, no explicit action is taken to disseminate information about new processes. Instead, processes get to know about new processes by simply receiving heartbeat messages. Each heartbeat that a process p sends to a process q includes some randomly chosen ids of K processes that p knows about. In a grid, it is important to quickly disseminate information about failed processes in order to initiate recovery as soon as possible and, when recovery is not possible and the application has to be re-initiated, to avoid wasting grid resources. On the other hand, information about new members is not so urgent, since not knowing about new members in general does not keep grid applications from making process.

InteGrade's group membership service is implemented in Lua (Ierusalimschy et al., 1996), an extensible and lightweight programming language. Lua makes it easy to use the proposed service from programs written in other programming languages, such as Java, C, and C++. Moreover, it executes in several platforms. Currently, we have successfully run the failure detector in Windows XP, Mac OS X, and several flavors of Linux. The entire implementation of the group membership service comprises approximately 80Kb of Lua source code, including comments.

4.2 Application failure handling

The main techniques used to provide application execution fault-tolerance can be divided in 2 levels: task level and workflow level (Hwang & Kesselman, 2003). At the task level, fault-tolerance techniques apply recovery mechanisms directly at the tasks, to masks the failures effects. At the workflow level, the recovery mechanisms creates recovery procedures directly in the workflow execution control.

4.2.1 Task-level techniques

There are 3 task-level techniques are frequently used in computational grids: retrying, replication and checkpointing.

Retrying is the simplest technique and consists in restarting the execution of the task after a failure. The task can be schedule at the same resource or at another one. Several scheduling can be used, such as FIFO (First-In First-Out), or algorithms that select resources with more computational power, more idleness or credibility (regarding security).

Replication consists in executing several replicas of the task on different resources, with the expectation that at least one of them finishes the execution successfully. The replicas can be scheduled to machines from the same or from different domains. Since networks failures can make an entire domain inaccessible, executing replicas in different domains improves the reliability. Replication is also useful to guarantee the integrity of the task execution results, since defective or malicious nodes can produce erroneous results. To prevent these errors, it is possible to wait until all executing tasks finish and apply a Byzantine agreement algorithm to compare the results.

Checkpointing consists in periodically store the application state in a way that, after a failure, the application can be restarted and continue its execution from the last saved state. The checkpointing mechanisms can be classified on how the application stated is obtained. There are two main approaches, called system-level and application-level checkpointing.

When using system-level checkpointing, the application state is obtained directly from the process memory space, together with some register values and state information from the operating system (Litzkow et al., 1997; Plank et al., 1998). This may require modifications in the kernel of the operating system, which may not be possible due to security reasons, but has the advantage that the checkpointing process can be transparent to the application. Some implementations permits the applications to be written in several program languages and used without recompilation. An important disadvantage of this approach for computational grids is that the checkpoints are not portable and is useful only in homogeneous clusters.

With application-level checkpointing, the application provides the data that will be stored in the checkpoint. It is necessary to instrument the application source-code so that the application saves its state periodically and, during recovery, reconstruct its original state from the checkpoint data (Bronevetsky et al., 2003; de Camargo et al., 2005; Karablieh et al., 2001; Strumpen & Ramkumar, 1996). Manually inserting code to save and recover an application state is a very error prone process, but this problem can be solved by providing a precompiler which automatically inserts the required code. Other drawbacks of this approach are the need to have access to the application source-code and that the checkpoints can be generated only at specified points in the execution. But this approach has the advantage that semantic information about memory contents is available and, consequently, only the data necessary to recover the application state needs to be saved. Moreover, the semantic information permits the generation of portable checkpoints (de Camargo et al., 2005; Karablieh et al., 2001; Strumpen & Ramkumar, 1996), which is an important advantage for heterogeneous grids.

In the case of coupled parallel applications, the tasks may exchange messages, which can be in transit during the generation of local checkpoints by the application processes. The content of these messages, including sending and delivery ordering, must also be considered as part of the application state. To guarantee that the global state (which includes the local state of all tasks) is consistent, it is necessary to use checkpointing protocols, which are classified as non-coordinated, coordinated and communication induced (Elnozahy et al., 2002).

The parallel checkpointing protocols differ in the level of coordination among the processes, from the non-coordinated protocols, where each process of the parallel application generates its local checkpoint independently from the others, to fully coordinated protocols, where all the processes synchronize before generating their local checkpoints. The communication induced protocol is similar to the non-coordinated one, with the difference that, to guarantee the generation of global checkpoints with consistent states, processes may be required to generate additional checkpoints after receiving or before sending messages.

4.2.2 Workflow-level techniques

Workflow-level techniques are based on the knowledge of the execution context of the tasks and on the flow control of the computations. They are applied to grids that support workflow-based applications and the more common techniques are: alternative task, redundancy, user defined exception handling and rescue workflow.

The basic idea of the *alternative task* technique consists in using a different implementation of the task to substitute the failed one. It is useful when a task has several implementations with distinct characteristics, such as the efficiency and reliability.

The *redundancy* technique is similar to the alternative task, with the difference that the distinct implementations of the task are executed simultaneously. When the first one finishes, the task is considered complete, and the remaining tasks are killed.

The *user defined exception handling* allows the user to provide the handling procedure for specific failures of particular tasks. This approach will usually be more efficient, since the user normally has specific knowledge about the tasks.

Finally, the last approach consists in generating a new workflow, called *rescue workflow*, to execute the tasks of the original flow that failed and the ones that could not be executed due to task dependencies. If the rescue workflow fails, a new workflow can be generated (Condor_Team, 2004).

4.2.3 InteGrade application failure handling

InteGrade provides a task-level fault tolerance mechanism. In order to overcome application execution failures, this mechanism provides support for the most used failure handling strategies: (1) **retrying**: when an application execution fails, it is restarted from scratch; (2) **replication**: the same application is submitted for execution multiple times, generating various application replicas; all replicas are active and execute the same code with the same input parameters at different nodes; and (3) **checkpointing**: periodically saves the process' state in stable storage during the failure-free execution time. Upon a failure, the process restarts from the latest available saved checkpoint, thereby reducing the amount of lost computation. As part of the application submission process, users can select the desired technique to be applied in case of failure. These techniques can also be combined resulting in four more elaborate failure handling techniques: *retrying* (without checkpoint and replication), *checkpointing* (without replication), *replication* (without checkpointing), and *replication with checkpointing*.

InteGrade includes a portable application-level checkpointing mechanism (de Camargo et al., 2005) for sequential, bag-of-tasks, and BSP parallel applications written in C. This portability allows an application's stored state to be recovered on a machine with a different architecture from the one where the checkpoint was generated. A precompiler inserts, into the application code, the statements responsible for gathering and restoring the application state from the checkpoint. On BSP applications, checkpoints are generated immediately after the end of a BSP synchronization phase. For MPI parallel applications, we provide a system-level checkpointing mechanism based on a coordinated protocol (Cardozo & Costa, 2008). For storing the checkpointing data, InteGrade uses a distributed data storage system, called OppStore (Section 4.3.1).

InteGrade allows replication for sequential, bag-of-tasks, MPI and BSP applications. The amount of generated replicas is currently defined during the application execution request, issued through the Application Submission and Control Tool (ASCT). The request is forwarded to the Global Resource Manager (GRM), which runs a scheduling algorithm that guarantees that all replicas will be assigned to different nodes. Another InteGrade component, called Application Replication Manager (ARM), concentrates most of the code responsible for managing replication. In case of a replica failure, the ARM starts its recovery process. When the first application replica concludes its job, the ARM kills the remaining ones, releasing the allocated grid resources.

4.3 Stable storage

To guarantee the continuity of application execution and prevent loss of data in case of failures, it is necessary to store the periodical checkpoints and application temporary, input, and output data using a reliable and fault-tolerant storage device or service, which is called stable storage. The reliability is provided by the usage of data redundancy and the system can determine the level of redundancy depending on the unavailability rate of the storage devices used by the service.

A commonly used strategy for data storage in computational grids usually store several replicas of files in dedicated servers managed by replica management systems (Cai et al., 2004; Chervenak et al., 2004; Ripeanu & Foster, 2002). These systems usually target high-performance computing platforms, with applications that require very large amounts (petabytes) of data and run on supercomputers connected by specialized high-speed networks.

When dealing with the storage of checkpoints of parallel applications in opportunistic grids, a common strategy is to use the grid machines used to execute applications to store checkpoints. It is possible to distribute the data over the nodes executing the parallel application that generates the checkpoints, in addition to other grid machines. In this case, data is transfered in a parallel way to the machines. To ensure fault-tolerance, data must be coded and stored in a redundant way, and the data coding strategy must be selected considering its scalability, computational cost, and fault-tolerance level. The main techniques used are *data replication*, *data parity*, and *erasure codes*.

Using data replication, the system stores full replicas of the generated checkpoints. If one of the replicas becomes unaccessible, the system can easily find another. The advantage is that no extra coding is necessary, but the disadvantage is that this approach requires the transfer and storage of large amounts of data. For instance, to guarantee safety against a single failure, it is necessary to save two copies of the checkpoint, which can generate too much local network traffic, possibly compromising the execution of the parallel application. A possible approach to adopt is to store a copy of the checkpoint locally and another remotely (de Camargo et al., 2006). Although a failure in a machine running the application makes one of the checkpoints unaccessible, it is still possible to retrieve the other copy. Moreover, the other application processes can use their local checkpoint copies. Consequently, this storage mode permits recovery as long as one of the two nodes containing a checkpoint replica is available.

The two other coding techniques decompose a file into smaller data segments, called stripes, and distribute these stripes among the machines. To ensure fault-tolerancy, redundant stripes are also generated and stored, permitting the original file to be recovered even if a subset of the stripes is lost. There are several algorithms to code the file into redundant fragments. A commonly used one is the use of data parity (Malluhi & Johnston, 1998; Plank et al., 1998; Sobe, 2003), where one or more extra stripes are generated based on the evaluation of the parity of the bits in the original fragments. It has the advantage that it is fast to evaluate and that the original stripes can be stored without modifications. But they have the disadvantage that data cannot be recovered if two or more fragments are lost and, consequently, cannot be used for storage in devices with higher rates of unavailability.

The other strategy is to use erasure coding techniques, which allow one to code a vector U of size n, into $m + k$ encoded vectors of size n/m, with the property that one can regenerate U

using only m of the $m+k$ encoded vectors. By using this encoding, one can achieve different levels of fault-tolerance by tuning the values of m and k. In practice, it is possible to tolerate k failures with an overhead of only $k/m * n$ elements. The information dispersal algorithm (IDA) (de Camargo et al., 2006; Malluhi & Johnston, 1998; Rabin, 1989) is an example of erasure code that can be used to code data. IDA provides the desired degree of fault-tolerance with lower space overhead, but it incurs a computational cost for coding the data and an extra latency for transferring the fragments from multiple nodes. But analytical studies (Rodrigues & Liskov, 2005; Weatherspoon & Kubiatowicz, 2002) show that, for a given redundancy level, data stored using erasure coding has a mean availability several times higher than using replication.

The checkpointing overhead in the execution time of parallel applications when using erasure coding, data parity and replication was compared elsewhere (de Camargo et al., 2006). The replication strategy had the smallest overhead, but uses more storage space. Erasure coding causes a larger overhead, but uses less storage space and is more flexible, allowing the system to select the desired level of fault-tolerance.

4.3.1 InteGrade stable storage

InteGrade implements a distributed data repository called OppStore (de Camargo & Kon, 2007). It is used for storing the application's input and output files and checkpointing data. Access to this distributed repository is performed through a library called *access broker*, which interacts with OppStore.

OppStore is a middleware that provides reliable distributed data storage using free disk space from shared grid machines. The goal is to use this free disk space in an opportunistic way, i.e., only during the idle periods of the machines. The system is structured as a federation of clusters and is connected by a Pastry peer-to-peer network (Rowstron & Druschel, 2001) in a scalable and fault-tolerant way. This federation structure allows the system to disperse application data throughout the grid. During storage, the system slices the data into several redundant, encoded fragments and stores them in different grid clusters. This distribution improves data availability and fault-tolerance, since fragments are located in geographically dispersed clusters. When performing data retrieval, applications can simultaneously download file fragments stored in the highest bandwidth clusters, enabling efficient data retrieval. This is OppSore standard storage mode, called perennial. Using OppStore, application input and output files can be obtained from any node in the system. Consequently, after a failure, restarting of an application execution in another machine can be easily performed. Also, when an application execution finishes, the output files uploaded to the distributed repositories can be accessed by the user from any machine connected to the grid.

OppStore also has an ephemeral mode, where data is stored in the machines of the same cluster where the request was issued. It is used for data that requires high bandwidth and only needs to be available for a few hours. It is used to store checkpointing (de Camargo et al., 2006; Elnozahy et al., 2002) data and other temporary application data. In this storage mode, the system stores the data only in the local cluster and can use IDA or data replication to provide fault-tolerance. For checkpointing data, the preferred strategy is to store two copies of each local checkpoint in the cluster, one in the machine where it was generated and the other on another cluster machine. During the recovery of failed parallel application, most of the processes will be able to recover their local checkpoints from the local machine.

The system stores most of the generated checkpoints using the ephemeral mode, since the usage of local networks generates a lower overhead. To prevent losing the entire computation due to a failure or disconnection of the cluster where the application was executing, periodically, the checkpoints are also stored in other clusters using the perennial storage mode, for instance, after every *k* generated checkpoints. With this strategy, InteGrade can obtain low overhead and high availability at the same time for checkpoint storage.

5. Conclusion

Corporations and universities typically have hundreds or thousands of desktop machines, which are used by workers as their personal workstations or by students in instructional and research laboratories. When analyzing the usage of each of these machines one concludes that they sit idle for a significant amount of time. Even when the computer is in use, it normally has a large portion of idle resources. When we consider the night period, we conclude that most of the times they are not used at all. This situation lives in contradiction with the growing demand for highly intensive computational power required by several fields of research, including physics, chemistry, biology, and economics. Several corporations also rely on the intensive use of computing power to solve problems such as financial market simulations and studies for accurate oil well drilling. The movie industry makes intensive use of computers to render movies using an increasing number of special effects.

Opportunistic grid middleware enables the use of the existing computing infrastructure available in laboratories and offices in universities, research institutes, and companies to execute computationally intensive parallel applications. Nevertheless, executing this class of applications on such a dynamic and heterogeneous environment is a daunting task, especially when non-dedicated resources are used, as in the case of opportunistic computing. In an opportunistic grid middleware resources do not need to be dedicated for executing grid applications. The grid workload coexist with local applications executions, submitted by the nodes regular users. The middleware must take advantage of idle computing cycles that arise from unused time frames of the workstations that comprise the grid.

An opportunistic grid middleware must provide innovative solutions to circumvent problems arising from the heterogeneity, high scalability and dynamism of the execution environment. Among the several aspects that must be considered, central issues are related to the support for a variety of programming models, highly scalable distributed resource management, application scheduling and execution management, and fault tolerance, since opportunist grid environments are inherently prone of errors. In this chapter, we provided a comprehensive description of reputable solutions found in the literature to circumvent the above described problems, emphasizing the approaches adopted in the InteGrade middleware, an open-source multi-university effort to build a robust and flexible middleware for opportunistic grid computing available at `http://www.integrade.org.br`.

6. References

Barbosa, R. M. & Goldman, A. (2004). Framework for mobile agents on computer grid environments, *First International Workshop on Mobility Aware Technologies and Applications (MATA 2004)*, Springer LNCS No 3284, Florianópolis, Brazil, pp. 147–157.

Barlow, H. B. (1999). *Unsupervised learning: Foundations of Neural Computation*, MIT Press.

Bisseling, R. H. (2004). *Parallel Scientific Computation: A Structured Approach using BSP and MPI*, Oxford University Press.

Bosilca, G., Bouteiller, A., Cappello, F., Djilali, S., Fedak, G., Germain, C., Herault, T., Lemarinier, P., Lodygensky, O., Magniette, F., Neri, V. & Selikhov, A. (2002). Mpich-v: toward a scalable fault tolerant mpi for volatile nodes, *Proceedings of the 2002 ACM/IEEE Conference on Supercomputing*, IEEE Computer Society Press, Baltimore, Maryland, USA, pp. 1–18.

Bronevetsky, G., Marques, D., Pingali, K. & Stodghill, P. (2003). Automated application-level checkpointing of MPI programs, *PPoPP '03: Proceedings of the 9th ACM SIGPLAN Symposium on Principles and Practice of Parallel Programming*, pp. 84–89.

Cai, M., Chervenak, A. & Frank, M. (2004). A peer-to-peer replica location service based on a distributed hash table, *SC '04: Proceedings of the 2004 ACM/IEEE conference on Supercomputing*, IEEE Computer Society, Washington, DC, USA, p. 56.

Cardozo, M. C. & Costa, F. M. (2008). Mpi support on opportunistic grids based on the integrade middleware, *2nd Latin American Grid International Workshop (LAGrid)*, Campo Grande, Brazil.

Chervenak, A. L., Palavalli, N., Bharathi, S., Kesselman, C. & Schwartzkopf, R. (2004). Performance and scalability of a replica location service, *HPDC '04: Proceedings of the 13th IEEE International Symposium on High Performance Distributed Computing (HPDC'04)*, IEEE Computer Society, Washington, DC, USA, pp. 182–191.

Condor_Team (2004). *Online Manual of Condor Version 7.4.4*, University of Wisconsin-Madison, http://www.cs.wisc.edu/condor/manual/v7.4.

da Silva e Silva, F. J., Kon, F., Goldman, A., Finger, M., de Camargo, R. Y., Filho, F. C. & Costa, F. M. (2010). Application execution management on the integrade opportunistic grid middleware, *Journal of Parallel and Distributed Computing* 70(5): 573 – 583.

de Camargo, R. Y., Cerqueira, R. & Kon, F. (2006). Strategies for checkpoint storage on opportunistic grids, *IEEE Distributed Systems Online* 18(6).

de Camargo, R. Y. & Kon, F. (2007). Design and implementation of a middleware for data storage in opportunistic grids, *CCGrid '07: Proceedings of the 7th IEEE/ACM International Symposium on Cluster Computing and the Grid*, IEEE Computer Society, Washington, DC, USA.

de Camargo, R. Y., Kon, F. & Goldman, A. (2005). Portable checkpointing and communication for BSP applications on dynamic heterogeneous Grid environments, *SBAC-PAD'05: The 17th International Symposium on Computer Architecture and High Performance Computing*, Rio de Janeiro, Brazil, pp. 226–233.

de Ribamar Braga Pinheiro Júnior, J. (2008). *Xenia: um sistema de segurança para grades computacionais baseado em cadeias de confianą*, PhD thesis, IME/USP.

de Ribamar Braga Pinheiro Júnior, J., Vidal, A. C. T., Kon, F. & Finger, M. (2006). Trust in large-scale computational grids: An SPKI/SDSI extension for representing opinion, *4th International Workshop on Middleware for Grid Computing - MGC 2006*, ACM/IFIP/USENIX, Melbourne, Australia.

Dong, F. & Akl, S. G. (2006). Scheduling algorithms for grid computing: State of the art and open problems, *Technical Report 2006-504*, School of Computing, Queens University, Kingston, Ontario.

El-Rewini, H., Lewis, T. G. & Ali, H. H. (1994). *Task scheduling in parallel and distributed systems*, Prentice-Hall, Inc., Upper Saddle River, NJ, USA.

Elnozahy, M., Alvisi, L., Wang, Y.-M. & Johnson, D. B. (2002). A survey of rollback-recovery protocols in message-passing systems, *ACM Computing Surveys* 34(3): 375–408.

Everitt, B., Landau, S. & Leese, M. (2001). *Cluster Analysis*, 4th edn, MIT Press.

Filho, F. C., Castro, R., Marques, A., Neto, F. S., de Camargo, R. Y. & Kon, F. (2008). A group membership service for large-scale grids, *6th International Workshop on Middleware for Grid Computing*, Leuven, Belgium.

Filho, F. C., Castro, R., Marques, A., Soares-Neto, F., de Camargo, R. Y. & Kon, F. (2009). A robust and scalable group membership service for large-scale grids *(in portuguese)*, *SBRC'2009 Workshop on Grid Computing and Applications*, Recife, Brazil.

Finger, M., Bezerra, G. C. & Conde, D. M. R. (2008). Resource use pattern analysis for opportunistic grids, *6th International Workshop on Middleware for Grid Computing (MGC 2008)*, Leuven, Belgium.

Finger, M., Bezerra, G. C. & Conde, D. M. R. (2010). Resource use pattern analysis for predicting resource availability in opportunistic grids, *Concurrency and Computation: Practice and Experience* 22(3).

Ganesh, A. J., Kermarrec, A.-M. & Massoulie, L. (2003). Peer-to-peer membership management for gossip-based protocols, *IEEE Transactions on Computers* 52(2): 139–149.

Goel, A., Steere, D. C., C, C. P. & Walpole, J. (1999). Adaptive resource management via modular feedback control, *Technical report*, Oregon Graduate Institute, Department of Computer Science and Engineering.

Goldchleger, A., Goldman, A., Hayashida, U. & Kon, F. (2005). The implementation of the bsp parallel computing model on the integrade grid middleware, *3rd International Workshop on Middleware for Grid Computing*, ACM Press, Grenoble, France.

Goldchleger, A., Kon, F., Goldman, A., Finger, M. & Bezerra, G. C. (2004). Integrade: Object-oriented grid middleware leveraging idle computing power of desktop machines, *Concurrency and Computation: Practice and Experience* 16(5): 449–459.

Grandinetti, L. (2005). *Grid Computing: The New Frontier of High Performance Computing*, Elsevier.

Hwang, S. & Kesselman, C. (2003). Gridworkflow: A flexible failure handling framework for the grid, *hpdc* 00: 126.

Ibarra, O. H. & Kim, C. E. (1977). Heuristic algorithms for scheduling independent tasks on nonidentical processors, *Journal of the ACM (JACM)* 24(2): 280–289.

Ierusalimschy, R., de Figueiredo, L. H. & Filho, W. C. (1996). Lua - an extensible extension language, *Software: Practice Experience* 26(6): 635–652.

Karablieh, F., Bazzi, R. A. & Hicks, M. (2001). Compiler-assisted heterogeneous checkpointing, *SRDS '01: Proceedings of the 20th IEEE Symposium on Reliable Distributed Systems*, New Orleans, USA, pp. 56–65.

Karonis, N., Toonen, B. & Foster, I. (2003). Mpich-g2: a grid-enabled implementation of the message passing interface, *Journal of Parallel and Distributed Computing (JPDC)* 63(3): 551–563.

Lee, C. & Talia, D. (2003). Grid programming models: Current tools, issues and directions, *Grid Computing*, Wiley Online Library, pp. 555–578.

Litzkow, M., Tannenbaum, T., Basney, J. & Livny, M. (1997). Checkpoint and migration of UNIX processes in the Condor distributed processing system, *Technical Report UW-CS-TR-1346*, University of Wisconsin - Madison Computer Sciences Department.

Liu, Y. (2004). Grid scheduling, *Technical report*, Department of Computer Science, University of Iowa. http://www.cs.uiowa.edu/ yanliu/QE/QEreview.pdf, Acessado em: 22/01/2009.

Lopes, R. F., Silva, F. J. S. & Souza, B. B. (2005). Mag: A mobile agent based computational grid platform, *Proceedings of the 4th International Conference on Grid and Cooperative Computing (GCC 2005)*, Springer LNCS Series, Beijing, China.

Maheswaran, M., Ali, S., Siegel, H. J., Hensgen, D. & Freund, R. F. (1999). Dynamic matching and scheduling of a class of independent tasks onto heterogeneous computing systems, *HCW '99: Proceedings of the Eighth Heterogeneous Computing Workshop*, IEEE Computer Society, Washington, DC, USA, p. 30.

Maia, R., Cerqueira, R. & Cosme, R. (2006). Oil: an object request broker in the lua, *5th Tools Session of the Brazilian Simposium on Computer Networks (SBRC2006)*, Curitiba, Brazil.

Malluhi, Q. M. & Johnston, W. E. (1998). Coding for high availability of a distributed-parallel storage system, *IEEE Transactions Parallel Distributed Systems* 9(12): 1237–1252.

Medeiros, R., Cirne, W., Brasileiro, F. V. & Sauvé, J. P. (2003). Faults in grids: why are they so bad and what can be done about it?, *4th IEEE International Workshop on Grid Computing (GRID 2003)*, Phoenix, USA, pp. 18–24.

MPI (1997). *MPI-2: extensions to the Message-Passing Interface.*
URL: *http://www.mpi-forum.org/docs/mpi-20-html/mpi2-report.html*

MPI (2009). *MPI: A Message-Passing Interface Standard Version 2.2.*
URL: *http://www.mpi-forum.org/docs/mpi22-report/mpi22-report.htm*

OMG (2011). *Common Object Request Broker Architecture (CORBA) Specification, Version 3.1.1*, Object Management Group (OMG).
URL: *http://www.omg.org/spec/CORBA/3.1.1/*

Pham, V. A. & Karmouch, A. (1998). Mobile software agents: An overview, *Communications Magazine* 7(36): 26–37.

Pinheiro, V. G., Goldman, A. & Kon, F. (2011). Adaptive fault tolerance mechanisms for opportunistic environments: a mobile agent approach, *Concurrency and Computation: Practice and Experience* .

Plank, J. S., Li, K. & Puening, M. A. (1998). Diskless checkpointing, *IEEE Transactions on Parallel and Distributed Systems* 9(10): 972–986.

Rabin, M. O. (1989). Efficient dispersal of information for security, load balancing, and fault tolerance, *Journal of the ACM* 36(2): 335–348.

Ripeanu, M. & Foster, I. (2002). A decentralized, adaptive replica location mechanism, *HPDC '02: Proceedings of the 11 th IEEE International Symposium on High Performance Distributed Computing*, IEEE Computer Society, Washington, DC, USA.

Rodrigues, R. & Liskov, B. (2005). High availability in DHTs: Erasure coding vs. replication, *IPTPS '05: Revised Selected Papers from the Fourth International Workshop on Peer-to-Peer Systems*, Springer-Verlag, London, UK, pp. 226–239.

Rowstron, A. I. T. & Druschel, P. (2001). Pastry: scalable, decentralized object location, and routing for large-scale peer-to-peer systems, *Middleware 2001: IFIP/ACM International Conference on Distributed Systems Platforms*, Heidelberg, Germany, pp. 329–350.

Schopf, J. M. (2004). Ten actions when grid scheduling: the user as a grid scheduler, *Grid resource management: state of the art and future trends* pp. 15–23.

Sobe, P. (2003). Stable checkpointing in distributed systems without shared disks, *IPDPS '03: Proceedings of the 17th International Symposium on Parallel and Distributed Processing*, IEEE Computer Society, Washington, DC, USA, p. 214.2.

Steere, D. C., Goel, A., Gruenberg, J., McNamee, D., Pu, C. & Walpole, J. (1999). A feedback-driven proportion allocator for real-rate scheduling, *OSDI âĂŹ99: Proceedings of the Third Symposium on Operating Systems Design and Implementation*, USENIX Association, New Orleans, LA, USA, pp. 145–158.

Strumpen, V. & Ramkumar, B. (1996). Portable checkpointing and recovery in heterogeneous environments, *Technical Report UI-ECE TR-96.6.1*, University of Iowa.

Subramani, V., Kettimuthu, R., Srinivasan, S. & Sadayappan, P. (2002). Distributed job scheduling on computational grids using multiple simultaneous requests, *HPDC '02: Proceedings of the 11th IEEE International Symposium on High Performance Distributed Computing*, IEEE Computer Society, Washington, DC, USA, p. 359.

Theodoridis, S. & Koutroumba, K. (2003). *Pattern Recognition*, Elsevier Academic Press.

Valiant, L. G. (1990). A bridging model for parallel computation, *Communications of the ACM* 33(8): 103 – 111.

van Renesse, R., Minsky, Y. & Hayden, M. (1998). A gossip-style failure detection service, *Proceedings of the IFIP International Conference on Distributed Systems Platforms and Open Distributed Processing (Middleware 1998)*, Lake District, England.

Weatherspoon, H. & Kubiatowicz, J. (2002). Erasure coding vs. replication: A quantitative comparison, *IPTPS '01: Revised Papers from the First International Workshop on Peer-to-Peer Systems*, Springer-Verlag, London, UK, pp. 328–338.

Wilkinson, B. (2009). *Grid Computing: Techniques and Applications*, Chapman & Hall/CRC.

Zhu, Y. (2003). A survey on grid scheduling systems, *Technical report*, Computer Science Department, University of Science and Technology, Hong Kong.

7

Research and Implementation of Parallel Cache Model Through Grid Memory

Qingkui Chen, Lichun Na, He Jia,
Song Lin Zhuang and Xiaodong Ding
School of Computer Engineering,
University of Shanghai for Science and Technology
China

1. Introduction

With the rapid development of the information techniques and the Internet popular applications, the demand for the high performance processing devices is becoming more and more vehement, such as the server construction of HDTV or IPTV for large scale VOD, and the parallel file system of grid computing. These applications need the ability to process the concurrent peak access. The parallel file system (J.Carretero, F. Perez, P. de Miguel& L.Alonso, 1996; P.F. Corbett & D. G, 1996; Craig S. Freedman, Josef Burger, & David J, 1996; Seogyun Kim, Jiseung Nam & Soon-ja Yeom, 2002) has become the very important research areas, and the parallel cache (Horst Eidenberger, 2005; J. Fernandez,J. Carretero, F. Garcia-Carballeira, A. Calderon & J. M. Perez-Menor, 2005; T. Kimbrel et. AI,1996; Pal Halvorsen, Carsten Griwodz, Vera Goebel, Ketil Lund, Thomas Plagemann & Jonathan Walpole,2006) is playing the key roles in these applications. At the same time, the numbers of the Intranet composed of computer clusters are quickly increasing, and a great deal of cheap personal computers are distributed everywhere, but the utilization of their resources is very low(E. P. Markatos & G. Dramitions,1996; Anurag Acharya & Sanjeev Setia,1998). Through mining and adopting these idle resources, we can get a lot of large-scale high performance computation, storage and communication resources which are not special. How to use these idle memories to construct the parallel cache for supporting the large scale applications, such as VOD for hot segments, is very interesting. It not only improves their performance, but also increases the utilization of these idle resources. However, the heterogeneous, dynamic and unstable characteristic of these resources brings a huge obstacle for us. The grid (I. Foster & C. Kesselman, 1999) techniques and multi-agents (E. Osawa, 1993; Wooldridge, M, 2002) become the main approaches to effectively use these resources, and the multi-agents have already become the feasible solutions for grid applications. There are many successful examples (O.F. Rana & D.W. Walker, 2000; J.O. kephart & Chess, D.M, 2003) of applications which are in conjunction with the automatic multi-agents system. But, the research of construction cache model for hot segment through grid idle memory is still not much. At the same time, the high performance cluster techniques (Rajkumar Buyya, 1999) are already mature and can be the foundation for supporting the parallel cache based on grid memory.

This book chapter introduced a Parallel Cache Model Based on Grid Memory (PCMGM) in the dynamic network environment (DNE). Through building an open grid environment, using the idle memory resources of DNE, adopting the multi-agents, the fuzzy theory and the self-learning methods, we designed the PCMGM model that can support the concurrent peak access for the hot segments in large scale internet applications, such as the large scale VOD system. The experimental results show that PCMGM can improve response time of the large scale application system for hot segments. It can be fit for the grid computing and the large scale VOD system in internet.

2. Architecture of PCMGM

PCMGM includes two parts: one is DNE that is the physical computing devices for the parallel cache, and DNE is composed of computer clusters connected through LAN and Intranet, and all the cache computers are not special, the other is the agent system, and we call it GMG (Global Management Group). GMG is composed of a management agent system (MAS), the application agent (AA), and a lots of cache agents (CA). The architecture is presented in figure1, and the definitions of NA, CA, CN, GA, SA are described as the definition 1 ~7 and the section 3.

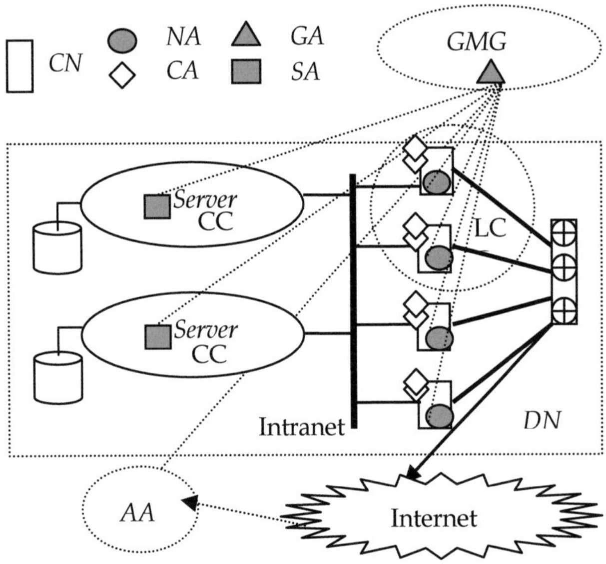

Fig. 1. The architecture of PCMGM

2.1 DNE

Definition.1. Cache node (CN) is a computer and it is defined as CN (id, AS, RSV, st), where id is the identifier of CN; AS is the set of agents running on CN; RSV(r_{cpu}, r_{mem}, r_{disk}, r_{net}) denotes its resource support vector, r_{cpu} is the power of its CPU, r_{mem} is the power of its memory storage, r_{disk} is the power of its hard-disk , and r_{net} is the power of its network adapter; st$\in${"Local", "Idle", "Caching"} is its states, "Local" denotes that this computer is working for local tasks, "Idle" denotes that this computer is not working , and "Caching" denotes that this computer is working for Grid in the form of cache.

Definition.2. Computer cluster (CC) is defined as CC (Master, CS), where Master is the main computer of CC; CS= {CN1, CN2 ... CNp} is the set of all cache nodes in computer cluster.

Definition.3. Logical computer cluster (LCC) is defined as LCC (id, LCS, B, CC), where id denotes the identifier of LCC; LCS is the set of cache nodes of LCC; CC is the computer cluster which comprises LCC. Network bandwidth of LCC denotes as B.

So, the dynamic network environment (DNE) can be defined as DNE (Master, CCS, SVS, N, R), where Master is the main computer of DNE; CSS is the set of all computer clusters in DNE; SVS is the set of file servers to storage the files; N is its network set; R is the connection rules. All the free memories of the idle cache nodes in DNE are called the grid memory.

Definition. 4. Basic memory unit (BMU) is the uniform size of basic memory block as the allotting unit in PCMGM, and its unit is MB.

Definition. 5. Grid memory capacity (Gmc) is the total numbers of BMU provided by all cache nodes in DNE. The Gmc value is dynamic changed.

2.2 Management Agents System (MAS)

The main functions of MAS are the computation resource management, the DNE monitoring and the task scheduler. MAS include four parts: The first part is the global control agent (GA) for managing PCMGM. The second part is the agent for managing one file server, and it is called as the server agent (SA). The third part is the agents for managing the cache nodes, and they are called as the node agents (NA), and each cache node has a NA. The last part is the application agent (AA) that is the connection manager between the users and PCMGM. The MAS structure is presented in figure 1.

The main functions of GA are as follows: (1) Control and manage DNE; (2) Receive and dispatch the caches; (3) control and monitor the file access process; (4) load balance; (5) Control all the cache nodes in DNE; (6) Calculate the idle resources; (7) Monitor the states all computing nodes and node agents ;

The main functions of SA are as follows: (1) File operations; (2) The hot segment 27 management; (3) File transfer;

The main functions of NA are as follows: (1) Control the cache node to join or disjoin the DNE in dynamic; (2) Calculate the idle resources, and report them to GA; (3) Monitor the states and events in CN, and make the response adjustments; (4) Control the cache agents (CA) to complete the file access task.

2.3 Cache file and cache agent

The large file is always divided into a series of segments (SEG) in the file server and the access frequency of each segment is different, so the high access frequency segment is called as the hot segment. If the hot segment is duplicated into the grid memory, the access efficiency will be improved greatly. For describing this mechanism, we introduce some conceptions.

Definition.6. Duplication Segment (DSEG) is the SEG (definition 5) duplication stored in Grid memory, and it can be defined as DSEG (SEG-id, CA, CN, ST), where SEG-id is the identifier of its SEG; CA is the cache agent for managing and accessing the DSEG; CN is the cache node on which the DSEG is stored. ST∈ {"Memory", "Disk"} is its states, and "Memory" denotes that the DSEG is in the memory of cache node, and "Disk" denotes that the DSEG is in the local disk of cache node. In the follow, we will give the detail definition about SEG.

Definition.7. Segment (SEG) is the file basic unit and it can be defined as SEG (SEG-id, File, DSEGS, LOC), where SEG-id is the identifier of SEG; File is the file that includes this SEG; DSEGS = {DSEG1, DSEG2 … DSEGd} is the set of all its active DSEGs; LOC is its server address. |SEG | is the numbers of DSEGS elements and it is called the duplication width of the SEG.

So, the file in PCMGM can be presented as a SEG sequence {SEG1, SEG2 … SEGf}, and the length of all SEGs is a constant Segl, and it is called the segment length, and its measure unit is BMU. Each file has its private segment length by its characteristic. The SEG duplication stored in Grid memory is called as duplication segment (DSEG). We call this structure file as the cache file.

Definition.8. Cache agent (CA) is defined as CA (id, DSEG, RDV, PRG, BDI, KS, CE), where id is the identifier of CA; DSEG is the duplication segment which is managed by CA; RDV (d_{cpu}, d_{disk}, d_{net}) is the resource demand vector of CA and it is the need rate for CPU, DISK and NET ; PRG is the executable program set of CA; BDI is the description of its BDI; KS is its knowledge set; CE is its configuration environment.

CA is the basic element to manage DSEG, and a CA can serve for a group of users; the relations between CA, SEG, DSEG, and cache file is presented in figure 2.

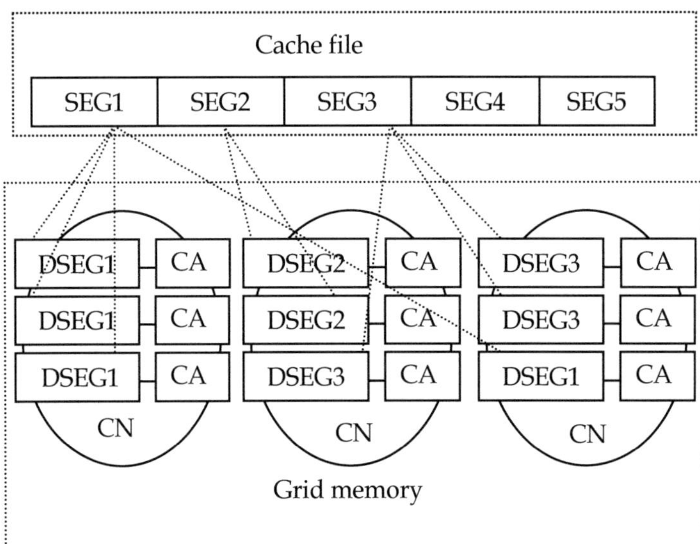

Fig. 2. The relations between CA, DSEG, SEG and the cache file

Defination.9. Cache node ability (CNA) is defined as CNA (CN-id, Ma, Ca), where CN-id is the identifier of CN; Ma is the memory storage ability for storing DSEG in its memory and $Ma=\left\lfloor \frac{CN.RSV.r_{mem}}{BMU} \right\rfloor$, Ca is its computing ability for supporting the cache agent and

$$Ca=.minimum\ \{ \left\lfloor \frac{CN.RSV.r_{cpu}}{CA.RDV.d_{cpu}} \right\rfloor, \left\lfloor \frac{CN.RSV.r_{disk}}{CA.RDV.d_{disk}} \right\rfloor, \left\lfloor \frac{CN.RSV.r_{net}}{CA.RDV.d_{net}} \right\rfloor \}$$

3. Construction of logical cluster

When GA received the information from all cache nodes in DNE, the logical computer cluster will be constructed for Parallel Cache Model. Here PCS={ $CN_i(id_i, CT_i, AS_i, RSV_i, st_i) \mid 1 \le i \le n$ } is the set of all cache nodes in DNE. Actually, as different cache node may provide different resources, we must classify the cache nodes to different power logical computer clusters according to their power. Therefore, the principle of classification is based on their power of CPU, Memory, Disk, and Net adapter. In order to solve this problem, we should firstly discrete the power data, and fuzzy relation theory is employed to represent the data.

3.1 Resource matrix

Suppose that MR= (r_{ij}) $(1 \le i \le n, 1 \le j \le 4)$ is the resource matrix in DNE. F_i denotes as CPU frequency of CN_i, here it is measured in MHZ; M_i denotes as memory capacity of CN_i, and it is measured in MB; R_i indicates Disk speed of CN_i, and it is measured in RPM; N_i indicates communication power of CN_i, and it is measured in MBS; The resource matrix elements are determined by the real ability of cache nodes, and the calculation method is as follows:

$$r_{i1}=\left\lfloor \frac{F_i}{500MHZ} \right\rfloor +1\ ;$$

$$r_{i2}=\left\lfloor \frac{M_i}{128MB} \right\rfloor +1\ ;$$

$$r_{i3}=\begin{cases} 1, when\ R_i = 5400RPM; \\ 2, when\ R_i = 7200RPM; \\ 3, when\ R_i = 10000RPM; \end{cases}$$

$$r_{i4}=\begin{cases} 1, when\ N_i = 10MBS; \\ 2, when\ N_i = 100MBS \\ 3, when\ N_i = 1000MBS; \end{cases}$$

3.2 Partition for logical computer cluster

It is very important to divide different logical computer clusters, then the LCC division algorithm as follows:

Algorithm 3.1 Partition method for LCC.

1. $MR = (r_{ij})$ $(1 \le i \le n, 1 \le j \le 4)$ is the resource matrix in *DNE*, where n is the numbers of all cache nodes; T is a parallel cache mode task.
2. Construct the fuzzy matrix $FM = (f_{ij})$ $(1 \le i \le n, 1 \le j \le n)$, where $f_{ii} = 1$;

$f_{ij} = 1 - \beta(x_1|r_{i1} - r_{j1}| + x_2|r_{i2} - r_{j2}| + x_3|r_{i3} - r_{j3}| + x_4|r_{i4} - r_{j4}|)$, when $i \ne j$, and $0 < \beta < 1$, and $x_1 + x_2 + x_3 + x_4 = 1$, $x_k > 0$ $(1 \le k \le 4)$;

3. build the fuzzy equivalence matrix;

Repeat do
FT=*FM* ⊙ *FM*; //⊙ is the operation theorem to take the maximum and minimum
If *FT*=*FM* then goto (4);
FM=FT;
End do;

4. Calculate the c-cut matrix FM_c;
5. Divide the cache nodes of *PCS* into several equivalence class $LCC_1 \cup LCC_2 \cup \ldots LCC_e$ by FM_c;
6. Choose a *LCC* for T according to its resource demand vector by algorithm3.2.

3.3 Choose LCC for parallel cache mode task

Suppose that $LCCS = LCC_1 \cup LCC_2 \cup \ldots \cup LCC_e$ is the set of all logical computer clusters which are built through algorithm3.1, and T is a parallel cache mode task.

Algorithm 3.2. Choose LCC method for parallel cache mode task.

1. Get the resource demand vector RDV (w1, w2, w3, w4) of T;

mine=∞;

2. While $LCCS \ne \phi$ do

{Get $S \in LCCS$; /* S is a logical computer cluster */
Calculate total resource vector $(ar_{Cpu}, ar_{mem}, ar_{disk}, ar_{net})$ of all cache nodes of S, it is as follows:

$$\{ar_{Cpu} = \sum_{CN\ in\ S} CN.RSV.r_{cpu}; \quad ar_{mem} = \sum_{CN\ in\ S} CN.RSV.r_{mem};$$

$$ar_{disk} = \sum_{CN\ in\ S} CN.RSV.r_{disk}; \quad ar_{net} = \sum_{CN\ in\ S} CN.RSV.r_{net};$$

$$y_1 = ar_{Cpu}/(ar_{Cpu} + ar_{mem} + ar_{disk} + ar_{net}); \quad y_2 = ar_{mem}/(ar_{Cpu} + ar_{mem} + ar_{disk} + ar_{net});$$

$$y_3 = ar_{disk}/(ar_{Cpu} + ar_{mem} + ar_{disk} + ar_{net}); \quad y_4 = ar_{net}/(ar_{Cpu} + ar_{mem} + ar_{disk} + ar_{net});$$

};
Construct the vector Y（y1,y2,y3,y4）;
e=|y1-w1|+|y2-w2|+|y3-w3|+|y4-w4|;
if mine<e then {LCC=S; mine=e};
LCCS=LCCS-{S};
}; // end while

3. Choose LCC as the logical computer cluster for T;
4. End.

3.4 Optimized LCC

Obviously, the *LCC* may span many different networks in *DNE*, so *LCC* can be optimized through the network skip distance, network bandwidth, and the resource demand vector of *T*. Suppose that $NSET=\{N_i\ (bw_i)\ |\ 1\leq i\leq m\}$ is the network set in *LCC*. bw_i indicates bandwidth of N_i, and m indicates the numbers of network. $RDV\ (w_1, w_2, w_3, w_4)$ indicates the resource demand vector of task *T*. The process is described as follows:

1. Construct network matrix $NM=(s_{ij})$ $(1\leq i\leq m,\ 1\leq j\leq m)$ that is composed of the factors of the network skip distance and bandwidth. The construction method for *NM* is as follows:

$s_{ii}=1$;

$s_{ij}=1-\gamma\ (distance(N_i - N_j)+|\ bw_i - bw_j\ |)$, when $i\neq j$, and $0<\gamma<1$;

Where,

When the network skip distance between N_i and N_j is 1, distance $(N_i, N_j)=1$;

When the network skip distance between N_i and N_j is 2, distance $(N_i, N_j)=3$;

When the network skip distance between N_i and $N_j > 2$, distance $(N_i, N_j)=6$;

When the bandwidth of N_i is 10MB, $bw_i=1$;

When the bandwidth of N_i is 100MB, $bw_i=3$;

When the bandwidth of N_i is 1000MB, $bw_i=6$;

If $N_i.bw_i=1$ and $(N_j.bw_j=3$ or $N_j.bw_j=6)$ then distance$(N_i, N_j)=6$

If $N_i.bw_i=3$ and $(N_j.bw_j=1$ or $N_j.bw_j=6)$ then distance$(N_i, N_j)=6$

If $N_i.bw_i=6$ and $(N_j.bw_j=1$ or $N_j.bw_j=3)$ then distance$(N_i, N_j)=6$

2. Build the fuzzy equivalence matrix:

Repeat do

$FT=NM \odot NM$; // $\odot$ is the operation theorem to take the maximum and minimum

If $FT=NM$ then goto (4);

NM=FT;

End do;

3. calculate the *c*-cut matrix FM_c by w_4 of resource demand vector of *T*;
4. Divide the cache nodes of *LCC* into several equivalence class $SLCCS=SLCC_1\cup SLCC_2\cup\ldots\cup SLCC_e$ by FM_c;
5. *SLCCS* is the set of optimized *LCC* according to the network factors.

4. Description of agent learning model

Because of the difference resources which *CC*, *CN*, and the network provided in *DNE*, their types must be considered. These types are described as follows:

Definition.10.Cache node type (CNT) can be defined by RSV $(r_{cpu}, r_{mem}, r_{disk}, r_{net})$ of the cache node. According to the real conditions of each CN in DNE, the CN types can be divided into the cache node type set CTS= $\{CT_1, CT_2,\ldots,CT_{ct}\}$.

Definition.11.Network type (NT) is defined as *NT* (*B*, *PRT*), where *B* denotes as the network bandwidth of *CC*; *PRT* indicates network protocols of *CC*. According to the real condition of networks, network types can be divided into the network type set $NTS=\{NT_1, NT_2,\ldots,NT_{nt}\}$.

The agent rules are described as follows:

1. **Basic rule (br)** is defined as *br* (*id, rul, MRS*), where *id* is its identifier; *rul* is the description of *br*; *MRS* is the meta-rules set for revising *br*; The **basic rule set (BRS)** is the set of all basic rules that *GMG* includes;
2. **Dynamic rule (dr)** is defined as dr (ct, nt, br, rul, w, sta, life), where ct ∈ CTS, nt ∈ NTS, br ∈ BRS; rul is the formalization description of dr; w is the its weight value; and sta is its state, and sta ∈ {"Naive", "Trainable", "Stable"}; "Naive" denotes that the dr is a new rule; "Trainable" denotes that the dr is revising rule; "Stable" denotes that the dr is a mature rule; life is the its life value;
3. If *dr* is a dynamic rule and *dr.w>MaxWeight*, which *MaxWeight* is a constant in *GMG*, we call *dr* as the **static rule (sr)**, its state is *"Static"*;
4. If *dr* is a dynamic rule and *dr.w<MinWeight*, which *MinWeight* is a constant in *GMG*, we call *dr* as **castoff rule (cr)**. Its state is *"Castoff"*.

The state graph of rules is presented in figure 3.

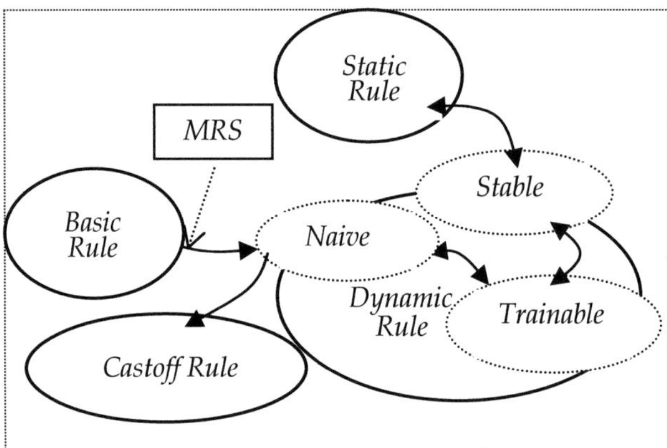

Fig. 3. The state graph of rules

The dynamic knowledge is the set of all the dynamic rules in *GMG*. The static knowledge is the set of all static rules. The basic knowledge can be earned by passive learning. To adapt the variety of cache resources, the dynamic rules must be generated at the start of the cache and revised during the caching process. Therefore, reinforcement learning can be adopted in the revising mechanism. Resources utilization for cache is very important reinforcement factors.

Suppose that Y_1 is the *castoff threshold,* and Y_2 is the *mature threshold; Q (urt)* denotes as the *reinforcement function,* and *Q(urt)* >0.*urt* indicates resources utilization rate; *MaxWeight* is the maximum of the rule weight, and *MinWeight* is the minimum of the rule weight, and let $MinWeight<Y_1<Y_2< MaxWeight$; *MaxLife* be the maximum of life value. The revising process is as follows:

1. Suppose that a cache agent *CA* adopted a dynamic rule *dr* of *CA.KS*;
2. *dr.life* + +; //increase the value of life
3. wait for the *urt* from *MAS*;
4. If *urt* >0 then *dr.w=dr.w* + *Q*(*urt*); //increase weight

If *urt* <0 then *dr.w=dr.w-Q* (*urt*); //decrease weight

5. If dr.w>MaxWeight then dr.w=MaxWeight;

If dr.w<MinWeight then dr.w=MinWeight;

6. If $dr.w<Y_1$ and $dr.life>MaxLife$ then *dr.sta="Castoff"*; //Castoff rule
If $Y_2<$ dr.w < MaxWeight then dr.sta="Stable"; //Stable rule
If dr.w >= MaxWeight then dr.sta="Static"; //Static rule
If $Y_1<$dr.w$<Y_2$ then dr.sta="Trainable"; //Trainable rule
If MinWeight <dr.w$<Y_1$ then dr.sta="Naive".

5. Cache allocation methods

For designing the allocation methods, we introduce some parameters firstly.

5.1 Parameters

Suppose that there are p cache nodes $CN_1, CN_2 \ldots CN_p$, and their memory storage ability are $Ma_1, Ma_2 \ldots Ma_p$, their computing ability are $Ca_1, Ca_2 \ldots Ca_p$; so, the total memory storage ability is Gmc= $\sum_{1 \le i \le p} Ma_i$, and the total computing ability is Gcc= $\sum_{1 \le i \le p} Ca_i$; and, there are m cache files $\{CF_1, CF_2 \ldots CF_m\}$ in PCMGM and their segment lengths are $\{Segl_1, Segl_2 \ldots Segl_m\}$. The parameters are as follows:

Average segment length is Asl= $(\sum_{1 \le i \le m} Segl_i)/m$;

Total cache ability of Grid memory is Tc= $\left\lfloor \frac{Gmc}{Asl} \right\rfloor$, and Tc denotes that the total numbers of DSEG can be stored by grid memories at one moment;

Average cache ability of cache node is Ac= $\lfloor Tc/p \rfloor$, and Ac denotes that the average numbers of DSEG can be stored by one cache node memory at one moment;

Average computing ability demand of cache agent is Ada that can be determined by the RDV of all cache nodes.

Total cache agent ability is Tca= $\left\lfloor \frac{Gcc}{Ada} \right\rfloor$, and Tca denotes that the total numbers of cache agent can be supported by PCMGM at one moment;

Average cache agent ability of cache node is Aca= $\lfloor Tca/p \rfloor$, and Aca denotes that the total numbers of cache agents can be supported by one cache node at one moment;

Hot segment threshold is a constant H in PCMGM, and if the duplication width of a segment is more than H, we call it as the hot segment. The file which includes the hot segment is called as the hot file.

5.2 Construction for cache demand matrix

According to the parameters described in Section 5.1, we can construct the cache demand matrix, which is the total cache needing of all cache files, and as followings:

1. For CFi ($1 \le i \le m$) do
{Calculate the duplication width vector

DWVi (|SEGi1|, |SEGi2| … |SEGiw|) for CFi by Segli , where iw is the numbers of the segment of CFi, and |SEGij| is the duplication width of j th segment of CFi};

2. Look for the cache file which has the maximal segment number in all cache files, and the maximal segment number is k;
3. Through the vector set DWV1, DWV2 … DWVm and k, we construct the cache demand matrix: CDM= (qij) ($1 \le i \le m$, $1 \le j \le k$), Where qij is the duplication width of the jth segment of CFi, and qij ≥0; If the jth segment of CFi is not existed, then qij=0.

In CDM, the sum value Tcd= $\sum_{1 \le i \le m,\, 1 \le j \le k} q_{ij}$ is the total cache demand of all cache files, and we hope the formula (1) is true. In fact, it is not possible.

$$Tcd \le Tc \tag{1}$$

When $Tcd \ge Tc$, we can processes the *CDM* by the techniques of cut-matrix and compress in order to make the formula (1) is true.

5.3 Cut-matrix and compress technique

The *cut-matrix* is a special $m \times k$ matrix $CM=(cq_{ij})$ ($1 \le i \le m$, $1 \le j \le k$), where $cq_{ij}=Cut\text{-}v$ and *Cut-v* is a integer. The process is presented as follows:

```
NCDM=CDM; /* NCDM is the cut CDM that can
                 satisfy the formula (1)*/
Cut-v=0;
Repeat do
   Cut-v++;
   Set all elements of CM as Cut-v;
   NCDM=NCDM-CM;
     /* - is the subtraction of Matrixes and if
       NCDM=0, then NCDM-CM=0, 0 is zero-matrix
       */
   Calculate the Tcd by NCDM;
            Until the formula (1) is true;
```

The *NCDM* is the new cache demand matrix and all its *DSEG*s can be cached in grid memory. The demand of *CDM-NCDM* will be save the disk. The cut-matrix is presented in the figure 4.

According to the *CA* conception, the corresponding relation between a *CA* and a *DSEG* is one to one. But if a set of duplications of the same segment of be stored in the same cache node, the duplication will be stored one time in the cache node. The corresponding cache agent is established many times in the cache node, so this mechanism can improve the use rate of memory resources, but the computing ability of the cache node may be overload. The average ratio of the *CA* numbers and the *DSEG* numbers is called as the *cache agent density* (CAD). The compress principle is presented in the figure 4.

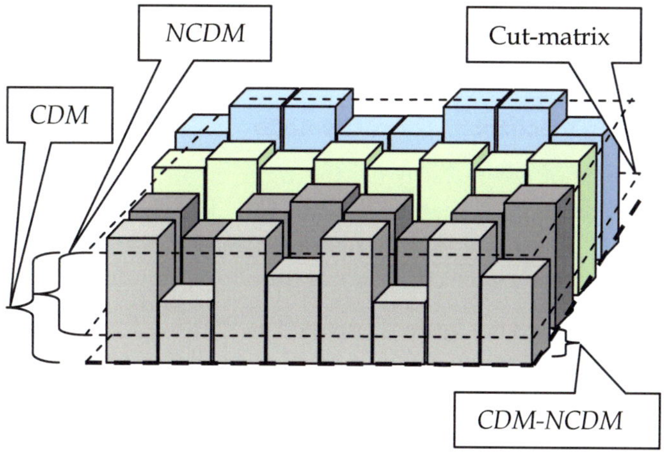

Fig. 4. The relations between CDM, Cut-matrix, and NCDM

Strategy 1. *d-density* **allocation strategy** means that the allocation ratio between the numbers of *CA* and the numbers of their *DSEG* for one segment in the same cache node is *d*. Namely, one *DSEG* has *d CA*s in the same cache node. *d* is the average in PCMGM.

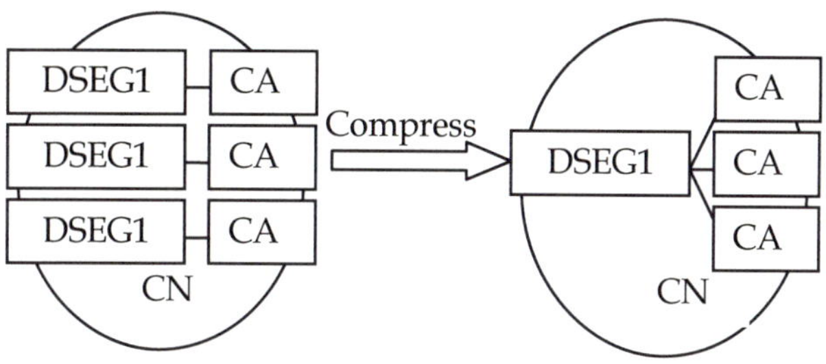

Fig. 5. This is the compress storage in a cach node for the same duplication and it is the 3-density allocation strategy.

In order to use the storage of grid memory effectively, we hope *CDM=NCDM*. Through the *d-density* allocation strategy, we can make the formula (2) is true, where *Tcd(NCDM)* means that the total cache demand of *NCDM*.

$$\mathrm{Tcd(NCDM)} < \mathrm{Tc} \times \mathrm{d} \tag{2}$$

5.4 Cache allocation

For all cache nodes CN_k $(1 \le k \le p)$, we get a subset of *NCDM* elements SE to make the formula (3) is true. ε is a small constant. For each *DSEG*s, we adopt the d-density allocation strategy to appoint CA.

$$\sum_{1\le i\le p,} Ma_i - \varepsilon \le \sum_{q_{ij}\in SE,} q_{ij} \le \sum_{1\le i\le p,} Ma_i + \varepsilon \tag{3}$$

The *DSEG*s in *CDM-NCDM* will be written into the local disk of cache node.

5.5 Dynamic adjusting mechanism for cache node

Because of the unstable of the cache node, the cache node can be joined or disjoined in dynamic. So the grid memory is changed in PCMGM. The dynamic adjusting mechanism for cache node must be discussed. We call the cache node which can't work for grid as the *failure cache node* and the new joined computer as the *new cache node.*

Definition.8. Computing density vector is defined as $CDV= (cd_1, cd_2\ldots cd_p)$, where cd_i is the value of density allocation strategy of CN_i. If $cd_i < d$, we call CN_i as the *low-density cache node;* If $cd_i > d$, we call CN_i as the *high-density cache node;*

Definition.9. Failure storage matrix is defined as $FSM= (fq_{ij})$ ($1\le i\le m$, $1\le j\le k$), where fq_{ij} *is DSEG* numbers of the *j* th segment of CF_i, which *DSEG*s are stored in the *failure cache node.*

Definition.10. effective storage matrix is defined as $ESM= (eq_{ij})$ ($1\le i\le m$, $1\le j\le k$), and *ESM=NCDM-FSM.*

Definition.11. Migration storage matrix is defined as $MSM= (mq_{ij})$ ($1\le i\le m$, $1\le j\le k$), where mq_{ij} is *DSEG* numbers of the *j* th segment of CF_i, which *DSEG*s are stored in the *failure (or overload) cache node* , and the *DSEG*s of *MSM* will be migrated.

5.5.1 Failure process

The failure process description is as follows:

1. Calculate the *DSEG*s which the current failure cache nodes include, and Construct the failure migration storage matrix *MSM;*
2. Look for the low-density cache node by *CDV*, and get the free cache resources for *MSM;* Calculate the acceptable cache matrix *AMSM* by these resources, and *AMSM* will be migrated the new cache node; *MSM* - *AMSM* will be added into the failure storage matrix *FSM* and *FSM* will be stored into the local disk which they are.
3. Revise the computing density vector *CDV;*

5.5.2 Joining process of new cache node

The new cache joining process description is as follows:

1. Calculate the ability of *new cache nodes;*
2. If the failure storage matrix is existed, we construct the migration storage matrix *MSM* by *FSM;*
3. Look for the high-density cache node by *CDV*, and add their *DSEG*s information into *MSM;*
4. *MSM* will be migrated into the new cache nodes;
5. Revise the computing density vector *CDV;*

6. Process of PCMGM

The PCMGM process is as follows:

1. AA do the statistics work from user information and report them to GA; GA calculates the cache demand matrix CDM by the statistics information, and get a LCC (That is constructed by GA through fuzzy partition method);
2. All NAs, which LCC includes, calculate its memory storage ability Ma and its computing ability Ca;
3. GA receives the idle resource information from LCC and calculates the total computing ability Gcc and the total memory storage ability Gmc;
4. GA constructs the NCDM according to the cut-matrix and d-density allocation strategy;
5. GA allots DSEGs for all CNs;
6. All NAs of CN transfer the segments form the file server into grid memory in order to form the DSEGs; then, construct CAs for each DSEG;
7. All CAs in PCMGM start the hot segment service;
8. All users commit its access sequences to AA, AA redirect the connections to build the relations between the users and CAs;
9. All CAs and users start the file operation in Parallel and PCMGM start the dynamic adjusting mechanism by the migration.

7. Experiments

In order to test this model, we built a *DNE* that is composed of 2 file servers and 8 cache nodes (personal computer), and 16 client computers, and they are connected by LAN. Each server has 4 disks, and the segments of large file are distributed in all disks in balance. There are 4 files and the length of all them is about 1GB. The segment length is 48MB. The cache nodes are classified into 2 types according to their types of cpu, memory, disk, and net adapter. The types of computers are *RSV* (2400MHZ, 768MB, 7200RPM, 100M) and *RSV* (1800MHZ, 512MB, 7200RPM, 100M). The operating systems of the computers are the LINUX. In order to test the peak access ability about the hot segment, we ignore the net factors. So, the test agent running on client end only sends the access command timely and the *CA* does the file operations and the data will be not transferred to the client end. The average value of *d*-density allocation strategy is 6.

Experiment 1. The experimentation includes two kinds: the one is the response time testing in the condition that all *DSEGs* are stored in the file server disks; the other is the response time testing in the condition that all *DSEGs* are stored in Grid memory. We calculate the average ratios of response time of this two kinds. The tests include 6 times according to the *DSEG* scales. The total number of *DSEGs* is the *Tc*, 2*Tc*... 6*Tc* during the 6 times testing. In each test, we adopt the three access method for the *DSEGs*: the random access, the sequence access, and the mix access composed of the random and sequence. The test results are shown in figure 6(a), and the results show that PCMGM is high efficiency compared with the disk cache method.

Experiment 2. We had tested the variety of PCMGM performance during d is 1, 2, 3, 4, 5, and 6 (The total number of DSEGs is the Tc, 2Tc… 6Tc). The test results are shown in figure

6(b), and the results show that the key influence factor about PCMGM performance is the capacity of Grid memory. So, mining large scale idle computer to construct the grid memory can improve the concurrent access response time for the hot segments during the peak access.

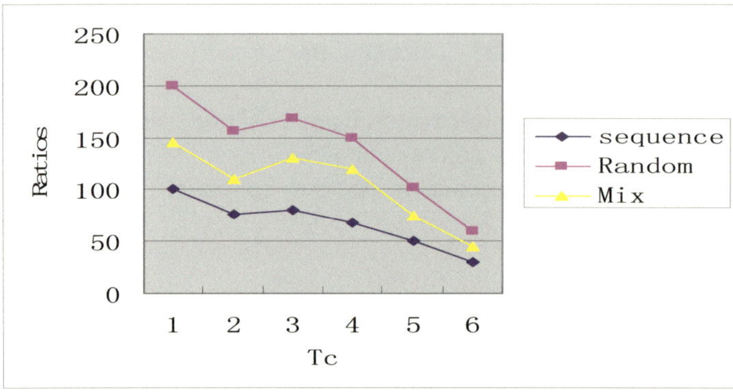

(a)

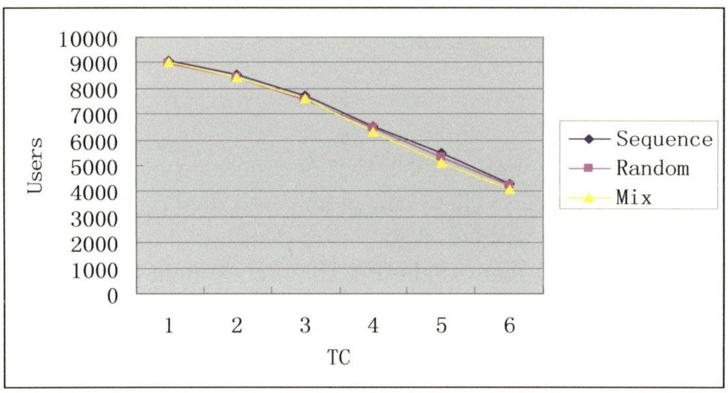

(b)

Fig. 6. The test results

8. Conclusions

For supporting the concurrent access for the hot segments of large files during the peak access phase in Internet, a parallel cache model based on the grid memory (PCMGM) was proposed in this paper. The concurrent accessing of hot segments depends on the disk performance greatly during the peak access. Through the grid technique, we can mine a lot of idle computers to construct the grid memory in order to store the duplications of hot segments. Because of the heterogeneous resources and the unstable catachrestic, the effective cache model is very difficult in the dynamic network environment. Through the techniques of *CA*, *DSEG*, the dynamic learning and the logical computer cluster partition based on fuzzy theory, PCMGM can support the parallel cache. These approaches can raise the peak access performance for hot segment of large files. It can fit for the grid computing and the large scale VOD in internet.

9. Acknowledgement

We would like to thank the support of National Nature Science Foundation of China (No.60573108), Shanghai Leading Academic Discipline Project (No.T0502) and Shanghai Education Committee Foundation (No. 06QZ002, 07ZZ92).

10. References

Anurag Acharya and Sanjeev Setia: Using Idle Memory for Data-Intensive Computations. In proceedings of the 1998 ACM SIGMETRICS Conference on Measurement and Modeling of Computer Systems, (1998):278-279

Craig S. Freedman, Josef Burger, and David J. Dewitt: SPIFFI-a Scable Parallel File System for the Intel Paragon. IEEE Transactions on Parallel and Distributed System, Vol.7 (11), (1996):1185-1200

E. Osawa: A Scheme for Agent Collaboration in Open MultiAgent Environment .Proceeding of IJCAI'93, (1993):352-358

E. P. Markatos and G. Dramitions: Implementation of Reliable Remote Memory Pager. In proceedings of the 1996 Usenix technical Conference, (1996):177-190

Horst Eidenberger: Gigabit Ethernet-Based Parallel Video Processing, Proceedings of 11th International Multimedia Modelling Conference (MMM'05), IEEE Computer Society, (2005):358-363

I. Foster, C. Kesselman: The Grid: Blueprint for Future Computing Infrastructure. San Francisco, USA: Morgan Kaufmann Publishers, (1999)

J. Fernandez,J. Carretero, F. Garcia-Carballeira, A. Calderon, J. M. Perez-Menor: New Stream Caching Schemas for Multimedia Systems, In Proceedings of First International Conference on Automated Production of Cross Media Content for Multi-Channel Distribution (AXMEDIS'05),IEEE Computer Society,(2005): 77-84

J. O. Kephart, Chess, D. M: The Vision of Autonomic Computing, IEEE Computer, (2003): 41-50

J. Carretero, F. Perez, P. de Miguel, and L.Alonso: ParFiSys: A Parallel File System for MPP. Operating System review, Vol.30 (2), (1996):74-80

O. F. Rana and D.W. Walker: The Agent Grid: Agent-based resource integration in PSEs, In proceedings of the 16th IMACS World congress on Scientific Computing, Applied mathematics and Simulation, Lausanne, Switzerland, (2000)

P. F. Corbett and D. G. Feitelson: The Vesta Parallel File System. ACM transaction on Computer Systems, Vol.14 (3), (1996):225-264

Pal Halvorsen, Carsten Griwodz, Vera Goebel, Ketil Lund, Thomas Plagemann, Jonathan walpole: Storage System Support for Continuous Media Applications, Part2: Multiple Disks, Memory, and Integration, IEEE Distributed systems online 1541-4922,vol.5(2), (2004)

Rajkumar Buyya: High performance Cluster Computing Architectures and Systems, Prentice Hall, (1999)

Seogyun Kim, Jiseung Nam, Soon-ja Yeom:Effective delivery of Virtual Class on Parallel Media Stream Server, Proceedings of the International Conference on Computers in Education, IEEE press,2002

T. Kimbrel et. Al: A Trace-Driven Comparison of Algorithms for Parallel Prefetching and Caching. In Proceedings of the 2nd International Symposium on Operating System Design and Impletation, USENIX Association, (1996):19-34

Wooldridge, M.: An Introduction to Multivalent System, John Wiley & Sons (Chichester, England). ISBN 0 47149691X, (2002)

8

Hierarchy-Aware Message-Passing in the Upcoming Many-Core Era

Carsten Clauss, Simon Pickartz, Stefan Lankes and Thomas Bemmerl
Chair for Operating Systems, RWTH Aachen University
Germany

1. Introduction

The demands of large parallel applications often exceed the computing and memory resources a local computing site offers. Therefore, by combining distributed computing resources as provided by Grid environments can help to satisfy these resource demands. However, since such an environment is a heterogeneous system by nature, there are some drawbacks that, if not taken into account, are limiting its applicability. Especially the inter-site communication often constitutes a bottleneck in terms of higher latencies and lower bandwidths than compared to the site-internal case. The reason for this is that the inter-site communication is typically handled via wide-area transport protocols and respective networks; whereas the internal communication is conducted via fast local-area networks or even via dedicated high-performance cluster interconnects. That in turn means that an efficient utilization of such a hierarchical and heterogeneous infrastructure demands a Grid middleware that provides support for all these different kinds of communication facilities (Clauss et al., 2008). Moreover, with the upcoming Many-core era a further level of hierarchy gets introduced in terms of *Cluster-on-Chip* processor architectures. The Single-chip Cloud Computer (SCC) experimental processor is a *concept vehicle* created by Intel Labs as a platform for Many-core software research (Intel Corporation, 2010). This processor is indeed a very recent example for such a Cluster-on-Chip architecture. In this chapter, we want to discuss the challenges of hierarchy-aware message-passing in distributed Grid environments in the upcoming Many-core era by taking the example of the SCC. The remainder of this chapter is organized as follows: Section 2 initially reviews the basic knowledge about parallel processing and message-passing. In Section 3, the demands for parallel processing and message-passing especially in Grid computing environments are detailed. Section 4 focuses on the Intel SCC Many-core processor and how message-passing can be conducted with respect to this chip. Afterwards, Section 5 discusses how the world of chip-embedded Many-core communication can be integrated into the macrocosmic world of Grid computing. Finally, Section 6 concludes this chapter.

2. Parallel processing using message-passing

With a rising amount of cores in today's processors, parallel processing is a prevailing field of research. One approach is the *message-passing paradigm*, where parallelization is achieved by having processes with the capability of exchanging messages with other processes. Instead of sharing common memory regions, processes perform send and receive operations for data and information transfer. In high-performance computing the message-passing paradigm is well established. However, this programming model gets more and more interesting also for the consumer sector. The message-passing model is mostly architecture independent, but it may profit from underlying hardware that supports the shared-memory model in terms of more performance. It is accompanied by a strictly separated address space. Therefore erroneous memory reads and writes are easier to locate than it would be with shared memory programming (Gropp et al., 1999).

2.1 Communication modes

The inter-process communication for synchronization and data exchanges has to be performed by calling send and received functions in an explicit manner. In doing so, the parallelization strategy is to divide the algorithm into independent subtasks and to assign these tasks to parallel processes. However, at the end of these independent subtasks intermediate results need commonly to be exchanged between the processes in order to compute the overall result.

2.1.1 Point-to-point communication

In point-to-point communication several different communication modes have to be distinguished: *buffered* and *non-buffered*, *blocking* and *non-blocking*, *interleaved* and *overlapped*, *synchronous* and *asynchronous* communication. First of all, *non-buffered* and *buffered* communication has to be differentiated. The latter requires an intermediate data buffer through which sender and receiver perform communication. A send routine will send a message to a buffer that may be accessed by both the sending and the receiving side. Calling the respective receive function, the message will be copied out of that buffer and stored locally at the receiving process. Figure 1(a) shows sender *A* transmitting a message to an intermediated buffer and returning after completion. The buffer holds the message until receiver *B* posts the respective receive call and completes the data transfer to its local buffer. In addition to that, the terms *blocking* and *non-blocking* related to message-passing have to be defined. They relate to the semantics of the respective send and receive function calls. A process that calls a blocking send function remains in this function until the transfer is completed. Whether this is associated with the arrival of the according message at the receiving side or only with the completion of the transmission on the sender side, has to be defined in the context where the function is used. Figure 1(b) shows an example where the completion of a blocking send call is defined as the point in time after the whole message arrived at the receiver and is stored in a local buffer. For this period, *A* is blocked even if *B* has not posted the respective receive call yet. On the contrary, a non-blocking send routine returns immediately regardless whether the message arrived at the receiver or not. Thus, the sender has to ensure with other mechanisms that a message was successfully transmitted before reusing its local send buffer. With non-blocking routines it is possible to perform *interleaved* but also *overlapped* communication and computation. Overlapped communication results in real parallelism where the data delivery occurs autonomously after being pushed by the sending process. Meanwhile, the sender is able to perform computation that is independent from the transmitted data. The same applies to the receiving side. With interleaved communication, message dependencies may be broken up, but there is still a serialized processing which requires a periodical alternating between computation and communication.

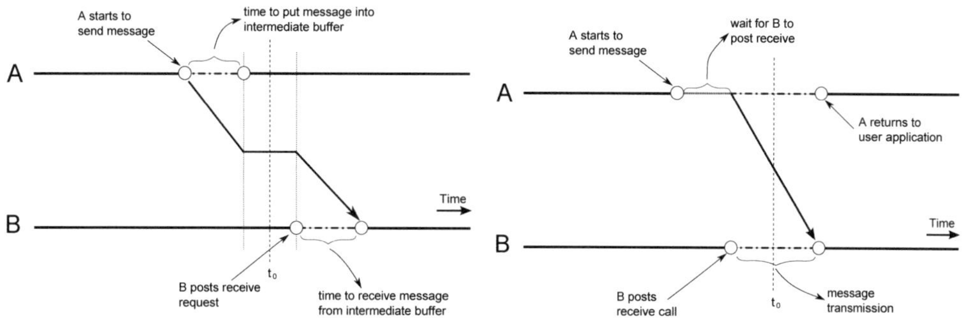

(a) Example: Buffered and Asynchronous (b) Example: Blocking and Synchronous

Fig. 1. Comparison of Asynchronous and Synchronous Communication

This may increase the application's performance if a resource is currently not available. Instead of waiting for the opponent to be ready, time is used to perform other tasks. Thus, the application itself has to check from time to time if the communication process is still stuck, by calling functions to query the status of the respective *request handle*. These are objects which are commonly being passed back for this purpose by a non-blocking function call. Although often used as a synonym for blocking/non-blocking function calls (Tanenbaum, 2008), *synchronous* and *asynchronous* communication primitives should be further distinguished. Facilitated by buffered communication, asynchronous message-passing enables the sender to complete the send routine without having the receiver posted a respective receive call. Thus, it is not necessary to have a global point in time when sender and receiver are coevally within their respective function calls. In Figure 1(a) A returns from the send call and *locally* completes the message transfer before the matching receive routine is posted. In contrast to that, in non-buffered mode where no intermediate communication buffer is available, it is not possible to perform asynchronous message-passing. That is because data transfer only occurs when both, sender and receiver, are situated in the communication routines at the same time. Referring to Figure 1(b) it becomes clear what is meant by *one point in time*. At time t_0 both, sender and receiver, are in the respective communication routines what is necessary in order to complete them.

2.1.2 Collective communication operations

Collective operations are communication functions that have to be called by all participating processes. These functions help the programmer to realize more complex communication patterns than simple point-to-point communication within a single function call. Moreover, it must be emphasized that using such collective operations not only simplifies the application programming, but also enables the lower communication layer to implement the collective communication patterns in the most efficient way. For that reason, application programmers should utilize offered collective operations instead of implementing the patterns by means of point-to-point communication whenever possible. However, a possible drawback of collective operations is that they may be synchronizing what means that the respective function may only return when all participating processes have called it. In case of unbalanced load, processes possibly have to wait a long time within the function, not being able to progress with the computation. In the following, some important examples of collective communication

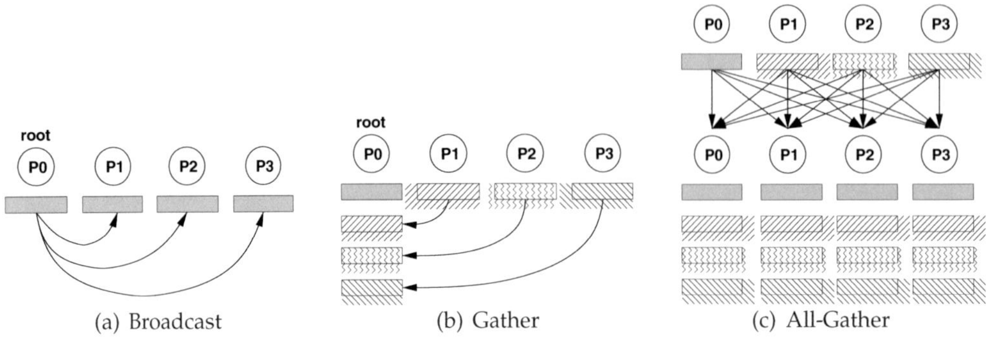

Fig. 2. Examples of Collective Communication Patterns

patterns are shown. Although important, not nearly all communication libraries provide collective functions for these patterns. If a process needs to send a message to all the other processes, a *broadcast* function (if provided by the communication library) can be utilized. In doing so, all participating processes have to call this function and have to state who is the initial sender (the so-called *root*, see Figure 2(a)) among them. In turn, all the others realize that they are eventual receivers so that the communication pattern can be conducted. However, during the communication progress of the pattern every process can become a sender and/or receiver. That means that the internal implementation of the pattern is up to the respective library. For example, internally this pattern may be conducted in terms of a loop over all receivers, or even better tree-like achieving higher performance. In many parallel algorithms, a so-called *master* process is used to distribute subtasks among the other processes (the so-called *worker*) and to coordinate the collection of partial results later on. Therefore, such a master may initially act as the root process of a broadcast operation distributing subtask-related data. Afterwards, a *gather* operation then may be used at the master process to collect partial results generating the final result with the received data. Figure 2(b) shows the pattern of such a gather operation. Besides this asymmetric master/worker approach, symmetric parallel computation (and hence communication) schemes are common, too. This means, regarding collective operations, that for example during a gather operation *all* processes obtain *all* partial datasets (a so-called *all-gather* operation). Internally, this may be for example implemented in terms of an initial gather operation to one process, followed by a subsequent broadcast to all processes. However, the internal implementation of such communication patterns can also be realized in a symmetric manner, as Figure 2(c) shows for the all-gather example.

2.2 Process topologies

A process topology describes the logical and/or physical arrangement of parallel processes within the communication environment. Thus, the *logical* arrangement represents the communication pattern of the parallel algorithm, whereas the *physical* arrangement constitutes the assignment of processes to physical processors. Of course, in hierarchical (or even heterogeneous) systems, the logical process topology should be mapped onto the underlying physical topology in such a way that they are as congruent as possible. For example, and as already noted in the last section, collective communication patterns should be adapted to the underlying hardware topologies. This may be done, for instance, by an optimized communication library as it is described for hierarchical systems in the later Section 3.2.2. Moreover, even an adaptation of the parallel algorithm itself to the respective hardware topology may become necessary in order to avoid unnecessary network contention. Therefore, a likewise hierarchical algorithm design would accommodate such systems. However, in homogeneous environments, the algorithm design can still be kept flat and process topologies are mapped almost transparently onto the hardware.

2.2.1 Programming paradigms

Based on the consideration where to place the processes and which part of a parallel task each of them should process, two programming paradigms can be distinguished (Wilkinson & Allen, 2005): the *Multiple-Program Multiple-Data* (MPMD) and the *Single-Program Multiple-Data* (SPMD) paradigm. According to the MPMD paradigm, each process working on a different subtask within a parallel session processes an individual program. Therefore, in an extreme case, all parallel processes may run different programs. However, usually this paradigm is not that distinctive. A very common example for MPMD is the master/worker approach where just the master runs a different program than the workers. In contrast to this, in a session according to the SPMD paradigm, all processes run only one single program. That in turn implies that the processes must be able to identify themselves[1] because otherwise all of them would work on the same subtask.

2.2.2 Session startup and process spawning

Considering the question which process should work on which subtask leads to a further question: When shall the processes of a session be created? Regarding this problem, two approaches can be distinguished: In the case of a *static* startup, all the processes are created at the beginning of a parallel run and are normally bound to their respective processors during runtime. Such a static startup is usually conducted and supported by a job scheduler detecting and assigning idle processors. However, in the case of a *dynamic* process startup, further processes can be spawned by already running processes even at runtime. This approach is commonly combined with the MPMD paradigm. So for example, when a master process running a master program spawns worker processes running subtask-related subprograms. However, this approach demands for an additional interaction between spawning processes and the runtime environment during execution, in order to place spawned processes onto free processors. That is the reason why this approach is more complicated in most cases.

2.3 Programming interfaces

The actual handling of a message transfer, that is the execution of the respective communication protocols through the different networking layers, is much too complex and too hardware-oriented to be done at application level. Therefore, the application programmer is usually provided with appropriate communication libraries that hide the hardware-related part of message transfers and hence allow the development of platform-independent parallel applications.

[1] for example by means of *process identifiers*

2.3.1 The Berkeley Socket API

A very common communication interface is the Berkeley Socket API, also known as BSD Sockets. A *socket* is a communication termination endpoint that facilitates the access to various transport layer protocols, such as TCP and UDP (Winett, 1971). Although usable to communicate between processes on the same machine, their intention is to enable the inter-process communication over computer networks. This can be done either first establishing a connection via creating a stream socket for the TCP protocol, or connectionless using datagram sockets for the UDP protocol. The sockets are managed by the operating system which organizes the access to the underlying network. They are used in a Client-Server manner, what means that the connection establishment between a pair of processes must be triggered in an asymmetric way, starting from the client side. Afterwards, messages may be exchanged bidirectional via the socket by using simple send and receive functions (Stevens et al., 2006).

2.3.2 Communication libraries for parallel environments

Besides simple send and receive functions, communication libraries especially for parallel environments do not only offer simple Client-Server relations, but rather provide support for a session management covering all parallel processes, including process startup and an all-to-all connection establishment. Commonly such libraries also offer additional features, as for example, for conducting collective operations or for transparent data conversion. In the course of time, several of such communication libraries had been developed, usually driven by the demand for new libraries in connection with new hardware platforms. Examples are: *NX, NX/2* and *NX/M* that are libraries developed by Intel for a past generation of dedicated multi-computers (Pierce, 1988), *Zipcode* is a software system for message-passing developed by the California Institute of Technology (Skjellum & Leung, 1990), *P4: Portable Programs for Parallel Processors* is a socket-based communication library by Argonne National Laboratory (Butler & Lusk, 1994), *Chameleon* is no communication library by itself but rather a macro-based interface to several underlying communication libraries (Gropp & Smith, 1993), and *PVM: Parallel Virtual Machine* is still a very common communication library (Dongarra et al., 1993) that has also been extended by the ability to be runnable in Grid environments (Geist, 1998).

2.3.3 The Message-Passing Interface (MPI)

When looking at the diversity of communication libraries listed in the last section, it becomes obvious that writing portable parallel applications was hardly possible in those days. Hence, there was a strong demand for the creation of a unified interface standard for parallel communication libraries in the early 1990s. This demand for an easy portability of parallel applications to always new generations of parallel machines eventually led in 1993 to the definition of such a unified library interface by the so-called Message-Passing Interface Forum. The goal was to define a communication standard that is hardware and programming language independent but still meets the requirements of high-performance computing. The result was the Message-Passing Interface Standard (MPI), which is a specification of a library interface (Message Passing Interface Forum, 2009). The main objective is that users do not need to compromise among efficiency, portability and functionality without having to abstain from advantages of specialized hardware (Gropp et al., 1999). Although MPI is, in contrast to the libraries mentioned in the last section, *not* a specific implementation but just an interface standard, the standardizing processes was accompanied by the development of a prototype and reference implementation: MPICH (Gropp et al., 1996).[2]

Today, two different compatibility levels can be distinguished:[3] Compatibility with MPI-1 means that an MPI implementation provides support for all features specified in the MPI standard Version 1.3. And compatibility with MPI-2 means as opposed to MPI-1 that the respective MPI implementation also provides support for the extensions specified up to the MPI standard Version 2.2. Altogether, these two levels incorporate a function set of about 280 MPI functions. However, many MPI applications just use a handful of them, mostly focusing on the actual message handling. To begin with the term of a message, the tuple (*address*, *count*, *datatype*) defines an MPI message buffer, in which *count* describes the amount of elements of *datatype* beginning at *address*. Thus, it is ensured that the receiving side obtains the same data even if it uses another data format than the sending side. To distinguish between several messages, a *tag* is introduced that represents the message type defined by the user application. Furthermore, MPI defines the concepts of the *context* and *groups* aggregated in a so-called *communicator*. Only messages with a valid context (that is in terms of a matching communicator) will be received and processes may be combined to logical groups by means of the communicator. In addition to these basic concepts, a wide range of further mechanism like non-blocking, buffered or synchronizing communication, as well as collective operations and a particular error handling is provided. Although most MPI applications are written according to the SPMD paradigm, MPI-2 also features process spawning and support for programs written according to the MPMD paradigm.

2.3.4 The Multicore Communications API (MCAPI)

The MCAPI, recently developed by the Multicore Association, resembles an interface for message-passing like MPI. However, in contrast to MPI and sockets which were primely designed for inter-computer communication, the MCAPI intends to facilitate lightweight inter-core communication between cores on one chip (Multicore Association, 2011). These may be even those which execute code from chip internal memory. Therefore the MCAPI tries to avoid the von Neumann bottleneck[4] using as less memory as it is necessary to realize communication between the cores. According to this, the two main goals of this API are extremely high-performance and low memory footprint of its implementations. In order to achieve these principals, the specification sticks to the KISS[5] principal. Only a small number of API calls are provided that allow efficient implementations on the one hand, and the opportunity to build other APIs that have more complex functionality on top of it, on the other hand. For an inter-core communications API, such as MCAPI, it is much easier to realize these goals because an implementation does not have to concern issues like reliability

[2] Nowadays, two more popular and also freely available MPI implementations exist: Open MPI (Gabriel et al., 2004) and MPICH2 (Gropp, 2002).

[3] Currently, the specifications of the upcoming MPI-3 standard are under active development by the working groups of the Message-Passing Interface Forum.

[4] It describes the circumstance that program memory and data memory share the same bus and thus result in a shortage in terms of throughput.

[5] Keep It Small and Simple

and packet loss which is the case in computer networks for example. In addition to that, the interconnect between cores on a chip offered by the hardware facilitates high-performance data transfer in terms of latency and throughput. Although designed for communication and synchronization between cores on a chip in embedded systems, it does not require the cores to be homogeneous. An implementation may realize communication between different architectures supported by an arbitrary operating system or even bare-metal. The standard purposely avoids having any demands to the underlying hardware or software layer. An MCAPI program that only makes use of functions offered by the API should be able to run in thread-based systems as well as in process-based systems. Thus, existing MCAPI programs should be easily ported from one particular implementation to another without having to adapt the code. This is facilitated by the specification itself. Only semantics of the function calls are described without any implementation concerns. Although MCAPI primarily focuses on on-chip core-to-core communication, when embedded into large-scale but hierarchy-aware communication environments, it can also be beneficial for distributed systems (Brehmer et al., 2011).

3. Message-passing in the grid

When running large parallel applications with demands for resources that exceed the capacity the local computing site offers, the deployment in a distributed Grid environment may help to satisfy these demands. Advances in wide-area networking technology have fostered this trend towards geographically distributed high-performance parallel computing in the recent years. However, as Grid resources are usually heterogeneous by nature, this is also true for the communication characteristics. Especially the inter-site communication often constitutes a bottleneck in terms of higher latencies and lower bandwidths than compared to the site-internal case. The reason for this is that the inter-site communication is typically handled via wide area transport protocols and respective networks, whereas the internal communication is conducted via fast local-area networks or even via dedicated high-performance interconnections. That in turn means that an efficient utilization of such a hierarchical and heterogeneous infrastructure demands a communication middleware providing support for all these different kinds of networks and transport protocols (Clauss et al., 2008).

3.1 Clusters of clusters

The basic idea of cluster computing is to link multiple independent computers by means of a network in such a way that this system can then be used for efficient parallel processing. Practically, such a cluster of computers constitutes a system that exhibits a NoRMA[6] architecture where each network node possesses its own private memory and where messages must be passed explicitly across the network. However, a major advantage of such systems is that they are much more affordable than dedicated supercomputers because they are usually composed of standard hardware. For this reason, cluster systems built of common *components off the shelf* (COTS) have already become prevalent even in the area of high-performance computing and datacenters. Moreover, this trend has been fostered in the last decades also by the fact that common desktop or server CPUs have already reached the performance class

[6] No Remote Memory Access

of former dedicated but expensive supercomputer CPUs.[7] This idea of linking common computing resources in such a way that the resulting system forms a new machine with an even higher degree of parallelism just leads to the next step (Balkanski et al., 2003): building a *Cluster of Clusters* (CoC). Such systems often arise inherently when, for example in a datacenter, new cluster installations are combined with older ones. This is because datacenters usually upgrade their cluster portfolio periodically by new installations, while not necessarily taking older installations out of service. On the one hand, this approach has the advantage that the users can chose that cluster system out of the portfolio that fits best for their application, for example, in terms of efficiency. On the other hand, when running large parallel applications, older and newer computing resources can be bundled in terms of cluster of clusters in order to maximize the obtainable performance. However, at this point also a potential disadvantage becomes obvious: While a single cluster installation usually constitutes a homogeneous system, a coupled system built from clusters of different generations and/or technologies exhibits a heterogeneous nature which is much more difficult to be handled.

3.1.1 Wide area computing

When looking at coupled clusters *within* a datacenter, the next step to an even higher degree of parallelism suggests itself: linking clusters (or actually cluster of clusters) in *different* datacenters in a wide area manner. However, it also becomes obvious that the interlinking wide area network poses a potential bottleneck with respect to inter-process communication. Therefore, the interlinking infrastructure as well as its interfaces and protocols of such a wide area Grid environment play a key role regarding the overall performance. Obviously, TCP/IP is the standard transport protocol used in the Internet, and due to its general design, it is also often employed in Grid environments. However, it has been proven that TCP has some performance drawbacks especially when being used in high-speed wide area networks with high-bandwidth but high-latency characteristics (Feng & Tinnakornsrisuphap, 2000). Hence, Grid environments, which are commonly based on such dedicated high-performance wide area networks, often require customized transport protocols that take the Grid-specific properties into account (Welzl & Yousaf, 2005). Since a significant loss of performance arises from TCP's window-based congestion control mechanism, several alternative communication protocols like FOBS (Dickens, 2003), SABUL (Gu & Grossman, 2003), UDT[8] (Gu & Grossman, 2007) or PSockets (Sivakumar et al., 2000) try to circumvent this drawback by applying their own transport policies and tactics at application level. That means that they are implemented in form of user-space libraries which in turn have to rely on standard kernel-level protocols like TCP or UDP, again. An advantage of this approach is that there is no need to modify the network stack of the operating systems being used within the Grid. The disadvantage is, of course, the overhead of an additional transport layer on top of an already existing network stack. Nevertheless, a further advantage of such user-space communication libraries is the fact that they can offer a much more comprehensive and customized interface to the Grid applications than the general purpose OS socket API does. However, in the recent years, a third kernel-level transport protocol has become common and available (at least within the

[7] The other way around, this trend can also be recognized when looking at today's multicore CPUs, making most common desktops or even laptops already being a parallel machine.

[8] UDT: a UDP-based Data Transfer Protocol

Linux kernel): the Stream Control Transmission Protocol (SCTP) which provides, similar to TCP, a reliable and in-sequence transport service (Stewart et al., 2007). Additionally, SCTP offers several features not present in TCP, as for example the *multihoming* support. This means that an endpoint of a SCTP association (SCTP uses the term *association* to refer to a connection) can be bound to more than one IP address at the same time. Thus, a transparent fail-over between redundant network paths becomes possible. Furthermore, it can be shown that SCTP *may* also perform much better than TCP especially in heterogeneous wide area networks due to a faster congestion control recovery mechanism (Nagamalai et al., 2005). For that reasons, employing SCTP also in Grid environments can be beneficial compared to common TCP (Kamal et al., 2005).

3.1.2 Grid-services and session layers

When looking at this diversity of alternative transport protocols, the question arises which one should be used by the bridging session layer of a message-passing library in Grid computing environments? The answer is that this depends on the properties of the actual environment. In fact, the best solution may differ even within the Grid, due to its heterogeneous nature. Moreover, since Grid resources can be volatile, the optimal protocol to be used may also vary in the course of time, as an initially assigned bandwidth does not necessarily be granted during a whole session for example. For that reason, an efficient session layer for message-passing-based Grid computing should be capable of supporting more than one transport facility at the same time. Nevertheless, such a session layer should also be aware of the inter-site communication overhead by being and acting as resource-friendly as possible in this respect. In order to exploit a Grid environment at its full potential, the underlying network must be a managed resource, just like computing and storage resources usually are. As such, it should be manages by an intelligent and autonomic Grid middleware (Hessler & Welzl, 2007). Such a middleware, like a Grid scheduler, needs to retrieve runtime information about the current capacity and quality of the communication infrastructure, as well as information about the communication patterns and characteristics of the running Grid applications. For that purpose, the possibility of a dynamic interaction between this scheduling middleware and the respective application would be very desirable. Therefore, a session layer for message-passing in Grid environments should also provide *Grid service interfaces* in order to make such information inquirable at runtime. Moreover, a dedicated interface that also allows to access and even to reconfigure the session settings at runtime would help to exploit the Grid's heterogeneous network capabilities at their best. Consequently, a session layer for an actual efficient message-passing should provide such integrated services to the Grid environment.

3.2 Grid-enabled message-passing interfaces

Since MPI is the most important API for implementing parallel programs for large-scale environments, also some MPI libraries have already been extended meeting these demands of distributed and heterogeneous computing. Those libraries are often called *Grid-enabled* because they do not only use plain TCP/IP (which is obviously the lowest common denominator) for all inter-process communication, but are also capable of exploiting fast but local networks and interconnect facilities accommodating the hierarchy of the Grid. Hence, for being able to provide support for the various high-performance cluster networks and

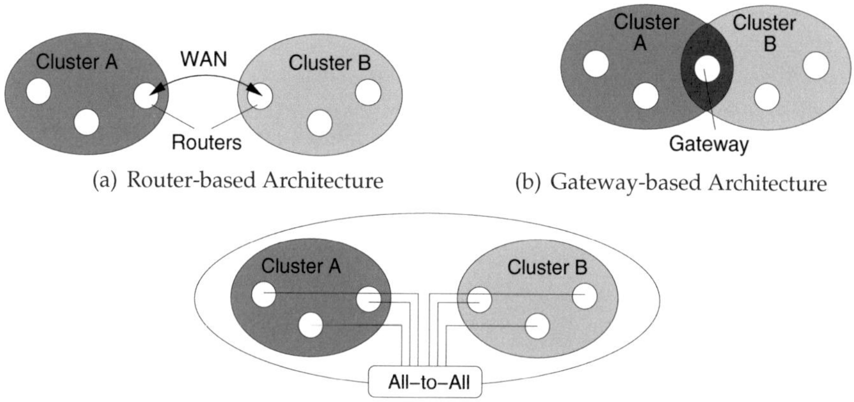

(a) Router-based Architecture

(b) Gateway-based Architecture

(c) All-to-all Architecture

Fig. 3. Different Topology Approaches regarding the Interlinking Network

their specific communication protocols, most of those libraries in turn rely on other high-level communication libraries (like site-*native* MPI libraries), rather than implementing this support inherently. Therefore, Grid-enabled MPI libraries can be understood as a kind of a *meta-layer* bridging the distributed computing sites. For that reason their application area is also referred to as a so-called *meta-computing* environment. The most common Grid-enabled MPI libraries are MPICH-G2 (Karonis et al., 2003), PACX-MPI (Gabriel et al., 1998), GridMPI (Matsuda et al., 2004), StaMPI (Imamura et al., 2000), MPICH/Madeleine (Aumage et al., 2001) and MetaMPICH (Pöppe et al., 2003), which are all proven to run large-scale applications in distributed environments. Although these meta-MPI implementations usually use native MPI support for site-internal communication, as for example provided by a site-local vendor MPI, they must also be based on at least a transport layer being capable of wide area communication for bridging and forwarding messages also to the remote sites. However, since regular transport protocols like TCP/IP are commonly point-to-point-oriented, it is a key task of such a bridging layer to setup all the required inter-site connections and thus acting as a session layer for the wide area communication.

3.2.1 Hardware topologies

When establishing the inter-site connections, a session layer has to take the actual hardware topologies into account in order to enable an efficient message-passing later on. With respect to topologies, three different linking approaches can be differentiated: *router*-based architectures, *gateway*-based architectures and finally a so-called *all-to-all* structures (Bierbaum, Clauss, Pöppe, Lankes & Bemmerl, 2006). In a router-based architecture, only certain cluster nodes have a direct access to the interlinking network. That means that all inter-site messages have to be routed through these special cluster nodes which then forward the messages to the remote clusters (see Figure 3(a)). This routing can either be done *transparently* concerning the MPI library, for example by means of the underlying transport protocol like TCP/IP. Or the MPI library itself has to perform this message routing, for example due to an incompatibility between the cluster internal and the external transport layer. In a gateway-based architectural approach, one or more cluster nodes are part of two or more clusters (see Figure 3(b)). That way, these nodes can act as gateways for

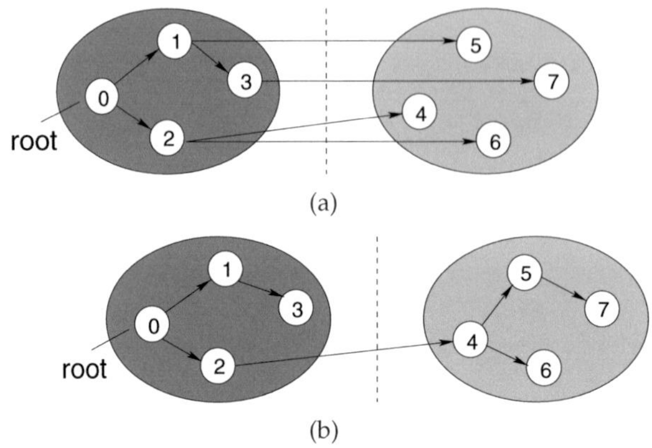

Fig. 4. Bad (a) and Good (a) Implementation of a Broadcast Operation on Coupled Clusters

messages to be transferred from one cluster to another. However, this approach is only suitable for locally coupled clusters, due to a missing wide area link. Finally, when using a fully connected interlinking network, all nodes in one cluster can directly communicate with all nodes in the other clusters. Actually, such a all-to-all topology only needs to be *logically* full connected, for example realized by means of switches (see Figure 3(c)). Not all Grid-enabled MPI libraries provide support for all these topologies. While router-based architectures are supported e.g. by PACX-MPI and MetaMPICH, the gateway approach is only supported by MPICH/Madeleine, whereas all-to-all topologies are supported by almost all above mentioned libraries.

3.2.2 Collective communication patterns

An efficient routing of messages through hierarchical topologies needs to take the underlying hardware structures accordingly into account. Moreover, this is especially true for collective communication operations because bottlenecks and congestion may arise, due to a high number of participating nodes. As already mentioned in Section 2.1.2, there exist a lot of collective communication operations and it is up to the respective communication library to map their patterns onto the hardware topologies in a most optimal way. So a broadcast operation for example may be optimally conducted in a *homogenous* system in terms of a binomial tree. However, in a *hierarchical* system, using just the same pattern would lead to redundant inter-site messages, as shown in Figure 4. Therefore, to avoid unnecessary inter-site communication, the following two rules should be observed: Send no messages with the same content more than once from one to another cluster, and each message must take at most one inter-site hop. The first rule helps to save inter-site bandwidth, whereas the second rule limits the impact of the inter-site latency on the overall communication time. An auxiliary communication library, especially designed for supporting optimized collective operations in hierarchical environments, is the so-called MagPIe library (Kielmann et al., 1999). This library is just an auxiliary library in this respect that is an extension to the well-known MPI implementation MPICH. Figure 5 shows as an example the broadcast pattern implemented by MagPIe for a system of four coupled clusters.

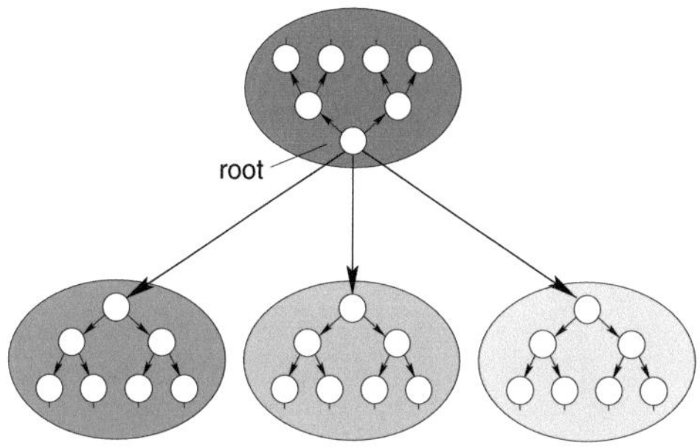

Fig. 5. Communication Pattern implemented by the MagPIe Library for a Broadcast Operation

3.3 The architecture of MetaMPICH

In this section, we detail the architecture of the Grid-enabled MPI implementation developed at the Chair for Operating Systems of the RWTH Aachen University: MetaMPICH which is derived, like many other MPI implementations, from the original MPICH implementation by Argonne National Laboratory (Gropp et al., 1996).

3.3.1 Session configuration

One key strength of MetaMPICH is that it can be configured in a very flexible manner. For that purpose, MetaMPICH relies on a dedicated configuration file that is parsed before each session startup. This configuration file contains information about the communication topologies as well as user-related information about the requested MPI session. The information must be coded in a special description language customized to coupled clusters in Grid environments. Such a configuration file is structured into three parts: a header part with basic information about the session, a part describing the different clusters and a part specifying the overall topology. The header part gives, for example, information about the number of clusters and the number of nodes per cluster and thus the total number of nodes. The second part describes each participating cluster in terms of access information, environment variables, node and router lists as well as information about type and structure of the cluster-internal network. In the third part, the individual links between router nodes in case of a router-based architecture are described in terms of protocols and addresses. The same applies to clusters that are connected in an all-to-all manner: Here, a transport protocol must be specified[9] and additional netmasks may be stated, too. Moreover, MetaMPICH even supports mixed configurations, where some clusters are connected via an all-to-all network, whereas others are simultaneously connected via router nodes. Figure 6 shows an example for such a mixed session configuration.

3.3.2 Internal message handling

Since MetaMPICH is derived from MPICH, it also inherits major parts of its layered architecture, which is shown here in Figure 7. Both supported interlinking approaches of

[9] MetaMPICH provides support for TCP, UDT and SCTP as the interlinking transport layers.

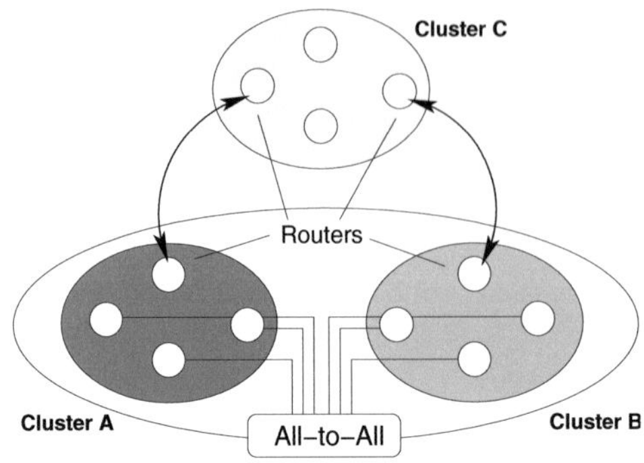

Fig. 6. Example for a Mixed Configuration Supported by MetaMPICH

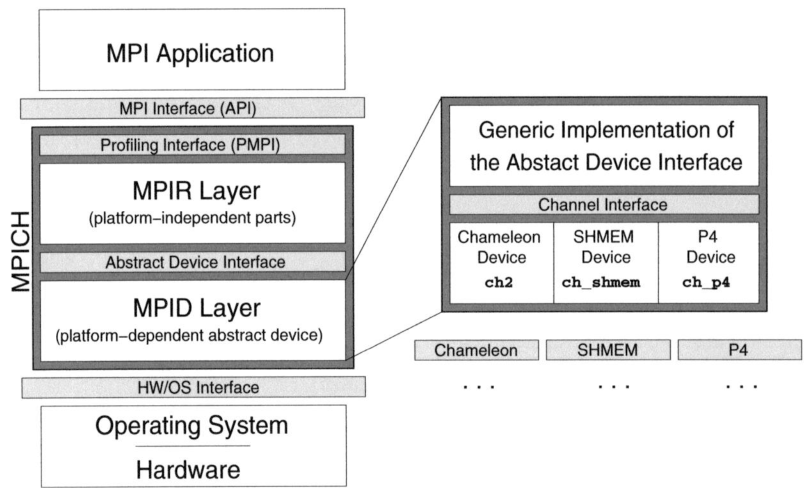

Fig. 7. The Layer Model of MPICH that enables the Multi-Device Support of MetaMPICH

MetaMPICH (the all-to-all approach as well as the router-based approach) in turn, rely on the so-called *multi-device* feature of MPICH. This feature allows the utilization of multiple *abstract communication devices*, which are data structures representing the actual interfaces to lower level communication layers, at the same time. That way, for example, communication via both TCP and shared memory within one MPI session becomes possible. MetaMPICH in turn uses this feature to directly access the interfaces of cluster-internal high-speed interconnects like SCI, Myrinet or InfiniBand via customized devices, while other devices are used to link the clusters via TCP, UDT[10] or SCTP. However, when running a router-based configuration, certain cluster nodes need to act as routers. That means that messages to remote clusters are at first forwarded via the cluster-native interconnect (and thus by means of a customized communication device) to a router node. The router node then sends the message to a corresponding router node at the remote site that finally tunnels the message via that cluster-native interconnect to the actual receiver.

[10] UDT: a UDP-based Data Transfer Protocol, see Section 3.1.1.

3.3.3 The integrated service interface

A further key strength of MetaMPICH is an integrated service interface that can be accessed within the Grid environment via *remote procedure calls* (RPC). Although there exist several approaches for implementing RPC facilities in Grid environments, we have decided to base our implementation on the raw XML-RPC specification (Winer, 1999). Therefore, all service queries have to be handled via XML-coded remote method invocations. Simple services just provide the caller with status information about the current session, as for instance whether a certain connection has already been established, which transport protocol is in use, or how many bytes of payload have already been transfered on this connection. However, also quality-of-service metrics like latency and bandwidth of a connection can be inquired. All these information can then be evaluated by an external entity like a Grid monitoring daemon in order to detect bottlenecks or deadlocks in communication. Besides such query-related services, MetaMPICH also offers RPC interfaces that allow external entities actually to control session-related settings. In doing so, external monitoring or scheduling instances are given the ability to reconfigure an already established session even at runtime. Besides such external control capabilities, also *self-referring* monitoring services are supported by MetaMPICH. These services react automatically on session-internal events, as for instance the detection of a bottleneck or the requirement of a cleanup triggered by a timeout (Clauss et al., 2008).

4. Message-passing on the chip

Since the beginning of the multicore era, parallel processing has become prevalent across-the-board. While previously parallel working processors almost exclusively belonged to the domain of datacenters, today nearly every common desktop PC is already a multiprocessor system. And according to Moore's Law, the number of compute cores per system will continue to grow on both the low end and the high end. Already at this stage, there exist multicore architectures with up to twelve entire cores. However, this high degree of parallelism poses an enormous challenge in particular for the software layers.

4.1 Cluster-on-chip architectures

On a traditional multicore system, a single operating system manages all cores and schedules threads and processes among them with the objective of load balancing. Since there is no distinction between the cores of a chip, this architecture type is also referred to as symmetric multiprocessing (SMP). In such a system, the memory management can be handled nearly similar to a single-core but multi-processing system because the processor hardware already undertakes the crucial task of cache coherency management. However, a further growth of the number of cores per system also implies an increasing chip complexity, especially with respect to the cache coherence protocols; and this in turn may cause a loss of the processors' capability and verifiability. Therefore, a very attractive alternative is to waive the hardware-based cache coherency and to introduce a software-oriented message-passing based architecture instead: a so-called *Cluster-on-Chip* architecture. In turn, this architecture can be classified into two types: The first resembles a homogeneous cluster where all cores are identically, whereas the second exhibits a heterogeneous design. Therefore, the second type is commonly referred to as asymmetric multiprocessing (AMP).

4.2 The Intel SCC Many-core processor

The Intel SCC is a 48-core experimental processor built to study Many-core architectures and how to program them, concerning parallelization capabilities (Intel Corporation, 2010). With this architecture, Many-core systems may be investigated that do not make use of a hardware based cache coherent *shared-memory* programming model but use the *message-passing* paradigm instead. For this purpose, a new memory type is introduced that is located on the chip itself.

4.2.1 Top level view

The 48 cores are arranged in a 6x4 array of 24 tiles with two cores on each of them. They are connected by an on-die 2D mesh that is used for inter-core data transfer but also to access the four on-die memory controllers. These address up to 64 GiB of DDR3 memory altogether which can be used as private but also shared among the cores. The SCC system contains a *Management Console PC* (MCPC) that is used to control the SCC being connected to an FPGA[11] on the SCC board using the PCIe bus. The FPGA controls all off-die data traffic and provides a method to extend the SCC system by new features. Programs may be loaded by the MCPC into the SCC's memory. The same applies to operating systems that shall be booted. The MCPC can be used to read the content of the memory. For this purpose the SCC's memory regions may be mapped into the MCPC's address space. Figure 8 gives a schematic view of the architecture described above. Furthermore the SCC introduces a concept to govern the energy consumption of the chip. It is divided into 7 voltage and 24 frequency domains that can be adjusted independently. Thus, the programmer has the opportunity to influence the software's power consumption. This may be achieved for example by throttling down a core that currently does not have any tasks.

4.2.2 Tile level view

The cores are based on the Intel P54C architecture, an x86 design used for the Intel Pentium I. They contain 16 KiB integrated L1 data and instruction cache each. Apart from the two cores, a tile holds an additional L2 cache of 256 KiB per core to cache the off-die private memory. In addition to that, the so-called *message-passing buffer* (MPB) is provided, a fast on-die shared memory of 16 KiB per tile whereby 8 KiB may logically be assigned to each core. Since the SCC does not provide any cache coherency between the cores, the MPB is intended to realize explicit message-passing among the cores. The so-called *Mesh Interface Unit* (MIU) on each tile handles all memory requests which may be those for message-passing via MPB or accesses to the off-die memory. According to Figure 8, the MIU is the only instance that interacts with the router constituting the connection to the mesh and therefore to the other tiles. For synchronization purposes each tile provides two *Test-and-Set registers*. They are accessible by all cores competitively and guarantee an atomic access. In addition to that, configuration registers are supplied that may be used to modify the operating modes of the on-tile hardware elements.

[11] Field-Programmable Gate Array

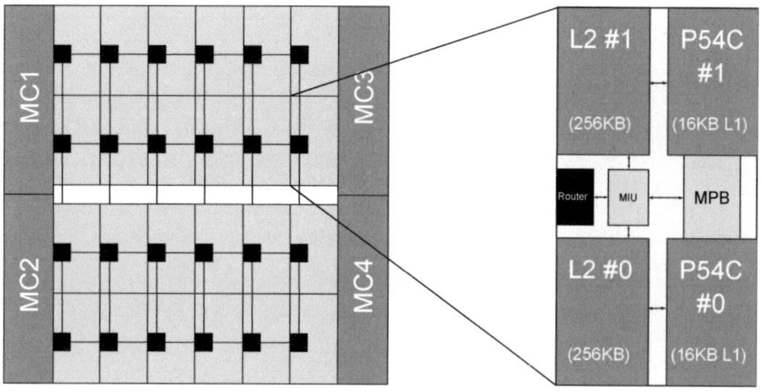

Fig. 8. Block Diagram of the SCC Architecture: a 6x4 mesh of tiles with two cores per tile

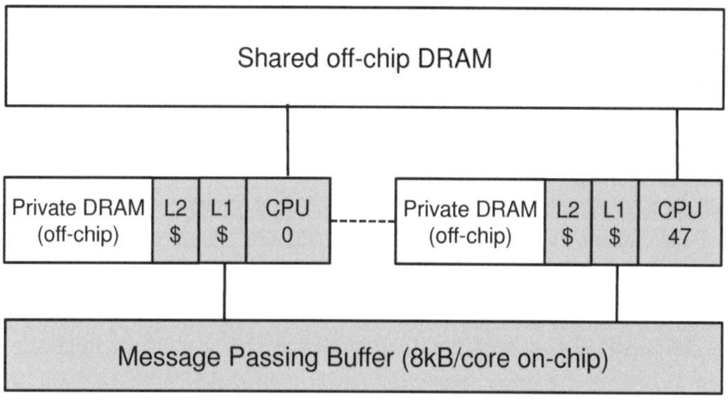

Fig. 9. Logical Software View onto the SCC's Memory System

4.2.3 Software level view

In order to avoid problems due to the missing cache coherency, the off-die memory of the SCC is logically divided into 48 private regions (one per core) plus one global region for all cores. Since for all cores an exclusive access to their private regions is guaranteed, the caches can be enabled for these regions per default. In doing so, each core can then boot its own operating system, usually a Linux kernel (Mattson et al., 2010). Therefore, the SCC is able to run 48 Linux instances simultaneously, actually resembling a cluster on the chip. Moreover, it is also possible to share data between the cores, since all cores have concurrent access to the additional global memory region. However, because of the missing cache coherency, the caches are disabled for this shared region per default. This logical software view onto the memory is illustrated in Figure 9.

4.3 SCC-customized message-passing interfaces

The memory architecture of SCC facilitates various programming models (Clauss, Lankes, Reble & Bemmerl, 2011), where the cores may interact either via the on-die MPBs or via the off-die shared memory. However, due to the lack of cache coherency, message-passing seems to be the most efficient model for the SCC.

4.3.1 RCCE: the SCC-native communication layer

The software environment provided with the SCC, called RCCE (Mattson & van der Wijngaart, 2010), is a lightweight communication API for explicit message-passing on the SCC. For this purpose, basic send and receive routines are provided that support *blocking* point-to-point communication which are based on one-sided primitives (put/get). They access the MPBs and are synchronized by the send and receive routines using flags, introduced with this API. Although used library internal in this case, the flags are also available to the user application. They can be accessed with respective write and read functions and may be used to realize critical sections or synchronization between the cores. Both at the sending and at the receiving side matching destination/source and size parameters have to be passed to the send and receive routine. Otherwise this will lead to unpredictable results. Communication occurs in a *send local, receive remote* scheme. This means that the local MPB, situated at the sending core, is used for the message transfer. The communication API is used in a static SPMD manner. So-called *Units of Execution* (UEs) are introduced that may be associated with a thread or process. Being assigned to one core each, with an ID out of 0 to #cores−1, all UEs form the program. As it is not sure when a UE exactly starts the execution, the programmer may not expect any order within the program. To encounter this, one may use functions to synchronize the UEs, like a barrier for example. Inspired by MPI, there is a number of collective routines (see Section 2.1.2). For example a program, in which each UE makes a part of a calculation, may use a all-reduce to update the current result on all UEs instead of using send/receive routines. A wider range of collectives is provided with the additional library *RCCE_comm* (Chan, 2010) that includes functions like *scatter*, *gather*, etc. With RCCE a fully synchronized communication environment is made available to the programmer. It is possible to gain experience in message-passing in a very simple way. However, if one wants to have further control over the MPB, the so-called *non-gory* interface of RCCE described above is not sufficient anymore. Thus, Intel supplies a *gory* version which offers the programmer more flexibility in using the SCC. Asynchronous message-passing using the one-sided communication functions is now possible, however it has to be considered that cache coherency must not be expected. Therefore the programmer has to make sure by himself that the access to shared memory regions is organized by the software. Although, a very flexible interface for one-sided communication is made available with the gory version, the lack of non-blocking functions concerning two-sided communication forces to look for alternatives.

4.3.2 iRCCE: a non-blocking extension to RCCE

At the Chair of Operating Systems of RWTH Aachen University an extension to the RCCE communications API called *iRCCE* has been developed (Clauss, Lankes, Bemmerl, Galowicz & Pickartz, 2011). It offers a *non-blocking* communication interface for point-to-point communication. Now interleaved communication and computation is possible. Due to the fact that the SCC does not supply asynchronous hardware to perform the message exchange, functions to push the pending requests are provided. To make sure the communication progress has completed, a test or wait function has to be called. To be able to process multiple communication requests, a queuing mechanism is implemented that handles posted requests in a strict FIFO manner. According to the definitions made in Chapter 2.1.1, iRCCE offers a non-blocking but still synchronized communication interface. Since messages may exceed the available MPB space, it can only be used to transfer data chunk-wise from sender to the receiver. Furthermore, the library itself does not perform overlapped but just interleaved message transfer from sender to receiver. Therefore, the transfer progress has to be actively fostered by the user application. Hence, even with this approach it is not possible to realize real asynchronous message-passing between the cores. While offering a wide range of functions that facilitate non-blocking communication between the cores of the SCC, iRCCE just as RCCE is still a low-level communications API which allows other APIs, like MPI for example, to be built on top of it. That is also reflected in the application programmer interface. It is kept very simple and one who is experienced in message-passing will not have any problems working with it. Due to the simplicity, the functionality is limited, compared to MPI for example.[12] No buffer management has been implemented with the consequence that the send and receive buffers have to be provided by the programmer. Furthermore, there is no mechanism to differ between different message types, like it is possible with tags in MPI.

4.3.3 An MCAPI implementation for the SCC

A *proof of concept* for an MCAPI implementation for the SCC has been developed at the Chair of Operating Systems of RWTH Aachen University, too. The approach that was made is to layer it on top of iRCCE including the features offered by an additional *mailbox system*[13]. This approach does not endeavor to be a highly optimized communication interface. However, it should be sufficient to investigate the usability of the communication interface offered by the MCAPI for future Many-core systems. The MCAPI defines a communication topology that consists of *domains*, *nodes* and *endpoints*. A domain contains an arbitrary number of nodes. The specification does not oblige what to associate with a domain. However, in this SCC-specific implementation, a core is defined as a node and the whole SCC chip as a domain. For now only one domain is supported, however further versions may connect different SCCs and thus offering more than one domain (see also Section 5). An endpoint is a communication interface that may be created at all nodes. Each node internally holds two endpoint lists, one for the local endpoints and one for the remote ones. As the specification requires, the tuple (*domain,node,port*) defining an endpoint is globally unique within the communication topology. The iRCCE communication interface only provides one physical channel for sending purpose (that is the local MPB). In contrast to that the MCAPI allows an arbitrary amount of endpoints to be created at each node. Thus, the approach made by this implementation has to supply a multiplex mechanism as well as a demultiplex mechanism that organizes the message transfer over the channel provided by iRCCE at each node.

5. Message-passing in future Many-core Grids

In the previous sections, we have considered the demands of message-passing in Grid environments as well as in Many-core systems. However, we have done this each apart from the other. Now, in this section we want to discuss how these two worlds can eventually be combined.

[12] MPI actually provides functions for real asynchronous two-sided communication.

[13] This is an asynchronous extension to iRCCE that may be used additionally to the functionality offered by iRCCE itself.

5.1 Bringing two worlds together

When looking at Section 3 and Section 4, it becomes obvious that the two worlds there described will inevitably merge in the near future. The world of chip-embedded Many-core systems will have to be incorporated into the hierarchies of distributed Grid computing. However, the question is how this integration step can be conducted in such a way that both worlds can benefit from this fusion. In doing so, especially the communication interfaces between these two worlds will play a key role regarding their interaction.

5.1.1 The macrocosmic world

In the world of Grid computing as well as in the domain of High-Performance Computing (HPC), MPI has become the prevalent standard for message-passing. The range of functions defined by the MPI standard is very large and an MPI implementation that aims to provide the sheer magnitude has to implement way above 250 functions.[14] In turn, this implies that such an MPI library tends to become heavyweight in terms of resource consumption, as for example in terms a large memory footprint. However, this is definitely tolerable concerning the HPC domain; at least as long as the resources deployed lead to a high performance as for example in the form of low latencies, high bandwidth and optimal processor utilization. Furthermore, a Grid-enabled MPI implementation must also be capable of dealing with heterogeneous structures and it must be able to provide support for the varying networking technologies and protocols of hierarchical topologies. Moreover, it becomes clear how complex and extensive the implementation of such a library might get if besides the MPI API additional service interfaces for an interaction between the MPI session and the Grid environment come into play. However, when looking at the application level it can be noticed that many MPI applications just make use of less than 10 functions from the large function set offered. On the one hand, this is due to the fact that already a handful of core functions are sufficient in order to write a vast number of useful and efficient MPI programs (Gropp et al., 1999). On the other hand, knowledge of and experience with *all* offered MPI functions are not very common even within the community of MPI users. Therefore, many users rely on a subset of more common functions and implement less common functionalities at application level on their own.[15]

5.1.2 The microcosmic world

Currently, there does not exist one uniform and dominant standard for message-passing in the domain of Many-cores and cluster-on-chip architectures. Although MPI can basically also be employed in such embedded systems, customized communication interfaces, as for example RCCE for the SCC, are predominant in this domain. The reason for this is that MPI is frequently too heavyweight for pure on-chip communication because major parts of an MPI implementation would be superfluous in such systems, as for example the support for unreliable connections, different networking protocols or heterogeneity in general. However, a major drawback of customized libraries with proprietary interfaces is that applications get bound to their specific library and thus become less portable to other platforms. Therefore, a unified and widespread *interface standard* for on-chip communication in multicore and

[14] That is an MPI implementation compliant with the compatibility level MPI-2.

[15] An example for this is the comprehensive set of *collective operations* offered by MPI (see Section 2.1.2).

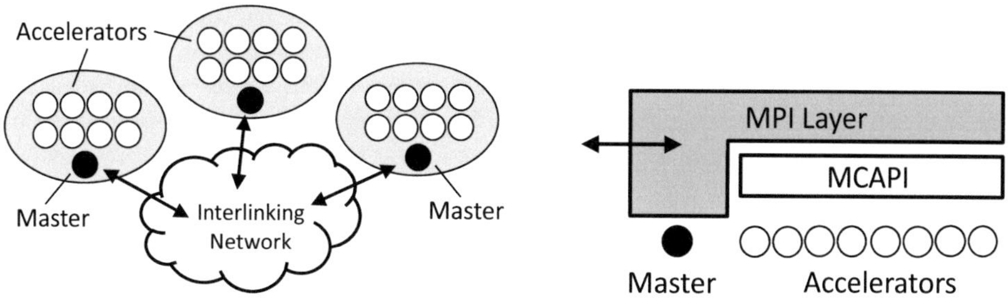

(a) Three Linked AMP Many-core Systems (b) MPI for On-die Communication

Fig. 10. Many-core Systems According to the AMP Approach

Many-core systems, as the MCAPI promises, would certainly be a step in the right direction. Actually, the MCAPI specification aims to facilitate lightweight implementations that can handle the core-to-core communication in embedded systems with limited resource but less requirements (Brehmer et al., 2011),

5.1.3 The best of both worlds

Several approaches for Many-core architectures follow the asymmetric multiprocessing approach (AMP) where one core is designated to be a master core whereas the other cores act as accelerator cores (see Section 4.1). Examples for this approach are the Cell Broadband Engine or Intel's Knights Corner (Vajda, 2011). One way to combine the macrocosmic world of Grid computing with the microcosmic world of Many-cores in terms of message-passing is using MPI for the off-die communication between multiple master cores and customized communication interfaces, as for example MCAPI, for the on-die communication between the masters and their respective accelerator cores. In this *Multiple-Master Multiple-Worker* approach, the master cores not only act as dispatchers for the local workload but must also act as routers for messages to be sent from one accelerator core to another one on a remote die (see Figure 10(a)). This approach can be arranged with the MPMD paradigm (see Section 2.2.1), where the master cores run a different program (based on MPI plus e.g. MCAPI calls for the communication) than the accelerator cores (running e.g. a pure MCAPI-based parallel code). In addition, the master cores may spawn the processes on the local accelerator cores at runtime and in an iterative manner, in order to assign dedicated subtasks to them. However, one drawback of this approach is the need for processes running on the master cores to communicate via two (or even more) application programming interfaces. A further drawback is the fact, that the master cores are prone to become bottlenecks in terms of inter-site communication. Another approach would be to base all communication calls of the applications upon the MPI API so that all cores become part of one large MPI session. However, also this approach has some drawbacks that, if not taken into account, threaten to limit the overall performance.

5.1.4 The demand for hierarchy-awareness

First of all, when running one large MPI session that covers all participating cores in a Many-core Grid, one has to apply a Grid-enabled MPI library that is not only capable of routing messages to remote sites but that also must be able to handle the internal on-die communication in a fast, efficient and thus lightweight manner. Hence, in a first instance such an MPI library must be able to differentiate between on-die messages and messages to remote destinations. Moreover, in case of an AMP system, the MPI library should be available in two versions: a lightweight one (possibly just featuring a subset of the comprehensive MPI functionalities) customized to the respective Many-core infrastructure, and a fully equipped one (but possibly quite heavyweight) running on the master cores that also offers, for example, Grid-related service interfaces (see Section 3.1.2). That way, on-die messages can be passed fast and efficient via a *thin* MPI layer that in turn may be based upon another Many-core related communication interface like MCAPI (see Figure 10(b)). At the same time, messages to remote sites can be transferred via appropriate local or wide area transport protocols (see Section 3.1.1) and Grid-related service inquiries can be served. So far, the considered hierarchy is just two-tiered in terms of communication: on-die and off-die. However, with respect to hierarchy-awareness, a further level can be recognized when building local clusters of Many-cores and then interlinking multiple of those via local and/or wide area networks.[16] In that case, the respective MPI library has to distinguish between three (or even four) types of communication: on-die, cluster-internal, (local area) and wide area. Additionally, at each of these levels, hierarchy-related information should be exploited in order to reduce the message traffic and to avoid the congestion of bottlenecks. So, for example, the implementation of *collective operations* has to take the information about such a deep hierarchy into account (see Section 3.2.2).

5.2 SCC-MPICH: A hierarchy-aware MPI library for the SCC

Considering the Intel SCC as a prototype for future Many-core processors, the question is: How can we build clusters of SCCs and deploy them in a Grid environment? In this section, we want to introduce SCC-MPICH that is a customized MPI library for the SCC developed at the Chair for Operating Systems of RWTH Aachen University.[17] Since SCC-MPICH is derived from the original MPICH library, just the same as MetaMPICH, it is possible to plug the SCC-related part of SCC-MPICH[18] into MetaMPICH. That way, the building of a prototype for evaluating the opportunities, the potentials as well as the limitations of future Many-core Grids should become possible.

5.2.1 An SCC-customized abstract communication device

Although the semantics of RCCE's communication functions are obviously derived from the MPI standard, the RCCE API is far from implementing all MPI-related features (see Section 4.3). And even though iRCCE extends the range of supported functions (and thus the provided communication semantics), a lot of users are familiar with MPI and hence want to use its well-known functions also on the SCC. A very simple way to use MPI functions on the SCC is just to port an existing TCP/IP-capable MPI library to this new target platform. However, since the TCP/IP driver of the Linux operating system image

[16] The resulting architecture may be called a *Cluster-of-Many-core-Clusters*, or just a true *Many-core Grid*.

[17] At this point we want to mention that by now there also exists another MPI implementation for the SCC: RCKMPI by Intel (Urena et al., 2011).

[18] This is actually an implementation of the non-generic part of an *abstract communication device* customized to the SCC (see Section 3.3).

for the SCC does not utilize the fast on-die message-passing buffers (MPBs), the achievable communication performance of such a ported TCP/IP-based MPI library lags far behind the MPB-based communication performance of RCCE and iRCCE. For this reason, we have implemented SCC-MPICH as an SCC-optimized MPI library which in turn is based upon the iRCCE extensions of the original RCCE communication library.[19] In doing so, we have added to the original MPICH a new abstract communication device (refer back to Figure 7 in Section 3) that utilizes the fast on-die MPBs of the SCC as well as the off-die shared-memory for the core-to-core communication. In turn, this new SCC-related communication device provides four different communication protocols: *Short*, *Eager*, *Rendezvous* and a second Eager protocol called *ShmEager* (Clauss, Lankes & Bemmerl, 2011). The Short protocol is optimized in order to obtain low communication latencies. It is used for exchanging message headers as well as header-embedded short payload messages via the MPBs. Bigger messages must be sent either via one of the two Eager protocols or via the Rendezvous protocol. The main difference between Eager and Rendezvous mode is that Eager messages must be accepted on the receiver side even if the corresponding receive requests are not yet posted by the application. Therefore, a message sent via Eager mode can implicate an additional overhead by copying the message temporarily into an intermediate buffer. However, when using the ShmEager protocol, the off-die shared-memory is used to pass the messages between the cores. That means that this protocol does not require the receiver to copy unexpected messages into additional *private* intermediate buffers unless there is no longer enough *shared* off-die memory. The decision which of these protocols is to be used depends on the message length as well as on the ratio of expected to unexpected messages (Gropp & Lusk, 1996).

5.2.2 Integration into MetaMPICH

By integrating the SCC-related communication device of SCC-MPICH into MetaMPICH, multiple SCCs can now be linked together according to the all-to-all approach as well as to the router-based approach (see Section 3.3.1). However, at this point the question arises how the SCC's frontend, that is the so-called *Management Console PC* (MCPC), has to be considered regarding the session configuration (see Section 4.2.1). In fact, the cores of the MCPC[20] and the 48 cores of the SCC are connected via an FPGA in such a way that they are contained within a private TCP address space. That means that all data traffic between the SCC cores and the outside world has to be routed across the MCPC. In this respect, an SCC system can be considered as an AMP system where the CPUs of the MCPC represent the master cores while the SCC cores can be perceived as 48 accelerator cores. In turn, a session of two (or more) coupled SCC systems must be based on a three-tiered mixed configuration: 1. On-die communication via the customized communication device of SCC-MPICH; 2. System-local communication within the private TCP domain; 3. Router-based communication via TCP, UDT or SCTP as local or wide area transport protocols to remote systems. Figure 11 shows an example configuration of two linked SCC systems.

[19] In fact, the development of iRCCE was driven by the demand for a non-blocking communication substrate for SCC-MPICH because one cannot layer non-blocking semantics (as supported by MPI) upon just blocking communication functions (as provided by RCCE), see also Section 2.1.1.

[20] Actually, the MCPC is just a common server equipped with common multicore CPUs.

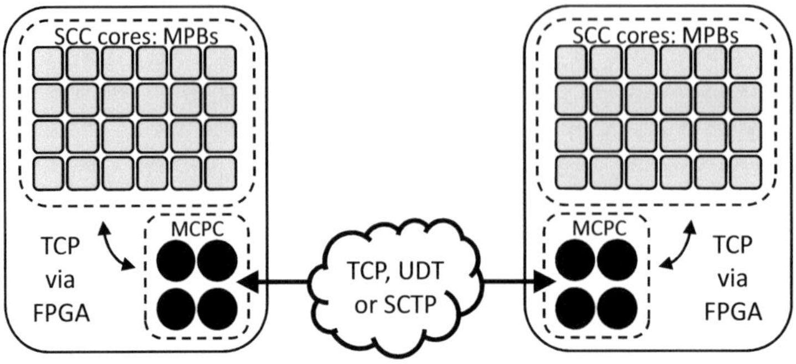

Fig. 11. Two Linked SCC Systems: Each Consisting of 4 MCPC Cores and 48 SCC Cores

5.2.3 Future prospects

The next step would be to link more than two SCC systems to a real cluster of SCCs and to deploy them in a Grid environment. However, one major problem is that currently the SCC cores are not able to communicate directly with the outside world. That means that all messages must be routed across the MCPC nodes which in turn may become bottlenecks in terms of communication. Although MetaMPICH supports configurations with more than one router node per site and allows for a static balancing of the router load, a second major problem is the link between the MCPC and the SCC cores: Because due to this link, each message to a remote site has to take two additional process-to-process hops. Therefore, a smarter solution might be to enable the SCC cores to access the interlinking network in a direct manner. However, this in turn implies that the processes running on the SCC cores have then to handle also the wide area communication. So, for example, when performing collective communication operations, a router process running on the MCPC can be used to collect and consolidate data locally before forwarding messages to remote sites, thereby relieving the SCC cores from this task. Without a router process, the SCC cores have to organize the local part of the communication pattern on their own. Hence, a much smarter approach might be hybrid: allow for direct point-to-point communication between remote SCC cores and use additional processes running on the MCPCs to perform collective operations and/or to handle Grid-related service inquiries. All the more so because such hierarchy-related interaction with other Grid applications will play an important part towards a successful merge of both worlds. Although the runtime system of MetaMPICH has already been extended by the ability to interact with a *meta-scheduling service* in UNICORE-based Grids (Bierbaum, Clauss, Eickermann, Kirtchakova, Krechel, Springstubbe, Wäldrich & Ziegler, 2006), the integration into other existing or future Grid middleware needs to be considered.

6. Conclusion

It is quite obvious that the world of chip-embedded Many-core systems on the one hand and the world of distributed Grid computing on the other hand will merge in the near future. With the Intel SCC as a prototype for future Many-core processors, we have even today the opportunity to investigate the requirements of such Many-core equipped Grid environments. In this chapter, we have especially focused on the challenges of message-passing in this upcoming new computing era. In doing so, we have presented the two MPI libraries

MetaMPICH and SCC-MPICH and we have shown how both can be combined in order to build a Grid-enabled message-passing library for coupled Many-core systems. By means of this prototype implementation, the evaluation of opportunities, potentials as well as limitations of future Many-core Grids becomes possible. We have especially pointed out the demand for hierarchy-awareness to be included into the communication middleware in order to reduce the message traffic and to avoid the congestion of bottlenecks. As a result, this approach requires knowledge about the hardware structures and thus related information and service interfaces. Moreover, even a likewise hierarchical algorithm design for the parallel applications will probably become necessary. However, in order to keep this chapter focused, a lot of other very interesting and important aspects could not be covered here. So, for examples, it is still quite unclear how such hardware-related information can be handled and passed in a standardized manner. Although the MPI Forum is currently fostering the upcoming MPI-3 standard, it looks quite unlikely that already the next standard will give answers to these questions.

7. References

Aumage, O., Mercier, G. & Namyst, R. (2001). MPICH/Madeleine: A True Multi-Protocol MPI for High Performance Networks, *Proceedings of the 15th International Parallel and Distributed Processing Symposium (IPDPS'01)*, IEEE CS Press, San Francisco, CA, USA.

Balkanski, D., Trams, M. & Rehm, W. (2003). Heterogeneous Computing With MPICH/Madeleine and PACX MPI: a Critical Comparison, *Chemnitzer Informatik-Berichte* CSR-03-04: 1–20.

Bierbaum, B., Clauss, C., Eickermann, T., Kirtchakova, L., Krechel, A., Springstubbe, S., Wäldrich, O. & Ziegler, W. (2006). Reliable Orchestration of distributed MPI-Applications in a UNICORE-based Grid with MetaMPICH and MetaScheduling, *Proceedings of the 13th European PVM/MPI Users' Group Meeting (EuroPVM/MPI'06)*, Vol. 4192 of *Lecture Notes in Computer Science*, Springer-Verlag, Bonn, Germany.

Bierbaum, B., Clauss, C., Pöppe, M., Lankes, S. & Bemmerl, T. (2006). The new Multidevice Architecture of MetaMPICH in the Context of other Approaches to Grid-enabled MPI, *Proceedings of the 13th European PVM/MPI Users' Group Meeting (EuroPVM/MPI'06)*, Vol. 4192 of *Lecture Notes in Computer Science*, Springer-Verlag, Bonn, Germany.

Brehmer, S., Levy, M. & Moyer, B. (2011). Using MCAPI to Lighten an MPI Load, EE Times Design Article (online).

Butler, R. & Lusk, E. (1994). Monitors, Messages and Clusters: The P4 Parallel Programming System, *Parallel Computing* 20(4): 547–564.

Chan, E. (2010). RCCE_comm: A Collective Communication Library for the Intel Single-Chip Cloud Computer, *Technical report*, Intel Corporation.

Clauss, C., Lankes, S. & Bemmerl, T. (2008). Design and Implementation of a Service-integrated Session Layer for Efficient Message Passing in Grid Computing Environments, *Proceedings of the 7th International Symposium on Parallel and Distributed Computing (ISPDC'08)*, IEEE CS Press, Krakow, Poland.

Clauss, C., Lankes, S. & Bemmerl, T. (2011). Performance Tuning of SCC-MPICH by means of the Proposed MPI-3.0 Tool Interface, *Proceedings of the 18th European MPI Users Group Meeting (EuroMPI 2011)*, Vol. 6960, Springer, Santorini, Greece.

Clauss, C., Lankes, S., Bemmerl, T., Galowicz, J. & Pickartz, S. (2011). iRCCE: A Non-blocking Communication Extension to the RCCE Communication Library for the Intel Single-Chip Cloud Computer, *Technical report*, Chair for Operating Systems, RWTH Aachen University. Users' Guide and API Manual.

Clauss, C., Lankes, S., Reble, P. & Bemmerl, T. (2011). Evaluation and Improvements of Programming Models for the Intel SCC Many-core Processor, *Proceedings of the International Conference on High Performance Computing and Simulation (HPCS2011), Workshop on New Algorithms and Programming Models for the Manycore Era (APMM)*, Istanbul, Turkey.

Dickens, P. M. (2003). FOBS: A Lightweight Communication Protocol for Grid Computing, *Processing of the 9th International Euro-Par Conference (Euro-Par'03)*, Austria.

Dongarra, J., Geist, A., Mancheck, R. & Sunderam, V. (1993). Integrated PVM Framework Supports Heterogeneous Network Computing, *Computers in Physics* 7(2): 166–175.

Feng, W. & Tinnakornsrisuphap, P. (2000). The Failure of TCP in High-Performance Computational Grids, *Proceedings of the Supercomputing Conference (SC2000)*, ACM Press and IEEE CS Press, Dallas, TX, USA.

Gabriel, E., Fagg, G., Bosilca, G., Angskun, T., Dongarra, J., Squyres, J., Sahay, V., Kambadur, P., Barrett, B., Lumsdaine, A., Castain, R., Daniel, D., Graham, R. & Woodall, T. (2004). Open MPI: Goals, Concept, and Design of a Next Generation MPI Implementation, *Proceedings of the 11th European PVM/MPI Users' Group Meeting (EuroPVM/MPI'04)*, Vol. 3241 of *Lecture Notes in Computer Science*, Springer-Verlag, Budapest, Hungary.

Gabriel, E., Resch, M., Beisel, T. & Keller, R. (1998). Distributed Computing in a Heterogeneous Computing Environment, *Proceedings of the 5th European PVM/MPI Users' Group Meeting (EuroPVM/MPI'97)*, Vol. 1497 of *Lecture Notes in Computer Science*, Springer-Verlag, Liverpool, UK.

Geist, A. (1998). Harness: The Next Generation Beyond PVM, *Proceedings of the 5th European PVM/MPI Users' Group Meeting (EuroPVM/MPI'98)*, Vol. 1497 of *Lecture Notes in Computer Science*, Springer-Verlag, Liverpool, UK.

Gropp, W. (2002). MPICH2: A New Start for MPI Implementations, *Proceedings of the 9th European PVM/MPI Users Group Meeting (EuroPVM/MPI'02)*, Vol. 2474 of *Lecture Notes in Computer Science*, Springer-Verlag, Linz, Austria.

Gropp, W. & Lusk, E. (1996). MPICH Working Note: The Implementation of the Second-Generation MPICH ADI, *Technical Report* , Mathematics and Computer Science Division, Argonne National Laboratory (ANL).

Gropp, W., Lusk, E., Doss, N. & Skjellum, A. (1996). A High-Performance, Portable Implementation of the MPI Message Passing Interface Standard, *Parallel Computing* 22(6): 789–828.

Gropp, W., Lusk, E. & Skjellum, A. (1999). *Using MPI: Portable Parallel Programming with the Message-Passing Interface*, Scientific and engineering computation, second edn, The MIT Press.

Gropp, W. & Smith, B. (1993). Chameleon Parallel Programming Tools – User's Manual, *Technical Report ANL-93/23*, Argonne National Laboratory.

Gu, Y. & Grossman, R. (2003). SABUL: A Transport Protocol for Grid Computing, *Journal of Grid Computing* 1(4): 377–386.

Gu, Y. & Grossman, R. (2007). UDT: UDP-based Data Transfer for High-Speed Wide Area Networks, *Computer Networks* 51(7): 1777–1799.

Hessler, S. & Welzl, M. (2007). Seamless Transport Service Selection by Deploying a Middleware, *Computer Communications* 30(3): 630–637.

Imamura, T., Tsujita, Y., Koide, H. & Takemiya, H. (2000). An Architecture of STAMPI: MPI Library on a Cluster of Parallel Computers, *Proceedings of the 7th European PVM/MPI Users' Group Meeting (EuroPVM/MPI'00)*, Vol. 1908 of *Lecture Notes in Computer Science*, Springer-Verlag, Balatonfüred, Hungary.

Intel Corporation (2010). SCC External Architecture Specification (EAS), *Technical report*, Intel Corporation.

Kamal, H., Penoff, B. & Wagner, A. (2005). SCTP versus TCP for MPI, *Proceedings of the ACM/IEEE Conference on Supercomputing (SC'05)*, ACM Press and IEEE CS Press, Seattle, WA, USA.

Karonis, N., Toonen, B. & Foster, I. (2003). MPICH-G2: A Grid-enabled implementation of the Message Passing Interface, *Journal of Parallel and Distributed Computing* 63(5): 551–563.

Kielmann, T., Hofmann, R., Bal, H., Plaat, A. & Bhoedjang, R. (1999). MagPIe: MPI's Collective Communication Operations for Clustered Wide Area Systems, *Proceedings of the 7th ACM SIGPLAN Symposium on Principles and Practice of Parallel Programming*, ACM Press, Atlanta, GA, USA.

Matsuda, M., Ishikawa, Y., Kaneo, Y. & Edamoto, M. (2004). Overview of the GridMPI Version 1.0 (*in Japanese*), *Proceedings of Summer United Workshops on Parallel, Distributed and Cooperative Processing (SWoPP'04)*.

Mattson, T. & van der Wijngaart, R. (2010). RCCE: a Small Library for Many-Core Communication, *Technical report*, Intel Corporation. Users' Guide and API Manual.

Mattson, T., van der Wijngaart, R., Riepen, M., Lehnig, T., Brett, P., Haas, W., Kennedy, P., Howard, J., Vangal, S., Borkar, N., Ruhl, G. & Dighe, S. (2010). The 48-core SCC Processor: The Programmer's View, *Proceedings of the 2010 ACM/IEEE Conference on Supercomputing (SC10)*, New Orleans, LA, USA.

Message Passing Interface Forum (2009). *MPI: A Message-Passing Interface Standard – Version 2.2*, High-Performance Computing Center Stuttgart (HLRS).

Multicore Association (2011). *Multicore Communications API (MCAPI) Specification*, The Multicore Association.

Nagamalai, D., Lee, S.-H., Lee, W. G. & Lee, J.-K. (2005). SCTP over High Speed Wide Area Networks, *Proceedings of the 4th International Conference on Networking (ICN'05)*, Vol. 3420, Springer-Verlag, Reunion, France.

Pierce, P. (1988). The NX/2 Operating System, *Proceedings of the 3rd Conference on Hypercube Concurrent Computers and Applications*, ACM Press, Pasadena, CA, USA.

Pöppe, M., Schuch, S. & Bemmerl, T. (2003). A Message Passing Interface Library for Inhomogeneous Coupled Clusters, *Proceedings of the 17th International Parallel and Distributed Processing Symposium (IPDPS'03)*, IEEE CS Press, Nice, France.

Sivakumar, H., Bailey, S. & Grossman, R. L. (2000). PSockets: The Case for Application-level Network Striping for Data Intensive Applications using High Speed Wide Area Networks, *Proceedings of the High Performance Networking and Computing Conference (SC2000)*, ACM Press and IEEE CS Press, Dallas, TX, USA.

Skjellum, A. & Leung, A. (1990). Zipcode: a Portable Multicomputer Communication Library atop the Reactive Kernel, *Proceedings of the 5th Distributed Memory Concurrent Computing Conference*, IEEE CS Press, Charleston, SC, USA.

Stevens, R., Fenner, B. & Rudoff, A. (2006). *UNIX Network Programming – The Socket Networking API*, Vol. 1, third edn, Addison-Wesley.

Stewart, R., Xie, Q., Morneault, K., Sharp, C., Schwarzbauer, H., Taylor, T., Rytina, I., Kalla, M., Zhang, L. & Paxson, V. (2007). Stream Control Transmission Protocol, *Request for Comments (RFC) 4960*, Network Working Group.

Tanenbaum, A. (2008). *Modern Operating Systems*, third edn, Prentice-Hall.

Urena, I. A. C., Riepen, M. & Konow, M. (2011). RCKMPI - Lightweight MPI Implementation for Intel's Single-Chip Cloud Computer (SCC), *Proceedings of the 18th European MPI Users Group Meeting (EuroMPI 2011)*, Vol. 6960, Springer, Santorini, Greece.

Vajda, A. (2011). *Programming Many-Core Chips*, Springer.

Welzl, M. & Yousaf, M. (2005). Grid-Specific Network Enhancements: A Research Gap?, *International Workshop on Autonomic Grid Networking and Management (AGNM'05)*, IEEE CS Press, Spain.

Wilkinson, B. & Allen, M. (2005). *Parallel Programming: Techniques and Applications Using Networked Workstations and Parallel Computers*, second edn, Prentice-Hall.

Winer, D. (1999). *XML-RPC Specification*, UserLand, Inc.

Winett, J. M. (1971). The Definition of a Socket, *Request for Comments (RFC) 147*, Massachusetts Institute of Technology, USA.

Section 4

Grid Applications

9

Grid Computing in High Energy Physics Experiments

Dagmar Adamová[1] and Pablo Saiz[2]
[1]*Nuclear Physics Institute, Řež near Prague*
[2]*CERN*
[1]*Czech Republic*
[2]*Switzerland*

1. Introduction

The High Energy Physics (HEP) [1] – often called Particle Physics – is one of the research areas where the accomplishment of scientific results is inconceivable without the infrastructure for distributed computing, the Computing Grid. The HEP is a branch of Physics that studies properties of elementary subatomic constituents of matter. It goes beyond protons and neutrons to study particles which existed only a fraction of a second after the Big Bang and quarks and gluons in the so-called Quark Gluon Plasma (QGP) [2]. These studies are based on experiments with particles colliding at very high energies, at speeds almost equal to the speed of light.

The world's leading Particle Physics research laboratory is CERN [3], the European Center for Nuclear and Particle Physics near Geneva, Switzerland. The CERN latest particle accelerator (see Fig. 1), the Large Hadron Collider (LHC) [4], installed in a 27 km long tunnel located about 100 m underground and crossing the Swiss - French border, uses counter-rotating beams of protons or lead ions (Pb) to collide at 4 points, inside large particle detectors: ALICE [5], ATLAS [6], CMS [7] and LHCb [8]. There are also another two smaller experiments, TOTEM [9] and LHCf [10]. These are much smaller in size and are designed to focus on

Fig. 1. LHC@CERN

"forward particles". These are particles that just brush past each other as the beams collide, rather than meeting head-on.

The energy of the protons is currently 3.5 TeV (1 Tera eV= 1 million MeV) and that of the Pb ions is 1.38 TeV, so the collision energies are 7 TeV for the protons and 2.76 TeV for the Pb ions.

The phrase often used to summarize the mission of the LHC is, that with the LHC we are going back in time very close to the Big Bang, as close as about 10^{-10} seconds. In terms of length it represents about 10^{-16} cm (compared to the dimensions of the Universe of about 10^{28} cm). At this scale, the matter existed in a form of a "soup" made of the quarks and gluons, the Quark Gluon Plasma. The quarks are objects protons and neutrons are made of, so the LHC represents in a sense a huge extremely complicated microscope enabling the study of the most basic elements of matter.

There are several major questions which scientists hope to get answered with the help of the LHC.

- What is the origin of mass, why do elementary particles have some weight? And why do some particles have no mass at all? At present, we have no established answers to these questions. The theory offering a widely accepted explanation, the Standard Model [11], assumes the existence of a so-called Higgs boson, a key particle undiscovered so far, although it was first hypothesized in 1964. One of the basic tasks of the LHC is to bring an established statement concerning the existence of the Higgs boson.
- Where did all the anti-matter disappear? We are living in the World where everything is made of matter. We suppose that at the start of the Universe, equal amounts of matter and antimatter were produced in the Big Bang. But during the early stages of the Universe, an un-known deviation or in-equilibrium must have happened, resulting in the fact that in our world today hardly any antimatter is left.
- What are the basic properties of the Quark-Gluon Plasma, the state of the matter existing for a tiny period of time after the Big Bang? Originally, we thought it would behave like a plasma, but the latest scientific results including those delivered by the LHC suggest that it behaves like a perfect liquid [2], which is somewhat surprising for us.
- What is the universe made of? At the moment, the particles that we understand create only 4 % of the universe. The rest is believed to be made out of dark matter and dark energy. The LHC experiments will look for supersymmetric particles, which would confirm a likely hypothesis for the creation of dark matter.

From the experiments analyzing the data from the LHC collisions, ATLAS and CMS are the largest. They were nominally designed to look for the Higgs boson but in fact these are general purpose detectors for the study of all kinds of Physics phenomena at the LHC energy range. The ALICE detector is a dedicated heavy ions detector to study the properties of the Quark Gluon Plasma formed in the collisions of lead ions at the LHC energies. The LHCb is much smaller detector and its mission is to study the asymmetry between matter and antimatter. Although all these experiments are designed for Particle Physics research, the scientific programs they follow actually cross a border between Particle Physics, Astrophysics and Cosmology.

Now, where does the Computing Grid show up in this scientific set-up? The LHC is the world's largest particle accelerator. The protons and lead ions are injected into the accelerator in bunches, in counter-rotating beams. According to the original design proposal, there should be 2808 bunches per a beam. Each bunch of protons contains 10^{11} protons. the design beam energy is 7 TeV and the design luminosity is 10^{34} $cm^{-2}s^{-1}$. The bunch crossing rate is 40 MegaHz and the proton collisions rate $10^7 - 10^9$ Hz.

However, the new phenomena looked for by the scientists appear at a rate of 10^{-5} Hz. So the physicists must analyze 10^{13} collision events/sec to have a chance to discover a New Physics phenomenon. At present, the machine has not yet reached the full number of bunches per beam and is operating at half of the originally proposed energy, but the luminosity is getting rapidly to the goal value. The LHC team has been increasing the number of bunches gradually reaching 1380 bunches/beam at the time of writing. The full beam energy will be reached in 2014, after one year of a technical stop to arrange for this increase. The machine has already beaten some world records which we will mention in section 5. Let us just mention the one concerning the stored energy: at the end of 2010, the energy stored in the accelerator ring was about 28 MegaJoules (MJ). At the target full intensity, this energy will reach about 130 MJ which is an equivalent of 80 kg of TNT.

In any case, the volume of data necessary to analyze to discover New Physics was already in the original proposal estimated to be about 15 PetaBytes (PB, 1PB=1 million GB) per data taking year. The number of the processor cores, CPUs, needed to process this amount of data was estimated to be about 200 thousands. And here, the concept of a distributed data management infrastructure comes into the scenario, because there is no single computing center within the LHC community/collaboration to offer such massive computing resources, even not CERN. Therefore in 2002, the concept of the Worldwide LHC Computing Grid (WLCG) [12] was launched to build a distributed computing infrastructure to provide the production and analysis environments for the LHC experiments.

In the present chapter, we give a short overview of the Grid computing for the experiments at the LHC and the basics of the mission of the WLCG. Since we are members of the ALICE collaboration, we will also describe some specific features of the ALICE distributed computing environment.

In section 2, we will describe the architecture of the WLCG, which consist of an agreed set of services and applications running on the Grid infrastructures provided by the WLCG partners. In section 3, we will mention some of the middleware services provided by the WLCG which are used for the data access, processing, transfer and storage. Although WLCG depends on the underlying Internet - computer and communications networks, it is the special kind of software, so-called middleware, that enables the user to access computers distributed over the network. It is called "middleware" because it sits between the operating systems of the computers and the Physics applications that solve particular problems. In section 4, the Computing model of the ALICE experiment will be briefly described. It provides guide lines for the implementation and deployment of the ALICE software and computing infrastructure over the resources within the ALICE Grid and includes planning/estimates of the amount of needed computing resources. Section 5 will be devoted to the ALICE-specific Grid services and the ALICE Grid middleware AliEn. It is a set of tools and services which represents an implementation of the ALICE distributed computing environment integrated in the WLCG environment. In section 6, an overview will be given of the experience and performance of the WLCG project and also of the ALICE Grid project in particular during the real LHC data taking. The continuous operation of the LHC started in November 2009.

When the data started to flow from the detectors, the distributed data handling machinery was performing almost flawlessly as a result of many years of a gradual development, upgrades and stress-testing prior to the LHC startup. As a result of the astounding performance of WLCG, a significant number of people are doing analysis on the Grid, all the resources are being used up to the limits and the scientific papers are produced with an unprecedented speed within weeks after the data was recorded.

Section 7 contains a short summary and an outlook. This chapter is meant to be a short overview of the facts concerning the Grid computing for HEP experiments, in particular for the experiments at the CERN LHC. The first one and half a year of the LHC operations have shown that WLCG has built a true, well functioning distributed infrastructure and the LHC experiments have used it to rapidly deliver Physics results. The existing WLCG infrastructure has been and will be continuously developing into the future absorbing and giving rise to new technologies, like the advances in networking, storage systems, middleware services and inter-operability between Grids and Clouds.

2. WLCG

As mentioned in section 1, the LHC experiments are designed to search for rare events with the signal/noise ratio as low as 10^{-13}. This Physics requires a study of enormous number of pp and Pb-Pb collisions resulting in the production of data volumes of more than 10 PetaBytes per one data taking year. The original estimates elaborated when the LCG TDR [13] was put together were about $\sim$ 15 PetaBytes (PB) of new data each year which translates into $\sim$ 200 thousands of CPUs/processor cores and 45 PB of disk storage to keep the raw, processed and simulated data.

Nowadays, 200 thousands cores does not sound like much and one can find them in large computer centers. 50 PB of a disk storage is however not that common. In any case, at the time the LHC Computing Grid was launched there was no single site within the LHC community able to provide such computing power. So, the task of processing the LHC data has been a distributed computing problem right from the start.

2.1 WLCG mission

The Worldwide LHC Computing Grid (WLCG) project [13] was launched in 2002 to provide a global computing infrastructure to store, distribute and process the data annually generated by the LHC. It integrates thousands of computers and storage systems in hundreds of data centers worldwide, see Figure 2. CERN itself provides only about 20% of the resources needed to manage the LHC data. The rest is provided by the member states' national computing centers and research network structures supported by national funding agencies. The aim of the project is the "collaborative resource sharing" between all the scientists participating in the LHC experiments, which is the basic concept of a Computing Grid as defined in [14]. The infrastructure is managed and operated by a collaboration between the experiments and the participating computer centers to make use of the resources no matter where they are located.

The collaboration is truly worldwide: it involves 35 countries on 5 continents and represents 49 funding agencies having signed the WLCG Memorandum of Understanding on Computing (WLCG MoUC) [15]. The distributed character has also a sociological aspect: even if the contribution of the countries depends on their capabilities, a member of any institution involved can access and analyze the LHC data from his/her institute.

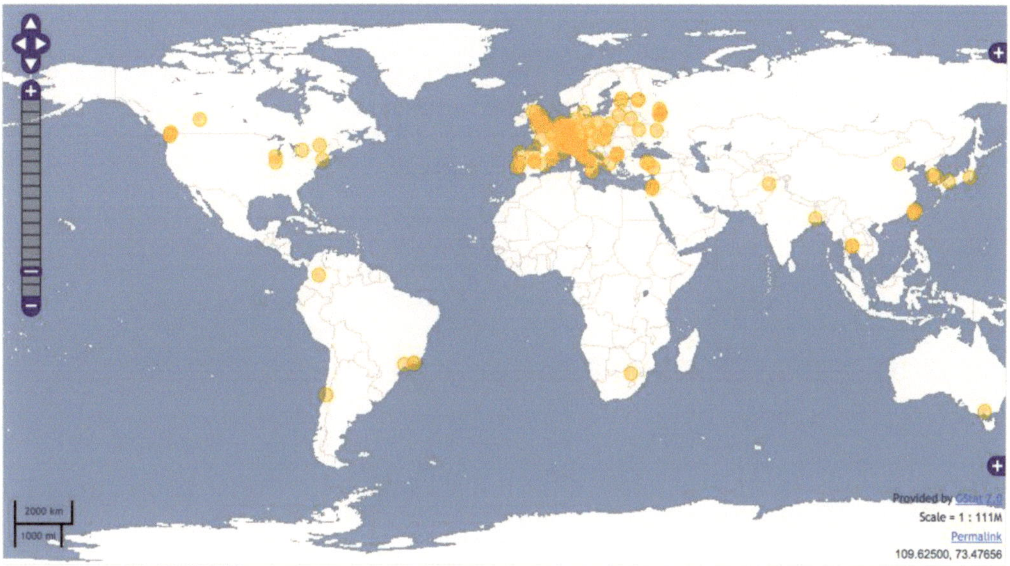

Fig. 2. Distribution of WLCG computing centers

Currently, the WLCG integrates over 140 computing sites, more than 250 thousands CPU cores and over 150 PB of disk storage. It is now the world's largest computing grid: the WLCG operates resources provided by other collaborating grid projects: either the two main global grids, EGI [16] and OSG [17], or by several regional or national grids.

2.2 Hierarchical (Tier) structure, the roles of different Tier-sites

The WLCG has a hierarchical structure based on the recommendations of the MONARC project [18], see Figure 3. The individual participating sites are classified according to their resources and level of provided services into several categories called Tiers. There is one Tier-0 site which is CERN, then 11 Tier-1 centers, which are large computing centers with thousands of CPUs, PBs of disk storage, tape storage systems and 24/7 Grid support service (Canada: TRIUMF, France: IN2P3, Germany: KIT/FZK, Italy: INFN, Netherlands: NIKHEF/SARA, Nordic countries: Nordic Datagrid Facility (NDGF), Spain: Port d'Informació Científica (PIC), Taipei: ASGC, United Kingdom: GridPP, USA: Fermilab-CMS and BNL ATLAS). Then there are currently about 140 Tier-2 sites covering most of the globe. The system also recognizes Tier-3 centers, which are small local computing clusters at universities or research institutes.

The raw data recorded by the LHC experiments (raw data) is shipped at first to the CERN Computing Center (CC) through dedicated links. CERN Tier-0 accepts data at average of 2.6 GBytes(GB)/s with peaks up to 11 GB/s. At CERN, the data is archived in the CERN tape system CASTOR [19] and goes through the first level of processing - the first pass of reconstruction. The raw data is also replicated to the Tier-1 centers, so there are always 2 copies of the raw data files. CERN serves data at average of 7 GB/s with peaks up to 25 GB/s [20]. The Tier-0 writes on average 2 PB of data per month to tape in pp running, and double that in the 1 month of Pb-Pb collisions, (cf. Figures 4,5). At Tier-1 centers, the raw data replicas are permanently stored as mentioned before and several passes of the data re-processing are performed. This multiple-stage data re-processing is performed using methods to detect

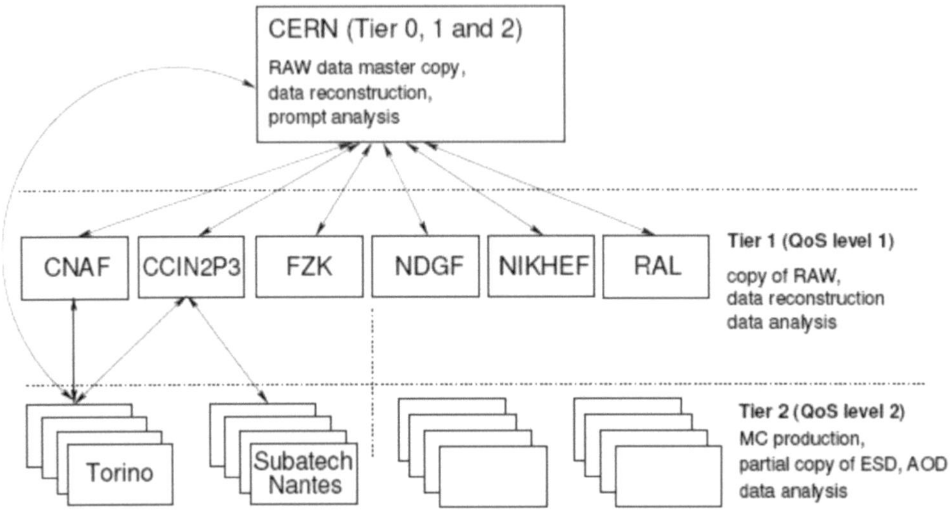

Fig. 3. Schema of the hierarchical Tier-like structure of WLCG

interesting events through the processing algorithms, as well as improvements in detector calibration, which are in continuous evolution and development. Also, the scheduled analysis productions as well as some of the end user analysis jobs are performed at Tier-1s.

Tier-2 centers (more than 130 in the WLCG, integrated within 68 Tier-2 federations) are supposed to process simulation (Monte Carlo simulations of the collision events in the LHC detectors) and end-user analysis jobs. The load of simulations needed to correctly interpret the LHC data is quite sizeable, close to the raw data volume. The number of end users regularly using the WLCG infrastructure to perform analysis is larger than expected in the beginning of the LCG project, it varies from about 250 to 800 people depending on the experiment. This is certainly also a result of the experiments' effort to hide the complexity of the Grid from the users and make the usage as simple as possible. Tier-2 sites deliver more than 50% of the total CPU power within the WLCG, see Figure 6.

2.3 Network

The sustainable operation of the data storing and processing machinery would not be possible without a reliable network infrastructure. In the beginning of the WLCG project there were worries that the infrastructure would not be able to transfer the data fast enough. The original estimates of the needed rate were about 1.3 GB/s from CERN to external Tiers. After the years spent with building the backbone of the WLCG network, CERN is able to reach rates about 5 GB/s to Tier-1s, see Figure 7. The WLCG networking relies on the Optical Private Network (OPN) backbone [21], see Figure 8, which is composed of dedicated connections between CERN Tier-0 and each of the Tier1s, with the capacity of 10 Gbit/s each. The original connections proliferated into duplicates or backroutes making the system considerably reliable. The OPN is then interconnected with national network infrastructures like the GEANT [22] in Europe or the US-LHCNet [23] and all the National Research and Education Networks (NRENs) in other countries.

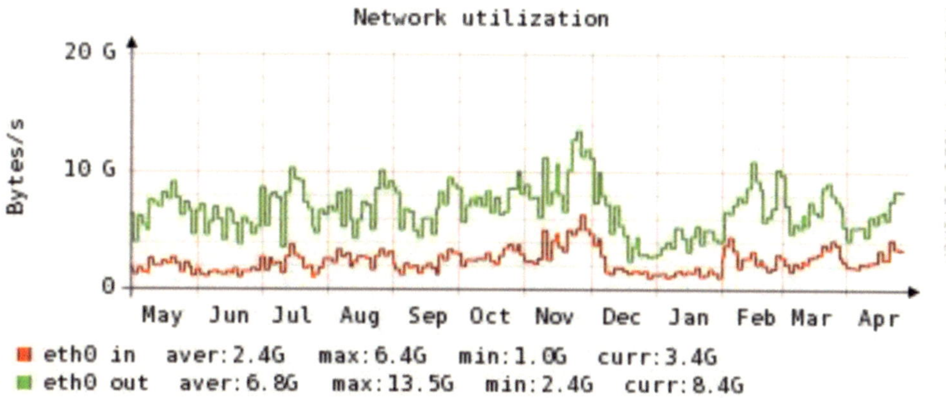

Fig. 4. CERN Tier-0 Disk Servers (GB/s), 2010/2011

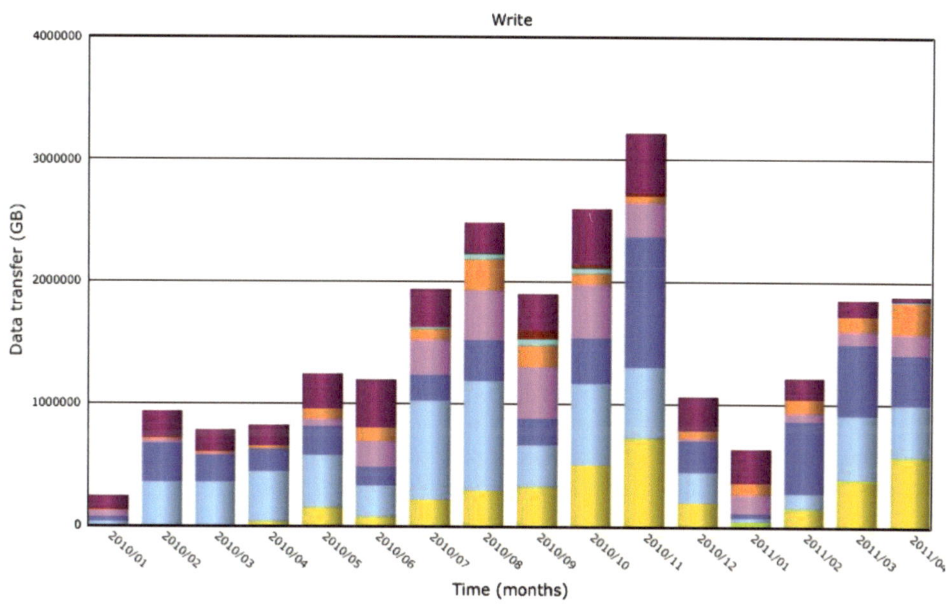

Fig. 5. Data written to tape at the CERN Tier-0 (GB/month)

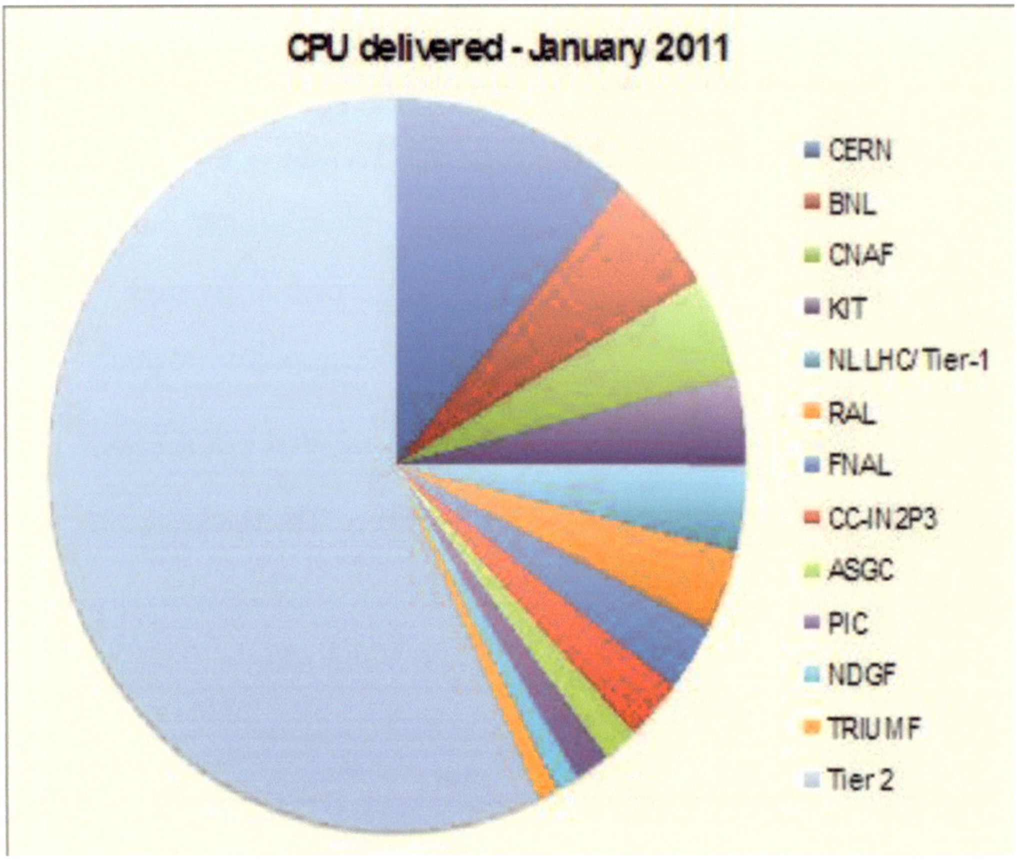

Fig. 6. CPU resources in WLCG, January 2011. More than 50% was delivered by Tier-2s.

There exists a concept of so-called LHCONE [24], which should enable a good connectivity of Tier-2s and Tier-3s to the Tier-1s without overloading the general purpose network links. It will extend and complete the existing OPN infrastructure to increase the interoperability of all the WLCG sites.

2.4 Data and Service challenges

As we will describe in section 6, the WLCG data management worked flawlessly when the real data started to flow from the detectors in the end of 2009. This was not just a happy coincidence. There were over 6 years of continuous testing of the infrastructure performance. There was a number of independent experiments' so-called Data Challenges which started in 2004, when the "artificial raw" data was generated in the Monte Carlo productions and then processed and managed as if it was the real raw data. Moreover, there was a series of WLCG Service Challenges also starting in 2004, with the aim to demonstrate WLCG services aspects: data management, scaling of job workloads, security incidents, interoperability, support processes and all was topped with data transfers exercise lasting for weeks. The last test was the Service Challenge STEP'09 including all experiments and testing full computing models. Also, the cosmic data taking which started in 2008 has checked the performance of the data processing chain on a smaller scale.

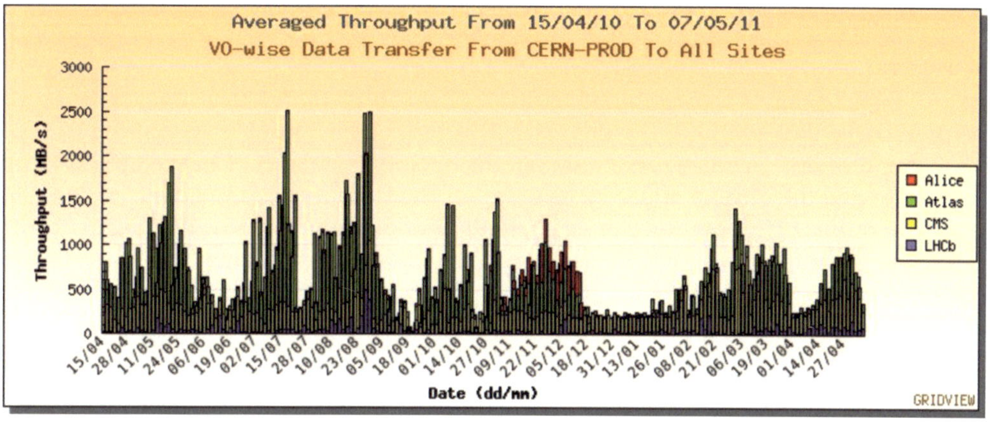

Fig. 7. CPU resources in WLCG, January 2011. More than 50% was delivered by Tier-2s.

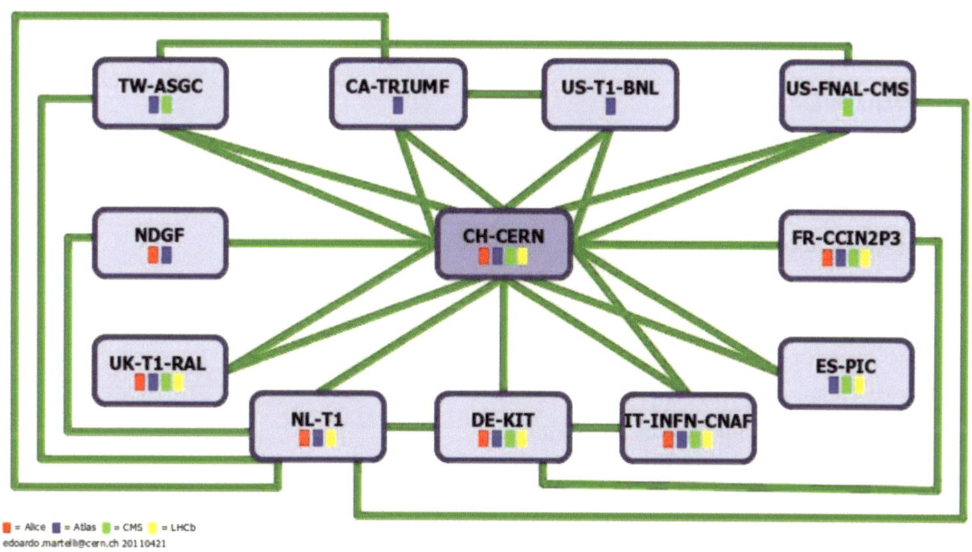

Fig. 8. LHCOPN

Currently, whether the data taking is going on or not, the network, especially the OPN, and the sites are under continuous checking: there are automatically generated test jobs periodically sent over the infrastructure to test the availability and functioning of the network and on-site services.

2.5 Concluding remarks

The WLCG integrates and operates resources distributed all over the world and its task is to make all these resources accessible and usable for the LHC experiments to distribute, archive and process the data produced by the LHC. This task is done using a specialized software called "middleware" because it sits between the operating systems of the computers at the WLCG sites and the Physics applications software used for the reconstruction, analysis and simulation of the LHC data (or any other application software layer). The middleware is a collection of protocols, agents and programs/services which we describe in the following section.

3. Middleware

As we already mentioned, the Worldwide LHC Computing Grid is a distributed computing infrastructure that spans over five continents managing resources distributed across the world (due to funding, operability and access reasons). The resources operated by the WLCG belong either to the two main global grids, EGI [16] and OSG [17], or to other collaborating regional or national grids. To make this diverse variety of resources globally available for all the WLCG users, the WLCG has been developing its own middleware, a software layer that "brings all the resources together": a collection of programs, services and protocols to manage and operate the entire WLCG infrastructure (see Figure 9).

3.1 Overview of Grid services

The WLCG middleware is a complex suite of packages which includes (see also Figure 10):

- Data Management Services:
  - Storage Element
  - File Catalogue Service
  - Grid file access tools
  - File Transfer Service
  - GridFTP service
  - Database and DB Replication Services
  - POOL Object Persistency Service
- Security Services:
  - Certificate Management Service
  - Virtual Organization [25] Management Registration Service (VOMRS)
  - Authentication and Authorization Service (the X509 infrastructure)
- Job Management Services:
  - Compute Element
  - Workload Management

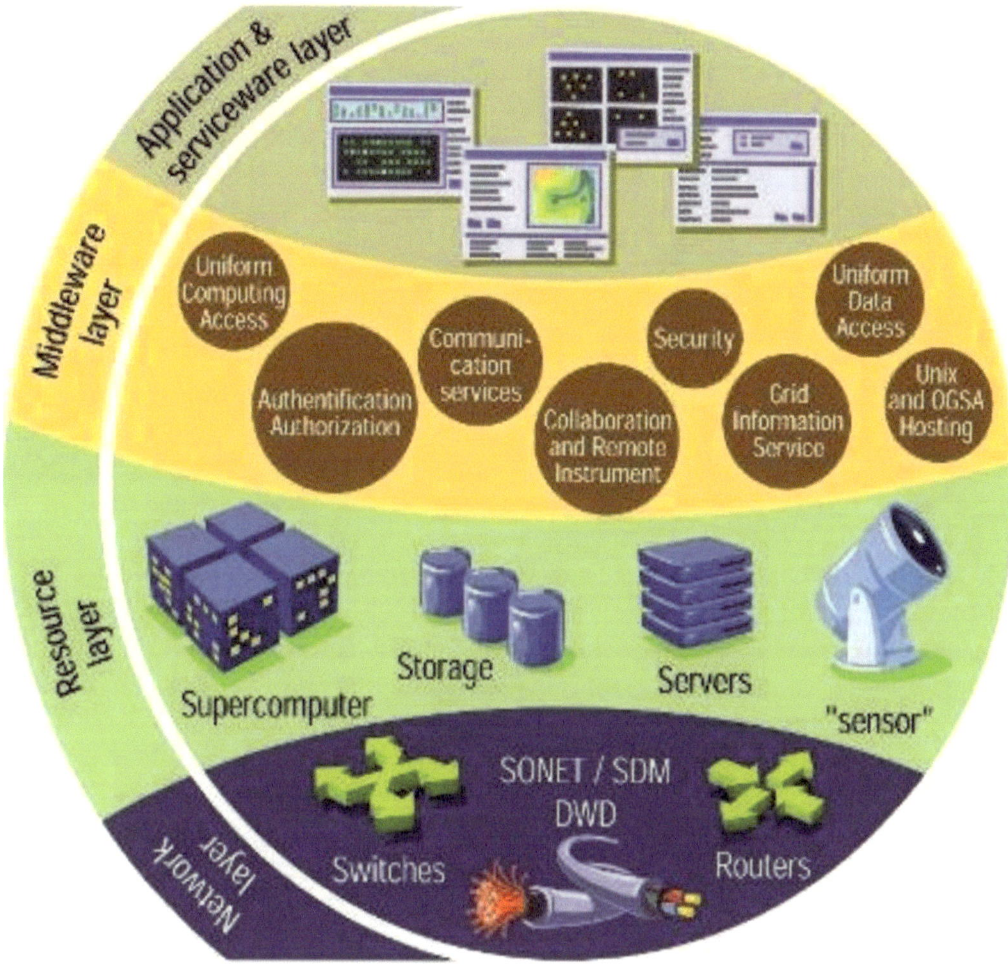

Fig. 9. Grid Layers

- Service VO Agent Service
- Application Software Install Service

- Information Services:
  - Accounting Service
  - Site Availability Monitor
  - Monitoring tools: experiment dashboards; site monitoring

The WLCG middleware has been built and further developed using and developing some packages produced by other projects including, e.g.:

- EMI (European Middleware Initiative) [26], combining the key middleware providers of ARC, gLite, UNICORE and dCache

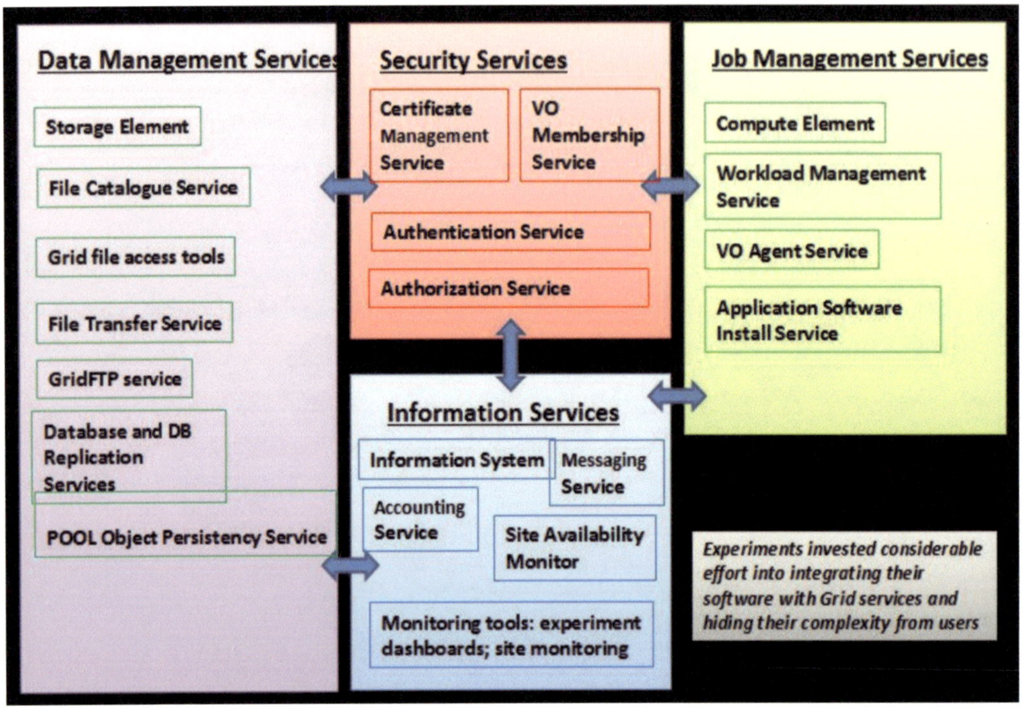

Fig. 10. Schema of Grid services

- Globus Toolkit [27] developed by the Globus Alliance
- OMII from the Open Middleware Infrastructure Institute [28]
- Virtual Data Toolkit [29]

3.2 Experiments' specific developments

All the LHC experiments created their own specific Computing models summarized in the individual Computing Technical Design Reports (TDRs). They do not rely only on the WLCG-provided middleware packages but are also developing some specific components tailored to better comply with their Computing models.

For example, the ALICE experiment has developed a grid middleware suite AliEn (AliCE Environment [30]), which provides a single interface for a transparent access to computing resources for the ALICE community. AliEn consists of a collection of components and services which will be described in the next section. AliEn, together with selected packages of the WLCG-provided middleware, gives a complete framework to the ALICE community to manage and process the data produced by the LHC according to the ALICE Computing model.

All the LHC experiments invested a considerable effort into shielding the users from the underlying complexity of the Grid machinery, trying to provide relatively simple entry points into the Grid. This effort has payed off and is reflected in a considerable number of physicists actually using the WLCG for their analysis.

3.3 Selected WLCG-provided services

In the following section, we will describe as an example the Computing model of the ALICE experiment. The WLCG services used in this model include the Computing Element (CE), the Storage Element (SE) and the VOBOX.

3.3.1 Computing Element

The Computing Element (CE) [31] is a middleware component/grid service providing an entry point to a grid site. It authenticates users and submits jobs to Worker Nodes (WN), aggregates and publishes information from the nodes. It includes a generic interface to the local cluster called Grid Gate (GG), Local Resource Management System (LRMS) and the collection of Worker Nodes.

Originally, the submission of jobs to CEs was performed by the Workload Management System (WMS) [32], a middleware component/grid service, that also monitors jobs status and retrieves their output. WLCG (gLite) CE is a computing resource access service using standard grid protocols. To improve the performance, the CREAM (Computing Resource Execution And Management) Computing Element [33] has replaced the gLite-CE in production since about 2009. It is a simple, lightweight service for job management operation at the Computing Element level. CREAM-CE accepts job submission requests (described with the same files as used for the Workload Management System) and other job management requests like, e.g., job monitoring. CREAM-CE can be used by a generic client, e.g., an end-user willing to directly submit jobs to a CREAM-CE, without the WMS component.

3.3.2 Storage Element (XRootD)

The Storage Element (SE) [34] provides storage place and access for data. Important variables apart from available storage space, read/write speeds and bandwidth concern reliability against overload, percentage of failed transfers from/to SE and percentage of lost/corrupted files.

WLCG (gLite) provides dCache [35] and DPM [36] storage management tools used by the LHC experiments. However within the ALICE infrastructure, the preferred storage manager is the Scalla/XRootD package [37] developed within a SLAC [38] - CERN collaboration (originally, it was a common project of SLAC and INFN [39]). After CERN got involved, the XRootD was bundled in ROOT [40] as a generic platform for distributed data access, very well suited for the LHC data analysis.

The primary goal has been the creation of data repositories with no reasonable size limit, with high data access performance and linear scaling capabilities. The framework is a fully generic suite for fast, low latency and scalable data access, which can serve any kind of data, organized as a hierarchical filesystem-like namespace, based on the concept of directory.

"xrootd" is just the name of the data access daemon. Although fundamental, it is just a part of the whole suite. The complete suite is called Scalla/XRootD, Scalla meaning Structured Cluster Architecture for Low Latency Access.

The manager exhibits important features including:

- High speed access to experimental data

- High transaction rate with rapid request dispersement (fast open, low latency)
- Write once read many times processing mode
- Fault tolerance (if servers go, the clients do not die)
- Fault tolerance (able to manage in realtime distributed replicas)
- Integrated in ROOT

From the site administrator point, the following features are important:

- No database requirements (no backup/recovery issues, high performance)
- Resources gentle, high efficiency data server (low CPU/byte overhead, small memory footprint)
- Simple installation
- Configuration requirements scale linearly with site complexity
- No 3rd party software needed (avoids messy dependencies)
- Low administration costs
- Self-organizing servers remove need for configuration changes in big clusters

Additional features:

- Generic Mass Storage System Interface (HPSS, CASTOR, etc)
- Full POSIX access
- Server clustering for scalability, supports large number of clients from a small number of servers
- Up to 262000 servers per cluster
- High WAN data access efficiency (exploit the throughput of modern WANs for direct data access, and for copying files as well)

3.3.3 VOMS

VOMS [41] stands for Virtual Organization Management Service and is one of the most commonly used Grid technologies needed to provide user access to Grid resources. It works with users that have valid Grid certificates and represents a set of tools to assist authorization of users based on their affiliation. It serves as a central repository for user authorization information, providing support for sorting users into a general group hierarchy - users are grouped as members of Virtual Organizations (VOs). It also keeps track of users' roles and provides interfaces for administrators to manage the users. It was originally developed for the EU DataGrid project.

3.3.4 VOBOX

The VOBOX [42] is a standard WLCG service developed in 2006 in order to provide the LHC experiments with a place where they can run their own specific agents and services. In addition, it provides the file system access to the experiment software area. This area is shared between VOBOX and the Worker Nodes at the given site. In the case of ALICE, the VOBOX is installed at the WLCG sites on dedicated machines and its installation is mandatory for sites to enter the grid production (it is an "entry door" for a site to the WLCG environment). The access to the VOBOX is restricted to the Software Group Manager (SGM) of the given Virtual Organization. Since 2008, this WLCG service has been VOMS-aware [42]. In the following section, we will describe the services running on the VOBOX machines reserved at a site for the ALICE computing.

4. ALICE computing model

In this section, we will briefly describe the computing model of the ALICE experiment [43].

ALICE (A Large Ion Collider Experiment) [5] is a dedicated heavy-ion (HI) experiment at the CERN LHC which apart from the HI mission has also its proton-proton (pp) Physics program. Together with the other LHC experiments, ALICE has been successfully taking and processing pp and HI data since the LHC startup in November 2009. During the pp running, the data taking rate has been up to 500 MB/s while during the HI running the data was taken with the rate up to 2.5 GB/s. As was already mentioned, during 2010 the total volume of data taken by all the LHC experiments reached 15 PB, which corresponds to 7 months of the pp running and 1 month of the HI running (together with 4 months of an LHC technical stop for maintenance and upgrades this makes up for one standard data taking year (SDTY)).

The computing model of ALICE relies on the ALICE Computing Grid, the distributed computing infrastructure based on the hierarchical Tier structure as described in section 2. ALICE has developed over the last 10 years a distributed computing environment and its implementation: the Grid middleware suite AliEn (AliCE Environment) [30], which is integrated in the WLCG environment. It provides a transparent access to computing resources for the ALICE community and will be described in the next section.

4.1 Raw data taking, transfer and registration

The ALICE detector consists of 18 subdetectors that interact with 5 online systems [5]. During data taking, the data is read out by the Data Acquisition (DAQ) system as raw data streams produced by the subdetectors, and is moved and stored over several media. On this way, the raw data is formatted, the events (data sets containing information about individual pp or Pb-Pb collisions) are built, the data is objectified in the ROOT [40] format and then recorded on a local disk. During the intervals of continuous data taking called runs, different types of data sets can be collected of which the so-called PHYSICS runs are those substantial for Physics analysis. There are also all kinds of calibration and other subdetectors' testing runs important for the reliable subsystems operation.

ALICE experimental area (called Point2 (P2)) serves as an intermediate storage: the final destination of the collected raw data is the CERN Advanced STORage system (CASTOR) [19], the permanent data storage (PDS) at the CERN Computing center. From Point2, the raw data is transferred to the disk buffer adjacent to CASTOR at CERN (see Figure 11). As mentioned before, the transfer rates are up to 500 MB/s for the pp and up to 2.5 GB/s for the HI data taking periods.

After the migration to the CERN Tier-0, the raw data is registered in the AliEn catalogue [30] and the data from PHYSICS runs is automatically queued for the Pass1 of reconstruction, the first part of the data processing chain, which is performed at the CERN Tier-0. In parallel with the reconstruction, the data from PHYSICS runs is also automatically queued for the

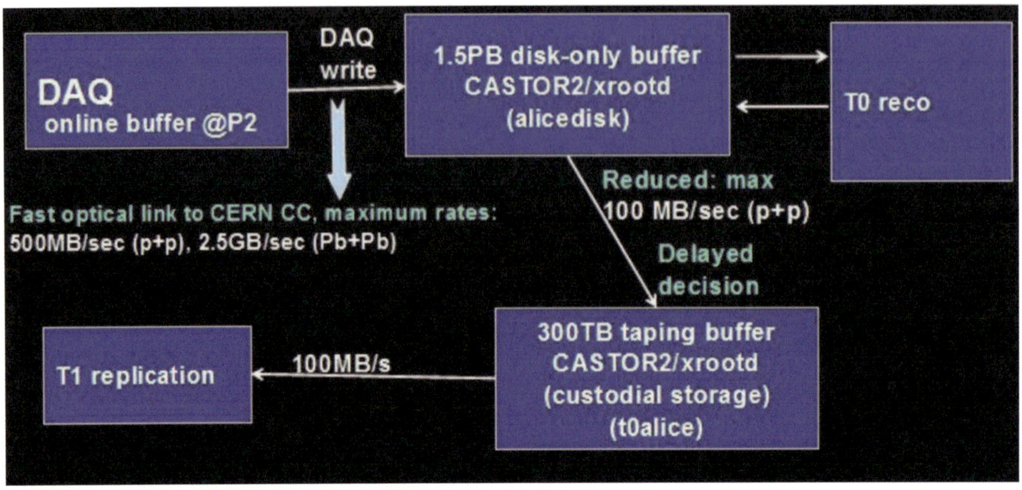

Fig. 11. Data processing chain. Data rates and buffer sizes are being gradually increased.

replication to external Tier-1s (see Figure 11). It may happen that the replication is launched and finished fast and the data goes through the first processing at a Tier-1.

The mentioned automated processes are a part of a complex set of services deployed over the ALICE Computing Grid infrastructure. All the involved services are continuously controlled by automatic procedures, reducing to a minimum the human interaction. The Grid monitoring environment adopted and developed by ALICE, the Java-based MonALISA (MONitoring Agents using Large Integrated Services Architecture) [44], uses decision-taking automated agents for management and control of the Grid services. For monitoring of raw data reconstruction passes see [45].

The automatic reconstruction is typically completed within a couple of hours after the end of the run. The output files from the reconstruction are registered in AliEn and are available on the Grid (stored and accessible within the ALICE distributed storage pool) for further processing.

4.2 AliRoot

AliRoot [46] is the ALICE software framework for reconstruction, simulation and analysis of the data. It has been under a steady development since 1998. Typical use cases include detector description, events generation, particle transport, generation of "summable digits", event merging, reconstruction, particle identification and all kinds of analysis tasks. AliRoot uses the ROOT [40] system as a foundation on which the framework is built. The Geant3 [47] or FLUKA [48] packages perform the transport of particles through the detector and simulate the energy deposition from which the detector response can be simulated. Except for large existing libraries, such as Pythia6 [49] and HIJING [50], and some remaining legacy code, this framework is based on the Object Oriented programming paradigm and is written in C++.

AliRoot is constituted by a large amount of files, sources, binaries, data and related documentation. Clear and efficient management guidelines are vital if this corpus of software should serve its purpose along the lifetime of the ALICE experiment. The corresponding policies are described in [51]. For understanding and improvement of the

AliRoot performance, as well as for understanding the behavior of the ALICE detectors, the fast feedback given by the offline reconstruction is essential.

4.3 Multiple reconstruction

In general, the ALICE computing model for the pp data taking is similar to that of the other LHC experiments. Data is automatically recorded and then reconstructed quasi online at the CERN Tier-0 facility. In parallel, data is exported to the different external Tier-1s, to provide two copies of the raw data, one stored at the CERN CASTOR and another copy shared by all the external Tier-1s.

For HI (Pb-Pb) data taking this model is not viable, as data is recorded at up to 2.5 GB/s. Such a massive data stream would require a prohibitive amount of resources for quasi real-time processing. The computing model therefore requires that the HI data reconstruction at the CERN Tier-0 and its replication to the Tier-1s be delayed and scheduled for the period of four months of the LHC technical stop and only a small part of the raw data (10-15%) be reconstructed for the quality checking. In reality, comparatively large part of the HI data (about 80%) got reconstructed and replicated in 2010 before the end of the data taking due to occasional lapses in the LHC operations and much higher quality of the network infrastructure than originally envisaged.

After the first pass of the reconstruction, the data is usually reconstructed subsequently more times (up to 6-7 times) for better results at Tier-1s or Tier-2s . Each pass of the reconstruction triggers a cascade of additional tasks organized centrally like Quality Assurance (QA) processing trains and a series of different kinds of analysis trains described later. Also, each reconstruction pass triggers a series of the Monte Carlo simulation productions. All this complex of tasks for a given reconstruction pass is launched automatically as mentioned before.

4.4 Analysis

The next step in the data processing chain is then the analysis. There are two types of analysis: a scheduled analysis organized centrally and then the end-user, so-called chaotic analysis. Since processing of the end-user analysis jobs often brings some problems like a high memory consumption (see Figure 12) or unstable code, the scheduled analysis is organized in the form of so-called analysis trains (see [52]). The trains absorb up to 30 different analysis tasks running in succession with one data set read and with a very well controlled environment. This helps to consolidate the end-user analysis.

The computing model assumes that the scheduled analysis will be performed at Tier-1 sites, while the chaotic analysis and simulation jobs will be performed at Tier-2s. The experience gained during the numerous Data Challenges, the excellent network performance, the stable and mature Grid middleware deployed over all sites and the conditions at the time of the real data taking in 2010/2011 progressively replaced the original hierarchical scenario by a more "symmetric" model often referred to as the "cloud model".

4.5 Simulations

As already mentioned, ever since the start of building the ALICE distributed computing infrastructure, the system was tested and validated with increasingly massive productions

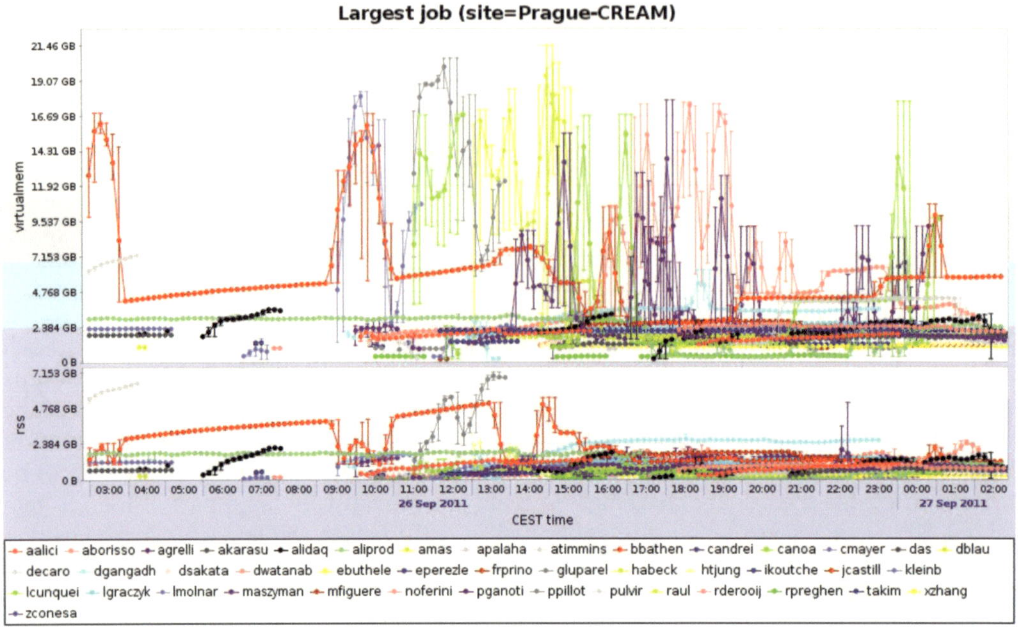

Fig. 12. End-user analysis memory consumption: peaks in excess of 20 GB

of Monte Carlo (MC) simulated events of the LHC collisions in the ALICE detector. The simulation framework [53] covers the simulation of primary collisions and generation of the emerging particles, the transport of particles through the detector, the simulation of energy depositions (hits) in the detector components, their response in form of so-called summable digits, the generation of digits from summable digits with the optional merging of underlying events and the creation of raw data. Each raw data production cycle triggers a series of corresponding MC productions (see [54]). As a result, the volume of data produced during the MC cycles is usually in excess of the volume of the corresponding raw data.

4.6 Data types

To complete the description of the ALICE data processing chain, we will mention the different types of data files produced at different stages of the chain (see Figure 13).

As was already mentioned, the data is delivered by the Data Acquisition system in a form of raw data in the ROOT format. The reconstruction produces the so-called Event Summary Data (ESD), the primary container after the reconstruction. The ESDs contain information like run and event numbers, trigger class, primary vertex, arrays of tracks/vertices, detector conditions. In an ideal situation following the computing model, the EODs should be of 10% size of the corresponding raw data files.

The subsequent data processing provides so-called Analysis Object Data (AOD), the secondary processing product, which are data objects containing more skimmed information needed for final analysis. According to the Computing model, the size of AODs should be 2% of the raw data file size. Since it is difficult to squeeze all the information needed for the Physics results in such small data containers, this limit was not yet fully achieved.

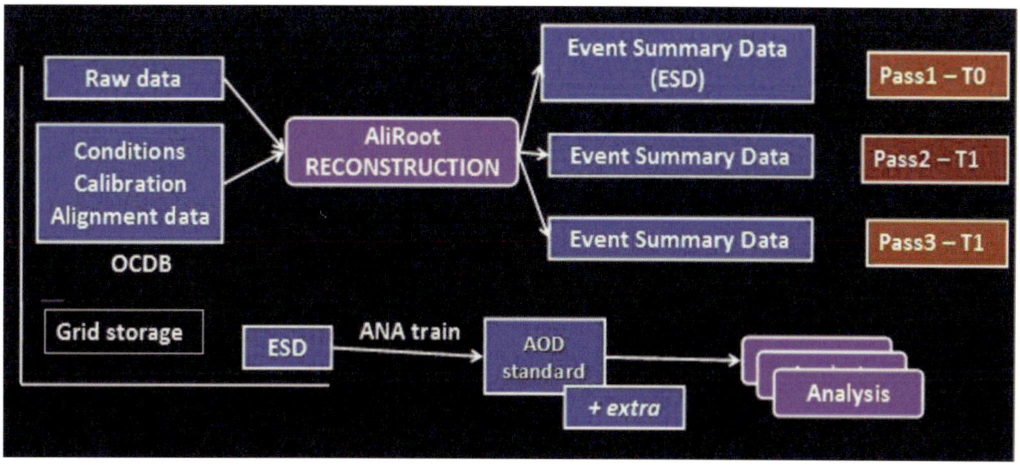

Fig. 13. Data types produced in the processing chain

4.7 Resources

The ALICE distributed computing infrastructure has evolved from a set of about 20 computing sites into a global world-wide system of distributed resources for data storage and processing. As of today, this project is made of over 80 sites spanning 5 continents (Africa, Asia, Europe, North and South America), involving 6 Tier-1 centers and more than 70 Tier-2 centers [55], see also Figure 14. Altogether, the resources provided by the ALICE

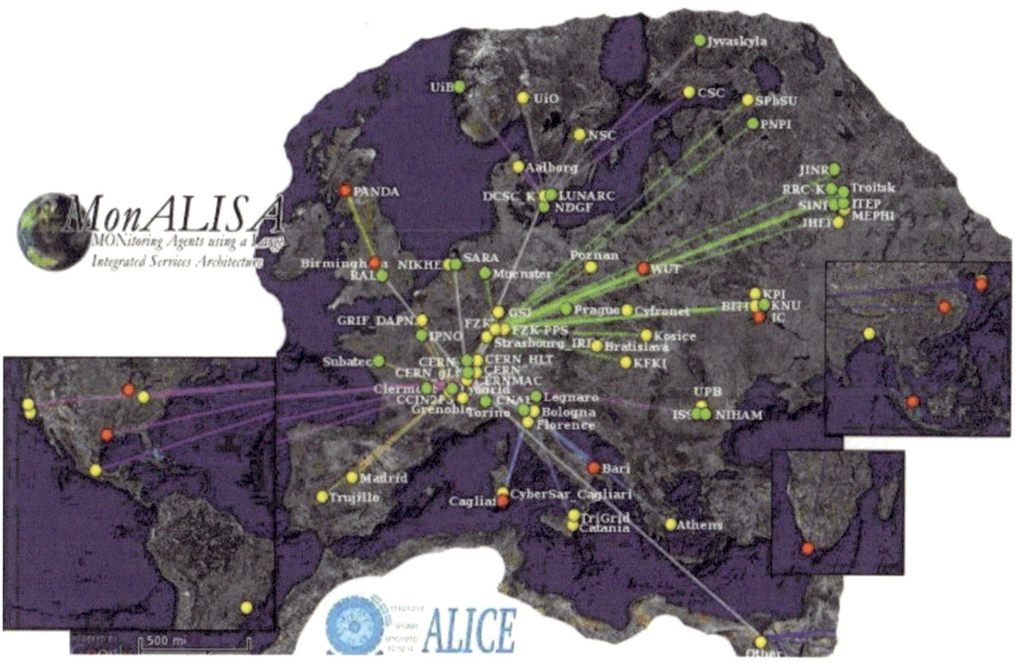

Fig. 14. ALICE sites

sites represent in excess of 20 thousands of CPUs, 12 PB of distributed disk storage and 30 PB of distributed tape storage, and the gradual upscale of this capacity is ongoing. Similar to other LHC experiments, about half of the CPU and disk resources is provided by the Tier-2 centers. For the year 2012, ALICE plans/requirements for computing resources within WLCG represent 211.7 of kHEP-SPEC06 CPU capacity, 38.8 PB of disk storage and 36.6 PB of tapes [56].

4.8 Concluding remarks

The concept of the ALICE computing model was officially proposed in 2005. Since then, it has been used for massive Monte Carlo event productions, for end-user analysis and for the raw data management and processing. The strategy has been validated under heavy load during a series of Data Challenges and during the real data taking in 2010/2011. The model provides the required Grid functionality via a combination of the common Grid services offered on the WLCG resources and the ALICE-specific services from AliEn. Today's computing environments are anything but static. Fast development in Information Technologies, commodity hardware (hardware being constantly replaced and operating systems upgraded), Grid software and networking technologies inevitably boosted also further development of the ALICE computing model. One of the main effects is a transformation of the model from the strictly hierarchical Tier-like structure to a more loose scenario, a "cloud-like" solution.

5. AliEn

AliEn [30] is a set of middleware tools and services which represents an implementation of the ALICE distributed computing environment integrated in the WLCG environment. AliEn has been under a constant development by ALICE since 2001 and was deployed over the ALICE Grid infrastructure right from the start. One of the important features is the set of interfaces to other Grid implementations like gLite [57], ARC [58] and OSG [17].

AliEn was initially developed as a distributed production environment for the simulation, reconstruction, and analysis of Physics data. Since it was put in the production in 2001, ALICE has been using AliEn before the start of the real data taking for distributed production cycles of Monte-Carlo simulated raw data, including subsequent reconstruction and analysis, during the regular Physics Data Challenges. Since 2005, AliEn has been used also for end-user analysis. Since December 2007, when the ALICE detector started operation taking cosmic data, AliEn has been used also for management of the raw data. Since the LHC startup in 2009, millions of jobs have been successfully processed using the AliEn services and tools.

AliEn developers provided the users with a client/interface - "alien shell" [59] and a set of plugins designed for the end users' job submission and handling. These tools together with the tools provided by the ALICE Grid monitoring framework MonALISA [44], hide the complexity and heterogenity of the underlying Grid services from the end-user while facing the rapid development of the Grid technologies.

AliEn is a lightweight Open Source Grid framework built around Open Source components using the combination of standard network protocols, a Web Service and Distributed Agent Model. The basic AliEn components include:

- AliEn File Catalogue with metadata capabilities
- Data management tools for data transfers and storage

- Authentication, authorization and auditing services
- Job execution model
- Storage and computing elements
- Information services
- Site services
- Command line interface - the AliEn shell aliensh
- ROOT interface
- Grid and job monitoring
- Interfaces to other Grids

AliEn was primarily developed by ALICE, however it was adopted also by a couple of other Virtual Organizations like PANDA [60] and CBM [61].

5.1 File Catalogue (FC)

The File Catalogue is one of the key components of the AliEn suite. It provides a hierarchical structure (like a UNIX File system) and is designed to allow each directory node in the hierarchy to be supported by different database engines, running on different hosts. This building on top of several databases allows to add another database to expand the catalogue namespace and assures scalability of the system and allow growth of the catalogue as the files accumulate over the years.

Unlike real file systems, the FC does not own the files; it is a metadata catalogue on the Logical File Names (LFN) and only keeps an association/mapping between the LFNs and (possibly multiple) Physical File Names (PFN) of real files on a storage system. PFNs describe the physical location of the files and include the access protocol (rfio, xrootd), the name of the AliEn Storage Element and the path to the local file. The system supports file replication and caching.

The FC provides also a mapping between the LFNs and Globally Unique Identifiers (GUID). The labeling of each file with the GUID allows for the asynchronous caching. The write-once strategy combined with GUID labeling guarantees the identity of files with the same GUID label in different caches. It is possible to automatically construct PFNs : to store only the GUID and Storage Index and the Storage Element builds the PFN from the GUID. There are two independent catalogues: LFN->GUID and GUID->PFN. A schema of the AliEn FC is shown in Figure 15.

The FC can also associate metadata to the LFNs. This metadata is a collection of user-defined key value pairs. For instance, in the case of ALICE, the current metadata is the software version used to generate the files, number of events inside a file, or calibration files used during the reconstruction.

5.2 Job execution model

AliEn's Job execution model is based on the pull architecture. There is a set of central components (Task Queue, Job Optimizer, Job Broker) and another set of site components (Computing Element (CE), Cluster Monitor, MonALISA, Package Manager). The pull

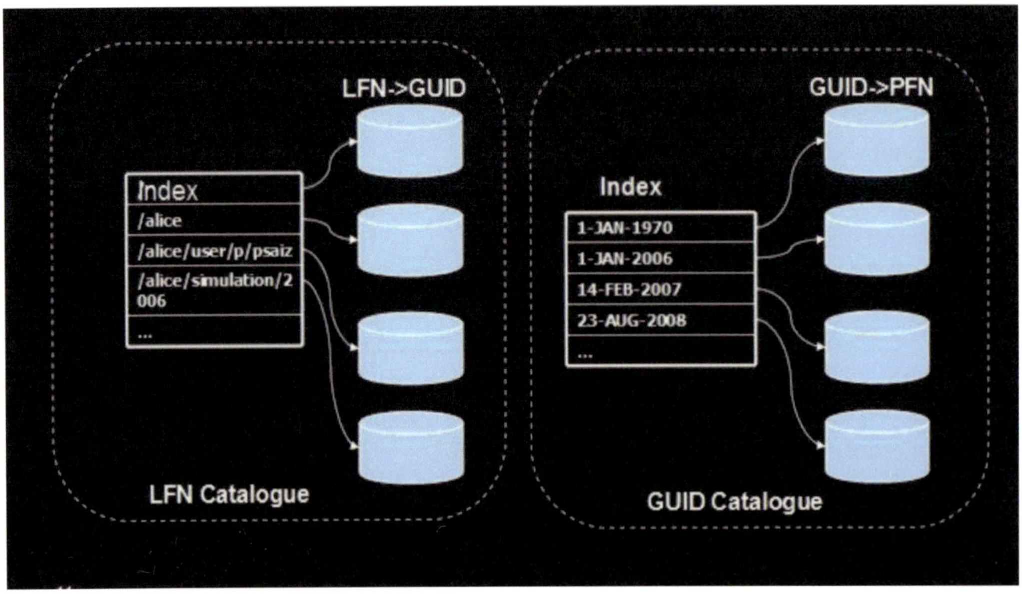

Fig. 15. AliEn File Catalogue

architecture has one major advantage with respect to the push one: the system does not have to know the actual status of all resources, which is crucial for large flexible Grids. In a push architecture, the distribution of jobs requires to keep and analyze a huge amount of status data just to assign a job, which becomes difficult in the expanding grid environment.

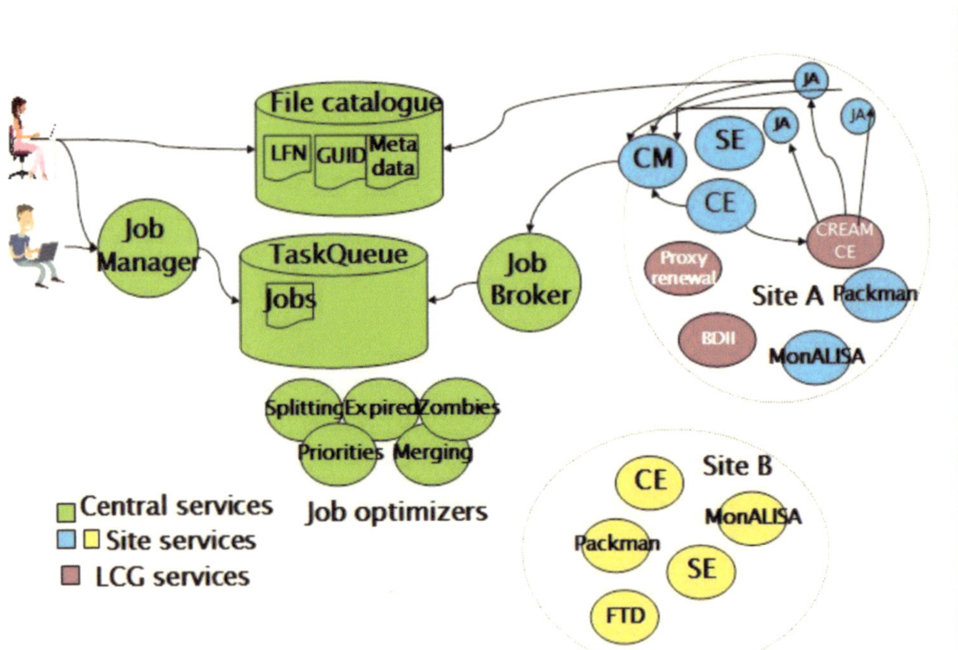

Fig. 16. AliEn + WLCG services

In the pull architecture, local agents (pilot status-checking test jobs) running at individual sites ask for real jobs after having checked the local conditions and found them appropriate for the processing of the job. Thus, AliEn only deals with the requests of local pilot jobs, so-called Job Agents (JA), to assign appropriate real jobs. The descriptions of jobs in the form of ClassAds are managed by the central Task Queue.

Each site runs several AliEn services: CE, ClusterMonitor, Package Manager (PackMan) and a MonALISA client. The AliEn CE automatically generates Job Agents and submits them to the local batch system. The ClusterMonitor manages the connections between the site and central services, so there is only one connection from each site. The AliEn CE can also be submit to the CREAM-CE, ARC, OSG or even the WMS, and delegate the communication with the local batch system to such a service. Schemas of the job submission procedure in AliEn are shown in Figures 16 and 17.

5.3 Jobs

When a job is submitted by a user, its description in the form of a ClassAd is kept in the central TQ where it waits for a suitable Job Agent for execution. There are several Job optimizers that can rearrange the priorities of the jobs based on the user quotas. These optimizers can also split jobs, or even suggest data transfers so it would be more likely that some Job Agent picks up the job. After it has been submitted, a job gets through several stages [62]. The information about running processes is kept also in the AliEn FC. Each job is given a unique id and a corresponding directory where it can register its output. The JAs provide a job-wrapper, a standard environment allowing a virtualization of resources. The whole job submission and

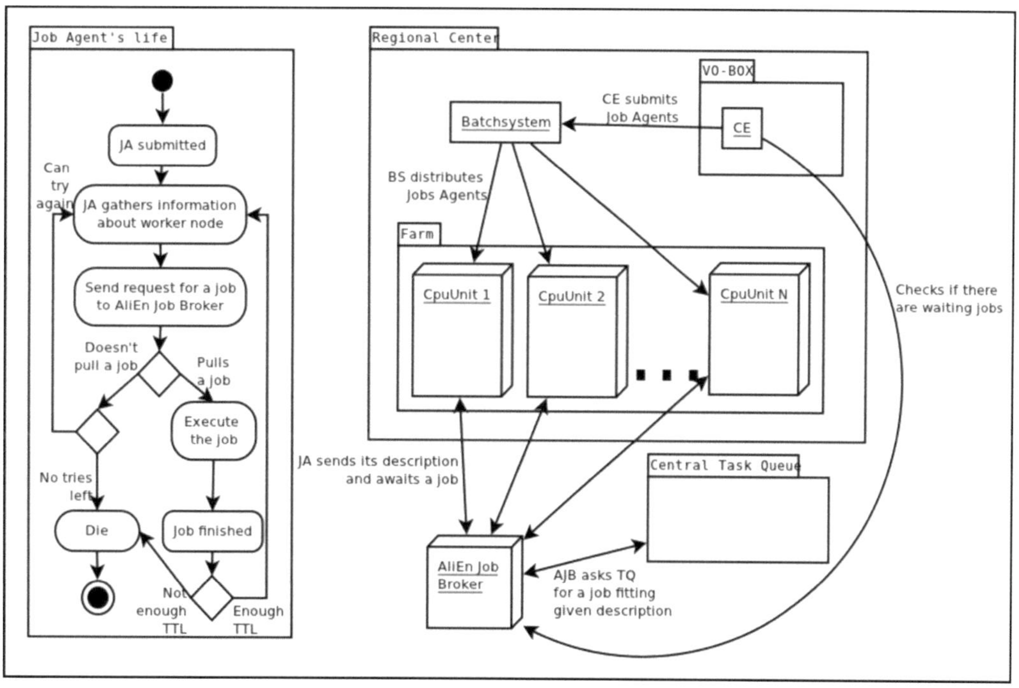

Fig. 17. The Job Agent model in AliEn: the JA does five attempts to pull a job before it dies.

processing chain is extensively monitored so a user can any time get the information on the status of his/her jobs.

5.4 Site services

As mentioned before, there are several AliEn services running at each ALICE site: CE, ClusterMonitor, PackMan and MonALISA. These services are running on a dedicated machine, so-called VOBOX described in section 3.

The AliEn site CE is usually associated with the local batch system. It is periodically submitting testing pilot jobs (Job Agents) to the local WLCG CE or an appropriate external Resource Broker or WMS. The role of the Job Agents is to verify the local hardware and software capacities at the site. After the usual matchmaking procedure, the JA is sent, through the site CE, into the local batch queue and then to a local Worker Node (WN). After its startup, the JA performs its task and in the case of a positive checkup, the JA requests a "real" job from the central Task Queue via the AliEn Job Broker, or dies otherwise. The PackMan automates the process of installation, upgrades, configuration and removal of the ALICE software packages from the shared software area on the site. It also advertises known/installed packages. The packages are installed on demand, when requested by a Job Agent running on a Worker Node or during the central software deployment over the Grid sites. If a package is not already installed the PackMan would install it along with its dependencies and return a string with commands that client has to execute to configure the package and all its dependencies. The PackMan manages the local disk cache and cleans it, when it needs more space to install newer packages. The Cluster Monitor handles communication with the AliEn Job Broker and gives configuration to JAs. It gets "heartbeats" from the JAs. If it gets no heartbeats from a JA, the existing job will get into the ZOMBIE status (after 1.5 hours) and then it will expire (after 3 hours).

5.5 Monitoring

Since the AliEn Workload Management does not depend directly on sophisticated monitoring, no special monitoring tools were developed in AliEn. As the monitoring solution, ALICE has adopted and further developed the Java-based MonALISA framework [44] mentioned already in the previous section. The MonALISA system is designed as an ensemble of autonomous multithreaded, self-describing agent-based subsystems which are registered as dynamic services, and together can collect and process large amounts of information.

The collected monitoring information is published via Web Service for use by AliEn Optimizers or for visualization purposes. An extension of the network simulation code which is a part of MonALISA can provide a tool for optimization and understanding of the performance of the AliEn Grid system.

5.6 Storage

Experience with the performance of different types of storage managers shows that the most advanced storage solution is the native XRootD manager [37] described in section 3. It has been demonstrated that with all other parameters being equal (protocol access speed and security) the native XRootD storage clusters exhibit substantially higher stability and availability. The ALICE distributed system of native XRootD clusters is orchestrated by the global redirector which allows interacting with the complete storage pool as a unique storage. All storages are on WAN (Wide Area Network).

5.7 AliEn Shell - aliensh

To complete the brief description of AliEn, we mention the client called AliEn shell. It provides a UNIX-shell-like environment with an extensive set of commands which can be used to access AliEn Grid computing resources and the AliEn virtual file system. There are three categories of commands: informative and convenience commands, File Catalogue and Data Management commands and TaskQueue/Job Management commands. The AliEn shell has been created about 4 years ago and become a popular tool among the users for job handling and monitoring.

5.8 Concluding remarks

AliEn is a high-level middleware adopted by the ALICE experiment, which has been used and validated in massive Monte Carlo events production since 2001, in end-user analysis since 2005 and during the real data management and processing since 2007. Its capabilities comply with the requirements of the ALICE computing model. In addition to modules needed to build a fully functional Grid, AliEn provides interfaces to other Grid implementations enabling the true Grid interoperability. The AliEn development will be ongoing in the coming years following the architectural path chosen at the start and more modules and functionalities are envisaged to be delivered.

The Grid (AliEn/gLite/other) services are many and quite complex. Nonetheless, they are working together, allowing to manage thousands of CPUs and PBs of various storage types. The ALICE choice of single Grid Catalogue, single Task Queue with internal prioritization and a single storage access protocol (xrootd) has been beneficial from user and Grid management viewpoint.

6. WLCG and ALICE performance during the 2010/2011 LHC data taking

In this section, we will discuss the experience and performance of the WLCG in general and the ALICE Grid project in particular during the real LHC data taking both during the proton and the lead ion beam periods.

6.1 LHC performance

The LHC delivered the first pp collisions in the end of 2009, and the stable operations startup was in March 2010. Since then, the machine has been working amazingly well compared to other related facilities. Already in 2009, the machine beaten the world record in the beam energy and other records have followed. In 2010, the delivered integrated luminosity was 18.1 pb^{-1} and already during the first months of operation in 2011, the delivered luminosity was 265 pb^{-1}. This is about a quarter of the complete target luminosity for 2010 and 2011 [63], which is supposed to be sufficient to get the answer concerning the existence of the Higgs boson. Also, as mentioned in section 1, the machine has beaten the records concerning the stored energy and also the beam intensity.

The target number of bunches per a beam of protons stated for 2011 was reached already in the middle of the year: 1380 bunches. The final target luminosity of 10^{34} cm^{-2}s^{-1} is being approached rapidly, at present it is about 10^{33} cm^{-2}s^{-1} [64].

6.2 WLCG performance

The performance of the data handling by the WLCG has also been surprisingly good. This wrapped up several years to the LHC startup, when the WLCG and the experiments themselves were regularly performing a number of stress-tests of their distributed computing infrastructure and were gradually upgrading the systems using new technologies. As a result, when the data started to flow from the detectors, the performance of the distributed data handling machinery was quite astounding. All aspects of the Grid have really worked for the LHC and have enabled the delivery of Physics results incredibly quickly.

During 2010, 15 PetaBytes of data were written to tapes at the CERN Tier-0 reaching the level expected from the original estimates for the fully-tuned LHC operations, a nominal data taking year. As mentioned in section 2, in average 2 PB of data per a month were written to tapes at Tier-0 with the exception of the heavy ions period when this number got about doubled and a world record was reached with 225 TB written to tapes within one day, see Figure 18. The CERN Tier-0 moved altogether above 1 PB of data per day.

As mentioned in section 2, the mass storage system at the CERN Tier-0 supported data rates at an average over the year of 2.5 GB/s IN with peaks up to 11 GB/s, and data was served at an average rate of $\sim$ 7 GB/s with peaks up to 25 GB/s.

The data processing went on without basic show-stoppers. The workload management system was able to get about 1 million of jobs running per day, see Figure 19, and this load is gradually going up. This translates into significant amounts of computer time. Towards the end of 2010 there was a situation when all of the available job slots at Tier-1s and Tier-2s were often fully occupied. This has been showing up also during 2011, so the WLCG collaboration has already now fully used all the available computing resources. During 2010, the WLCG delivered about 100 CPU-millennia.

As also briefly mentioned in section 2, the WLCG was very successful concerning the number of individuals really using the grid to perform their analysis. At the start of the project, there was a concern that end users will be discouraged from using the grid due to complexity of its structure and services. But thanks to the effort of the WLCG and experiments themselves a reasonably simple access interfaces were developed and the number of end users reached up to 800 in the large experiments.

The distribution of the delivered CPU power between sites has been basically according to the original design, but the Tier-2s provided more than the expected 40%: it was in fact 50% or more of the overall delivery, see section 2. Member countries pledged different amounts of resources according to their capacities and have been delivering accordingly. So the concept of collaborative Grid resource sharing really works and enables institutes worldwide to share data, and provide resources to the common goals of the collaboration.

6.2.1 Network performance

The key basis for building up a distributed system is the data transfer infrastructure. The network which the WLCG operates today is much in advance of what was anticipated in

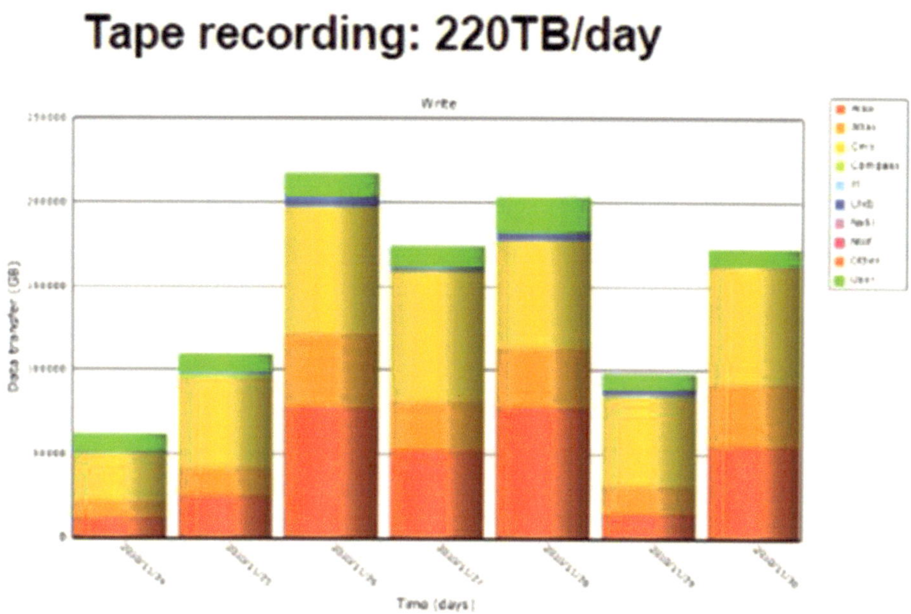

Fig. 18. A record in data tape recording: over 220 TB/day.

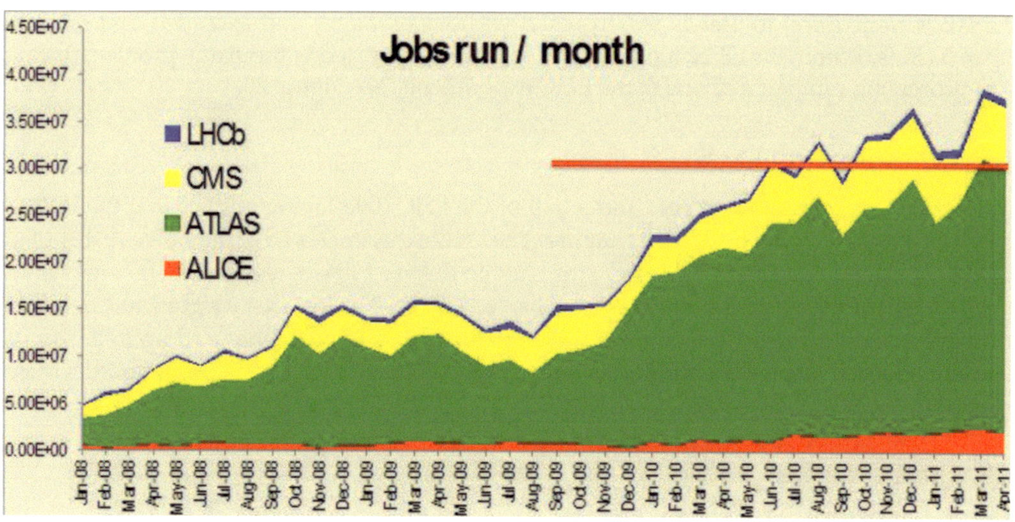

Fig. 19. WLCG job profile

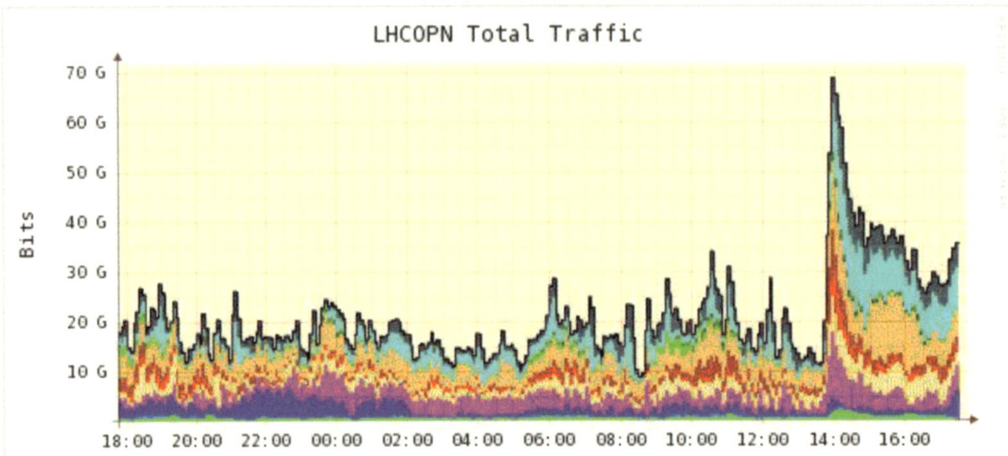

Fig. 20. WLCG OPN traffic in 2010 with a peak of 70 Gbit/s

the time of writing the WLCG TDR. The OPN, see also section 2, started as dedicated fiber links from CERN to each of the Tier-1s with the throughput 10 Gbit/s. Today, there is a full redundancy in this network with the original links doubled and with back-up links between Tier-1s themselves. The OPN is a complicated system with many different layers of hardware and software and getting it into the current shape was a difficult task, which evidently paid-off.

The original concerns about the possible network unreliability and insufficiency were not realized. The network infrastructure relying on the OPN and the complementary GEANT, US-LHCNet and all the R&E national network infrastructures, extensively monitored and continuously checked with the test transfer jobs, has never been a problem in the data transfer except for occasional glitches. The originally estimated sustained transfer rate of 1.3 GB/s from Tier-0 to Tier-1s was reached without problems and exceeded and reached up to 5 GB/s. Within the OPN, a peak of 70 Gb/s was supported without any problem during a re-processing campaign of one of the LHC experiments, see Figure 20.

6.2.2 Concluding remarks - WLCG

The experience from the first year and a half of the LHC data taking implies that the WLCG has built a truly working grid infrastructure. The LHC experiments have their own distributed models and have used the WLCG infrastructure to deliver Physics results within weeks after the data recording which has never been achieved before. The fact that a significant numbers of people are doing analysis on the Grid, that all the resources are being used up to the limits and the scientific papers are produced with an unprecedented speed is proving an evident success of the WLCG mission.

6.3 ALICE performance

To conclude this section, we will briefly summarize the experience and performance of the ALICE experiment. ALICE started extremely successfully the processing of the LHC data in 2009: the data collected during the first collisions delivered by the LHC on November 23rd

(2009) got processed and analyzed so fast that within one week the article with the results from the first collisions was accepted for publication as the first ever scientific paper with the Physics results from the LHC collisions [65].

6.3.1 Jobs

During the data taking in 2010, ALICE collected 2.3 PB of raw data, which represented about 1.2 million of files with the average file size of 1.9 GB. The data processing chain has been performing without basic problems. The Monte Carlo simulation jobs together with the raw data reconstruction and organized analysis (altogether the organized production) represented almost 7 millions of successfully completed jobs, which translates into 0.3 jobs/second. The chaotic (end user) analysis made for 9 millions of successfully completed jobs, which represents 0.4 jobs/s, consuming approximately 10% of the total ALICE CPU resources (the chaotic analysis jobs are in general shorter than the organized processing jobs). In total, there were almost 16 millions of successfully done jobs, which translates to 1 job/s and 90 thousands jobs/day. The complimentary number of jobs which started running on the Grid but finished with an error was in excess of this.

The running jobs profile got in peaks to 30 thousands of concurrently running jobs (see Figure 21) with more than 50% of the CPU resources delivered by the Tier-2 centers. About 60% of the total number of jobs represented the end user analysis (see Figure 22). In general, the user analysis already in 2010 was a resounding success, with almost 380 people actively using the Grid. Since the chaotic analysis brings sometimes problems concerning not completely perfect code resulting, e.g., in a high memory consumption (cf. section 4), ALICE was running a mixture of the organized production and end user jobs at all its sites, and this scenario was working well.

6.3.2 Storage-2010

The distributed storage system endured and was supporting an enormous load. During 2010/2011, 25.15 PB of data (raw, ESDs, AODs, Monte Carlo productions) was written to xrootd Storage Elements with the speed maximum of 621.1 MB/s. 59.97 PB of data was read from the xrootd Storage Elements, with the speed maximum of 1.285 GB/s, see Figure 23.

6.3.3 Data taking 2011

Constantly upgrading and extending its hardware resources and updating the grid software, ALICE continued a successful LHC data handling campaign in 2011. By September, the total volume of the collected raw data was almost 1.7 PB with the first reconstruction pass completed. The year 2011 was marked by massive user analysis on the Grid. In May, the most important conference in the Heavy Ion Physics community, Quark Matter 2011 (QM2011) [66], took place and was preceded by an enormous end user analysis campaign. In average, 6 thousands end-user jobs were running all the time, which represents almost 30% of the CPU resources officially dedicated to ALICE (The number of running jobs is higher than that most of the time due to use of opportunistic resources). During the week before the QM2011, there was a peak with 20 thousands of concurrently running end-user jobs, see Figures 23,24. The number of active Grid users reached 411.

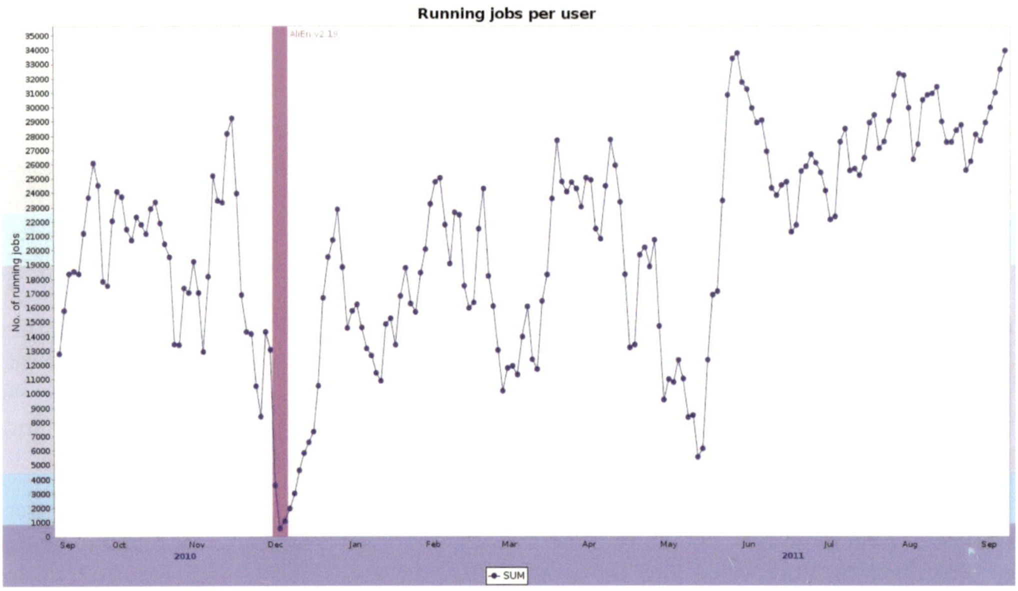

Fig. 21. ALICE running jobs profile 2010/2011.

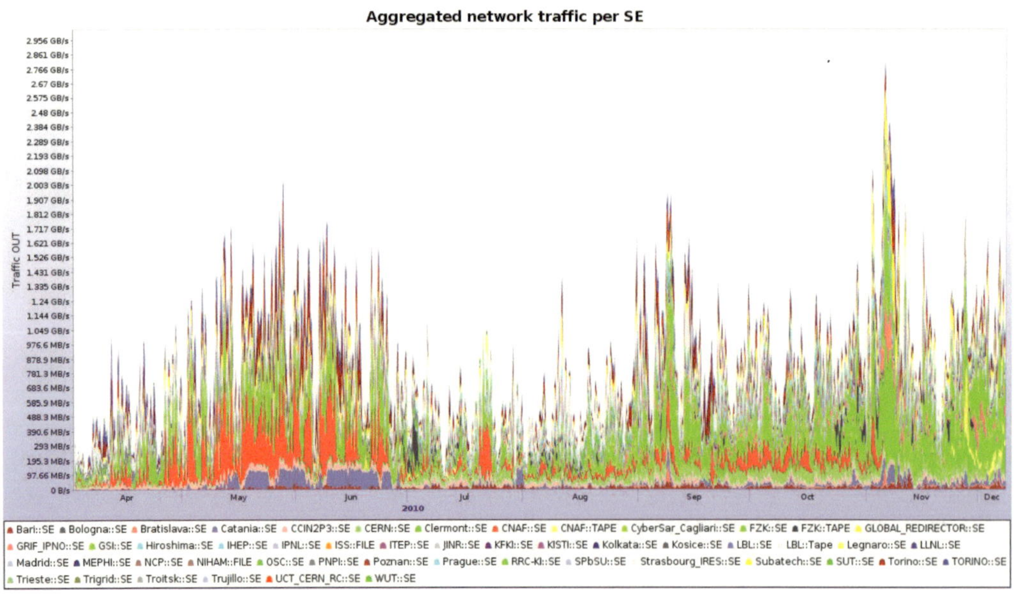

Fig. 22. Network traffic OUT by analysis jobs - 2010

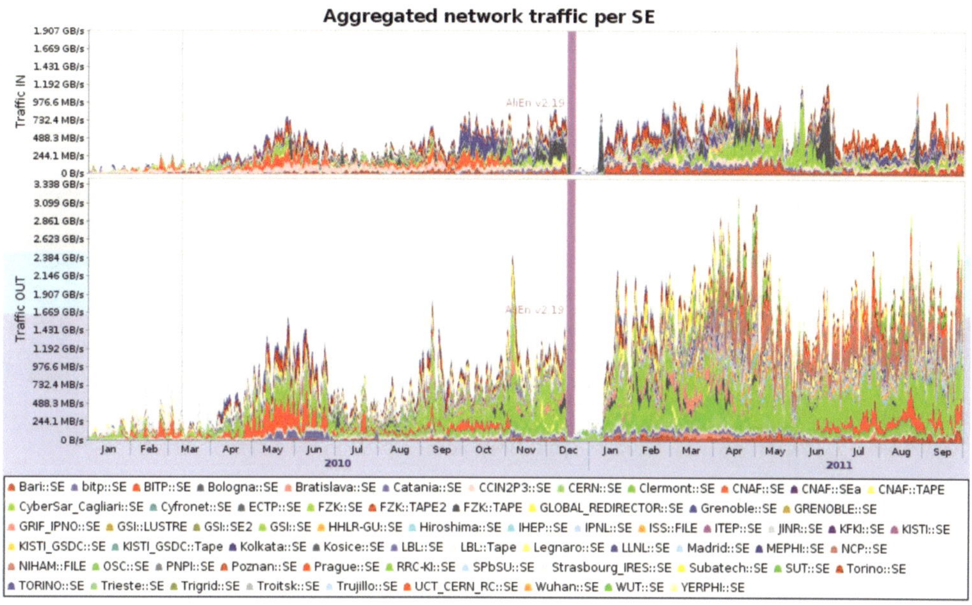

Fig. 23. Total network traffic at the ALICE Storage Elements - 2010/2011

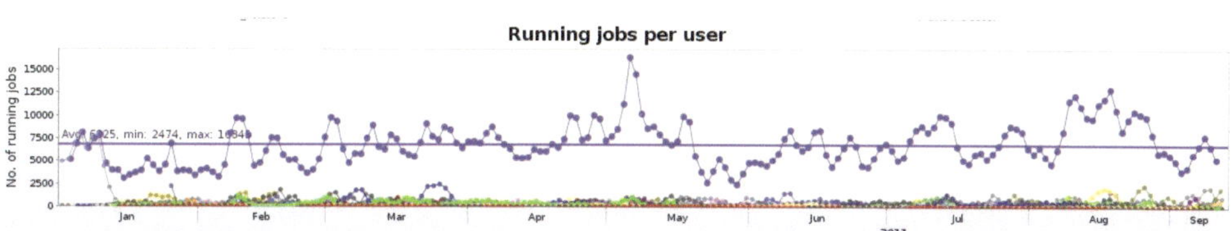

Fig. 24. End-user jobs profile - 2011

In total, the ALICE sites were running in average 21 thousands of jobs with peaks up to 35 thousands (Figure 21). The resources ratio remained 50% delivered by Tier-0 and Tier-1s to 50% delivered by Tier-2s. Altogether, 69 sites were active in the operations. The sites' availability and operability kept very stable throughout the year. The gLite (now EMI) middleware, see section 3, is mature and only a few changes are necessary.

In the beginning of the 2011 campaign, there was a concern that the storage would be saturated. In fact the storage infrastructure was performing basically without problems supporting the enormous load from the end-user analysis and was getting ready for the Pb-Pb operations. The network situation, as was already mentioned for the WLCG in general, has been excellent and allowed for the operation scenario where the hierarchical tiered structure got blurred, the sites of all levels were well interconnected and running a similar mixture of jobs. As a result, the ALICE Grid in a sense has been working as a cloud.

6.4 Concluding remarks - ALICE

In general, similar to the overall characteristics of the WLCG performance also the ALICE operations and data handling campaigns were notably successful right from the beginning of the LHC startup, making the Grid infrastructure operational and supporting a fast delivery of Physics results. By September 2011, ALICE has published 15 scientific papers with the results from the LHC collisions and more is on the way. Two papers [67,68] were marked as "Suggested reading" by the Physical Review Letters editors and the later was also selected for the "Viewpoint in Physics" by Physical Review Letters.

The full list of the ALICE papers published during 2009-2011 can be found on [69]. One of the Pb-Pb collision events recorded by ALICE is shown on Figure 25.

Fig. 25. Pb-Pb collision event recorded by ALICE

7. Summary and outlook

This chapter is meant to be a short overview of the facts concerning the Grid computing for HEP experiments, in particular for the experiments at the CERN LHC. The experience gained during the LHC operations in 2009-2011 has proven that for this community, the existence of a well performing distributed computing is necessary for the achievement and fast delivery of scientific results. The existing WLCG infrastructure turned up to be able to support the data production and processing thus fulfilling its first-plan mission. It has been and will be continuously developing into the future absorbing and giving rise to new technologies, like the advances in networking, storage systems and inter-operability between Grids and Clouds [70,71].

7.1 Data management

Managing the real data taking and processing in 2009-2011 provided basic experience and a starting point for new developments. The excellent performance of the network which was by far not anticipated in the time of writing the WLCG (C)TDR shifted the original concept of computing models based on hierarchical architecture to a more symmetrical mesh-like scenario. In the original design, the jobs are sent to sites holding the required data sets and there are multiple copies of data spread over the system due to anticipation that network will be unreliable or insufficient. It turned out that some data sets were placed on sites and never touched.

Based on the existing excellent network reliability and growing throughput, the data models start to change along a dynamical scenario. This includes sending data to a site just before a job requires it, or reading files remotely over the network, use remote (WAN) I/O to the running processes. Certainly, fetching over the network one needed data file from a given data set which can contain hundreds of files is more effective than a massive data sets deployment and will spare storage resources and bring less network load.

The evolution of the data management strategies is ongoing. It goes towards caching of data rather than strict planned placement. As mentioned, the preferences go to fetching a file over the network when a job needs it and to a kind of intelligent data pre-placement. The remote access to data (either by caching on demand and/or by remote file access) should be implemented.

7.2 Network

To improve the performance of the WLCG-operated network infrastructure, the topology of LHC Open Network Environment (LHCONE [24]) is being developed and built. This should be complementary to the existing OPN infrastructure providing the inter-connectivity between Tier-2s and Tier-1s and between Tier-2s themselves without putting an additional load on the existing NREN infrastructures. As we learned during the last years, the network is extremely important and better connected countries do better.

7.3 Resources

During the 2010 data taking the available resources were sufficient to cover the needs of experiments, but during 2011 the computing slots as well as the storage capacities at sites started to be full. Since the experience clearly shows that delivery of the Physics results is limited by resources, the experiments are facing a necessity of more efficient usage of existing resources. There are task forces studying the possibility of using the next generations computing and storage technologies. There is for instance a question of using multicore processors which might go into the high performance computing market while WLCG prefers usage of commodity hardware.

7.4 Operations

Another important issue is sustainability and support availability for the WLCG operations. The middleware used today for the WLCG operations is considerably complex with many services unnecessarily replicated in many places (like, e.g., databases) mainly due to original worries concerning network. The new conception is to gradually search for more standard solutions instead of often highly specialized middleware packages maintained and developed by WLCG.

7.5 Clouds and virtualization

Among the new technologies, the Clouds is the right buzzword now and the virtualization of resources comes along. The virtualization of WLCG sites started prior to the first LHC collisions and has gone quite far. It helps improving system management, provision of services on demand, can make use of resources more effective and efficient. Virtualization also enables to make use of industrial and commercial solutions.

But, no matter what the current technologies advertise, the LHC community will always use a Grid because the scientists need to collaborate and share resources. No matter what technologies are used underneath the Grid, the collaborative sharing of resources and the network of trust and all the security infrastructure developed on the way of building the WLCG is of enormous value, not only to WLCG community but to e-science in general. It allows people to collaborate across the infrastructures.

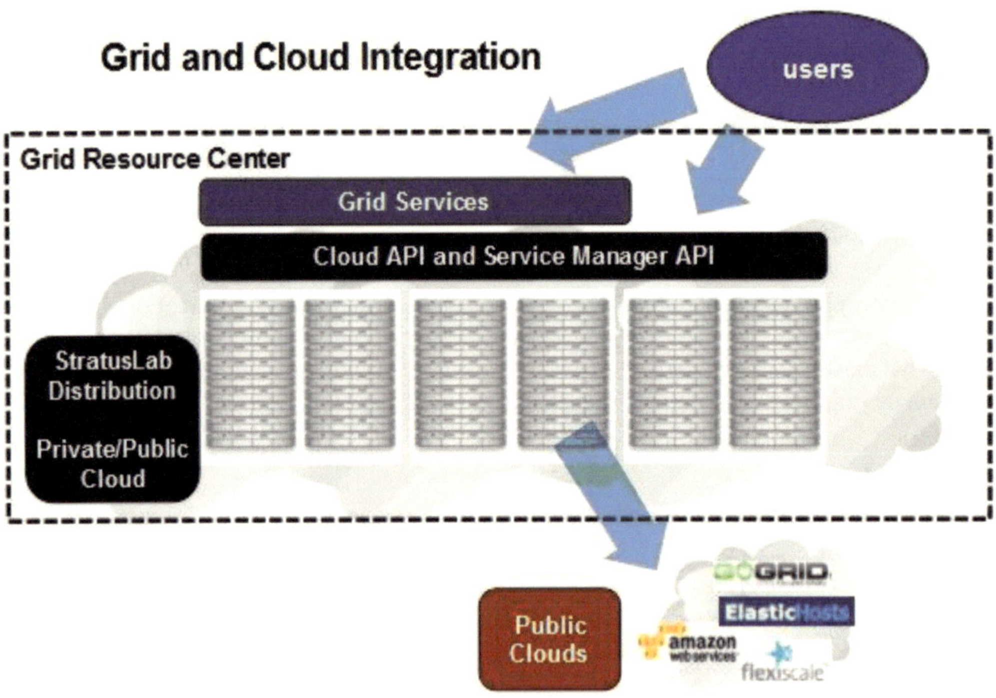

Fig. 26. Schema of StratusLab IaaS Cloud interoperability with a Grid

The basic operations like distributed data management, the high data throughput and the remote job submission can probably be more cloud-like. There is a great interest among people to use commercial Clouds resources, especially when the experiments see their resources becoming full.

So, can we use Amazon or Google to do processing of data from LHC? The point is, one cannot be sure what the level of services will be and what the IN/OUT bandwidth will be. This can in principle be negotiated with these companies and may bring some level of agreement. That in principle is doable.

7.6 Grids and Clouds

As argued in [70], "Cloud Computing not only overlaps with Grid Computing, it is indeed evolved out of Grid Computing and relies on Grid Computing as its backbone and infrastructure support. The evolution has been a result of a shift in focus from an infrastructure that delivers storage and compute resources (in the case of Grids) to one that is economy based ....". Both the Grids and the Clouds communities are facing the same problems like the need to operate large facilities and to develop methods by which users/consumers discover, request and use resources provided by the centralized facilities.

There exist a number of projects looking into and developing Cloud to Grid interfaces with the idea that Grid and Cloud Computing serve different use cases and can work together improving Distributed Computing Infrastructures (see, e.g., [71]). Also CERN is involved in this activity together with other international laboratories in Europe.

With the WLCG resources becoming used up to their limits, using commercial Clouds to process the LHC data is a strategy that should be assessed. Several of the LHC experiments have done tests whether they can use commercial Clouds. But today, the cost is rather high. Also, there are issues like whether academic data can be shipped through academic networks to a commercial provider or how to make sure what happens to this data.

Nevertheless the strategy towards deployment over the WLCG resources Cloud interfaces, managed with high level of virtualization, is under evaluation. Some level of collaboration with industry would provide the understanding how to deploy this properly and what would be the cost. The Cloud and Grid interfaces can be deployed in parallel or on top of each other. This development might also give a way to evolve into a more standardized infrastructure and allow to make a transparent use of commercial Clouds.

A testbed of such an architecture is the CERN LXCloud [72] pilot cluster. Implementation at CERN allows to present a Cloud interface or to access other public or commercial Clouds. This is happening with no change to any of the existing Grid services. Another interesting example is the development of a comprehensive OpenSource IaaS (Infrastructure as a Service) Cloud distribution within the StratusLab project [71], see Figure 26. Anyone can take the code and deploy it on his site and have IaaS Cloud running on his site. The project is focused on deploying Grid services on top of this Cloud, 1) to be a service to existing European Grid infrastructures and to enable these people to use Cloud-operated resources and 2) because the developers consider the Grid services very complex and making sure they run safely on this Cloud should guarantee that also other applications will run without problems.

7.7 Physics results achieved by the LHC experiments

Before we bring the final concluding remarks for our chapter, we will briefly summarize the Physics results delivered by the LHC experiments by the time of writing this document.

In addition to many specific new results describing different Physics phenomena in the energy regime never explored before, there have been new findings concerning some of the major issues addressed by the LHC research.

- ATLAS and CMS experiments have been delivering results concerning the energy regions excluding the mass of the Higgs boson. The latest results on the topic of Higgs boson searches exclude a wide region of Higgs boson masses: ATLAS excludes Higgs boson masses above 145 GeV, and out to 466 GeV (apart from a couple of points in-between, which are however excluded by CMS studies). For some of the latest references see [73-75].
- To contribute new results on the topic of the dominance of matter over antimatter in the present Universe, the LHCb experiment has been pursuing studies of phenomena demonstrating the so-called CP-symmetry violation. Violation of this symmetry plays an important role in the attempts of Cosmology to explain the dominance of matter over antimatter in our world. The latest LHCb results concerning the demonstration of the existence of the CP-violation can be found, e.g., in [76].
- The study of properties of the Quark Gluon Plasma (QGP), the phase of matter which existed in a fraction of a second after the Big Bang, is the mission of the ALICE experiment. During the lead-lead collisions at the LHC energies, the individual collisions can be seen as "little Big Bangs". The matter produced in these collisions is under extreme conditions: the energy density corresponds to a situation when 15 protons are squeezed into the volume of one proton and the temperature reaches more than 200000 times the temperature in the core of the Sun. ALICE has confirmed the previous findings of the STAR experiment at the Relativistic Heavy Ion Collider (RHIC) at Brookhaven that this QGP behaves like an ideal liquid [68] even at the LHC energies.

7.8 Concluding remarks

As we already stressed, the WLCG performance during the LHC data taking in 2009-2011 was excellent and the basic mission of the WLCG has been fulfilled: the data taking and processing is ongoing without major show-stoppers, hundreds of people are using the Grid to perform their analysis and unique scientific results are delivered within weeks after the data was recorded. In addition, the experience gained during this data taking .stress test. launched new strategies to be followed on the way of the future WLCG development. There are fundamental issues like the approaching lack of WLCG resources and the expansion of new technologies like the Cloud computing. In the time of writing this chapter it looks like we will see in the future some combination of Grid and Cloud technologies will be adopted to operate the distributed computing infrastructures used by the HEP experiments.

8. Acknowledgements

We would like to thank Jiri Adam for a critical reading of the manuscript and for a great help with the LaTeX matters. The work was supported by the MSMT CR contracts No. 1P04LA211 and LC 07048.

9. References

[1] D.H. Perkins: Introduction to High Energy Physics, Cambridge University Press, 4th edition (2000), ISBN-13: 978-0521621960.
Procedings of 35th International Conference of High Energy Physics, July 22-28, 2010, Paris, France, Proceedings of Science (PoS) electronic Journal: ICHEP 2010

[2] STAR Collaboration: Experimental and theoretical challenges in the search for the quark gluon plasma: The STAR Collaboration's critical assessment of the evidence from RHIC collisions, Nucl. Phys. A757 (2005) 102-183.

[3] CERN - the European Organization for Nuclear Research; `http://public.web.cern.ch/public/`

[4] The Large Hadron Collider at CERN; `http://lhc.web.cern.ch/lhc/`; `http://public.web.cern.ch/public/en/LHC/LHC-en.html`

[5] ALICE Collaboration: `http://aliceinfo.cern.ch/Public/Welcome.html`

[6] ATLAS Collaboration: `http://atlas.ch/`

[7] CMS Collaboration: `http://cms.web.cern.ch/`

[8] LHCb Collaboration: `http://lhcb-public.web.cern.ch/lhcb-public/`

[9] TOTEM Experiment: `http://cern.ch/totem-experiment`

[10] LHCf Experiment: `http://cdsweb.cern.ch/record/887108/files/lhcc-2005-032.pdf`

[11] W.N. Cottingham and D.A. Greenwood: An Introduction to the Standard Model of Particle Physics, Cambridge University Press, 2nd edition (2007), ISBN-13: 978-0521852494

[12] Worldwide LHC Computing Grid: `http://public.web.cern.ch/public/en/lhc/Computing-en.html`

[13] LHC Computing Grid: Technical Design Report, `http://lcg.web.cern.ch/LCG/tdr/`

[14] I. Foster and C. Kesselman. The Grid: Blueprint for a New Computing Infrastructure. Morgan Kaufmann, 1999;
I. Foster et al: The Anatomy of the Grid: Enabling Scalable Virtual Organizations, International Journal of High Performance Computing Applications Vol.15(2001), p.200.

[15] WLCG Memorandum of Understanding, `http://lcg.web.cern.ch/lcg/mou.htm`

[16] EGI - The European Grid Initiative; `http://web.eu-egi.eu/`

[17] OSG - The Open Science Grid, `http://www.opensciencegrid.org/`; `https://osg-ress-1.fnal.gov:8443/ReSS/ReSS-prd-History.html`

[18] I. Legrand et al: MONARC Simulation Framework, ACAT'04, Tsukuba, Japan,2004; `http://monarc.cacr.caltech.edu:8081/www_monarc/monarc.htm`

[19] CERN Advanced Storage Manager: `http://castor.web.cern.ch/castor/`

[20] I. Bird: LHC Computing: After the first year with data, TERENA Networking Conference (TNC2011), Prague, 2011, `https://tnc2011.terena.org/web/media/archive/7A`

[21] LHCOPN - The Large Hadron Collider Optical Private Network, `https://twiki.cern.ch/twiki/bin/view/LHCOPN/WebHome`

[22] The GEANT Project, `http://archive.geant.net/`

[23] USLHCNet: High speed TransAtlantic network for the LHC community, http://lhcnet.caltech.edu/
[24] LHCONE-LHC Open Network Environment: http://lhcone.net/
[25] Virtual Organisation: http://technical.eu-egee.org/index.php?id=147
[26] The European Middleware Initiative: http://www.eu-emi.eu/home
[27] The Globus Toolkit: http://www-unix.globus.org/toolkit/
[28] OMII - The Open Middleware Infrastructure Institute: http://www.omii.ac.uk/
[29] The Virtual Data Toolkit, http://vdt.cs.wisc.edu/
[30] P. Saiz et al., AliEn-ALICE environment on the GRID, Nucl. Instrum. Meth. A502 (2003) 437; http://alien2.cern.ch/
[31] Computing Element: http://glite.cern.ch/lcg-CE/
[32] Workload Management System: http://glite.cern.ch/glite-WMS/
[33] The CREAM (Computing Resource Execution And Managemen) Service, http://glite.cern.ch/glite-CREAM/
[34] Storage Element: http://glite.cern.ch/glite-SE_dpm_mysql/
[35] dCache: http://www.dcache.org/
[36] The Disk Pool Manager: https://www.gridpp.ac.uk/wiki/Disk_Pool_Manager; https://twiki.cern.ch/twiki/bin/view/LCG/DataManagementTop
[37] XRootD: http://project-arda-dev.web.cern.ch/project-arda-dev/xrootd/site/index.html
[38] SLAC (Stanford Linear Accelerator Center): http://slac.stanford.edu/
[39] INFN - The National Institute of Nuclear Physics: http://www.infn.it/indexen.php
[40] R. Brun and F. Rademakers, ROOT: An object oriented data analysis framework, Nucl. Instrum. Meth. A389 (1997) 81; http://root.cern.ch
[41] VOMS-Virtual Organization Membership Service: http://glite.web.cern.ch/glite/packages/R3.1/deployment/glite-VOMS_mysql/glite-VOMS_mysql.asp
[42] The VO-box: http://glite.cern.ch/glite-VOBOX/
[43] ALICE Experiment Computing TDR: http://aliceinfo.cern.ch/Collaboration/Documents/TDR/Computing.html
[44] Monitoring Agents using a Large Integrated Services Architecture: http://monalisa.cern.ch/monalisa.html;
C. Grigoras et al., Automated agents for management and control of the ALICE Computing Grid, Proceedings of the 17th Int. Conf. CHEP 2009, Prague, March 21-27, 2009, J. Phys.: Conf. Ser. 219, 062050.
[45] ALICE raw data production cycles: http://alimonitor.cern.ch/production/raw.jsp
[46] AliRoot: http://aliceinfo.cern.ch/Offline/AliRoot/Manual.html
[47] GEANT3-Detector Description and Simulation Tool: http://wwwasd.web.cern.ch/wwwasd/geant/
[48] FLUKA-Particle Physics MonteCarlo Simulation package: http://www.fluka.org/fluka.php

[49] Pythia6: http://projects.hepforge.org/pythia6/;
Pythia8: http://home.thep.lu.se/~torbjorn/pythiaaux/present.html
[50] Xin-Nian Wang and Miklos Gyulassy: HIJING: A Monte Carlo model for multiple jet production in pp, pA and AA collisions,
Phys. Rev. D44 (1991), 3501;
http://www-nsdth.lbl.gov/~xnwang/hijing/
[51] ALICE Offline policy:
http://aliceinfo.cern.ch/Offline/General-Information/Offline-Policy.html
[52] Monitoring of Analysis trains in ALICE:
http://alimonitor.cern.ch/prod/
[53] ALICE simulation framework:
http://aliceinfo.cern.ch/Offline/Activities/Simulation/index.html
[54] ALICE MC simulation cycles:
http://alimonitor.cern.ch/job_details.jsp
[55] ALICE Computing sites:
http://pcalimonitor.cern.ch:8889/reports/;
ALICE Distributed Storage:
http://pcalimonitor.cern.ch/stats?page=SE/table
[56] Yves Schutz: Computing resources 2011-2013, ALICE Computing Board Sept. 1st, 2011:
http://indico.cern.ch/materialDisplay.py?contribId=3&materialId=2&confId=153622;
https://twiki.cern.ch/twiki/bin/view/FIOgroup/TsiBenchHEPSPEC
[57] gLite-Lightweight Middleware for Grid Computing,
http://glite.cern.ch/
[58] ARC-The Advanced Resource Connector middleware,
http://www.nordugrid.org/arc/about-arc.html
[59] The AliEn Shell-aliensh, AliEn User Interfaces:
http://project-arda-dev.web.cern.ch/project-arda-dev/alice/apiservice/guide/guide-1.0.html#_Toc156731986;
ALICE Grid Analysis:
http://project-arda-dev.web.cern.ch/project-arda-dev/alice/apiservice/AA-UserGuide-0.0m.pdf
[60] The PANDA Experiment: http://www-panda.gsi.de/
[61] The CBM Experiment: http://www-cbm.gsi.de/
[62] Job statuses in AliEn:
http://pcalimonitor.cern.ch/show?page=jobStatus.html
[63] LHC Design Report: http://lhc.web.cern.ch/lhc/LHC-DesignReport.html
[64] LHC Performance and Statistics:
https://lhc-statistics.web.cern.ch/LHC-Statistics/
[65] The ALICE Collaboration: First proton-proton collisions at the LHC as observed with the ALICE detector: measurement of the charged-particle pseudorapidity density at $\sqrt{s} = 900$ GeV, Eur. Phys. J. C65 (2010), 111-125.
[66] Quark Matter 2011: http://qm2011.in2p3.fr/
[67] The ALICE Collaboration: Charged-Particle Multiplicity Density at Midrapidity in Central Pb-Pb Collisions at $\sqrt{s_{NN}} = 2.76$ TeV, Phys. Rev. Lett. 105 (2010), 252301.

[68] The ALICE Collaboration: Elliptic Flow of Charged Particles in Pb-Pb Collisions at $\sqrt{s_{NN}} = 2.76$ TeV, Phys. Rev. Lett. 105 (2010), 252302.
[69] Physics Publications of the ALICE Collaboration in Refereed Journals, http://aliceinfo.cern.ch/Documents/generalpublications
[70] I. Foster et al: Cloud Computing and Grid Computing 360-Degree Compared, Proc. of the Grid Computing Environments Workshop, 2008. GCE '08, Austin, Texas, http://arxiv.org/ftp/arxiv/papers/0901/0901.0131.pdf
[71] C. Loomis: StratusLab: Enhancing Grid Infrastructures with Cloud and Virtualization Technologies, TERENA Networking Conference (TNC2011),Prague, 2011, https://tnc2011.terena.org/web/media/archive/11C
[72] LXCloud: https://twiki.cern.ch/twiki/bin/view/FIOgroup/LxCloud
[73] The ATLAS Collaboration: Search for the Higgs boson in the $H \rightarrow WW \rightarrow lvjj$ decay channel in pp collisions at $\sqrt{s} = 7$ TeV with the ATLAS detector; arXiv:1109.3615v1, Sep. 2011.
[74] The ATLAS Collaboration: Search for a Standard Model Higgs boson in the $H \rightarrow ZZ \rightarrow llvv$ decay channel with the ATLAS detector; arXiv:1109.3357v1, Sep. 2011.
[75] The CMS Collaboration: New CMS Higgs Search Results for the Lepton Photon 2011 Conference; http://cms.web.cern.ch/news/new-cms-higgs-search-results-lepton-photon-2011-conference
[76] The LHCb Collaboration: A search for time-integrated CP violation in $D^0 \rightarrow h^+h^-$ decays and a measurement of the D0 production asymmetry; http://cdsweb.cern.ch/record/1349500/files/LHCb-CONF-2011-023.pdf
The LHCb Collaboration: Measurement of the CP Violation Parameter A_Γ in Two-Body Charm Decays; http://cdsweb.cern.ch/record/1370107/files/LHCb-CONF-2011-046.pdf

10

Using Grid Computing for Constructing Ternary Covering Arrays

Himer Avila-George[1], Jose Torres-Jimenez[2], Abel Carrión[1] and Vicente Hernández[1]

[1]*Instituto de Instrumentación para Imagen Molecular (I3M), Centro Mixto CSIC - Universitat Politècnica de València - CIEMAT, Valencia*

[2]*CINVESTAV-Tamaulipas, Information Technology Laboratory, Km. 5.5 Carretera Victoria-Soto La Marina, Ciudad Victoria, Tamaulipas*

[1]*Spain*

[2]*Mexico*

1. Introduction

To continue at the forefront in this fast paced and competitive world, companies have to be highly adaptable and to suit such transforming needs customized software solutions play a key role. To support this customization, software systems must provide numerous configurable options. While this flexibility promotes customizations, it creates many potential system configurations, which may need extensive quality assurance.

A good strategy to test a software component involves the generation of the whole set of cases that participate in its operation. While testing only individual values may not be enough, exhaustive testing of all possible combinations is not always feasible. An alternative technique to accomplish this goal is called combinatorial testing. Combinatorial testing is a method that can reduce cost and increase the effectiveness of software testing for many applications. It is based on constructing economical sized test-suites that provide coverage of the most prevalent configurations. Covering arrays (CAs) are combinatorial structures which can be used to represent these test-suites.

A covering array (CA) is a combinatorial object, denoted by $CA(N;t,k,v)$ which can be described like a matrix with $N \times k$ elements, such that every $N \times t$ subarray contains all possible combinations of v^t symbols at least once. N represents the rows of the matrix, k is the number of parameters, which has v possible values and t represents the strength or the degree of controlled interaction.

To illustrate the CA approach applied to the design of software testing, consider the Web-based system example shown in Table 1, the example involves four parameters each with three possible values. A full experimental design ($t = 4$) should cover $3^4 = 81$ possibilities, however, if the interaction is relaxed to $t = 2$ (pair-wise), then the number of possible combinations is reduced to 9 test cases.

	Browser	OS	DBMS	Connections
0	Firefox	Windows 7	MySQL	ISDN
1	Chromium	Ubuntu 10.10	PostgreSQL	ADSL
2	Netscape	Red Hat 5	MaxDB	Cable

Table 1. Parameters of Web-based system example.

Fig. 1 shows the CA corresponding to $CA(9;2,4,3)$; given that its strength and alphabet are $t = 2$ and $v = 3$, respectively, the combinations that must appear at least once in each subset of size $N \times 2$ are $\{0,0\}$, $\{0,1\}$, $\{0,2\}$, $\{1,0\}$, $\{1,1\}$, $\{1,2\}$, $\{2,0\}$, $\{2,1\}$, $\{2,2\}$.

$$\begin{pmatrix} 0\ 0\ 0\ 0 \\ 0\ 1\ 1\ 1 \\ 0\ 2\ 2\ 2 \\ 1\ 0\ 1\ 2 \\ 1\ 1\ 2\ 0 \\ 1\ 2\ 0\ 1 \\ 2\ 0\ 2\ 1 \\ 2\ 1\ 0\ 2 \\ 2\ 2\ 1\ 0 \end{pmatrix}$$

Fig. 1. A combinatorial design, $CA(9;2,4,3)$.

Finally, to make the mapping between the CA and the Web-based system, every possible value of each parameter in Table 1 is labeled by the row number. Table 2 shows the corresponding pair-wise test suite; each of its nine experiments is analogous to one row of the CA shown in Fig. 1.

Experiments				
1	Firefox	Windows 7	MySQL	ISDN
2	Firefox	Ubuntu 10.10	PostgreSQL	ADSL
3	Firefox	Red Hat 5	MaxDB	Cable
4	Chromium	Windows 7	PostgreSQL	Cable
5	Chromium	Ubuntu 10.10	MaxDB	ISDN
6	Chromium	Red Hat 5	MySQL	ADSL
7	Netscape	Windows 7	MaxDB	ADSL
8	Netscape	Ubuntu 10.10	MySQL	Cable
9	Netscape	Red Hat 5	PostgreSQL	ISDN

Table 2. Test-suite covering all 2-way interactions, $CA(9;2,4,3)$.

When a CA contains the minimum possible number of rows, it is optimal and its size is called the *Covering Array Number* (CAN). The CAN is defined according to

$$CAN(t,k,v) = \min_{N \in \mathbb{N}} \{N : \exists\, CA(N;t,k,v)\}.$$

The trivial mathematical *lower bound* for a covering array is $v^t \leq CAN(t,k,v)$, however, this number is rarely achieved. Therefore determining achievable bounds is one of the main research lines for CAs. Given the values of t, k, and v, the optimal CA construction problem (CAC) consists in constructing a $CA(N;t,k,v)$ such that the value of N is minimized.

The construction of $CAN(2,k,2)$ can be efficiently done according with Kleitman & Spencer (1973); the same is possible for $CA(2,k,v)$ when the cardinality of the alphabet is $v = p^n$, where p is a prime number and n a positive integer value (Bush, 1952). However, in the general case determining the *covering array number* is known to be a hard combinatorial problem (Colbourn, 2004; Lei & Tai, 1998). This means that there is no known efficient algorithm to find an optimal CA for any level of interaction t or alphabet v. For the values of t and v that no efficient algorithm is known, we use approximated algorithms to construct them. Some of these approximated strategies must verify that the matrix they are building is a CA. If the matrix is of size $N \times k$ and the interaction is t, there are $\binom{k}{t}$ different combinations which implies a cost of $O(N \times \binom{k}{t})$ for the verification (when the matrix has $N \geq v^t$ rows, otherwise it will never be a CA and its verification is pointless). For small values of t and v the verification of CAs is overcame through the use of sequential approaches; however, when we try to construct CAs of moderate values of t, v and k, the time spent by those approaches is impractical. This scenario shows the necessity of Grid strategies to construct and verify CAs.

Grid Computing is a technology which allows sharing resources between different administration domains, in a transparent, efficient and secure way. The resources comprise: computation hardware (supercomputers or clusters) or storage systems, although it is also possible to share information sources, such as databases or scientific equipment. So, the main concept behind the Grid paradigm is to offer a homogeneous and standard interface for accessing these resources. In that sense, the evolution of Grid Middlewares has enabled the deployment of Grid e-Science infrastructures delivering large computational and data storage capabilities. The current infrastructures rely on Globus Toolkit (Globus Alliance, 2011), UNICORE (Almond & Snelling, 1999), GRIA (Surridge et al., 2005) or gLite (gLite, 2011) mainly as core middleware supporting several central services dedicated to: user management, job metascheduling, data indexing (cataloguing) and information system, providing consolidated virtual view of the whole or larger parts of the infrastructure. The availability of hundreds and thousands of processing elements (PEs) and the efficient storage of Petabyes of data is expanding the knowledge on areas such as particle physics, astronomy, genetics or software testing. Thus, Grid Computing infrastructures are the cornerstone in the current scientific research.

In this work is reported the use of Grid Computing by means of the use of the European production infrastructure provided by the European Grid Infrastructure (EGI) (EGI, 2011) project. The availability of this kind of computing platforms makes feasible the execution of computing-intensive applications, such as the construction and verification of CAs. In this work we focus on the construction of ternary CAs when $5 \leq k \leq 100$ and $2 \leq t \leq 4$.

The chapter is structured as follows. First, Section 2 offers a review of the relevant related work. Then, the algorithm for the verification of CAs is exposed in Section 3. Moreover, Section 4 details the algorithm for the construction of CAs by using a simulated annealing algorithm. Next, the Section 5 explains how to parallelize the previous algorithm using a master-slave approach. Taking the previous parallelization, Section 6 describes how to develop a Grid implementation of the construction of CAs. The results obtained in the experiments performed in the Grid infrastructure are showed in Section 7. Finally, Section 8 presents the conclusions derived from the research presented in this work.

2. Relevant related work

Because of the importance of the construction of (near) optimal CAs, much research has been carried out in developing effective methods for construct them. There are several reported methods for constructing these combinatorial models. Among them are: (a) direct methods, (b) recursive methods, (c) greedy methods, and d) meta-heuristics methods. In this section we describe the relevant related work to the construction of CAs.

Direct methods construct CAs in polynomial time and some of them employ graph or algebraic properties. There exist only some special cases where it is possible to find the covering array number using polynomial order algorithms. Bush (1952) reported a direct method for constructing optimal CAs that uses Galois finite fields obtaining all $CA(q^t; t, q+1, q)$ where q is a prime or a prime power and $q \leq t$. Rényi (1971) determined sizes of CAs for the case $t = v = 2$ when N is even. Kleitman & Spencer (1973) and Katona (1973) independently determined covering array numbers for all N when $t = v = 2$. Williams & Probert (1996) proposed a method for constructing CAs based on algebraic methods and combinatorial theory. Sherwood (2008) described some algebraic constructions for strength-2 CAs developed from index-1 orthogonal arrays, ordered designs and CAs. Another direct method that can construct some optimal CAs is named zero-sum (Sherwood, 2011). Zero-sum leads to $CA(v^t; t, t+1, v)$ for any $t > 2$; note that the value of degree is in function of the value of strength. Recently, cyclotomic classes based on Galois finite fields have been shown to provide examples of binary CAs, and more generally examples are provided by certain Hadamard matrices (Colbourn & Kéri, 2009).

Recursive methods build larger CAs from smaller ones. Williams (2000) presented a tool called TConfig to construct CAs. TConfig constructs CAs using recursive functions that concatenate small CAs to create CAs with a larger number of columns. Moura et al. (2003) introduced a set of recursive algorithms for constructing CAs based on CAs of small sizes. Some recursive methods are product constructions (Colbourn & Ling, 2009; Colbourn et al., 2006; Martirosyan & Colbourn, 2005). Colbourn & Torres-Jimenez (2010) presented a recursive method to construct CAs using *perfect hash families* for CAs contruction. The advantage of the recursive algorithms is that they construct almost minimal arrays for particular cases in a reasonable time. Their basic disadvantage is a narrow application domain and impossibility of specifying constraints.

The majority of commercial and open source test data generating tools use greedy algorithms for CAs construction (AETG (Cohen et al., 1996), TCG (Tung & Aldiwan, 2000), IPOG (Lei et al., 2007), DDA (Bryce & Colbourn, 2007) and All-Pairs (McDowell, 2011)). AETG popularized greedy methods that generate one row of a covering array at a time, attempting to select the best possible next row; since that time, TCG and DDA algorithms have developed useful variants of this approach. IPOG instead adds a factor (column) at a time, adding rows as needed to ensure coverage. The greedy algorithms provide the fastest solving method.

A few Grid approaches has been found in the literature. Torres-Jimenez et al. (2004) reported a mutation-selection algorithm over Grid Computing, for constructing ternary CAs. Younis et al. (2008) presented a Grid implementation of the modified IPOG algorithm (MIPOG).

Calvagna et al. (2009) proposed a solution for executing the reduction algorithm over a set of Grid resources.

Metaheuristic algorithms are capable of solving a wide range of combinatorial problems effectively, using generalized heuristics which can be tailored to suit the problem at hand. Heuristic search algorithms try to solve an optimization problem by the use of heuristics. A heuristic search is a method of performing a minor modification of a given solution in order to obtain a different solution.

Some metaheuristic algorithms, such as TS (Tabu Search) (Gonzalez-Hernandez et al., 2010; Nurmela, 2004), SA (Simulated Annealing) (Cohen et al., 2003; Martinez-Pena et al., 2010; Torres-Jimenez & Rodriguez-Tello, 2012), GA (Generic Algorithm) and ACA (Ant Colony Optimization Algorithm) (Shiba et al., 2004) provide an effective way to find approximate solutions. Indeed, a SA metaheuristic has been applied by Cohen et al. (2003) for constructing CAs. Their SA implementation starts with a randomly generated initial solution M which cost $E(M)$ is measured as the number of uncovered t-tuples. A series of iterations is then carried out to visit the search space according to a neighborhood. At each iteration, a neighboring solution M' is generated by changing the value of the element $a_{i,j}$ by a different legal member of the alphabet in the current solution M. The cost of this iteration is evaluated as $\Delta E = E(M') - E(M)$. If ΔE is negative or equal to zero, then the neighboring solution M' is accepted. Otherwise, it is accepted with probability $P(\Delta E) = e^{-\Delta E/T_n}$, where T_n is determined by a cooling schedule. In their implementation, Cohen et al. use a simple linear function $T_n = 0.9998T_{n-1}$ with an initial temperature fixed at $T_i = 0.20$. At each temperature, 2000 neighboring solutions are generated. The algorithm stops either if a valid covering array is found, or if no change in the cost of the current solution is observed after 500 trials. The authors justify their choice of these parameter values based on some experimental tuning. They conclude that their SA implementation is able to produce smaller CAs than other computational methods, sometimes improving upon algebraic constructions. However, they also indicate that their SA algorithm fails to match the algebraic constructions for larger problems, especially when $t = 3$.

Some of these approximated strategies must verify that the matrix they are building is a CA. If the matrix is of size $N \times k$ and the interaction is t, there are $\binom{k}{t}$ different combinations which implies a cost of $O(N \times \binom{k}{t})$ (given that the verification cost per combination is $O(N)$). For small values of t and v the verification of CAs is overcame through the use of sequential approaches; however, when we try to construct CAs of moderate values of t, v and k, the time spent by those approaches is impractical, for example when $t = 5, k = 256, v = 2$ there are $8,809,549,056$ different combinations of columns which require days for their verification. This scenario shows the necessity of grid strategies to solve the verification of CAs.

The next section presents an algorithm for the verification of a given matrix is a CA. The design of algorithm is presented for its implementation in grid architectures.

3. An algorithm for the verification of covering arrays

In this section we describe a grid approach for the problem of verification of CAs. See (Avila-George et al., 2010) for more details.

A matrix $\mathcal{M}$ of size $N \times k$ is a $CA(N;t,k,v)$ iff every t-tuple contains the set of combination of symbols described by $\{0,1,...,v-1\}^t$. We propose a strategy that uses two data structures called P and J, and two injections between the sets of t-tuples and combinations of symbols, and the set of integer numbers, to verify that $\mathcal{M}$ is a CA.

Let $\mathcal{C} = \{c_1, c_2, ..., c_{\binom{k}{t}}\}$ be the set of the different t-tuples. A t-tuple $c_i = \{c_{i,1}, c_{i,2}, ..., c_{i,t}\}$ is formed by t numbers, each number $c_{i,1}$ denotes a column of matrix $\mathcal{M}$. The set $\mathcal{C}$ can be managed using an injective function $f(c_i) : \mathcal{C} \to \mathcal{I}$ between $\mathcal{C}$ and the integer numbers, this function is defined in Eq. 1.

$$f(c_i) = \sum_{j=1}^{t} \binom{c_{i,j} - 1}{i + 1} \tag{1}$$

Now, let $\mathcal{W} = \{w_1, w_2, ..., w_{v^t}\}$ be the set of the different combination of symbols, where $w_i \in \{0, 1, ..., v-1\}^t$. The injective function $g(w_i) : \mathcal{W} \to \mathcal{I}$ is defined as done in Eq. 2. The function $g(w_i)$ is equivalent to the transformation of a v-ary number to the decimal system.

$$g(w_i) = \sum_{j=1}^{t} w_{i,j} \cdot v^{t-i} \tag{2}$$

The use of the injections represents an efficient method to manipulate the information that will be stored in the data structures P and J used in the verification process of $\mathcal{M}$ as a CA. The matrix P is of size $\binom{k}{t} \times v^t$ and it counts the number of times that each combination appears in $\mathcal{M}$ in the different t-tuples. Each row of P represents a different t-tuple, while each column contains a different combination of symbols. The management of the cells $p_{i,j} \in P$ is done through the functions $f(c_i)$ and $g(w_j)$; while $f(c_i)$ retrieves the row related with the t-tuple c_i, the function $g(w_i)$ returns the column that corresponds to the combination of symbols w_i. The vector J is of size t and it helps in the enumeration of all the t-tuples $c_i \in \mathcal{C}$.

Table 3 shows an example of the use of the function $g(w_j)$ for the Covering Array $CA(9; 2, 4, 3)$ (shown in Fig. 1). Column 1 shows the different combination of symbols. Column 2 contains the operation from which the equivalence is derived. Column 3 presents the integer number associated with that combination.

$\mathcal{W}$	$g(w_i)$	$\mathcal{I}$
w_1 ={0,0}	$0 \cdot 3^1 + 0 \cdot 3^0$	0
w_2 ={0,1}	$0 \cdot 3^1 + 1 \cdot 3^0$	1
w_3 ={0,2}	$0 \cdot 3^1 + 2 \cdot 3^0$	2
w_4 ={1,0}	$1 \cdot 3^1 + 0 \cdot 3^0$	3
w_5 ={1,1}	$1 \cdot 3^1 + 1 \cdot 3^0$	4
w_6 ={1,2}	$1 \cdot 3^1 + 2 \cdot 3^0$	5
w_7 ={2,0}	$2 \cdot 3^1 + 0 \cdot 3^0$	6
w_8 ={2,1}	$2 \cdot 3^1 + 1 \cdot 3^0$	7
w_9 ={2,2}	$2 \cdot 3^1 + 2 \cdot 3^0$	8

Table 3. Mapping of the set $\mathcal{W}$ to the set of integers using the function $g(w_j)$ in $CA(9; 2, 4, 3)$ shown in Fig. 1.

The matrix P is initialized to zero. The construction of matrix P is direct from the definitions of $f(c_i)$ and $g(w_j)$; it counts the number of times that a combination of symbols $w_j \in \mathcal{W}$ appears in each subset of columns corresponding to a t-tuple c_i, and increases the value of the cell $p_{f(c_i),g(w_j)} \in P$ in that number.

Table 4(a) shows the use of injective function $f(c_i)$. Table 4(b) presents the matrix P of $CA(9;2,4,3)$. The different combination of symbols $w_j \in \mathcal{W}$ are in the first rows. The number appearing in each cell referenced by a pair (c_i, w_j) is the number of times that combination w_j appears in the set of columns c_i of the matrix $CA(9;2,4,3)$.

(a) Applying $f(c_i)$.

c_i		
index	t-tuple	$f(c_i)$
c_1	{1,2}	0
c_2	{1,3}	1
c_3	{1,4}	3
c_4	{2,3}	2
c_5	{2,4}	4
c_6	{3,4}	5

(b) Matrix P.

	$g(w_j)$								
$f(c_i)$	{0,0}	{0,1}	{0,2}	{1,0}	{1,1}	{1,2}	{2,0}	{2,1}	{2,2}
0	1	1	1	1	1	1	1	1	1
1	1	1	1	1	1	1	1	1	1
2	1	1	1	1	1	1	1	1	1
3	1	1	1	1	1	1	1	1	1
4	1	1	1	1	1	1	1	1	1
5	1	1	1	1	1	1	1	1	1

Table 4. Example of the matrix P resulting from $CA(9;2,4,3)$ presented in Fig. 1.

In summary, to determine if a matrix $\mathcal{M}$ is or not a CA the number of different combination of symbols per t-tuple is counted using the matrix P. The matrix $\mathcal{M}$ will be a CA iff the matrix P contains no zero in it.

The grid approach takes as input a matrix $\mathcal{M}$ and the parameters N, k, v, t that describe the CA that $\mathcal{M}$ can be. Also, the algorithm requires the sets $\mathcal{C}$ and $\mathcal{W}$. The algorithm outputs the total number of missing combinations in the matrix $\mathcal{M}$ to be a CA. The Algorithm 1 shows the pseudocode of the grid approach for the problem of verification of CAs; particularly, the algorithm shows the process performed by each core involved in the verification of CAs. The strategy followed by the algorithm 1 is simple, it involves a block distribution model of the set of t-tuples. The set $\mathcal{C}$ is divided into n blocks, where n is the processors number; the size of block $\mathcal{B}$ is equal to $\lceil \frac{\mathcal{C}}{n} \rceil$. The block distribution model maintains the simplicity in the code; this model allows the assignment of each block to a different core such that SA can be applied to verify the blocks.

Algorithm 1: Grid approach to verify CAs. This algorithm assigns the set of t-tuples $\mathcal{C}$ to *size* different cores.

Input: A covering array file, the number of processors (*size*) and the current processor id (*rank*).
Result: A file with the number of missing combination of symbols.

```
begin
    readInputFile()                          /* Read M, N, k, v and t parameters.   */
    B ← ⌈ (k choose t) / size ⌉              /* t-tuples per processor.             */
    K_l ← rank · B                           /* The scalar corresponding to the first t-tuple. */
    K_u ← (rank + 1) · B − 1                 /* The scalar corresponding to the last t-tuple.  */
    Miss ← t_wise(M, N, k, v, t, K_l, K_u)   /* Number of missing t-tuples.         */
end
```

The *t_wise* function first counts for each different t-tuple c_i the times that a combination $w_j \in \mathcal{W}$ is found in the columns of $\mathcal{M}$ corresponding to c_i. After that, it calculates the missing combinations $w_j \in \mathcal{W}$ in c_i. Finally, it transforms c_i into c_{i+1}, i.e. it determines the next t-tuple to be evaluated.

The pseudocode for *t_wise* function is presented in Algorithm 2. For each different t-tuple (lines 5 to 28) the function performs the following actions: counts the expected number of times a combination w_j appears in the set of columns indicated by J (lines 6 to 14, where the combination w_j is the one appearing in $\mathcal{M}_{n,J}$, i.e. in row n and t-tuple J); then, the counter *covered* is increased in the number of different combinations with a number of repetitions greater than zero (lines 10 to 12). After that, the function calculates the number of missing combinations (line 15). The last step of each iteration of the function is the calculation of the next t-tuple to be analyzed (lines 16 to 27). The function ends when all the t-tuples have been analyzed (line 5).

Algorithm 2: Function to verify a CA.

```
   Output: Number of missing t-tuples.
1  t_wise (M, N, k, v, t, K_l, K_u)
2  begin
3      Miss ← 0, iMax ← t − 1, P ← 0
4      J ← getInitialTuple(k, t, K_l)
5      while J_t ≤ k and f(J) ≤ K_u do
6          covered ← 0
7          for n ← 1 to N do
8              P_{f(J),g(M_{n,J})} ← P_{f(J),g(M_{n,J})} + 1
9          end for
10         for j ← 1 to v^t do
11             if P_{f(J),j} > 0 then
12                 covered ← covered + 1
13             end if
14         end for
15         Miss ← Miss + v^t − covered
           /* Calculates the next t-tuple */
16         J_t ← J_t + 1
17         if J_t > k and iMax > 0 then
18             J_iMax ← J_iMax + 1
19             for i ← iMax + 1 to t do
20                 J_i ← J_{i−1} + 1
21             end for
22             if J_iMax > k − t + iMax then
23                 iMax ← iMax − 1
24             else
25                 iMax ← t
26             end if
27         end if
28     end while
29     return Miss
30 end
```

To make the distribution of work, it is necessary to calculate the initial t-tuple f for each core according to its ID (denoted by *rank*), where $F = rank \cdot \mathcal{B}$. Therefore it is necessary a method to convert the scalar F to the equivalent t-tuple $c_i \in \mathcal{C}$. The sequential generation of each t-tuple c_i previous to c_F can be a time consuming task. There is where lies the main contribution of our grid approach; its simplicity is combined with a clever strategy for computing the initial t-tuple of each block.

We propose the *getInitialTuple* function as a method that generates c_F (see Algorithm 3), according to a lexicographical, without generating its previous t-tuples c_i, where $i < F$. To explain the purpose of the *getInitialTuple* function, lets consider the $CA(9;2,4,3)$ shown in Fig. 1. This CA has as set $\mathcal{C}$ the elements found in column 1 of Table 4(a). The *getInitialTuple* function with input $k = 4,\ t = 2,\ F = 3$ must return $J = \{1,4\}$, i.e. the values of the t-tuple c_3. The *getInitialTuple* function is optimized to find the vector $J = \{J_1, J_2, ..., J_t\}$ that corresponds to F. The value J_i is calculated according to

$$J_i = \min_{j \geq 1} \left\{ \Delta_i \leq \sum_{l=J_{i-1}+1}^{j} \binom{k-l}{t-i} \right\}$$

where

$$\Delta_i = F - \sum_{m=1}^{i-1} \sum_{l=J_{m-1}+1}^{J_m - 1} \binom{k-l}{t-m}$$

and

$$J_0 = 0.$$

Algorithm 3: Get initial t-tuple to PA.

Input: Parameters k and t; the scalar corresponding to the first t-tuple ($\mathcal{K}_l$).
Output: The initial t-tuple.

```
getInitialTuple ( k, t, K_l )
begin
    Θ ← K_l, iK ← 1, iT ← 1
    kint ← C(k−iK, t−iT)
    for i ← 1 to t do
        while Θ > kint do
            Θ ← Θ − kint
            iK ← iK + 1
            kint ← C(k−iK, t−iT)
        end while
        J_i ← iK
        iK ← iK + 1
        iT ← iT + 1
        kint ← C(k−iK, t−iT)
    end for
    return J
end
```

In summary, the Algorithm 3 only requires the computation of $O(t \times k)$ binomials to compute the n initial t-tuples of the PA. This represents a great improvement in contrast with the naive approach that would require the generation of all the $\binom{k}{t}$ t-tuples, as done in the SA.

The next three sections presents a simulated annealing approach to construct CAs. Section 4 describes in depth the components of our algorithm. Section 5 presents a method to parallelizing our SA algorithm. Section 6 describes how to implement our algorithm on a grid architecture.

4. An algorithm for the construction of covering arrays using a simulated annealing technique

Often the solution space of an optimization problem has many local minima. A simple local search algorithm proceeds by choosing random initial solution and generating a neighbor from that solution. The neighboring solution is accepted if it is a cost decreasing transition. Such a simple algorithm has the drawback of often converging to a local minimum. The simulated annealing algorithm (SA), though by itself it is a local search algorithm, avoids getting trapped in a local minimum by also accepting cost increasing neighbors with some probability. SA is a general-purpose stochastic optimization method that has proven to be an effective tool for approximating globally optimal solutions to many types of NP-hard combinatorial optimization problems. In this section, we briefly review SA algorithm and propose an implementation to solve CAC problem.

SA is a randomized local search method based on the simulation of annealing of metal. The acceptance probability of a trial solution is given by Eq. 3, where T is the *temperature* of the system, ΔE is the difference of the costs between the trial and the current solutions (the cost change due to the perturbation), Eq. 3 means that the trial solution is accepted by nonzero probability $e^{(-\Delta E/T)}$ even though the solution deteriorates (*uphill move*).

$$(P) = \begin{cases} 1 & if \Delta E < 0 \\ e^{(-\frac{\Delta E}{T})} & otherwise \end{cases} \tag{3}$$

Uphill moves enable the system to escape from the local minima; without them, the system would be trapped into a local minimum. Too high of a probability for the occurrence of uphill moves, however, prevents the system from converging. In SA, the probability is controlled by temperature in such a manner that at the beginning of the procedure the temperature is sufficiently high, in which a high probability is available, and as the calculation proceeds the temperature is gradually decreased, lowering the probability (Jun & Mizuta, 2005).

4.1 Internal representation

The following paragraphs will describe each of the components of the implementation of our SA. The description is done given the matrix representation of an CA. An CA can be represented as a matrix M of size $N \times k$, where the columns are the parameters and the rows are the cases of the test set that is constructed. Each cell $m_{i,j}$ in the array accepts values from the set $\{1, 2, ..., v_j\}$ where v_j is the cardinality of the alphabet of jth column.

4.2 Initial solution

The *initial solution* M is constructed by generating M as a matrix with maximum Hamming distance. The Hamming distance $d(x, y)$ between two rows $x, y \in M$ is the number of elements in which they differ. Let r_i be a row of the matrix M. To generate a random matrix M of maximum Hamming distance the following steps are performed:

1. Generate the first row r_1 at random.
2. Generate two rows c_1, c_2 at random, which will be candidate rows.
3. Select the candidate row c_i that maximizes the Hamming distance according to Eq. 4 and added to the ith row of the matrix M.

$$g(r_i) = \sum_{s=1}^{i-1} \sum_{v=1}^{k} d(m_{s,v}, m_{i,v}), \textbf{where } d(m_{s,v}, m_{i,v}) = \begin{cases} 1 \textbf{ if } m_{s,v} \neq m_{i,v} \\ 0 \textbf{ Otherwise} \end{cases} \quad (4)$$

4. Repeat from step 2 until M is completed.

An example is shown in Fig. 2; the number of symbols different between rows r_1 and c_1 are 4 and between r_2 and c_1 are 3 summing up 7. Then, the hamming distance for the candidate row c_1 is 7.

$$Rows \begin{cases} r_1 = \{2\,1\,0\,1\} \\ r_2 = \{1\,2\,0\,1\} \\ c_1 = \{0\,2\,1\,0\} \end{cases} \qquad Distances \begin{cases} d(r_1, c_1) = 4 \\ d(r_2, c_1) = 3 \\ g(c_1) = 7 \end{cases}$$

Fig. 2. Example of the hamming distance between two rows r_1, r_2 that are already in the matrix $\mathcal{M}$ and a candidate row c_1.

4.3 Evaluations function

The *evaluation function* $E(M)$ is used to estimate the goodness of a candidate solution. Previously reported metaheuristic algorithms for constructing CA have commonly evaluated the quality of a potential solution (covering array) as the number of combination of symbols missing in the matrix M (Cohen et al., 2003; Nurmela, 2004; Shiba et al., 2004). Then, the expected solution will be zero missing.

In the proposed SA implementation this evaluation function definition was used. Its computational complexity is equivalent to $O(N\binom{k}{t})$.

4.4 Neighborhood function

Given that our SA implementation is based on Local Search (LS) then a neighborhood function must be defined. The main objective of the neighborhood function is to identify the set of potential solutions which can be reached from the current solution in a LS algorithm. In case two or more neighborhoods present complementary characteristics, it is then possible and interesting to create more powerful compound neighborhoods. The advantage of such an approach is well documented in (Cavique et al., 1999). Following this idea, and based on the results of our preliminary experimentations, a neighborhood structure composed by two different functions is proposed for this SA algorithm implementation.

Two *neighborhood functions* were implemented to guide the local search of our SA algorithm. The neighborhood function $\mathcal{N}_1(s)$ makes a random search of a missing t-tuple, then tries by setting the jth combination of symbols in every row of M. The neighborhood function $\mathcal{N}_2(s)$ randomly chooses a position (i, j) of the matrix M and makes all possible changes of symbol. During the search process a combination of both $\mathcal{N}_1(s)$ and $\mathcal{N}_2(s)$ neighborhood functions is employed by our SA algorithm. The former is applied with probability P, while the latter is employed at an $(1 - P)$ rate. This combined neighborhood function $\mathcal{N}_3(s, x)$ is defined in Eq. 5, where x is a random number in the interval [0, 1).

$$\mathcal{N}_3(s,x) = \begin{cases} \mathcal{N}_1(s) & \text{if } x \leq P \\ \mathcal{N}_2(s) & \text{if } x > P \end{cases} \tag{5}$$

In the next section it is presented our parallel simulated annealing approach for solving CAC problem.

4.5 Cooling schedule

The *cooling schedule* determines the degree of uphill movement permitted during the search and is thus critical to the SA algorithm's performance. The parameters that define a cooling schedule are: an initial temperature, a final temperature or a stopping criterion, the maximum number of neighboring solutions that can be generated at each temperature, and a rule for decrementing the temperature. The literature offers a number of different cooling schedules, see for instance (Aarts & Van Laarhoven, 1985; Atiqullah, 2004). In our SA implementation we preferred a geometrical cooling scheme mainly for its simplicity. It starts at an initial temperature T_i which is decremented at each round by a factor α using the relation $T_k = \alpha T_{k-1}$. For each temperature, the maximum number of visited neighboring solutions is L. It depends directly on the parameters (N, k and v is the maximum cardinality of M) of the studied covering array. This is because more moves are required for CAs with alphabets of greater cardinality.

4.6 Termination condition

The *stop criterion* for our SA is either when the current temperature reaches T_f, when it ceases to make progress, or when a valid covering array is found. In the proposed implementation a lack of progress exists if after ϕ (frozen factor) consecutive temperature decrements the best-so-far solution is not improved.

4.7 SA Pseudocode

The Algorithm 4 presents the simulated annealing heuristic as described above. The meaning of the four functions is obvious: INITIALIZE computes a start solution and initial values of the parameters T and L; GENERATE selects a solution from the neighborhood of the current solution, using the neighborhood function $\mathcal{N}_3(s, x)$; CALCULATE_CONTROL computes a new value for the parameter T (cooling schedule) and the number of consecutive temperature decrements with no improvement in the solution.

5. Parallel simulated annealing

In this section we propose a parallel strategy to construct CAs using a simulated annealing algorithm.

A common approach to parallelizing simulated annealing is to generate several perturbations in the current solution simultaneously. Some of them, those with small variance, locally explore the region around the current point, while those with larger variances globally explore the feasible region. If each process has got different perturbation or move generation, each

Algorithm 4: Sequential simulated annealing for the CAC problem

```
INITIALIZE(M,T,L) ;                          /* Create the initial solution.  */
M* ← M ;                                     /* Memorize the best solution.  */
repeat
    for i ← 1 to L do
        M_i ← GENERATE(M) ;                   /* Perturb current state.  */
        ΔE ← E(M_i) − E(M) ;                  /* Evaluate cost function.  */
        x ← random ;                          /* Range [0,1).  */
        if ΔE < 0 or e^(−ΔE/T) > x then
            M ← M_i ;                         /* Accept new state.  */
            if E(M) < E(M*) then
                M* ← M ;                      /* Memorize the best solution.  */
            end if
        end if
    end for
    CALCULATE_CONTROL(T,φ)
until termination condition is satisfied;
```

process will probably get a different solution at the end of iterations. This approach may be described as follows:

1. The *master* node set $T = T_0$, generates an *initial_solution* using the Hamming distance algorithm (See Section 4.2) and distributes them to each workers.
2. At the current temperature T, each worker begins to execute iterative operations (L).
3. At the end of iterations, the *master* is responsible for collecting the solution obtained by each process at current temperature and broadcasts the best solution of them among all participating processes.
4. If the termination condition is not met, each process reduces the temperature and goes back to step 2, else algorithm terminates.

Algorithm 5 shows the pseudocode for *master* node. The function INITIALIZE computes a start solution (using Hamming distances algorithm) and initial values of the parameters T and L. The *master* node distributes the initial parameters to slave nodes, and awaits the results. Each L iterations, the slaves send their results to the master node (See Algorithm 6). The master node selects the best solution. If the termination criterion is not satisfied, the master node computes a new value for the parameter T (cooling schedule) and the number of consecutive temperature decrements with no improvement in the solution.

Algorithm 5: Simulated annealing for the master node

```
INITIALIZE(M,T,L) ;                          /* Create the initial solution.  */
M* ← M ;                                     /* Memorize the best solution.  */
repeat
    M ← annealing_worker(M*,T,L) ;            /* Call workers */
    if E(M) < E(M*) then
        M* ← M ;                              /* Memorize the best solution.  */
    end if
    CALCULATE_CONTROL(T,φ)
until termination condition is satisfied;
```

Algorithm 6: Worker algorithm

Input: *best_solution*, Temperature (T) and the number of perturbations (L).
Output: *best_local_solution*.

annealing_worker(M, T, L **)**
for $i \leftarrow 1$ **to** L **do**
  $M_i \leftarrow GENERATE(M)$ `/* Perturb current state. */`
  $\Delta E \leftarrow E(M_i) - E(M)$ `/* Evaluate cost function. */`
  $x \leftarrow random$ `/* Range [0,1). */`
  if $\Delta E < 0$ **or** $e^{(-\frac{\Delta E}{T})} > x$ **then**
    $M \leftarrow M_i$ `/* Accept new state. */`
  end if
end for
return M

6. Grid Computing approach

Simulated annealing (SA) is inherently sequential and hence very slow for problems with large search spaces. Several attempts have been made to speed up this process, such as development of special purpose computer architectures (Ram et al., 1996). As an alternative, we propose a Grid deployment of the parallel SA algorithm for constructing CAs, introduced in the previous section. In order to fully understand the Grid implementation developed in this work, this subsection will introduce all the details regarding the Grid Computing Platform used and then, the different execution strategies will be exposed.

6.1 Grid Computing Platform

The evolution of Grid Middlewares has enabled the deployment of Grid e-Science infrastructures delivering large computational and data storage capabilities. Current infrastructures, such as the one used in this work, EGI, rely on gLite mainly as core middleware supporting several services in some cases. World-wide initiatives such as EGI, aim at linking and sharing components and resources from several European NGIs (National Grid Initiatives).

In the EGI infrastructure, jobs are specified through a job description language (Pacini, 2001) or JDL that defines the main components of a job: executable, input data, output data, arguments and restrictions. The restrictions define the features a resource should provide, and could be used for meta-scheduling or for local scheduling (such as in the case of MPI jobs). Input data could be small or large and job-specific or common to all jobs, which affects the protocols and mechanisms needed. Executables are either compiled or multiplatform codes (scripts, Java, Perl) and output data suffer from similar considerations as input data.

The key resources in the EGI infrastructure are extensively listed in the literature, and can be summarized as:

1. WMS / RB (Workload Management System / Resource Broker): Meta-scheduler that coordinates the submission and monitoring of jobs.
2. CE (Computing Elements): The access point to a farm of identical computing nodes, which contains the LRMS (Local Resource Management System). The LRMS is responsible for scheduling the jobs submitted to the CE, allocating the execution of a job in one

(sequential) or more (parallel) computing nodes. In the case that no free computing nodes are available, jobs are queued. Thus, the load of a CE must be considered when estimating the turnaround of a job.

3. WN (Working Nodes): Each one of the computing resources accessible through a CE. Due to the heterogeneous nature of Grid infrastructure, the response time of a job will depend on the characteristics of the WN hosting it.
4. SE (Storage Element): Storage resources in which a task can store long-living data to be used by the computers of the Grid. This practice is necessary due to the size limitation imposed by current Grid Middlewares in the job file attachment (10 Megabytes in the gLite case). So, use cases which require the access to files which exceed that limitation are forced to use these Storage Elements. Nevertheless, the construction of CAs is not a data-intensive use case and thus the use of SEs can be avoided.
5. LFC (Logic File Catalog): A hierarchical directory of logical names referencing a set of physical files and replicas stored in the SEs.
6. BDII (Berkley Database Information System): Service point for the Information System which registers, through LDAP, the status of the Grid. Useful information relative to CEs, WNs and SEs can be obtained by querying this element.
7. R-GMA (Relational Grid Monitoring Architecture). Service for the registration and notification of information in most of the EGI services.
8. VOMS (Virtual Organisation Management System). Authorization infrastructure to define the access rights to resources.

Some of this terms will be referenced along the following sections.

6.2 Preprocessing task: Selecting the most appropriate CEs

A production infrastructure such as EGI involves tens of thousands of resources from hundreds of sites, involving tens of countries and a large human team. Since it is a general-purpose platform, and although there is a common middleware and a recommended operating system, the heterogeneity in the configuration and operation of the resources is inevitable. This heterogeneity, along with other social and human factors such as the large geographical coverage and the different skills of operators introduces a significant degree of uncertainty in the infrastructure. Even considering that the service level required is around 95%, it is statistically likely to find in each large execution sites that are not working properly. Thus, prior to beginning the experiments, it is necessary to do empirical tests to define a group of valid computing resources (CEs) and this way facing resource setup problems. These tests can give some real information like computational speed, primary and secondary memory sizes and I/O transfer speed. These data, in case there are huge quantities of resources, will be helpful to establish quality criteria choosing resources.

6.3 Asynchronous schema

Once the computing elements, where the jobs will be submitted, have been selected, the next step involves correctly specifying the jobs. In that sense, it will be necessary to produce the specification using the job description language in gLite. An example of a JDL file can be seen in the Fig. 3.

```
Type = "Job";
VirtualOrganisation = "biomed";
Executable = "test.sh";
Arguments = "16 21 3 2";
StdOutput = "std.out";
StdError = "std.err";
InputSandbox = {"/home/CA_experiment/gridCA.c","/home/CA_experiment/N16k21v3t2.ca","/home/CA_experiment/test.sh"};
OutputSandbox = {"std.out","std.err","N16k21v3t2.ca"};
```

Fig. 3. JDL example for the case of $N = 16, k = 21, v = 3, t = 2$.

As it can be seen in Fig. 3, the specification of the job includes: the virtual organisation where the job will be launched (VirtualOrganisation), the main file that will start the execution of the job (Executable), the arguments that will used for invoking the executable (Arguments), the files in which the standard outputs will be dumped (StdOutput y StdError), and finally the result files that will be returned to the user interface (OutputSandBox).

So, the most important part of the execution lies in the program (a shell-script) specified in the *Executable* field of the description file. The use of a shell-script instead of directly using the executable (gridCA) is mandatory due to the heterogeneous nature present in the Grid. Although the conditions vary between different resources, as it was said before, the administrators of the sites are recommended to install Unix-like operative systems. This measure makes sure that all the developed programs will be seamlessly executed in any machine of the Grid infrastructure. The source code must be dynamically compiled in each of the computing resources hosting the jobs. Thus, basically, the shell-script works like a wrapper that looks for a *gcc*-like compiler (the source code is written in the C language), compiles the source code and finally invokes the executable with the proper arguments (values of N, k, v and t respectively).

One of the most crucial parts of any Grid deployment is the development of an automatic system for controlling and monitoring the evolution of an experiment. Basically, the system will be in charge of submitting the different gLite jobs (the number of jobs is equal to the value of the parameter N), monitoring the status of these jobs, resubmitting (in case a job has failed or it has been successfully completed but the SA algorithm has not already converged) and retrieving the results. This automatic system has been implemented as a master process which periodically (or asynchronously as the name of the schema suggests) oversees the status of the jobs.

This system must possess the following properties: completeness, correctness, quick performance and efficiency on the usage of the resources. Regarding the completeness, we have take into account that an experiment will involve a lot of jobs and it must be ensured that all jobs are successfully completed at the end. The correctness implies that there should be a guarantee that all jobs produce correct results which are comprehensive presented to the user and that the data used is properly updated and coherent during the whole experiment (the master must correctly update the file with the .ca extension showed in the JDL specification in order the Simulated Annealing algorithm to converge). The quick performance property implies that the experiment will finish as quickly as possible. In that sense, the key aspects are: a good selection of the resources that will host the jobs (according to the empirical tests performed in the preprocessing stage) and an adequate resubmission policy (sending new jobs to the resources that are being more productive during the execution of the experiment). Finally, if the on-the-fly tracking of the most productive computing resources is correctly done, the efficiency in the usage of the resources will be achieved.

Due to the asynchronous behavior of this schema, the number of slaves (jobs) that can be submitted (the maximum size of N) is only limited by the infrastructure. However, other schemas such as the one showed in the next point, could achieve a better performance in certain scenarios.

6.4 Synchronous schema

This schema a sophisticated mechanism known, in Grid terminology, as submission of *pilot jobs*. The submission of pilot jobs is based on the master-worker architecture and supported by the DIANE (DIANE, 2011) + Ganga (Moscicki et al., 2009) tools. When the processing begins a master process (a server) is started locally, which will provide tasks to the worker nodes until all the tasks have been completed, being then dismissed. On the other side, the worker agents are jobs running on the Working Nodes of the Grid which communicate with the master. The master must keep track of the tasks to assure that all of them are successfully completed while workers provide the access to a CPU previously reached through scheduling, which will process the tasks. If, for any reason a task fails or a worker losses contact with the master, the master will immediately reassign the task to another worker. The whole process is exposed in Fig. 4. So, in contrast to the asynchronous schema, in this case the master is continuously in contact with the slaves.

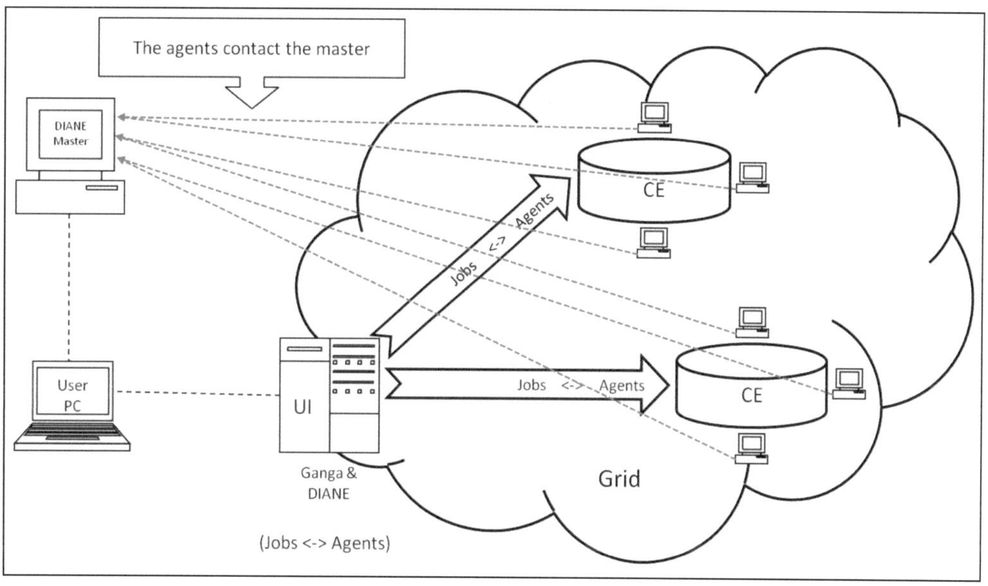

Fig. 4. Pilot jobs schema offered by DIANE-Ganga.

However, before initiating the process or execution of the master/worker jobs, it is necessary to define their characteristics. Firstly, the specification of a run must include the master configuration (workers and heartbeat timeout). It is also necessary to establish master scheduling policies such as the maximum number of times that a lost or failed task is assigned to a worker; the reaction when a task is lost or fails; and the number of resubmissions before a worker is removed. Finally, the master must know the arguments of the tasks and the files shared by all tasks (executable and any auxiliary files).

At this point, the master can be started using the specification described above. Upon checking that all is right, the master will wait for incoming connections from the workers.

Workers are generic jobs that can perform any operation requested by the master which are submitted to the Grid. In addition, these workers must be submitted to the selected CEs in the pre-processing stage. When a worker registers to the master, the master will automatically assign it a task.

This schema has several advantages derived from the fact that a worker can execute more than one task. Only when a worker has successfully completed a task the master will reassign it a new one. In addition, when a worker demands a new task it is not necessary to submit a new job. This way, the queuing time of the task is intensively reduced. Moreover, the dynamic behavior of this schema allows achieving better performance results, in comparison to the asynchronous schema.

However, there are also some disadvantages that must be mentioned. The first issue refers to the unidirectional connectivity between the master host and the worker hosts (Grid node). While the master host needs inbound connectivity, the worker node needs outbound connectivity. The connectivity problem in the master can be solved easily by opening a port in the local host; however the connectivity in the worker will rely in the remote system configuration (the CE). So, in this case, this extra detail must be taken into account when selecting the computing resources. Another issue is defining an adequate timeout value. If, for some reason, a task working correctly suffers from temporary connection problems and exceeds the timeout threshold it will cause the worker being removed by the master. Finally, a key factor will be to identify the rightmost number of worker agents and tasks. In addition, if the number of workers is on the order of thousands (i.e. when N is about 1000) bottlenecks could be met, resulting on the master being overwhelmed by the excessive number of connections.

7. Experimental results

This section presents an experimental design and results derived from testing the approach described in the section 6. In order to show the performance of the SA algorithm, two experiments were developed. The first experiment had as purpose to fine tune the probabilities of the neighborhood functions to be selected. The second experiment evaluated the performance of SA over a new benchmark proposed in this chapter. The results were compared against two of the well-known tools in the literature that constructs CAs, the TConfig[1] (recursive constructions) and ACTS[2] (a greedy algorithm named IPOG-F) respectively.

In all the experiments the following parameters were used for our SA implementation:

1. Initial temperature $T_i = 4.0$
2. Final temperature $T_f = 1.0E - 10$
3. Cooling factor $\alpha = 0.99$
4. Maximum neighboring solutions per temperature $L = (N \times k \times v)^2$

---

[1] TConfig: `http://www.site.uottawa.ca/~awilliam/TConfig.jar`
[2] ACTS: `http://csrc.nist.gov/groups/SNS/acts/index.html`

5. Frozen factor $\phi = 11$
6. According to the results shown in section 7.1, the neighborhood function $\mathcal{N}_3(s, x)$ is applied using a probability $P = 0.3$

Moreover, the characteristics of the Grid infrastructure employed for carrying the experiments are:

1. Infrastructure's name: EGI (European Grid infrastructure)
2. Virtual Organisation: biomed
3. Middleware: gLite
4. Total number of WNs available: 281.530

7.1 Fine tuning the probability of execution of the neighborhood functions

It is well-known that the performance of a SA algorithm is sensitive to parameter tuning. In this sense, we follow a methodology for a fine tuning of the two neighborhood functions used in our SA algorithm. The fine tuning was based on the next linear Diophantine equation,

$$P_1x_1 + P_2x_2 = q$$

where x_i represents a neighborhood function and its value set to 1, P_i is a value in $\{0.0, 0.1, .., 1.0\}$ that represents the probability of executing x_i , and q is set to 1.0 which is the maximum probability of executing any x_i. A solution to the given linear Diophantine equation must satisfy

$$\sum_{i=1}^{2} P_i x_i = 1.0$$

This equation has 11 solutions, each solution is an experiment that test the degree of participation of each neighborhood function in our SA implementation to accomplish the construction of an CA. Every combination of the probabilities was applied by SA to construct the set of CAs shows in Table 5(a) and each experiment was run 31 times, with the data obtained for each experiment we calculate the median. A summary of the performance of SA with the probabilities that solved the 100% of the runs is shown in Table 5(b).

Finally, given the results shown in Fig. 5 the best configuration of probabilities was $P_1 = 0.3$ and $P_2 = 0.7$ because it found the CAs in smaller time (median value). The values $P_1 = 0.3$ and $P_2 = 0.7$ were kept fixed in the second experiment.

In the next subsection, we will present more computational results obtained from a performance comparison carried out among our SA algorithm, a well-known greedy algorithm (IPOG_F) and a tool named TConfig that constructs CAs using recursive functions.

7.2 Comparing SA with the state-of-the-art algorithms

For the second of our experiments we have obtained the ACTS and TConfig software. We create a new benchmark composed by 60 ternary CAs instances where $5 \leq k \leq 100$ and $2 \leq t \leq 4$.

The SA implementation reported by (Cohen et al., 2003) for solving the CAC problem was intentionally omitted from this comparison because as their authors recognize this algorithm fails to produce competitive results when the strength of the arrays is $t \geq 3$.

(a)

Id	CA description
ca_1	$CA(19;2,30,3)$
ca_2	$CA(35;3,5,3)$
ca_3	$CA(58;3,10,3)$
ca_4	$CA(86;4,5,3)$
ca_5	$CA(204;4,10,3)$
ca_6	$CA(243;5,5,3)$
ca_7	$CA(1040;5,15,3)$

(b)

p_1	p_2	ca_1	ca_2	ca_3	ca_4	ca_5	ca_6	ca_7
0	1	4789.763	3.072	46.989	12.544	3700.038	167.901	0.102
0.1	0.9	1024.635	0.098	0.299	0.236	344.341	3.583	0.008
0.2	0.8	182.479	0.254	0.184	0.241	173.752	1.904	0.016
0.3	0.7	224.786	0.137	0.119	0.222	42.950	1.713	0.020
0.4	0.6	563.857	0.177	0.123	0.186	92.616	3.351	0.020
0.5	0.5	378.399	0.115	0.233	0.260	40.443	1.258	0.035
0.6	0.4	272.056	0.153	0.136	0.178	69.311	2.524	0.033
0.7	0.3	651.585	0.124	0.188	0.238	94.553	2.127	0.033
0.8	0.2	103.399	0.156	0.267	0.314	81.611	5.469	0.042
0.9	0.1	131.483	0.274	0.353	0.549	76.379	4.967	0.110
1	0	7623.546	15.905	18.285	23.927	1507.369	289.104	2.297

Table 5. (a) A set of 7 CAs configurations; (b) Performance of SA with the 11 combinations of probabilities which solved the 100% of the runs to construct the CAs listed in (a).

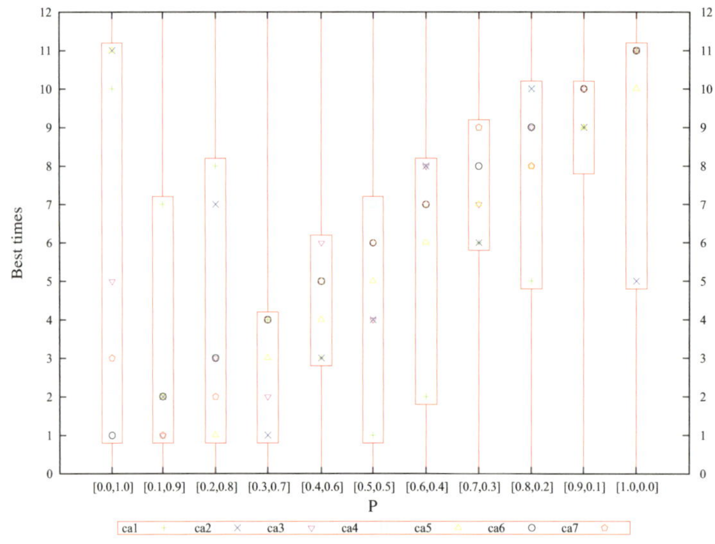

Fig. 5. Performance of our SA with the 11 combinations of probabilities.

The results from this experiment are summarized in Table 6, which presents in the first two columns the strength t and the degree k of the selected benchmark instances. The best size N found by the TConfig tool, IPOG-F algorithm and our SA algorithm are listed in columns 3, 4 and 5 respectively. Next, Fig. 6 compares the results shown in Table 6.

From Table 6 and Fig. 6 we can observe that our SA algorithm gets solutions of better quality than the other two tools. Finally, each of the 60 ternary CAs constructed by our SA algorithm have been verified by the algorithm described in Section 3 . In order to minimize the execution time required by our SA algorithm, the following rule has been applied when choosing the rightmost Grid execution schema: experiments involving a value of the parameter N equal or less than 500 have been executed with the synchronous schema while the rest have been performed using the asynchronous schema.

(a) $CAN(2,k,3)$

t	k	TConfig	IPOG-F	Our SA
	5	15	13	11
	10	15	19	14
	15	17	20	15
	20	21	21	15
	25	21	21	17
	30	21	23	18
	35	21	23	19
	40	21	24	20
	45	23	25	20
2	50	25	26	21
	55	25	26	21
	60	25	27	21
	65	27	27	21
	70	27	27	21
	75	27	28	21
	80	27	29	21
	85	27	29	21
	90	27	30	21
	95	27	30	22
	100	27	30	22

(b) $CAN(3,k,3)$

t	k	TConfig	IPOG-F	Our
	5	40	42	33
	10	68	66	45
	15	83	80	57
	20	94	92	59
	25	102	98	72
	30	111	106	87
	35	117	111	89
	40	123	118	89
	45	130	121	90
3	50	134	126	101
	55	140	131	101
	60	144	134	104
	65	147	138	120
	70	150	141	120
	75	153	144	120
	80	155	147	129
	85	158	150	130
	90	161	154	130
	95	165	157	132
	100	167	159	133

(c) $CAN(4,k,3)$

t	k	TConfig	IPOG-F	Our
	5	115	98	81
	10	241	228	165
	15	325	302	280
	20	383	358	330
	25	432	405	400
	30	466	446	424
	35	518	479	475
	40	540	513	510
	45	572	533	530
4	50	581	559	528
	55	606	581	545
	60	621	596	564
	65	639	617	581
	70	657	634	597
	75	671	648	610
	80	687	663	624
	85	699	678	635
	90	711	690	649
	95	723	701	660
	100	733	714	669

Table 6. Comparison among TConfig, IPOG-F and our SA to construct ternary CAs when $5 \leq k \leq 100$ and $2 \leq t \leq 4$.

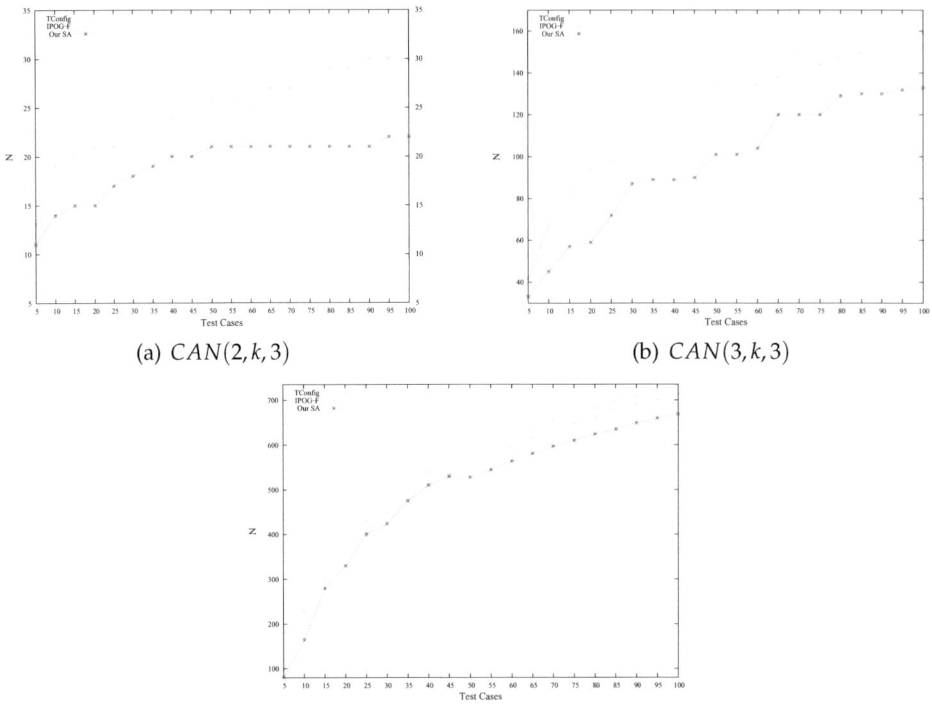

(a) $CAN(2,k,3)$ (b) $CAN(3,k,3)$

(c) $CAN(4,k,3)$

Fig. 6. Graphical comparison of the performance among TConfig, IPOG-F and our SA to construct ternary CAs when $5 \leq k \leq 100$ and $2 \leq t \leq 4$.

8. Conclusions

In large problem domains, testing is limited by cost. Every test adds to the cost, so CAs are an attractive option for testing.

Simulated annealing (SA) is a general-purpose stochastic optimization method that has proven to be an effective tool for approximating globally optimal solutions to many types of NP-hard combinatorial optimization problems. But, the sequential implementation of SA algorithm has a slow convergence that can be improved using Grid or parallel implementations

This work focused on constructing ternary CAs with a new approach of SA, which integrates three key features that importantly determines its performance:

1. An efficient method to generate initial solutions with maximum Hamming distance.
2. A carefully designed composed neighborhood function which allows the search to quickly reduce the total cost of candidate solutions, while avoiding to get stuck on some local minimal.
3. An effective cooling schedule allowing our SA algorithm to converge faster, producing at the same time good quality solutions.

The empirical evidence presented in this work showed that SA improved the size of many CAs in comparison with the tools that are among the best found in the state-of-the-art of the construction of CAs.

To make up for the time the algorithm takes to converge, we proposed an implementation of our SA algorithm for Grid Computing. The main conclusion extracted from this point was the possibility of using two different schemas (asynchronous and synchronous) depending on the size of the experiment. On the one hand, the synchronous schema achieves better performance but is limited by the maximum number of slave connections that the master can keep track of. On the other hand, the asynchronous schema is slower but experiments with a huge value of N can be seamlessly performed.

As future work, we aim to extend the experiment where $100 \leq k \leq 20000$ and $2 \leq t \leq 12$, and compare our results against the best upper bounds found in the literature (Colbourn, 2011).

Finally, the new CAs are available in CINVESTAV Covering Array Repository (CAR), which is available under request at `http://www.tamps.cinvestav.mx/~jtj/CA.php`.

9. Acknowledgments

The authors thankfully acknowledge the computer resources and assistance provided by Spanish Supercomputing Network (TIRANT-UV). This research work was partially funded by the following projects: CONACyT 58554, Calculo de Covering Arrays; 51623 Fondo Mixto CONACyT y Gobierno del Estado de Tamaulipas.

10. References

Aarts, E. H. L. & Van Laarhoven, P. J. M. (1985). Statistical Cooling: A General Approach to Combinatorial Optimization Problems, *Philips Journal of Research* 40: 193–226.

Almond, J. & Snelling, D. (1999). Unicore: Uniform access to supercomputing as an element of electronic commerce, *Future Generation Computer Systems* 613: 1–10. `http://dx.doi.org/10.1016/S0167-739X(99)00007-2`.

Atiqullah, M. (2004). An efficient simple cooling schedule for simulated annealing, *Proceedings of the International Conference on Computational Science and its Applications - ICCSA 2004*, Vol. 3045 of *Lecture Notes in Computer Science*, Springer-Verlag, pp. 396–404. `http://dx.doi.org/10.1007/978-3-540-24767-8_41`.

Avila-George, H., Torres-Jimenez, J., Hernández, V. & Rangel-Valdez, N. (2010). Verification of general and cyclic covering arrays using grid computing, *Proceedings of the Third international conference on Data management in grid and peer-to-peer systems - GLOBE 2010*, Vol. 6265 of *Lecture Notes in Computer Science*, Springer-Verlag, pp. 112–123. `http://dx.doi.org/10.1007/978-3-642-15108-8_10`.

Bryce, R. C. & Colbourn, C. J. (2007). The density algorithm for pairwise interaction testing, *Softw Test Verif Rel* 17(3): 159–182. `http://dx.doi.org/10.1002/stvr.365`.

Bush, K. A. (1952). Orthogonal arrays of index unity, *Ann Math Stat* 23(3): 426–434. `http://dx.doi.org/10.1214/aoms/1177729387`.

Calvagna, A., Gargantini, A. & Tramontana, E. (2009). Building T-wise Combinatorial Interaction Test Suites by Means of Grid Computing, *Proceedings of the 18th IEEE International Workshops on Enabling Technologies: Infrastructures for Collaborative Enterprises - WETICE 2009*, IEEE Computer Society, pp. 213–218. `http://dx.doi.org/10.1109/WETICE.2009.52`.

Cavique, L., Rego, C. & Themido, I. (1999). Subgraph ejection chains and tabu search for the crew scheduling problem, *The Journal of the Operational Research Society* 50(6): 608–616. http://www.ingentaconnect.com/content/pal/01605682/1999/00000050/00000006/2600728.

Cohen, D. M., Dalal, S. R., Parelius, J. & Patton, G. C. (1996). The combinatorial design approach to automatic test generation, *IEEE Software* 13(5): 83–88. http://dx.doi.org/10.1109/52.536462.

Cohen, M. B., Colbourn, C. J. & Ling, A. C. H. (2003). Augmenting simulated annealing to build interaction test suites, *Proceedings of the 14th International Symposium on Software Reliability Engineering - ISSRE 2003*, IEEE Computer Society, pp. 394–405. http://dx.doi.org/10.1109/ISSRE.2003.1251061.

Colbourn, C. (2004). Combinatorial aspects of covering arrays, *Le Matematiche* 58: 121–167.

Colbourn, C. J. (2011). Covering array tables for t=2,3,4,5,6. Accessed on April 20, 2011. URL: *http://www.public.asu.edu/ ccolbou/src/tabby/catable.html*

Colbourn, C. J. & Kéri, G. (2009). Binary covering arrays and existentially closed graphs, *Proceedings of the 2nd International Workshop on Coding and Cryptology - IWCC 2009*, Vol. 5557 of *Lecture Notes in Computer Science*, Springer-Verlag, pp. 22–33. http://dx.doi.org/10.1007/978-3-642-01877-0_3.

Colbourn, C. J. & Ling, A. C. H. (2009). A recursive construction for perfect hash families, *Journal of Mathematical Cryptology* 3(4): 291–306. http://dx.doi.org/10.1515/JMC.2009.018.

Colbourn, C. J., Martirosyan, S. S., Mullen, G. L., Shasha, D., Sherwood, G. B. & Yucas, J. L. (2006). Products of mixed covering arrays of strength two, *J. Combin. Designs* 12(2): 124–138. http://dx.doi.org/10.1002/jcd.20065.

Colbourn, C. J. & Torres-Jimenez, J. (2010). Error-Correcting Codes, Finite Geometries and Cryptography. Chapter: Heterogeneous Hash Families and Covering Arrays, *Contemporary Mathematics* 523: 3–15. ISBN-10 0-8218-4956-5.

DIANE (2011). Distributed analysis environment. Accessed on June 6, 2011. URL: *http://it-proj-diane.web.cern.ch/it-proj-diane/*

EGI (2011). European grid initiative. Accessed on September 6, 2011. URL: *http://www.egi.eu/*

gLite (2011). Lightweight middleware for grid computing. Accessed on June 6, 2011. URL: *http://glite.cern.ch/*

Globus Alliance (2011). Globus toolkit. Accessed on May 21, 2011. URL: *http://www.globus.org/toolkit/*

Gonzalez-Hernandez, L., Rangel-Valdez, N. & Torres-Jimenez, J. (2010). Construction of mixed covering arrays of variable strength using a tabu search approach, *Proceedings of the 4th international conference on Combinatorial optimization and applications - COCOA 2010*, Vol. 6508 of *Lecture Notes in Computer Science*, Springer-Verlag, pp. 51–64. http://dx.doi.org/10.1007/978-3-642-17458-2_6.

Jun, Y. & Mizuta, S. (2005). Detailed analysis of uphill moves in temperature parallel simulated annealing and enhancement of exchange probabilities, *Complex Systems* 15(4): 349–358. URL: *http://www.complexsystems.com/abstracts/v15_i04_a04.html*

Katona, G. O. H. (1973). Two applications (for search theory and truth functions) of sperner type theorems, *Periodica Math.* 3(1-2): 19–26. http://dx.doi.org/10.1007/BF02018457.

Kleitman, D. J. & Spencer, J. (1973). Families of k-independent sets, *Discrete Math* 6(3): 255–262. http://dx.doi.org/10.1016/0012-365X(73)90098-8.

Lei, Y., Kacker, R., Kuhn, D. R., Okun, V. & Lawrence, J. (2007). IPOG: A general strategy for t-way software testing, *Proceedings of the 14th Annual IEEE International Conference and Workshops on the Engineering of Computer-Based Systems - ECBS 2007*, IEEE Computer Society, pp. 549–556. http://dx.doi.org/10.1109/ECBS.2007.47.

Lei, Y. & Tai, K.-C. (1998). In-parameter-order: A test generation strategy for pairwise testing, *Proceedings of the 3rd IEEE International Symposium on High-Assurance Systems Engineering - HASE 1998*, IEEE Computer Society, pp. 254–261.

Martinez-Pena, J., Torres-Jimenez, J., Rangel-Valdez, N. & Avila-George, H. (2010). A heuristic approach for constructing ternary covering arrays using trinomial coefficients, *Proceedings of the 12th Ibero-American Conference on Artificial Intelligence - IBERAMIA 2010*, Vol. 6433 of *Lecture Notes in Computer Science*, Springer-Verlag, pp. 572–581. http://dx.doi.org/10.1007/978-3-642-16952-6_58.

Martirosyan, S. S. & Colbourn, C. J. (2005). Recursive constructions of covering arrays, *Bayreuth. Math. Schr.* 74: 266–275.

McDowell, A. G. (2011). All-pairs testing. Accessed on June 21, 2011.
URL: *http://www.mcdowella.demon.co.uk/allPairs.html*

Moscicki, J., Brochu, F., Ebke, J., Egede, U., Elmsheuser, J., Harrison, K., Jones, R., Lee, H., Liko, D., Maier, A., Muraru, A., Patrick, G., Pajchel, K., Reece, W., Samset, B., Slater, M., Soroko, A., Tan, C., van der Ster, D. & Williams, M. (2009). Ganga: A tool for computational-task management and easy access to grid resources, *Comput Phys Commun* 180(11): 2303–2316. http://dx.doi.org/10.1016/j.cpc.2009.06.016.

Moura, L., Stardom, J., Stevens, B. & Williams, A. (2003). Covering arrays with mixed alphabet sizes, *Journal of Combinatorial Designs* 11(6): 413–432. http://dx.doi.org/10.1002/jcd.10059.

Nurmela, K. J. (2004). Upper bounds for covering arrays by tabu search, *Discrete Appl. Math.* 138: 143–152. http://dx.doi.org/10.1016/S0166-218X(03)00291-9.

Pacini, F. (2001). Job description language howto. Accessed on October 10, 2011.
URL: *http://server11.infn.it/workload-grid/docs/DataGrid01TEN01020_2-Document.pdf*

Ram, D. J., Sreenivas, T. H. & Subramaniam, K. G. (1996). Parallel simulated annealing algorithms., *Journal of Parallel and Distributed Computing* 37(2): 207–212.

Rényi, A. (1971). *Foundations of Probability*, John Wiley & Sons, New York, USA.

Sherwood, G. (2011). On the construction of orthogonal arrays and covering arrays using permutation groups. Accessed on June 20, 2011.
URL: *http://testcover.com/pub/background/cover.htm*

Sherwood, G. B. (2008). Optimal and near-optimal mixed covering arrays by column expansion, *Discrete Mathematics* 308(24): 6022 – 6035. http://dx.doi.org/10.1016/j.disc.2007.11.021.

Shiba, T., Tsuchiya, T. & Kikuno, T. (2004). Using artificial life techniques to generate test cases for combinatorial testing, *Proceedings of the 28th Annual International Computer Software and Applications Conference - Volume 01 - COMPSAC 2004*, IEEE Computer Society, pp. 72–77. http://dx.doi.org/10.1109/CMPSAC.2004.1342808.

Surridge, M., Taylor, S., Roure, D. D. & Zaluska, E. (2005). Experiences with gria - industrial applications on a web services grid, *Proceedings of the First International Conference on e-Science and Grid Computing*, IEEE Computer Society, pp. 98–105. http://dx.doi.org/10.1109/E-SCIENCE.2005.38.

Torres-Jimenez, J., De Alfonso, C. & Hernández, V. (2004). Computation of ternary covering arrays using a grid, *Proceedings of the Second Asian Applied Computing Conference - AACC 2004*, Vol. 3285 of *Lecture Notes in Computer Science*, Springer-Verlag, pp. 240–246. http://dx.doi.org/10.1007/978-3-540-30176-9_31.

Torres-Jimenez, J. & Rodriguez-Tello, E. (2012). New bounds for binary covering arrays using simulated annealing, *Information Sciences*, 185(1): 137–152. http://dx.doi.org/10.1016/j.ins.2011.09.020.

Tung, Y. & Aldiwan, W. S. (2000). Automating test case generation for the new generation mission software system, *Proceedings of the IEEE Aerospace Conference*, Vol. 1, IEEE Press, pp. 431–437. http://dx.doi.org/10.1109/AERO.2000.879426.

Williams, A. W. (2000). Determination of test configurations for pair-wise interaction coverage, *Proceedings of the IFIP TC6/WG6.1 13th International Conference on Testing Communicating Systems: Tools and Techniques - TestCom 2000*, Kluwer, pp. 59–74.

Williams, A. W. & Probert, R. L. (1996). A practical strategy for testing pair-wise coverage of network interfaces, *Proceedings of the The Seventh International Symposium on Software Reliability Engineering - ISSRE 1996*, IEEE Computer Society, pp. 246–256. http://dx.doi.org/10.1109/ISSRE.1996.558835.

Younis, M., Zamli, K. & Mat Isa, N. (2008). IRPS - An Efficient Test Data Generation Strategy for Pairwise Testing, *Proceedings of the 12th International Conference on Knowledge-Based and Intelligent Information & Engineering Systems - KES 2008*, Vol. 5177 of *Lecture Notes in Computer Science*, Springer-Verlag, pp. 493–500. http://dx.doi.org/10.1007/978-3-540-85563-7_63.

11

Grid Infrastructure for Domain Decomposition Methods in Computational ElectroMagnetics

Olivier Terzo, Pietro Ruiu, Lorenzo Mossucca,
Matteo Alessandro Francavilla and Francesca Vipiana
Istituto Superiore Mario Boella (ISMB)
Italy

1. Introduction

The accurate and efficient solution of Maxwell's equation is the problem addressed by the scientific discipline called Computational ElectroMagnetics (CEM). Many macroscopic phenomena in a great number of fields are governed by this set of differential equations: electronic, geophysics, medical and biomedical technologies, virtual EM prototyping, besides the traditional antenna and propagation applications. Therefore, many efforts are focussed on the development of new and more efficient approach to solve Maxwell's equation. The interest in CEM applications is growing on. Several problems, hard to figure out few years ago, can now be easily addressed thanks to the reliability and flexibility of new technologies, together with the increased computational power. This technology evolution opens the possibility to address large and complex tasks. Many of these applications aim to simulate the electromagnetic behavior, for example in terms of input impedance and radiation pattern in antenna problems, or Radar Cross Section for scattering applications. Instead, problems, which solution requires high accuracy, need to implement full wave analysis techniques, e.g., virtual prototyping context, where the objective is to obtain reliable simulations in order to minimize measurement number, and as consequence their cost. Besides, other tasks require the analysis of complete structures (that include an high number of details) by directly simulating a CAD Model. This approach allows to relieve researcher of the burden of removing useless details, while maintaining the original complexity and taking into account all details. Unfortunately, this reduction implies: (a) high computational effort, due to the increased number of degrees of freedom, and (b) worsening of spectral properties of the linear system during complex analysis. The above considerations underline the needs to identify appropriate information technologies that ease solution achievement and fasten required elaborations. The authors analysis and expertise infer that Grid Computing techniques can be very useful to these purposes. Grids appear mainly in high performance computing environments. In this context, hundreds of off-the-shelf nodes are linked together and work in parallel to solve problems, that, previously, could be addressed sequentially or by using supercomputers. Grid Computing is a technique developed to elaborate enormous amounts of data and enables large-scale resource sharing to solve problem by exploiting distributed scenarios. The main advantage of Grid is due to parallel computing, indeed if a problem can be split in smaller tasks, that can be executed independently, its solution calculation fasten up considerably. To exploit this advantage, it is necessary to identify a technique able to split original electromagnetic task into a set of smaller subproblems. The Domain Decomposition (DD) technique, based on the block generation algorithm introduced in Matekovits et al.

(2007) and Francavilla et al. (2011), perfectly addresses our requirements (see Section 3.4 for details). In this chapter, a Grid Computing infrastructure is presented. This architecture allows parallel block execution by distributing tasks to nodes that belong to the Grid. The set of nodes is composed by physical machines and virtualized ones. This feature enables great flexibility and increase available computational power. Furthermore, the presence of virtual nodes allows a full and efficient Grid usage, indeed the presented architecture can be used by different users that run different applications.

The chapter is organized as follow, Section 2 briefly explains author's contribution. Section 3 describes technologies used and summarized Domain Decomposition principles. The architecture is shown in Section 4, while the advantages derived by its adoption are illustrated in Section 5 and Section 6 draws conclusions and gives hints for future works.

2. Motivation

Due to the decomposition of the original problems into a larger number of subproblems, the scheme is well suited to a parallelization approach, since the subproblems (which will be referred to as blocks in the following) are disjoint, and the elaboration of the blocks is intrinsically a parallelizable operation. Since the generation of the entire domain basis functions on each block is independent from the other blocks, a high scalability is expected. As an example, Figure 1 shows a fighter subdivided into 4 different blocks, identified by different colors. The four blocks can be processed in parallel by four different processes, in order to generate the basis functions describing each block. Parallelization can be achieved using two different techniques: parallel programming or Grid Computing. Parallel programming is the technique by which have been obtained the best results in this field (500 billion of unknowns) Mouriño et al. (2009). There are important barriers to the broader adoption of these methodologies though: first, the algorithms must be modified using parallel programming API like MPI (2011) and OpenMP (2011), in order to run jobs on selected cores. The second aspect to consider is the hardware: to obtain results of interest supercomputers with thousands of cores and thousands of GB of RAM are required. Typically these machines are made by institutions to meet specific experiments and do not always allow public access. Grid Computing is a rather more easily applicable model for those who do not fulfill the requirements listed above Foster & Kesselman (2003). For its adoption the only requirement is to have at disposal computers to use within the grid. The machines may be heterogeneous, both in terms of the types (workstations, servers) and hardware resources of each machine (RAM, CPU, HD); besides they can also be recovery machines. With the Virtualization technology the number of processes running on each machine (for multicore ones) can be optimized by instantiating multiple virtual nodes on the same physical machine. The real advantage of this model, however, is that researchers do not have to worry about rewriting code to make their application parallelizable. One of the drawbacks in the adoption of this model is the addition of overhead introduced by the grid (e.g., inputs time transfer) and by the hypervisor that manages the virtual machines. It has been shown, however, that the loss of performance due to the hypervisor is not particularly high, usually not exceeding 5% Chierici & Verald (2010). For the above reasons, in our case it was decided to grid infrastructure, composed of heterogeneous recovery machines, both physical and virtual, on which to run scientific applications without the need to modify the source codes of the used algorithms. The ultimate goal is the reduction of execution times of CEM applications.

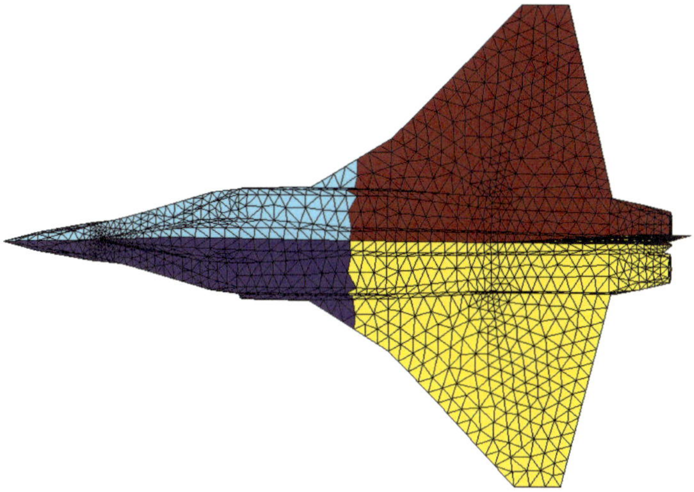

Fig. 1. A fighter discretized with 4774 triangles is subdivided into 4 blocks, shown with different colors.

3. Background

The rapid technology growth in the recent years has helped the development and rapid expansion of Grid Computing. "The roots of Grid Computing can be traced back from the late 80s when the research about scheduling algorithms for intensive applications in distributed environments accelerated considerably" Kourpas (2006). In the late 1990s began to emerge, a more generalized framework for accessing high performance computing systems, and at the turn of the millennium, the pace of change was accelerated by the recognition of potential synergies between the grid and the emerging Service Oriented Architectures (SOA) through the creation of the Open Grid Services Architecture (OGSA) Kourpas (2006). "The Open Grid Services Architecture is a set of standards defining the way in which information is shared among several components of large, heterogeneous grid systems. The OGSA is, in effect, an extension and refinement of the Service Oriented Architecture" OGSA (2007). The Open Grid Services Architecture is a standard created by the Open Grid Forum (OGF) OGF (2011). OGF was founded in 2006 from the Global Grid Forum (GGF) and the Enterprise Grid Alliance (EGA). GGF had a rich background and established international presence within the academic and research communities while EGA was focused on developing and promoting enterprise grid solutions. The OGF community now counts thousands of members working in research and industry, representing more than 400 organizations in 50 countries.

3.1 Grid Computing technologies

Grid Computing is often described by referring to the analogy between electrical networks and grid. When people access to electric network they use wall sockets with no care about where or how electricity is actually generated. This relation underlies that computing becomes pervasive thanks to Grid Computing diffusion. Therefore, individual users (or client applications) can access computing resources (processors, storage, data, applications, etc..) when needed with little or no knowledge about where those resources are located or what underlying technologies, hardware, operating system are used. A further definition is given by "Grid is an infrastructure that involves the integrated and collaborative use of computers, networks, databases and scientific instruments owned and managed by multiple organizations" Asadzadeh et al. (2005). Grid Computing is based on these technology principles Oracle (2009):

Standardization on operating systems, servers, storage hardware, middleware components, and network components extends interoperability and reduce system management overhead. It also improves operational complexity reduction in data center by simplifying application deployment, configuration, and integration.

Virtualization of resources means that applications are not bound to a specific server, storage, or network components but can be used in any virtualized resource. Virtualization is realized thanks to a sophisticated software layer that hides the underlying complexity of hardware resources and presents a simplified interface used by applications and other resources (see Section 3.2).

Automation Grid Computing requires large-scale automation of IT operations due to the potentially very high number of components, both virtual and physical. Each component requires configuration management, on-demand provisioning, top-down monitoring, and other management tasks. Combining these capabilities into a single, automated, integrated solution for managing grids enables organizations to maximize their return of investment.

3.1.1 The Globus Toolkit

The Globus Toolkit (Globus (2010)) developed by the Globus Alliance, is an open source software toolkit used for building grid systems and applications. The Globus Alliance includes ISI, the University of Chicago, the University of Edinburgh, the Royal Institute of Technology in Sweden, the National Center for Supercomputing Applications, and Univa Corporation. Sponsors include federal agencies such as DOE, NSF, DARPA, and NASA, along with commercial partners such as IBM and Microsoft.

The Globus Toolkit includes software for security, information infrastructure, resource management, data management, communication, fault detection, and portability. It is packaged as a set of components that can be used either independently or together to develop applications. It is used by various companies and organizations as the basis for grid implementations of various types.

Globus Toolkit is composed by four main components (shown in Figure 2):

- Security (GSI: Grid Security Infrastructure). It is a set of tools, libraries and protocols used in Globus to allow users and applications to securely access resources. GSI is based on a public key infrastructure, (PKI) with certificate authorities (CA) and (X509) certificates. GSI uses (SSL) for authentication and message protection and enables user to create and delegate proxy credentials to processes running on remote resources;
- Resource Management (GRAM: Grid Resource Allocation Manager). It provides the user to access the grid in order to run, terminate and monitor jobs remotely;
- Information Services are for providing configuration and adaptation capabilities for heterogeneous resources:
  - MDS: Monitoring and Discovery Service: provides information about the available resources on the Grid and their status;
  - GRIS: Grid Resource Information Service: is associated with each resource and answers queries from client for their current configuration, capabilities and status;

- GIIS: Grid Index Information Service: is a directory service that pulls information for GRIS's. It is a "caching" service which provides indexing and searching functions.

- Data Management GridFTP: is a protocol that provides for the secure, robust, fast and efficient transfer of data.

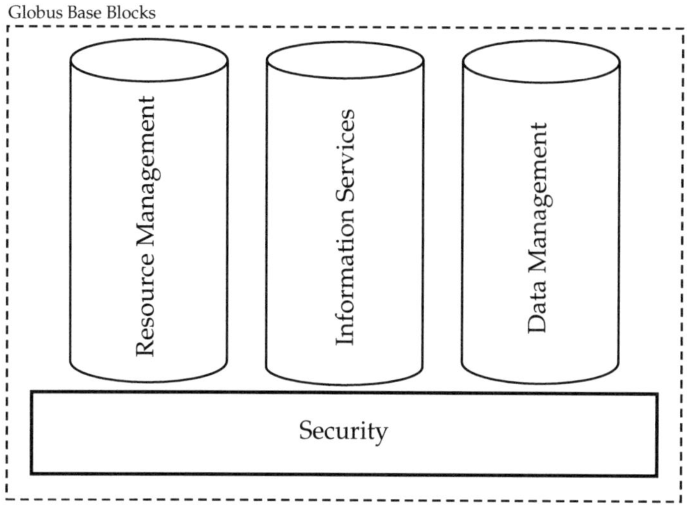

Fig. 2. Globus Toolkit Protocols.

3.2 Virtualization technologies

The idea of computer system virtualization is not new, the earliest examples dates back to the 60s when IBM introduced the IBM 7044 and when Manchester University presented the Atlas project (one of the first world's supercomputers). These systems present the first rudimental example of demand paging and supervisor calls.

However, in the last ten years, the use of virtualization in modern data centers increased mainly due to contain operating. Virtualization is a technology that allows running several concurrent Operating System (OS) instances inside a single physical machine called host. The physical device is divided into multiple isolated virtual environments called guest system. A Virtual Machine (VM) is an instance of the physical machine and gives users the illusion of accessing the physical machine directly and each VM is a fully protected and isolated copy of the underlying system. Virtualization is thus used to reduce the hardware costs on one side and to improve the overall productivity by letting many more users work on it simultaneously. Moreover the global cost and electricity power consumption makes the virtualization adoption convenient. Furthermore, the server number can rationalized, while maintaining the functional capacity of the system. A virtualization layer provides the required infrastructural support exploiting lower-level hardware resources in order to create multiple independent virtual machines that are isolated from each other. This layer, traditionally called Virtual Machine Monitor, usually sits on top of the hardware and below the operating system.

The hypervisor, or Virtual Machine Manager (VMM), allows multiple operating systems to concurrently run on a single host computer. It is so named because it is conceptually one level higher than a supervisory program. A supervisory program or supervisor is usually part of an operating system, that controls the execution of other routines and regulates work

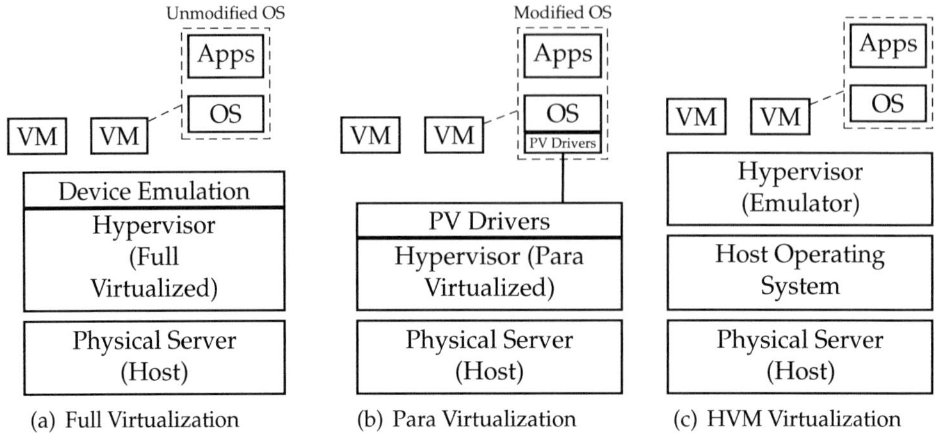

Fig. 3. Virtualization approaches.

scheduling, input/output operations, error actions, and similar functions and regulates the flow of work in a data processing system. The supervisor is generally called kernel. The hypervisor presents to the guest OS a virtual hardware platform and manages the execution of the guest OS. Multiple instances of different operating systems may share the virtualized hardware resources. Hypervisors are installed on server hardware whose only task is to run guest operating systems. Non hypervisor virtualization systems are used for similar tasks on dedicated server hardware, but also commonly on desktop, portable and even handheld computers. There are three popular approaches to server virtualization: Full Virtualization, Para Virtualization and virtualization with hardware support (Hardware Virtual Machine, or HVM).

Full Virtualization provides emulation of the underlying platform on which a guest operating system and application set run without modifications and unaware that the platform is virtualized. This approach is idealistic, in real world scenarios virtualization comes with costs.

Providing a Full Virtualization implies that every platform device is emulated with enough details to permit the guest OS to manipulate them at their native level (such as register-level interfaces). Moreover, it allows administrators to create guests that use different operating systems. These guests have no knowledge about the host OS since they are not aware that the hardware they see is not real but emulated. The guests, however, require real computing resources from the host, so they use a hypervisor to coordinate instructions to the CPU. The hypervisor provides virtual machine to show all the needed hardware to start and run the operating system. Via a virtual bios, it shows CPU, RAM and storage devices. The main advantage of this paradigm concerns the ability to run virtual machines on all popular operating systems without requiring them to be modified since the emulated hardware is completely transparent.

Para Virtualization Machine approach is based on the host-guest paradigm and uses a virtual machine monitor. In this model the hypervisor modifies the guest operating system's code in order to run as a guest operating system in a specific virtual machine environment. Like virtual machines, Para Virtual Machines are able to run multiple operating systems. The main advantage of this approach is the execution speed, always faster than HVM and Full Virtualization approach. The Para Virtualization method uses a hypervisor for shared access to the underlying hardware but integrates virtualization aware code into the OS itself. In a context of Para Virtualization the guest operating system must be aware of being run in a virtual environment. So the original operating system, in particular its kernel, is modified to run in a Para Virtualized environment.

Hardware Virtual Machine (HVM) Hardware-assisted virtualization is a virtualization approach that enables efficient Full Virtualization using help from hardware capabilities. Last innovations in hardware, mainly in CPU, MMU and memory components (notably the Intel VT-x and AMD-V architectures), provide direct platform-level architectural support for OS virtualization. For some hypervisors (like Xen and KVM) it is possible to recompile Para Virtualized drivers inside the guest machine running in HVM environment and load those drivers into the running kernel to achieve Para Virtualized I/O performance within an HVM guest.

3.2.1 Virtualization considerations

As anticipated, several advantages ensue from virtualization use. The number reduction of physical servers is one of the most evident: the hardware (software) solution for virtualization allows multiple virtual machines running on one physical machine, moreover additional advantages are power consumption reduction, better fault tolerance, optimization of time needed for device installation and of the number of cabinets. Another advantage is that virtualization can be used to abstract hardware resources, since operating systems are closely related to the underlying hardware, several issues need to be taken into account when a server is moved or cloned, e.g., incompatible hardware, different drivers and so on. Another virtualization feature is the creation of abstraction levels such that the operating system does not see the actual physical hardware, but a virtualized one. Administrator can move or clone a system on other machines that run the same virtualization environment without worrying about physical details (network and graphics cards, chipsets, etc.).

Another important aspect is adaptability: if a company changes its priorities and needs, a service may become more important than another or may require more resources. Virtualization allows resource allocation to virtual hardware easily and quickly. Some companies maintain old servers with obsolete operating systems that cannot be moved to new servers as these OS would not be supported. In virtualized environments it is possible to run legacy systems allowing IT managers to get rid of old hardware no longer supported, and more prone to failure. In many cases it is appropriate to use virtualization to create test environments. It frequently happens that production systems need to be changed without knowledge about consequences, i.e., installing an operating system upgrade or a particular service pack is not a risk-free. Virtualization allows immediate replication of virtual machines in order to run all necessary tests.

Like any other technology, the virtualization gives disadvantages that depends on the application scenario. The most important are performance overhead and presence of hardware virtualization. Each virtualization solution is decreasing the overall performance, such as disk access times or access to memory. Some critical applications may suffer from this overhead introduced by virtualization. Depending on the products used, some devices may not be used by virtual machines, such as serial and parallel ports, USB and Bluetooth interfaces, or graphics acceleration hardware.

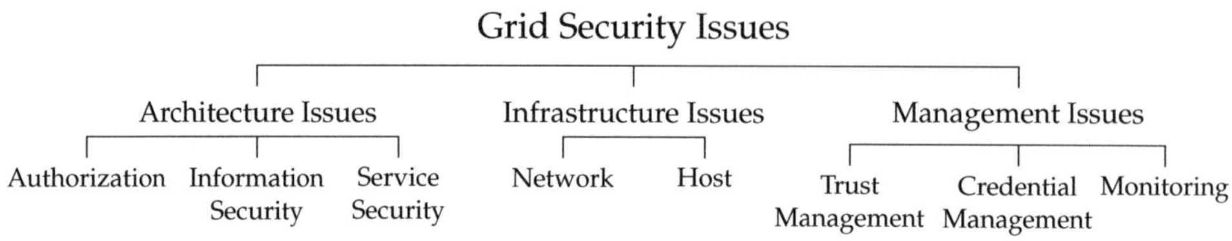

Fig. 4. Taxonomy of grid security issues.

3.2.2 Xen and KVM based virtualization

Xen is a Virtual Machine Monitor that allows several guest operating systems to be executed on the same computer hardware concurrently. A Xen system is structured with the Xen hypervisor as the lowest and most privileged layer. Above this layer are located one or more guest operating systems, which the hypervisor schedules across the physical CPUs. Xen can work both in Para Virtualized or HVM mode; in the first the guest operating system must be modified to be executed. Through Para Virtualization, Xen can achieve very high performance. The HVM mode offers new instructions to support direct calls by a Para Virtualized guest/driver into the hypervisor, typically used for I/O or other so-called hypercalls. KVM is a Full Virtualization solution for Linux on x86 hardware containing virtualization extensions (Intel VT or AMD-V). KVM is implemented as a module within the Linux kernel. A hypervisor hosts the virtual machine images as regular Linux processes, so that each virtual machine image can use all of the features of the Linux kernel, including hardware, security, storage, and applications. KVM supports I/O Para Virtualization using the so called VIRTIO subsystem consisting of 5 kernel modules IBM (2010).

3.3 Security overview

The basis idea of pooling has been always employed by humans. Its most evident and valuable advantage is cost and resource optimization, but it hides facets that may shadows its benefits. Whenever we share something we are worried since our goods may not be handle properly and may be manipulated by strangers. Moreover when we use someone else stuff we worry about safety since objects may be dangerous, broken or compromised.

The above concept perfectly fits grid system since grid can be seen as a mechanism to pool resources to optimize system utilization. Therefore we can state that security and trust, together with resource monitoring, authentication and authorization of users, and data protection, are essential to Grid Computing. In the following we give an overview of security in Grid Computing by using the classification proposed by Chakrabarti (2007). As shown in Figure 4, he categorized grid security issues into three main categories: architecture, infrastructure, and management related issues.

3.3.1 Architecture issues

Architecture level issues concerns threats - pertaining information security (e.g., data confidentiality and integrity), authorization, and service level security - that impact the whole grid system.

Information Security is defined as the security properties of data transmission between hosts, that is, mainly, secure communication and authentication. These aspects involve confidentiality (i.e., the data can be accessed only by legitimate users) and integrity (i.e., the data has not been modified during transmission). These aspects are essential security requirements in all information and communication areas, but become extremely critical in distributed and heterogeneous environment like grids. The Open Grid Forum released an open standard called Open Grid Standards Architecture OGSA (2007) which is the referring point for worldwide researchers. OGSA specifies a layer called Grid Security Infrastructure GSI (2010) which aim is to undertake these matters, for further details see Section 3.3.4. The GSI is based on X.509 infrastructure and Secure Socket Layer (SSL) protocol, and uses public key cryptography and certificates for creating secure grid and application level data encryption. The X.509 certificates are used to ensure authentication: every user or service owns a certificate which contains needed information to identify and authenticate the owner.

Authorization is a security feature that implies the definition of "who" can access "what", clearly this definition can be extended by adding "when", "how", "how long", and so on. In the grid environment authorization is very important as resources are shared between several users and services. The Authorization Systems (AS) can be classified into two groups: (1) Virtual Organization (VO) Level and (2) Resource Level Systems. The former is centralized AS for an entire VO: when an user needs to access a resource of Resource Provider (RP) he requests for credentials to the AS and presents them to the RP which allows/denies rights to the user. The latter, instead, specifies the authorization to a set of resources, these systems allow the (authenticated) users to access the resources based on the credentials he presents. Examples of the first authorization systems are Community Authorization Service CAS (2010) and Virtual Organization Membership Service VOMS (2003), while example of the second are Privilege and Role Management Infrastructure Standards Validation PERMIS (2002), and the GridMap system.

Service Security entails the implementation of protection mechanisms focussed to guarantee the availability of services. Attack class examples are QoS violation and Denial-of-Service (DoS). The first is achieved through traffic congestion, packet delay or drop, while the second aims to cause software crash and to completely disrupt the service. The countermeasures to contain these attacks are mainly based on prevention and monitoring in order to limit damages and to raise alarms. Some approaches also try to detect the source, but an effective defense against these attacks is really hard to achieve.

3.3.2 Infrastructure issues

Infrastructure threats regards network and host devices that form the grid infrastructure and are classified in Host level and Network level. These issues impact data protection, job protection, host availability, access control functionalities, secure routing and all the communication aspects.

Host Security impacts data protection and job starvation. The former regards the protection of data already stored in the host, in fact the host submitting the job may be untrusted and the job code may be malicious. The latter is a scenario in which resources assigned to a job are denied to the original job and assigned to a different (malicious) job. The most effective countermeasures to limit data threats are: (1) application level sandboxing, (2) virtualization, and (3) sandboxing. The first approach uses proof carrying code (PCC), the compiler creates proofs of code-safeness and embed those in the executable binary. The second solution is based on the creation of Virtual Machines upon the physical host, this technique ensures strong isolation between different VMs and the host system. The third method confines system calls and sandboxes (isolates) the applications to avoid data and memory access not allowed. The solution adopted to avoid job starvation are based on resource booking or priority reduction for long running jobs, in order to reduce starvation likelyhood.

Network Security is a core requirement in grid scenario due to high speed needs and host heterogeneity. Access control and isolation are fundamental to the grid networks. Solutions for Grid Computing may not work effectively with existing firewalls and virtual private networks (VPN), for this reason researcher developed solutions like Adaptive Grid Firewalls (AGF) and Hose. Moreover routing attacks can be very dangerous for grid working, countermeasures to these threats came from the traditional networking research and foresee the deploy of secure routing protocol.

3.3.3 Management issues

Management issues are very delicate as the grid is an heterogeneous environment composed of several entities, users, domains, and policies. The management problem can be seen as three distinct, but correlated, points: (1) credential management, (2) trust management, and (3) monitoring.

Credential Management is a complex and delicate task due to the distributed and numerous components that form the grid. Each of these requires rights to access resources that need to be trusted and non compromised. This aim is achieved by using credential management mechanisms that securely store, grant, revoke, and renew credentials for user and system. Some solutions move the burden to store credential from the user to the system, e.g., by using smart cards. Other approaches resort to the federated identity paradigm to manage credentials, across different systems, domains, and frameworks. Implementation example of the first family is MyProxy, while KX.509 (a protocol which enables interoperability between X.509 and Kerberos), Liberty Framework and Shibboleth are examples of the second one.

Trust Management is a critical aspect in grid since nodes and users continuously join and leave the system. Therefore a mechanism to manage trust levels of users, nodes and the grid itself is mandatory. Different trust management solutions have been developed, their key features are scalability, reliability, and security and can be grouped into two main categories: reputation based and policy-based systems. The formers are based on trust metrics taken from local and global reputation of a resource or an host. In the latter approach, the different units that compose the system, exchange and manage credentials to create trust connections given a set policies.

Monitoring of resources is necessary in grid due to two main reasons. Firstly, organizations can be charged according to grid utilization, and, secondly, resource information can be logged for auditing, debugging, testing and security purposes. Different monitoring system are available in literature and can be grouped into three categories: (1) system level, (2) cluster level, and (3) grid level. The first systems collect and transmit data related to standalone systems or networks. The second ones require deployment across clusters and gather information upon the cluster itself. The thirds are more flexible than the formers because they can be deployed on top of other monitoring systems and may provide interfaces for querying, and displaying data in standard formats.

3.3.4 Grid Security Infrastructure (GSI)

The definition and implementation of a robust infrastructure is one of the main issue when the problem of securing grid is investigated. The Grid Security Infrastructure GSI (2010) addresses exactly this issue, it defines security requirements and provides a framework to provide security in Virtual Organization based grid systems. GSI has been provided by the Global Grid Forum (GGF) that is a forum of researchers and practitioners with the aim to exchange information and to define standards for Grid Computing. One of the most important aspects of GSI is that it is not only a theoretical definition, but it is implemented and used worldwide thanks to Globus Toolkit Globus (2010). GSI handles different security requirements, that can be summarized in: authentication, integrity, confidentiality, and delegation. The most prevalent mechanisms of authentication in a GSI based on grid is the certificate based on authentication (X.509) mechanism where a public key infrastructure (PKI) is assumed to exist which allows the trusted authority to sign information to be used for authentication purposes, by using these mechanisms it is also possible to ensure integrity. In addition to certificate based mechanism, it supports password based authentication, and research efforts are underway to integrate One Time Password (OTP) and Kerberos authentication with GSI.

Confidentiality are supported through transport level security using SSL/TLS protocols, and message level security using Web services standards. It is worth notice that Globus Toolkit is one of the few implementations where message level security is used for grid confidentiality purposes.

Delegation is especially important in case of grid because of the possibility of multiple resources involved in grid based transactions. It may be unnecessary or very expensive to authenticate each and every time a resource is accessed. On the other hand, if the user issues a certificate allowing the resource to act on its behalf then the process will become a lot simpler. This type of certificate issued by the user to be used by some other entity is called a proxy certificate. A proxy is made up of a new certificate containing two parts, a new public and a new private key. The proxy certificate has the owner's identity, with a slight change to show that it is a proxy certificate. The certificate owner will sign the proxy certificate. As part of the proxy certificate there is an entry with a timestamp, which indicates at what time the proxy certificate expires.

3.4 Computational ElectroMagnetics description

A complete discussion about the EM modeling and the mathematical aspects of the formulation goes beyond the scope of this paper; only a short summary of the problem will be presented in the following. In order to simplify the mathematical model, in the following the analysis of the electromagnetic behavior of Perfectly Electric Conducting (PEC) objects in a free space environment will be briefly introduced. Nevertheless, the authors would like to point out that the described approach is not limited to PEC objects in free space, in fact it is applicable to different formulations as well (dielectric objects or layered media problems for instance): in other terms it is a kernel free method. Besides, the focus of this chapter will be on a Grid Computing approach applied to computationally demanding electromagnetic problems: rather than considering more complicate approaches, that would divert the attention from the subject of this chapter, we prefer to introduce and apply the method to PEC objects in a homogeneous background, but we stress that it can be applied to other formulations as well. The Electric Field Integral Equation (EFIE) is a very versatile approach to the full-wave analysis of complex electromagnetic problems: for PEC objects the EFIE can be written by enforcing the boundary condition on the surface of the object, i.e. the tangential component of the electric field vanishes on the surface S:

$$\hat{n} \times \underline{E}|_{\Sigma} = \hat{n} \times \left(\underline{E}^{scat} + \underline{E}^{inc}\right)|_{\Sigma} = 0 \tag{1}$$

The surface S is discretized by a mesh with triangular cells, over which a usual system of RWG functions $\underline{f}_n$ is defined. The unknown surface current $\underline{J}$ is approximated by the above set of RWG basis functions

$$\underline{J}(\underline{r}) \approx \sum_{n=1}^{N} I_n \underline{f}_n(\underline{r}) \tag{2}$$

A Galerkin testing is used to convert the EFIE into the MoM linear system; hence we obtain the matrix equation

$$[Z] \cdot [I] = \left(\left[Z^{\Phi}\right]\left[Z^{A}\right]\right) \cdot [I] = [V] \tag{3}$$

where a generic element of the scalar potential and of the vector potential matrix, $\left[Z^{\Phi}\right]$ and $\left[Z^{A}\right]$ respectively, is expressed as

$$Z^{\Phi}_{m,n} = \frac{1}{4\pi j\omega\epsilon_0} \iint_{S_m} dS\, \nabla_s \cdot \underline{f}_m(\underline{r}) \iint_{S_n} dS'\, G(\underline{r},\underline{r}')\, \nabla_s \cdot \underline{f}_n(\underline{r}') \tag{4}$$

$$Z^{A}_{m,n} = \frac{j\omega\mu_0}{4\pi} \iint_{S_m} dS\, \underline{f}_m(\underline{r}) \cdot \iint_{S_n} dS'\, G(\underline{r},\underline{r}')\, \underline{f}_n(\underline{r}') \tag{5}$$

where: $G(\underline{r},\underline{r}') = \frac{e^{-jk_0R}}{R}$, $k_0 = \omega\sqrt{\epsilon_0\mu_0}$, $R = |\underline{r} - \underline{r}'|$, and S_m is the definition domain of the function $\underline{f}_m$. The coefficients I_n in (2) are collected in the vector $[I]$, and the mth element of $[V]$ is equal to

$$V_m = -\iint_{S_m} dS\, \underline{f}_m(\underline{r}) \cdot \underline{E}^i(\underline{r}) \tag{6}$$

where $\underline{E}^i$ is the impressed field in absence of bodies.

The first step of the Domain Decomposition approach is a subdivision of the overall geometry, breaking down the scatterer surface S into N_B sub-scatterers, which will be referred as *blocks* in the following. An example of the splitting of a sphere into 8 blocks is shown in Figure 5.

To subdivide the structure in blocks, on which entire domain synthetic functions will be generated, we use a fully automatic procedure. We would like to stress this aspect of our implementation, as it is of vital importance to be able to properly generate the subdomains for the synthetic function approach, and it is especially critical for arbitrary and complex structures. The block generation algorithm is based on the multi-level cell grouping described in Andriulli et al. (2008); Vipiana et al. (2009) for the generation of the Multi-Resolution basis functions. The starting point is the usual mesh for the analysis of the considered structure, without any constraint on the mesh properties and on the topology of the structure. Then a nested family of meshes, with non-simplex cells, is generated through subsequent groupings of the initial triangular mesh cells. We denote this initial mesh with M_0, and call it level-0 mesh. All other meshes will be composed of groups of adjacent cells of the initial mesh. We start by considering groupings of adjacent cells in M_0 formed so that their average area is about four times the average area of the cells in M_0. This covering will be called the level-1 mesh, M_1. The same procedure applied to M_1 will generate the generalized mesh M_2, and so forth. We stop grouping a cell with its adjacent cells when its size reaches a chosen threshold

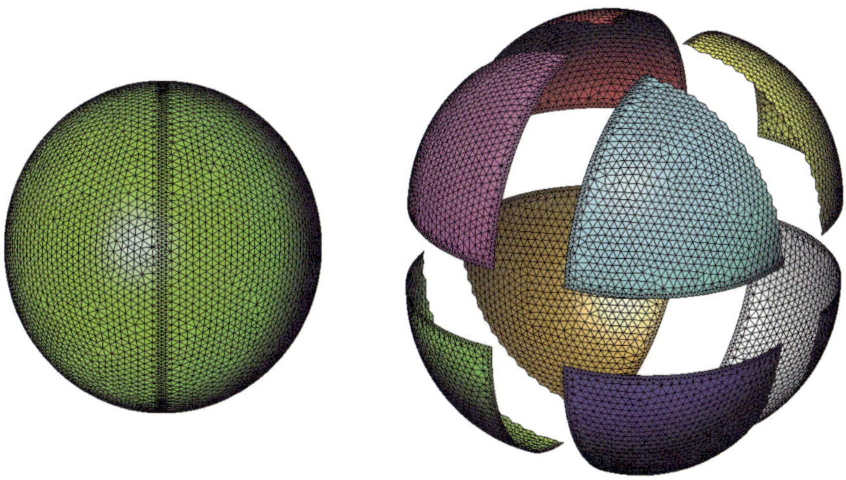

Fig. 5. Example of geometric block partitioning and definitions; a sphere is split into 8 blocks.

Δ; the algorithm stops when the last level L contains non-simplex cells with (linear) dimension around Δ. The non overlapping blocks, on which the synthetic functions will be generated, will then be the cells of the last level M_L. The only parameter the user has to control for the algorithm is the threshold where the grouping has to be stopped. We underline that the grouping procedure used to find the domains where the Synthetic Functions are defined has a $O(NlogN)$ complexity, where N is the number of initial mesh cells.

The next step consists in the generation of the basis functions to model the current distribution over each block; these will be referred as *synthetic functions* (SFs), whose support extends over the entire block. The synthetic functions are chosen in the set of responses to the required incident field, and to other sources placed at the borders of the block and around it, to make up the space of all (rigorous) solutions restricted to that block. Once the set of the solutions to all these sources is computed, the minimum number of necessary responses has to be determined. This is done through a combination of a Singular Value Decomposition (SVD) and a Gram-Schmidt (GS) procedure, applied to the matrix that collects the responses from all the sources: the functions are then selected with a proper thresholding on the associated singular value. Finally, the set of RWG functions defined over the connections of contacting blocks is added to the set of SFs in order to guarantee continuity across blocks. Since the SFs are expressed as a linear combination of the initial RWG functions, the scheme can be seen as a purely multiplicative algebraic compression of the standard MoM matrix.

It should be clear now that the process of generation of the synthetic functions is carried out independently on different blocks, i.e. the set of SFs is generated by solving the electromagnetic problem on each block in *isolation*. As a consequence, a Grid Computing approach is particularly well suited for the generation of the SFs: each block can be processed by a different node of the grid.

Finally, after the complete set of SFs is generated, the original system matrix is compressed, and the compressed system is inverted to yield the solution of the full problem. We underline that the goal of the synthetic functions approach is to accelerate the solution of the problem when a large number of excitation vectors (right hand sides, RHSs) is present, which is typical for Radar Cross Section (RCS) calculations. On the other hand, when a single RHS is present, approaches based on the combination of a fast factorization scheme and an iterative solver, are more efficient.

In order to exploit the Grid Computing approach, each node of the grid has to sequentially solve a number of blocks. The synthetic functions are chosen in the set of responses to the required incident field, and to other sources placed at the borders of the block and around it, to make up the space of all (rigorous) solutions restricted to that block. Since the grid is in general heterogeneous, i.e., the nodes have different processing and memory characteristics, the blocks should be properly dimensioned and assigned to the computing nodes. When the block dimensions are properly taken into account, the computation of the full MoM matrix and its handling do not pose a limitation within a single block.

However, once the full set of synthetic functions is generated, one needs to apply the basis change to the full system matrix related to the original structure, in order to compress the system and invert it. For practical problems this is not feasible though, due to the total dimension of the problem. Therefore we perform the compression within a fast scheme, which avoids computing the full system matrix and makes the solution of large problems possible. The compressed matrix in the new basis can be written as:

$$[Z_{SF}] = [T]\,[Z]\,[T]^H \tag{7}$$

where $[Z_{SF}]$ is the compressed matrix, $[T]$ is the change of basis matrix, whose dimensions are $N_{SF} \times N_{RWG}$ (the total number of synthetic functions and the total number of RWG functions, respectively), $[Z]$ is the MoM matrix in the RWG basis, and $[]^H$ represents the hermitian operator. The same change of basis is performed on the RHS, namely:

$$[V_{SF}] = [T]\,[V] \tag{8}$$

where $[V_{SF}]$ is the compressed RHS in the SF basis. Finally the compressed system is solved. At the present stage of the work, the compression and the solution of the complete system is not carried out in the grid though; this will be object of future research.

4. GridCEM architecture

The GridCEM project aims to improve performance of CEM application. This objective is achieved by the adoption of a grid architecture that exploits the benefits derived from the parallel computation. The proposed system manages data automatically and without impact for users. Furthermore, virtualized resources make system flexible, simplify the underlying infrastructure and improve scalability. To this aim an hybrid grid infrastructure was built and tests were performed in order to compare grid results to the ones of the same task executed on a single machine. The grid is composed of two types of nodes, a Master Node (MN) and Worker Nodes (WN). The Master Node is in charge to manage, control, and grant the security of the entire infrastructure. In addition, it coordinates other node operations. The middleware used to create the grid infrastructure is the Globus Toolkit (Globus (2010)). The toolkit, as explained in Section 3.1.1, includes functionalities for security, information systems, resource and data management, node communication, fault detection, portability and all the features need to safely deploy grid. The input data is a file that contains the mesh structure to analysis. It is split by the MN in smaller files, called blocks, that are distributed to WN. Since these blocks are generated according to Domain Decomposition technique and are independent, they can executed in parallel. The size of split blocks is not uniform but

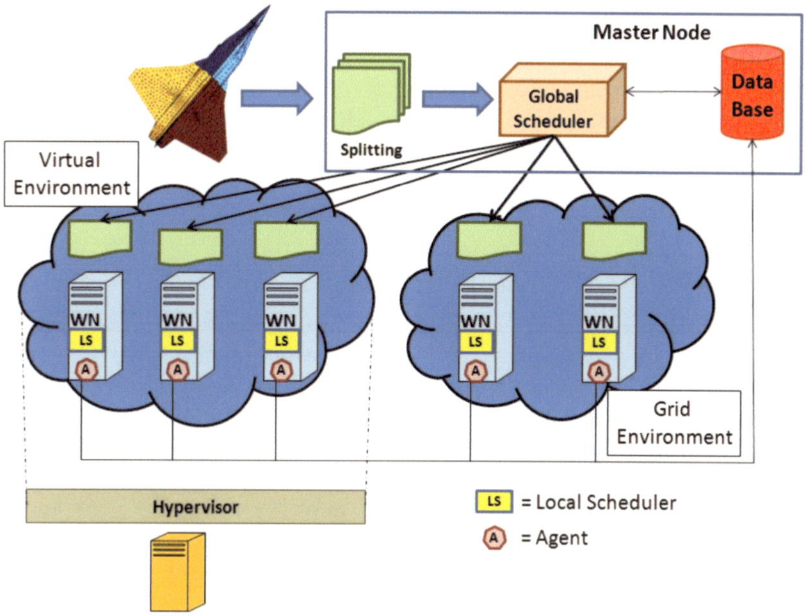

Fig. 6. GridCEM Architecture.

depends on the geometry of the structure. Moreover, the MN hosts the Global Scheduler (GS), that represents the smart component of the grid, and it holds information related to grid status, that are sent from each Worker Node, and stored in a database. The WN, instead, receives blocks, elaborates them and sends results to MN. The execution phase is managed by the Local Scheduler (LS) and the node status is monitored by an always active agent. The agent monitors the availability of each service on the node and sends periodically its status to the database on the MN. The agent role is crucial since the choice to send a job to a node depends on the information it gathers: if all services are available, the node is in condition to receive a job. All Worker Nodes have same operating system and are equipped with the same software: the middleware, the monitoring agents, the Local Scheduler and the code for execution.

4.1 Global Scheduler

As mentioned before the Master Node holds the brain of the grid that is represented by the Global Scheduler. It is a software module developed in Java responsible for the distribution of smaller parts of the input data (blocks) to each Worker Nodes. It communicates with other nodes thanks to grid services provided by the Globus Toolkit. The files are sent by the scheduler in order to balance the execution on each node: this is achieved by checking WNs availability and the number of files to sent. In order to know the overall status of the grid, the GS queries the database and transfers file only to nodes that have communicate their status within a specific time period. It is worth noting that this monitoring system that periodically push data into the database instead of gather information from each machine, allows to reduce time and computational wastes Gradwell (2003).

4.2 Local Scheduler

Each WN is provided with a Local Scheduler, developed in Java, that checks contents of its input folder: every time a new job file is detected it executes the task. In order to be recognized the filename must follow a predefined naming convention rules. During the execution the analyzed block is transformed into a Method of Moments (MOM) matrix. If the execution terminates successfully, the output is sent to the Master Node, that reassembles it with the outputs received from other nodes. Also the LS is in charge of tracking the status of job execution and sends information about start and stop time of each process.

4.3 Virtual environment

Since the code was not developed for parallel execution, it was decided to optimize resources by virtualizing nodes in order to run multiple processes on the same physical machine. In this way it was possible to create multiple virtual nodes on the same resource and increase the available nodes number, e.g., the parallelization of the system, instead of coding parallelization, to improve the overall performance. Virtualized systems also help to improve infrastructure management, allowing the use of virtual node template to create virtual nodes in a short time, speeding up the integration of new nodes on the grid and, therefore, improving the reactivity and the scalability of the infrastructure. Another advantage of virtual environment is the availability improvement, since in case of damage of a virtual node the system will be able to quickly restore it, reducing the downtime due to his recovery. The open source KVM (Hirt (2010)), has been used as hypervisor. It allows to create fully virtualized machines. The kernel component of KVM is included in mainline Linux. The basic requirements for the installation of this hypervisor is that the processor of the machine supports virtualization technology (Intel VT or AMD-V).

5. Test environment

In order to measure the gain in terms of time, some performances test were conducted. It has been compared the result times of the analysis of a model executed on the grid infrastructure with the sequential execution of the same model on a single computer. The experiment allowed verifying the practical usefulness of the adoption of distributed infrastructures in this kind of applications.

Node	Type	CPU model	Virtual CPU	RAM[GB]
master	physical	Intel Core Duo 2.66GHz		4
wn1	physical	Intel Pentium 4 @ 3.20GHz		3.5
wn2	physical	Intel Core 2 6420 @ 2.13GHz		2
wn3	virtualized	Intel Xeon E5440 @ 2.83GHz	2	4
wn4	virtualized	Intel Xeon E5440 @ 2.83GHz	2	4
wn5	virtualized	Intel Xeon X3470 @ 2.93GHz	2	4

Table 1. Grid Nodes Specifications.

The grid used for performance testing consists of hardware not purchased specifically for this purpose, but of computer available to researchers of Istituto Superiore Mario Boella(ISMB). For this reason, its composition is heterogeneous in terms of the machines types (workstations, servers) and in terms of view of hardware resources of each machine (RAM, CPU, HD). Within the pool of available machines, two machines met the criteria for virtualization: on

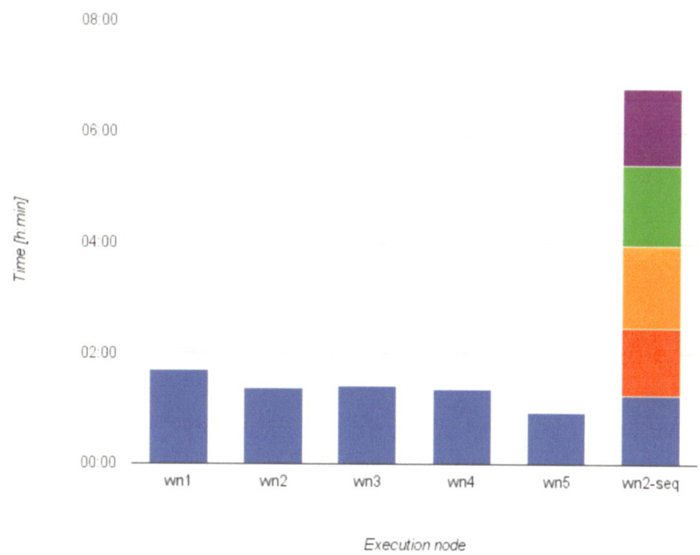

Fig. 7. Total execution time comparison between grid enviroment and sequential execution

these machines three VMs have been created. To run the tests six nodes with the following configuration have been used: a Master Node, two physical Worker Nodes (wn1, wn2) and three virtualized Worker Nodes (wn3, wn4, wn5). The details of the machines used for the experiment are shown in Table 1.

As a test-case a jet fighter aircraft (shown in Figure 1) has been discretized with a linear mesh density around 5 cm. The input file has a size of 17 MB and consists of about 156K unknowns. The plane is illuminated with a wave at the frequency of 600 MHz. The geometry has been subdivided into 67 blocks, each one described in a mesh file of about 7.5 MB. The first test performed was the execution of the entire process on a single physical machine. The node chosen for this test was the wn2: despite the smaller amount of RAM, the processing time of this machine is comparable to the average processing time of the other nodes. This node splits

Node	Executed blocks	Number of executed blocks	Time [h:min:s]
master		0	0:02:55
wn1	5 10 15 20 25 30 35 40 45 50 55 60 65	13	1:42:19
wn2	1 6 11 16 21 26 31 36 41 46 51 56 61 66	14	1:22:33
wn3	2 7 12 17 22 27 32 37 42 47 52 57 62 67	14	1:24:50
wn4	3 8 13 18 23 28 33 38 43 48 53 58 63	13	1:21:38
wn5	4 9 14 19 24 29 34 39 44 49 54 59 64	13	0:56:22
wn2	all	67	6:56:51

Table 2. Nodes Execution Time.

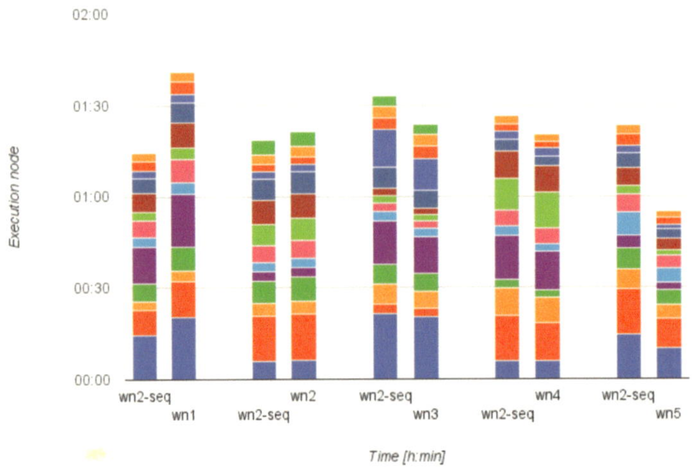

Fig. 8. Block execution time of each node compared to the same block executed in sequential mode (wn2-seq)

the main input into smaller chunks and ran the sequential execution of individual blocks: the total processing time for 67 blocks on wn2 was equal to 6h 56min 51s. In the second test the splitting was delegated to the Master Node, which has also been responsible for the distribution of the single blocks to different nodes. The execution time of the build process of the blocks and the file transfer is 2min 55s, and therefore it is negligible if compared to the total execution time. The execution times of different nodes are very similar, only the virtual machine wn5 has slightly better performance, probably due to the higher performance processor. The total execution time of the grid is equal to the maximum execution time of individual nodes, i.e., 1h 42min 19s of wn1. Table 2 summarizes the execution times. Figure 7 depicts total execution time comparison between grid environment and sequential execution on different nodes, on the grid and on sequential execution. The total time reduction is of 75%. Figure 7 shows the comparison between the processing times of individual nodes on the grid and the sequential execution: the colors of the column wn2-seq, correspond to the processing time of each node, through this comparison it can be appreciate the performance gain of the grid. In Figure 8 the comparison between the execution of individual blocks on the grid and in sequential mode is represented. The columns are divided into small parts that correspond to different executed blocks, each block is identified by a different color. The graph is useful for reasoning on the overhead introduced both by the grid and by the virtual machines. From the comparison between the execution of a group of blocks on the grid on a given node and sequentially on the same machine (i.e., the second pair of columns) it can be deduced that the grid introduces an overhead (equal to 2min 38s in this case) due to the transfer of files output, but negligible compared to the total execution time.

5.1 Application domains overview

More and more applications require high performance computing, flexibility and reduced processing time. The architecture explained before, can be useful in many fields i.e., in e-science applications (electronic, geophysics, biomedical domains). In our past studies, a similar grid infrastructure has been created for the analysis of Radio Occultation data. This project for the Italian Space Agency (ASI), allows to characterize the temperature, pressure and humidity (further details are available at Terzo et al. (2011)). In this project we have focused the attention on configuration and management problems due to distributed environment, scheduling of processes and resources, virtualization and Cloud environment. Another type of application, where the Grid Computing technique can be useful is in bioinformatic field, i.e., biological laboratories are producing a huge amount of DNA/RNA sequencing data and Next Generation Sequencing has proved to be extremely helpful in making the detection of various forms of disease. Unfortunately, this is reflected in a higher computational effort that must be faced by innovative computing infrastructure but in this case an hybrid infrastructure, composed of physical and virtualized resources and when it is necessary a Public Cloud (i.e., Amazon), is the best choice. An important feature is the application type that must allow to split a process in a smaller independent jobs in order to elaborate each single job in several resources reducing the elaboration time and increase the system flexibility.

6. Conclusion

The solution for CEM problems requires infrastructures based on high performance computing in order to reduce the execution time. However, it is not always possible to use supercomputers or parallelize algorithms code used for the calculation, a good solution may be represented by the Domain Decomposition technique, which allows the subdivision of the original complex problem into a set of smaller subproblems in a grid environment. In fact for this project, a grid infrastructure was carried out, that consists of 6 nodes (both physical and virtual). The results showed that the adoption of this infrastructure has reduced the execution time of 75% with respect to the sequential execution on a single machine. It was also noted that the overhead introduced by the grid is negligible when compared to the total execution time. The Virtualization has allowed optimizing the hardware resources of the machines, letting to run multiple blocks in parallel on the same physical machine, not introducing a significant overhead compared to the overall system performance. Studies are underway to improve the implementation of the scheduler, ensuring that blocks will be distributed to nodes most suitable for their execution. In particular, it will be developed a system that takes into account the weights of the jobs and the weights of the nodes available, assigned on the basis of predetermined criteria (e.g., file size, hardware resources, nodes availability, the average time of execution). The Scheduler will also be able to turn on and off virtual nodes according to the needs of the system, considering the load level of the grid. Furthermore the virtual nodes will be configured dynamically as needed to perform specific jobs (RAM, CPU and storage). A further improvement will be the integration of the system with Public Cloud Platforms (e.g., Amazon EC2) in order to increase the system scalability, asking for virtual nodes usage only when necessary.

7. References

Andriulli, F., Vipiana, F. & Vecchi, G. (2008). *Hierarchical bases for non-hierarchic 3D triangular meshes*, IEEE Trans. on Antennas and Propagation.

Asadzadeh, P., Buyya, R., Kei, C. L., Nayar, D. & Venugopal, S. (2005). *Global Grids and Software Toolkits: A Study of Four Grid Middleware Technologies*, available: http://www.buyya.com/papers/gmchapter.pdf.

CAS (2010). *Community Authorization Service*, available: http://globus.org/toolkit/ docs/4.0/security/cas.

Chakrabarti, A. (2007). *Grid computing security*, Springer.

Chierici, A. & Verald, R. (2010). *A quantitative comparison between xen and kvm*, 17th International Conference on Computing in High Energy and Nuclear Physics (CHEP09), IOP Publishing Journal of Physics.

Foster, I. & Kesselman, C. (2003). *The Grid2: Blueprint for a New Computing Infrastructure*, Morgan Kauffman.

Francavilla, M. A., Vasquez, J. A. T., Vipiana, F., Matekovits, L. & Vecchi, G. (2011). *Multi-level cell grouping scheme for an SFX/GIFFT approach for the analysis of electrically large 3D structures*, IEEE International Symposium on Antennas and Propagation.

Globus (2010). *Globus Toolkit*, available: http://www.globus.org.

Gradwell, P. (2003). *Grid scheduling with agents*, Proceedings of the Second International Joint Conference on Autonomous Agents and Multi-Agent Systems.

GSI (2010). *Grid Security Infrastructure*, available: http://www.globus.org/security/overview.html.

Hirt, T. (2010). *KVM-The Kernel-Based virtual machine*, available: http://www.cs. hs-rm. de/ linn/fachsem0910/hirt/KVM.pdf.

IBM (2010). *Virtual Linux*, available: http://www.ibm.com/developerworks/linux/library /l-linuxvirt/.

Kourpas, E. (2006). *Grid Computing:Past, Present and Future, An Innovation Perspective*, available: http://www.cnw.com.cn/cnw07/download/IBM.pdf.

Matekovits, L., Laza, V. A. & Vecchi, G. (2007). *Analysis of Large Complex Structures With the Synthetic-Functions Approach*, IEEE Trans on Antennas and Propagation.

Mouriño, J. C., Gómez, A., Taboada, J. M., Landesa, L., Bértolo, J. M., Obelleiro, F. & Rodríguez, J. L. (2009). *High scalability multipole method. Solving half billion of unknowns.*

MPI (2011). *Message Passing Interface Forum*, available: http://www.mpi-forum.org/docs/docs.html.

OGF (2011). *OGF Introduction*, available: http://www.gridforum.org/About/abt_introduction.php.

OGSA (2007). *Open Grid Services Architecture*, available: http://searchsoa.techtarget.com/definition/Open-Grid-Services-Architecture.

OpenMP (2011). *The OpenMP, API specification for parallel programming*, available: http://openmp.org/wp/.

Oracle (2009). *Oracle Grid Computing*, available: http://www.oracle.com/us/technologies/ grid/057123.pdf.

PERMIS (2002). *Privilege and Role Management Infrastructure Standards Validation*, available: www.permis.org.

Terzo, O., Mossucca, L., Cucca, M. & Notarpietro, R. (2011). *Data intensive scientific analysis with Grid Computing*, International Journal of "Applied Mathematics and Computer Science".

Vipiana, F., Andriulli, F. & Vecchi, G. (2009). *Two-tier non-simplex grid hierarchic basis for general 3D meshes*, Waves in Random and Complex Media.

VOMS (2003). *Virtual Organization Membership Service*, available: http://edg-wp2.web.cern.ch/edg-wp2/security/voms/voms.html.

12

Characterization of Hepatic Lesions Using Grid Computing (Globus) and Neural Networks

Sheng Hung Chung[1] and Ean Teng Khor[2]
School of Science and Technology, Wawasan Open University, Penang, Malaysia

1. Introduction

Magnetic Resonance Imaging (MRI) images have been widely used for liver disease diagnosis. Designing and developing computer-assisted image processing techniques to help doctors improve their diagnosis has received considerable interest over the past years. In this paper, a computer-aided diagnostic (CAD) system for the characterization of hepatic lesions, specifically cyst and tumor as well as healthy liver, from MRI images using texture features and implementation of grid computing (Globus approach) and neural networks (NN) is presented. Texture analysis is used to determine the changes in functional characteristics of organs at the onset of a liver disease, Region of interest (ROI) extracted from MRI images are used as the input to characterize different tissue, namely liver cyst and healthy liver using first-order statistics. The results for first-order statistics are given and their potential applicability in grid computing is discussed. The measurements extracted from First-order statistic include entropy and correlation achieved obvious classification range in detecting different tissues in this work.

In this chapter, texture analysis of liver MRI images based on the Spatial Grey Level Co-occurrence Matrix (SGLCM) [3] is proposed to discriminate normal, malignant hepatic tissue (i.e. liver tumor) and cysts in MRI images of the abdomen. SGLCM, also known as Grey Tone Spatial Dependency Matrix [3], is a tabulation of how often different combinations of pixel brightness values (i.e. grey-level) occur in an image. Regions of interest (ROI) from cysts, tumor and healthy liver were used as input for the SGLCM calculation. Second order statistical texture features estimated from the SGLCM are then applied to a Feed-forward Neural Network (FNN) and Globus toolkit for the characterization of suspected liver tissue from MRI images for hepatic lesions classification. This project proposed an automated distributed processing framework for high-throughput, large-scale applications targeted for characterization of liver texture statistical measurements mainly healthy liver, fatty liver, liver cyst for MRI (Magnetic Resonance Imaging) images.

Table 1 lists eight second-order statistical calculations based on SGLCM, namely, contrast, entropy, correlation, homogeneity, cluster tendency, inverse difference moment, energy, and angular second moment, which have shown useful results in hepatic lesions classification for liver tumor using Computed Tomography (CT), Ultrasonography (US) and

Properties	Valanis [4]	CHEN [5]	MIR [6]	MOUGIAKAKOU [7]
Contrast	√			√
Entropy		√	√	√
Correlation	√	√	√	√
Homogeneity			√	√
Cluster Tendency	√			
Inverse Difference Moment	√			√
Energy	√		√	√
Angular Second Moment	√	√		

Table 1. SGLCM properties for second-order statistical measurements. The features successfully examined in prior work are summarized in Table 1 below.

MRI. The measurements identified in various approaches are indicated by a tick. The SGLCM approach undertaken by Valanis et al. [4] was to classify three hepatic tissues: normal, hemangeoma and hepatocellular carcinoma on CT images with a resolution of 512 X 512 pixels and 8 bits per pixel (bpp) (256 grey levels). Correlation, inverse difference moment and cluster tendency were shown in the paper to achieve classification rates of up to 90.63% after being applied with feature selection based on a Genetic Algorithm (GA) approach. Of particular interest is an approach by Chen [5], using a modified probabilistic neural network (MPNN) to classify liver tumor, hepatoma and hemangeoma on CT images with 12 bpp representing 4096 grey levels and resolution of 320 X 320 pixels. The entropy and correlation showed better performance than other features extracted from co-occurrence matrices at directions $\theta = 0°, 45°, 90°$ and $135°$, resulting in a classification rate of 83% where the misclassification resulted from the tumor matrices block size. The classification rate could be increased by reducing the block size. Another approach was by Mir [6] to classify normal and malignant liver on 256 X 256 pixels CT images. Entropy and local homogeneity were found to be consistent within a class and most appropriate for discrimination of the malignant and normal liver. Mougiakakou [7] implemented an automated CAD system for characterization of liver CT images into cysts, hepatoma and hemangeoma using a multiple NN classification scheme. Contrast, entropy, correlation and homogeneity were the identified features based on feature selection using the Squared Mahalanobis Distance as the fitness function [8].

1.1 Image acquisition

MRI produces images of the insides of the body. Unlike an X-ray, MRI does not use radiation. Instead, a magnetic field is used to make the body's cells vibrate [1]. The vibrations give off electrical signals which are interpreted and turned into very detailed images of "slices" of the body. MRI may be used to make images of every part of the body, including the bones, joints, blood vessels, nerves, muscles and organs. Different types of tissue show up in different grayscale intensities on a computer-generated image. In this study, series of MRI images were acquired from the Diagnostic Imaging Department of Selayang Hospital, Malaysia, using a Siemens Magnetom Avanto, 1.5T MRI Scanner. The sample liver MRI images (256 X 256 pixels, 12 bps) were acquired consisting of sets of cyst, liver tumor and healthy liver, for training and testing.

2. Grid computing with globus

Grid Computing describes computation in which jobs are run on a distributed computational unit spanning two or more administrative domains. It has sparked tremendous excitement among scientists worldwide and has renewed the interest of the scientific community toward distributed computing, an area which was almost forgotten during the 90's.

The Globus toolkit [4] was created in the late 1990s as part of a joint research project between Argonne National Laboratory and the Information Sciences Institute at the University of Southern California. Its aim was to provide a solution to the computational needs of large virtual organizations [4] that span multiple institutional and administrative domains. Globus is a middleware toolkit that provides fundamental distributed computing services such as authentication, job starting and resource discovery.

Globus provides a collection of services [5] including: GSI, Grid Security Infrastructure which provides authentication based on a Certificate Authority trust model; GRAM, Grid Resource Allocation Manager which handles job starting or submission; GridFTP, providing extensions to the FTP standard to provide GSI authentication and high performance transfer; MDS, Monitoring and Discovery Service enabling remote resource discovery.

By itself Globus does not provide all of the tools and services required to implement a full featured distributed computing environment. Additional tools are available to fill some of the gaps. The National Center for Supercomputing Applications (NCSA) provides a patch to add GSI authentication to OpenSSH. This allows Globus environments to have terminal based single-signon. Globus does not provide any scheduling functionality, but rather relies on the client operating system scheduler or batch schedulers such as OpenPBS [6] to handle local scheduling activities.

Global scheduling between Globus processes can be provided by meta-schedulers, such as Condor-G [6]. Condor-G submits jobs to the GRAM service running on Globus nodes and GRAM handles the task of submitting the job to the local scheduling system.

3. Spatial grey level co-occurrence matrices

The SGLCM aspect of texture is concerned with the spatial distribution and spatial dependence among the grey levels in a local area. This concept was first used by Julesz [9] in texture discrimination experiments. Being one of the most successful methods for texture discrimination at present, we have investigated its effectiveness for use with MRI images in the present work. This method is based on the estimation of the second order joint conditional probability density function [10]

$$f(i,j\,|\,d,\theta) \tag{1}$$

where θ = 0°, 45°, 90°, 135°, 180°, 225°, 270°, and 315°.Each $f(i,j\,|\,d,\theta)$ is the probability of going from grey level i to grey level j, given that the inter-sample spacing is d and the direction is given by the angle θ. The estimated value for these probability density functions can thus be written in matrix form [11]

$$\phi(d,\theta) = [f(i,j,|\,d,\theta)]\,. \tag{2}$$

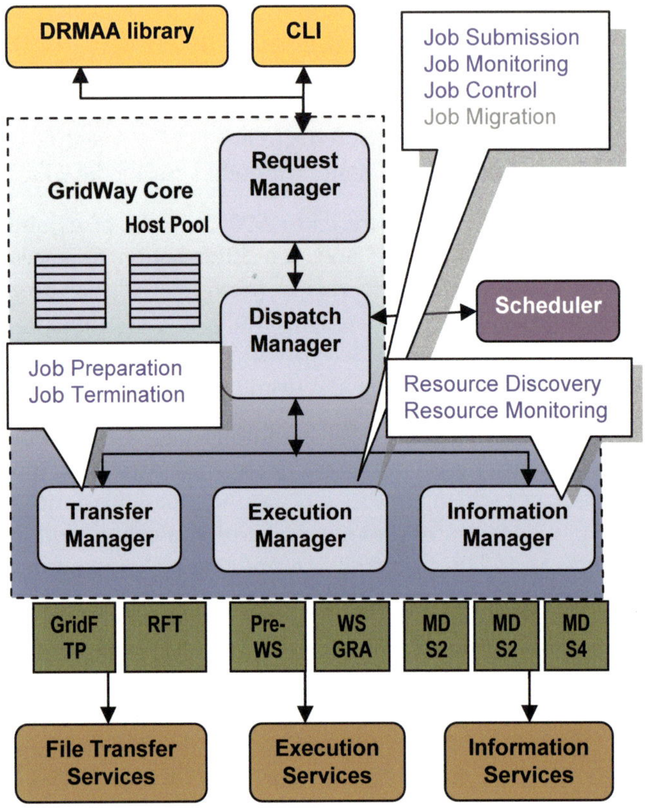

Fig. 1. Component of Gridway in Globus

For computing these probability distribution functions, scanning of the image in four directions has been carried out in this work, with θ = 0°, 45°, 90° and 135° sufficient, since the probability density matrix for the rest of the directions can be computed from these four basic directions, as denoted in the following [11]

$$\phi(d,0) = \phi^t(\mathrm{d},180)$$

$$\phi(d,45) = \phi^t(\mathrm{d},225)$$

$$\phi(d,90) = \phi^t(\mathrm{d},270)$$

$$\phi(d,135) = \phi^t(\mathrm{d},315) \quad (3)$$

where $\phi^t(\mathrm{d},\theta)$ denotes the transpose of the matrix for the inter-sample spacing *d*, and direction, θ.

3.1 Second-order statistical measurements

Findings by other researchers on SGLCM second-order feature extraction for use in statistical classification using neural networks (NN) has been shown to be efficient and very effective [4-7]. There are eleven general second-order statistic measurements, as illustrated in [12], which include energy, entropy, contrast, correlation, homogeneity, inverse different moment, inertia, skewness, kurtosis, angular second moment and cluster tendency. The second-order statistical measurements commonly used in most texture classification cases for hepatic tissues using SGLCM are energy, entropy, homogeneity, inertia, contrast and correlation.

Entropy is a notoriously difficult term to understand shown as follows[10].

$$H(S_\theta(d)) = \sum_{i=0}^{NG-1} \sum_{j=0}^{NG-1} S_\theta(i,j,d) \log S_\theta(i,j,d) \tag{4}$$

where $S_\theta(i,j,d)$ is the *(i, j)*th entry in a co-occurrence matrix, *NG* is the number of grey levels in the image from which the SGLCM matrices are extracted.

The concept of entropy comes from thermodynamics, referring to the quantity of energy that is permanently lost to heat ("chaos") every time a reaction or a physical transformation occurs. Entropy cannot be recovered to do useful work. Because of this, the term is used in non-technical speech to mean irremediable chaos or disorder. Also, as with Angular Second Moment [11], the equation used to calculate physical entropy is very similar to the one used for the texture measure. In image processing, entropy measures the disorder or randomness in an image. The smaller the value of entropy, $H(S_\theta(d))$, the less common is the occurrence of the pixel combinations [12]. Entropy measures the randomness of the elements of the matrix when all elements of the matrix are maximally random, entropy has its highest value. So, a homogeneous image has lower entropy than an inhomogeneous image.

Energy, the opposite of entropy, is, in this context denoted by.

$$E(S_\theta(d)) = \sum_{i=0}^{NG-1} \sum_{j=0}^{NG-1} [S_\theta(i,j)d]^2 \tag{5}$$

The energy of a texture describes the uniformity of the texture. In a homogeneous image there are very few dominant grey-tone transitions, hence the co-occurrence matrix of this image will have fewer entries of large magnitude. So, the energy of an image is high when the image is homogeneous. In that sense, it represents orderliness. Thus, energy is useful for measuring the texture orderness in the image.

Homogeneity is the dissimilarity and contrast result in larger numbers for more contrasty windows,

$$L(S_\theta(d)) = \sum_{i=0}^{NG-1} \sum_{j=0}^{NG-1} \frac{1}{1+(i-j)^2} S_\theta(i,j,d) \tag{6}$$

If weights decrease away from the diagonal, the result will be larger for images with little contrast. Homogeneity weights values by the inverse of the contrast weight, with weights decreasing exponentially away from the diagonal. When there is a large amount of contrast, weights are created in SGLCM so that the calculation results in a larger figure. Values on the SGLCM diagonal show contrast as follows,

$$Con(S_\theta(d)) = \sum_{i=0}^{NG-1} \sum_{j=0}^{NG-1} (i-j)^2 S_\theta(i,j,d,\theta) \tag{7}$$

For non-square matrices, the correlation function computes the linear Pearson correlation coefficient of two vectors or the correlation matrix of an *i* x *j* array,

$$C(S_\theta(d)) = \frac{\sum_{i=0}^{NG-1} \sum_{j=0}^{NG-1} (i-\mu_i)(j-\mu_j) S_\theta(i,j,d,\theta)}{\mu_i \mu_j} \tag{8}$$

where μ refers to the mean intensity value of the image in the x and y directions, respectively,

$$\mu_i = \sum_{i=0}^{NG-1} i \sum_{j=0}^{NG-1} S_\theta(i,j) \tag{9}$$

$$\mu_j = \sum_{i=0}^{NG-1} j \sum_{j=0}^{NG-1} S_\theta(i,j) \tag{10}$$

When correlation is high, the image will be more complex than when correlation is low. If vectors of unequal lengths are specified, the longer vector is truncated to the length of the shorter vector and a single correlation coefficient is returned. If an *i* x *j* array is specified, the result will be an *i* x *j* array of linear Pearson correlation coefficients, with the element *i,j* corresponding to correlation of the *i*th rows and *j*th column of the input array.

The inverse difference moment is defined as ,

$$IDM(S_\theta(d)) = \sum_{i=0}^{NG-1} \sum_{j=0}^{NG-1} \frac{1}{1+(i-j)^2} S_\theta(i,j,d,\theta) \tag{11}$$

It has a relatively high value when the high values of the matrix are near the main diagonal because the squared difference $(i, j)^2$ is then smaller, which increases the value of $\frac{1}{1+(i-j)^2}$.

The feature inertia defined as

$$I(S_\theta(d)) = \sum_{i=0}^{NG-1} \sum_{j=0}^{NG-1} (i-j)^2 S_\theta(i,j,d,\theta) \tag{12}$$

which gives the opposite effect as the inverse difference moment does; when the high values of the matrix are further away from the main diagonal, the value of inertia becomes higher.

So inertia and the inverse difference moment are measures for the distribution of grey values in the image.

The skewness feature, also known as cluster shade and cluster prominence, is the measure of the skewness of the matrix [10]

$$S(S_\theta(d)) = \sum_{i=0}^{NG-1} \sum_{j=0}^{NG-1} (i-\mu_i)^3 (j-\mu_j)^3 S_\theta(i,j,d) \tag{13}$$

When cluster shade and cluster prominence are high, the image is asymmetric.

4. Implementation of SGLCM, globus for hepatic lesions detection using region of interest

In constructing the sparse coding for SGLCM, the reduction of the number of intensity levels by quantizing the image to fewer levels of intensity [13] helps increase the speed of computation, with some loss of textural information. An interactive graphical user interface (GUI) region drawing tool was developed for image block size flexibility. Inter-sample distance of d = 1, image block size of 12 x 12 pixels and direction θ= 0°, 45°, 90° and 135°, were used in the experiment. Fig. 2 shows an ROI drawn on healthy liver texture for NN training. Fig. 3 and Fig. 4 show the ROI image block of 12 x 12 pixels drawn on suspected texture areas of cyst and liver tumor, respectively.

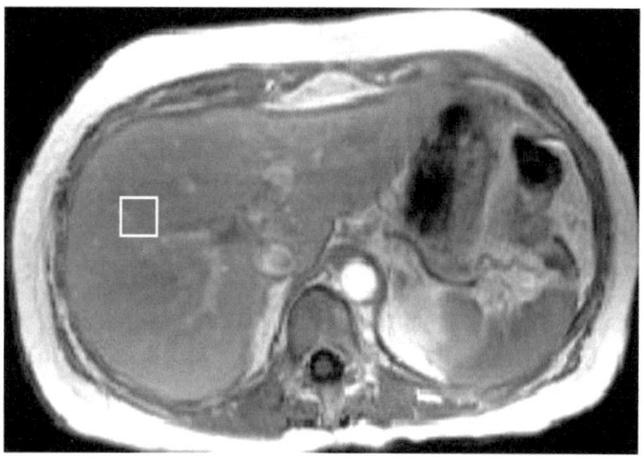

Fig. 2. 12 x 12 ROI block drawn on healthy liver in a MR image of the abdomen.

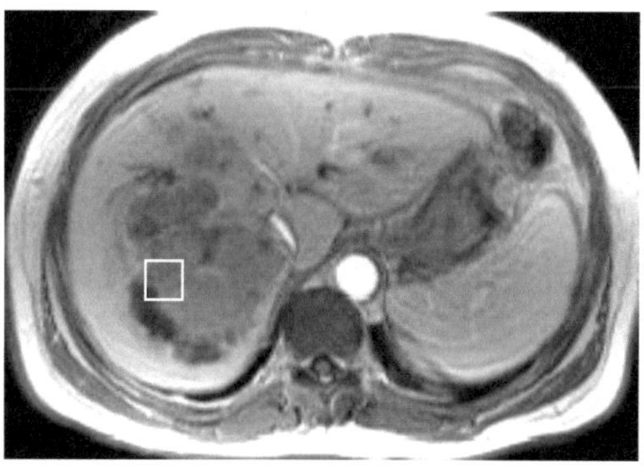

Fig. 3. 12 x 12 ROI block drawn on suspected liver tumor in a MR image of the abdomen. Liver tumor has irregular shape and has multiple growths tissue.

Co-occurrence matrices for the θ = 0° and θ = 90° are calculated as illustrated in Fig. 5 and Fig. 6, respectively. A test image of 4 x 4 pixels was used as the input to illustrate the sparse matrix construction. As observed in Fig. 4, each pixel within the test image window becomes the reference pixel in the position of the matrix, starting from the upper left corner and proceeding to the lower right. The pixels along the right edge of the image have no right hand neighbour, so they are not used in this count.

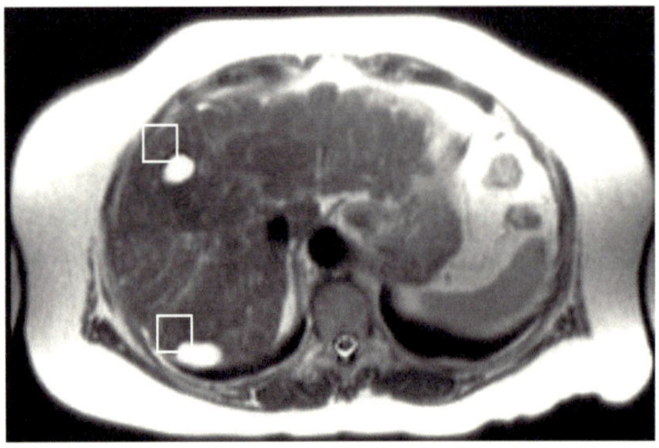

Fig. 4. 12 x 12 ROI block drawn on cyst in a MR image of the abdomen. cyst is a recently recognized genetic disorder characterized by the appearance of numerous cysts spread throughout the liver. A cyst may be identified as an abnormal fluid-filled sac-like structure.

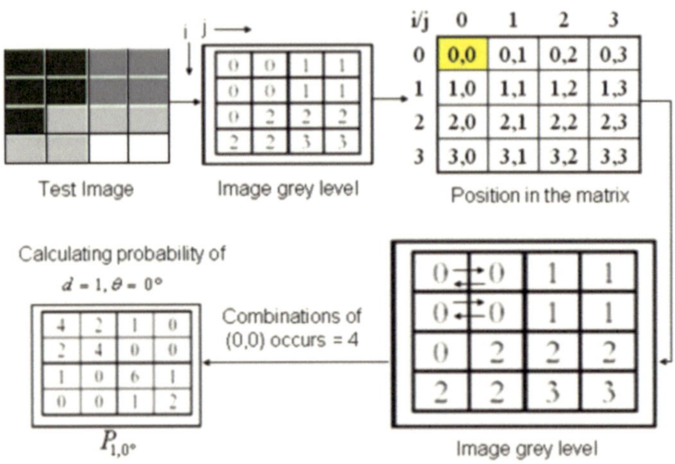

Fig. 5. Constructing SGLCM spatial matrix based on θ =0°, d=1, using 4 x 4 ROI block. Each pixel within the test image becomes the reference pixel of the position in the matrix of the direction of 0°. A reference pixel of 3 and its horizontal neighbour of 2 would contribute one count to the matrix element (3,2) and one count to the matrix element (2,3).

The spatial matrix, $P_{1,0^\circ}$ is constructed by filling in the probability of the combinations of pixels coordinate occurring in the window test image at the direction, denoted as angle, θ. The top cell of $P_{1,0^\circ}$ will be filled with the number of times the combination of (0,0) occurs (i.e. amount of times within the image area a pixel with grey level 0 neighboring pixels) falls to the left and right side of another pixel with grey level 0 as the reference pixel. The number of combination of (0,0) that occurs are 4 at the angle direction of 0° with the distance, d=1. As such, the sparse matrix constructed corresponds to the size of the test image.

Similar calculations using SGLCM are evaluated with θ=45°, 135°, 180°, 225°, 270°, and 315° as the direction of the reference pixel. If the test image is smaller (e.g 3 x 3 image block), the sum of all the entries in the SGLCM spatial matrix generated would be smaller.

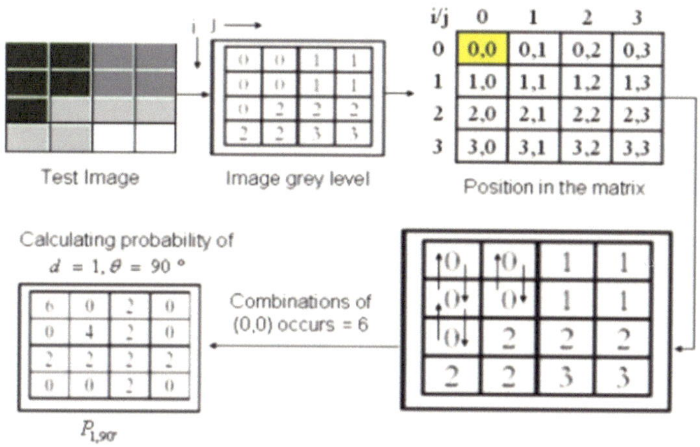

Fig. 6. Constructing SGLCM spatial matrix based on θ =90°, d=1, using 4 x 4 ROI block. A reference pixel of 0 and its neighbour of 0 at the direction of 90° will contribute one count to the matrix element (0,0). Similar to Fig. 4, a reference pixel of 3 and its vertical neighbour of 2 would contribute one count to the matrix element (3,2) and one count to the matrix element (2,3).

It is, in theory, possible to choose three or more pixels in a given direction [15]. However, this becomes extremely unwieldy for calculations and is not an operational procedure. Calculation involving three pixels would be third order, four pixels would be forth order and so forth.

4.1 Implementation of SGLCM for hepatic lesions using automated segmentation of the image block

An automated segmentation scheme using a flexible image block size for automated liver tissue characterization is shown in Fig. 7.

Square image blocks of widths of 5, 8 and 10 pixels were used within the liver boundary. The purpose of automated segmentation with these various block sizes was for preliminary diagnosis of the entire liver, without requiring intervention by the user in identifying an ROI.

4.2 Implementation and anlaysis

By using SGLCM, approximately two dozen co-occurrence features can be obtained [16]. Consideration of the number of distance angle relations also will lead to a potentially large number of dependent features. In this study, we restrict the representation to four features, which we hypothesize from Table 1 would provide useful information for texture characterization. These are entropy, correlation, contrast and homogeneity. For soft textures, the second order measurement distributions change very slightly with distance, while for coarse textures, the change in the distribution is rapid [16].

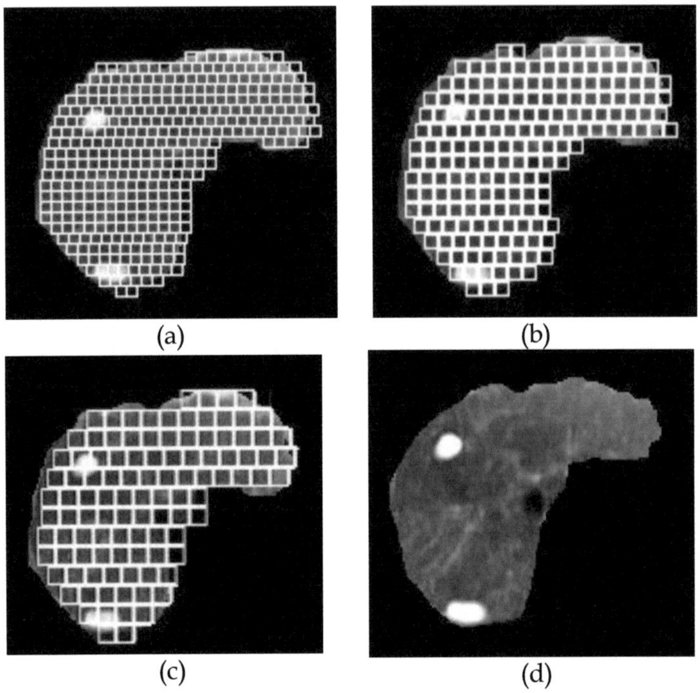

Fig. 7. Automated segmentation of image block in a cyst liver boundary using (a) 5 x 5 (b) 8 x 8 (c) 10 x 10 image block (d) shows the liver region in MRI abdomen image.

Table 2 shows the statistical results achieved for entropy calculated based on spatial co-occurrence matrices generated using SGLCM on cysts, tumor and healthy liver of the training set (*T1, T2, …, Tn*). Entropy is consistent within a specific range from 5.174-7.911 for cyst classification and 2.487- 4.291 for tumor classification. In healthy liver, entropy ranges from 0.054-1.954. As the entropy ranges are distinct for each of the 3 categories tested, entropy could be a suitable feature for successful liver lesions classification.

Table 3 provides the results for the correlation calculated using SGLCM. As observed, correlation is consistent within a specific range from 5.962-6.997 for cyst and 2.300-4.932 for tumor and 0.071-1.500 for healthy liver. Being different for the 3 categories, correlation may also be deemed a suitable classification feature.

The statistical results for two more features, homogeneity and contrast, calculated based on SGLCM on healthy liver ROI were inconsistent as shown in Table 4 and Table 5. As all the ranges for the 3 categories overlap, these features cannot be used to classify the liver MRI images.

4.3 Classification for hepatic lesions using neural networks and globus

The diagnostic value of MRI liver images has become increasingly important in liver disease detection. However, the interpretation effectiveness still relies heavily on experience and skill of the doctors. From the analysis of the SGLCM results obtained, only entropy and correlation are selected for classification for liver tumor and cyst.

ROI		Direction, θ				Entropy	
	ROI	0°	45°	90°	135°	Min	Max
Cyst	T1	5.802	5.724	6.425	6.484	5.802	6.484
	T2	5.487	5.524	5.925	6.183	5.487	6.183
	T3	5.477	6.554	6.072	7.854	5.477	7.854
	T4	5.339	6.774	6.241	7.692	5.339	7.692
	T5	5.174	6.694	6.131	7.911	**5.174**	**7.911**
	T6	5.477	5.884	6.082	7.054	5.477	7.054
	T7	5.884	6.145	6.281	7.692	5.884	7.692
Tumor	T8	2.802	2.724	2.925	4.284	2.802	4.284
	T9	2.487	2.719	2.919	4.183	**2.487**	4.183
	T10	2.677	2.794	2.999	4.254	2.677	3.254
	T11	2.539	2.724	2.802	4.192	2.539	4.192
	T12	2.494	2.894	2.994	4.291	2.494	**4.291**
	T13	3.327	3.484	3.792	4.054	3.327	4.054
	T14	3.124	3.145	3.381	4.102	3.124	4.102
Healthy	T15	0.054	0.692	1.054	1.692	**0.054**	1.692
	T16	0.082	0.281	1.082	1.954	0.082	**1.954**
	T17	0.554	0.784	1.054	1.281	0.554	1.281
	T18	0.887	0.231	1.607	1.784	0.887	1.784
	T19	0.574	0.884	1.177	1.231	0.574	1.231
	T20	0.114	0.145	1.484	1.884	0.114	1.884
	T21	0.774	0.954	1.074	1.145	0.774	1.145

Table 2. Entropy results for cyst, tumor and healthy liver.

ROI		Direction, θ				Correlation	
	ROI	0°	45°	90°	135°	Min	Max
Cyst	T1	5.962	6.403	6.825	6.854	**5.962**	6.854
	T2	6.127	6.241	6.325	6.483	6.127	6.483
	T3	6.493	6.554	6.610	6.854	6.493	6.854
	T4	6.384	6.774	6.941	6.997	6.384	**6.997**
	T5	6.128	6.694	6.910	6.111	6.128	6.910
	T6	6.773	6.884	6.904	6.341	6.773	6.904
	T7	6.237	6.345	6.431	6.562	6.237	6.562
Tumor	T8	2.302	2.924	3.164	4.269	2.302	4.269
	T9	2.300	2.811	3.119	4.702	**2.300**	4.702
	T10	2.321	2.703	2.321	4.164	2.321	4.164
	T11	2.370	2.718	3.860	4.718	2.370	4.718
	T12	2.410	2.843	2.994	4.932	2.410	**4.932**
	T13	3.156	3.481	3.494	4.156	3.156	4.156
	T14	2.186	2.916	3.994	4.321	2.186	4.321
Healthy	T15	0.110	0.241	1.314	1.500	0.110	**1.500**
	T16	0.120	0.231	1.312	1.431	0.120	1.431
	T17	0.152	0.214	1.224	1.322	0.152	1.322
	T18	0.133	0.231	1.167	1.311	0.133	1.311
	T19	0.142	0.284	1.437	1.410	0.142	1.410
	T20	0.071	0.145	1.224	1.374	**0.071**	1.374
	T21	0.140	0.254	1.284	1.350	0.140	1.350

Table 3. Correlation results for cyst, tumor and healthy liver.

ROI		Direction, θ				Contrast	
	ROI	0°	45°	90°	135°	Min	Max
Cyst	T1	4.120	0.242	4.527	0.242	0.242	4.527
	T2	0.872	10.51	2.520	11.21	0.872	11.21
	T3	7.711	16.50	0.721	16.30	0.721	16.50
	T4	0.091	7.741	2.411	17.41	0.091	**17.41**
	T5	1.746	6.942	13.14	6.042	1.746	13.14
	T6	14.01	5.841	0.821	0.841	0.821	14.01
	T7	3.341	1.206	0.011	1.210	**0.011**	1.206
Tumor	T8	0.103	0.212	0.527	0.242	0.103	0.527
	T9	0.872	11.31	2.520	12.21	0.872	11.21
	T10	0.001	17.20	0.761	13.40	**0.001**	**17.20**
	T11	0.004	0.741	2.411	0.411	0.004	2.411
	T12	0.246	6.842	8.104	0.052	0.052	8.104
	T13	0.071	0.771	0.811	0.101	0.071	0.811
	T14	1.345	1.216	0.081	1.210	0.081	1.345
Healthy	T15	12.10	0.222	1.021	2.230	0.222	12.10
	T16	3.212	0.141	12.02	11.21	0.141	12.02
	T17	0.701	1.110	0.001	16.30	**0.001**	**16.30**
	T18	1.091	0.011	2.017	12.41	0.011	12.41
	T19	5.342	0.442	1.014	1.042	0.442	5.342
	T20	1.121	5.821	0.123	10.31	0.123	10.31
	T21	1.341	1.306	1.011	12.10	1.306	12.10

Table 4. Contrast Results for cyst, tumor and healthy liver.

ROI		Direction, θ				Homogeneity	
	ROI	0°	45°	90°	135°	Min	Max
Cyst	T1	3.015	0.101	12.98	2.045	0.101	12.98
	T2	5.178	1.087	0.251	1.101	0.251	5.178
	T3	0.018	1.679	1.022	0.667	0.667	1.679
	T4	10.54	12.05	11.02	1.668	1.668	12.05
	T5	5.890	0.014	12.98	1.031	0.014	**12.98**
	T6	0.012	11.02	0.023	0.098	0.012	11.02
	T7	0.001	11.78	0.078	1.189	**0.001**	11.78
Tumor	T8	0.040	1.212	5.527	2.142	0.040	5.527
	T9	0.012	12.31	2.320	10.17	0.012	12.31
	T10	0.007	11.30	12.61	13.24	0.007	**13.24**
	T11	0.001	11.01	0.401	0.011	**0.001**	11.01
	T12	11.20	0.047	10.14	0.009	0.009	11.20
	T13	2.001	0.731	0.011	0.001	**0.001**	2.001
	T14	2.562	3.691	0.001	0.001	**0.001**	3.691
Healthy	T15	1.133	1.895	1.021	2.230	1.021	2.230
	T16	0.112	0.141	6.027	11.21	0.112	6.027
	T17	0.001	0.140	0.001	12.31	**0.001**	12.31
	T18	0.001	0.011	2.028	0.480	**0.001**	2.028
	T19	11.30	0.442	1.134	0.001	**0.001**	11.30
	T20	12.01	0.821	0.123	2.078	0.123	12.01
	T21	0.001	0.002	1.011	13.28	**0.001**	**13.28**

Table 5. Homogeneity results for cyst, tumor, and healthy liver.

The texture features obtained were then applied to the NN classifier and Globus automated scheduling for the detection. The final decisions of the NN classifier was generated by combining the diagnostic output using the input layer consisting of a number of input neurons equal to the number of features fed into the NN. (i.e. 2, namely entropy and correlation. Training and testing of the NN classification was based on the use of sample MRI abdomen images for all 3 categories as observed in Table 6.

	Entropy		Correlation	
	Min	Max	Min	Max
Cyst	5.174	7.911	5.962	6.997
Tumor	2.487	4.291	2.300	4.932
Healthy	0.054	1.954	0.071	1.500

Table 6. Classification of hepatic lesions using entropy and correlation.

5. Conclusion

In the approach described above, it should be noted that, resolution, ROI image block size and sampling space used for calculation of SGLCM are important considerations in statistical feature extraction. The present study has shown promising results in the use of texture for the extraction of diagnostic information from MR images of the liver. Two features were selected using SGLCM, namely entropy and correlation, whilst it was shown that homogeneity and contrast were unsuitable to differentiate between cyst, tumor and healthy liver. In our experiment, the same features were used as input to the NN with the aid of Globus automated scheduling for hepatic liver tissue characterization of MRI images. In particular, this paper provides results of successful preliminary diagnosis of cyst and liver tumor in the liver tissue.

6. References

[1] Carrillo, J. L. Duerk, J. S. Lewin, D. L. Wilson, "Semiautomatic 3-D image registration as applied to interventional MRI liver cancer treatment." *IEEE Transactions on Information Technology in Biomedicine*, vol. 19, pp. 175-185, 2000.

[2] M. Gletsos, S. G. Mougiakakou, G. K. Matsopoulus, K. S. Nikita, A. S. Nikita and D. Kelekis, "A Computer-aided Diagnostic System to Characterize CT Focal Liver Lesions: Design and Optimization of a Neural Network Classifier", *IEEE Transactions on Information Technology in Biomedicine*, vol. 7, no. 3, pp. 153-162, 2003.

[3] S. Kitaguchi, S. Westland and M. R. Luo, "Suitability of Texture Analysis Methods for Perceptual Texture", Proceedings, *10th Congress of the International Colour Association*, vol. 10, pp. 923-926, 2005.

[4] Valanis, S. G. Mougiakakou, K. S. Nikita and A. Nikita, "Computer-aided Diagnosis of CT Liver Lesions by an Ensemble of Neural Network and Statistical Classifiers", *Proceedings of IEEE International Joint Conference on Neural Networks*, vol. 3, pp. 1929-1934, 2004.

[5] E. L. Chen, P. C. Chung, C. L. Chen, H. M. Tsai and C. L. Chang, "An automatic diagnostic system for CT liver image classification", *IEEE Transactions on Biomedical Engineering*, vol. 45, no. 6, pp. 783-794, 1996.

[6] H. Mir, M. Hanmandlu and S. N. Tandon, "Texture Analysis of CT Images", *IEEE Transactions on Computers*, vol. 42, no. 4, pp. 501-507, 1993.
[7] S. G. Mougiakakou, I. Valanis, K. S. Nikita, A. Nikita and D. Kelekis, "Characterization of CT Liver Lesions Based on Texture Features and a Multiple Neural Network Classification Scheme", *Proceedings of the 25th Annual International Conference of the IEEE EMBS*, vol. 2, no. 3, pp. 17-21, 2001.
[8] D. Goldberg, "Genetic Algorithms in Search, Optimization and Machine Learning", *Addison-Wesley*, 1989.
[9] Julesz, "Experiments in the Visual Perception of Texture", *Scientific American*, vol. 232, no. 4, pp. 34-43, 1975.
[10] Materka and M Strzelecki, "Texture Analysis Method-A Review", *COSTB11 Report*, pp. 1-33, 1998.
[11] G. D. Kendall and T. J. Hall, "Performing fundamental image processing operations using quantized neural networks", *International Conference on Image Processing and its Applications*. vol. 4, no. 1, pp. 226-229, 2002
[12] R. Haralick, "Statistical and Structural Approaches to Texture", *Proceedings of IEEE*, vol. 67, no. 5, pp. 786-804, 1979.
[13] Kyoung, "An Adaptive Resource-Allocating Network for Automated Detection, Segmentation, and Classification of Breast Cancer Nuclei Topic Area", *Image Processing and Recognition, Neural Networks*, Israel, 2003.
[14] L.L Lanzarini, A.C. Camacho, A. Badran and D. G. Armando, "Images Compression for Medical Diagnosis using Neural Networks", *Processing and Neural Networks*, vol. 10, no. 5, pp. 13-16, 1997.
[15] Lauterbach, "A Neural Network Based Recognition of Complex Two-Dimensional Objects", *IEEE Transaction on Computers*, vol. 1, no.6, pp. 203-210, 1996.
[16] S. I. Kim, K. C. Choi and D. S. Lee, "Texture classification using run difference matrix", *Proceedings of Ultrasonics Symposium*, vol. 2, no. 10, pp. 1097-1100, 1991.

Section 5

International Widespread of Grid Technology

13

Applications Exploiting e-Infrastructures Across Europe and India Within the EU-IndiaGrid Project

Alberto Masoni[1] and Stefano Cozzini[2]
[1]*INFN Sezione di Cagliari, Cittadella Universitaria di Monserrato, Monserrato,*
[2]*CNR/IOM Democritos National Simulation Centre, Trieste, Italy*

1. Introduction

In the last few years e-Infrastructures across Europe and India faced remarkable developments. Both national and international connectivity improved considerably and Grid Computing also profited of significant developments.

As a consequence scientific applications were in the position of taking substantial benefits from this progress. The most relevant cases are represented by High Energy Physics (with the contribution to the program of Large Hadron Collider at CERN, Geneva) and Nano Science (exploiting NKN-TEIN3-GEANT interconnection for crystallography experiments with the remote access & control of experimental facility at the ESRF Synchrotron based in Grenoble, France directly from Mumbai, India). Other relevant application areas include Climate Change research, Biology, and several areas in Material Science.

Within this framework, in the last five years period two specific EU funded projects (the EU-IndiaGrid and EU-IndiaGrid2) played a bridging role supporting several applications that exploited these advanced e-Infrastructures for the benefit of Euro-India common research programs. EU-IndiaGrid2 - Sustainable e-infrastructures across Europe and India - is a project funded by European Commission under the Research Infrastructure Programme of the Information and Society Directorate General with the specific aim of promoting international interoperation between European and Indian e-Infrastructures. The project started in January 2010 and will close at the end of 2011. EU-IndiaGrid2 strongly bases and capitalizes on the achievement of its precursor the EU-IndiaGrid project (lasting from 2006 to 2009), whose contribution in bringing forward EU-Indian collaboration in e-Science and effectively mobilising actors on both sides, was widely recognised both in Europe and India. A crucial important part in the project activity was the support offered to selected applications which ranges from the training the user communities behind up to the porting of their scientific applications on the grid computing infrastructure.

This article aims to present and review the main e-Infrastructures development in India and their full exploitation by scientific applications with a focus on the role played by the EU-IndiaGrid and EU-IndiaGrid2 projects.

The paper is organized as follow: in the next section we will present and discuss the Indian scenario about the e-infrastructure while in section three we will discuss the role of the two EU funded projects for the Europe-India collaboration. In section four we present some significant technical achievements that made possible a full exploitation of scientific applications on the Euro-Indian infrastructure. In section five we will introduce the activities performed to promote applications and users communities within the e-infrastructure and will highlight some key examples of the scientific application ported and successfully exploited within the project and their interesting results. Some conclusions are then presented in the last section.

2. Indian e-infrastructures scenario

In this section we discuss both the network and the grid infrastructure scenario, which had, in the last few years a rapid and important evolution.

The most prominent landmarks in the connectivity area since 2006 have been:

- The establishment of the 45 Mbps ERNET - GÉANT link and routing of regional WLCG data to CERN and subsequently EU-IndiaGrid traffic to EGEE in 2006;
- The establishment of a dedicated 1 Gbps TIFR-CERN link for LHC research in 2008 and peering with GÉANT in 2009;
- The establishment of the National Knowledge Network (NKN) in April 2009;
- The connectivity of the TransEurasia Information Network (TEIN3): 2.5 Gbps Geant link to India in February 2010.
- The establishment of the Indian Grid Certification Authority recognised by APGRIDPMA, by CDAC.
- The GARUDA transition for Proof-of-Concept to Foundation Phase, in April 2008 and currently is in the third phase namely Grid Technology Services for Operational Garuda.
- The interoperation between GARUDA and worldwide Grid infrastructure after GARUDA transition to NKN.

In the following sections we will provide a brief description of NKN and TEIN3 initiatives together with an overview of the Indian National Grid Initiatives.

2.1 The NKN project

The National Knowledge Network (NKN, www.nkn.in) represents the main innovation in the Indian e-Infrastructure scenario. NKN is a high bandwidth and low latency network, with three layers. A powerful CORE with 7 Supercore locations with fully meshed multi-10Gbps connectivity and 26 Core locations having multi-10Gbps partially meshed connectivity with Supercore locations. A Distribution layer connected to the network core using multiple links at 2.5/10 Gbps. The Edges networks that connect institutions at 1 Gbps.

The creation of NKN was recommended by the Office of the Principal Scientific Adviser to Government of India and the National Knowledge Commission and obtained full approval with a budget of over 1 billion euro and a duration of 10 years by Government of India in March 2010. The National Informatics Centre (NIC) a premier Government Institution, is in charge of the implementation. NKN project is aimed at establishing a strong and robust internal Indian network capable of providing secure and reliable connectivity. NKN brings together all the main stakeholders from Higher Education, Science, Technology, Healthcare, Agriculture, Grid Computing, e-Governance. The project aims also at facilitating connection between different sectorial networks in the field of research, education, health, commerce and governance.

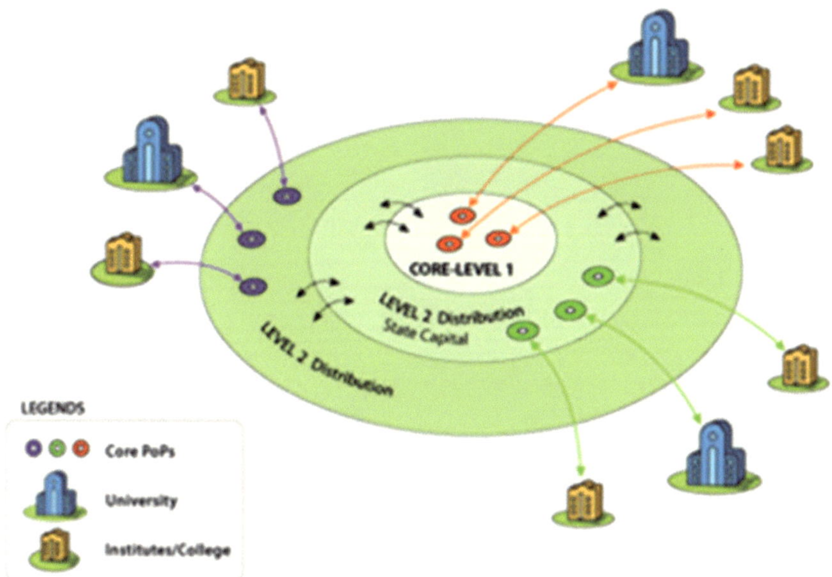

Fig. 1. NKN Layers

This approach responds to a vision where different activities in the research domain but also other areas as Healthcare, or e-Governance can move from a silos-like structure to a gradual share of the upper layers from the network to the computing (grid and HPC) and the data management. This e-Infrastructure can provide a core of services not affordable to an individual application jumping across geographical, administrative and academic boundaries (see figure2).

The NKN infrastructure is entirely fiber based and owned by Government of India. It relies on a high capacity highly scalable backbone and covers the entire country. NKN will connect more than 5000 sites across the country serving million of end-users and all major e-science projects. In the vision of Prof. Raghavan, Scientific Secretary to Principal Scientific Adviser to Government of India and Chief Architect and Chairman of Technical Advisory Committee of NKN, NKN represents for education a great integrator, making reachable and available the collective wisdom of institutions and laboratories with every Indian, irrespective of the geographical location, being able to benefit by accessing this vast

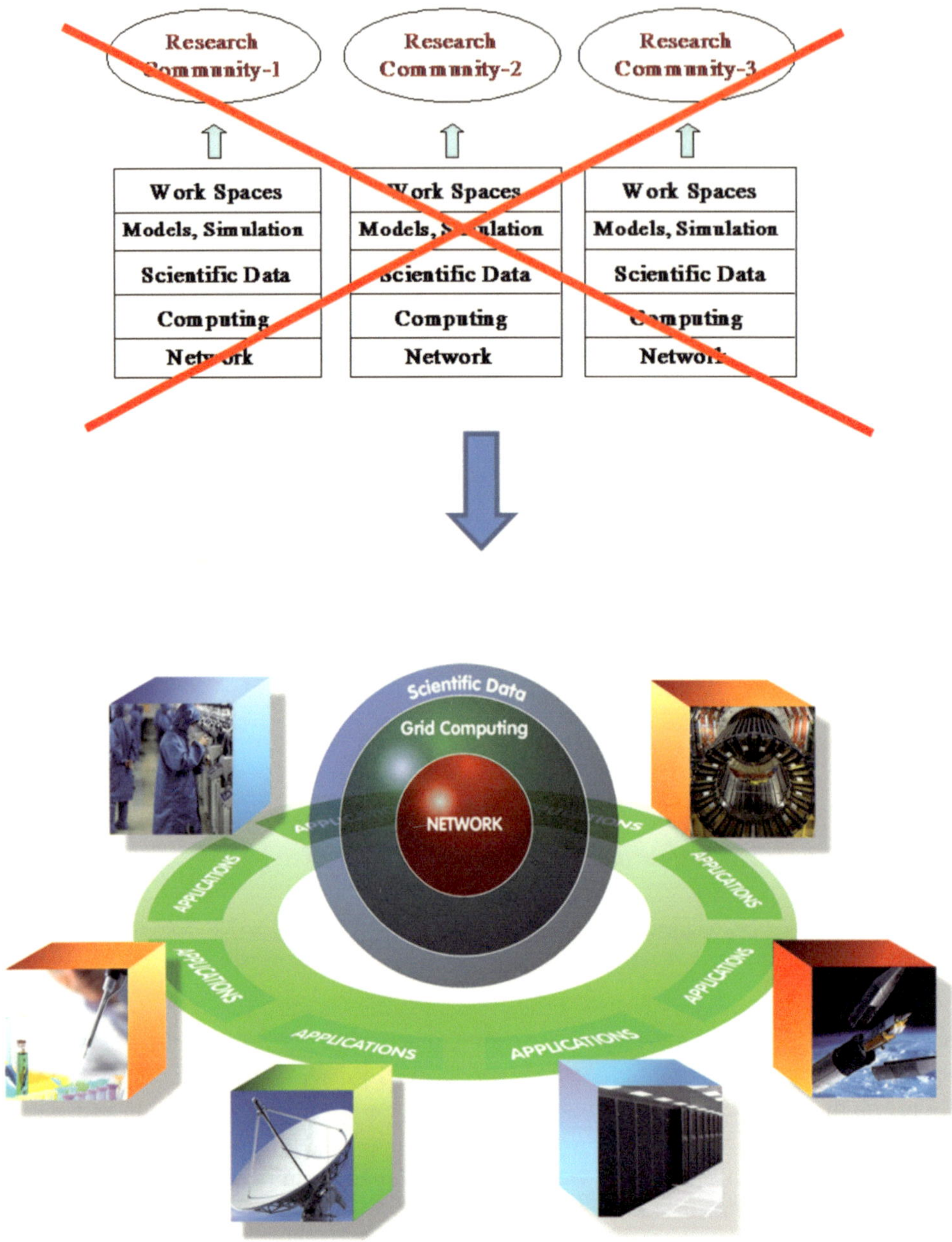

Fig. 2. From a silos-like to integrated core of shared advanced services.

intellectual resource. These features are also of paramount impact for research and for health related applications. In this case NKN provides is "Clear Visibility" of whatever medical records are generated at the remote end X Rays, 2D and 3D,MRIs, CT Scans, PETs and so on. Moreover thanks to the very high bandwidth and very low latency a patient requiring critical attention and an expert opinion can be remotely seen, examined, diagnosed, and treated.

NKN implementation strategy consists of two phases the initial phase and the final phase. Initial phase is already operational with a fully meshed core backbone spanning across the country with twenty-three points of presence (PoPs) and connecting 90 institutions. Efforts are underway to scale the number of institutions connected to 550 in the next future.

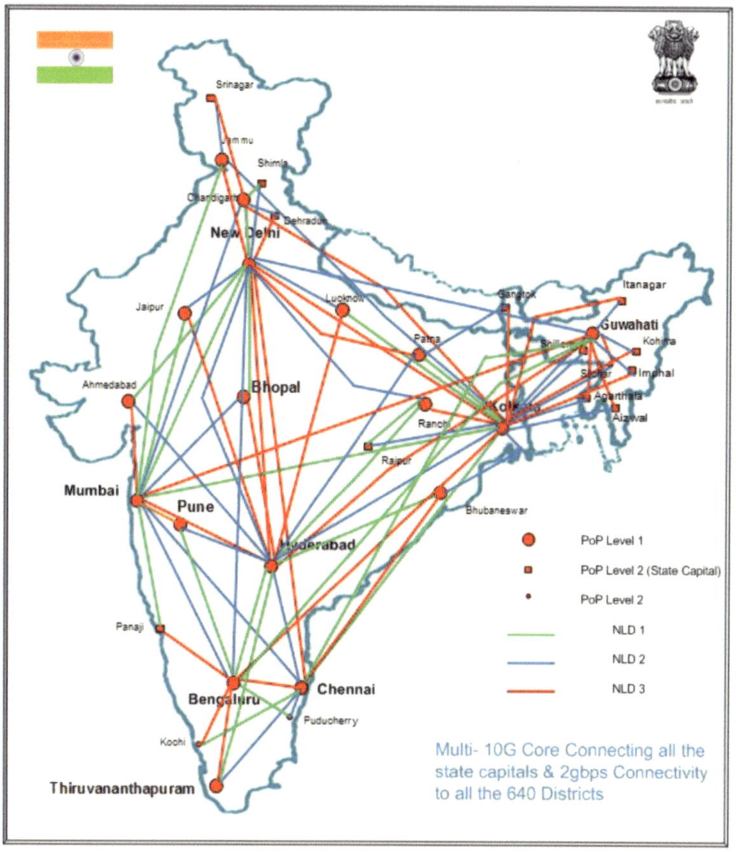

Fig. 3. NKN Phase 1

In the initial phase NKN is already providing services for virtual classrooms and grid computing applications such as High Energy Physics to Climate modelling and Health care as well as collaborative design of advanced complex engineering systems.

2.2 International connectivity

NKN is connected to the Pan-European Research network, GÉANT (www.geant.net), by means of a 2-5 Gbps link co-funded by Government of India and the European Commission within the framework of the TransEurasia Information Network project phase 3 (TEIN3, http://www.tein3.net). TEIN3 provides Internet network to the research and education communities in the Asia-Pacific area serving more than 8000 research and academic centre and 45 million users. TEIN3 includes 19 partners and rely on four hubs: Mumbai, Singapore, Hong Kong, Beijing (see Figure 4). For India TEIN3 provides a 2.5 Gbps link from Europe to Mumbai and also a 2.5 Gbps link from Mumbai to Singapore.

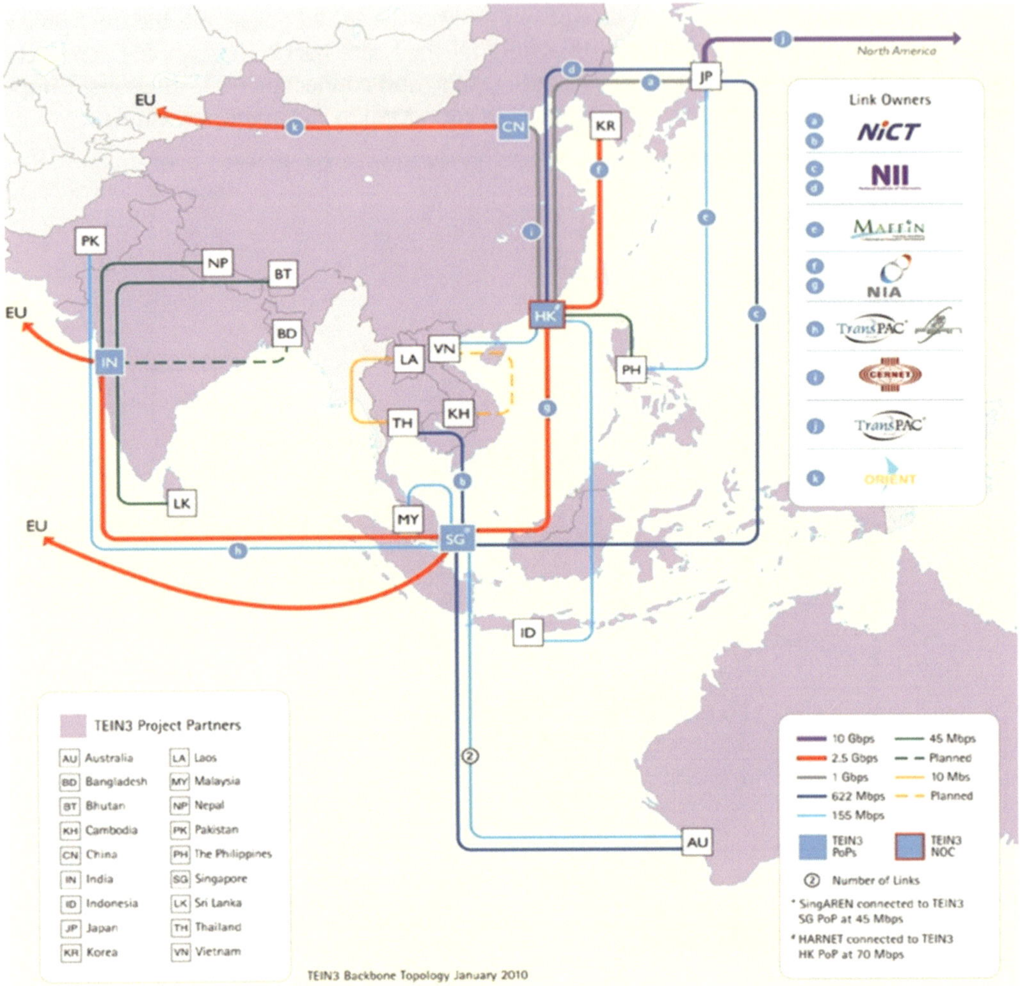

Fig. 4. TEIN3 Topology

In this vision, for research collaborations, Mumbai represents, at the same time, the Gate of India and the gateway to Asia-Pacific area.

In addition it is under way an agreement to connect the Open Science Grid in the USA in cooperation with the USA National Science Foundation and to connect to Japan a dedicated high speed link from Chennai. The NKN-TEIN3 connectivity is successfully exploited by several research applications as described in the sections below.

2.3 Grid infrastructures

Two main Grid Initiatives are present in India: the Regional Component of the WorldWide LHC Computing Grid (WLCG, http://lcg.web.cern.ch/LCG/) and the GARUDA National Grid Initiative (http://www.garudaindia.in/). Both are strongly connected with the EU-IndiaGrid2 project thanks to the presence, as project partners, of the leading actors of both initiatives.

Fig. 4. GARUDA Grid and WLCG Tier2 sites

2.3.1 The Worldwide LHC Computing Grid in India

WLCG represents the world largest grid infrastructure and with the start of data taking at the CERN Large Hadron Collider (LHC) WLCG entered the full production phase (Bonacorsi, 2011). The data from the LHC experiments will be distributed around the globe, according to a four-tiered model. India participates with two Tier2 centres supported by the Department of Atomic Energy (DAE). One at the Tata Institute for Fundamental Research (TIFR) Mumbai provides the services for the CMS experiment. The other one, dedicated to the ALICE experiment, is located in Kolkata and managed by the Saha Institute of Nuclear Physics in collaboration with the Variable Energy Cyclotron Centre (VECC).

These Tier2 centres provide access to CMS & ALICE users working from Tier III centres of Universities and national labs and LCG Data Grid services for analysis. TIFR is presently connected to CERN with the 2.5 Gb/s TEIN3 link via NKN. The ALICE TIER2 centre is also connected via NKN at 1 Gb/s. Thanks to a coordinated action of the main actors involved participating also to the EU-IndiaGrid2 project TIFR is successfully exploiting the TEIN3 connectivity for LHC data transfer since December 2010.

2.3.2 GARUDA: The national grid initiative of India

GARUDA is India's first national grid initiative bringing together academic, scientific and research communities for developing their data and compute intensive applications with guaranteed Quality of Service. The project is coordinated by Centre for Development of Advanced Computing (CDAC) under the funding of Department of Information Technology (DIT) of Government of India. GARUDA involves 36 Partner institutions with 45 research and academic centres. GARUDA ended its Proof of Concept phase in 2008 and concluded the Foundation Phase in August 2009.

Afterwards GARUDA has moved successfully to the Operational phase, thereby providing sustainable production grade computing infrastructure as a service to its partners. With this endeavour, the GARUDA grid is playing a key role in accelerating the research work by inter-connecting academicians, researchers, policy makers and the masses at large. Applications of national importance are being hosted on the vast infrastructure offered by the GARUDA grid, to solve grand challenge problems of national priority as Disaster Management (DMSAR) and Bio informatics. At present GARUDA network infrastructure is provided by NKN (see section 2.1), consolidating this way the integration between NKN and Indian grid infrastructures and related applications.

Within the grid infrastructure various resources such as High Performance Computing systems (HPC) and satellite based communication systems have been committed by different centres of C-DAC and GARUDA partners. GARUDA Grid is composed of various heterogeneous computing resources such as HPC clusters and SMP systems running on AIX, Linux and Solaris. At the moment GARUDA is offering several thousand of cores. The total computational power available today on Garuda is approximately 65 Teraflops.

GARUDA is well equipped with the provisioning of a customized middleware stack that can effectively harness this diverse range of resources being available on the grid. The middleware stack is enabled with CDAC's in-house developed, efficient reservation managers that ensure high availability & reliability of the resources to the applications running on the production grid infrastructure. Basic grid middleware services are provided by GlobusToolkit -4.0.8 on the top of which Gridway metascheduler has been enabled.

3. The role of EU-IndiaGrid & EU-IndiaGrid2 projects

As discussed in the sections above during the period of the EU-IndiaGrid project activity and right at the start of EU-IndiaGrid2 e-Infrastructures in India marked a considerable progress (Masoni, 2011). The leading responsibilities of EU-IndiaGrid Indian partners and the project bridging role between European and Indian e-Infrastructures gave to EU-IndiaGrid project the opportunity to be at the core of this development and to effectively contribute at improving cooperation between Europe and India in this domain.

In particular the activities related to the High Energy Physics applications were fully integrated in the framework of the Worldwide LHC Computing Grid Collaboration with particular concern with the ALICE and CMS experiments active in India.

Moreover a dedicated Virtual Organization (VO euindia) was made available by the project to the users from the beginning of 2006. Such a VO included several grid resources distributed across Europe and India and it was fundamental to allow users to deploy and then use the grid infrastructure for their research.

Grid resources available to the user communities via the dedicated VO comprises grid sites installed and configured mainly using gLite 3.2 middleware running on 64bit Linux Operating System. Available hardware is relatively recent and includes several multicore (4, 8,12,24 CPU-cores) Worker Nodes. A snapshot taken at end of December 2010 shows that VO members have at disposal , on a best effort basis, over about 7300 CPU-cores (1800 CPU-sockets) that represents a computing power of around 20 MSI00; on the storage side, the VO can use up to 44 TB of total space.

The EU-IndiaGrid2 project installed and currently maintains all the gLite central services needed to support the operational status of the user applications belonging to the EUIndia Virtual Organization.

As discussed in the next section on the top of this standard gLite infrastructure some advanced services have been installed and configured. We stress here the importance to have our own dedicated EUIndia services that allow the project to easily experiment and configure additional services on the request of users.

The increase of usage of the EU-IndiaGrid infrastructure, combined with scientific results obtained and presented at relevant international conferences or published on journals represent a clear measure of success of the user communities activity. The project Workshops and Conferences dedicated to the different applications were an important vehicle for the dissemination of results and for fostering the adoption of grid technology toward the scientific community and not only. In addition, supporting and addressing the problem of the interoperability at the application level further contributed to promote the use of advanced grid technology, and the cooperation between different projects and Institutes. Applications and user communities behind can thus be regarded as a key to sustainability, and they can help motivating the investment in e-Infrastructures.

EU-IndiaGrid2 which started on January 2010, leveraged on the EU-IndiaGrid project achievements and the strong cooperation links established with the foremost European and Indian e-Infrastructure initiatives and then paved the way for successful sustainable cooperation across European and Indian e-Infrastructures.

EU-IndiaGrid2 is strongly integrated in the Indian e-Infrastructure scenario. Its partners take leading roles in NKN, WLCG and GARUDA and a solid and fruitful cooperation has been established between these initiatives and the EU-IndiaGrid2 project.

EU-IndiaGrid2 provided specific support to ensure exploiting the progress in connectivity favouring Euro-India cooperation in e-Science. The project supports the interoperation and interoperability between the European and the Indian grid infrastructures as well as four main application areas in the domain of Biology, Climate Change, High Energy Physics and Material Science. The main landmarks during the time life of the projects includes:

- The interoperation between GARUDA and worldwide Grid infrastructure
- The exploitation of the TEIN3 link for LHC data transfer

- The exploitation of NKN-TEIN3-GÉANT connectivity for remote control and data collection at the Grenoble beam facility.
- The exploitation of grid services to study the Indian Monsoon
- The exploitation of grid services to develop advanced seismic hazard assessment in India

With the transition from ERNET to NKN for the network layer an interoperation problem occurred since all the nodes within the GARUDA grid became not visible to the external world. Thanks to the effort, coordinated by the EU-IndiaGrid2 project, ERNET, NIC and CDAC it was possible to solve this issue in the context of the EU-IndiaGrid2 Workshop in December in Delhi and since end 2010 all the GARUDA infrastructure is visible to worldwide grids. In addition the project supported the interoperability between the European Grid Initiative, EGI (www.eigi.eu) and the GARUDA grid infrastructure which is now possible using a metascheduler based on Gridway (Huedo 2005).

The TEIN3 link from Europe to Mumbai was commissioned in March 2010. However a number of issues related to the connectivity between the TEIN2 PoP and the WLCG Tier2 at TIFR needed to be solved. Again with the coordinated effort of NIC and EU-IndiaGrid2 partners it was possible since fall 2010 to exploit the TEIN3 links for LHC data transfers. Considering that the Academia Sinica Computing Centre acts as reference Tier1 for CMS Tier2 at TIFR both TEIN3 links (to Europe for CERN and to Singapore for Academia Sinica Tier1) are crucial for WLCG operation in India. In addition the commissioning of the 1 Gbps NKN connectivity from Kolkata to Mumbai makes the international connectivity available also for the ALICE experiment.

Finally the collaboration between Bhabha Atomic Research Centre (BARC) in Mumbai and Commissariat pour l' Energie Atomique (CEA) in Grenoble represents an excellent showcase for the usage of NKN-TEIN3-géant connectivity for remote control and data collection at the Grenoble beam facility. The BARC and CEA research groups collaborate in experiments dedicated to the study of crystallography of biological macromolecules. using protein crystallography beamlines. Two facilities have been set-up in India allowing to operate remotely the beamline FIP on ESRF, Grenoble. Good X-ray diffraction data has been collected on crystals of drug resistant HIV-1 protease enzyme. Both BARC and CEA are EU-IndiaGrid2 partners and this activity is fully supported by the EU-IndiaGrid2 project.

4. Tools and methodologies within EU-IndiaGrid projects

In this section we will briefly discuss some tools and some methodologies we successfully developed within the lifetime of the two EU-IndiaGrid projects in order to enable a full exploitation of the scientific applications we promoted. The motivations behind such development effort rely on the requirements of the user communities involved in the projects. User communities issued several requests. In particular users wanted:

i. Training additional tools and methods to learn how to use the Grid.
ii. Specific advanced service to better implement their computational scientific packages on the GRID.
iii. Tools to use easy and seamlessly all the grid infrastructures made available.

In the following subsection we will highlight three different actions, one for each category listed above.

4.1 Parallel support on GRID

Many scientific applications, like for instance climate modelling simulations, require a parallel computing approach and many tasks are also of the tightly coupled type. The question of how to run in parallel on the grid is therefore of great importance and we want to address here. Nowadays multicore architectures are widely available, even on the European GRID, but they are only suitable for small and medium size jobs. Distributed memory, multi-node clusters are still the only viable tool for serious scientific computing done generally through the MPI paradigm.

Our aim was thus to provide a simple, transparent and efficient mechanism to exploit MPI distributed memory parallelism over capable GRID CEs.

As of today, the gLite middleware does not yet provide proper MPI support. gLite is now integrating the MPI-start mechanism, a set of scripts, which should make it easy to detect and use site specific MPI-related configuration. In fact, it can select the proper MPI distribution, the proper batch scheduler and it can distribute the files if there is no shared disk space. The MPI-Start scripts will also handle user's pre/post execution actions. However from the point of view of users the JDL attributes that could characterize MPI enabled CEs in job descriptor files are misleading and they describe a wrong level of abstraction. The EGEE- MPI working group proposed (more than one year ago) three new attributes added to CPUnumber in order to request explicitly MPI-type distributed resources. These are

- WholeNodes: to ask for all the cores on a specified node
- SMPGranularity: to determine how many cores you would like to use on every single node
- HostNumber: to specify the total number of nodes you wish to run on

Even if it is still an open question, whether WholeNodes has priority over SMPGranularity and whether SMPGranularity has priority over CPUnumber, they could provide however a great improvement to submit parallel jobs on the gLite infrastructure. Unfortunately these attributes are still to be implemented on gLite middleware.

There are however some patches available to enable the WMS and the CREAM CE to recognize these new attribute. The EUIndia WMS and some computing elements CEs have been therefore patched and the patches are now available and distributed within our Virtual Organization. The new attributes allow the GRID users to submit transparently their MPI parallel jobs to the MPI capable resources and furthermore fine-tune their request matching it to the job requirements.

4.2 GRIDSEED training tool

The GRIDSEED tool (Gregori, 2011) , a set of virtual VM machines preconfigured with several grid services, is by far the most successful training tool developed within EuindiaGRID projects. GRIDSEED is not just a software package, but a complete training tool containing a software package and all the information to use it as training platforms, targeting different user community and different kind of aspects (users vs. sys administrator training).

The development of this tool, coordinated by CNR/IOM laboratory for e-science (eLab) continued after the closing of the first project and was quite active also during the EUIndiaGRID2 project. This tool was used in several ICTP training events and in the entire official training events of the projects. Gridseed is now an open laboratory where interoperability solutions and ideas are tested and experimented jointly by European and Indian partners (Amarnath, 2010). Version 1.6.2 was released in December 2010. This latest version includes not only gLite services but also Globus/GARUDA Services allowing setup a portable and interoperable environment between the two Grid infrastructures of the project. Components of GRIDSEED were downloaded more than 2000 times so far.

GRIDSEED provides a simple tool to setup a portable and interoperable Grid infrastructure based on virtual machines. The GRIDSEED tool was originally developed to easily deploy a training gLite Grid infrastructure almost everywhere in the world with a set of machines (simple PC's) locally connected among them as the only requirement. It uses standard virtualization tools (VirtualBox and/or VMmare) easily and widely available. Recently the virtual environment is enriched with other different middleware (Arc and Globus Toolkit) to make it the first virtual training laboratory for interoperability and interoperation among different middleware. GRIDSEED is therefore a complete training environment formed by a virtual infrastructure complemented by some demo applications and training materials ready to be used both in standard training events and advanced interoperation demo/events session.

4.3 General services toward interoperability: Milu software and Gridway installation

GARUDA and gLite users are using different method to access and use resources belonging to the two different infrastructure. To avoid this burden and to make the usage of both infrastructures as simple as possible the MILU tool, originally conceived as a portable gLite User Interface, was further developed and enhanced in collaboration with eLab .

Miramare Interoperable Lite User interface (MILU) is now a software tool which allows seamless usage of different grid infrastructures from the same Linux workstation.

MILU is a repackaging of the user-interface software provided by gLite, ARC and the Globus Toolkit (version 4), providing access to the functionality of all three middlewares concurrently. Extensive testing and an ingenious use of UNIX tricks allow MILU binaries to run on a large variety of Linux distributions (CentOS, Debian, Ubuntu, etc.), including some that are not supported by the original upstream middleware packages. MILU is packaged as a single archive that users can extract and install into their home directories by running a single shell script; no super-user privileges or technicalities are needed. MILU is distributed with a configuration ready for use for several VOs; new configurations can be added by the users (and we encourage submission upstream, so that more people can benefit from pre-packaged configuration).

MILU is already in use by the EU-IndiaGrid and the e-NMR VOs, plus other groups of local grid users.

We think that MILU could be interesting to community developers, in addition to non-technical users, who have been historically the target audience of MILU. Indeed, MILU can be the ideal tool for quickly enabling Grid client access on a Linux machine, for the purpose of rapid prototyping a new tool, or for deploying test/debug instances of running services.

We believe that MILU, possibly extended in the future to include the EMI "unified client" to be, can have an impact for the users and developers belonging to emerging communities, as a lower-level tool upon which more sophisticated Grid access mechanisms can be built. There is a clear need for a tool like MILU:

- To provide a smooth transition between different middleware systems, e.g., when the old software still needs to be around as the new one is too immature to completely replace it, or when two infrastructures with different access methods have to be bridged.
- To provide a preconfigured environment that can satisfy the needs of the average scientific user, who does not care about the technical details and only needs a tool that "just works".

Milu 1.1 is now distributed with Gridway middleware bundled together and properly configured to access both GARUDA and gLite infrastructure. User communities have therefore at disposal a simple and efficient interoperability tool to use both infrastructures at the same time. Milu was downloaded more that 2500 times so far.
(see http://eforge.escience-lab.org/gf/project/milu/)

5. Applications exploiting e-infrastructures

In the course of the last five years a specific effort was dedicated to the support of several user communities including Biology, High Energy Physics, Material Science, and Earth & Atmospheric Sciences.

For each user community specific applications were deployed on the grid infrastructure and each application was supported by a collaboration of European and Indian partners. Scientific and technical results were presented at relevant international conferences or published on journals and represent a clear measure of success of the user communities' activity.

A short guideline on how to enable applications on Grid infrastructure has been also drawn up by the EU-IndiaGrid projects based on the experience collected within various user communities. The document had the goal to offer a first support to users interested in using the EU-IndiaGrid infrastructure to its best. In such a document we propose that a successful procedure for Grid-enabling application should be performed in the following five major steps:

- Initial Step: Awareness of Grid computing opportunities/analysis of the computational requirements
- Step 1: Technical deployment on the infrastructure
- Step 2: Benchmarking procedures and assessment of the efficiency
- Step 3: Production runs and final evaluation
- Final Step: Dissemination of the results among peers.

At the end of each intermediate step an evaluation procedure takes place to understand if the action should move to the next step, should be stopped with the execution of the final step, or should go back and repeat the step previously done. It is worth to note that such procedure was elaborated keeping in mind the point of view of the users: this is why we insist that the procedure should have in any case (even if it is stopped after the initial step) a final dissemination phase. The results (even negative) can be of great importance for other users as initial input when starting the Grid-enabling procedure. Several successful porting stories followed this approach as reported in the EU-IndiaGrid deliverables dedicated to applications and in other publication as well, see e.g. a few papers in (Cozzini, 2009).

In the following subsection we report two successful and outstanding examples of scientific application within the project, which exploited at best the euro-Indian infrastructure in a joint collaboration among Indian and European partners.

5.1 Climate change simulations

Climate research activities were mainly conducted in a joint and strict collaboration among ICTP EU-IndiaGrid team and the Computational Atmospheric Science (CAS) Department at IIT Delhi lead by Professor Dash.

Climate modelling is among the most computational power and data intensive fields, it is one of the key users of High Performance Computing Infrastructure. Grid infrastructure could be suited well to perform climates experiments since it is the best alternative for HPC as it facilitates computing power and storage space required. Moreover, it allows running a full state-of-art model and store regular output information unlike the volunteer hosts. Grid usage for climate simulation is becoming more important but still has some big limitations:

- Limited MPI/parallel support
- Complexity and heterogeneity of middleware
- Data management issues: moving terabytes of data is not easy

Within EuindiaGrid2 project we address and analyse the issues above presenting novel methodology to overcome some of them (data management through opendap protocols, MPI support on multicore platforms using "relocatable package" mechanism, interoperability by means of Gridway to solve complexity and heterogeneity of middleware). Scientific work was then done in order to study Indian Moonson.

Monsoon is one of the most important phenomenon's that influences various aspects of India to a great extent. India has an agro-based economy and this fact makes it crucial and important that various facets of monsoon and the associated rains be predicted as accurately as possible. It is a challenging task to all scientists for developing and tuning models for obtaining beneficial forecasts. The Indian monsoon extends over a distance of nearly 3000 km, directed to the southwest from the Himalayas [13]. Monsoon lasts from June to September. The season is dominated by the humid southwest summer monsoon, which slowly sweeps across the country beginning in late May or early June. Monsoon rains begin to recede from North India at the beginning of October. South India typically receives more rainfall. Monsoon features are difficult to be simulated by Global Climate Model (GCM) primarily because of large temporal and spatial variations.

For this reason, the ICTP regional climate model named RegCM in its last version (4.1.1) was used to study the Indian Monsoon.

Specifically a careful tuning the RegCM4.1.1 package was performed to get the correct parameterization for Indian summer monsoon simulations.

In the following subsection we will discuss the porting strategy of the package toward the Euro -Indian infrastructures and the innovative solution we developed.

5.1.1 RegCM 4.1.1 exploitation on the GRID

RegCM4 is the fourth generation of the regional climate models originally developed at the National Centre for Atmospheric Research (NCAR) and currently being developed at ICTP, Trieste, Italy. It was released in June 2010 as a prototype version RegCM4.0 and as a complete version RegCM4.1 in May 2011 (Giorgi 2011). A bug fixing release RegCM4.1.1 was then released in June 2011.

The RegCM4.1 package now uses dynamic memory allocation in all its components. The whole output subsystem is now able to produce NetCDF format files, which is in better compliance with the standard Climate and Forecast Conventions.

The RegCM modelling system has four components namely Terrain,sst,ICBC, RegCM and some postprocessing utilities. Terrain sst and ICBC are the three components of RegCM pre-processor:

Th first step will define the domain of the simulation: the executable terrain horizontally interpolates the landuse and elevation data from a latitude-longitude grid to the cartesian grid of the chosen domain.

Sst executable then creates the Sea Surface Temperature file. Finally the ICBC program interpolates Sea Surface Temperature (SST) and global re-analysis data to the model grid. These files are used for the initial and boundary conditions during the simulation.

The pre-processing phase will therefore need to read global re-analysis data (size of the order of several dozen GB for each year of simulation) and will produce a large size of input data as well. RegCM itself produces than a large amount of output data.

As an example, a monthly run on domain of 160x192 points will produce around 10 GBytes of data, which means around 10 TBytes of data are produced for a climate simulation lasting a century. This data needs to be locally available, as a remote file system would slow the simulation down dramatically.

The greatest challenge in running RegCM on the GRID is therefore handling the data properly.

5.1.1.1 RegCM on gLite

The present day status of the RegCM software and the GRID gLite infrastructure makes it not really suitable for long production runs, which require a number of CPUs in the 64-256 range, but a well implemented MPI handling mechanism, such as MPI-Start, makes the running of small to medium size RegCM simulations feasible. The data transfer from and to the GRID Storage Elements is still a matter of concern and its impact on performance should be investigated thoroughly in the future.

The GRID could be therefore used with proficiency for physical and technical testing of the code by developers and users, as well as for "parametric" simulations, that is. running many shorter/smaller simulation with different parameterisation at the same time.

As said the RegCM preprocessing part requires a big data ensemble (several TBytes) to be locally available every time it is run. This is quite impossible to accomplish on the GRID so the preprocessing needs to be always performed locally before submitting the job. A typical run will be started by uploading the input data previously stored on a SE. This can be accomplished by a pre-run hook script. Afterwards the actual execution will be handled by MPI-Start in a transparent way on the appropriate resources requested. Once the execution is over the data produced by the simulation will be transferred on a SE and the job will terminate. This is accomplished by a post-run hook script. In this way a RegCM simulation can be run on GRID resources.

To run RegCM properly on a MPI-Start enabled resource will actually require a compilation to be performed in advanced. This means that the RegCM software should be made available on the Grid resources by means of the Vo software managers and the grid site will then publish the availability of such a software.

Not many CEs support MPI-Start and the new MPI-related attributes in the JDL script files so we provide the possibility to run RegCM (or any other MPI parallel application actually) through a "relocatable package" approach.

With this approach all the software needed, starting from an essential OpenMPI distribution, is moved to the CEs by the job. All the libraries needed by the program have to be precompiled elsewhere and packaged for easy deployability on any architecture the job will land on. The main advantage of this solution is that it will run on almost every machine available on the GRID and the user will not even need to know what the GRID will have assigned to him. The code itself will need to be compiled with the same "relocatable" libraries and shipped to the CE by the job.

This alternative approach allows a user to run a small RegCM simulation on any kind of resource available to him, even if not a MPI-Start enabled one, although it is actually aimed at SMP resources, which are quite widely available nowadays. The main drawback of this solution is that a precompiled MPI distribution will not take advantage of any high speed network available and will not be generally able to use more than one computing node. The "relocatable" solution will though be able to use an available SMP resource, making it a reasonably good solution to run small sized RegCM simulations on any GRID resource available.

RegCM4.1.1 manages all the I/O operation through netcdf data format, provided by the netcdf library. This allows the use of the OPeNDAP Data Access Protocol (DAP), which is a protocol for requesting and transporting data across the web. This means that all the RegCM input/output operations can be done remotely without no need to upload/download data through grid data tools. Any data server providing opendap protocol (for instance THREDDS Server) can therefore be used to provide global dataset for creating DOMAIN and ICBC without the need to download the global dataset, but just the required subset in space and time. This means that even pre-processing phase can be easily done on any e-infrastructure which provides outbound connectivity. The netCDF library is to be compiled with OpenDAP support to be able to use this approach The schema is therefore to just submit the correct input file where an an URL can be used as a path in the inpter and inpglob variables in the regcm.in file instead of the usual data path on the server itself. A command line web downloader such as curl is also to be installed on the system as pre-requisite, along with its development libraries to be used, to enable OpenDAP remote data access protocol capabilities of netCDF library.

We performed several experiments in order to estimate how feasible is to perform all the steps require to perform RegCM climate simulation on the grid hiding all the data management complexity within the netcdf library and the openDAP protocol. A detailed report is in preparation.

5.1.1.2 RegCM across Garuda and gLite by means of GridWay

On GARUDA grid infrastructure RegCM can be easily compiled by the user itself connecting to the MPI clusters she plans to use and once the executable is provided on the cluster as local software simulation can be submitted by means of Gridway metascheduler. There was however at the moment still a big concern about data storage and movement because data management tools and services on GARUDA still have to provided. At the moment users can only move simulation data back and forth from the grid resources to the local resources by means of globus-url-copy command, a solution far to be acceptable for large simulations which produce terabyte of data.

For this reason an approach based on netcdf opendap protocols allows us to run easily the model without any concerns about the status the data management.

As said the actual submission will then be done using the Gridway scheduler able to reach all the MPI resources made available on the Garuda GRID. Being now Gridway perfectly able to manage both gLite and globus resources it is clear that RegCM simulations can be easily and transparently submitted on both Indian and European GRID resources. A unique job description file can be used and modifying just the name of the hostname where you want to run.

This working environment is presently made available by MILU, the interoperable user interface and the GRIDWAY package preconfigured as discussed in the above sections.

5.1.2 Overall achievements

The regional climate model version 4.1.1 was ported and tested on both Indian and European infrastructure and the feasibility and performance of executing the code on both HPC and grid infrastructure has been tested. It has been observed that the performance of the code on different platforms is comparable considering the CPU cores. The performance has been measured in terms of execution speed and the time taken to complete one execution.

Data management issues has been solved by means of the openDAP approach that proved to be efficient and feasible. This marks a considerable result that allow to exploit in a similar manner all the available computational resources without the need to move back and forth terabyte of data.

Finally Different simulations has been performed on the South Asia CORDEX domain to find out the best suited configuration of parameters and tune the model to be able to get the best possible results for the Indian sub-continent. The tuning is being done by performing various experiments using different set of parameters each simulation, for instance, using different convective precipitation schemes on land and ocean, modifying the values of the parameters in the regcm.in file and changing the landuse pattern. Scientific results of Indian Summer Monsoon using RegCM4.1 compared with those of Global Climate models such as GPCP and CRU are under study and will published soon.

5.2 Advanced seismic hazard assessment in India

Another remarkable examples of fruitful collaborations established within EU-IndiaGrid is the activity performed on the EU-IndiaGrid computing infrastructure by ICTP/SANDs group and their Indian partners (Institute of Seismological Research (ISR), in Gujarat and CSIR Centre for Mathematical Modelling and Computer Simulation (C-MMACS) in Bangalore) in the area of advanced seismic hazard assessment in the Indian region of Gujarat.

Seismic risk mitigation is a worldwide concern and the development of effective mitigation strategies requires sound seismic hazard assessment. The purpose of seismic hazard analysis is to provide a scientifically consistent estimate of seismic ground shaking for engineering design and other considerations. The performances of the classical probabilistic approach to seismic hazard assessment (PSHA), currently in use in several countries worldwide, turned out fatally inadequate when considering the earthquakes occurred worldwide during the last decade, including the recent destructive earthquakes in Haiti (2010), Chile (2010) and Japan (2011).

Therefore the need for an appropriate estimate of the seismic hazard, aimed not only at the seismic classification of the national territory, but also capable of properly accounting for the local amplifications of ground shaking (with respect to bedrock), as well as for the fault properties (e.g. directivity) and the near-fault effects, is a pressing concern for seismic engineers.

Current computational resources and physical knowledge of the seismic waves generation and propagation processes, along with the improving quantity and quality of geophysical data (spanning from seismological to satellite observations), allow nowadays for viable numerical and analytical alternatives to the use of probabilistic approaches. A set of scenarios of expected ground shaking due to a wide set of potential earthquakes can be defined by means of full waveforms modelling, based on the possibility to efficiently compute synthetic seismograms in complex laterally heterogeneous anelastic media. In this way a set of scenarios of ground motion can be defined, either at national and local scale, the latter considering the 2D and 3D heterogeneities of the medium travelled by the seismic waves.

The considered scenario-based approach to seismic hazard assessment, namely the NDSHA approach (neo-deterministic seismic hazard assessment), builds on rigorous theoretical basis and exploits the currently available computational resources that permit to compute realistic synthetic seismograms. The integrated NDSHA approach intends to provide a fully formalized operational tool for effective seismic hazard assessment, readily applicable to compute complete time series of expected ground motion (i.e. the synthetic seismograms) for seismic engineering analysis and other mitigation actions.

e-Infrastructures represent a critical mean to provide access to important computing resources and specialized software to worldwide seismological community. In fact, e-science removes some of the infrastructural barriers that prevent collaborative work at the international level. Accordingly, the proposed scientific and computational tools and networking will permit a widespread application of the advanced methodologies for seismic hazard assessment, particularly useful for urban planning and risk mitigation actions in developing countries, and, in turn, will allow for a faster development and verification of the models.

The use of the mentioned seismological methodologies can be optimized by the use of modern computational infrastructures, based on GRID computing paradigms. Advanced computational facilities, in fact, may enable scientists to compute a wide set of synthetic seismograms, dealing efficiently with variety and complexity of the potential earthquake sources, and the implementation of parametric studies to characterize the related uncertainties.

The application of the NDSHA approach to the territory of India already started in the framework of long-term bilateral cooperation projects Italy-India, involving ICTP/Sand group and CSIR C-MMACS (Bangalore). In that framework, a neo-deterministic hazard map have been produced for India, and specific studies have been performed to estimate the ground motion amplifications along selected profiles in the cities of Delhi and Kolkata. The collaboration has been recently extended to the ISR, Institute of Seismological Research (Ghandinagar, Gujarat).

5.2.1 Porting and optimization of codes

Preliminary studies have been devoted to expose seismologists and seismic engineers to modern e-infrastructures (which includes both HPC and Grid environments) so that the potential provided by this infrastructure for seismic hazard assessment research can be assessed and exploited. These activities aim to enable the computational seismology user community to the use of modern e-infrastructure and acquire the core innovations emerging in this framework, for example the development of an European and worldwide e-infrastructure for advanced applications in seismic hazard assessment driven by European Union projects such as EU-IndiaGRID2. The major goals of this new collaboration are to:

- facilitate the development and application of a scientifically consistent approach to seismic hazard assessment;
- disseminate, in scientific and in engineering practice, advanced reliable tools for seismic hazard estimates;
- exploit, as much as possible, the advantages provided by computational resources and e-Infrastructures.

Activities carried out so far have been dedicated to a general introduction to the e-Infrastructures for Grid and HPC and to the preliminary assessment of their use in seismological research, with special emphasis on methods for advanced definition of ground shaking scenarios based on physical modelling of seismic waves generation and propagation processes. Researchers gained some practice on the use of the e-infrastructure for neo-deterministic seismic hazard assessment at different scales and level of detail, working actively on Italian data and testing the specialized seismological software running on an e-Infrastructure environment, leveraging on the work performed within the EU-IndiaGrid projects.

The use of the EU-India Grid infrastructure allows conducting massive parametric tests, to explore the influence not only of deterministic source parameters and structural models but also of random properties of the same source model, to enable realistic estimate of seismic hazard and their uncertainty. The random properties of the source are especially important in the simulation of the high frequency part of the seismic ground motion.

We have ported and tested seismological codes for national scale on the Grid infrastructure Flowchart of this code is illustrated in figure 5. The first step of the work, performed at a EU-IndiaGrid side-training event was the optimization of whole package by the identification of the critical programs and of the hot spots within programs. The critical point in the algorithm was the computation of synthetic seismograms. The optimization was performed in two ways: first by removing of repeated formatted disk I/O, second by sorting of seismograms by source depth, to avoid the repeated computation of quantities that are depth-dependent. Figure 6 show the remarkable improvement obtained in such work.

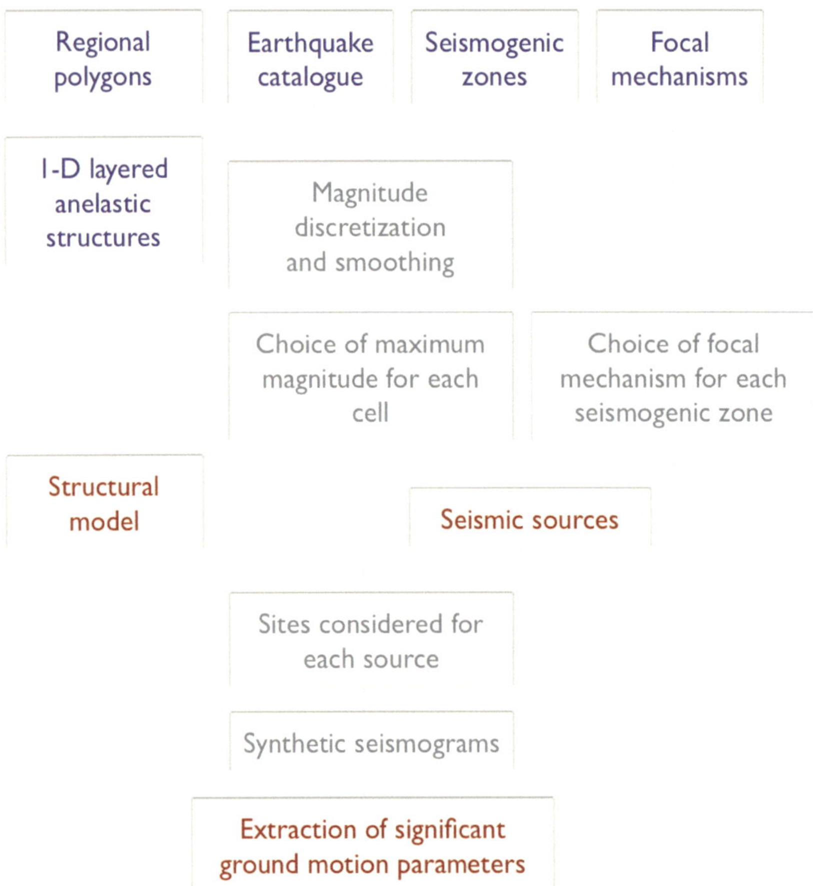

Fig. 5. Flow chart of national scale hazard package

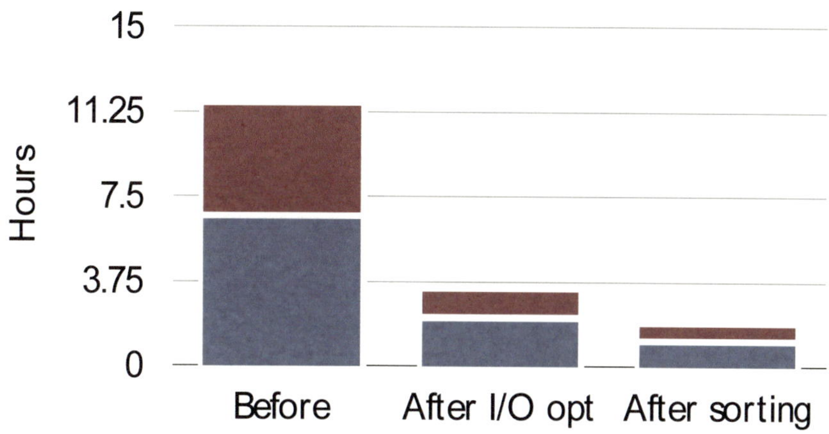

Fig. 6. Speedup of seismograms computation obtained on our local machine

The second step was porting the optimized hazard package on EU-IndiaGrid infrastructure. Two different types of parametric tests were developed: on the deterministic source parameters and on the random properties of the source model. The first experiment is performed by perturbing the properties of the seismic sources selected by the algorithm before the computation of synthetic seismograms. In the second test different sets of curves of source spectrum generated by a MonteCarlo simulation of the source model are used for scaling the seismograms. In both cases there are many independent runs to be executed, so a script for generation of the input and other scripts for checking the status of jobs, retrieving the results and relaunching aborted jobs were developed.

5.2.2 Preliminary results

Two preliminary tests over deterministic source parameter for a restricted area ("persut") and for whole Italy ("persut Italy"), and two different tests over random properties ("seed1Hz" and "seed10Hz") for the whole Italian territory, with different frequency content and different maximum distance for the computation of seismograms, were conducted. So the performance of the package over the grid in terms of computational time and number of successful jobs were tested, and submission of job and retrieval of its output were refined. The number of seismograms that must be computed determines the duration and the storage requirement of the run. This parameter seems critical for the success of the job. The test runs on the random component of the source gave an indication on the effective number of jobs that must be computed to have a good estimate of the distribution of the ground shaking peaks at each receiver.

The first runs have provided a preliminary evaluation of the uncertainty of the hazard maps due to the random representation of the source and to the uncertainty on source parameter. Figure 3 shows an example of results of the test on the random component of the source model. The variability on the different random realizations of the source model (right) is shown in terms of ratio between standard deviation and average at each receiver.

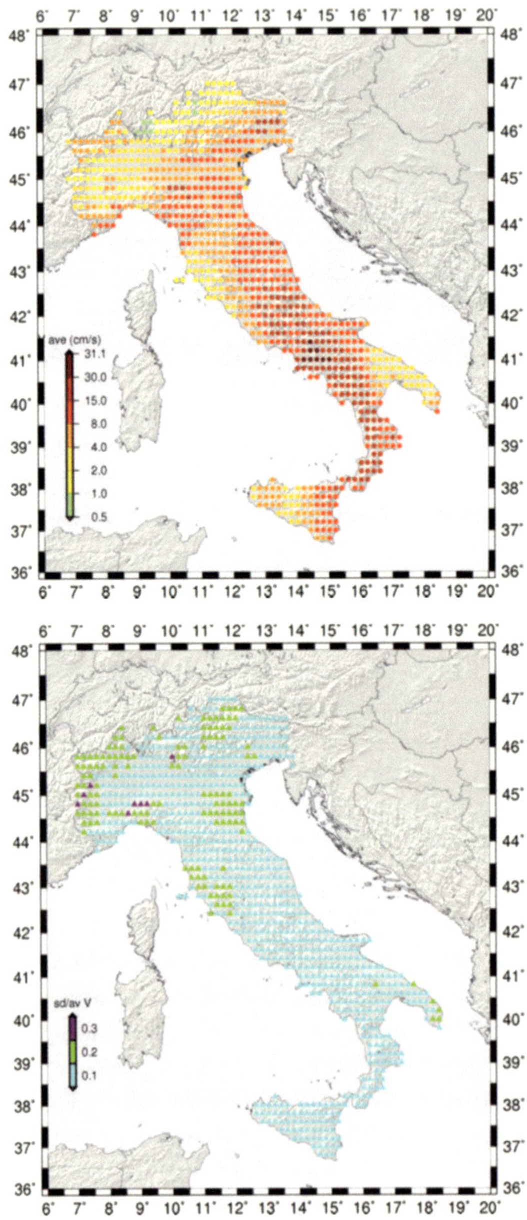

Fig. 7. Maps of average of PGV (peak ground velocity) on different random realizations of source model (left) and variability of the PGV in terms of ratio between standard deviation and average of the maximum peaks at each receiver.

	seed1Hz	persut Italy	seed10Hz	persut
type of submission	direct to CE	WMS	WMS	WMS
total n. of job	216	526	600	315
% of successful job	26	65	80	100
total time of computation of successful job	948 h	1200 h	791 h	14 h
average time of computation for one job	17 h	3.5 h	1.6 h	161 s

Table 1. Performance of the four test runs. From left to right number of seismograms for each run decreases

5.2.3 Future perspective

The NDSHA methodology has been successfully applied to strategic buildings, lifelines and cultural heritage sites, and for the purpose of seismic micro zoning in several urban areas worldwide. Several international projects have been carried out and are still in progress based on the NDSHA methodology, including: the "MAR VASTO" project, with the participation of Italian (ENEA, Universities of Ferrara and Padua, ICTP) and Chilean (University Federico Santa Maria in Valparaiso, University of Chile in Santiago) partners; the UNESCO/IUGS/IGCP projects "Realistic Modelling of Seismic Input for Megacities and Large Urban Areas", "Seismic Hazard and Risk Assessment in North Africa" and "Seismic microzoning of Latin America cities"; the multilateral-oriented network project "Unified seismic hazard mapping for the territory of Romania, Bulgaria, Serbia and Republic of Macedonia", supported by the CEI (Central European Initiative). The very positive outcomes from seismological collaborative research call for an improvement of such interactions; this is attained by integration and formalization of the existing scientific and computing networks. The e-Infrastructures provide an innovative and unique approach to address this problem. They demonstrated to be an efficient way to share and access resources of different types, which can effectively enhance the capability to define realistic scenarios of seismic ground motion, i.e. to compute the reliable seismic input necessary for seismic risk mitigation. Such facilities, in fact, may enable scientists to compute a wide set of synthetic seismograms, dealing efficiently with variety and complexity of the potential earthquake sources, and the implementation of parametric studies to characterize the related uncertainties.

A Cooperation Project, aimed at the definition of seismic and tsunami hazard scenarios by means of indo-european e-infrastructures in the Gujarat region (India), has been recently funded by the Friuli Venezia Giulia Region. This two-years project, starting in November 2011, involves three Italian partners (DiGeo, University of Trieste; ICTP SAND Group; CNR/IOM uos Democritos) and two Indian partners (ISR, Gujarat; CSIR C-MMACS, Bangalore). The project aims to set up a system for the seismic characterization, integrated with the e-infrastructures distributed amongst India and Europe, to allow for the optimization of the computation of the ground shaking and tsunami scenarios. This goal will be attained thanks to the strict connection with the European project EU-IndiaGrid2, which provides the necessary infrastructure. Thus, the project will permit developing an integrated system, with high scientific and technological content, for the definition of scenarios of ground shaking, providing in the same time to the local community (local authorities and engineers) advanced information for seismic and tsunami risk mitigation in the study region. Advanced services for the use of the computational resources will be developed, integrating the seismological computer codes inside the grid infrastructure of the EU-IndiaGrid Project. Synthetic seismograms, and the related ground shaking maps and microzonation analyses (that define the seismic input) will be generated using the above-mentioned advanced services.

6. Conclusions

e-Infrastructure progress in the last years in India impacted considerably in the evolution of grid computing with a significant benefit for scientific applications. Internal and international connectivity scaled up by two orders of magnitude, the National Grid Initiative moved from proof-of-concept to operational phase and essential services as a national grid certification authority, interoperability tools, MPI support, were established. This created the essential conditions for an effective use of these services by applications and the development of international cooperation in several strategic scientific areas.

Europe has a long-term, coordinated and shared e-Infrastructures R&D vision, mission, strategy, roadmap and funding, driven by the European Commission's Framework Programmes.

As clearly stated in the latest e-Infrastructures Roadmap released by the e-Infrastructures Reflection Group (e-IRG,2010), the fundamental contribution of research e-Infrastructure to European competitiveness is almost universally acknowledged. Sustainable and integrated networking, grid, data and high performance and commodity computing services are now essential tools for 40 million users in research and academia across Europe. The same document also remarks: Increasingly, new and diverse user communities are relying on e-Infrastructure services; as such, the common e-Infrastructure must cater to new and updated requirements. This junction between leading-edge research and the e-Infrastructure that supports it is an area where considerable socio-economic benefits can be realised.

This vision is also present in the Government of India policy driven by the Office of the Principal Scientific Adviser to Government of India. Thanks to this action a major e-Infrastructure programme, based on the Indian National Knowledge Network Project (NKN) has been launched and provides the high-speed network backbone to the Indian grid infrastructures as GARUDA NGI and the regional component of the LHC Computing Grid.

These developments are expected to impact in a substantial way on research applications in strategic and socially relevant domains as eHealth, climate change, study of of seismic hazard. For eHealth Europe and India are moving the first steps for the cooperation of e-Infrastructure-based neuroscience projects.

Climate simulation exploitation on Euro-Indian infrastructures is in perspective the driving application to integrate a mixed HPC/HTC paradigm across India and Europe. The variety and the complexity of the simulations that could be performed by means of regional climate can provide a dataset of unprecedented quality to assess the potential of global warming effects on the South Asia region and associated uncertainties, in particular as they relate to simulation aspects relevant to water, food and health security. Such an ambitious task clearly requires in the near future a seamless approach to both HPC and HTC infrastructures. Our experience and work described can be regarded as the starting point for such integration where the key role will be played by data management.

A similar line of reasoning could also be applied to the seismic hazard applications: in this moment EU-IndiaGrid computing infrastructure enables more detailed and complex computational investigations otherwise not possible. In perspective however the complexity of the simulation can easily grow when a 2D and 3D approaches will be used At this point, once again HPC resources will be needed and the seamless usage of them within the same Grid infrastructure will be necessary. Seismic hazard has some interesting perspective also for a future cloud computing exploitation with possible links to industry exploitation as well. The idea is to setup an advanced service where seismic hazard maps could be easily and seamlessly provided on demand could be of great appeal for industry players.

We remark as final note that the EU-IndiaGrid and EU-IndiaGrid2 projects played a crucial role in promoting fruitful international collaboration in grid computing involving Europe, India and Asia-Pacific countries. It is expected that driving key applications (like Climate simulations) established in the course of the project will enhance further such cooperation and extend it to HPC infrastructure as well.

7. Acknowledgments

The authors would like to acknowledge the valuable contribution of all members of EU-IndiaGrid2 Consortium and the support of the EU-IndiaGrid2 Project, Grant Agreement RI-246698

8. References

Aamodt K. et al. ALICE Collaboration (2008). *The ALICE experiment at the CERN LHC,* JINST, 3, S08 002.

CMS Collaboration. (2010). *Missing transverse energy performance of the CMS detector,* JINST, 6, P09001

Bonacorsi, D. (2011). Computing at LHC experiments in the first year of data taking at 7 TeV, *Proceedings of the International Symposium on Grids & Clouds (ISGC 2011),* Taipei Taiwan, March 2011, http://pos.sissa.it/cgi-bin/reader/conf.cgi?confid=133

e-IRG the e-Infrastructures Reflection Group (2011). e-IRG Roadmap 2010, http://www.e-irg.eu/images/stories/eirg_roadmap_2010_layout_final.pdf

Masoni A. (2011). EU-IndiaGrid2 sustainable e-Infrastructures across Europe and India, *Proceedings of the International Symposium on Grids & Clouds (ISGC 2011),* Taipei Taiwan, March 2011, http://pos.sissa.it/cgi-bin/reader/conf.cgi?confid=133

Huedo E et At (2005) The GridWay Framework for Adaptive Scheduling and Execution on Grids. *6(3)*:1-8, September 2005.

Gregori I. et al (2011) GRIDSEED: A Virtual Training Grid Infrastructure, *Proceedings of the CLCAR conference* (Colima,Mexico, September2011)

Amarnath, B.R. et al. EU-IndiaGrid interoperability experiments using GridSeed tool *Multiagent and Grid Systems – An International Journal 6 (2010) 1–9*

Cozzini S. and A. Lagana (2009) "Chemistry and Material science applications on Grid Infrastructures", ICTP Lecture Notes Series, ISBN 92-95003-42-X, Trieste 2009 http://publications.ictp.it/lns/vol024.html

Giorgi F. et al (2011) RegCM4: Model description and preliminary tests over multiple CORDEX domains. *Accepted for publication on Climate Research.*

Section 6

New Horizons for Grid Technology

14

Open Development Platform for Embedded Systems

E. Ostúa, A. Muñoz, P. Ruiz-de-Clavijo, M.J. Bellido,
D. Guerrero and A. Millán
Grupo de Investigación y Desarrollo Digital (ID2)
Dpto. Tecnología Electrónica, University of Seville
Spain

1. Introduction

Embedded systems are those that implement a specific function while satisfying a number of restrictions. These restrictions have evolved over time and today, the most common for this type of system are cost and low consumption, and minimum size and weight. Moreover, the demand for embedded systems for different functions, and also the complexity of these functions has increased significantly in recent years. Also, due to the high level of competition, is the need to significantly reduce development times of these systems (Sangiovanni-Vincentelli, 2001).

All these problems in the design of embedded systems have been giving rise to an evolution in design methodology, so it has passed from implementing them as an application specific hardware, to a methodology whose main part is software design.

This change in methodology has been possible thanks to advances in technology that allow a complete system to be included in a single chip (ie, System on Chip, SoC). The hardware architecture of Embedded systems in SoC technology consists of a microprocessor as a core, around which are the components or peripherals necessary to carry out the function of the system. This function is implemented through software running on the microprocessor (Beeckler, 2007; Atitallah, 2008).

For views of both cost reduction as well as development time, design methodologies of embedded systems have consisted of pre-built hardware platforms closed with a wide range of applications. This range of applications is achieved because these platforms have multiple ports that are able to package different types of signals. The most common platforms of this type are microcontrollers (MCUs) and digital signal processors (DSPs). With this type of component, the final application design consists primarily in the development of software running on them. In order to reduce development times as well as being able to use these platforms in highly complex functions, manufacturers have made an effort in software development environments (Salewski, 2005). Thus, in recent years, the new MCUs are characterized by supporting several operating system because they provide a convenient way for software applications development.

However, these type of closed platforms reduce the degree of freedom of the designer of embedded systems. This is so because the designer is not able to manipulate and adapt the hardware to the specific application. This could lead to an improved final performance of the system.

An alternative to closed hardware platforms is the use of FPGAs (Ostua, 2008; Muñoz, 2008; Eastman, 2005). The high capacity of integration, low cost on short runs, and high performance in terms of operating frequency and power consumption in FPGAs makes it possible to implement an entire microprocessor-based system in one of these programmable devices. This type of FPGA-based hardware platform has several advantages over closed platforms:

- SoC design adapted to the specific needs of embedded systems
- Ability to design and adapt the hardware components to specific application functionality, and include them in the SoC
- Dynamic reconfiguration capability of the SoC (Williams, 2004)

However, the use of FPGAs necessarily implies an effort to design the hardware architecture that makes the total development time of the system can be significantly higher than in the case of closed platforms. To make the design of embedded systems using a FPGA as central core of the system feasible, CAD tools are necessary to facilitate the construction of the hardware architecture quickly and efficiently. Indeed, nowadays, manufacturers are leveraging the SoC design tools on FPGAs and there is a level of competition for the best solution that combines both ease of construction of the complete architecture as the best performance of the final system implemented. Examples of these tools are, for example Xilinx EDK (Xilinx Inc., 2009), Altera ESD (Altera Inc., 2009), etc.

But in addition to facilitating the development of the hardware architecture it is also necessary to facilitate software development. This is the point where there is greater difference between the MCUs and FPGAs. The new MCUs are characterized by supporting operating systems. The introduction of the operating system level in an embedded system allows these to be used in applications of high complexity. In contrast, microprocessors used in FPGAs, are only now beginning to support operating systems (Henkel, 2004) such as the case with petalinux MicroBlaze (Petalogix Inc., 2010), or projects to port Linux to Altera's Nios (Altera Inc., 2010) or Lattice Mico32 (Lattice Inc., 2010).

In this chapter, we present a platform hw / sw open in the sense that it is technologically independent, and that it is implementable in low-cost FPGAs that meets both of the main features mentioned above: CAD tools that facilitate the development of SoC hardware architecture and, above all, a software development methodology comparable to the methods used in standard PCs.

The platform is based on the LEON3 processor (Gaisler, 2010) that implements the SPARC v8 architecture. The main advantage is that on this microprocessor a Debian Linux distribution (Debian, 2010) was implemented. Having not only a Linux operating system, but of all the components of a very mature distribution as Debian, gives rise to a great potential and easiness when developing software applications for embedded systems.

In what follows we describe the platform, starting with the hardware architecture. Then we describe the implementation process of the Debian distribution. In the 4th section, we detail a general development methodology for any application based on this platform. We show the advantages of the platform on a specific example of embedded system consisting of a terminal unit for location and positioning. Finally, are summarized the main points of work.

2. SoC hardware level

As we mentioned before, we chose LEON3 synthesizable microprocessor, that implements a SPARC architecture. The main features of this microprocessor are described as follows:

- The LEON3 32-bit core implements the full SPARC V8 standard
- It uses big-endian byte ordering and has 32- bit internal registers
- It has 72 instructions in 3 different formats and 3 different instruction addressing modes (immediate, displacement and indexed)
- Implements signed and unsigned multiply, divide and MAC operations and has a 7-stage pipeline instructions
- Also implements Harvard Architecture with two separate instruction and data cache interfaces

With final purpose in mind, Debian was chosen as the Linux distribution, since it has been adapted and compiled for many architectures such as x86 or SPARC v8 among other features. The microprocessor we want to use, must have the ability to run any of these sets of instructions and should be capable of running a Linux kernel 2.6 version. For this purpose, it requires some extra functional blocks, such as a memory management unit (MMU) and a floating point unit (FPU), and should be included within the microprocessor.

Moreover, the whole system must provide a minimum number of other functional blocks that enable a proper operating system support. These blocks are an interrupt controller and a timers unit. On the other hand, support for system memory and an alternative to connecting a mass storage medium should be included. The developed SoC includes a mixed memory control block, which allows access to both FLASH memory and SDRAM memory. It's memory map is assigned as follows: the lowest memory addresses point to the non-volatile memory, while the the rest of addresses cover the dynamic memory. In this way, the start of FLASH memory match the microprocessor boot vector, allowing one to store and run a boot loader in these positions.

In order to provide disk space for the operating system, the inclusion of an IDE interface controller was a good option. This controller has been connected to a Compact Flash card and, in addition, this medium is also used to provide swap memory to the system.

Finally, it is necessary to add some peripheral blocks for communication with the outside of the SoC. It is interesting to provide some kind of Internet access to fully exploit the advantages that the operating system as a development platform provides. Therefore, we have implemented both access methods: modem and Ethernet interfaces. It also includes other general-purpose and debug ports, such an UART blocks that provide RS232 communication.

In summary, figure 1 shows the block-level diagram of the system, where all functional blocks that have been included can be appreciated. Its interconnections has been made through open AMBA 2.0 Bus specification.

Most building blocks of this design are part of a set of libraries and IP cores (including LEON3 microprocessor) called Grlib (Gaisler, 2010). However, it is relatively easy to add new logic cores to the system. For example, a 16550 UART core have been added to support a modem GSM / GPRS communications. This core, wich is based on a model written in Verilog

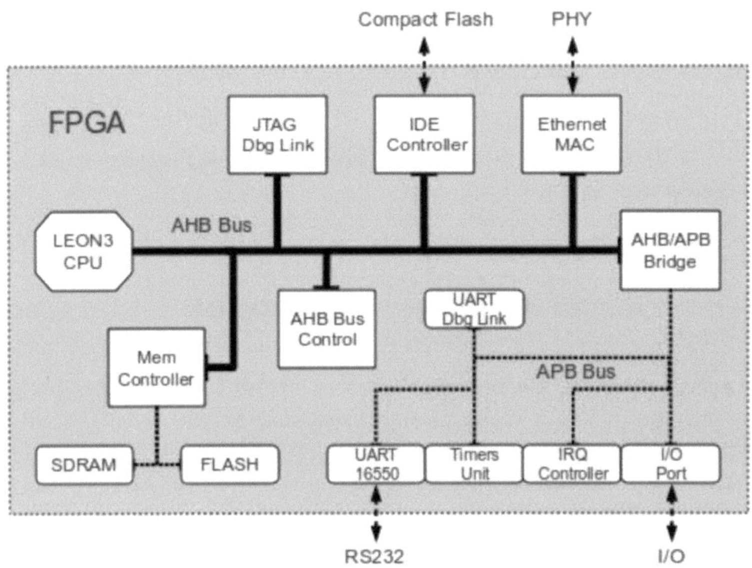

Fig. 1. SoC block-level diagram

language, is obtained from Opencores (OpenCores, 2010). It was necessary do some work to adapt its native intefarce to function properly with the AMBA APB bus.

The synthesis of this design can be accomplished with many software packages and may use different FPGA families and even ASIC as target.

Grlib includes some shell scripts for Linux that greatly facilitate this task. In this chapter, the Xilinx ISE package (Xilinx Inc, 2010) has been used, obtaining the results of compilation and synthesis for Spartan3 XC1500 shown at table 1.

These results are heavily dependent on the choices made when configuring the microprocessor. For example, the size of data and instructions caches, and the number and complexity of the peripherals that have been added to the system, will dramatically change these results.

3. SoC platform operating system

The main objective of this chapter is aimed at obtaining a development platform similar to those available on conventional workstations, but this one will run on top of the SoC platform itself. To accomplish this, and based on the exclusive use of open software, we will install a complete Linux distribution, allowing the use of all development tools, compilers and libraries and also take advantage of using open source code without restrictions.

We can divide our campaign into two main goals, as the SoC platform should first be able to boot a Linux kernel before a complete Linux distribution can be installed. The LEON3 core we

Device Utilization Summary		
Number of BUFGMUXs	4 out of 8	50%
Number of DCMs	2 out of 4	50%
Number of LOCed DCMs	2 out of 2	100%
Number of External IOBs	221 out of 333	66%
Number of LOCed IOBs	192 out of 221	86%
Number of MULT18X18s	1 out of 32	3%
Number of RAMB16s	14 out of 32	43%
Number of Slices	12809 out of 13312	96%
Number of SLICEMs	391 out of 6656	5%
Overall effort level (-ol):	High	
Router effort level (-rl):	High	
Timing summary		
Timing errors:	0	
Score:	0	
Constraints cover	21241138 paths, 0 nets and 106771 connections	
Design statistics		
Minimum period:	24.822ns	
Maximum frequency:	40.287MHz	
Minimum input required time before clock:	6.591ns	
Minimum output required time after clock:	12.193ns	

Table 1. Xilinx ISE compilation and synthesis

planned to synthesize meets all the requirements for the implementation of a modern Linux kernel 2.6, while a few adaptations are necessary to meet the particularities of its architecture.

3.1 SnapGear & boot-loader

Snapgear (SnapGear, 2010) is an open source specific Linux distribution for embedded systems. A fork of the main distribution was adapted by Gaisler Research for LEON3 systems, which have included various kernel patches and a few basic device drivers.

This software package also includes a fundamental and indispensable element in order to load the operating system, which is the boot loader. This small piece of software is usually stored at the beginning of the FLASH memory which must correspond to the memory address $0, so it's then executed by LEON3 processor on the startup process.

The first function of the boot loader is to initialize the basic hardware system, such as debugging console or memory chips. Then it proceeds to uncompress the software package you want to run to the RAM memory system, both a 2.6 Linux kernel and a small romfs filesystem, both Gzipped. On this read-only file system the Linux kernel mounts the root system, which includes all utilities and applications that we have decided to include in the software applications compilation.

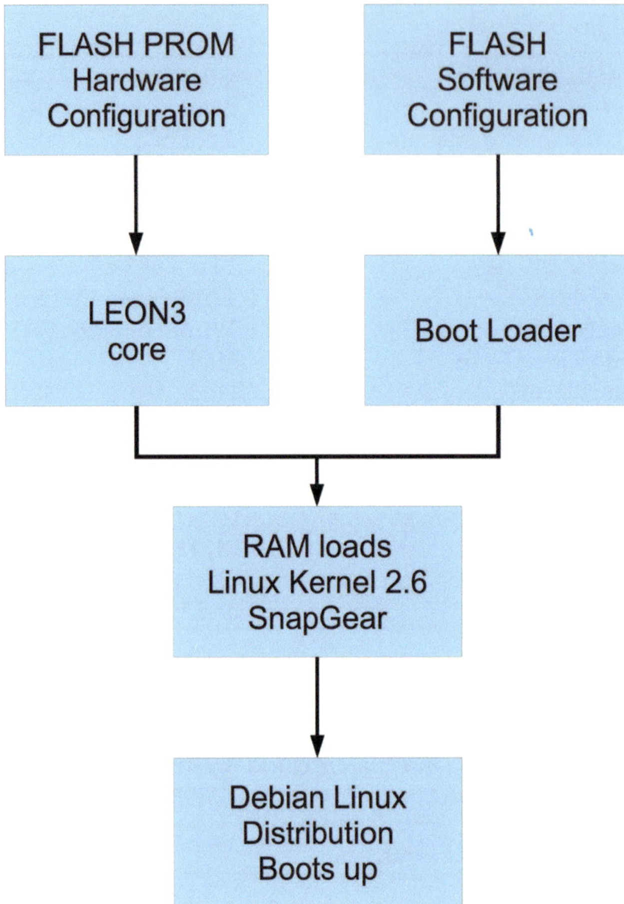

Fig. 2. SoC Boot Up

Another important ability of this small piece of software (boot loader) is to pass arguments to the Linux kernel, which avoids the need to use complex bootloaders such as LILO or GRUB, which are necessary in workstations.

The configuration of the Linux kernel and boot loader and the preparation of the romfs unit are performed by a few scripts. After this process, we proceed to compile the software system and so a set of software images (object files) are obtained.

With this set of object files generated we chose an image prepared for flash memory that contains the boot loader with the Linux kernel and the small romfs file system. Then we can program the flash memory using the Debug-Support Unit (DSU) within LEON3 core by interfacing with a JTAG or Ethernet connection, using the debugging application grmon from Gaisler Research.

Once the process is completed we have a functional Linux kernel with very basic core lightweight applications on top of our SoC platform. The complete programming and booting process of the SoC platform is shown in figure 2.

3.2 Debian

Once Snapgear Linux operating system is running on the system it's time to implement a complete Debian distribution, obtained directly from an official Debian repository. This distribution is precompiled for many platforms, including SPARC V8, which makes it mandatory to usage of Integer Multiplier (MUL) and a Floating Point Unit (FPU) hardware cores, which LEON3 provides.

There are a few ways to install this operating system, however we have chosen the defacto approach to use a small application called debootstrap, which takes care of the download, unzip and install all necessary packages for our target platform. A file system was created that includes such romfs application and its dependencies to other libraries and applications (such as wget and binutils) and they were integrated into the image we created for Snapgear in the previous step.

After the inclusion of the new file system in the romfs Snapgear compilation, it is possible to boot the Linux system and to prepare the installation process of the Debian distribution. In order to do so, having initialized the system and using the Linux shell, it proceeds to boot and configure the Ethernet interface to access the Internet and a DNS server.

Then comes the setup for the drive where you want to install the operating system, which in this case it's a portable solid state memory Compact Flash Card connected through an ATA Controller IP core, but also could have opted for a remote unit NFS hard disk drive IDE interface as a network booting solution.

It is desirable to have at least 1.5 GBytes free on the device to allow easy installation of those software packages and also in order to make use of swap space. Next, two partitions are created in the disk, one for the ext2 filesystem and one swap, with the commands fdisk, mke2fs and mkswap, which are then assembled and activated by the commands mount and swapon.

We must note that romfs is a read-only filesystem, so it has been necessary to have an empty path to mount the unit, in our case we have used the path /mnt/debinst. In this state, the system is ready to install Debian Operating System Cross. Simply run the setup application debootstrap like this:

```
# /usr/sbin/debootstrap -arch sparc stable /mnt/debinst
http://ftp.es.debian.org/debian
```

This command starts downloading packages from the Internet repository. These software packages are stored in the mass storage unit, to be validated and then installed in the system.

Once the process gets the basic installation of Debian on the drive, then it's necessary to configure certain aspects before its first use. At this point the use of chroot command proved quite useful to facilitate the entire process of design and preparation. This command allows the change of the root environment file system and keep running applications of the new distribution in the path that has been installed, allowing one to continue the setup process without restarting the whole system.

Firstly, the process was necessary to explicitly indicate the operating system to invoke a command line (shell) when booting the system (init process). To achieve this we simply modified the description file load during the boot process of the operating system, the file /etc/inittab, by adding the following line:

```
T0: 234: respawn:/sbin/getty -L ttyS0 38400 vt100
```

Thus, the getty application launched a shell connected to the serial port every time the system restarts.

Secondly, the network interface and the name servers (DNS) have to be configured in order to introduce a suitable network configuration, adjusting the files /etc/network/interfaces and /etc/resolv.conf . Also it's need to tell where the mount points of the units will be, such as the boot, root and swap file systems. Like in other standard distributions, one just has to edit the configuration file /etc/fstab.

Finally the /dev directory is empty in the new distribution installation and so it was necessary to create the block and character devices in order to let the kernel manage the peripherals, a task done using the mknod command.

Once the installation and configuration of the Debian Linux distribution is complete, it's time to recompile the kernel adapted to the LEON3 microprocessor. In this new compilation the romfs partition is removed and the kernel will take the parameters where to locate the actual root file system (the drives) by modifying the boot loader configuration.

This argument was necessary to provide the kernel to configure the system console through the serial port and to tell the kernel where the root filesystem was:

```
# console=ttyS0, 38400 root=/dev/hda1
```

Finally started, the system with the new kernel and the Debian Linux installation that, after loading, presented a console with all the benefits of this operating system.

Importantly, once complete the whole process of installation and configuration, has the tools Debian APT package installation, such as apt-get, which allow you to install many libraries and applications, such as compilers, servers, internet services, daemons, desktop environments, etc., and even full distribution upgrades quickly and conveniently.

4. Developing methodology

The previous sections have been devoted to describing the basic technical characteristics of the platform proposed. This section, however, is devoted to discuss the development methodology of embedded systems based on this platform. The developing methodology of SOCs is divided two main parts: hardware developing and software developing. Although both are interlaced, they are very different. With regard to hardware development, begin identifying the components needed for the specific embedded system will be implemented. These components will be the interface of the SoC with the ports needed by the system.

Once identified, we must make the complete design of SoC (as shown in Figure 1) including all necessary components. As mentioned in section 2, this process will be done with GRLIB library that comes with the development system LEON3 processor. GRLIB includes a large number of components common in embedded systems. One of the advantages of this platform is the possibility of designing a controller or peripheral specific for a particular application, which can be included in the SoC. It is also possible to reuse IP cores available for other systems. In these cases, it will make a design interface with the AMBA bus, which is the main bus that uses the hardware platform.

The most important improvement on this platform is under software developing since, the biggest effort in SOCs developing falls on the software and specifically in the interaction with peripherals. Our platform includes a operating system installed that solves the peripheral management through the device drivers. Even if a given driver is not avaliable for a new hardware, using Debian distribution we have tools to makes easy the developing. While with a conventional software developing methodology, some external tools are required: cross compilers, emulators, debug connection tools, etc., once installed the Debian distribution some advantages are achieved versus conventional software development methodologies of embedded systems.

We have achived significant improvements in the software tasks such as installing, compiling and developing, also, in the manage of devices drives or in high level applications. All this due some advantages of the using Debian as base software, it can be summarized as following:

- The Debian repositories has a large set of precompiled software that can be easily installed using the distribution tools. All is done inside of the platform without external tools.
- The distribution provides a the development environment and integrated debug tools that may be installed inside the platform. Also, without the need of external tools.
- Several improvements in the process of update firmware/software. The distribution adds tools to update all software installed inside in an automated mode.

Usually, is not an easy task to install any precompiled software in a SoC. Most medium-high complex software applications depend of other software as shared libraries or external tools. Software distributions give tools to solve applications dependences. Specifically, the main feature of Debian software distribution is the Debian package machinery. This resolves the software dependencies and creates a minimal configuration for each installed software. This minimal configuration allows the putting services on just after install processes and also, can be used as example of end software configuration.

Using precompiled software avoids the heavy task of compile software. Compile software for embeded systems is a heavy task due some of following reasons: one, is the dependence between applications and shared libraries making the compilation process complex. Usually one application needs an exact version of each required shared library. If there are several applications installed at the same time, the same library could appear several times, but with a different version number. In this situation install, upgrade and maintain the software is a tedious task.

Other reasons that make the task of compile software for SoCs complex is the use of cross compilers to generate software. Once compiled software, to test it, all necessary files must be transferred and installed: executable files, shared libraries, config files, etc. The steps of compiling and transference are repeated as many times as necessary to achieve the software to be ready. This process is improved when the Debian distribution is installed. It is possible to install all compiler tools in the platform and make the compilation process inside of platform. Also, this task is assisted by Debian tools since, it detects all dependencies between applications, source code, and shared libraries. Debian tools leave the software developer environment ready inside of platform and the software compilations can be made easily. At this point the software can be developed inside of SoC, the software is also able to be debugged inside using the debug tools included.

Once the developing process has finished, this platform has some advantages during its lifetime. Having the ability of upgrade in the field is a common task today and is an advantage over closed systems. Upgrading the software or fix critical bugs are easy tasks becouse Debian community maintains its repository and, the software upgrades are automated when packages machinary is used. Other embedded SoCs require external tools to update the firmware, instead, this platform has the ability of autoupgrade if its necessary, eg. using network connection.

Another important aspect is the improvement in the process of developing drivers for this platform. By running 2.6 kernels it is possible to load devices drivers in the kernel under demand. With this, we obtain two advantages, one concerning to the resources used and the other, in the devices drivers developing process. Both are now explained in detail.

One of improvements is the capacity to add all avaliable device drivers with the kernel. Although most of the device drivers are not necessary at same time, the capabilities of the platform is not affected by including all. In fact, only the necessary device drivers are loaded into memory on demand, while the rest of them remain stored at disk. With this, the system maintains all functionality and, it saves resources for the rest of the tasks. On the other hand, new device drivers are developed without touching the binary kernel that is running into platform. Since the new drivers are loaded and unloaded dynamically, the driver developer can debug inside the platform. This is an advantage over other SOCs where, the kernel must be fully recompiled and loaded into the SOC for each change in the drivers thus, making the debugging process of drivers difficult.

5. Sample system implemented with this hardware platform

This section presents a specific development of a Remote Terminal Unit (RTU) which implements the standard IEC-60870-5 application-layer protocol for telecontrol messaging stacks. Both the hardware and the operating system are based on the platform already presented in this chapter and we discuss the main tasks required to customize our developments to fit the target system and also describe some of the advantages of using our embedded platform.

In a typical telecontrol scenario one station (primary station, called CC), controls the communication with other stations (secondary stations, also called RTUs), so IEC 60870-5 specification allows online telecontrol applications to take place. In this sense, the IEC defines a set of functions (profiles) that performs standard procedures for telecontrol system. A typical scenario for this kind of communication is shown in figure 3.

The transmission channels available within the design RTU are RF (Radio Frequency), GSM (Global System Mobile) and GPRS (General Packet Radio System). We had to provide the hardware platform with these devices and to integrate everything in the kernel drivers so they were addressable by the user level applications.

For RF transmission an ICOM IC-V82 (VHF transceiver) device was used, with the digital unit UT-118. This device is D-star capable, and can be connected to any RS232 device for data

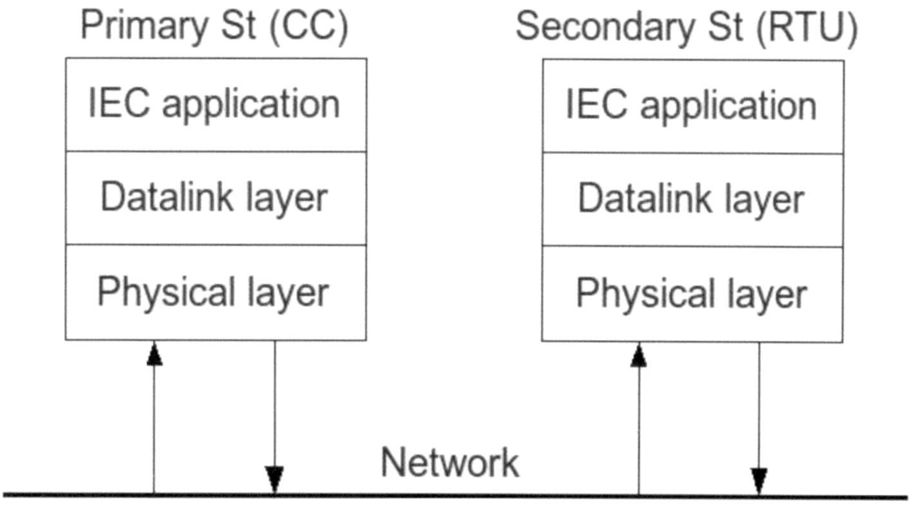

Fig. 3. IEC 60870-5 transmission scenario

transmission, with a data transmission speed of 1200bps. The GSM modem was a Wavecom Fastrack M1306B, which behaves as a standard AT-command modem via a RS232 port, so the modem is connected to the RTU this way. According to device specifications, it allows a data transmission of up to 14.400 bps for GSM but this feature depends on the GSM operator used, so it might not be available (in fact, our tests ran at 9600bps).

In order to get those devices into the design we needed some serial ports and so we integrated a fully capable UART 16550A compatible peripheral, which improves the default UART integrated with LEON microprocessor, by using all the transmit, receive & handshaking lines and also adding two onchip FIFO buffers for improved usability.

We started the development of the UART with one of the free IP cores from OpenCores community (written in Verilog) and we had to interface the Wishbone bus interconnection architecture to the AMBA-2.0 APB (ARM Corp., 1999) peripheral connection LEON manages (the one for relatively slow and simple devices like this). The main issue when interfacing those two protocols is that the AMBA-APB bus does not have a signal for acknowledgement, so every operation always has the same duration, while the Wishbone peripherals usually insert wait states in the communication to the bus master using that ACK line. Finally some Plug & Play information was added to the system so it enable the identification and allocation of the peripheral automatically on the LEON based system startup.

In figure 4 a picture of a prototype of the platform is shown, where you can see the GPS device, the GPRS modem fitted in a custom expansion card with some more serial ports, a compact flash card to hold the Linux local filesystems and the FPGA which holds the embedded design. The prototype has been implemented on the development board XC3S GR-1500. This board includes a Xilinx XC1500 FPGA Spartan3. Also, the board provide others features needed to run the system: 64Mbytes of SDRAM, 64 Mbit of Flash memory, Ethernet PHY transceivers R232, etc. In order to connect both the GPS and GSM modem and Compact Flash card has been necessary to develop adaptive PCBs as shown in figure 4.

Fig. 4. Hardware Platform Prototype

Regarding the software development, there is no open source applications available for the IEC standard protocols, so both the data-link layer and the application layer have to be implemented from scratch. Anyway, as we're using Linux on our platform we already have a TCP/IP stack and standard development tools and libraries, so the data transport and other concrete IEC specifications were built.

The software project was divided into a few different modules, but the most interesting one is the Remote Module, (RTU module). Modules have been developed in C++ language, under a typical software development IDE on a hardware platform x86 (PC) running Linux operating system. Only standard libraries have been used in the development. After the initial setup and debugging the software toolkit also has been compiled for LEON (SPARC) architecture. As LEON has a standard Linux Debian distribution with standard C++ libraries, getting a binary file running is as simple as compiling the same source code developed in the PC in the embedded Linux by using the standard C compilers for the architecture. A GCC compiler has been used to compile and link the RTU source code inside LEON.

In order to test the full system, two parameters were analyzed, initialization time (IT), mean time required to complete the initialization on a RTU, and Poll Time (PT), mean time required to complete a poll over a RTU. Also two scenarios were tested. In one the CC and RTU were PCs and in the other the RTU was LEON. Full details on the application solution implemented and main results were presented in (Medina, 2009).

6. Conclusions

The breakthrough in the capabilities and performance of FPGAs has made becoming an alternative to the MCU in the design and implementation of embedded systems. The main differences between the two alternatives are in fact that the design with FPGAs need to design not only the SoC software but also hardware. This can be very advantageous in many cases because the hardware can be adapted to the specific needs of an embedded system. However, there are still significant differences in the software design methodology due to the development tools available to the MCU are far more advanced than the software development environment for microprocessors that are implemented in FPGAs.

In this chapter we present a platform hw / sw implementable on FPGA which greatly facilitates the process of software development. This platform has several significant advantages such as it is based on open components (LEON3 microprocessor and operating system Linux, Debian), tools that facilitate the development of hardware platform, etc.. But, fundamentally, the main advantage is based on having implemented the Linux operating system with the Debian distribution. This distribution is prepared to run on a standard PC. This means that all the software available for Debian is easily installed. It also has a large set of libraries for developing software applications that can be implemented and used in the embedded system that is based on this platform.

To demonstrate the efficiency of embedded systems development based on this platform we have designed a terminal of geolocation. Thus, it has completed the design of both hardware platform and software applications running on the terminal unit. Software development has demonstrated the advantage and versatility that means having both a large set of available libraries and development environments equivalent to those of a standard PC.

7. Acknowledgements

This work has been partially supported by the Ministerio de Economía y Competitividad of the Spanish Government through project HIPERSYS (TEC2011-27936) and the European Regional Development Fund (ERDF).

8. References

Sangiovanni-Vincentelli, A. and Martin, G. 2001. "Platform-Based Design and Software Design Methodology for Embedded Systems" *IEEE Design & Test of Computers*, 18, 6 (Nov. 2001), 23-33. DOI:10.1109/54.970421

Beeckler, J.S. , Gross, W.J., 2007. "A Methodology for Prototyping Flexible Embedded Systems" *CCECE: Canadian Conference on Electrical and Computer Engineering*, 2007. pp. 1679-1682

A. Ben Atitallah, P. Kadionik, N. Masmoudi, H. Levi. "FPGA implementation of a HW/SW platform for multimedia embedded systems" *Design Automation for Embedded Systems* (2008) 12: 293âĂŞ311, DOI 10.1007/s10617-008-9030-2

Salewski, F., Wilking, D., and Kowalewski, S. 2005. "Diverse hardware platforms in embedded systems lab courses: a way to teach the differences" *SIGBED* Rev. 2, 4 (Oct. 2005), 70-74. DOI:10.1145/1121812.1121825

E. Ostua, J. Viejo, M. J. Bellido, A. Millan, J. Juan, A. Muñoz, 2008, "Digital Data Processing Peripheral Design for an Embedded Application Based on the Microblaze Soft Core",

4th Southern Conference on Programmable Logic (SPL 2008) ; San Carlos de Bariloche (Argentina), 2008
A. Muñoz, E. Ostua, M. J. Bellido, A. Millan, J. Juan, D. Guerrero, 2008, "Building a SoC for industrial applications based on LEON microprocessor and a GNU/Linux distribution", *IEEE International Symposium on Industrial Electronics (ISIE 2008)* pp. 1727-1732, Cambridge (United Kingdom)
J. Williams and N. Bergmann, "Embedded linux as a platform for dynamically self-reconfiguring systems-on-chip" *Proc. Eng. Reconfig. Syst. Algorithms (ERSA)*, Jun. 2004, pp. 171-176
Salewski, F. and Kowalewski, S. 2007. "Hardware platform design decisions in embedded systems: a systematic teaching approach" *SIGBED* Rev. 4, 1 (Jan. 2007), 27-35. DOI:10.1145/1217809.1217814
Nancy Eastman. 2005. "Moving Embedded Systems onto FPGAs" *00 Embedded Magazine* http://china.xilinx.com/publications/magazines/emb_02/xc_pdf/emb02-altium.pdf
Xilinx Inc. (2009) "EDK Concepts, Tools, and Techniques" http://www.xilinx.com/support/documentation/sw_manuals/xilinx11/edk_ctt.pdf
Altera Inc. (2009) "Nios II Processor Reference Handbook" http://www.altera.com/literature/hb/nios2/n2cpu_nii5v1.pdf
Joachim Henkel, Mark Tins (2004) "Munich/MIT Survey: Development of Embedded Linux" http://pascal.case.unibz.it/retrieve/1535/MunichMIT-Survey_Embedded_Linux_2004.pdf
Petalogix Inc. (2010), "Petalinux User Guide" http://www.petalogix.com/resources/documentation/petalinux/userguide
Altera Inc. (2010) "Nios Forum: Operative Systems" http://www.alteraforum.com/forum/forumdisplay.php?f=38
Lattice Inc. (2010) "uCLinux for LatticeMico32" http://www.latticesemi.com/products/intellectualproperty/ipcores/mico32/mico32uclinux.cfm
Jiri Gaisler, Sandi Habinc, 2010 "GRLIB IP Library User's Manual"
Debian (2010) "Debian SPARC Port" http://www.debian.org/ports/sparc/index.en.html
OpenCores.org, equivalent to ORSoC AB, all rights reserved. OpenCoresÂő, registered trademark http://www.OpenCores.org
Xilinx Inc. (2009) "ISE Design Suite Software Manuals and Help" http://www.xilinx.com/support/documentation/sw_manuals/xilinx11/manuals.pdf
Snapgear 2010, "SnapGear Embedded Linux Distribution" http://www.snapgear.org/
ARM Ltd. Corp. 1999, "AMBA(TM) Specification (Rev 2.0)" http://www.arm.com/products/solutions/AMBA_Spec.html
V. Medina, I. Gomez, E. Dorronzoro, D. Oviedo, S. Martin, J. Benjumea, G. Sanchez, 2009, "IEC-60870-5 application layer for an Open and Flexible Remote Unit" *IEEE International Symposium on Industrial Electronics (ISIE 2009)* ; Seoul Olympic Parktel, Seoul, Korea July 5-8, 2009

15

Potential of Grid Technology for Embedded Systems and Applications

Mona Abo El-Dahb[1,2] and Yoichi Shiraishi[2]
[1]*Department of Computer Science, Faculty of Engineering, Helwan University, Cairo,*
[2]*Department of Production Science and Technology, Graduate School of Engineering, Gunma University,*
[1]*Egypt*
[2]*Japan*

1. Introduction

First, this chapter offers a brief introduction for the grid computing and its potential in the embedded system design, embedded system definition the difference between the embedded system and the general purpose computer, embedded systems classification and the design challenges. Next, an embedded system design for inverter power supply is described as a case study. An embedded system can be simply defined as a combination of hardware (microprocessor) and software that is built into a product for purposes such as controlling, monitoring and communication without human intervention. Furthermore, embedded system is a special-purpose computing device designed to perform dedicated functions. The hardware includes a microprocessor or microcontroller with additional external memory, I/O, and other components such as sensors, keypad, LEDs, LCDs, and any kind of actuators. The embedded software is the driving force of the embedded system design. Once it is loaded, the embedded software will never be changed unless it needs to be reloaded or replaced (Turley, 2010 & Henzinger and Sifakis, 2006 & Hongxing and Thomas, 2006). Nowadays, embedded systems can be found in devices ranging from from digital watches to communication systems, transportation navigation systems, medical systems, and financial systems. Figure 1 shows some examples of the applications of embedded systems. The number of the embedded systems has increased rapidly in the last few decades to meet modern life demands.

2. Embedded system versus general-purpose system

An embedded system is usually classified as a system that has a set of predefined, specific functions to be performed and in which the resources are constrained (Stepner et al., 1999). For example, the mobile phone is an embedded system and it has several readily apparent functions as follows: the main function is to call and receive phone calls, along with perhaps several other functions such as a stopwatch, time-keeper, alarm, and camera and so on. A mobile phone also has several resource constraints as follows: firstly, the processor that is

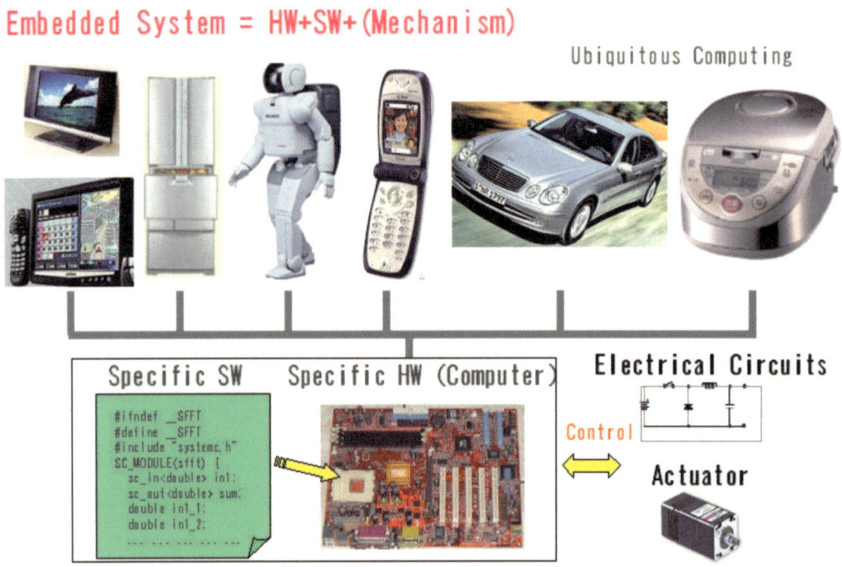

Fig. 1. Examples of embedded system

operating the mobile phone cannot be very large, or else no one would use it. Secondly, the power consumption must be minimal as only a small battery can be contained in a mobile phone. Finally, it must perform its function accurately. Each embedded system design satisfies its own set of functions and constraints. By comparing this example with the general propose computer we can see the differences. In this section, the main differences between both systems are described below:

1. Embedded systems are dedicated to specific tasks, where PCs are general computing platforms. An embedded system is programmed to perform specific tasks. Conversely, a general-purpose computer is able to perform unlimited tasks or one can install any software to do all kinds of tasks such as word processing, data sheet, database management, and others depending on one's purposes.
2. Embedded systems are usually cost-sensitive because the embedded system is only part of the whole product. Subsequently, if the cost of the embedded system reduces, one can potentially reduce the product cost.
3. The implication of software failure are much more severe in the embedded systems than the general propose computer. It is considered one of the most difficult technical and commercial environments because many critical systems are controlled by the embedded computer system. These include communication systems, transportation navigation systems, medical systems, and financial systems. Failure or compromise of such a system can have significant consequences including disruption of critical services, financial loss, and loss of life (Thomas, 2006).
4. Embedded systems have power constrains. This is not a practically serious constraint for the general-purpose computer system. However, consider an embedded system connected to medical system in the ambulance, so the system must work reliably and for a long time with a set of small batteries. So, it is very important issue to keep the embedded system running on a minute amount of power (Berger, 2002).

5. Embedded systems have real-time constraints. Real-time constraints generally are grouped into categories depending on the application as follows: the first category is time-sensitive constraints and; the second category is time-critical constraints. If the application has time-critical constraints the task must take place within a set window of time, controlling the flight worthiness of an aircraft is a good example of this.
6. Embedded systems must operate under different environmental conditions. The embedded systems are everywhere, so the system must be designed to work well in different environment conditions and in the harsh environment as well.
7. Embedded systems microprocessors often have debugging circuitry.

3. Challenges of embedded software design

Embedded system development tools have traditionally lagged behind tools for the development of general systems (ChristopherChristopher, 2000). Unlike general systems, the design space for embedded systems is extremely large, so it is difficult to contain all of the facilities to specify, design, and test embedded systems. The number of embedded systems increased rapidly year by year and then the designers of the embedded system face ever-increasing challenges in the design stage. Some of these challenges are listed below:

1. In the traditional design method of the embedded system, the hardware and the software of an embedded system are developed simultaneously, which is a sharp contrast to the general or business system. In the business system development, the hardware on which the software should be executed is available. Usually in the business software development, the software can be tested and modified in the computer. However, in the embedded software design, even the specifications of hardware are generally not completed. Therefore, embedded software cannot test on the actual platform until the completion of the hardware. This will cause the degradations of qualities of embedded software as well as increasing the process time (Woodward and Mosterman, 2007).
2. In the traditional development method, design took places early in the development process, and the software designer should wait until late in the process. Then the embedded software is tested in the actual prototype. So, revealing the errors in the embedded software is considered a critical step. Furthermore, the discovery of errors often resulted in production delay as well as the possibility of additional expenses to the product cost (Woodward and Mosterman, 2007 & Manfred, 2006).
3. One of the major challenges in the design process of embedded systems is to accurately predict performance characteristics of the final system implementation in the early design stages.
4. The complexity of the embedded system arises due to the combination of more and more functions onto a single system (Woodward and Mosterman, 2007 & Madhukar and Lee, 2008). For example, luxury vehicles produced today contain more than 90 embedded electronic control units (ECU), which execute more than 10 million lines of computer codes that control many different functions in a car (Ming-Shan, 2007). Increase of system complexity may also lead to the increase of a project time and the system design cost.
5. As aforementioned, the main difference between the conventional computer systems and the embedded computer systems is that the hardware on which the software

should be executed is unavailable. Therefore, a simulator of the embedded hardware is very useful for the development of the embedded software but it becomes a difficult matter because of the length of time required to build a simulator (Woodward and Mosterman, 2007 & Madhukar and Lee, 2008).

6. Verification is the process of determining whether a system satisfies a given property of interest or not. It is considered one of the most difficult challenges of the embedded system. Due to the fact that the embedded systems deal with very critical applications, a designer has to make sure that the system meets the required specification perfectly. It is reported that the verification takes more than 50 to 70% of the project time and the cost for verification of the embedded system is increasing rapidly (Christopher, 2000).
7. As a result, the competition among the companies to deliver the product to the market faster and with lower cost. In most cases, the embedded system is a part of the system. Thus, any delay in the embedded system development will cause overall delay in the project or products.

However, nowadays, embedded systems have garnered more interests in the research community, as well as there being an increased need for those embedded systems. The increase of the embedded system challenges opens a wide range of research in the development tools. Most of researchers try to find a design tool that can solve some of the challenges of embedded system design. Model Based Design method is one of the techniques for developing embedded software and it puts a system model at the center of the developing processes. For example, the environment supplied by MathWorks, Inc. allows engineers to mathematically model the behaviors of the physical system and re-use the program components in the library. This approach meets with significant success in some applications. This chapter will investigate the development of the inverter power supply as an example of the embedded system. The embedded software of the inverter power supply is optimized and tested using the Model Based Design (MBD) method. Moreover, the superiority of this method to the traditional design method is verified.

4. Grid technology for embedded system and application

Grid computing is another way of distributed computing. Distributed computing is a science which solves a large problem by giving small parts of the problem to many computers to solve and then combining the solutions for the parts into a solution for the problem. Grid Computing finds many potential opportunities and advantages in the fields of education, research, engineering, bio-medicine, pharmaceuticals, financial sector and government organizations(Mark,el.,2002). In the embedded system design the gird computing technology is used for improving the developing cycle of the embedded system . for example, GridSim is a toolkit for modeling and simulation of Grid resources and application scheduling. It provides a comprehensive facility for the simulation of different classes of heterogeneous resources, users, applications, resource brokers, and schedulers. It has facilities for the modeling and simulation of resources and network connectivity with different capabilities, configurations, and domains. It supports primitives for application composition, information services for resource discovery, and interfaces for assigning application tasks to resources and managing their execution. These features can be used to simulate resource brokers or Grid schedulers to evaluate performance of scheduling algorithms or heuristics(Buyya R, el.,2002). May programs are built based on the gird technology one of this program is the MATLAB and SimuLink which is used in this study.

MATLAB is a high-level technical computing language and interactive environment for algorithm development, data visualization, data analysis, and numeric computation. The MATLAB infrastructure design is based on the gird computing technology .MATLAB is used to solve problems in several application areas such as signal and image processing, communications, control design, test and measurement, financial modeling and analysis, and computational biology. Add-on toolboxes extend the MATLAB environment to solve particular classes of problems in different application areas.

Simulink is a companion product to MATLAB that offers an environment for multidomain simulation and Model-Based Design for dynamic and embedded systems. It provides an interactive graphical environment and a customizable set of block libraries that allows users to design, simulate, implement, and test a variety of time-varying systems.

In this chapter we used the Model Based Design method to eliminate some of the embedded system challenges. Model Based Design is a simulation based method so, if the embedded system becomes large and more complicated, its simulation time will be increased. To accelerate the simulation time of such embedded systems, some parallel and distributed systems (grid computing method) are necessary.

5. Model based design

Currently, many researches are focused on determining a good way to eliminate the challenges of the embedded systems design. Embedded systems have particularly tight performance, time to market and cost constraint. To meet these constraints, researchers try to find solutions to efficiently design the systems with required performances. Recently, the MBD method is considered to be one of the chief techniques in this field. The Model Based Design method is considered one of the leading techniques as a solution of those challenges. In this method, the model can be used to verify the plant design and the control algorithm. MBD method puts a system model at the center of the development process, from requirement development through design implementation (Woodward and Mosterman, 2007).

The system specifications phase is started by the analysis and the documentation of the system requirements. In the traditional method, this step is accomplished using the paper-based method which results in poor communication in the design process, errors in the design as well as limited traceability between the design and the requirements. In the MBD method, the model can provide an excellent virtual environment for high level descriptions of the embedded system, as shown in Figure 2. This figure illustrates the main four elements of the MBD method. The description for elements of Model Based Design method is presented below.

5.1 Executable specifications

As designs become larger and more complicated, it becomes necessary to first describe them at a high level of abstraction. For example, Simulink (The MathWork web site) can provide specific block-sets such as signal processing, communication, video and image processing block set to help the designer to build an abstraction model. This model provides a

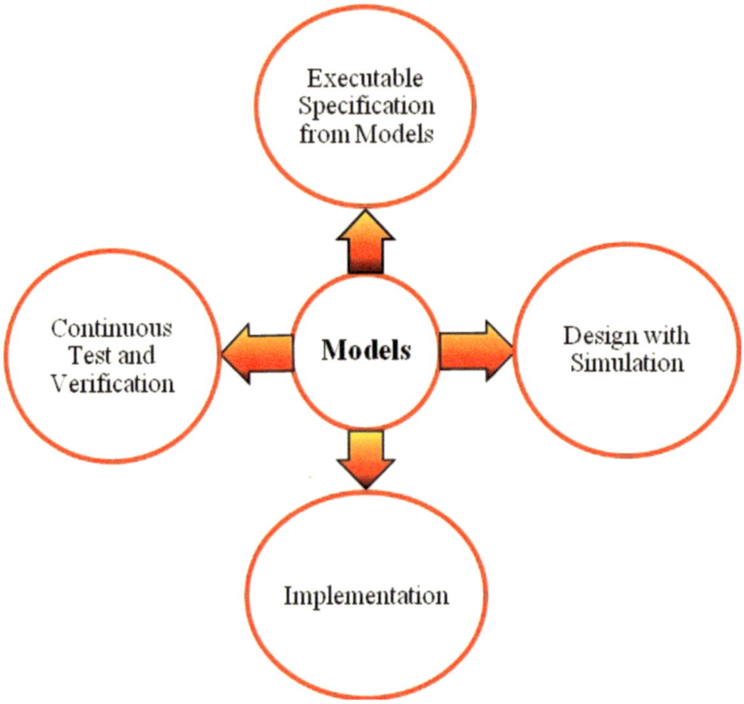

Fig. 2. Elements of Model Based Design

documented method for verifying and validating of design before move to the development in actual controllers and hardware (Woodward and Mosterman, 2007 & Manfred, 2006). System engineers usually develop this high-level description for several purposes as listed below:

1. It enables designers to perform simulations by directly executing the model.
2. It is used throughout the development process for testing, verification and implementation.
3. It allows for developers to identify bugs early on and avoid costly bug discovery towards the end of development.
4. It eliminates the need for paper-based specifications, which is easily prone to misinterpretations, and replaces it with the executable specification.
5. Each member of a design team can understand and execute the model and can focus in developing parts of the main model (Madhukar and Lee, 2008 & Ming-Shan, 2007).

A key point of shrinking the embedded life cycle by applying the MBD method is to begin developing the embedded control algorithm early in the design cycle as possible (Rautio, 2008). In this stage, the model provides the ability to begin simulation of the control behaviors while the hardware prototype is still under development. In addition, the model can be re-used for further modification of the same product which reduces the effort necessary to build the model again.

5.2 Design with simulation

When designing the executable specification, the system engineer generally does not keep the implementation details in mind, but rather designs the algorithm to match the behavioral requirements for the system. Once the system engineer submits the executable specification to the development team, the team may need to make modifications to it in order to fit the design into a real world that may have limited resources, such as memory or processing power. These modifications may cause the output of the new design to deviate from the original design. Design engineers should decide if the deviation is acceptable. In this section, modifications in the controlling algorithms will be done to make it suitable for hardware implementation and demonstrate how to continuously verify the design against the executable specifications. For example, if the designers need to change the controlling algorithm to meet the requirements, MBD method provides an environment where the designer can redesign the control algorithms and validate it in very short time comparing to traditional method of design (Ming-Shan, 2007).

5.3 Implementation and testing

The modern Model Based Design tools provide automatic generation for both prototype and production codes directly from the model. So, all the design changes automatically flow through the final implementation. This process results in significant time and cost saving due to the inherent reproducibility and testability of the generated codes and elimination of communication errors (Ming-Shan, 2007 & Rautio, 2008). In the Hardware In the Loop (HIL) Testing, the designer can test the real-time behaviors and characteristics of the final system to verify the system control without the need for the physical hardware or operational environment, as shown in Figure 3. HIL Testing can save the time with significant ratio comparing to the traditional design method. As well, it is easy to implement comparing to physical prototype production. Up to this moment, the Model Based Design process does not completely eliminate the need for testing in the actual prototype, but it offers several opportunities to reduce the time needed to the testing stage (Stepner et al., 1999 & Mosterman, 2010 & Behboodian, 2006 & Davey and Friedman, 2007).

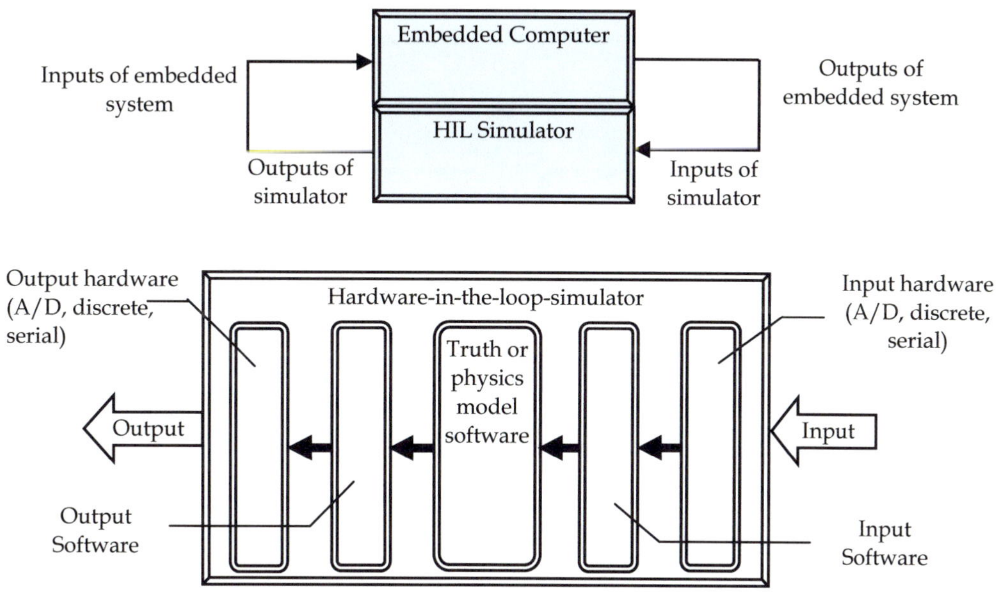

Fig. 3. Hardware In the Loop (HIL) Testing

Generally, it can be concluded that the Model Based Design method will reduce the number of the development stages by combining the design, implementation and testing into one process. The reduction of the required step comparing to the traditional method of design will result in better project management and mitigate the system development risk. The system design using this approach will reach the market faster and will cost less than that of the system designed using the traditional method. Subsequently, the use of the MBD method can provide numerous advantages over the traditional design method. Therefore, this study investigates how the Model Based Design method can provide such advantages by applying and building a new virtual environment for the embedded system design. Inverter power supply is used as a case study of the embedded system in this research.

6. Description of the inverter power supply

The development of new useful energy sources is the key to continued industrial progress. Discovering new sources of energy, obtaining an essentially inexhaustible energy source, making it available everywhere and converting it from one form to another without polluting or destroying the environment are some of the great challenges in the world today. One of the techniques to tackle these challenges is to produce AC (Alternative Current) from DC (Direct Current) generated by fuel cells or solar panels and such device is called an inverter power supply. An inverter power supply is a device which can convert DC to AC that can be used in various AC applications. Many topologies are considered to be candidates for the inverter design and there are many factors affecting the choice of such topology, such as the size and the required efficiency as well as the cost of the inverter. In this study, an inverter power supply configuration is broken into two stages. The first stage is to step up the DC voltage level by using DC/DC converter and the second stage is to invert DC to AC through a DC/AC inverter. The block diagram of the inverter power supply is shown in Figure 4.

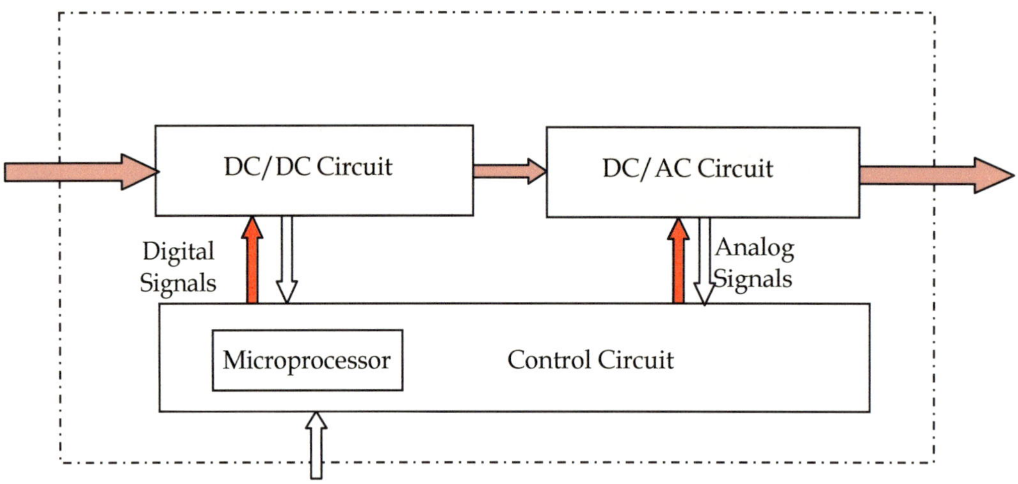

Fig. 4. Block diagram of inverter power supply

In this application, the operation of the electric circuit is controlled by the embedded system that includes the SH microprocessor and the embedded software. Development of the embedded software faces many challenges when using the traditional design method.

6.1 DC-DC conversion

The first step of the inverter power supply is to step up the DC voltage level which comes from a battery to higher DC level by using the DC/DC converter. DC/DC conversion revolves around the conversion of DC voltage level which comes from sources such as batteries, solar panels, fuel cells, or wind generations to a higher DC level. There are many different types of DC/DC converters, and each of which tends to be more suitable for some types of application than for others. For convenience, we can classify them into various groups. For example, some converters are only suitable for stepping down the voltage while others are only suitable for stepping it up; a third group can be used for both cases of stepping up and stepping down the voltage. Another important distinction among converters is which one offers full dielectric isolation between their input and output circuits. Dielectric isolation behavior may be important for some applications, although it may not be significant in many others. In this section we are going to look briefly at each of the main types of DC/DC converter in the current use as presented below:

- Non-isolating converter: The non-isolating type of converter is generally used where the voltage needs to be stepped up or down by relatively small value (less than 4:1), and there is no problem with the output and the input having dielectric isolation. Examples are the 24V/12V reducer, 5V/3V reducer, and 1.5V/3V step up converter (Mohan.N, 1995). There are five main types:
  1. Buck converter;
  2. Boost converter;
  3. Buck-boost converter;
  4. Cuk converter; and
  5. Charge-pump converter.
- Isolating converters: In many applications, the non-isolating converter is unsuitable where the output needs to be completely isolated from the input. Isolated converter topologies can provide advantages in applications which require large voltage conversion ratio. The transformer in the isolation type DC/DC converter can reduce switch and diode device stresses and allow multiple windings or taps to be used for multiple converter outputs (Mohan. N, 1995). Here are some examples of isolating converters:
  a. Half Bridge;
  b. Push-Pull; and
  c. Full Bridge DC-DC converter.

In this study, the isolation type DC/DC converter is used in the inverter power supply implementation. Figure 5 shows examples of the isolated converter.

The full-bridge is a popular design for both buck and boost applications. It is one of the simplest and most cost-effective configurations. Another advantage for using the full bridge converter is the fact that when higher power application are requested the full bridge converter can act as a modular block and that it is possible to stack up. For this purpose, the chosen topology for the converter to be used in this application is a full bridge phase shifted PWM converter (Mohan. N, 1995).

A schematic of DC/DC converter is shown in Figure 6. The major components are the four transistors (full bridge converter).

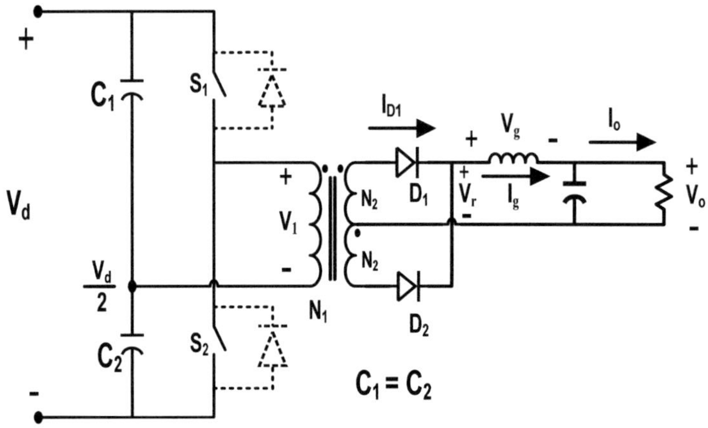

a) Half bridge

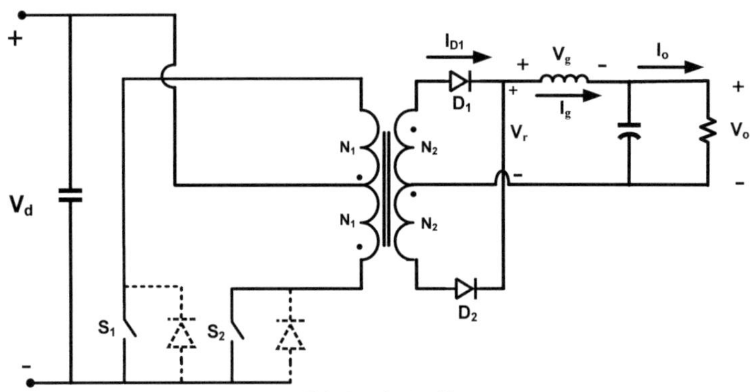

(b) Push-Pull

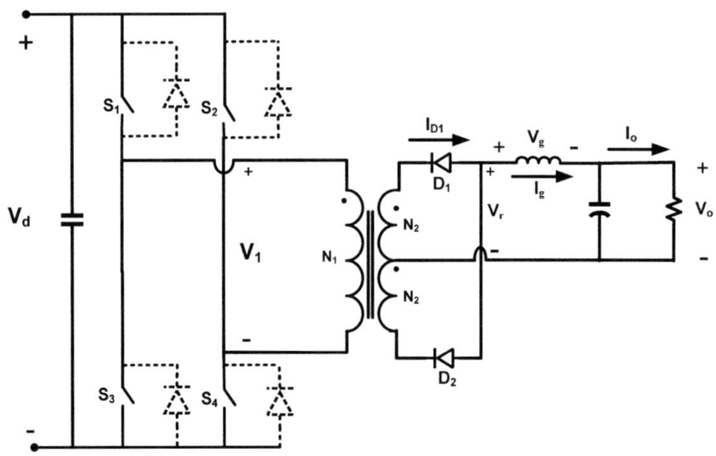

(c) Full bridge

Fig. 5. Examples of the isolated DC/DC converter

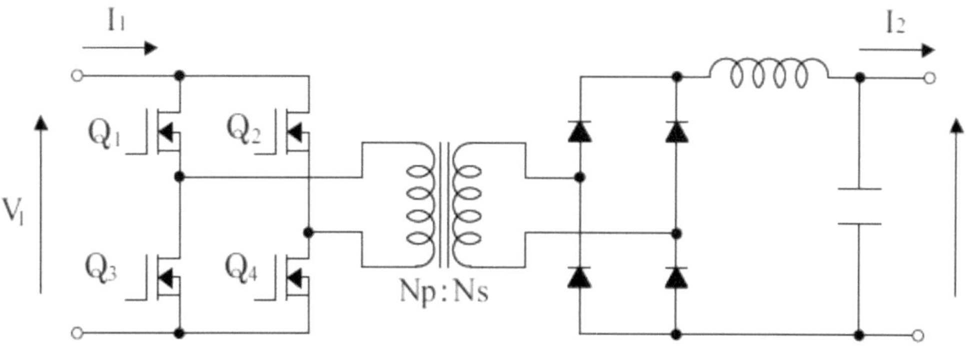

Fig. 6. Circuit schematic of DC/DC converter

The main purpose of this full bridge converter is to chop up the DC voltage so that AC is seen by the transformer. The current is forced across the primary side of the transformer when Q1 and Q4 are on and Q2 and Q3 are off, and the current in the primary of the transformer changes its polarity when Q2 and Q3 are on and Q1 and Q4 are off, as shown in Figure. 7.

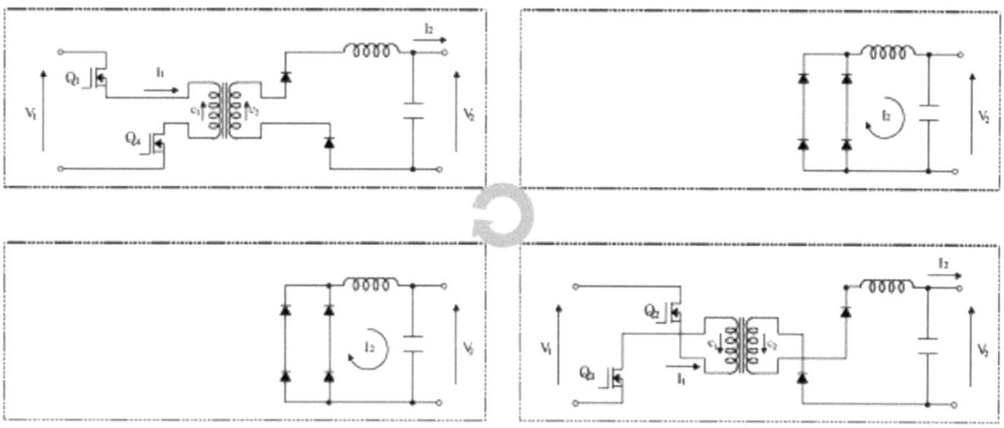

Fig. 7. Switching operation of DC/DC converter

The transformer is a part of the DC/DC circuit that is responsible for boosting the voltage V1 by means of a ferrite core, a primary winding and a secondary winding. It is important to note that the transformer does not create any power, and it only transforms or transfers the voltage. The transformer operates by inducing a magnetic flux on the core from the current flowing through the primary winding. The flux passing through the core is induced onto the secondary winding and the current flows out of the device. The transformer output will apply to the full bridge rectifier and the low pass filter, respectively, to get the stepped up DC voltage V2. The DC voltage is converted to a square wave signal due to the switching operation of the full bridge, as shown in Figure 8.

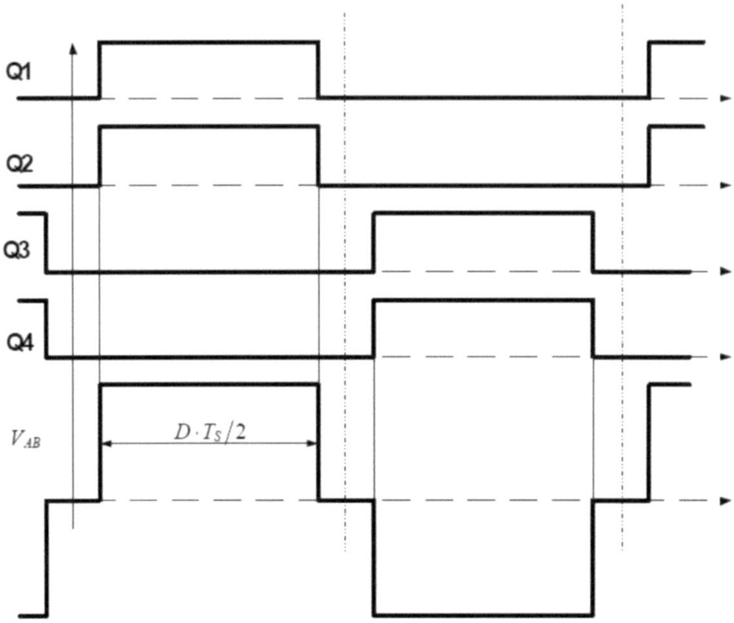

Fig. 8. DC/DC switching operation

The output of the transformer is rectified using the full bridge rectifier circuit and then filtered using low path filter. all the signals are shown in Figure 9.

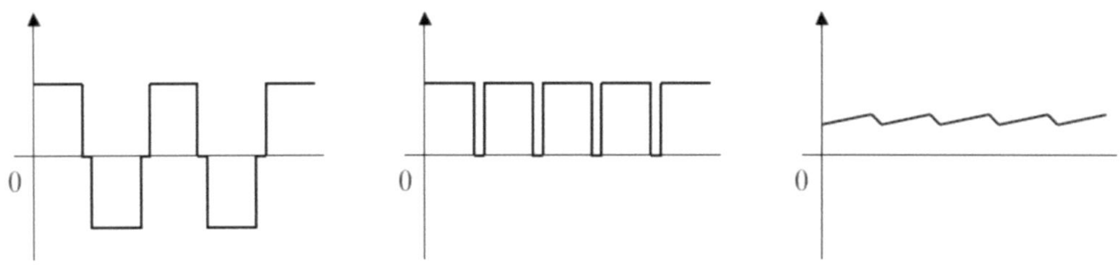

Fig. 9. DC/DC rectification and filtering operation

6.2 DC/AC inverter

The second stage of the inverter power supply is to invert the new DC level into AC voltage through DC/AC inverter. There are many different topologies for a DC/AC inverter. The most common topology is the full bridge configuration because of its easy filtering (Xue et al., 2004). The full-bridge inverter was chosen as the inverting output stage for a number of reasons. It is preferred over a half-bridge inverter because with an equivalent input voltage, the full-bridge inverter can provide twice the amount of output voltage. The full-bridge inverter is also significantly more controllable than other configurations. A single phase full bridge inverter is shown in Figure 10 and the function of the full bridge inverter is to convert the DC voltage supplied by DC/DC converter into a 100V, 60 Hz sine wave. The most important part of the DC/AC inversion process is in the generation of the sinusoidal input signals to the gates of the MOSFETs. This will be covered in the next section which focuses on microprocessor control systems and PWM.

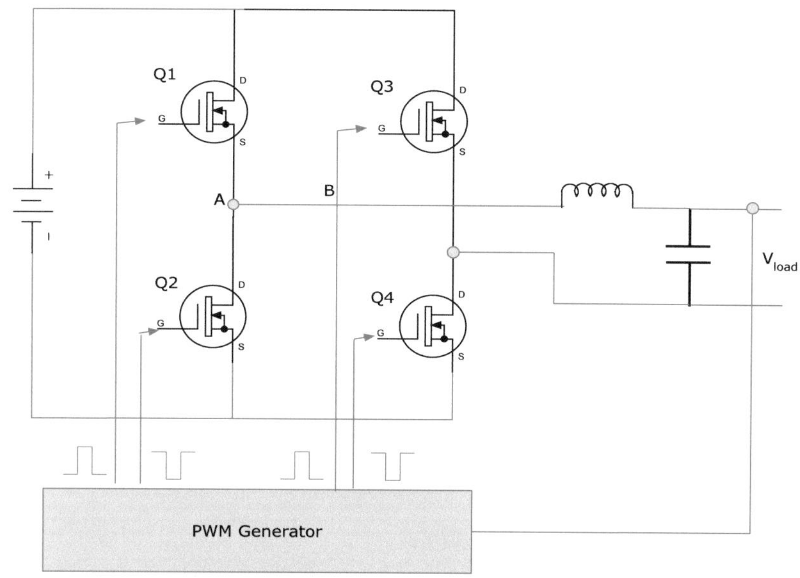

Fig. 10. Circuit schematic of DC/AC inverter

The PWM pulses which are generated by a microcontroller are fed into the gates of a full bridge inverter. Programming the microcontroller allows the transistors Q1 and Q4 to be on while Q2 and Q3 to be off and vice versa. Due to the limited response time and delay time of the transistors, two switches in one leg may be switched on at the same time then shoot through will occur and the switches may be damaged due to high short circuit current then the dead time is introduced in order to avoid the occurrence of the short circuit.

Figure 11 shows the ideal switching patterns and the drive signals containing the dead time for the inverter leg. The S_p and S_n are the ideal switching pattern of the positive device and the negative device of the full bridge DC/AC inverter, respectively. As mentioned before, the short time delay is used to avoid shoot-through, where the actual gate drive signals must be delayed by the dead time. The gate drive signals containing the dead time are denoted as S_{pd} and S_{nd} since the gate drive signals are shifted from the center of the sampling interval by the dead time. The generated phase voltage is also shifted as much as the delay time. It had been reported that the generated voltage pulses residing in the middle of the sampling interval contain the least amount of harmonics (Choi et al., 1999). Although the produced voltage pulses resulting from each of the gate drive signals during the sampling intervals are not much affected, the resultant voltage during an entire cycle is significantly reduced due to the dead time. In addition, those cumulated delays may distort the output waveform of the inverter.

In fact, the addition of the dead time can improve the performance of inverter power supply by preventing the short circuit current. However, the instability and harmonic distortion problem can be arising due to the incorrect selection of the sufficient dead time value.

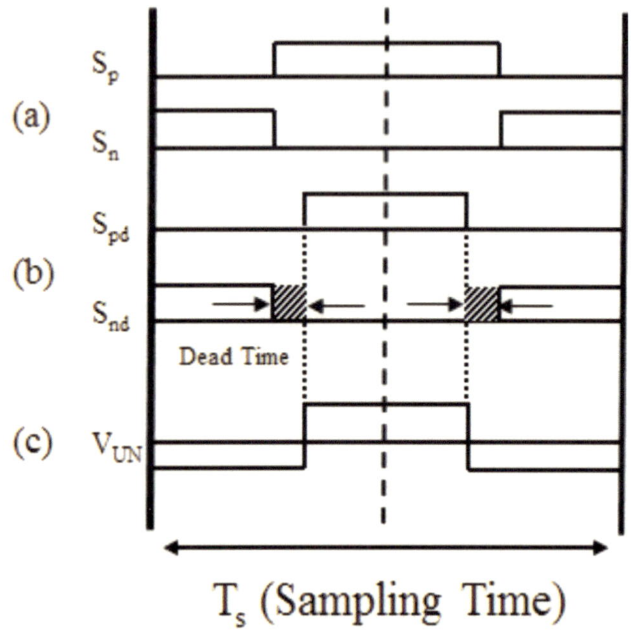

Fig. 11. Gate drive signals of the PWM inverters

6.3 SH microprocessor

In the inverter power supply application, the microprocessor is used to control the switching period of the transistor as a digital controller. Due to the fact that a digital PWM technique can provide the benefits which cannot be given by an analog one, a digital PWM technique starts to be used. The standard method for generating a PWM using a microcontroller or digital signal processing (DSP) is developed by using one of the built-in PWM modules. These modules operate by comparing a free running timer with a duty cycle and duty period register. When a match occurs between the timer and duty cycle register, the corresponding pin is either set to "high" or "low". The match between the timer and the duty cycle register also causes the timer to re-set to zero and then to restart counting (Behboodian, 2006). Depending on the type of microcontroller or DSP, the PWM can be classified into "left-aligned", "central-aligned" or "right-aligned". In this study, Renesas SH microprocessor is used. It is a Reduced Instruction Set Computer (RISC) integrating a Renesas original RISC CPU core with peripheral functions required for a system configuration. SH RISC is a microprocessor family and combines the computational ability of a high speed RISC core with embedded Multiply-Accumulate hardware and extensive on-board peripheral function to enable a virtual single chip PID controller (Sh-2Sh7047 Group Hardware Manual).

In the inverter power supply application, two separate control units in the SH microcontroller are used to generate the PWM signal and control the system operation. These two units are Motor Management Timer unit (MMT) which controls the generation of the PWM pulse in the DC/DC stage and Multi Function Timer Pulse Unit (MTU) which controls the generation of the PWM DC/AC stage. The block diagram of the entire microprocessor is shown in Figure 12.

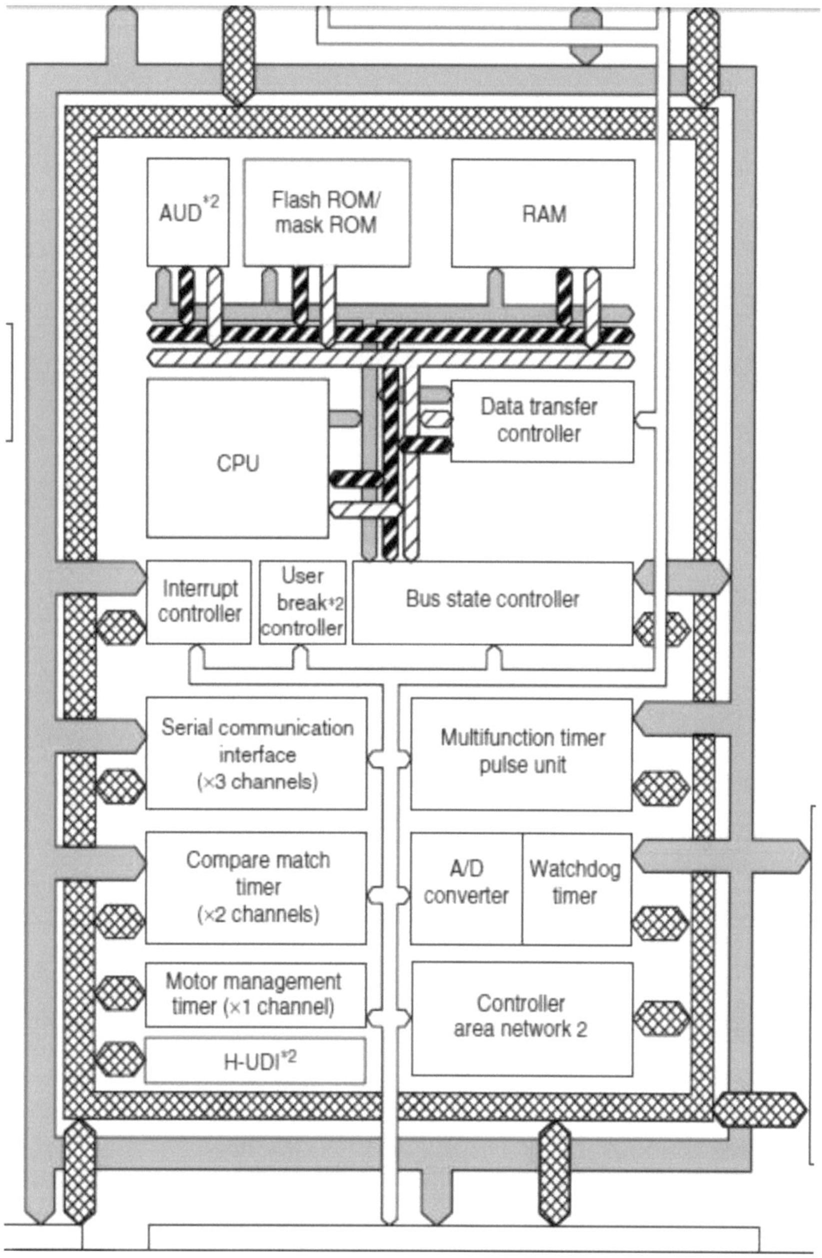

Fig. 12. Block diagram of SH microprocessor

6.3.1 Motor Management Timer (MMT)

Motor Management Timer (MMT) can output 6-phase PWM waveforms with non-overlap times. Figure 13 shows a block diagram of the MMT. In the inverter power supply application, the MMT unit is used to control the switching devices in the DC/DC stage by generating the PWM signal.

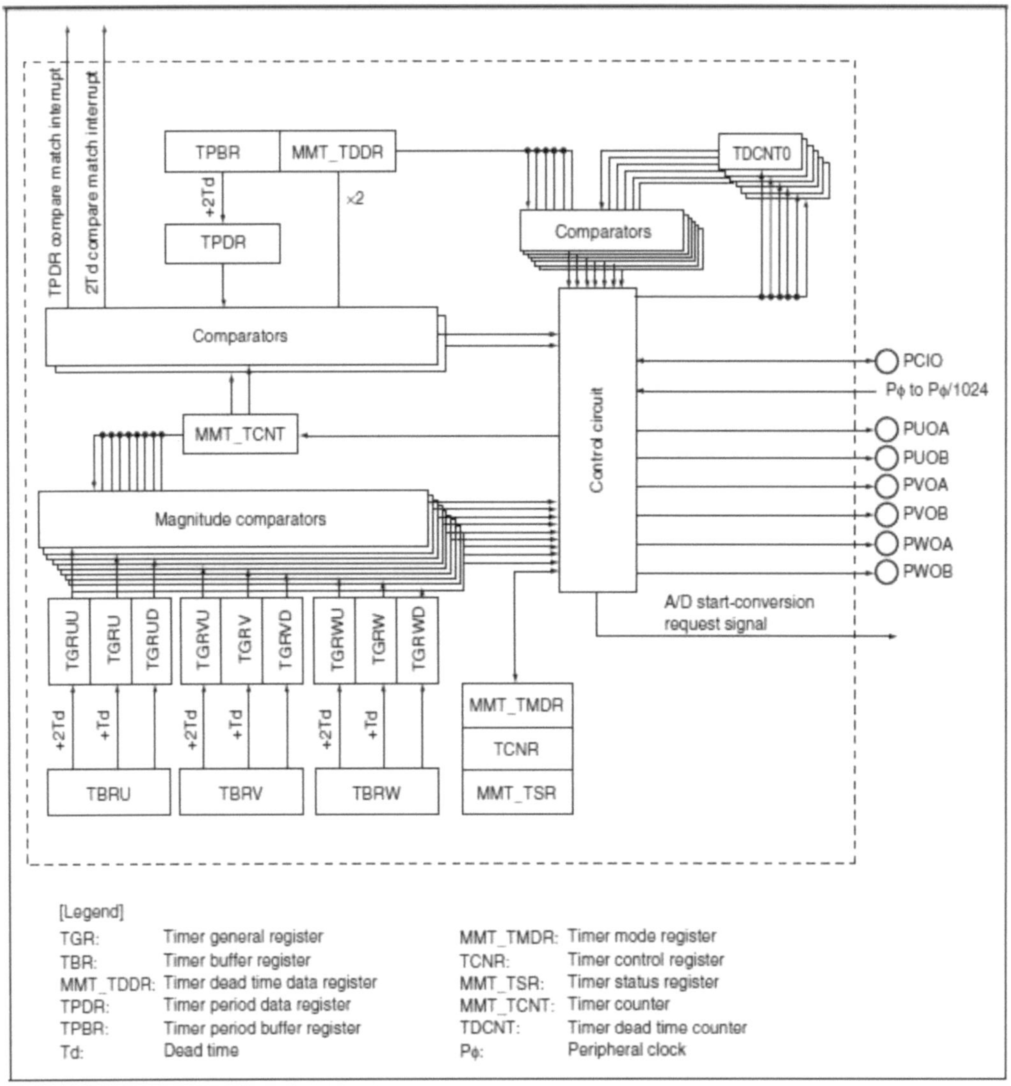

Fig. 13. Block diagram of MMT

Pin Configuration of the MMT unit is described in Table 1, as shown in Table 1, the PUOA, PUOB, PVOA, PVOB, PWOA, and PWOB pins are PWM output pins (Sh-2Sh7047 Group Hardware Manual).

Name	I/O	Function
PCIO	Input/Output	Counter clear signal input when set as an input by PAIORL register: toggle output in synchronization with the PWM cycle when set as output by PAIORL register.
PUOA	Output	PWMU phase output (positive phase)
PUOB	Output	PWMU phase output (negative phase)
PVOA	Output	PWMV phase output (positive phase)
PVOB	Output	PWMV phase output (negative phase)
PWOA	Output	PWMW phase output (positive phase)
PWOB	Output	PWMW phase output (negative phase)

Table 1. The pin configuration of the MMT

Figure 14 illustrates an example of the PWM pulse which is generated from the MMT unit. In this figure the PWM output waveform is generated by comparing the values in the Timer counter (TCNT) and the Timer general register (TGR) resulting in the compare output waveform. Then the dead time generation process is started using the TDCNT0 and TDCNT1 registers. The output generation wave form is generated by finally adding the compare output waveforms with the dead time signal. The PWM waveform is generated by converting the output generation waveform to the output PWM pins. In the operating modes, PWM waveforms with any duty cycle from 0% to 100% can be generated.

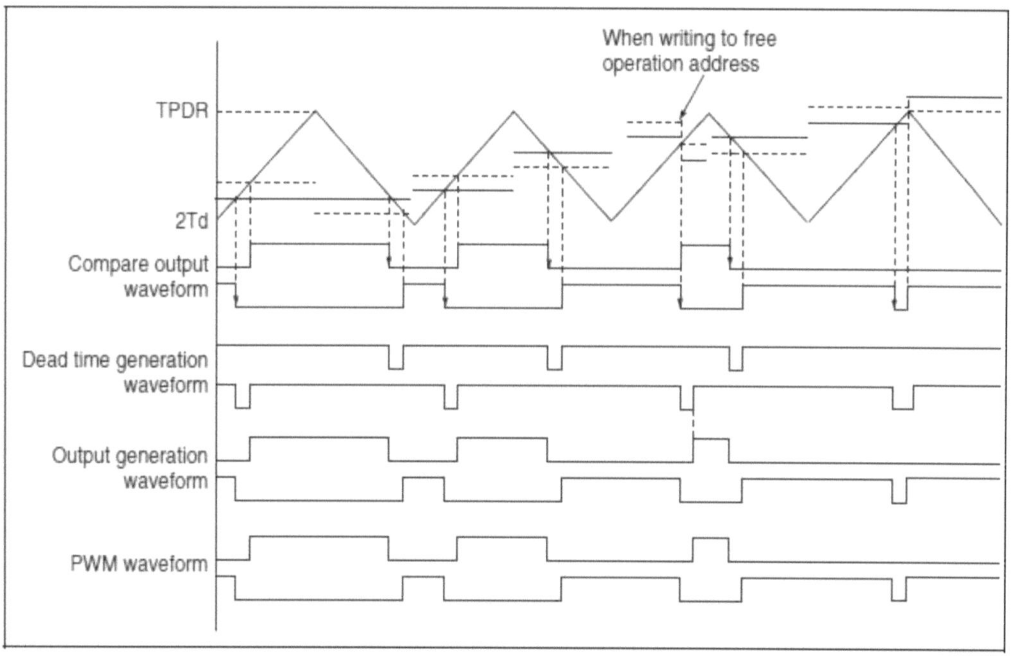

Fig. 14. Example of PWM waveform generation from MMT unit

6.3.2 Multi-Function Timer Pulse Unit (MTU)

MTU is the control unit which is used to generate the PWM pulses that control the operation of the DC/AC inverter stage. MTU comprises of five 16-bit timers, as shown in Figure 15, channels 3 and 4 of the MTU are used in complementary PWM mode with programmable dead time to generate the chopping waves for sinusoidal PWM.

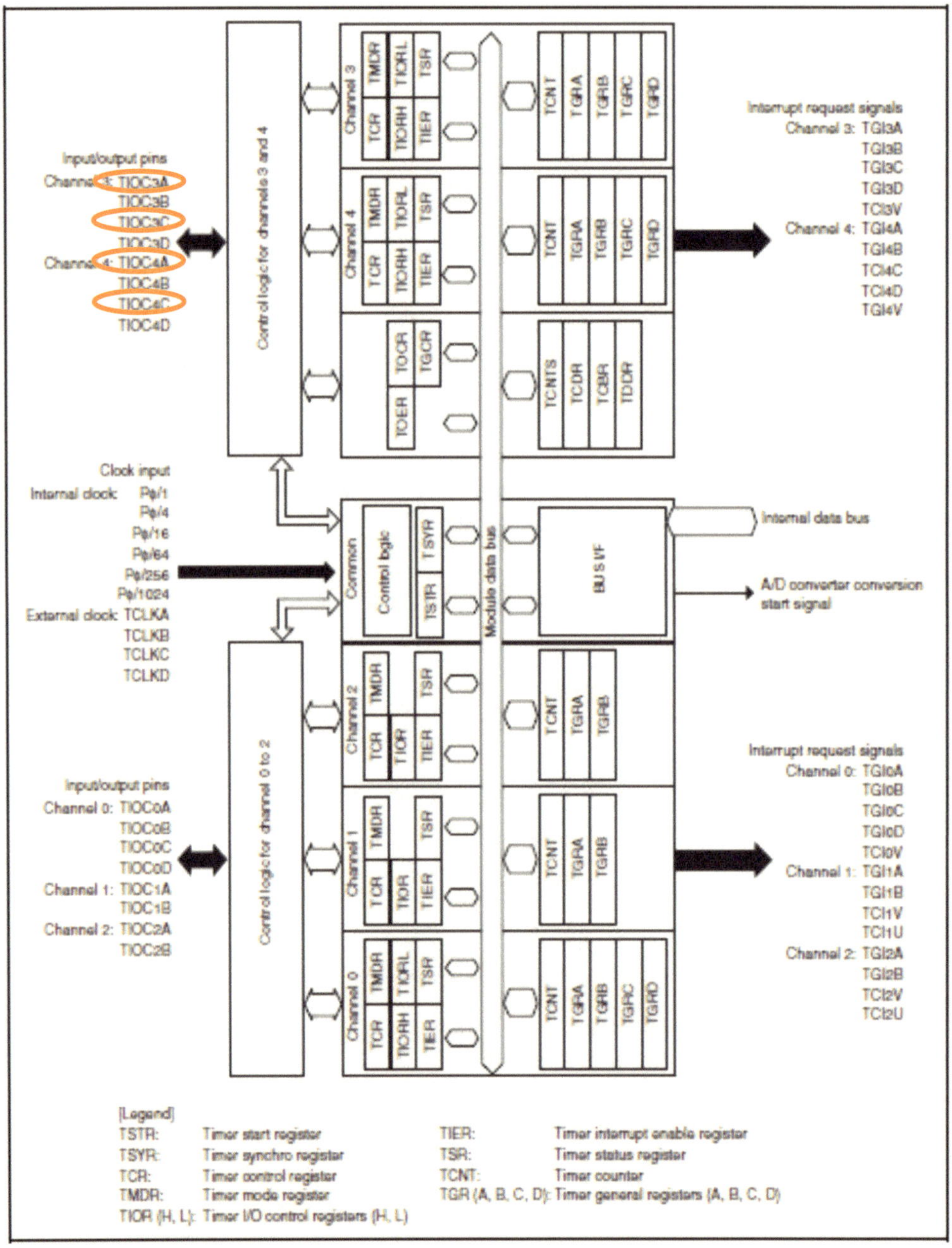

Fig. 15. Block diagram of MTU

In PWM mode, PWM waveforms can be generated from the output pins. The output level can be selected and TGR registers settings can be used to output a PWM waveform in the range of 0% to 100% duty. All channels can be independently designated for PWM mode (Sh-2Sh7047 Group Hardware Manual).

There are two PWM modes: in PWM mode 1, PWM output is generated from the TIOCA and TIOCC pins by pairing TGRA with TGRB and TGRC with TGRD. In PWM mode 2, PWM output is generated using one TGR as the cycle register and the others as duty registers. The output specified in TIOR is performed by means of compare matches. Upon counter clearing by a synchronization register compare match, the output value of each pin is the initial value set in TIOR. If the set values of the cycle and duty registers are identical, the output value does not change when a compare match occurs.

7. Model in the Loop Simulation (MILS)

This chapter proposes an entire virtual environment for the inverter power supply design to optimize and test the embedded software parameters. This environment is based on the Model Based Design method. The MATLAB and Simulink (MathWorks web site) environment is used for building such a virtual system which is divided in two main parts, the analog part (controlled part) and the digital (control) part which are described as follows. The analog part consists of electrical circuits of DC/DC converter and DC/AC inverter. The second part is the digital part (controller part) consisting of the microcontroller and the embedded software. The embedded software has two tasks which are the generation of the pulses to control the operations of the electrical circuits and to implement the control algorithm that is necessary for regulating the output voltage against any disturbance. The entire virtual environment of the inverter power supply is described below.

The topology of the inverter power supply is DC-DC-AC. MILS of the inverter process is done in two stages. The first stage is the DC/DC converter and in this stage, the input DC voltage is converted to higher level DC output. This new DC output acts as an input of the second stage which is the DC/AC inverter. SH 7047 was used as a digital controller to control the generation of the PWM pulses and control the inverter power supply operation. Both the DC/DC and DC/AC stages are controlled individually, as shown in Figure 16.

7.1 DC/DC and DC/AC circuit simulation

The hardware parts of the electric circuits are modelled using Simulink power block set. The power block set consists of the power electronic elements. Each element in this block set has its own block window which allows for the selection for the key parameters. At the bottom of the block parameter window is a pull down menu, which allows for the key voltage and current to be easily measured. In the first stage, the electrical circuit was modeled in an open loop system to determine the performance of each circuit separately. The PWM generation block was modeled for both DC/DC converter stage and DC/AC inverter stage. For example, the PWM model in the MTU microprocessor unit is illustrated in Figure 17. The PWM block compares both the sin wave signal with the required output frequency and the sawtooth signal with the carrier frequency equal to 10 kHz. Then the dead time is generated using the delay block and finally, the PWM pulse is generated and fed into the gates of the full bridge transistors.

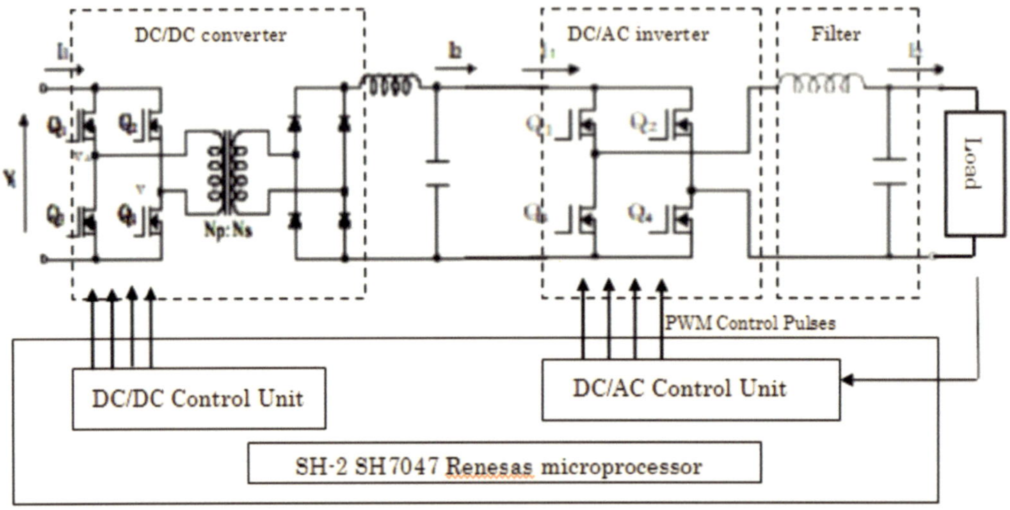

Fig. 16. Circuit schematic of inverter power supply

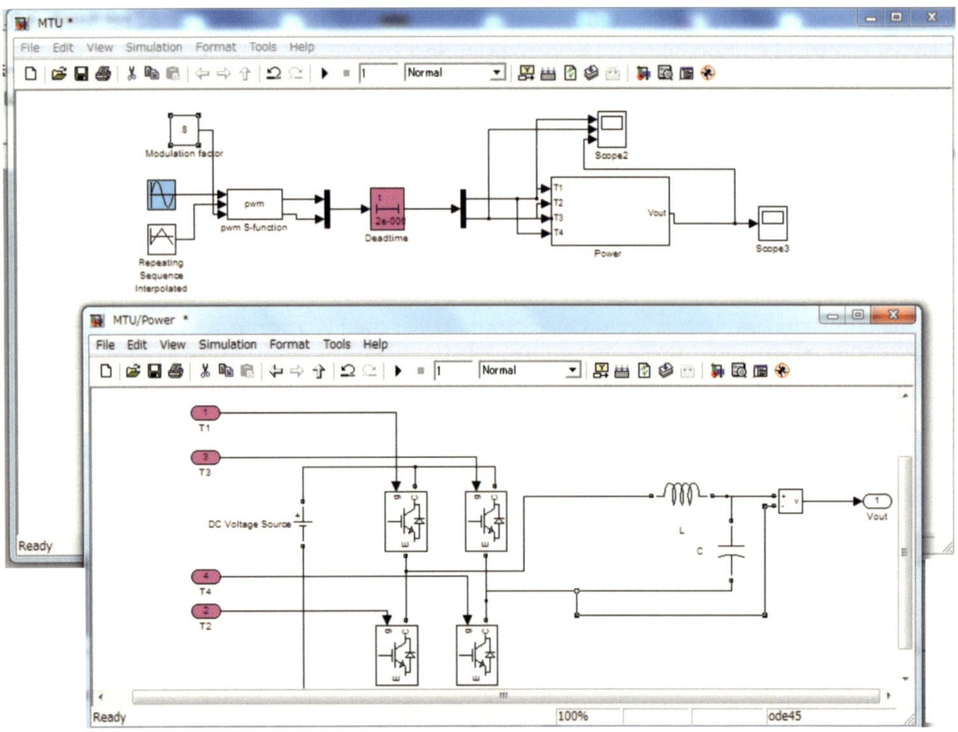

Fig. 17. PWM model in the MTU microprocessor unit

The modulation ratio, the carrier frequency, the reference frequency were changed manually. Equation (1) describes the relation among all three parameters.

$$m = VC / Vcarrier \tag{1}$$

Where: m: modulation index, VC: amplitude of the reference voltage, Vcarrier: amplitude of the carrier signal.

In the DC/AC stage, the carrier frequency is set equal to 10kHz and the reference frequency equal to the desired output frequency of 60 Hz. By changing the modulation factor, the duty of the PWM pulse is changed. The electric circuit specification of the two stages of the inverter power supply is described in Table 2. The signal is monitored using the scope and display blocks which allow us to figure the circuit outputs.

Parameter	Value	Unit
Output frequency	60	Hz
Output Voltage	100	RMS
Battery Voltage	24	V
Switching frequency	10	kHz
Filter inductor DC/DC	29	mH
Filter capacitor DC/DC	47	μF
Transformer turns ratio	7.2	
Filter inductor DC/AC	3	mH
Filter capacitor DC/AC	25	μF

Table 2. Specifications of the inverter circuits

7.2 Microprocessor simulation

In the inverter power supply applications, the microprocessor is used to control the switching period of the transistors as a digital controller. This microprocessor has two main units which are used to control both the DC/DC and DC/AC stages of the inverter power supply. Each unit is controlled by a software program; this embedded software function can be divided into two main parts which are the control program (control algorithm) and the PWM generation program.

7.2.1 Control algorithm

Traditionally, the implementation of switching type inverter power supply has been accomplished by using the analog technique. However, the analog technique has some drawbacks such as a number of parts required in the system and its susceptibility to ageing and environment variations, which lead to high cost of maintenance. Further, analog control once designed is inflexible and its performance cannot be optimized for various utility distortions. Now with the advent of high speed, lower cost digital signal processing (DSP) ICs, and microprocessors, digital control has become one effective candidate for inverter power supply.

Using a DSP or microprocessor has many benefits that make it attractive for use in control systems, such as:

- Flexibility of Control: When using analog circuits to perform control, the control algorithm is fixed, and is not easily modified. Using a microprocessor allows the designer to change the control code very quickly. It is often helpful to implement simple, slow control algorithms first to verify that the hardware is functioning correctly before moving to a higher performance or complex control algorithm. If hardware were used to do this, this would mean separate hardware designs and implementations for each algorithm. With the use of software, modifying the control algorithm means changing several lines of codes, which will take only several minutes.

- Parameter Adjustment: Once the control algorithm is fixed, it is easy to modify the values of references and constants in the control code by directly modifying memory locations. This can be performed while the system is operational, allowing for quick adjustments to be made. If the control algorithm were implemented in analog hardware, this would not be as easy to complete such a process.
- Backtracking: The use of software allows for easy backtracking when the control algorithm is not working. If the control were implemented in analog circuits, the physical modifications would need to be reversed, which may also introduce additional errors in the process.

Many control techniques have been applied to the inverter power supply as mentioned in previous works (Abo Eldahb, 2011). In this study, we newly apply a controlling algorithm which is a two layer control. This algorithm is a combined feed-forward control and feedback control. This control algorithm can significantly improve performances over simple feedback control whenever there is a major disturbance that can be measured before it affects the process output. The basic configuration of the proposed controlling algorithm is shown in Figure 18.

The Proportional Integral (PI) controller control algorithm has been one of the most utilized control techniques in the industry. It has proven its wide range of applications, and it was first introduced to the market in 1939 ((Ho. et al.1999). The main reasons for using PI controller are its simple structure, easy to implement in the practical applications and its flexibility.

To improve the accuracy of both the steady state response and transient response and to minimize the output disturbance, a feed-forward control is added to the classical PI controller. Then the controller equation can be described through equation (2).

$$u_{pi} = K_p e(k) + k_i T \sum_{n=1}^{k} e(n) + r(k) \tag{2}$$

Where: K_p and K_i, are the Proportional, Integral coefficient, respectively, upi is controller output , e(k) is the error signal and $r_{(k)}$ is the feed-forward signal.

When the switching time is coming, the deviation between the target output and the actual output is calculated and this deviation is used to modify the controller output. The output of the PI controller must be within specific interval in order to protect the circuits. The modulation factor m is calculated with respect to the controller output. The controller algorithm was applied to both the DC/DC converter and DC/AC inverter separately and it was implemented using the SH7047 microprocessor. In the MILS environment, S-Function Block is used as the interface block to test the embedded software and to optimize the parameters. Details of the S-Function will be described in the next section. Each of the inverter power supply stages has its own C-MEX file which describes part of the embedded software. This C-MEX file is compiled to the S-Function Block, and then the output of the S-Function block acts as the simulation of the microprocessor unit.

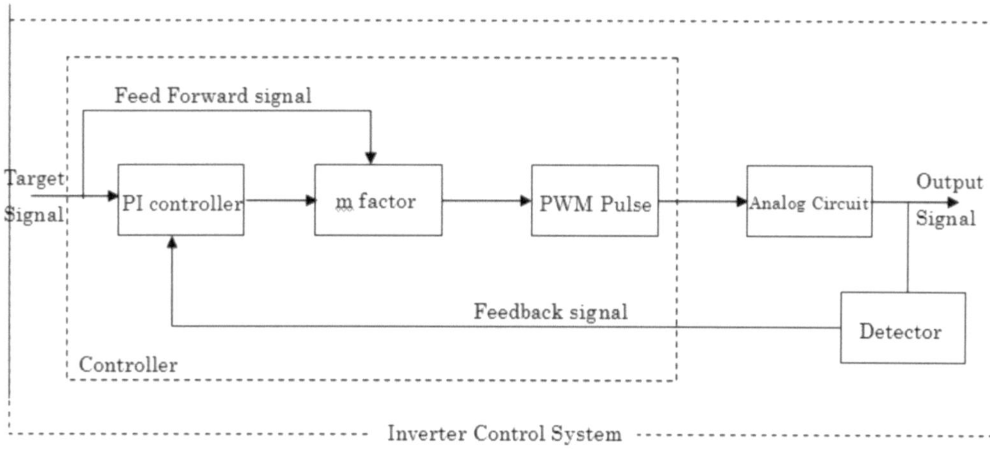

Fig. 18. Simplified block diagram of the proposed control system

7.2.2 PWM generation program

The standard method for generating PWM pulses by using a microprocessor or DSP is to utilize one of the built-in PWM modules. In our model, the System Function (S-Function) Block is used to compile the embedded system software to control DC/DC and DC/AC circuits. C programs implement the operations of the microcontroller's control units, that is, MMT which controls the generation of the PWM pulses in the DC/DC and MTU which controls the generation of the PWM in DC/AC stage. These programs are embedded into the S-Function Block, as shown in the lower part of Figure 21.

S-Function

The S-Function provides a powerful mechanism for extending the capabilities of the Simulink environment. It is a computer language description of the Simulink block written in MATLAB, C, C++, and/or FORTRAN. S-Functions are compiled as MEX-files using the MEX utility (The MathWorks web site). The S-Function uses a special calling syntax called the S-Function API (Application Program Interface) that enables the user to interact with the Simulink engine. The interaction is very similar to the interaction that takes place between the engine and the built-in Simulink blocks. S-Function follows a general form and it can accommodate continuous, discrete and hybrid systems. It allows the user to implement different algorithm and to add them to the Simulink model.

Two S-Function Blocks are designed: one to describe the DC/DC control unit, which is the MMT unit and the other S-Function is used for the MTU unit which controls the second stage, DC/AC stage. The embedded C codes are compiled to the S-Function Block, as shown in Figure 19. In the first step, all the electrical circuit parameters are tested and then, in the second step, the embedded software is tested using the S-Function.

The S-Function and the C-MEX file have the same name and if the MATLAB path includes a C-MEX file and M file having the same name, the S-Function uses the C-MEX file. After the S-Function name is set, then the S-Function parameters are defined. The parameters include the PI controller parameters which are the K_p and K_i, the proportional coefficient and the integral coefficient. Further, the dead time value (TD) is set. The parameters and the name of the S-Function are defined using the function block parameter then the main C code can be generated then the user can modified this C code until the embedded software is completed .So, the value of the parameters in the S-Function is initialized in the C-MEX file, and then this values will be updated during the simulation process. The updated values can be tested using the S-Function Block parameters for both DC/DC S-Function and DC/AC S-Function, as shown in Figure 20.

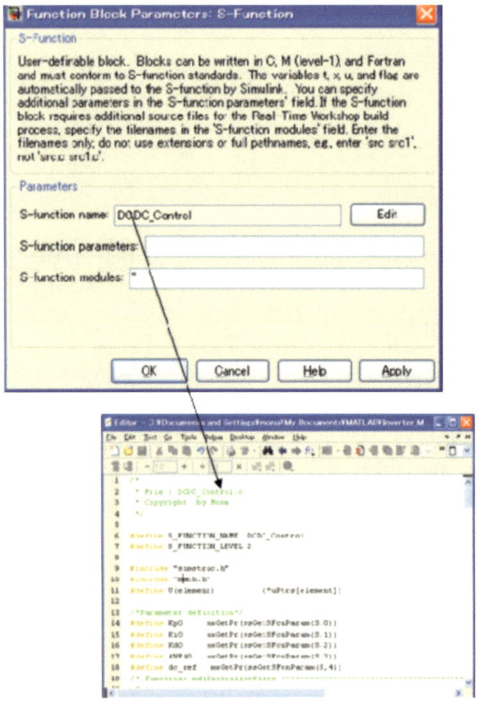

Fig. 19. Block parameter dialog box of DC/DC S-Function

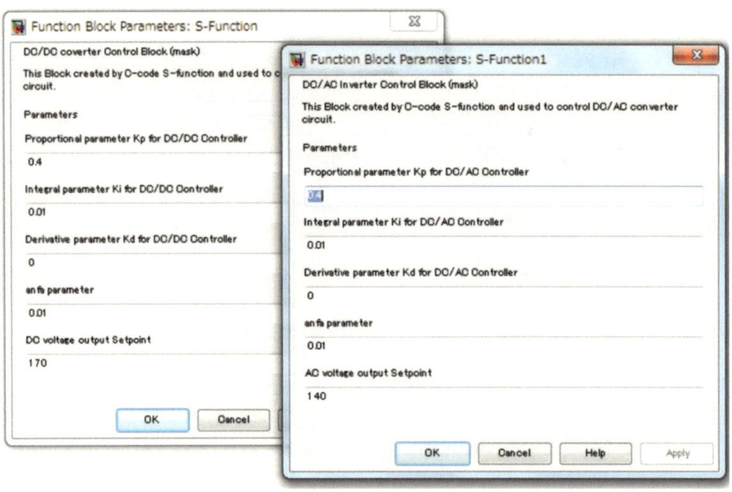

Fig. 20. S-Function parameter block

The data can be displayed and sent to the MATLAB workspace for further analysis by using the scope blocks. The scope block is used to measure and monitor the signal at each point in the model, which allows the user to check the model operation at each point, as shown in Figure 21. This figure presents the entire inverter power supply model which is the MILS environment. The embedded software parameters are optimized and the system performance is tested as well as the verification of the control algorithm is done.

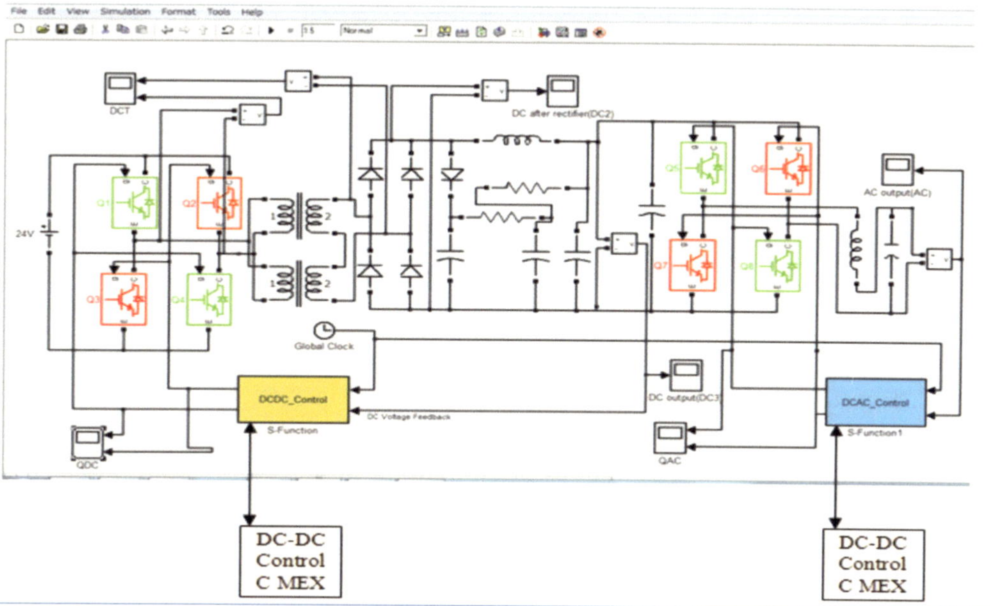

Fig. 21. Virtual environment of the inverter power supply

8. Experimental results

Actual prototype of inverter power supply has been fabricated using Renesas SH microprocessor. The output voltage and the frequency of the inverter power supply are verified and the responses of the inverter power supply in the existence of loads are checked to confirm the efficiency of the control algorithm. Some of the results are shown below in Figure 22.

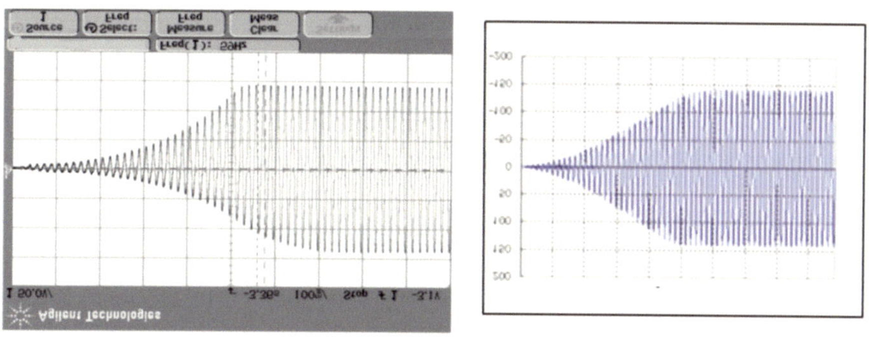

Fig. 22. Output of inverter power supply: (a) Actuals (b) Simulation

One of the effective parameters of the inverter power supply is the time it can reach its stationary value. Figure 22 describes this parameter and it is clear that the shapes of the wave are visually identical. We can conclude that the developed models can simulate the actual prototype in a good way within very short time comparing to the traditional method of design. The output voltage and frequency are tested, as shown in Figure 23 as well as the relationship between the output waves and the generated PWM signals which are generated by the microprocessor and controlled by the embedded software.

In Figure 23, comparing the two waveforms, it can be seen that the result obtained by the developed model is in a good agreement with the actual result in both frequency and voltage amplitude. It is apparent that the narrow pulse is generated when the modulating signal is at its maximum or minimum values.

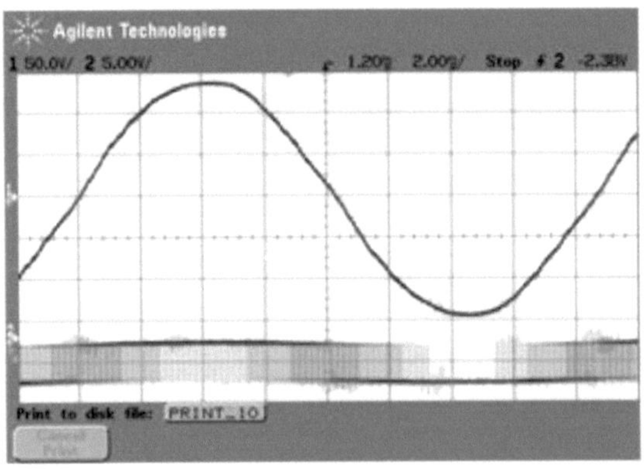

(a) Actual

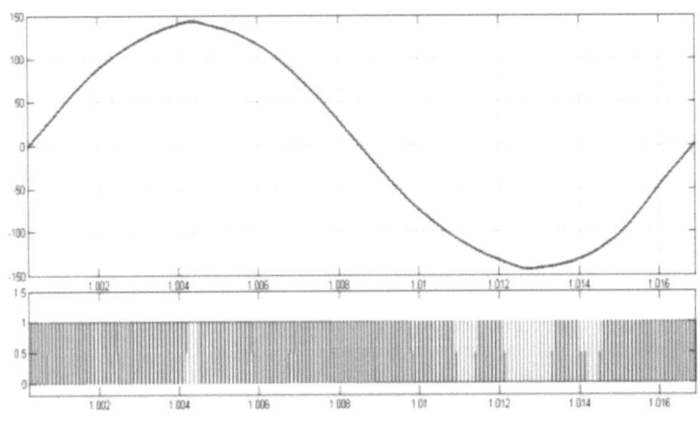

(b) Simulation

Fig. 23. Sin wave output of inverter power supply:

Response with linear load

The inverter power supply output distortion or the output voltage drop is considered a very important issue in the design of the inverter power supply. There are many regulations regarding the allowable voltage drop in the inverter power supply. For example, based on the standard IEC686, the allowed voltage drop is no more than 5% voltage against single parameter. Various techniques are used to compensate the effect of the voltage drop in the inverter power supply design. One of the main techniques is to apply the control system. The main duty of the inverter control system is to regulate the output voltage against the entire possible disturbance and the load variations. As mentioned before, the two layer control algorithm which consists of the feedback PI controller plus the feed-forward controller is proposed to control the inverter power supply. The validity and usefulness of this controlling algorithm are tested in the existence of linear load. Figures 24 and 25 show the output of the inverter power supply with no load and after connecting the load resistance Rl = 60Ω respectively. From Figure 25, we can see the voltage reduction at the moment when the resistance is connected but due to the control algorithm, the voltage can return to its value within a very short time. We can conclude that the proposed control algorithm is able to modify the distortion that occurred due to the load in a very short time. So, using the control algorithm can improve the inverter power supply's performances.

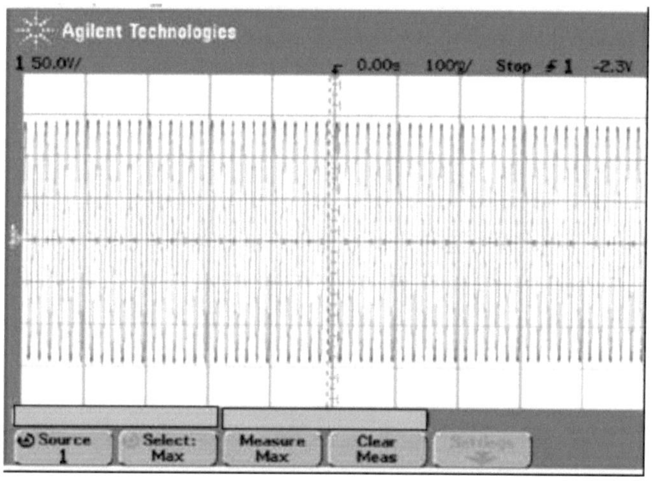

Fig. 24. Inverter power supply output with no load

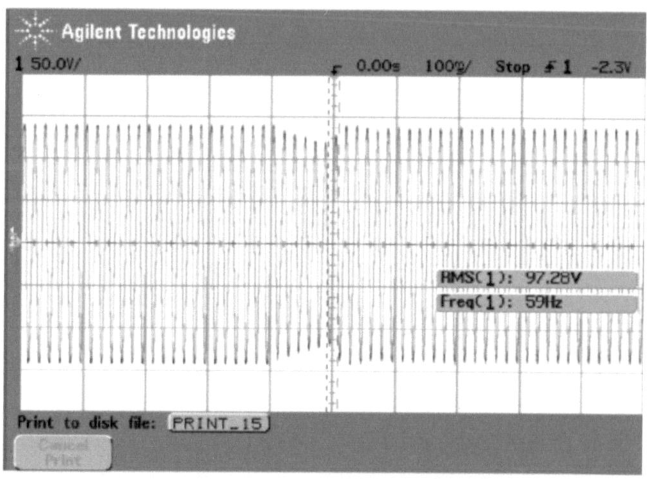

Fig. 25. Inverter power supply output with no load in the MILS

Comparing the result with no load and the result with load, it seems that the shapes of the wave forms are almost identical except in the moment that the load resistances are connected. The voltage decreased by about 2% of no load voltage for a very short time of approximately 100 msec, and then it returned to its normal value. So, we can conclude that the proposed controlling algorithm is working well, and it can maintain the disturbance occurred due to the load connection.

9. Conclusions

This research meets the challenges of the embedded system design by applying the Model Based Design (MBD) method in the early design stage. Furthermore, the main contribution of this research is to prove the potential of using the MBD method in the optimization and verification of the embedded system software development. This study proposed the functional model of a microprocessor in the early stage of the inverter power supply development, which allows the full simulation of the system in the virtual environment including the electrical circuit and software implementation. Inverter power supply was taken as a case study of the embedded system design. An entire model of the system was developed, including the electrical circuit and the microprocessor using the MATLAB and Simulink package. All the software parameters were optimized as well as a newly applied controlling algorithm was evaluated using the Model In the Loop Simulation (MILS) environment. The validity and the usefulness of the proposed model were tested comparing with the actual prototype of the inverter power supply. The developed model was shown to be well in agreement with the experimental results. This method can be used to optimize the software parameters before the actual design. Moreover, the models can be used to study and analyze the behaviors of the system which meet the challenges of designing the digital control system. The results show that the suggested models are promising and the models can be useful for optimizing the performances in developing the embedded software.

10. References

Abo Eldahb, M.A. (2011). *Model Based Design Environment for the Embedded System; Case study: Inverter Power supply*. Ph D Thesis, Production Science and technology Dept., Gunma University, Japan, Sept. 2011.

Abo Eldahb, M.A., Iino, S. Shirashi, Y.& Tatsumo, M.(2009).*Model Based Design of The inverter Power Supply*, In the Proceeding of ICCAS-SICE International Joint Conference, Fukuoka, Japan, August 17-21th, 2009.

Behboodian, A. (2006). *Model Based Design*. DSP Magazine, Vol.2, pp.52-56., May 2006.

Berger, A. S. (2002). *Embedded Systems Design: An Introduction to Processes, Tools & Techniques. Group West Publishers, USA.*

Buyya R, Murshed M. GridSim(2002): *A toolkit for the modeling and simulation of distributed resource management and scheduling for Grid computing.* Concurrency and Computation: Practice and Experience 2002

Christopher, M. (2000). *An Evaluation of Embedded System Behaviour"* M.Sc Thesis, Department of Electrical and Computing Engineering, University of Maryland, 2000.

Choi, S. Yong, Y. Lim W. & Young, S. (1999).*A Novel Dead Time Minimization Algorithm on the PWM Inverter*, In the Proceeding of the Industrial Application Conference, IEEE, Vol.4, pp.2188-2193, 3-7 October, 1999.

Davey, C. & Friedman, J. (2007). *Software Systems Engineering with Model-Based Design.* In the Proceedings of the Fourth International Workshop on Software Engineering for Automotive System, pp. 7, May 20-26, 2007.

Henzinger, T. & Sifakis, J. (2006). *The Embedded System Design Challenge.* In the Proceedings of the 14th International Symposium on Formal Methods (FM), May 2006.

Ho, W. K. Lee T. H. & Tay.(1999).Knowledge-Based Multivariable *PID Control.* Technical Notes, National University of Singapore, April, 1999.

Hongxing, W. & Tianmiao, W. (2006). *Curriculum of Embedded System for Software Colleges.* In the Proceedings of the 2nd IEEE, August 2006.

Madhukar, A. & Lee, I. (2008). *Challenges and Opportunities in Deeply Embedded System Security.* ACM SIGBED Journal, Vol. 5, January 2008.

Manfred, B. (2006). *Challenges in Automotive Software Engineering.* In the Proceedings of ICSE'06 Conference, May 20-28th, 2006.

Mark B., Rajkumar B. & Domenico L.(2002). *Grids and Grid technologies for wide-area distributed computing:* Software-Practice and Experience, Vol.32, issue 15, Pp 1437-1466, Dec., 2002

Ming-Shan, L. (2007). *Application of Embedded System in Construction Machinery.* In the Proceedings of the 8th ACIS International Conference, 30th July-1st August, 2007.

Mohan,T.M,(1995). *Power Electronic Converters: Applications and Design.* John Wiley &Sons Co., Ltd, 1995.

Mosterman, P.J., (2010). *Model Based Design for Embedded System.* Taylor &Francis Group Co., Ltd., New York, 2010.

Rautio, J. (2008). *Shortening the Design Cycle.* Microwave Magazine, IEEE, Vol.9, No.6, pp.86-96, Dec. 2008.

Sh-2Sh7047 Group Hardware Manual, Accessed in September 2009, http://www.renrsas.com.

Stepner, D., & Rajac, N. & Hui, D., "Embedded Application Design Using a Real-time OS", In proceeding of the 36th of Design Automation Conference, New Orleans UAS, pp. 151-156, 21-25, June 1999.

Stepner, D., & Rajan, N., & Hui, D. (1999). *Embedded Application Design Using a Real-time OS.* In the proceeding of 36th Design Automation Conference, pp.151-156, New Orleans, USA, 21-25, June 1999.

The MathWork web site, Accessed in December, 2010.http://www.mathworks.com/.

Thomas, B. (2006). *Embedded Robotics: Mobile Robot Design and Application with Embedded system.* Springer- Verlag Hiedelerg Ltd. Co., Year(2006).

Turley, J. (2010). *Embedded processors by the numbers.* Accesses in October, 2010, Available <http://vault.embedded.com/1999/9905/9905turley.htm>

Woodward, V. & Mosterman, J. (2007). *Challenges for Embedded Software Development*. In the Proceeding of Circuit and System, MWSCAS Conference, pp.630-633, 5-8th August, 2007.

Xue Y., Baekhy K. & Bordonau, J. (2004).*Topologies of Single Phase Inverter for Small Distributed Power Generators: An Overview*, Transactions, IEEE, Vol.19, No.5, September, 2004.